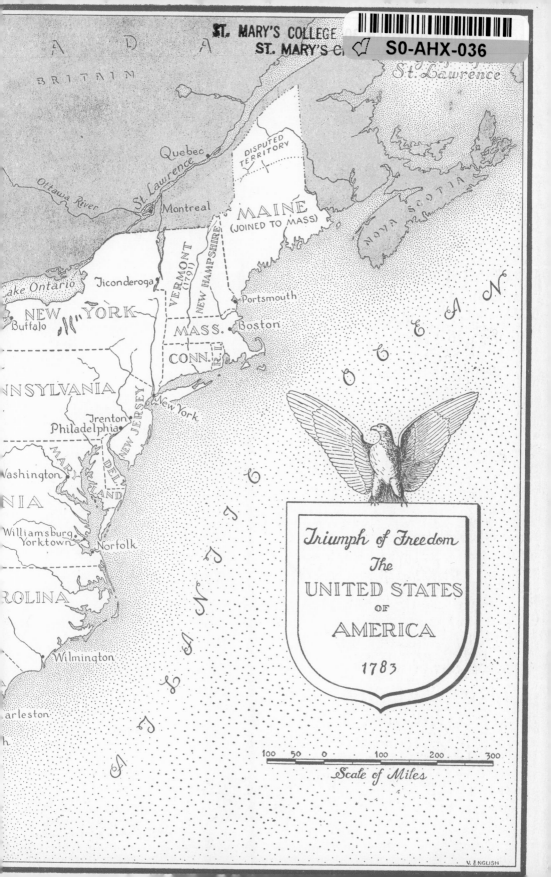

Triumph of Freedom
The
UNITED STATES
OF
AMERICA
1783

Scale of Miles

V. ENGLISH

BOOKS BY
JOHN C. MILLER

SAM ADAMS, *Pioneer in Propaganda*

ORIGINS OF THE AMERICAN REVOLUTION

TRIUMPH OF FREEDOM, 1775–1783

Triumph of Freedom

1775–1783

Triumph of Freedom

〰〰〰〰〰〰〰〰〰〰〰〰〰〰〰〰〰〰〰

1775–1783

〰〰〰〰〰〰〰〰〰〰〰〰〰〰〰〰〰〰〰

BY JOHN C. *hester* MILLER

WITH MAPS BY VAN H. ENGLISH

〰〰〰〰〰〰〰〰〰〰〰〰〰〰〰〰〰〰〰

AN ATLANTIC MONTHLY PRESS BOOK

LITTLE, BROWN AND COMPANY · BOSTON

ATLANTIC–LITTLE, BROWN BOOKS
ARE PUBLISHED BY
LITTLE, BROWN AND COMPANY
IN ASSOCIATION WITH
THE ATLANTIC MONTHLY PRESS

Published simultaneously
in Canada by McClelland and Stewart Limited

PRINTED IN THE UNITED STATES OF AMERICA

TO

CHARLES, JOHNNY, AND JEFFREY

"Posterity! you will never know how much it cost the present generation to preserve your freedom! I hope you will make a good use of it.
If you do not, I shall repent it in heaven that I ever took half the pains
to preserve it."

— JOHN ADAMS. *1777*

Chronology

1775

April 19. Skirmishes at Lexington and Concord.

May 10. Assembling of the Second Continental Congress in Philadelphia.

May 10. Capture of Ticonderoga by Ethan Allen and Benedict Arnold.

May 25. Arrival of the Three Major Generals in Boston.

May 31. Formation of the Continental army.

June 15. Washington appointed Commander-in-Chief of the Continental army.

June 17. Battle of Bunker Hill.

July 3. Washington assumes command of the Continental army at Cambridge.

July (to *March* 1776). Siege of Boston.

November 12. Capture of Montreal by General Montgomery.

December 31. Repulse of Montgomery and Arnold at Quebec.

1776

March 4. Occupation of Dorchester Heights by the American army.

March 17. British evacuation of Boston.

June 28. Repulse of the British at Charleston, South Carolina.

July 2. Arrival of the British fleet and army in New York Harbor.

July 4. Adoption of the Declaration of Independence.

August 27. Battle of Long Island.

September 12. Peace conference between Lord Howe and the American commissioners.

September 15. Occupation of New York City by the British.

October 11–13. Naval battle of Lake Champlain.

October 28. Battle of White Plains.

November 16. Capture of Fort Washington.

November 20. Capture of Fort Lee.

November 28. Washington's retreat across the Delaware.

December 26. Battle of Trenton.

1777

January 3. Battle of Princeton.
July 6. Fall of Fort Ticonderoga.
July 7. Battle of Hubbardton.
August 16. Battle of Bennington.
September 11. Battle of Brandywine.
September 18. Congress flees Philadelphia.
September 19. Battle of Freeman's Farm.
September 20. Paoli Massacre.
September 27. Sir William Howe occupies Philadelphia.
October 4. Battle of Germantown.
October 7. Battle of Bemis Heights.
October 17. Surrender of Burgoyne.
November 15. Articles of Confederation submitted to the states.

1778

February 6. Signing of the Franco-American treaties.
February 17. Lord North's Conciliatory Propositions presented to Parliament.
June 17. Rejection by Congress of Lord Carlisle's peace overtures.
June 18. Evacuation of Philadelphia by the British.
June 28. Battle of Monmouth Courthouse.
July 4. Wyoming Massacre.
July 8. Arrival of D'Estaing off Delaware Capes.
August. Siege of Newport.
November 11. Cherry Valley Massacre.
December 29. Capture of Savannah by the British.

1779

February 24. Capture of Vincennes by George Rogers Clark.
June 16. Spain declares war upon Great Britain.
July 5. Plundering of New Haven.
July 16. Storming of Stony Point.
September 23. Naval victory of John Paul Jones.
October 9. Franco-American repulse at Savannah.

1780

March 18. Devaluation of the dollar.
May 12. Fall of Charleston, South Carolina.
June 2–9. Lord George Gordon Riots.

July 10. Arrival of Rochambeau at Newport.
August 16. Battle of Camden.
August 18. Defeat of Sumter by Tarleton.
September 23. Treason of Benedict Arnold.
October 2. Execution of André.
October 7. Battle of King's Mountain.
December 30. Declaration of war by Great Britain upon Holland.

1781

January 1. Mutiny of the Pennsylvania Line.
January 17. Battle of Cowpens.
February 3. Congress proposes the first impost to the states.
February 20. Robert Morris elected Superintendent of Finance.
March 1. Formal ratification of the Articles of Confederation.
March 15. Battle of Guilford Courthouse.
June 15. Adoption by Congress of Instructions to American Peace Commissioners.
August 30. Arrival of De Grasse at the Chesapeake.
September 8. Battle of Eutaw Springs.
October 19. Surrender of Cornwallis.

1782

March 20. Fall of the Ministry of Lord North.
April 12. Battle of the Saints.
July 1. Death of Lord Rockingham; formation of the Ministry of Lord Shelburne.
November 30. Signing by the American commissioners of the Preliminary Articles of Peace between Great Britain and the United States.

1783

January 20. Cessation of hostilities between the United States and Great Britain.
March. The Newburgh Addresses.
April 18. Congress proposes the second impost to the states.
May 26. Congress votes to furlough the army.
June 24. Congress flees Philadelphia.
September 3. Definitive Treaty of Peace between the United States and Great Britain signed at Paris.
November 2. Washington's Farewell Address to the army.
November 25. British evacuation of New York.
December 23. Washington resigns his commission as Commander-in-Chief.

Preface

ANOTHER book about the American Revolution calls for a word of explanation. Few fields of history have been more intensively cultivated by successive generations of historians; few offer less reward in the shape of fresh facts or theories. Nevertheless, the lack of a one-volume history of our struggle for independence and the need of a concise restatement of the results of a century and a half of historical scholarship seem to warrant this addition to already crowded shelves.

Moreover, it is a story that bears retelling. American democracy will always profit by going back to its origins. The spirit and philosophy of the era that gave birth to the Declaration of Independence are perennial sources of strength to Americans in days of trial and doubt; to recapture this faith and resolution is a compulsive need of democracy in our time.

Yet this story is by no means wholly one of heroism and self-sacrifice: as the war progressed, lethargy, indifference, and the spirit of money-making began to supplant the earlier idealism. It is significant that this decline in morale coincides with the onset of inflation. Not even the spiritual values of the American Revolution could withstand the blighting influence of that inflation, the worst in American history.

Although this book is addressed to a larger audience than scholars and experts in the field, I have tried to abide by the canons of historical scholarship. It has been found advisable, however, to dispense with citations of sources. If I were to do full justice to my sources, there would be a lengthy footnote at the end of virtually every sentence — in which case, my text would be submerged in my footnotes. This I cannot bring myself to inflict upon readers already obliged to grapple with a book of formidable proportions. In compensation for this omission, I have appended a bibliography which, in a general way, will serve to indicate my sources and underscore the more important books relating to the American Revolution.

I am deeply indebted to Mr. Stanley Salmen for the invaluable editorial assistance he has given me in preparing this book for the press.

JOHN C. MILLER
Rosemont, Pennsylvania

Contents

Triumph of Freedom
1775–1783

CHAPTER I

A House Divided

IN 1775 the British Empire, long a house divided against itself, became
the scene of civil war. The American colonies rose in revolt, declared
their independence of the mother country, and fought a seven years' war
to make good that declaration. Beginning as a family quarrel within the
British Empire, the War of American Independence ultimately involved
the great powers, and both hemispheres felt the impact of war. For Great
Britain, the struggle became a war of survival against some of the most
formidable odds faced by the island kingdom since the days of the Spanish
Armada. "It is no longer our task," said Edmund Burke in 1775, "to
describe devastation in Poland, or slaughter on the Danube. The evil is
at home." Three years later, enemy fleets rode in the English Channel
and enemy armies were poised to invade England itself. That the British,
as a result of this conflict, lost no more than one third of their empire is
a tribute — scarcely less memorable than the Battle of Britain — to their
indomitable courage in adversity.

In the beginning, however, the odds favored Great Britain as heavily
as they later turned against her. With manufacturing and warmaking
resources that dwarfed those of her colonies; with nine million inhabitants
against two and one-half million; with a mighty fleet and army opposed
by militiamen and a few poorly armed naval vessels — only those blinded
by love of liberty would have gone to war with Great Britain upon such
terms. Moreover, for the first three years of the struggle, Great Britain
enjoyed virtually a free hand: her European rivals pursued a policy of
watchful waiting, secretly feeding the flames but refraining from forcing
Englishmen to fight the two-front war that alone seemed capable of saving
Americans from defeat.

England boasted a long and unbroken string of victories over its enemies.

So regularly had France, Spain, and Holland gone down to defeat that by the time of the American Revolution it was almost unthinkable to Englishmen that they could lose a war. Instead of counting the risks of war and appeasing their enemies, Englishmen were urged to "recollect the great, extensive, and successful wars, which this country carried on before America was known. . . . Shall we then be told, that this people of yesterday, whose greatness is the work of our own hands, can resist the powerful efforts of this nation?"

Since the fall of the Roman Empire, no colonial people had succeeded in throwing off the rule of the parent country. Americans took comfort in the example of the Dutch, who in the seventeenth century had won their independence of Spain; but the Dutch were not a colonial people and their struggle for freedom had been long and bloody. From a more recent instance of rebellion in Europe, Americans could draw no encouragement whatever. In 1769, a French army under Count de Vaux overran Corsica despite the heroic defense of Pasquale Paoli and his countrymen. Thus was confirmed the superiority of regular troops over untrained levies — a superiority which the advance of military science was steadily increasing. The high morale of men fighting for their homes and freedom was insufficient to withstand the artillery, bayonets, and discipline of the professional armies of Europe. A nation of farmers seemed unlikely to emerge victorious against troops as highly trained and as undeniably courageous as were British regulars.

For the first time in their history, Americans were meeting the British army as an enemy. Hitherto, they had fought alongside the redcoats, and less than fifteen years before, they had aided in driving the French from the North American continent. As allies, they had seen British troops under Wolfe storm the Heights of Abraham and capture the citadel of Quebec, toppling the military power of France in North America into the dust. After 1775, memories of these common triumphs were forgotten, and Americans comforted themselves with the idea that Englishmen had vastly degenerated and that the army was now composed of "six penny soldiers, picked up from prisons and dungeons, freed from transportation, the whipping post, and the gallows, fighting for the worst of causes, and for the worst of Kings." American propagandists made the British army appear to be an assemblage of rapists, plunderers, pickpockets, and murderers. Even their courage was suspect. "England was never famous by land," said Thomas Paine; "her officers have generally been suspected of cowardice, have more of the air of a dancing-master than a soldier"; the exploits they performed under the planet Venus were greater than those under Mars. As for the people as a whole, said Paine, it was their unhappy temper "to be pleased with any war, right or wrong, be it but successful; but they soon grow discontented with ill-fortune." Here was one war of which Americans intended to make Englishmen weary before they had fairly begun it.

Americans were soon to alter their opinion of their enemy's want of courage; yet it was undeniable that the British army labored under serious difficulties in carrying war to the rebels across the Atlantic. Although experienced in waging war overseas, the British army had always depended upon the colonists for aid; never before had it been obliged to fight its way into a hostile continent. Moreover, military science was still conceived largely in terms of European battlefields: the forests, mountains, rivers, and vast distances of America had hardly begun to modify the art of war. In conformity with the maxims of Frederick the Great, the greatest military genius of the age, British soldiers marched into battle in columns and attacked with almost as much formality as they displayed on the parade ground: war was governed by a minute and exacting etiquette admitting of little deviation from the rules. Although these methods had proved their worth in Europe, they were ill adapted to the conditions encountered in North America where, as Sir William Howe discovered, every movement of the war was "an act of enterprise, clogged with innumerable difficulties."

After the war was fairly launched and the full magnitude of the undertaking began to dawn upon Englishmen, William Eden [1] said that he heartily regretted that English statesmen "instead of making the Tour of Europe did not finish their Education by a Voyage round the Coasts & Rivers of the Western Side of the Atlantic." Had they done so, they might have been less optimistic of quick victory in America. But Englishmen knew little of this part of their empire; it was lost from ignorance of the nature of the country and people they governed.

Little attention was given to teaching British soldiers to shoot accurately. Marksmanship was in danger of becoming a lost art; the musket seemed to be valued more as a convenient means of carrying a bayonet than as a weapon in its own right. As they advanced to the attack, the soldiers fired their guns in volleys without taking aim; then, behind the smoke screen, they rushed upon their enemies and gave them cold steel. [2]

As a result, the musket remained relatively undeveloped as an implement of war. "Brown Bess" — the musket employed in the British army — was a heavy, unwieldy, and surprisingly harmless weapon. Loaded from the muzzle and ignited by a priming pan, it could be fired two or three times a minute when expertly handled. From a gun with such a staggering recoil, much might have been expected by way of execution, yet actually it had an effective range of only about a hundred yards, and lacking a rear

[1] An ancestor of Anthony Eden, former British Foreign Secretary.
[2] Against massed bodies of men the musket did considerable execution. But this kind of fighting was not generally sought by commanders in the eighteenth century.

sight it could not be accurately aimed. Little dreading the firepower of "Brown Bess," Americans quickly conceived a healthy respect for its bayonet.

In the eighteenth century, speed was given scant consideration in the British army. Weighted down with a backbreaking load of equipment, soldiers went into battle carrying sufficient supplies to last several days of hot campaigning. "Brown Bess" alone weighed fourteen pounds. Under these conditions, rapid movement could not be expected of the troops; a slow, methodical advance was favored by the leading tacticians of the day. The British army fought much in the manner of the bulldog which served to symbolize these determined but slow-moving islanders.

British officers and soldiers wore uniforms of the color most likely to make them conspicuous targets. When engaged with an enemy who, like themselves, did not take aim, this was not particularly disadvantageous. In America, however, where soldiers took aim and often hit the mark, uniforms that looked dashing in Hyde Park were woefully out of place. Moreover, British officers sported gold lace, epaulets, and ribbons, all of which served to advertise their presence to American sharpshooters, who always made it a point to pick off officers whenever they showed themselves.

A voyage across the Atlantic often left the troops almost as exhausted as though they had undergone a rough tour of duty. A soldier pictured life on board an army transport as "the pox above-board, the plague between decks, hell in the forecastle, the devil at the helm." Even if the men were not laid low by disease on the long voyage out, they faced the ordeal of becoming acclimated to the infectious maladies endemic in America. Most of the patients in British hospitals in this country, however, were newly arrived recruits; after a year in the United States, exposed to its extreme variations in temperature and its diseases, a British or German trooper was apt to be as healthy as an American soldier. In general, disease took a surprisingly light toll in the British army; during seven years of war, there were no serious epidemics.

In the train of the British army marched a large number of female camp followers, consisting of *filles du régiment* and fond wives who could not bear to part with their soldier husbands when they went overseas. The British government permitted officers and soldiers to take their wives on the campaign: they cooked, washed and mended clothes, tidied up quarters, and in general gave the camp a much-needed feminine touch. In return, they drew rations from army stores, thereby sometimes imposing a heavy drain upon the commissariat. In 1775, when the Americans captured a British fort, they found more women and children than soldiers in the garrison. Over two thousand women accompanied Burgoyne's army of seven thousand men. Had they been Amazons, no doubt the British general would have hewn his way to Albany and safety; instead, their presence helped to bog down Burgoyne in the wilderness while the Americans closed in for the kill.

As usual, Great Britain was unready for war when the crisis came to a head in its colonies. In every war, Englishmen risked disaster at the outset by unpreparedness; but the lesson that safety consisted in keeping their powder dry had not, luckily for the Americans, been assimilated. After the Peace of Paris (1763), although England had doubled its empire at the expense of France and Spain, the army had been permitted to revert to its peacetime basis — with the result that, in 1775, less than fifty thousand men were under arms to garrison the home islands, maintain the outposts of the empire, and subdue the rebellion in America. It was necessary, therefore, to resort to improvisation to repair the consequences of neglect; "desks, counting-houses, and public offices," it was said, "were stripped of their useful and peaceable occupiers, to supply a new race of commanders and generals" for British armies.

Nor did Great Britain, in embarking upon war with its transatlantic dominions, take fully into account the difficulty of equipping, transporting, and supplying an army three thousand miles from its base. Failing to provide for a long war against a stubborn foe, the mother country encountered transportation bottlenecks which, almost as much as American resistance itself, defeated the best-laid plans of British generals. In 1775–1776, more transports were required than even during the Seven Years' War (1756–1763) when England had been at war with France, Spain, and Austria; and before the struggle with the colonies was over, as many men were employed in bringing troops and supplies across the Atlantic as were serving in the army. Even so, operations were frequently held up by delays in transportation; time and space repeatedly seemed to league themselves against the success of British arms. Supply ships were delayed by bad weather; the Admiralty was slow in providing convoys; friction between the army and navy sometimes held up combined operations; and brass hats in high places refused to permit efficiency to supersede routine. Much of Sir William Howe's notorious slowness, it is fair to say, was owing to the failure of supplies to arrive on time. And always there was danger that by losing command of the sea even temporarily, the British army would be cut off from supplies and be starved into surrender.

Lord North later made a merit of the confusion, mismanagement, and divided counsels that obstructed the British war effort during the early part of the struggle. It proved, he asserted, that the mother country, far from planning to strip the colonies of their liberty by military force, was caught napping by the outbreak of rebellion in North America. England's only fault, lamented the Prime Minister, was that it trusted too implicitly in the loyalty of Americans and treated them with gentleness and forbearance when severity might have nipped the rebellion in the bud.

Unprepared as it was, the army suffered from a bad case of overconfidence. At the beginning of the war, British officers often spoke of disciplining the rebels with horsewhips; these "damned rebellious sons of bitches," they swore, were as cowardly as they were malicious. "Some few Virginians and Marylanders excepted," said a British officer, "they [the American soldiers] are the most dastardly wretches of the Almighty's creation." As for Yankees, in Englishmen's eyes they were a kind of Yahoo. A British general told Benjamin Franklin that with a thousand British grenadiers "he would undertake to go from one end of America to the other, and geld all the males, partly by force and partly by a little coaxing." Major Pitcairn of the British army declared that "if he drew his sword but half out of the scabbard, the whole banditti of Massachusetts Bay would flee before him." The major drew his sword entirely out of the scabbard — and was promptly killed by a Yankee sharpshooter.

The unmilitary appearance of the American army further swelled the disdain in which these true-born Britons held the rebels. An English official in America pronounced the American army to be "but a contemptible band of vagrants, deserters and thieves"; a general pardon to convicts, he predicted, would break up Washington's army in a trice. "The Flower of Mr. Washington's army," it was averred, "is composed of the Gleanings of British Prisons, transported to the Southern Colonies."

In short, the American Revolution seemed to prove the hazard of transporting felons to the colonies, where they became republicans and rebels and transferred to politics the talents that had made them redoubtable as highwaymen and housebreakers.

This "monstrous Pride and Insolence" (as Franklin called it) led some Englishmen to feel that a gentleman degraded himself by taking the field against American rebels. There was little satisfaction to be gained from killing such peasants — a fox hunt was infinitely more exhilarating. "I hope that we shall soon have done with these scoundrels," said Lord Rawdon, "for one only dirties one's fingers by meddling with them." "I shall be ashamed to reckon the beating such wretches among my annals," observed another British officer. "They are not fit for a Soldier's wrath — Jack Ketch should be the minister of vengeance to them." But to be killed by these skulking boors was an unspeakable indignity. "It grieves me," said an Englishman after Bunker Hill, "that gentlemen, brave British soldiers, should fall by the hands of such despicable wretches as compose the banditti of the country; amongst whom there is not one that has the least pretensions to be called a gentleman. They are a most rude, depraved, degenerate race, and it is a mortification to us that they speak English, and can trace themselves from that stock." Viewed in this light, the American war was far less glorious than a French or Spanish war, where an English gentleman had at least a chance of being killed by another gentleman.

Whatever may account for the failure of the British army to conquer the Americans, it was not owing to any lack of zeal on the part of the common soldiers. Their zest for battle was not lessened by any cousinly regard for the rebels. Lord Rawdon looked forward to the day when his men could be "let slip against a parcel of wretches whom they hate and despise, when no Officer will interpose to rescue the Victims from their Rage"; and Burgoyne declared that it was necessary to restrain the soldiers rather than to urge them on when they went into battle against the rebels. There were few advocates of a "soft peace" in the British army; indeed, among the obstacles to reconciliation, it was observed that "the contempt every Soldier has for an American is not the smallest. They cannot possibly believe that any good Quality can exist among them."

Even the British private, albeit he had come to the army straight from prison, was apt to conceive himself to be superior to any and all Americans. "The meanest person among us," said an Englishman, "is disposed to look upon himself as having a body of subjects in America, and to be offended at the denial of his right to make laws for them, though perhaps he does not know what colour they are of, or what language they talk." Closer acquaintance with their subjects overseas did not tend either to dispel prejudice or to persuade Englishmen that the colonists were their equals. In their own eyes, they came as conquerors and as superior beings commissioned to restore law, order, and civilization among these benighted outlanders. The primary cause of Britain's failure to overcome the rebellion, said a German officer, was "the confounded pride and arrogant bearing of the English, who treat every one that was not born upon their ragamuffin Island with contempt." Even the ardor of many Loyalists for the cause of King and country was seriously dampened by the manners of "this haughty America-despising people."

⌢ ⌢ ⌢

From top to bottom, the army faithfully reflected the well-defined class lines of English society. The highest ranks were pre-empted by the upper class, subalterns were generally of the middle class, and the common soldiers were recruited from the proletariat. From the peerage and nobility came the generals: holding seats in Parliament and moving in the lofty reaches of society, they made the upper ranks of the army indistinguishable from the social register. Advancement in the army was made easy for those whose way was smoothed by wealth. Commissions were bought and sold much like shares on the exchange: prudent parents provided for their children by purchasing them commissions in the army. The talents or inclinations of the young men themselves were unimportant — the army was expected to furnish them a comfortable living for life unless, as often happened, a bad run of cards or a major mistake in judgment at the race tracks forced them to sell their commissions to pay off their creditors. Sometimes mere children might bear the title of lieutenant or captain. Generally, however, commissions were not granted to boys under sixteen.

It would perhaps be unjust to say that the War of American Independence was lost upon the playing fields of Eton; yet it is certain that a large number of schoolboys took part in that struggle. During Burgoyne's invasion of the United States, a British soldier recorded that on one day he helped bury three officers of the 20th Regiment, "the age of the eldest not exceeding seventeen."

And little children shall lead them!

This system resulted in veterans of proved ability and valor being brushed aside to make room for younger men of long purses but slight experience. It created a large group of embittered, restless, and underpaid officers to whom the door of promotion was forever closed. While it brought blue blood into the army, the purchase and sale of commissions deprived the service of military skill and brains — qualities which it sorely needed.

Theoretically, the British army was maintained by volunteering. In practice, however, volunteering was often a euphemism for kidnaping, shanghaiing, conducting raids upon dives, and reprieving criminals on condition that they join the army. Getting drunk with a friendly stranger had peculiar hazards in eighteenth-century England: he might prove, the morning after, to be a recruiting officer. These officers could hardly complain that they were not given a wide latitude of choice in filling the ranks. "Any sturdy beggar," ran the law, "any fortune teller, any idle, unknown, or suspected fellow in a parish that cannot give an account of himself," was to be clapped into the army. Incorrigible rogues, poachers, catch-purses, and the like were fair game for recruiting officers, and a pardon was sometimes offered to convicted felons if they would enlist in the army. Three British regiments were composed entirely of reprieved criminals. "If there be no other consequence from raising Regiments," remarked an Englishman, "there will be this at Least, that you will have fewer Thieves." Since Great Britain at the time of the American Revolution was one of the most lawless nations in the world, the British army possessed a large reservoir of manpower from which to fill its ranks. Long accustomed to dump its criminal population upon the colonies, Great Britain was now putting its undesirables into uniform in order to teach Americans the virtues of loyalty and obedience.

Manifestly, these men were not likely to diffuse sweetness and light among the erring brethren in America. Their basic training had been picked up in street brawls, snatching purses, matching wits with the police, and making quick getaways after a holdup. Prone to pillage and loot, they were kept under the control of their officers with great difficulty. Sir William Howe estimated that it took ten years to discipline a soldier. In 1758, General James Wolfe described conditions in the British army: "Sergeants drunk upon duty, sentries upon their posts and the rest wallowing in the dirt. . . . I believe," he added, "no nation ever paid so many bad soldiers at so high a rate." Yet they were stout-hearted fellows ready to follow their officers into the jaws of death. And although, in the War of American Independence, they were fighting against an enemy who professed to be upholding the rights of mankind against tyrants, they — the outcasts, the oppressed, the scourings and scrapings of the nation — remained indifferent to American propaganda and fought as though they were the sovereigns of the empire.

Despite the apparently inexhaustible supply of criminals at its disposal, the British army found it impossible to procure sufficient soldiers during the War of American Independence. Bounties were raised, the standard was lowered to five feet three inches in height and sixteen years of age, a vigorous recruiting drive was made among the Irish Catholics; but still the army failed to attain its required strength. Only Scotland seemed eager to send its sons to war: by 1779, over thirty thousand Scotchmen were serving in the British army.

The reluctance of Englishmen to take an active part in the struggle against the colonists does not necessarily prove that the war was unpopular. Englishmen usually held back until they were satisfied that matters were critical; they prided themselves upon losing the first battles but always winning the war; and they rose to their full stature only when their backs were against the wall. Foreigners frequently observed that Englishmen liked to be told that they were ruined; then, inspired by disaster, they confounded the prophets by rising up in their wrath and overwhelming the enemy. This — except for the glorious finish — was the course followed by the War of American Independence. Not until 1778 did Englishmen begin to fight in earnest, but by that late hour they were confronted by such an array of enemies that victory could not be snatched from defeat.

Moreover, for generations Englishmen had been taught to expect others to do much of the soldiering for them — their task was to man the navy, serve on board British merchantmen, conquer their enemies' colonies, and keep the factories humming to increase the national wealth. This freedom from militarism was made possible by England's insular position and by the government's policy of subsidizing its European allies to take the field against the common enemy — usually the dominant power on the continent. Thus it was English pounds and shillings rather than Englishmen themselves that went to war in Europe. The armies that England raised and sent to the continent were usually small and highly professional; the bulk of the manpower of the coalitions sponsored by England was furnished by her continental allies. Thanks to their navy, Englishmen were able to continue their peacetime pursuits and to extend their manufacturing, commerce, and empire while Europe was shattered by internal conflict.

Recognizing that Great Britain was not likely to provide the manpower necessary to crush the American revolt, the government, as was its wont, began to scour Europe for soldiers. Russia was asked for twenty thousand troops — who, it was sardonically remarked in the House of Commons, would civilize Americans wonderfully. No force was too insignificant to be overlooked by the British in their quest for manpower: a brigade of Scots serving with the Dutch was ordered home to take the field against the rebels. Neither the Russians nor the Dutch, however, were inclined to help England pull its chestnuts from the fire; and from neither country did the government receive aid or comfort.

But the German states — an unfailing reservoir — were willing to furnish soldiers, at a price. For hundreds of years, Germany had supplied warring European states with mercenaries who, indifferent to the causes for which they fought, were nevertheless reckoned among the best soldiers in Europe. This system of barter and sale of German manpower was made possible by the fact that Germany was not a united country but a congeries of small states, numbering about three hundred all told. The rulers of some of these principalities, eager to emulate in their own courts the splendors of Versailles and the *Grand Monarque*, made a practice of selling their subjects abroad as soldiers. In several smaller German states, men became one of the chief articles of export. It was a remunerative, albeit unsavory, business; when volunteering failed to produce the desired number of men for foreign service, man hunts were staged by the princes to round up recruits.[3] As usual, British guineas worked wonders; over thirty thousand German troops were supplied Great Britain during the War of American Independence, and of this number, eighteen thousand saw service in North America. It was, of course, the princes who reaped the profits of this traffic, and there was no customer with whom they more delighted to do business than Great Britain.

By the terms of their contracts with the British government, the princes were allowed a lump sum for every man killed, and every three men wounded were reckoned as a man killed. Thus, every time an

[3] None knew better than the Landgraves of Hesse-Cassel the value of a recruit; they had sold men to Venice to fight the Turks and to the Italian states to fight other Italian states. Of course, such prodigality threatened to depopulate the country, but the Landgraves set their subjects an admirable example by begetting scores of children: Frederick II, Landgrave at the time of the American Revolution, was the proud father of more than one hundred children.

Although Americans called all German troops "Hessians," actually Hesse-Cassel furnished only about twelve hundred men to the British army during the war.

American bullet went home, the princes' cash register rang up a sale. After a battle, American soldiers sometimes counted the score in dead and wounded Germans to determine how much profit had accrued to the princes from the blood shed by their subjects.

When it came to selling their subjects to the British, the German princes were not above palming off as first-class soldiers men tottering under the infirmities of old age or disease. The British asked for prime human flesh, but the princes gave them inferior cuts. "Only picture to your imagination," said a British officer upon surveying several regiments of German troops, "ensigns of forty and fifty, commanding troops not much younger, and judge how proper they are for an active and vigorous campaign in the thick woods of America." Among these soldiers were to be found one-eyed veterans, broken-down ne'er-do-wells, students, renegade priests, and many others who found it convenient to leave the country in the shortest possible order. Some had never carried a musket or pitched a tent. On the other hand, there were crack regiments, such as the Prince of Hesse's Bodyguards, that compared favorably with the best in the British army.

Off duty, the Germans seemed hardly to merit the reputation for fierceness that they won for themselves early in the war. Quiet and peaceable, they spent a good part of their time singing hymns — in which, remarked a British officer, they were "as bad as the Yankees, though it must be owned they have not the godly twang through the nose which distinguishes the faithful." It also distinguished them from the British troops, who were seldom found at their devotions. This difference between the two nations was strikingly revealed when the British and Hessians went into action together against the Americans on Manhattan Island. Finding themselves in a tight spot, the Hessians began immediately to sing hymns, whereas the British "expressed their feelings as strongly, though in a different manner, by damning themselves and the enemy indiscriminately with wonderful fervency."

Hurling mercenaries against free men struggling for liberty! In the eyes of the English Whigs, England had never sunk so low. Edmund Burke was agonized to see "the liberal government of this free nation" seeking the aid of "a few traders in human flesh" and thrusting "the hireling sword of German boors and vassals" against Englishmen guilty of no greater crime than raising the standard of freedom. Lord Chatham declared that "40,000 German boors can never conquer ten times the number of British freemen; they may ravage; they can never conquer." These mercenaries, the Whigs warned, might soon be turned against English as well as American liberty: victorious over the colonists, the King might make himself absolute by means of foreign mercenaries, and Englishmen would learn too late that the rights of Americans were the first line of defense of English freedom.

From the point of view of British commanders in America, however, the government was at fault not in employing mercenaries but in failing to provide them in greater numbers. Constantly they implored the home government to send more mercenaries, without whose aid they held out no prospect of vanquishing the rebellion. Sir William Howe much preferred Germans and Russians to American Loyalists as soldiers — give him ten thousand Russians, he exclaimed in 1777, and he would guarantee to end the war in a single campaign. General Sir Henry Clinton fretted that more Germans were not sent to America; and General Burgoyne, after the battle of Bunker Hill, declared that there was no prospect of speedy victory unless large numbers of foreign mercenaries, Canadians, Indians, and Negroes were thrown into battle. With the aid of these redoubtable allies the British army, he said, "might possibly do the business in one campaign." All these generals agreed that "such a pittance of troops as Great Britain and Ireland can supply will only serve to protract the war, to much fruitless expense, and ensure disappointment." And even if Great Britain could furnish the manpower, it would be better, they reasoned, to employ experienced veterans from the European continent than raw, undisciplined levies from the home islands.

In answer to the Whigs' squeamishness over employing German mercenaries against Americans, it was pointed out that Great Britain had utilized mercenaries in many previous wars without incurring moral opprobrium — in 1745, Germans had been brought into Great Britain itself to aid in smothering rebellion in the Highlands. It was argued that German mercenaries would restore peace to America quicker and cheaper than could Englishmen alone: no pensions or half pay needed to be paid them, thus relieving Great Britain of the obligation of paying for the war long after the last shot had been fired. If the Germans proved ruthless and brutal, rebels deserved nothing better. As for destroying liberty in the empire by means of mercenaries, this objection, in George III's opinion, did not apply to the business in hand: the mother country was seeking to free Americans from the tyranny of demagogues and republicans, and surely it mattered little to the colonists if their deliverers happened to be paid for the job and their manners left something to be desired.

The spectacle of the mother country rounding up hirelings to do the dirty work of tyranny convinced thousands of Americans, hitherto loyal to Great Britain, that independence offered the only security to liberty. Moreover, it proved to the satisfaction of the rebellious elements in the colonies that Great Britain by itself was incapable of overcoming American resistance. However loudly it might roar, the British lion seemed so toothless and infirm that it was forced to depend upon "German Blood-hounds hired from all the German Traffickers in Blood, in all the petty Principalities of Germany." Let George III employ "Hes-

s not an empty title but the very foundation of England's greatness,
e source of the strength that enabled it to stand against its enemies.
To permit "a few hardy ringleaders of an unnatural rebellion" to de-
roy this rich inheritance was intolerable to Englishmen. "Our stately
brick is too well founded and compactly built," it was pointed out,
to be pushed down by a few *Rebel Yankeys*, who, like frogs in the sun,
ave grown wanton and petulant, under its *too benign* influence." That
he upheaval was the work of a few demagogues and fanatics was a set-
led conviction among many Englishmen; in their eyes, the causes of the
Revolution lay solely in the perversity of its leaders. Of the members
of the Continental Congress, an Englishman remarked that the "Arrogance assumed by the Offspring of Regicides, Convicts, and transported
Slaves, to me is grating." General Burgoyne conceded that John Adams
was "as great a conspirator as ever subverted a state," but he was not
prepared to admit the New Englander's title to statesmanship.

Moreover, if Englishmen tamely swallowed insults and permitted their
mastery of the empire to be called into question, the laws overthrown,
and the royal governors forced to flee in terror of their lives, "what
would in that event all Europe think of us'? Presumably, Europe would
rejoice in the humiliation of the mistress of the seas and prepare to lend
a hand in pulling down the British Empire.

Thus national interest, pride, and prestige demanded that England
move without delay to suppress sedition in its colonies and punish the
leaders. Although few except true-blue Tories rejoiced in this struggle,
most Englishmen admitted its necessity. With much justice, Lord North
declared that the majority of his countrymen regarded the conflict as
"a war founded in right, and dictated by necessity . . . a truly British
war, carried on upon British principles, and for the true and ultimate
interests of Britain."

The necessity of keeping the colonies in subjection was manifest; yet
to hold them against their will seemed to call for justification. In part,
this was provided by drawing an analogy between parental authority and
the rights of a mother country over its colonies; it was no less justifiable,
said the apologists of coercion, to retain the colonies in constitutional
subordination to the mother country than for parents to maintain authority over their children. In this conception of empire there was, however, one important flaw: colonies, unlike children, were never permitted to grow up and break away from the maternal apron strings.

Americans had a very different conception of their rights within the
empire, and against filial obedience they set the right of self-determination. Nor did they believe that in their struggle for freedom, victory
would necessarily incline to the side of the heaviest battalions. Despite
the disparity in strength of the combatants, they took comfort in the
fact that geography was on the side of the rebellion: separated from

sians, Tories, Negroes, Japanese, Moors, Esquim
Laplanders, Feejee Islanders," and any others he m
"heroes of liberty" could whip them all!

Despite these brave words, Americans had high
not be necessary to fight the German mercenaries
no quarrel with the colonists and fought for pay rat
viction, and who were kinsmen of many thousand (
The mercenaries, in short, seemed to be the weakest
armor. "If we can alienate the foreign troops from th
said General Nathanael Greene, "we inevitably ruin (
her own natural strength is totally insufficient." Therefc
them that Americans directed their most potent propag
moment they arrived in America, the Germans were ex
side to temptations to desert to the rebels. Land, oxen,
complete farm except for the *Frau* — were offered them
and besides these material rewards, they were promised reli
and the guarantees of liberty and property enjoyed by eve
Washington recommended that companies of German-A
raised and sent among the German mercenaries "for excitin
disaffection and desertion"; and in 1778, Congress authorizec
tion of a corps of German Volunteers consisting of desertec
German troops in British service. German prisoners of war w
far more leniently than were British prisoners: the Hessians, saic
sylvania Council of Safety, ought to be regarded "as a people
wish to unite with ourselves in improving the fertile forests of
extending its manufactures & Commerce, and maintaining its Lil
independency." Even their plundering was forgiven: it was tl
ple of the British, the patriots chose to believe, that had led th
mable Germans astray.

⌢ ⌢ ⌢

In the mother country, the revolt of the colonies was often pic
as a struggle between Great Britain and America for supremacy i
English-speaking world. If Britain triumphed, the center of politica
economic authority would remain in the Old World; but if the col
were victorious, the inexhaustible resources and rapidly growing pe
lation of the United States seemed destined ultimately to overwhe
Great Britain and to make the island kingdom "a vassal to her own
bellious colonies" — in which event, it could hardly be expected that En
land would be spared the final abomination of democracy. Seldom ha
Great Britain gone to war in a cause more vital, in its own eyes, t
its survival as a great power than when it took up arms against its rebellious American colonists. To Englishmen, the sovereignty of America

the mother country by three thousand miles of ocean requiring at least six weeks to traverse, some Americans concluded that they might safely defy all Europe. The scale of the country to be conquered by British arms afforded added confidence to the patriots. In the thirteen revolted provinces there were no large cities the capture of which would put an end to the rebellion; and Americans were far too provincial a people to look upon any one city as the capital of the country. Lacking a nerve center, the rebellion could not be struck a vital blow. How, it was asked, could the power of the British army be brought to bear against "farmers and farm-houses, scattered through a wild waste of continent"?

Although numerically inferior to the British, Americans did not expect to stand alone against the mother country. Their strategy was to involve the entire empire in resistance to the centralizing policy of the King and Ministry. By means of the doctrine of no taxation without representation — the watchword of the American Revolution — the patriots hoped to bring down the empire about the heads of their oppressors. To that end, they attempted to enlist the aid of Irishmen, Canadians, West Indians, and even the English people themselves. The cause of America was proclaimed to be the cause of liberals everywhere in the British Empire; and it was confidently expected that the British government would be forced either to yield to the patriots or to face the consequence of civil war in all quarters of the empire. In this spirit Benjamin Franklin, in July 1775, submitted to the Continental Congress a plan of confederation providing that Ireland, the British West Indies, Quebec, St. John's, Nova Scotia, Bermuda, and East and West Florida were free to join the American union on terms of equality with the original thirteen colonies. Unless the British government withdrew its troops from America and made full reparation for the damage they had committed, Franklin proposed that this confederation be made perpetual — a new American Empire, composed of free men, rising on the ruins wrought by the misgovernment of England.

But the greatest strength of the colonists seemed to reside in the fact that they were fighting for freedom on their home soil. "It is not a field or a few acres of ground, but a cause, that we are defending," said Thomas Paine. ". . . We fight not to enslave, but to set a country free and to make room upon the earth for honest men to live in." Like other patriots, Paine pinned his faith to his countrymen's morale, which, it was supposed, was immeasurably superior to that of the enemy. In the American creed, free men always triumphed over the foes of liberty; and believing themselves to be fighting "the powers of Darkness on this Globe," they did not doubt of victory. The American soldier was expected to surmount such handicaps as shortages of arms, clothing, medicine, and every other essential of war; simply by resolving to conquer or to die he would vanquish the enemies of freedom. Congress gave expression to this prevailing belief in the omnipotence of morale when it assured the people that "Courage warmed with Patriotism" would conquer all; and, in like spirit, Washington urged his countrymen to remember "what a few brave men contending in their own land, and in the best of causes can do, against base hirelings and mercenaries."

Certainly the goal of the Revolution was one of the loftiest ever held up to men: to create a country, and a world, where liberty and justice would prevail for all time. "The Blood and treasure of the Choicest and best Spirits of this Land is but a trifling Consideration for this rich Inheritance," said Anthony Wayne; for out of this conflict was to emerge "a new empire . . . which will rise superior to all that have gone before it, and extend human happiness to its utmost possible limits." Thomas Jefferson predicted that America would give "liberty to half the globe" and that millions who had never seen the republic would one day rise up and call it blessed.

This new world was to be called into being not by the conquering armies but by the more powerful principles which Americans upheld. Americans would conquer the world by the force of their ideas; they would work a revolution in the minds of men. Tyranny could not successfully compete with freedom for the allegiance of mankind: ultimately the world itself must become free. Moreover, by serving as a refuge to the oppressed people of the earth, America would powerfully abet the eventual triumph of freedom. By drawing unto itself the best of humanity — those who loved liberty above all else — America would become a stronghold of democracy, and the "industry, the virtue and the wisdom of the world will centre in these free and independent States."

This was the philosophy of 1776.

No doubt, in contemplating the future glory of the United States, some Americans permitted their imaginations to run away with them. For example, in the vision of a patriot of '76, the "imperial Americans" of 1980, when going abroad to inspect the ruins of Rome and Athens, include a side trip to the ruins of London. A voyage to Great Britain is like a slumming expedition, all the best Englishmen having long since emigrated to "the empire of America . . . which now gives laws to so many regions," and those who remain are starving and in rags. It was difficult for Americans of the revolutionary era to believe that the grandeur of the United States was compatible with a strong and vigorous Britain.

If Englishmen did not fear Americans as fighting men, they might justly fear them as husbands and fathers. Enthusiastically obeying the Biblical injunction, the colonists doubled their numbers every twenty years by natural means. Americans boasted that their climate — a perhaps too modest explanation of this phenomenon — was in all the world "the most favourable to the propagation of human species." In striking contrast Englishmen, denied the exhilarating effects of the American climate, doubled their numbers (at the then prevailing rate of increase) in little less than five hundred years. From these statistics, it could be readily seen where the course of empire was tending. Englishmen might well have concluded that the time to settle matters with these spawning republicans across the Atlantic was before they had inherited the earth by dint of numbers.

John Adams calculated that about twenty thousand fighting men were added annually to the population of the United States — from whence Benjamin Franklin drew the moral that it was hopeless for Great Britain to wage war against the republic. Thanks to the stout loins of its sons, he said to an Englishman, the United States "grows faster than you can diminish her and will outgrow all the mischief you can do her." The British might defeat the armies but they never could conquer the nurseries of America: like "another Hercules in its cradle, contending with another serpent," the infant republic would triumph. "Oppression may retard their progress, while it increases their hatred," it was said, "but grow they must, though a *Pharaoh* were their despot."

In part, the secret of this abounding fecundity was early marriages. Girls were frequently married at the age of thirteen. Child brides were distinctly in favor among the revolutionary fathers. Launched into marriage — and usually maternity — at such a tender age, it was inevitable that they looked old before they were thirty; and at forty, travelers observed, they were sometimes toothless hags.[4]

Yet, unless Americans were willing to fight as well as to replenish the earth, there was little hope that they could stave off the enemy. Heedful of this necessity, the patriots declared that any American who was not willing to die to save his country was unworthy of liberty. They anticipated no dearth of heroes in the United States. It was generally expected that hundreds of thousands of Americans would spring to arms, and some spoke confidently of raising an army of half a million men.

The outpouring of manpower in 1775 justified the high hopes of the patriot leaders. In New England, almost fifty thousand men were under arms; in Pennsylvania, some twenty-five thousand volunteers, including "the men of best fortune and character in the province," joined the colors. Farmers, town workers, and college students turned out in response to the call for men; in May 1775, the Princeton students formed a military company composed entirely of officers. Whether privates or officers, in their first flush of martial enthusiasm, Americans asked only for an opportunity to meet "the ministerial butchers," "the bloody instruments of tyranny," in fair fight. "If we turn aside," they vowed, "may God shut the Door of Mercy on us." There were seemingly no privations or sacrifices which Americans were not ready to undergo in the cause of freedom. To those

---

[4] The early decay of the teeth of American women was often remarked by travelers in the colonies. Some ascribed it to the practice, general in colonial America, of drinking copious quantities of hot tea.

who had never seen a battlefield, what could be more glorious – in anticipation – than to die for liberty?

Although few Englishmen realized it in 1775, they were fighting against a skilled and resourceful enemy. The training Americans had received in warfare was along the lines of frontier fighting: they were more indebted to the Indians than to Frederick the Great. Instead of employing the stiff, formal maneuvers of European armies, Americans fought from behind trees and houses, converting them into temporary fortresses. From logs they constructed blockhouses which proved invulnerable to artillery fire. It was in the forests of America that these methods had proved their merit; and it was here that Americans expected to write the doom of the British armies sent against them. It would be Braddock's defeat over again, but this time on a far greater scale. "In the Woods," said an American officer, "we shall be a Match for them, and was their number trebled have I the least doubt, but we should be superior to them in force as we are in Virtue." [5]

Although it was hardly true – as was sometimes claimed – that every American was a sharpshooter capable of hitting a British officer between the eyes at a hundred paces, the colonists were certainly more experienced in the use of firearms than were the English. In the mother country, the common people were forbidden to use guns, whereas in the colonies, particularly along the frontier, there was a close connection between longevity and quickness on the draw. The rawest recruits in the American army were often better marksmen than were veterans in the British army; Lafayette once said that American soldiers, even the greenest hands, knew more about handling a gun than did three quarters of the soldiers of Europe.

[5] Most of the soldiers on the American side in the War of Independence saw action for the first time in that struggle, and almost half the generals received their training in the war itself. Of the generals who had prior military training, over half were Englishmen who had held commissions in the British army and subsequently settled in the colonies.

CHAPTER II

The Leaders

THE Continental Congress, the head and front of colonial resistance to Great Britain, was composed of representatives elected by the legislatures or conventions of the thirteen revolted colonies. Summoned to deal with the crisis precipitated by the Boston Tea Party, the Continental Congress first met in Philadelphia in 1774. Upon it were centered the hopes of American freedom and American nationalism. Thanks to British "tyranny," Americans learned, albeit at first imperfectly, that only in union were to be found strength and salvation.

Despite the fact that the Continental Congress was unsanctioned by King or Parliament and therefore enjoyed no constitutional standing, Lord Chatham pronounced it to be the most distinguished assemblage of men in the English-speaking world. In this verdict, posterity has concurred; but unfortunately for the British Empire, the Englishmen who discerned elements of greatness in these transatlantic statesmen were out of power in 1776. The party in office was little disposed to attribute talents, or even probity, to the American revolutionaries: Lord North and his colleagues were fond of disparaging the "vagrant Congress" and the "demagogues" and "intriguing republicans" who presided over its councils. It is fair to say that the rulers of England were wholeheartedly committed to the proposition that no good could come out of the Continental Congress.

The age of most members of Congress was little more than forty; in 1776, when he wrote the Declaration of Independence, Thomas Jefferson was only thirty-three. A study of vital statistics of the membership of this body might well have persuaded Englishmen that their chief enemy was the ardor of youth. In Congress, as all over America, young men were responding to the exhilarating impact of a new humane philosophy, and to the confidence and optimism engendered by contact with a country of boundless resources. It augured well for the future of the American republic that in the beginning its destinies were guided by men of such enlightened outlook as those who met in the State House in Philadelphia. Standing on the fringes of western civilization, these men were in the vanguard of a movement destined in the next century to remake that civilization in the image of democracy. The state papers that issued from the Continental Congress laid the foundations of a new order that was to sweep the world.

Many members of Congress came from the top layer of colonial society — the conservative, propertied group which, had Great Britain pursued a different colonial policy, might have remained sturdy upholders of the empire. Men whose natural bent led them to support the established order, and who loved the British Empire as a great conservative institution, reluctantly helped to cut the connection between mother country and colonies. Gouverneur Morris, whose father was a lord of the manor in New York and who always favored strong government against the "riotous mob"; James Duane, a New York lawyer, conservative to the core; John Jay, whose family was among the social leaders of New York and who faithfully reflected in Congress the conservative point of view of American businessmen; Henry Laurens of South Carolina, merchant and planter, one of the wealthiest men in that colony; George Washington, whose wealth and social position were at first better known to the delegates than were his military talents; John and Edward Rutledge, South Carolinians who had studied at the Middle Temple and had been admitted to the English bar and who feared the "low Cunning, and those levelling Principles" of New Englanders; Charles Carroll of Maryland, educated in France and England, one of the wealthiest men in the country — these are hardly the stuff of which revolutionaries are made. Certainly they gave the lie to the sneer that the American Revolution was the work of a "rabble in arms"; from the British point of view, the most menacing aspect of the upheaval was that so many of the wealthiest, most vigorous, and most talented men in the colonies were on the side of rebellion. British policy, it is true, had helped to put them there, but Englishmen could scarcely acclaim this as an achievement.

In this select circle of the well-born and opulent, Sam Adams of Boston was regarded by some as an unwelcome intruder. Older than most of the delegates, Adams brought to the Continental Congress well-known talents as a propagandist and politician that had made him a terror to the Tories of New England. Adams's virtuosity in manipulating mobs and delving in backstairs politics sharply distinguished him from his cousin, John Adams, and indeed from all other Adamses; but it must be borne in mind that his cousinship with John was distant and that Sam, unlike his Braintree relatives, was a Bostonian born and bred. Adroit, patient, and persevering, he moved with single-minded devotion to his goal: to make the United States independent and to establish the sovereignty of the people.

⌢ ⌢ ⌢

In holding George III personally and solely responsible for the American Revolution, Americans did their sovereign a palpable injustice. It was good propaganda but poor history to portray George as the chief culprit and number one enemy of liberty in the British Empire. In writing the Declaration of Independence, Thomas Jefferson was too concerned with making out a case for his own theory of empire, and too intent upon demolishing the reputation of the King — in itself a formidable obstacle to independence — to deal fairly with George III. Seen from this side of the Atlantic, George was — and still is — a monster among British Kings. It is fair to say, however, that Americans have seldom received an unprejudiced view of the last King to reign over the thirteen colonies. Perhaps it is not too late to remedy some of the defects of the portrait of George III that has been handed down to Americans.

George III was eminently fitted to adorn private life. Seldom have the domestic virtues had a more brilliant exemplification in a British monarch. Those who saw him in his family circle, surrounded by his progeny — neatly arranged in gradations — beheld an aspect of his character unrevealed to most of his subjects in America. "It is impossible," exclaimed an American Loyalist after meeting the King, " — a man of his fine feelings, so good a husband, so kind a Father, *cannot be a Tyrant*." His domestic blessings were undeniably numerous — his fifteenth child was born in 1783, the year he lost the thirteen colonies. The King, it can be said, was doing his utmost to replenish the empire.

Moreover, he was a serious-minded, diligent, and conscientious ruler. He took his duties solemnly and had little time for levity. Indeed, it required a great deal of hard work on the part of the King and his ministers to lose the empire.

The monarch was never able to fathom why Englishmen, upon emigrating to America, degenerated into rebels and republicans. Far from admitting that they were "poor mild persons who after unheard of and repeated grievances had no choice but Slavery or the Sword," he regarded them as born rebels who took advantage of England's leniency and good nature. The wickedness of Cromwellian times, he once remarked, seemed to have crossed the Atlantic and to have grown rankly in the English colonies. "They are a sad nest," was his considered opinion.

It was not George III's intention to reduce the colonies to his personal rule, as the Declaration of Independence implies; he proposed rather to restore the authority of the British Parliament over the revolted regions of the empire, assured that in so doing he was carrying out the ordinances of God. "I feel the justness of our cause," he declared; "I put the greatest confidence in the valour of both Navy and Army and above all in the Assistance of Divine Providence." Yet, despite his anxiety to restore the empire, the King proved to be one of the greatest obstacles to reunion. Although once revered in the American colonies as a guileless young man unhappily in the grip of wicked ministers, after 1776 he bore the reputation, among many of his former subjects, of "the cruel and bloody *Nero* of Britain"; "a Blood thirsty inhuman Scoundrel that . . . can hear of the Slaughter of his Subjects and laugh at it." Benjamin Franklin said that when the history of the Revolution came to be written, George III would "stand foremost in the list of diabolical, bloody, and execrable tyrants." The war was a "devilish contest," said Franklin — thanks largely to the King's rancor against Americans.

Lord North, the wartime Prime Minister and confidant of George III, sprang from one of those honorable families that composed the governing class of eighteenth-century England. North had served his apprenticeship under Charles Townshend, a brilliant but erratic Chancellor of the Exchequer, and having won the reputation of being an able and diligent man of business, succeeded to the chancellorship after Townshend's death. A few years later, in 1770, when the Duke of Grafton "suddenly threw up the seals and retired to his diversions and his mistress at Newmarket," North became Prime Minister.

The head of the government was a stout, hearty Englishman — a beefeater who might have passed for John Bull himself. A contemporary summed up his impression of Lord North in these words: "large legs, walks heavily, manner clumsy, very large featured, thick lips, wide mouth, high forehead, large nose, eyes not lively." He bore a close resemblance to his master, George III, and gossip did not overlook that his mother had been a close friend of the father of George III. Like the King, he was a good family man: those who knew him best said that he was "formed for the enjoyment of domestic comforts, and to shine in the most elegant societies."

Like many fat men, Lord North was easygoing and good-humored — valuable qualities for a man who, during the twelve years he served as Prime Minister, was denounced by some of the greatest orators in English history: Barré, Chatham, Fox, Sheridan, and Burke. Probably no English Prime Minister has ever taken more abuse over a longer period of time. For the most part, North bore this vilification in silence — he left the speechmaking to the Whigs and, while the storm of words swirled and raged about him, sat like a rock which only at intervals appeared above the froth. He listened to the Whig orators — when he was not dozing — with an equanimity gained from long experience as a butt of masters of invective; and he even learned to admire their flights of vituperation. Appreciative of crack marksmanship even when he was the target, he was known to applaud a particularly telling insult hurled at him. Invective "always seemed to sink into him, like a Cannon Ball into a Wool Sack." In perfect command of his temper, North seldom gave the Whigs the satisfaction of seeing that he was hurt: they hit him often but rarely drew blood.

North's habit of dozing quietly through long-winded orations in the House of Commons made him the object of much raillery among the members. Burke, for example, once said that he "hoped that government was not dead, but only asleep." At this moment he looked directly at Lord North, who was asleep, and said, in the Scripture phrase, 'Brother Lazarus is not dead, but sleepeth.' " The Prime Minister entered heartily into the laugh "as soon as he was sufficiently awake to understand the course of the joke." Threatened with impeachment and death, he was roused from his cat nap by the thunderous declamations hurled against him, but only to complain that he was denied "a solace which other criminals so often enjoyed, that of having a night's rest before their fate." On another occasion, North remarked to Fox after that Whig orator had delivered a particularly stinging attack upon Lord George Germain: "Charles, I am glad you did not fall on me to-day, for you was in full feather."

To these engaging traits, North joined considerable skill as a party manager: he was at his best in distributing patronage where it would do the most good, smoothing over personal differences between party members, and keeping the King's followers in Parliament contented. Possessed of only a small estate with which to support his large and growing family, North was seldom free from financial worry; yet, although he practised wholesale corruption in Parliament, he himself was not corrupt. Vast amounts of public money passed through his hands, but even his enemies did not allege that the Prime Minister pocketed any part of these funds. As First Lord of the Treasury, he lived beyond his income, but he eked out by borrowing rather than by resorting to graft. On one occasion, the harassed Prime Minister, bursting into tears, told the House of Commons that "naked he came into the world, naked he should go out of it."

The qualities of amiability and temperateness which endeared Lord North even to his critics did not distinguish the character of Lord George Germain, the Colonial Secretary upon whom devolved a large part of the conduct of the war. Harsh, domineering, and autocratic, Lord George Germain seemed to epitomize the most objectionable traits of the "tyrannical Britons" against whom Amercians rebelled. His career was marked by spectacular ups and downs. Born George Sackville, the son of the Duke of Dorset, he entered the army, rose rapidly in rank, and in 1756 attained command of the British forces fighting under the leadership of Prince Ferdinand of Brunswick against the French. At the battle of Minden, Sackville refused to lead his forces into action at the orders of the allied commander; and for this dereliction of duty he was court-martialed, expelled from the Privy Council, and declared unfit to serve the King. Branded as a coward, cut in society, and debarred from high office, George Sackville seemed consigned to oblivion.

And so he was; but he rose again under the name Germain. Gradually he fought his way back into favor, and in 1765 he was restored his seat in the Privy Council. It was the outbreak of civil war in the empire, however, that gave Germain his opportunity to redeem his reputation: he now emerged as the most vindictive and implacable enemy of the American colonists, the foremost to demand "Roman severity" towards the rebels. In 1775, sixteen years after his disgrace at Minden, he rode into office as Secretary of State for the Colonies, on the crest of the wave of anger toward the American rebels that swept England in that year.

Germain quickly emerged as the "strong man" of the Ministry. Lord North's fondness for taking his ease, and his reluctance to act the part of Prime Minister, gave Germain a free hand in his office. The new Colonial Secretary entered with zest upon his duties; he was quite prepared to take upon his own shoulders the entire direction of the war. And he was not, the Tories thanked God, a puling Methodist like Lord Dartmouth, his predecessor in office, but a red-blooded Englishman, keenly resentful of the slightest insult to the majesty of Great Britain. Germain would have no truck with rebels, and his prescription for settling the rebellion — unconditional surrender and a Draconic peace — delighted the hearts of the Tories, in whose eyes he loomed as a tower of strength. In Parliament, he revealed himself to be a man of great vigor and firmness, untroubled by doubts as to the rightness of his course. Among the wavering and timid members he radiated confidence; and even the cautious and uncertain Prime Minister found comfort in Germain's air of assurance and illimitable strength of purpose.

Germain took office in 1775 little doubting that a vigorous prosecution of the war would quickly wind up the rebellion in North America. By gathering the full force of Great Britain in one mighty effort, he expected to end the war in one campaign; by his reckoning, 1776 was to be the year of decision. "Nothing," he declared, "is so much to be wished for as a decisive Action. . . . One decisive blow by land is absolutely necessary. After that, the whole will depend upon the diligence and activity of the officers of the Navy." From his headquarters in London, Germain annihilated the American army many times over, executing prodigies of maneuvers that baffled and dismayed Washington and finally ended the rebellion in utter rout. Unfortunately for Great Britain, these triumphs existed only on paper; and Germain's bold and brilliant strokes of war were sometimes found, on execution, to have failed to take into account such relevant matters as geography and transport.

It must be confessed that few English ministers succumbed so completely to their prejudices, their insularity, and their pride in being "true-born Britons" as did Lord George Germain. The Colonial Secretary, in fact, glorified these weaknesses into virtues — and at the very time when Englishmen most needed wisdom, forbearance, and a conciliatory frame of mind. He pandered to every failing of Englishmen: he told them that they did right to hold the colonists in contempt, to ignore their grievances, and to exalt prejudice over reason. Whenever conciliation was mentioned, Germain began to talk about England's honor; to renounce even the right of taxation, he declared, would be to abandon sovereignty over the colonies. Every gesture of appeasement made by Great Britain was accomplished over Germain's bitter opposition.

Germain was in his best form when jeering at the courage of Americans. In his opinion, the distinguishing features of Americans were cowardice, moral depravity, and boorishness; he declined to acknowledge them as *his* cousins and he strongly implied that if they were Englishmen at all, they were a lesser breed than those who had remained at home. His confidence in the superiority of British troops over such "peasants" was unshakable; indeed, it transcended that of English generals in the field, whom he frequently found it necessary to remind that the troops they commanded were invincible. "The Spirit & Intrepidity of the King's Troops," he assured Sir Henry Clinton, "will always triumph over them [the Americans], and . . . however they may exceed in Numbers, the Vigor and Perseverance of the British Soldiers will overcome all Resistance." Sir Henry was expected to be properly thankful for such invaluable information; nevertheless, Sir Henry continued to ask for reinforcements.

In this labor of reviling Americans, Germain was ably abetted by Lord Sandwich, the First Lord of the Admiralty. In Lord Sandwich's words, Americans were "the most treacherous, infamous, worthless race of men that God ever permitted to inhabit the earth" — which raises the question why he was so anxious to have them back in the empire. If the First Lord was to be believed, the American army would hardly serve as a breakfast for the redcoats; nor could the battle be regarded as a sporting event, so overwhelming would be the rout of the rebels. In the fullness of his illusion, he predicted that the Americans would "never meet our people in fair conflict": only when firing from behind rocks or trees or when raised to frenzy by their poisonous rum would they offer any semblance of battle. "Have we not conquered the French and the Spaniards," he asked rhetorically; "and shall we be afraid of a body of *fanatics* in New-England, who will bluster and swell when danger is at a distance, but when it comes near, will like all other mobs throw down their arms and run away?" In short, they would behave in the same manner as did those people to whom they bore such close resemblance — the natives of Bengal. The Bengalese, said Sandwich, "are also fanatics; but it is well-known that a few of our troops will rout the greatest number of them; and were I," he added, "in General Gage's situation [in Boston] and heard that 20,000

New-England men were coming against me, I should wish that they were rather thirty or forty thousand" — the more rebels, the greater the stampede when they came up against the British.

Lord Sandwich told the French ambassador that the English were at a cruel disadvantage in making peace with their revolted provinces because they were "embarrassed by the word 'liberty' " and impeded by "the difficulties of the English Constitution with regard to the administration of the Colonies." Germain's plans for reconstructing the British Empire, however, would have made the "tyranny" against which the Americans rebelled seem insignificant. He would have stripped the colonies of their representative form of government and held them down by military force — Rhode Island, the most democratic of the colonies, was scheduled to become an army base. And prominent in Germain's agenda was the establishment of an hereditary aristocracy in the American colonies "for the purpose of creating distinctions of ranks, and to draw them nearer to the model of the British government."

Whatever may be said of Germain, he was a stalwart Englishman to whom strife was a delight. It was by means of the American war, after all, that he hoped to restore his reputation and to make his name in history; therefore, it is not surprising that he displayed toward that war all the fondness of a parent for an ailing child; as other Englishmen lost their affection for this ill-starred stripling, Germain's increased apace. Being an experienced gamester, he knew that a run of bad luck does not last forever. "There is," he said in 1778, "a great deal due to us from fortune, and I hope our luck will turn before we are quite ruin'd." This was hardly the language he had used in 1776; yet, for the most part, Germain lived in almost daily expectation of witnessing the collapse of the rebellion.

Although the tight little island bred tight little minds, it also produced minds of a liberal and progressive cast which, had they been given free play, might have solved the problems of empire. Most men of the first magnitude — those whose names are most often remembered today — opposed the government's policy toward the colonies and, after the outbreak of war, took the side of the Americans. With few exceptions, these men were Whigs.[1]

Traditionally, the leadership of the Whig Party was recruited from the aristocracy. Although there were such notable exceptions as Lord Shelburne and Lord Chatham — who, as William Pitt, had led England to victory in the Seven Years' War — for the most part the Whig lords were a horsy set, deeply concerned with such momentous subjects as "the difficult pedigree of a promising filly," the likely winners at Newmarket, and the fine points of a hound. Many were better acquainted with "the jockey scales, than with the balance of Europe." Prodigally they devoted to

---

[1] The name "Tory" was going out of use in England, and I use the name to denote conservatives, as did the liberal branch of the Whig Party.

horses, the gaming table, and dissipation talents which properly belonged to the country of which they were the ruling class.

Edmund Burke was the oracle of the Rockingham Whigs [2] — a scholar and philosopher in politics. Born in Dublin, the son of a Protestant attorney, he entered English politics without the passport of a noble lineage or an education at Oxford or Cambridge. Literature and philosophy were his early interests: his first book was a disquisition upon the "Origin of our Ideas of the Sublime and Beautiful" — a subject which hardly prepared him for what he found in English politics. In 1765 he became secretary to Lord Rockingham, who had just become Prime Minister, and Rockingham gave Burke a seat in Parliament from a pocket borough belonging to the Rockingham family. To the end of his life, Burke made the House of Commons a second home and gave to politics an erudition and eloquence which made him the best-informed and the most powerful — but by no means the most graceful — speaker in Parliament. His speeches were in themselves a liberal education, although some of his fellow members, devoted neither to liberalism nor to education, pronounced him to be the greatest bore in Parliament. Not least among Burke's services to the Whig cause was his skill in gilding the rule of the Whig aristocracy as the perfect consummation of English liberty, although Burke himself, as an Irishman and a commoner, was debarred from leadership of his party.

Burke's Irish brogue — as thick "as if he had never quitted the banks of the Shannon" — and his somewhat uncouth mannerisms often grated upon the House, while his sternness, reserve, and intractableness repelled many who admired his erudition and ability. Moreover, his speeches, although masterpieces when read as literature, were less effective when delivered in the House of Commons; it was frequently complained that he stuffed his addresses with involved metaphors and allegories "spun out to a wearisome length." Burke's brilliant wit, his command of ridicule, satire, mockery, and pathos, were often lost upon the members, who objected to his long-windedness. Moreover, he was sometimes guilty, when overcome by emotion, of displaying intemperance and violence out of keeping with the code of the House; occasionally, his friends had to hold him down by the skirts of his coat in order to prevent him from giving vent to an uncontrollable outburst of passion. He was not a natural leader of men; he lacked the amiability and good fellowship that take a man farther in politics than do scholarship, honesty of purpose, and a masterly English prose style.

Charles James Fox began his parliamentary career as a conservative, and won his spurs by jibes at Edmund Burke that sent the whole House, and particularly the ministerial benches, into roars of laughter at the Irish-

[2] At this period the Whigs were divided into factions. The Rockingham Whigs (so called) followed the leadership of the Marquis of Rockingham. Lord Chatham refused to associate himself with any of the Whig factions.

man's expense. In those days, the Tories loved Fox; and in later years they always said of him that he had "when he was younger, been much wiser." Fox was a little Tory who grew up to be a Whig. His sojourn in the Tory camp was brief: the struggle between Great Britain and her colonies awakened the liberalism that was to be his distinguishing characteristic as an English statesman. Believing that the cause of America was "the cause of freedom, the cause of the constitution, the cause of whiggism," Fox parted company with the administration and threw in his lot with the Whigs.

Fox lacked the grand presence of Lord Chatham: short and fat, harsh of voice, haggard from dissipation, and clad in stained and threadbare clothes, he bore little resemblance to the conventional idea of a British statesman. From his father, who as paymaster of the forces during the Seven Years' War had amassed a fortune from the perquisites of that office and had been raised to the peerage as Lord Holland, Fox inherited great wealth. But in the eighteenth century a craze for gambling seized upon the British aristocracy; faro, whist, and other games of chance proved almost as effective as high taxes in reducing peers to a level with their butchers and bakers. Among the victims of this vice was Charles James Fox.

It has been said of Fox that he loved passionately three things: women, gambling, and politics. Ironically, he was seldom happy, during his early career at least, in his mistresses; he lost a fortune at play; and practically his entire political life was spent in opposition. No doubt it was his passion for gambling that brought upon him the greatest portion of unhappiness. Faro almost ruined his health and his public career. Englishmen were accustomed to seeing their statesmen at the gambling tables, but Fox devoted himself so wholeheartedly to play that it became difficult to regard him as anything more than a gambler. It might be true, as was said, that Fox, from long experience, knew how to borrow money on better terms than did Lord North and was therefore better qualified for the post of Chancellor of the Exchequer; but Englishmen might be forgiven for doubting if Fox, on his record, was a proper person to be entrusted with control of the country's finances.

Had Fox been content to confine himself to whist or piquet, at which he was singularly expert, he might have prospered: but he insisted upon trying his hand at faro, a game which to him was nemesis. On several occasions he lost so heavily that he was obliged to borrow money from the waiters at Brooks's to pay for his dinner. He admitted that gaming was a vice, "and a vice which carried with it its own punishment, and entailed a curse upon those who were addicted to it," but he could not free himself from the obsession: immediately after finishing a hard session in the House, he hurried to Brooks's to spend the night in frenzied play.

Fox not only ran through his own fortune: he began to borrow from any who would trust him. As a result, he could scarcely walk the streets

without being dunned for debt: moneylenders, chairmen, tailors, haber-
dashers swarmed around him until it seemed that a small riot was in
progress. And as his fortunes declined, Fox's appearance began to alter
for the worse: from a dandy he became a seedy-looking ne'er-do-well; his
clothes were neither new nor clean, and his hair was often uncombed.
Certainly there was nothing in his appearance to remind his friends of
the young fop who had driven across France in search of new patterns
for his waistcoats, and who had made a sartorial Grand Tour of Europe.

Having lost a fortune in play, Fox resolved not to give up gambling,
but to make it a profession. Experience had taught him that it was the
bankers who prospered — so why should he not change places at the board
and take other people's money instead of losing his own? Accordingly,
he organized a faro bank at Brooks's and set about relieving young Whigs
of their money. Charles and his brother Richard were the dealers or
bankers, and by doing shifts, they ran their table continuously. "The
vestal fire is perpetually kept up," it was said, "and they, like Salamanders,
owe their existence to and flourish in the flame."

As a faro banker, Fox's fortunes underwent a happy change. His patrons,
indeed, began to complain of that "damned Pharo bank which swallows
up everybody's cash that comes to Brooks's," but Fox was at last in his
glory. His affluence was reported to be prodigious; he bought race horses,
acquired a new mistress, and became again the swell of his younger days.

Charles Fox was saved from his vices by a fortunate choice in mistresses.
In 1782, he met Mrs. Armistead, who took him under her wing, weaned
him from gambling, and finally succeeded in domesticating him. Under
her benign influence, Fox's idea of bliss changed from a lucky winning
streak at Brooks's to a little cottage in the country, where he could live
surrounded by his books and listen to the nightingales in the garden.

Fox was one of the first Whigs to demand the recognition of American
independence. It was not, it is true, a consummation ardently desired by
him — for Fox was a good Englishman, George III's opinion notwithstanding — but early in the struggle he became convinced that there was
no feasible alternative. Like Burke, he believed that Englishmen could
"expect ten times more benefit to this kingdom from the affection of
America, though under a separate establishment, than from her perfect
submission to the crown and Parliament, accompanied with her terror,
disgust, and abhorrence."

Indeed, Fox and other Whigs exhibited such joy upon learning of British
defeats in America that the King swore they were no better than rebels
and traitors to their country. When Howe was victorious over the Americans, Fox spoke of "the terrible news from Long Island"; and Burke
remarked that "nothing but the success of Burgoyne's army could be more
deplorable than its capture." John Wilkes declared in Parliament that he
regarded British victories in America as losses "and our cause as an unjust

one," and he refused to thank British generals for their triumphs over the rebels, on the ground that they were not victories over "the natural enemies of Britain." Every British soldier who was killed in America ought to have inscribed upon his grave, said Wilkes, the statement that he had died because he had violated the "holy constitution" of England — "the best constitution on earth." Chatham rejoiced in Saratoga as though it were an English victory; what chiefly struck him in Burgoyne's downfall was the "nobleness, dignity, and humanity" of the victorious Americans.

Fox carried his opposition to the war to such lengths that administration supporters inquired whether he intended "to draw the sword, put on the American uniform, and enlist under Washington, to fight the battles of America, and point his sword against the breast of his countrymen." In the blue and buff of the Continental army which he affected, Fox's worn and haggard appearance might have led one to mistake him for some hard-bitten veteran of Long Island and Brandywine. His conduct, he was well aware, might bring him to the traitor's dock. "Who knows," he once remarked, "but the ministers, in the fullness of their malice, may take it into their heads, that I have served on Long Island, under General Washington?" Nevertheless, though the Tories screamed that "there never was a war waged by us before this in which a numerous and able Opposition, favoured, defended, abetted, justified, and encouraged THE ENEMY," Fox was not silenced: the government of George III, against which Americans rebelled as the worst of tyrannies, tolerated a freedom of opinion that no government today, under the stress of war, would endure.

During virtually the entire War of American Independence, Lord North, despite the vicissitudes of the struggle, remained in power as Prime Minister and the government was supported by large majorities in both houses of Parliament. While the Whig opposition charged that North was maintained in power by means of corruption emanating from the Crown, even the Whigs admitted that North owed his long tenure of office not merely to the purchase of votes of members of Parliament and of the electorate — although the King was indubitably a master of that art — but to the much more powerful force of public opinion. Outside London and a number of the larger commercial cities, the people generally supported the policy of coercing the colonies. Although elected by a small minority of the population, the House of Commons, at least as regards the war with the colonies, was not an unfaithful mirror of the public mind. The empire could not be given up without a struggle: had Parliament tamely yielded to the Americans, it would have forfeited the support of the British people.

The American Revolution, it should be borne in mind, occurred at a time when Great Britain was passing through a period of moral and spiritual letdown. For seven years — from 1756 to 1763 — the kingdom had waged war in both hemispheres against France, Spain, and Austria, and although the British emerged triumphant, they fell victim to the post-war enervation that sometimes overcomes the victors.

The upper classes tended to become soft, pleasure-loving, and indifferent to public affairs; and it was in this atmosphere of lassitude and heedlessness that they lost the fruits of victory. With their empire at the highest pitch of grandeur, all classes wished to relax. Discontent in such "far away regions" of the earth as America came as an unwelcome intrusion upon what had promised to be a long period of peace and prosperity. It was remarked that the British were "almost indifferent whether the French, the Pope, the Pretender, or the Devil, should take the reins of Government." Lord North they gladly endured.

This indifference or want of vigor could not be alleged against the British squirearchy, by far the most inveterate enemies of the American rebels. It was not necessary to buy the votes of the country gentlemen: staunch and intractable Tories, they voted from conviction on the side of government. Moreover, the squires supported the war not only by their votes but by their pocketbooks, for under the prevailing system of taxation the burden of the war fell upon the land. Sir Robert Walpole remarked, some years before, that "the landed gentlemen were like the flocks upon the plains; they suffered themselves to be shorn without resistance; while the trading part of the nation resembled the boar, who would not let a bristle be plucked from his back without making the whole parish echo with his complaint." On the other hand, the squires expected to be the chief gainers by a British victory: upon the colonists would be thrust part of the tax load under which English landowners staggered.

The country gentlemen composed the hard, impermeable core of English Toryism. Rallying round the King in defense of the rights of the mother country, they formed a phalanx of honest John Bulls. To the end, they persisted in coercing the colonies, unmindful of the warnings of the Whigs that the cost of the war would ultimately fall upon landowners of England. Appeasement found no favor among the country gentlemen: they were the last to support Lord North's peace offers. Any show of leniency toward the rebels disgusted the squires: their only criticism of Lord North was that he was not sufficiently severe. These hard-riding squires halloed the Ministry against the rebels as vigorously as they urged their hounds after a fox. To no avail, liberals raged that the squirearchy was a great dumb beast that fetched and carried for the Ministry. "The most short-sighted of all animals is undoubtedly our country gentleman of the true Tory breed," said John Wilkes. "He has scarcely the sagacity of his pointer. Formerly he was very stubborn and restive, and would not be driven forward. Now he is perfectly tame, fawns on his feeder, and is easily managed." Under this storm of invective, the squires sat dumb; but when the division came, they invariably sided with the Ministry.

With the notable exceptions of Dr. Johnson and Edward Gibbon, most eminent Englishmen were ranged against the government of Lord North.[3] But Gibbon and Johnson made up in zeal what they lacked in numbers: Johnson pamphleteered against the American rebels, and Gibbon, on one occasion, had himself carried to the House, swathed in flannel and supported by crutches, and sat up all night in order to cast his vote for the administration in an important division.

Americans in Great Britain warned their countrymen not to expect assistance from the English people. Franklin pronounced them as rancorous towards the rebels as even the King could wish. Except for reserving to themselves "the precious privilege of calling their King a fool, and his mother a w——e," Englishmen seemed content to give the Ministry a free hand. Franklin finally concluded that only a revolution could save England, but he doubted if the people had sufficient "virtue" to begin one; it was more probable, he remarked, that they would always have a King who ruled by bribery and corruption while the people were "obliged to pay by Taxes the Plunderers for Plundering and Ruining."

In this environment, the talents of the Whigs were frittered away in oratory: their finest flights of fancy were spent upon the desert air of a Tory Parliament. More and more, they began to appear like professional crapehangers, and their speeches to sound like funeral orations over the British Empire. Many times has that monumental institution been pronounced dead and buried and as often has it risen stronger than before — but the Whigs had no faith in miracles, certainly not as long as the Tories remained in power.

The Whigs got more satisfaction from the Tories by challenging them to duels: if the Tories dodged debate, let them dodge bullets! Fox, Shelburne, and other Whig leaders settled their affairs of honor regularly in Hyde Park. But Burke refused all duels — which, not being a gentleman born, he could do with impunity. He came very close to such an affair, however, when, during a debate in the House, he, "in the warmth of his indignation, threw the book of estimates at the Treasury bench, which, taking the candle in its way . . . nearly struck Mr. Ellis' shins."

Could the Whigs have enjoyed the consolation — sometimes vouchsafed unsuccessful politicians — that they had the people on their side, they might have borne their lot with greater equanimity. In the state of mind

---

[3] Boswell disagreed with Dr. Johnson over the American Revolution. He upheld the right of Americans to freedom from taxation by the British Parliament, but he always considered himself a good Tory. In his opinion, the colonists were bound to the mother country through the King, not through Parliament. "I am persuaded," he said, "that the power of the Crown, which I wish to encrease, would be greater when in contact with all its dominions, than if 'the rays of regal bounty' were to 'shine' upon America through that dense and troubled body, a modern British Parliament."

of the English people in 1776 it seemed probable, however, that the Whigs would be obliged to wait for posterity to accord them the popularity and esteem which they believed their due. Yet the Whigs could not tarry for posterity; George III and the Tories seemed to be steering straight for the breakers.

CHAPTER III

The Volcano Erupts

To PRESERVE order in Boston after the uproarious Tea Party of 1773, the British government dispatched several regiments to the Puritan metropolis. These troops soon found themselves in the position of hostages to fortune, for two thousand British regulars could not rule a population of four hundred thousand unruly Yankees and enforce the laws of Parliament which stripped them of liberties they had enjoyed for generations.[1] There were unmistakable signs that this handful of British soldiers was sitting on a volcano. All over the countryside, New Englanders were getting under arms and practising military exercises, including sharpshooting, on their village commons; and although they spoke of resisting a French invasion, it was strongly suspected that the "Frenchmen" wore red coats. Even children began to play, not at hunting Indians as had once been their pastime, but at mowing down British regulars. "Bang! And another redcoat bit the dust." Boston boasted a company of boys from ten to fourteen years of age who, in the opinion of the city fathers, could "go thro the whole military exercise much more dexterously than a very great part of the regulars" of the British army.

But the British were daunted by neither the embattled children nor the adults of New England: expeditions frequently sallied into the country from Boston to destroy stores of powder and arms and to overawe the patriots. Few British officers believed that the "peasants" would actually dare to fire upon the British uniform and thereby bring down upon their heads the wrath of the mother country. Knowing the temper of New Englanders, it might easily have been foreseen that sooner or later these

[1] This was the effect of the so-called "Coercive" or "Intolerable" Acts passed by the British Parliament in 1774 to punish Boston for the Tea Party.

raids would stir up a hornets' nest and that the British might not march back to Boston as bravely as they had marched out of the city.

The British, having got wind of a large store of powder and arms laboriously collected by the patriots at Concord, set out on the night of April 18, 1775, to destroy it. In this raid, however, the redcoats conspicuously lacked the element of surprise that might have made the march to Concord another routine foray: thanks to the hard riding of Paul Revere and William Dawes the countrypeople were warned of the danger. Before he completed his famous ride, Revere was captured by a small detachment of British troops who released him after cutting his girths and stirrups. The damage, however, had been done and the patriots were ready at Lexington to contest the advance of the British raiders.

But the British, too, were warned: on the march to Lexington, "a very genteel man" riding in a carriage informed them that about six hundred armed men were gathered on Lexington Common. On every hand were evidences that trouble was brewing: church bells were ringing, firing was heard in the woods near by, and as the British cautiously approached the village of Lexington, bullets were fired at them from houses on the outskirts. As they had been warned, a large number of Americans were drawn up on the Common. When British officers called out, "Throw down your Arms & you shall come to no harm," the only answer was the ominous clicking of firelocks. Thereupon British cavalry rode in among the rebels to disperse them, while Major Pitcairn, in command of the expedition, instructed his men: "Soldiers, don't fire, keep your Ranks, form & surround them." Instantly bullets began to fly, presumably from the guns of the rebels, for the British troops could not fire without danger of killing their own officers who had galloped among the "armed mob."

Once their officers were out of the line of fire, however, the British troops quickly drove the rebels into the woods and continued their march to Concord. But they had by no means seen the last of the embattled farmers; although they succeeded in destroying some of the military stores at Concord (most had already been removed to safety), the redcoats encountered stiff resistance when they prepared to return to Boston. At the Old North Bridge in Concord, there was a sharp exchange of fire — "the shot heard round the world." As the British marched down the country lanes they were subjected to a grueling fire from rebels fighting like Indians, concealed in houses and behind trees and stone walls. To the hard-pressed troopers, it began to seem that the whole country had turned out to have a shot at them. Only the timely arrival of Lord Percy with reinforcements enabled the weary regulars, their powder spent and their bodies bleeding from wounds inflicted by an enemy they had hardly seen, to stagger into Charlestown.

At least some British soldiers who saw action at Concord and Lexington experienced a rude awakening to the magnitude of the task of coercing the colonies. Lord Percy, a high-ranking officer who had hitherto held the provincials in contempt, now warned his countrymen they were in for a rough time. "Whoever looks upon them [the New Englanders] as an irregular mob," he declared, "will find himself much mistaken": men who had braved death by rushing to within ten yards of British officers to shoot them down were assuredly not the cowards that Englishmen had supposed. These Yankees, Lord Percy decided, were fanatics ready to sacrifice their lives for something they called liberty. Their fanaticism did not make them more admirable in his eyes, but it did make them infinitely more dangerous.

"A single drop of blood may be considered as the Signal of civil war," exclaimed Edward Gibbon when he learned of the fray at Lexington. The verdict of the great historian, a specialist in the decline and fall of empires, was borne out to the full.

∩   ∩   ∩

With the outbreak of fighting at Lexington and Concord began the rapid collapse of British authority in the thirteen colonies. Unprepared to put down rebellion in America, the mother country could do little to halt the spread of sedition. Most of the troops in the colonies were stationed in frontier outposts, hundreds of miles from the trouble spots. The royal governors lacked even arms and ammunition to distribute among the Loyalists; when they called for aid from General Gage in Boston, the headquarters of the British army, invariably they were told that no troops were available and that they must find their own salvation. The empire was tottering and there were neither men nor weapons to sustain it.

Although, until July 1776, Americans professed to be loyal British subjects, in actuality they had long before stripped the mother country of power and taken into their own hands all the real authority in the colonies. The King and the British Parliament were sovereign only by sufferance. American patriots might love "good King George" and empty their bumpers in his honor, but they did not carry their allegiance to the point of yielding him obedience. In place of government by King and Parliament, Americans established government by committees. These committees, dominated in every case by radical patriots, called up the militia, directed military operations, hunted down Loyalists, and enforced the decrees of the Continental Congress — and in the process gave Americans a taste of stronger government than they had ever known as British subjects.[2]

Thanks to the committees and to the spontaneous support of the people,

[2] Committees of Safety were appointed by the provincial congresses to carry out their mandates. They were considered as the executive power in the colonies; and while the congresses were in recess, the recommendations of the Committees of Safety carried the same force as the acts and resolves of the congresses themselves.

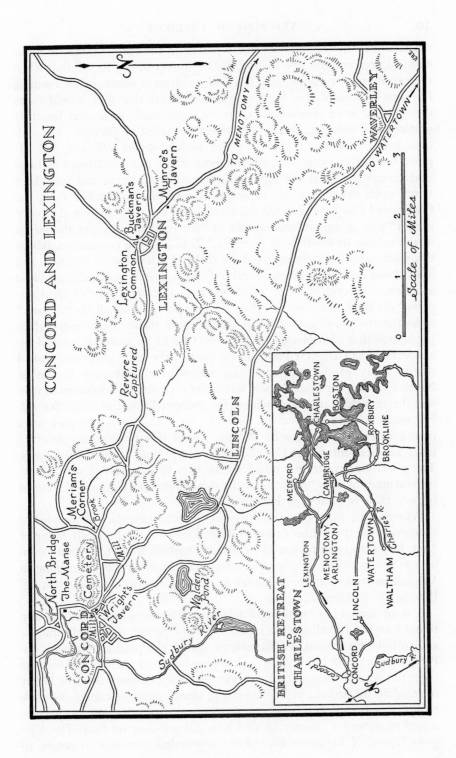

CONCORD AND LEXINGTON

North Bridge
The Manse
Meriam's Corner
Brook
Mill
CONCORD
Cemetery
Mill
Wright's Tavern
Walden Pond
Sudbury River

Revere Captured

LINCOLN

Lexington Common
Buckman's Tavern
Munroe's Tavern
LEXINGTON

TO MENOTOMY

TO WATERTOWN
WAVERLEY

Scale of Miles
0 1 2 3

BRITISH RETREAT
TO
CHARLESTOWN

MEDFORD
CHARLESTOWN
BOSTON
CAMBRIDGE
ROXBURY
BROOKLINE
LEXINGTON
MENOTOMY
(ARLINGTON)
CONCORD
LINCOLN
WATERTOWN
WALTHAM Charles R.
Concord
Sudbury R.

the Continental Congress became a power in the land: indeed, it never enjoyed greater authority than at the beginning of the Revolution when the committees made its writ law and its name a terror to its enemies. Loyalists who scoffed at the Congress and swore that they would do as they pleased were summoned before the committees to answer for their opinions and conduct; and if the committees failed to persuade, the mob took over. Thus was created a police system, secret, efficient, and all-powerful. Letters were seized in the post office, those addressed to England receiving special attention from the committeemen; and spies kept watch upon the movements of suspected persons. In October 1775, the Continental Congress directed the committees to take into custody every person "who, going at large, might in their opinion endanger the safety of the colony or liberties of America." Zealously the committees fell to this work; suspects were rounded up, oaths of fidelity were imposed, and in stubborn cases imprisonment and disfranchisement were inflicted. "It is as much as a person's life is worth to speak disrespectfully of the Congress," declared a Loyalist in 1775. "The people . . . are all liberty mad."

As for the royal governors of the thirteen revolted provinces, their plight was that of orphans in the storm. Chased by mobs or assailed by hundreds of hair-triggered militiamen, most of the royal governors rushed to the safety of the nearest British man-of-war. Governor Martin of North Carolina, for example, was left under no misapprehension as to who was the real ruler of the province. He entreated General Gage for aid. For many months he received no reply until he chanced to pick up a patriot newspaper and, to his dismay, found that Gage's long-deferred letter had been intercepted by the rebels and printed in their newspapers. The governor prudently made his way to a British man-of-war where, he lamented, he was "reduced to the deplorable and disgraceful state of being a tame Spectator of Rebellion."

Whether the royal governors fought or ran away, they accomplished little good for the British cause. William Franklin, the royal governor of New Jersey and natural son of Benjamin Franklin, stood his ground until he was put in prison by the rebels; and Lord Dunmore, by remaining in Virginia, stirred up more animosity against the mother country than did Patrick Henry himself.

A stouthearted but bumbling Englishman, Dunmore attempted to rally round him the Loyalists of Virginia — chiefly Scotch and Englishmen — and to hold the capital, Williamsburg, against the patriot militia led by Patrick Henry. But besieged by a champing legion of planters and farmers eager to add a royal governor to their trophies, Dunmore thought better of standing his ground in Williamsburg; abandoning the capital, he took refuge on a British ship lying near Yorktown. From this position he presumed to govern a country in which he did not dare set foot. The Virginia House of Burgesses invited the absconded governor to return to

Williamsburg and resume the exercise of his duties. Dunmore politely declined, inviting in turn the burgesses to meet with him on board the British man-of-war. Neither side was deceived by the other's show of hospitality — the burgesses had no more desire to take an enforced journey to England than had Lord Dunmore to make himself a martyr to British authority.

The governor, however, had not played his last card: desperately in need of armed men to support his authority, he promised freedom to all indentured servants and Negro slaves who took up arms in the name of the King.

Except for Norfolk and its environs, Dunmore's jurisdiction did not extend over the land; on the Chesapeake he was master. His navy consisted only of a tender and a few other small ships but it was sufficient to give him control of the sea. Lord Dunmore, like many other lords, was known to be fond of his bottle, and Richard Henry Lee suggested that he might be taken in liquor by a few chosen men; but, unfortunately for this plan, the governor did his heavy drinking on shipboard. With his partisans, consisting of about two hundred British regulars, together with a few Scotch and Negroes, Lord Dunmore maintained control over Norfolk; but the patriots finally forced him to abandon even this slender foothold and to retreat to his ships. Still Dunmore held on; with the aid of his fleet he burned plantations, carried off tobacco, and finally, by a cannonade from his ships, set fire to the Norfolk waterfront.[2a] He even opened negotiations with the Indians to ravage the frontier while he kept the patriots engaged along the seacoast. But none of the governor's schemes prospered. The Loyalists, except those who joined him aboard ship, fell into the hands of the rebels, and many of his Negroes died of fever. Had it not been for the unlucky epidemic that carried off his blacks, Dunmore declared that he would have had an "Ethiopian corps" of two thousand men with which to carry war into the heart of the country.

By attempting to enlist Negroes in the British cause, Dunmore brought upon himself and upon the country he represented the full weight of Virginians' wrath: Southerners did not take lightly incitements to racial war. And the alleged burning of Norfolk aroused such anger that a Philadelphia patriot remarked that the British had "nothing more to do than burn a Town in each Province & we shall bring Matters to a short Issue." Dunmore's next step, it was predicted, would be to poison the wells and springs: there was no enormity of which Virginians were not prepared to believe their governor guilty.

Meanwhile, in Great Britain, Lord North had taken two steps — one in the direction of peace, the other towards war — in the hope of averting

---

[2a] The British began the burning of the town, but it was the Americans who, moving into Norfolk shortly after its evacuation by the invaders, were responsible for most of the destruction.

the impending conflict. Before the battle of Lexington, the Prime Minister submitted to Parliament a plan of conciliation, and at almost the same time he sent three major generals, together with considerable reinforcements of British troops, to Boston. Lord North did not conceal his hope that the use of force might be averted; the three major generals and the British troops who accompanied them were intended chiefly to awe Americans into accepting a peaceful settlement of the quarrel.

Lord North was not slow to perceive that he had blundered into a most unpromising dispute with the colonies, and, as was his custom, he sought to placate the furies he had helped arouse. It had never been his intention, he now declared, "to impose on our fellow-subjects in America any terms inconsistent with the most perfect liberty." Fair words, but they sounded to Americans like the deathbed repentance of a hardened sinner against the rights of man.

Lord North's peace plan — passed by Parliament in February 1775 — offered freedom from taxation by the British Parliament to any colony voluntarily making a fair contribution to imperial expenses. This proposal, it is plain, did not go to the heart of the dispute between Great Britain and its colonies: instead of receiving exemption from parliamentary taxation as they demanded, Americans were simply permitted to convert their colonial legislatures into taxgatherers for the British Parliament. Moreover, this scheme left unaltered the question of fundamental right. "An armed robber who demands my money," exclaimed an indignant American, "might as well pretend he makes a concession, by suffering me to take it out of my own pocket, rather than search there for it himself." The Continental Congress was pointedly ignored in Lord North's peace plan.

Despite these objections, the government's plan was accepted by the legislature of Nova Scotia and might have made headway in the thirteen revolted provinces had it been proposed at a more opportune time. But Lord North was never happy in the timing of his peace offers: Conciliatory Propositions of 1775 reached New York the day after news of the battle of Lexington. With the colonists in this warlike frame of mind, it required greater art than Lord North or the British Parliament was capable of to calm the tempest produced in America by the fighting at Lexington. Doomed to failure, the peace plan of 1775 served to indicate that the British government, although not bent upon war with the colonies, was determined to retain intact the right of taxation which was the ostensible cause of the quarrel between Englishmen and Americans.

Among Lord North's own followers, more good was expected from the three major generals than from the Prime Minister's peace overtures. Much difficulty was experienced in persuading the Tory members of Parliament to vote for North's peace plan — in striking contrast to the enthusiastic support they accorded the proposal of sending the major generals to America.

The three major generals were carefully chosen by the government as the most brilliant officers in the army and as the most likely to discourage Americans from any ideas they might entertain of rebellion. All three became notable figures in the American war, and two of them served as commander-in-chief of the British army in North America. They came to America in 1775: the last member of the triumvirate left the country in 1782, after the British army had lost the war. They came as comparatively young men, full of ambition and vigor: they left as disillusioned and embittered veterans.

If any general could, Sir William Howe might have been expected to strike terror among the rebels. Reputed to be one of the ablest officers in the army, his admirers saw in him a future Wolfe or Marlborough. As a dashing young officer, he had served under Wolfe at Quebec where, in his enthusiasm, he had stripped off his coat and led his men to the charge. In 1774, he had been picked to train the light troops of the British army — a corps designed to apply to British strategy the lessons learned from warfare against the French and Indians in North America. Howe was a leader in the most advanced military ideas of the times and he personally instructed the light troops in the new tactics and in the use of an improved type of musket. Unlike the rest of the troops in the British army, these men were trained to shoot accurately: every man was a marksman. On almost every score, Howe seemed an excellent choice; the only criticism advanced against him was that he might prove too rash.

Sir William enjoyed the family background and social prestige necessary to a British general. He was reputed to be descended — illegitimately, as was so often true of the best families — from George I, the great-grandfather of the reigning sovereign. And, indeed, he bore a noticeable resemblance to George III: the puffy, heavy face, the thick lips and dull eyes, indicated that he and the King might properly call each other cousin.

There was, in short, only one thing wrong with Howe: his politics were not right from the point of view of George III. He and his brother, Lord Howe, the admiral, were staunch Whigs and had distinguished themselves by their opposition to George's efforts to rule the country through Parliament. Such uncousinly conduct did not endear the Howes to their sovereign, who much preferred to send a Tory general to chastise the Americans; but unhappily for the King, there was a painful shortage of Tories in the armed forces. Tory policies had helped precipitate the American Revolution, but it was left largely to the Whigs to lead the armed forces.

Acquiring the services of the Howes was vital to George III because many Whigs had proclaimed their refusal to take part in the coercion of the colonies. Keppel, an admiral of the Whiggish persuasion, flatly refused to serve against the Americans; Whig peers when ordered to America threw up their commissions; and Lord Chatham refused to permit Lord Pitt, his son, to serve in the army. Sir William Howe, in his capacity as member of Parliament, had assured his constituents that he would never accept a command against the Americans, for whom, he remarked, he had nothing but affectionate regard. But he soon thought better of this promise: his fortune was not great, he was eager for preferment, and he brought himself to believe that his acceptance was essential to the preservation of the empire. Only an enlightened Whig, he reasoned, could stamp out rebellion and at the same time reconcile the Americans to returning to the empire. In Sir William's opinion, the American rebels might yet be redeemed by kindness and good will. He therefore entered the struggle quite as much to make peace as to make war.

Sir Henry Clinton, the second major general and the least colorful of the three, was an able officer whose extreme sensitivity made his life a torment. A soldier, like a politician, ought perhaps to be impervious to barbs of critics, but Clinton was thin-skinned and disposed to brood over the slights and rebuffs that he experienced during his military career in America. He ended by conceiving himself to be one of the most unfortunate men in history; his only hope was that posterity, fully informed of his merits (he left a great mass of manuscript to that end), would do him justice.

Sir John Burgoyne, the youngest of the major generals, was a fashionable man about town, a playwright, wit, and soldier. "Gentleman Johnny" had come a long way by his wits. From his father, it was said, he had inherited little except extravagant tastes; but he had helped to put himself in a position to gratify those tastes by eloping with the daughter of one of England's wealthiest peers. Thereafter he joined the army as a captain (his commission was purchased) and won distinction in Portugal during the Seven Years' War as the colonel in command of "Burgoyne's Light Horse." But Burgoyne, unlike most military men, was nagged by an ambition to shine in literary circles. He was fond of writing, although he was apt to mistake bombast for eloquence and loved words not for their fitness but for those sonorous qualities in which the eighteenth century delighted. In his hands, literature was less light and agile swordplay than a heavy bombardment in which the senses were stunned in the roll of majestic epithets. A handsome man, a bit on the florid side, a lion in the drawing rooms and, if rumor spoke true, in the boudoir, Burgoyne seemed to be bent upon giving up to literature and social life talents which had made him one of the most spirited and capable officers in the British army. Had it not been for the American war, Burgoyne might today have been remembered chiefly as one of the lesser eighteenth-century playwrights. His first play was performed at Drury Lane in 1775; and after meeting with disaster at Saratoga, he resumed his literary labors and scored his greatest success in 1785 with the production of *The Heiress.*

At the outbreak of the Revolution he was living comfortably in London, moving in the best circles, gambling heavily, and enjoying a sinecure from the King which was expected to induce him to vote on the right side in Parliament, although he was known on occasion to vote as he pleased. His attitude toward the colonies was more liberal than might have been expected of one so closely connected with the court. He called America a spoiled child that richly deserved punishment, but he was eager to stop short of bloodshed, and no sooner did he arrive in America than he began to try to settle the dispute peacefully.

The reputations of the three major generals were as awe-inspiring as any to be found in the army. It was no doubt with this in mind that Lord North is said to have exclaimed, "I do not know whether our generals will frighten the Americans, but they certainly frighten me." And when they boarded H.M.S. *Cerberus* for America, a London wit remarked:

> "Behold the *Cerberus* the Atlantic plow,
> Her precious cargo — Burgoyne, Clinton, Howe,
> Bow, wow, wow." [3]

The three major generals were not Happy Warriors: they were plagued by doubts and apprehensions which ought not to have entered the minds of conquerors. None was particularly eager to go to America; none relished the idea of making war upon fellow citizens struggling for liberty. Burgoyne had felt obliged to apologize in the House of Commons for accepting the command, and to the King he said that he had received with regret his orders to go to America. None believed that dragooning Americans was a solution of the problems that bedeviled the British Empire; as members of Parliament they regarded the dispute with the colonies from the point of view of statesmen as well as that of militarists. It was necessary, they recognized, not merely to beat the Americans but to win their loyalty to the mother country; and to that end they favored negotiation and compromise rather than war and bloodshed. Burgoyne lamented that he, the junior major general, would have nothing to do at Boston except perhaps to inspect a brigade and make sure that the soldiers "boiled their kettles regularly." Rather than sink into such insignificance, Burgoyne asked to be given a separate command at New York or to undertake a peace mission to Philadelphia —

[3] In Greek mythology, Cerberus was the dog who guarded the entrance to the lower world. He allowed all to enter but none escaped. He was finally tamed by Hercules.

anything, in short, except the deadly dullness of garrison duty in Boston.

Unhappily for the government's plan of frightening the rebels with the major generals, it was the major generals themselves, rather than the Americans, who were struck with consternation upon their arrival in Boston in May 1775. Here they found a British army smarting under a reverse administered by the colonists and cooped up in Boston by twenty thousand provincials. Flushed by their success at Lexington and Concord, the rebels had pushed their lines to within musket shot of the British outposts. The fleet in the harbor lay perilously near American cannon; the troops of the garrison were disgusted at the caution of General Thomas Gage and burning to exact retribution for the British soldiers "murdered" by rebel snipers on April 19. It was clear to the major generals that they were in for some hard fighting and that it would take powder and shot, rather than gold braid and resounding titles, to frighten the Americans into surrender. Reinforcements instead of generals were urgently needed; unless the home government sent more troops, said a British officer in Boston, the three major generals would bring the British "no more authority than we had before, which was none at all."

In the haste and confusion of their retreat from Concord, the redcoats had abandoned Charlestown and the peninsula upon which it stood. Plunging across the bay that separated Charlestown from Boston, they had not stopped until they were safe within the city — a precipitance that was to cost them dear. For the Charlestown isthmus was the key to Boston: whoever held Bunker Hill controlled the metropolis. After the battle of Lexington, the British were too weak to attempt to take possession of the heights above Charlestown. As a result, the way was left open for the rebels to make Boston untenable by the British fleet and army. The Americans had only to mount heavy cannon on the hills across the bay to dislodge the enemy from his last refuge in New England.

Yet neither were the Americans in position to move in force onto the Charlestown isthmus: their victory on the nineteenth of April had not wholly overcome their sense of caution in engaging British regulars. So Charlestown and its environs became a no man's land, and each side waited until it should be strong enough to venture upon this disputed ground.

It was the British who made the first move. The major generals were eager to win laurels in North America, and heartened by the reinforcements which had begun to reach the besieged city from England, they planned to occupy the Charlestown isthmus on June 18, 1775.[4]

In this emergency, the American spy service functioned to perfection;

---

[4] The British commanders planned that the first attack should be made upon Dorchester Heights, which likewise commanded Boston. Then, seizing Bunker Hill before the rebels could recover from their surprise, they might have succeeded in making Boston secure.

just as they had learned beforehand of the British intention to march to Concord on April 19, so now they were informed of the designs of the British command to occupy the Charlestown isthmus. Thus forewarned, the Americans prepared to anticipate the enemy by seizing Bunker Hill on the night of June 16. The surprise party was to be given by the Americans, not by the British.

But it was not Bunker Hill that the Americans fortified. Ordered to take a position on Bunker Hill, General Israel Putnam impetuously led his men to Breed's Hill, closer to Boston, but more exposed to British fire and farther from safe retreat. At best, the expedition was hazardous. The Americans were venturing upon a peninsula connected with the mainland by a narrow isthmus. This corridor, the only means of retreat open to the Americans, might easily be raked with fire from British ships or be closed by British landing parties. Apparently "Old Put" was not content merely to thrust his head into the lion's mouth; he felt impelled to twist its tail at the same time.

The noise made by the Americans on Breed's Hill was clearly audible in Boston, for the rebels were under no orders to conduct their operations silently. British sentries reported to headquarters that suspicious sounds were coming from across the bay, but although General Clinton was alarmed, Howe merely yawned and went up to bed. He could not be bothered at that late hour to talk about the war; if the Americans were on the hill, they would not remain there long after the British army went into action. In his overconfidence, Howe did not even consider it necessary to ready the army for the next day's work; no alarm was sounded and no preparations were made to drive the rebels from their position.[5]

While Sir William Howe slumbered the Americans worked like beavers, constructing a redoubt and digging trenches on the summit of the hill preparatory to installing heavy guns with which they could batter Boston to rubble about the heads of the British. By morning the Americans were "almost suffocated with dust & choak'd for want of liquor." They expected to be relieved and to go back to camp to quench their thirst, but these plans went awry. No relief appeared, and as a result the men who had spent half the night digging were obliged to withstand the British onslaught almost unaided by the American army stationed a few miles away in Cambridge.

With the coming of daylight, the Americans were plainly visible on Breed's Hill, throwing up dirt as though realizing their lives depended

---

[5] General Thomas Gage, although commander-in-chief of the British army in Boston, allowed himself to be dominated by the newcomers. He was likewise undisturbed by the activity of the patriots above Charlestown. The story that the British generals were not informed of what was going on is, according to Clinton's notes, apparently unfounded.

on it. Refreshed by a good night's sleep, Sir William Howe quickly went into action. Trumpets sounded, the streets were filled with troops hurrying to the water front, and in a short time over fifteen hundred men had been packed in barges and were on their way across the bay to give battle to the Americans.

It is clear that, when finally roused, Sir William Howe displayed no hesitation. But in all this activity there is nothing to show that he ever sat down to study the situation. He reacted quickly when he saw his danger, yet he ignored — perhaps deliberately — the advantages he enjoyed. The patriots had rushed into a trap; the British, instead of closing the trap upon them, proceeded to fall in themselves.

It would have been an easy matter for Howe to have cut off the retreat of the American force on Breed's Hill: he had at his disposal a fleet of gondolas — large flatboats, with musket-proof side walls — which, placed in the Mystic River, might have poured grape and shot into the Americans' flank at musket range and have made impassable the narrow isthmus by which Charlestown peninsula was connected with the mainland. In short, here was a way of annihilating the Americans on Charlestown peninsula without risk of heavy loss to the British. This was the strategy advocated by Clinton. Reconnaissance had convinced him that the American position was strong and could not be carried without heavy casualties. Howe waved these objections aside; the hill, he declared, was an easy ascent and the Americans had no fortifications that would stand a moment against the King's troops.

Under this persuasion, Howe decided to make a frontal attack upon the Americans' position on the heights. Disdaining strategy, he even discarded the caution ordinarily employed by a military commander. He attacked the Americans without reconnoitering, he formed no reserves, his troops advanced in line rather than in columns, and he threw the weight of his forces against the strongest part of the American defenses. Although he had been in charge of the training of the light infantry in England, he signally failed at Bunker Hill to make effective use of them; nor did he utilize the new ideas in tactics of which he was England's leading exponent.

In part, Howe's purpose in coming to America was to persuade Americans of the hopelessness of resistance because, no matter how strong their position, the courage and discipline of British regulars would always carry the field. He wanted, at least at Bunker Hill, to win his battles the hard way and, by deliberately courting difficulties, to make his victory over the rebels the more convincing. It was as though Sir William Howe believed that a British general ought not stoop to strategy against the rebels. But something went wrong — terribly wrong — at Bunker Hill.

Under cover of heavy fire from the fleet, the British troops landed on

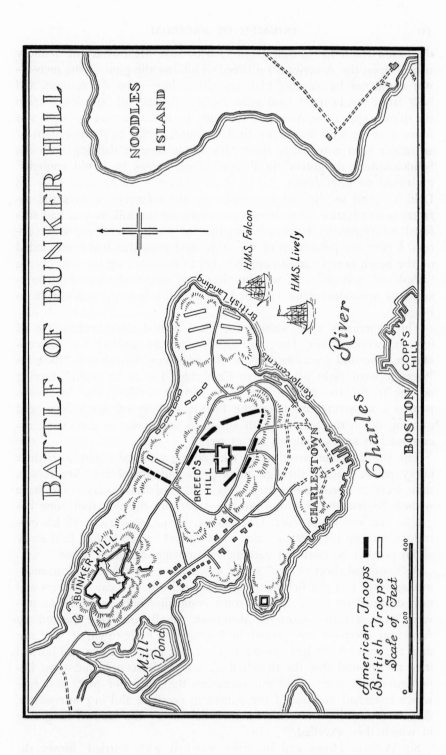

BATTLE OF BUNKER HILL

NOODLES ISLAND

Mill Pond

BUNKER HILL

BREED'S HILL

British Landing

H.M.S. Falcon

H.M.S. Lively

Reinforcements

CHARLESTOWN

Charles River

BOSTON

COPP'S HILL

American Troops
British Troops
Scale of Feet

0   200   400

the beach about half a mile from Charlestown. Meanwhile the artillery turned upon the Americans on Breed's Hill, but the guns of the men-of-war could not be elevated high enough to bear upon the summit, and balls from the heaviest land guns merely glanced off harmlessly from the thick walls of the American redoubt. To make matters worse, it was found that the balls would not fit the cannon, owing to the oversight of an officer who notoriously spent "his whole time in dallying with the Schoolmaster's daughters" in Boston. "God knows he is old enough," exclaimed an Englishman; " — he is no Samson — yet he must have his Delilah." And so the call was made for the infantry — always the infantry — to advance even though the rebels on the hill, as yet, had suffered no distress by bombardment. But the soldiers were eager for action. Under the protection of fire from land guns that had been landed on the beach near Charlestown, they began to march up the hill, crying " 'Push on! Push on!' . . . with infinite spirit" and in full view of the thousands of spectators who crowded every hill, rooftop, and steeple in Boston.

The Americans were waiting for them behind their breastworks of hay and wooden rails. They had also brought up artillery but the captain in command gave one look at the advancing British and "took his Pieces & went right off home to Cambridge fast as he could," leaving no one to fire the cannon. Yet even without artillery, the Americans poured a withering fire upon the British, picking off the officers and mowing down the privates with almost as much ease as they were accustomed to knock squirrels out of trees.

The British made no effort to take cover; weighed down with their heavy packs, wading through thick grass and scrambling over fences, they were as conspicuous targets as Yankee sharpshooters could have wished. So fast and furiously did the Americans fire that they soon began to run low on powder. One patriot, having shot away all his cartridges, tore up his shirt to make wadding and "when he had fir'd away all his powder he retreated without hat or wigg, & almost naked."

A "continual sheet of fire" swept down from the American entrenchments; never had the British troops sustained a hotter day. Officers and men dropped on every side; in some companies only sergeants or privates were left to command. Moreover, the British were flanked by American sharpshooters posted in houses in Charlestown; it was not until the men-of-war had thrown red-hot shot into the town and burned it to the ground that the British flank was made secure. But, most important of all, they could not surmount the fences of posts and rails which stretched in front of the American position; and in consequence, they were unable to attack with their bayonets — the kind of infighting in which they excelled.

Sir William Howe and his suite watched with startled dismay the red lines growing thinner and thinner. To rally the faltering redcoats, Howe, attended by a servant carrying liquor for the refreshment of the general and his staff, moved so close to the Americans' lines that a bottle was shot out of the servant's hand by an American marksman. But the situation was past saving by any inspiration that Howe might have drawn from a bottle: he needed reinforcements to take the places of the hundreds of men whose bodies dotted the hillside. Fortunately for the British, Clinton arrived with five hundred fresh men in the nick of time; the lines were re-formed, and again the redcoats flung themselves against the American entrenchments.[6]

Their assault carried them to the summit. In the redoubt, General Joseph Warren and a handful of Americans, using their guns as clubs, fought to almost the last man, holding up the British while the rest of the Americans made good their escape. But the fighting in the redoubt was soon over: although the Americans fought with a ferocity that surprised the British — for whom, indeed, this was a day of surprises — they were no match for regulars in hand-to-hand combat. The bayonet here proved its worth, and the Americans were quickly overwhelmed.

The British were in possession of Breed's and Bunker Hills but there were no bands in Boston that night playing "Yankee Doodle" in derision of the rebels. Instead of a victory celebration, there were "wounded and dead officers in every street . . . wounded soldiers lying in their tents and crying for assistance to remove some men who had just expired." Few preparations had been made to receive the wounded; the workhouse and almshouse had to be hurriedly converted into hospitals; wood carts and coaches and chaises were pressed into service to bring the dead and wounded from Charlestown.

The British had paid a fearful price for their victory at Breed's Hill: of the twenty-five hundred men engaged, over a thousand were casualties, against five hundred on the American side. Another such victory as this, it was said, and there would be no one left alive to carry the good news home. Particularly heavy was the loss in officers: some of the best blood in England was spilled by American sharpshooters on June 17. Certainly the British could not afford to purchase American soil at this rate: a few acres of real estate had cost the flower of the British army. England had seldom so grieved over a victory. "Poor little Mrs. Howe," her friends reported, "fainted away with only the shock of the word *action*" and could scarcely be persuaded that her husband had survived the slaughter.

To account for this staggering casualty list, British officers concluded that the rebels must have enjoyed a vast superiority in numbers: Lord

---

[6] Contrary to the opinion of early historians, it seems clear that there were not three distinct attacks by the British upon the American lines. In some places the British held their ground; elsewhere they were driven back.

Rawdon estimated that there were between fourteen and fifteen thousand Americans on Breed's Hill "entrenched up to their chins." [7] Accordingly, Englishmen made a slight concession to American courage: Yankees would fight, it was now admitted, when they were on a hill and protected by entrenchments.

Nonetheless, many officers who had seen action at Bunker Hill were disturbed by the "enthusiasm" and "frenzy" displayed by the Americans, particularly in that last battle in the redoubt. "Damn the rebels," exclaimed a British officer, "that they would not flinch." Even granting American numerical superiority and advantages of terrain, Burgoyne admitted that "the defence was well conceived and obstinately maintained; the retreat was no flight: it was even covered with bravery and military skill."

Bunker Hill proved the valor and discipline of British troops; Burgoyne declared that "no men on earth ever behaved with more spirit and perseverance" than the redcoats. But it also proved that, in war, courage was not enough and that generalship could not be dispensed with, even against American "peasants." As an officer said, the action had revealed "a gross ignorance of the most common rules of the profession, and gives us, for the future, anxious foreboding"; the lives of brave men had been wantonly thrown away — "our conductor as much murdered them as if he had cut their throats himself, on Boston Common." General Clinton acidly remarked that he never saw "so great a want of order and more luck than skill."

On the strength of the casualties they had inflicted, Americans claimed a victory at Bunker Hill — a victory, moreover, which seemed to open a new age of freedom for mankind. For here embattled farmers fighting for liberty had defeated a "brave Army of Veterans, commanded by the most experienced Generals, but employed by bad Men in the Worst of Causes."

But if Bunker Hill revealed that Americans could fight, it also brought to light numerous defects in the New England army. To this day, it is not known with certitude who was in command of the Americans at Bunker Hill; as General Charles Lee said, the troops were "composed, in part of raw lads and old men, half armed, with no practice or discipline, commanded without order, and God knows by whom." It was clearly a case of every man for himself; the Yankees were on their own, and it was the pluck and resourcefulness of individuals, rather than inspired leadership or military organization, that made Bunker Hill such a costly victory for the British. Yet, since every battle has to have a hero, General Putnam was awarded the palm; he was, it was said, "inspired by God Almighty with a military genius, and formed to work

[7] Actually, there were not more than fifteen hundred Americans on Breed's Hill.

wonders in the sight of those uncircumcised Philistines, at Boston and Bunker Hill." On the strength of this unmistakable indication of divine favor, "Old Put" was placed in command of "Putnam's Impregnable Battery," a huge brass mortar captured from the British and first used by the Americans as a punch bowl.

IN taking up arms against the mother country, Americans expected that Great Britain would be crippled by civil war: mobs of honest Englishmen would storm Parliament and the King's palace, overthrow the government, and make a just peace with the colonies. In actuality, Americans themselves were more sharply divided by the revolt than were Englishmen. As the patriots admitted, it was necessary for one part of the American people "to dragoon another at the same time that they are opposing a most powerful external foe," and in 1776 a committee of the Continental Congress declared that "if America falls, it will be owing to such divisions more than the force of our enemies." The opponents of the Revolution — totaling perhaps as much as a third of the population — were known as Tories or Loyalists. A large number were gentry: lawyers, doctors, clergymen, governmental officials, merchants, and large landowners.

Many well-to-do Americans were reluctant to embark their persons and their worldly goods upon the troubled waters where Sam Adams and his fellow radicals swam boldly; having much to lose, they hesitated to take the risks that poorer members of the community could scorn. Harvard graduates — a more reliable index of social acceptability during the revolutionary period than at the present time — made up a considerable part of the Massachusetts Loyalists. On the other hand, Harvard as well as Yale and Princeton contributed numerous leaders to the Revolution, Hancock and "the brace of Adamses" being the most notable of the Harvard revolutionaries.

In the North, it is fair to say, more of the gentry opposed the Revolution than in the Southern states. Sitting down to dinner with a Southern gentleman in 1776, one might assume that he was a patriot — with almost as fair certainty as today one might assume that he is a member of the Democratic Party. A Northern gentleman, however, presented a more ticklish problem; it was advisable to sound him out carefully before proposing as a toast "Damnation to King George!" or "A pox to the Congress!"

Because many Loyalists were "the first people," it does not necessarily follow that all the poor were rebels. The American Revolution was never a clear-cut struggle between the haves and the have-nots: the underprivileged and the overprivileged, as well as a great mass of middle-class citizens, joined forces in defense of British sovereignty.

Most of the Loyalists who took the hard and thorny road to exile came from the Middle states — New York, New Jersey, Pennsylvania, Maryland, and Delaware. Of these states, New York furnished the largest number of émigrés — almost half the total. Nearly as numerous was the Pennsylvania contingent — far more Pennsylvanians went into exile than served at any one time in the Pennsylvania Line of the Continental army. With good reason, the patriots spoke of New York, New Jersey, and Pennsylvania as "the enemy's country." In these states, the Revolution was the work of a resolute and organized minority opposed by a disorganized, floundering, leaderless majority. It was by the pressure of Virginia and New England, and by the activity and zeal of comparatively few patriots within these states themselves, that the conservatives were overthrown and the Revolution was carried to its consummation.

Probably no group in the colonies was under more suspicion of unpatriotic activities than the Quakers. For the most part prosperous merchants and farmers, the Quakers were inclined to adopt a conservative point of view. Moreover, instead of oppression, they had received from the British government protection against sectarian persecution; and their religious principles made them averse to supporting actively a rebellion which employed armed force to achieve its ends. In 1776, the Quakers voted to remain neutral in the dispute, but their neutrality was not acceptable to the patriots. "In Politicks," said John Adams, "the Middle Way is none at all — If we finally fail in this great and glorious Contest, it will be by bewildering ourselves in groping after the Middle Way." Some Quakers, it is true, renounced their conscientious objections to war and joined the American army — for which backsliding they were read out of meeting — but on the whole the Quakers were regarded by the patriots as Tories of a particularly dangerous and malignant type.[1] Hiding under their religious immunities, they were suspected of reporting American troop movements to the enemy, acting as guides and informers, and refusing to accept paper money. "A rigid old Quaker and of course a Damn'd Tory" was the way a patriot described a Quaker acquaintance.

[1] Generals Nathanael Greene of Rhode Island and Thomas Mifflin of Pennsylvania were both Quakers.

It is probably true that the Quakers, taken as a group, were more friendly to the British cause than to the American; but the practice of British spies disguising themselves in the costume of the Society of Friends in order to pass through American lines made the Quakers appear blacker than the facts warranted. And it must be acknowledged that although the members of the Society of Friends generally abstained from active participation in the war, they were among the leaders in the humanitarian reforms wrought by the Revolution — the emancipation of slaves, the improvement of prison conditions, and the mitigation of punishment for minor breaches of the law.

In the western sections of the Southern states, Loyalism existed among some of the most democratic groups in the population. Hatred of the ruling clique of planters and merchants of the seaboard — the leaders of the Revolution in the South — eclipsed, for many westerners, the menace of tyranny from overseas. Only from the eastern "oligarchs" had they experienced ill treatment; from the British Crown, on the other hand, they had received protection against the Indians, secure land titles, and honest dealing. Naturally, therefore, they looked to the mother country for relief against the unfair system of representation by which they were taxed without their consent, and against the judicial system which denied them adequate courts. For these Americans, tyranny began at home.

The British government embarked upon the war under the persuasion that the majority of Americans were loyal at heart. Two thirds of the people, it was commonly said, were on the British side and only awaited the presence of a British army to rise up against the tyranny of the Continental Congress. Accordingly, the American war was conceived of as a large-scale rescue to free the people from the power of a small group of desperate rebels. It was admitted that if the colonists were united in seeking independence, there was little hope of reducing them to subjection or making them good subjects. "I never had an idea of subduing the Americans," said a British general. " — I meant to assist the good Americans to subdue the bad ones." Lord George Germain declared that victory by Great Britain was impossible unless steps were taken "to engage the people of America in support of a cause which is equally their own and ours," and that "he trusted rather to the good sense and feelings of the people of America than to the force of arms." This had profound effect upon British military strategy — every commander sought in America a Shangri-la, the fabulous land of Tories where British sovereignty might be re-established upon a solid foundation of popular support.

Unfortunately for their own cause, the Loyalists encouraged the home government to believe that they outnumbered the rebels, that the rebellion was at its last gasp, and that the people as a whole yearned to return to the mild and just rule of Great Britain. Germain lent a willing ear to American Loyalists who drew rosy pictures of the progress of the war and bore tales against British commanders. Sometimes, indeed, he seemed to put more credence in the tales of the Tories than in the reports of his own generals.

During the first years of the war, the British made little effort to enlist the active military aid of the Tories. Although Germain advocated as early as 1775 that they be utilized on a large scale, the army leaders were not eager to share the glory of crushing the rebellion with "colonials." Sir William Howe, moreover, was reluctant to invite Americans to shed the blood of their fellow Americans; as he was well aware, civil war in the colonies meant defeat for his plans of reuniting the colonies to Great Britain in affection and understanding. And even after he had been compelled by lack of regular troops to employ Loyalists, he used them principally for garrison duty, as laborers on fortifications, and as reserves.[2]

Tories, it can be safely said, were more bitterly hated by the patriots than were the British themselves. In a civil war, no one is hated so venomously as the brother who takes the opposite side. Upon the Tories was saddled the war guilt: it was they, declared the patriots, who had persuaded the British government to begin the war, and they were blamed for the worst atrocities that marked its course. At the door of the Loyalists, exclaimed a member of Congress, could be placed responsibility for "the greatest part of the miseries of this cruel war": they had induced the British to conduct the war "in a manner before unknown to civilized nations, and shocking even to barbarians"; they had incited the Indians to take the warpath; they had assisted the braves in lifting the scalp from "the aged matron, the blooming fair one, the helpless infant, and the dying hero"; they had burned American cities, ravaged the country, and violated women. "Were it not for these miscreants," said Governor Livingston of New Jersey, "we should have thought that for

[2] By the end of 1778, almost seventy-five hundred Loyalists were under arms in the service of George III — a host which, had it been added to Washington's army, might have brought victory at that time. The Continental army was hardly as numerous as were the Loyalist troops in British pay. In 1779, Lord George Germain boasted in the House that more Americans were enlisted in the British service than were to be found in Washington's entire army and that the British could raise men in America for five or six pounds, whereas the Continental Congress could not procure recruits for less than two hundred and fifty dollars. Altogether, between twenty-five and thirty thousand Loyalists were on the rolls of the British army, or served in the forty-odd Loyalist military organizations or in the Loyalist militia. By the end of the war, it was said that the King's American Dragoons, composed of Loyalists, was one of the crack corps of the British army; its commander remarked that the appearance of his troops was such that he would not be ashamed to show the regiment in Hyde Park. It is not remarkable, therefore, that Englishmen were encouraged to continue the war despite its unfavorable turnings, sustained by the hope that the majority of the American people were on the British side.

cool, deliberate cruelty, and unavailing, undecisive havoc, the sons of Britain were without parallel"; but the Tories had plumbed new depths of hellishness and had given Americans a fresh perspective on the horrors of war.

Standing chargeable with such a catalogue of crimes, it is understandable why Loyalists should have been made the object of a witch hunt. On the ground that they were not worth hanging and that there were not enough prisons in the country to contain them, Elbridge Gerry of Massachusetts recommended that they be exiled to Great Britain where they might enjoy to the full the slavery they loved so well. Other patriots swore that Tories deserved death. "A Tory," said Governor Livingston, "is an incorrigible Animal: And nothing but the Extinction of Life, will extinguish his Malevolence against Liberty." Even Washington, usually more troubled by the derelictions of the patriots than by the iniquities of the Loyalists, said that the most notorious offenders ought to be hanged as an example to the rest.

Under this sanction, the patriots zealously fell to terrorizing suspected Loyalists, riding them on rails, varnishing them with tar and feathers, making them targets for a barrage of rotten eggs, driving them at the cart's tail, and lashing them through the streets.[3] At the hands of the sovereign mob they were forced to go down on their knees and to beg forgiveness of the sovereign people and to "damn Bute, North, and their brethren." A Tory desirous of saving his skin was well advised to tread softly in the presence of the patriots. "I have had the misfortune," lamented a Tory, "to affront one of the Committee men, by not giving his Daughter a kiss when I was introduced to her. This has offended the old man so much, that . . . he has several spys to watch my actions. Sorry I did not give the ugly Jade a kiss." Of course, unpopular individuals — especially those to whom money was owing — often found themselves denounced as Tories and haled before a patriot committee. Few people love their creditors, and it is not difficult to believe the worst of them. Informers were well rewarded, and the committees were soon swamped with cases of suspected treason. "It is a fine time to gratify low private revenge," it was observed, "& few opportunities are lost."

To force the Tories to declare themselves, the patriots rigorously imposed oaths of loyalty to the United States. Those who refused to swear allegiance to the republic were punished with fines, imprisonment, and the loss of civil rights. Before the war was over, every state had begun to confiscate the property of notorious Loyalists, particularly those who had fled to the British for protection or had taken up

[3] Some unfortunates were sent to the notorious Simsbury Mines in Connecticut — abandoned copper mines where cells had been hewn out one hundred and fifty feet below the surface. So many Loyalists died in this black and noisome hole that it was called "the catacomb of Loyalty."

arms against the United States. Inevitably, it was the well-to-do who bore the brunt of these losses: a rich Tory had little chance of escaping the vigilance of the patriots. Thomas Paine rejoiced in this work of dispossessing the enemies of freedom; by distributing the property of great Tory landowners among needy patriots, he believed that the economic basis of American democracy would be strengthened. Justice, he said, required that those who fought in defense of liberty should be rewarded with the property of its enemies. Nor was it overlooked that the worldly goods of exiled Loyalists would powerfully aid Americans in carrying on the struggle with Great Britain.

In a revolution, many seek only to survive: safety rather than glory is the greatest good. And so, during the War of American Independence, thousands of Americans were content to take comfortable seats on the side lines, cheer for both sides, and be the first to congratulate the winner. By passing as a Loyalist with the British and as a patriot with the Americans, one possessed double-barreled insurance against molestation or property loss. Of these trimmers, Thomas Paine said that all they asked was: *"Give me peace in my day."* In private they made themselves "as merry as Whiskey, Toddy, and good company will afford," damning the rebels with fine gusto and weeping upon each other's shoulders over the degeneracy of the times. But in public they were willing to empty their bumpers, depending upon the company, to the toast "GOD SAVE GREAT WASHINGTON! GOD DAMN THE KING!" or "GOD SAVE THE KING! GOD DAMN THE REBELS!"

HE American army that fought at Bunker Hill was in reality four different armies composed of militiamen, minutemen, and any others willing to wield a musket, drawn from the four New England colonies. Within an amazingly short time after the battles of Lexington and Concord, over twenty thousand men had laid siege to Boston. Yet, despite the urgency of the occasion, colonial distinctions were not wholly laid aside. Massachusetts, Connecticut, Rhode Island, and New Hampshire each sent its own army to the scene of action, and each colony refused to admit any but its own citizens to the ranks. Although, in May 1775, General Artemas Ward of Massachusetts was placed in command of these four armies, there was no general staff and no close integration of the various provincial contingents. It was not until the battle of Bunker Hill that the shortcomings of this imperfect merger of forces were fully revealed.

Even before that battle, Massachusetts, recognizing that the task of confining the British army to Boston and withstanding the inevitable onslaught from Great Britain was beyond the power of New England alone, urged the Continental Congress to take over control of the army besieging Boston and to appoint a commander-in-chief of this "continental" army. By this means, New Englanders foresaw, all the colonies would be directly involved in the struggle with Great Britain – a consummation essential to the success of American resistance.

In June 1775, the Continental Congress responded to the pleas of Massachusetts by assuming direction of the military resistance to Great Britain. The Continental army was created, the New England troops then engaged in besieging Boston forming the nucleus of the new army. But in appointing a commander-in-chief of the Continental army, Congress found itself obliged to steer a course between personal and sectional aspirations and jealousies that for some time left the issue in doubt.

Because the army was composed largely of New Englanders, it seemed fitting to the Yankees that one of their countrymen should be given the command. In fact, it was extremely doubtful whether New Englanders would fight under a commander who did not come from that favored region. In particular, the screams that would arise from the Yankees if a New Yorker were chosen to lead the army promised to split the union wide open. There was no dearth of candidates: Congress might choose between such heroes and would-be heroes as John Hancock (whose military experience consisted largely in parading the cadets on Boston Common); Artemas Ward, the commander of the New England army around Boston; and Israel Putnam, the hero of Bunker Hill.

It was at this moment that John Adams, among others, decided that the finger of expediency pointed to a Southerner for that office. The objective of New Englanders was to get the boys from the Middle and Southern colonies into the trenches around Boston. In John Adams's opinion, the aid of the rest of the colonies was worth the commandership of the Continental army.

What is more, John Adams had already spotted his man. Among the delegates to the Continental Congress, a tall, rangy Virginian stood out from the rest of the members partly by reason of the fact that he alone attended the sessions dressed in military uniform. Clad in civilian clothing, George Washington would have made a striking figure in any assemblage; but to the Continental Congress, seeking a commander for the Continental army, he looked like the answer to its prayers.[1]

Distrustful of militarists and eager to keep the newly organized Continental army under its control, Congress was strongly inclined to look among its own membership for a commander-in-chief. The military reputation, large fortune, and aristocratic lineage of George Washington made him by all odds the leading candidate in the field. As head of the military forces of the United Colonies, he would give the rebellion a respectability which it badly needed. But none of these considerations carried as much weight in Congress as did the fact that he was the outstanding military man of Virginia, the largest colony in the union, the support of which was essential to the American cause. Politically speaking, Washington was eminently "available" for the post of commander-in-chief. And, as he well knew, he was elected to that post for the same reason that a great many presidential candidates have been nominated by their

[1] With fighting going on in New England, Washington did not propose to remain on the side lines. No doubt he wore his uniform in Congress to signify his conviction that the struggle had entered the "shooting stage" for all Americans, whether Southerners or Northerners, and to indicate that he was ready to do his part in the struggle. That he was angling for the command of the as yet unformed Continental army is not credible.

party: he came from the right state. The finger of Providence not merely pointed at Washington: it reached out and tapped him on the shoulder. Congress could hardly ignore such explicit directions.

Thus a body of civilians, for the most part ignorant of military matters, took upon themselves to elect the military leader of the Revolution. Seldom has the democratic process been carried to greater lengths, and seldom has it resulted in a happier choice.

Washington had no dazzling qualities to attract the attention of his contemporaries; it was by strength of character, by a fierce will to surmount all difficulties, and by the solidity of his personality that he inspired confidence. The key to his character is self-discipline; cold, imperturbable, aloof, and slow to unbend, he was a man who never swerved from his purpose. He lived by the code of a gentleman, and it is right to regard him as the fairest flower of the Virginia gentry. Few leaders have been less enamored of fame and adulation. In his selflessness, his willingness to subordinate personal renown to the winning of the war, he resembles Abraham Lincoln. The great aristocrat and the great commoner of American history were of the same fiber.

Washington was a big, heavy-jawed man who did not bother with unnecessary talk — which made him a great favorite among congressmen who liked to do most of the talking themselves. But his silence did not make him dull and heavy; rather, it seemed to betoken wisdom and calm. His grave, reserved manner inspired confidence; if he said little, what he said had substance and was to the point. For example, in 1774 he had quietly remarked that "if the English should attack the People of Boston, he would raise a thousand Men at his own expense and march at their head to New England to their aid."

Besides, Washington enjoyed the inestimable advantage of being cast in a heroic mold: if not a great general, he certainly looked like one. Tall, dignified, cold in manner though courteous, his long thin face marked by smallpox, he was every inch the soldier. The revolutionary patriots liked to think of themselves as Old Romans — and few could deny that Washington seemed to be the noblest Roman of them all. Indeed, to some congressmen, he appeared to be some austere figure of antiquity risen to save his country's liberties. Although it was perhaps premature to press the analogy, it was observed that like Cincinnatus he was a farmer.

Washington owed much of his early rise in the military and civic life of Virginia to the fact that he belonged to the clique of Virginia aristocrats that supported the royal governor. Another faction of the aristocracy opposed the governor and sought to curtail British authority and win a larger measure of home rule, but the members of this group paid the penalty of being excluded from the choice political jobs and military commissions in the gift of the King's representative. The party of which Washington was a member was composed largely of "old and judicious" aristocrats, well-seasoned conservatives who believed that British authority offered the best guarantee of the perpetuation of the old order. Most of the young men, ardent and rebellious against authority, were in the opposition. Washington was clearly an exception: although a young man of considerable talent, he preferred to follow the leadership of the great magnates of Virginia. Accordingly, he was regarded with special benignity by his elders: this promising young man, so wise for his years, ought to be boosted up the ladder as quickly as possible.

Enjoying the backing of the right people, chief among them being the royal lieutenant governor of Virginia, Washington was put in command of an expedition in 1754 to warn the French off territory claimed by Virginia west of the Appalachians. It was not merely as English soil violated by foreigners that this region attracted the attention of the government and citizens of Virginia: land companies, in which the lieutenant governor and the gentry were financially concerned, had claims to these lands over which the French were seeking to extend their jurisdiction. Washington himself had a financial stake in Western lands, for this kind of speculation came naturally to a well-born Virginian. On this expedition, with the aid of Indians, Washington wiped out a French scouting party and was himself shortly after besieged by the French at Fort Necessity. Here Washington gave the first evidence of his skill in extricating himself from tight situations — a talent of which he was required to make full use during the War of American Independence. He surrendered the fort to the French after extracting a promise from the French commander that the garrison, together with Washington himself, would be permitted to return to Virginia.

To rid the American West of these unwelcome French neighbors, General Braddock at the head of a British army was sent to the colonies by the British government in 1755. Leading a party of Virginia Rangers, Washington accompanied Braddock in his march through the wilderness to Fort Duquesne; but despite the advice of the young Virginia colonel, Braddock bumbled into disaster, his army being ambushed and thrown into utter rout. Here Washington saw British regulars struck with a "deadly Panick." "The dastardly behaviour of the English Soldiers," he said, "expos'd all those who were inclin'd to do their duty to almost certain Death. . . . Despite of every effort to the contrary," he added, the British regulars "broke and run as Sheep before the Hounds. . . . When we endeavour'd to rally them . . . it was with as much success as if we had attempted to have stop'd the wild Bears of the Mountains." Washington's own courage is incontestable: in attempting to stop the rout, he had four bullets through his coat and two horses shot under him. Manifestly, British regulars were fighting at a serious disadvantage in the American wilderness; at no other time during the war did Washington find reason to question their courage.

It was not until three years after Braddock's defeat that the British army finally succeeded in capturing Fort Duquesne. During these years of preparation and waiting, Washington, in command of the Virginia militia, was engaged in whipping an effective fighting force out of the inadequate material at his disposal. In so doing, he made himself unpopular in the colony: Virginia civilians did not submit easily to dictation from a military man, no matter how menacing their enemies. Moreover as commander of the Virginia militia, Washington was plagued by shortages of powder and food, was obliged to go into action with half the men he deemed necessary, and had to deal with a currency — the colonial paper money of Virginia — that was almost worthless. He was also confronted by a deep-rooted provincialism — it sometimes happened that one Virginia county would protest against sending men or supplies to the defense of another county. And he was compelled to deal with a militia that seemingly thought only of home and mother, and with a people whose timidity, he remarked, was "equalled by nothing but their perverseness." Calling upon them to show "the heroic spirit of every free-born Englishman," he met with a niggardliness and preoccupation with private affairs which, however disheartening at the time, taught him how to contend with the same spirit during the War of American Independence.

For his pains in trying to save the colony, Washington was attacked in the newspapers and was vilified by politicians who professed themselves the defenders of the common people against military despotism. Perhaps for this reason, after the fall of Fort Duquesne in 1758, Washington threw up his command; the war went on, but Washington, bruised by the buffeting he had received at the hands of the politicians, retired to his estate.

Washington took time out from the war to marry the richest woman in Virginia, spending his honeymoon upon his wife's plantation. Washington's own fortune was considerable, having come to him by the death of an older brother. Although not particularly successful as a money-maker, Washington was a good administrator; he conducted his affairs prudently and avoided "those foolish, giddy and expensive frolics natural to a Virginian" which ruined many of the young blades of the Old Dominion. He was quick to adopt new ways; when tobacco became unprofitable, for example, he was among the first to turn his tobacco lands into wheat fields. But neither his marriage nor his economies freed Washington from financial worry. His capital was largely tied up in land and slaves, and though on paper he was a wealthy man, he was, like most of his fellow planters, chronically short of ready money. Expenses, he complained, "swallowed up before I well knew where I was, all the money I got by Marriage, nay more, brought me into Debt." It was the fate of a Virginia planter to struggle endlessly with bills, mortgages, and taxes; and Washington was hard pressed to keep his head above water.

With the ending of the French and Indian War, Washington settled down to a round of duties and pleasures which did not greatly distinguish him from other Virginia aristocrats, unless perhaps it was that he took his pleasures more temperately than most of his companions. He entertained frequently at Mount Vernon, went to the races, played cards, attended cockfights and the theater, danced extremely well, and played a conspicuous part in the social whirl of eighteenth-century Virginia. He was elected to the House of Burgesses, almost a social obligation to men in society. Mrs. Washington was a lively companion, and if her husband was apt to lapse into gravity and reserve, she brought the good man out of his solemn moods.

A member of the ruling clique and supporter of the royal governor, Washington was jolted from his complacency by the outbreak of the revolutionary movement. Like other Virginia planters, he ascribed his financial difficulties to the craft and greed of English and Scottish merchants who paid him low for his tobacco and charged him high for the merchandise he bought. When the British Parliament attempted to tax Americans in 1765 — a step certain to strip their colonial assemblies of all real power — Washington emerged as a resistance leader. Casting off his earlier conservatism, he now joined forces with the dissatisfied elements in the province in opposition to the royal government; as early as 1768, he declared that he was ready to take up arms against British tyranny. He became friendly with Patrick Henry, the leader of the democratic westerners whose aspirations to office Washington had always opposed; and Henry was favored with an invitation to visit Mount Vernon. For the first time, Washington became popular with all groups in Virginia, and in 1774 he was elected to the Continental Congress.

Although, by 1775, Washington had been long absent from the field, he was not so rusty as might have been supposed. Behind the erect military bearing and officer's uniform that helped make him a man of mark in Philadelphia lay the student of the art of war. When he retired from the army in 1759 he by no means abandoned his interest in military affairs. He diligently collected and read the best manuals and textbooks of the day, and although he was not a bookish man, his library was well stocked with military books. It is significant that when Charles Willson Peale painted his portrait in 1772, Washington sat, not in the finery of a Virginia gentleman, but in the uniform of a Virginia colonel of militia. When he learned of the battle of Lexington, he closely studied all the available accounts of the engagement to get the facts "stripped of all colouring." And as a member of the Continental Congress, he turned his military knowledge to account by helping to plan the defense of New York City, formulate army regulations, and obtain much-needed war supplies.

In accepting command of the Continental army, Washington acknowledged that his greatest shortcoming was his lack of experience in moving troops on a large scale. The conditions of warfare around Boston were unfamiliar to a man who had specialized in frontier fighting and whose command had consisted of a few hundred men. Nevertheless, he believed that this deficiency would be outweighed by "sound judgment, and some knowledge of Men and Books; especially when accompanied by an enterprizing genius." But Washington would have been the first to admit that he knew vastly more about running a farm than organizing an army and fighting a battle; he was primarily a civilian rather than a military man. Against Howe, Burgoyne, and Clinton, he could pit only a comparatively slender store of military knowledge; it was the familiar story of the amateur versus the professional, meeting in a contest in which the amateur seldom carries off the honors.

In appointing Washington, a comparatively untried man, to the chief command, Congress was taking a risk; but to men who had taken many risks and who lived with halters around their necks, Washington seemed worth the chance. Courage, coolness, and tenacity were qualities which Washington had frequently shown in action; and these characteristics might well compensate for his relative inexperience in actual command. Jonathan Boucher, a Loyalist clergyman who had been friendly with Washington, warned the British government to expect no quick victory over this Virginia tobacco planter. The only hope of defeating him, said Boucher, lay in outgeneraling him: "in a regular action, he may, by his steadiness and extreme care, acquit himself well; but against the manoeuvres of art, I am satisfied he is defenceless."

Never disposed to overrate his abilities or to believe in his star, Washington made no promises of victory: on the contrary, he cautioned Congress against the strong inclination of civilians to expect miracles from their generals. He declared that he "never assumed the Character of a Military genius and the Officer of experience" and that he might prove unequal to his responsibilities — in which case, he wanted Congress to remember that he had been virtually drafted into the post of commander-in-chief. His resolution to defend American liberty was tinged with foreboding of disaster; as he told Patrick Henry, he might well date his fall and the ruin of his reputation from his assumption of the military leadership of the rebellion. All that he was sure of was his devotion to the cause of American freedom.

Certainly, Washington did not gloss over the difficulties that lay ahead; yet he was hardly prepared for the situation he found in the

American camp around Boston. Congress had commissioned him to command the American army; he now learned that he must first create an army out of the raw materials, supply it with necessities that were almost unobtainable, and simultaneously wage war by land and sea against the enemy. In such an emergency, there was little in the text-books to guide him.

The troops of the army over which Washington assumed command early in July 1775 were undisciplined, poorly officered, and lacking in the organization necessary to maintain a large body of men in the field. Moreover, he was obliged to deal with a species of man unfamiliar to a Virginia gentleman — the Yankees. It was the New Englanders, rather than the British, who first gave Washington an inkling of the trials and tribulations he was to encounter as commander-in-chief. Indeed, before he met the enemy in battle, Washington's morale had been severely shaken by his experiences in attempting to make soldiers out of New England democrats.

At Bunker Hill, the privates had displayed exemplary spirit and gallantry, but many of their officers had run away at the first sign of danger. It was largely owing to the cowardice of the officers that so few reinforcements reached the defenders of Breed's Hill during the battle. Troops ordered to relieve the Americans who had labored on the fortifications all night reached the scene just as the action was beginning, but the major in command "no sooner came in sight of the enemy than a tremor seiz'd him & he began to bellow, 'Retreat! Retreat! or you'll all be cut off' " — which so frightened the troops that many ran for dear life. One captain ordered his men to march to Bunker Hill, then excused himself, saying that he would overtake them immediately. He did not turn up until the next day. Under such leaders, it is not surprising that some soldiers lacked courage to meet the enemy. During the battle, it was observed that "if a man was wounded twenty more were glad of an Opportunity to Carry him away when not more than three could take hold of him to advantage." One company in retreat was stopped by a threat of being fired upon by another company — "the Poor Dogs were forced to Come back like Dogs that had been stealing sheep." It is probable that if the American officers had acted differently, and if reinforcements and ammunition had been brought up promptly, the British would never have carried Bunker Hill.[2]

Before he joined the army at Cambridge, Washington was resolved to love New Englanders as he loved his fellow Virginians; he would

[2] Even New Englanders were sometimes critical of their countrymen: General Nathanael Greene of Rhode Island admitted that "the sentiment of honor, the true characteristic of a soldier, has not yet got the better of interest"; and General Sullivan of New Hampshire, finding that his troops were clamorous for their pay before they went home, remarked that "these worthless Scoundrels Though willing to Sacrifice their Liberties could not Suffer the Least Delay of payment for their Services."

prove himself to be above sectional partialities by showing equal consideration to all Americans. But his contact with New Englanders in
the flesh shook this resolve, and despite his good intentions, he became
the Virginia aristocrat looking down his nose at the unsavory Yankees.
They were, he said, "an exceeding dirty and nasty people" and there
seemed uncommonly few gentlemen among them. But they might have
been forgiven their low birth had they lived by high ideals. It was here
that Washington believed that their greatest shortcoming lay. They
seemed to make self-interest their god; from them could be expected
shrewd bargains but not heroic actions or self-sacrifice.[3] They took advantage of the necessities of the army by raising the prices for provisions and wood; barrels were sometimes only half full; "beef" proved
to be horse meat, and bread was sometimes moldy and unfit to be
eaten.

Washington had come to New England with very definite ideas regarding the kind of men he wanted as officers in the army. "None but
Gentlemen," in his opinion, ought to hold rank in the army. The true
criterion of judgment "when past Services do not enter into the Competition," he said, "is, whether the Candidate for Office has a just pretension to the Character of a Gentleman, a proper sense of Honor, and
some reputation to lose." Above all, he wanted no officers who, having
been raised from the masses, "placed themselves upon a level with the common Soldiery"; such familiarity he regarded as subversive of all order
and discipline. He believed that rank in civil life ought to be carried
over into the army, and that soldiers were more likely to respect and obey
men who came from the upper class than those who had been their
equals.

Washington set great store by the quality of his officers: they could
make or break an army. "It would be a mere phenomenon in nature,"
he said, "to find a well disciplin'd Soldiery, where Officers are relax'd
and tardy in their duty." It was therefore shocking to find the New
Englanders over whom he had assumed command officered to a large
degree by incompetents, rogues, and cowards who, "seeking by dirty
and base means, the promotion their own dishonest gain," had brought
dishonor upon an army created to defend the liberties of mankind. Immediately, he began to weed out these undesirables, making, as he said,
"a pretty good slam" among the New Englanders. One captain, for
example, dressed in woman's clothing, was drummed out of camp; sev-

[3] Washington, it is fair to say, did not harbor long this low opinion of New Englanders. Their good points grew upon him with longer acquaintance; by 1777, he was
singing their praises. "I do not believe that any of the states produce better men, or
persons capable of making better soldiers," he declared; ". . . no people fly to arms
readier, or come better equipped, or with more regularity into the field than they."
In fact, he acknowledged that they were the most dependable troops under his
command.

eral were horsewhipped, and others were stripped of their commissions and run out of the army.

The American commander recognized that it was not sufficient to break unworthy officers: they must be prevented from attaining rank. In his opinion, the root of the trouble was insufficient distinction between the common soldiers and their officers; their pay was too nearly on a level; their uniforms — when they had such — were too much alike; and they came from equally humble walks of life. The common people of New England, he found, lacked a proper sense of subordination to the gentry; levelers at heart, they denied that pre-eminence to family, breeding, and wealth upon which Southern aristocrats set such store. Their equalitarianism, objectionable in everyday life, became intolerable when they tried to apply it to the army. They considered tailors, shoemakers, and dirt farmers as perfectly eligible to command: indeed, they seemed to have a definite partiality for such men when conferring rank.

New Englanders were apt to take the position that no officers except those chosen in a fair and free election had any authority over them. Nor did they tolerate high and mighty airs in their officers. Tailor Jones might be Colonel Jones, thanks to his skill in getting out the vote, but to his men he was Tailor Jones still. He was given unmistakably to understand not to presume upon his rank; a bit of gold braid did not make him any better than the men he commanded. Many officers, preferring the emoluments and honor — such as it was — of rank to the dubious and painful joys of authority, wisely bowed to the will of their constituents. They cultivated the back-slapping, good-fellow practices of politicians; their orders were given as requests; and, on occasion, they proved their capacity to hold liquor — in itself a weighty recommendation — by drinking and carousing with their men. In some instances, candidates for officer's rank were obliged to promise to pool their pay with that of their men and share alike; and officers sometimes cut the soldiers' hair and mended their boots. It was all very democratic and extraordinarily pleasant for the enlisted man, but it emphatically did not make for subordination or efficiency in the army.

Washington's second-in-command was General Charles Lee, an Irishman who, from the tender age of twelve years, had held a commission in the British army. Serving in America during the French and Indian War, he had been called "Boiling Water" by the Indians, a name which proved the redskins no mean judges of character. After the war, despairing of advancement in the British army, he had gone to Poland, where he had risen to rank of general in the Polish army and had become the confidant of the Polish King. But the props were kicked from this promising career when the great powers began to move in on Poland and carve up that helpless kingdom among themselves. If worst came to worst, Lee could no doubt have made a living with his pen; a literary man of some distinction, he was thought in certain quarters to be "Junius" — and, indeed, his work is reminiscent of that master of the poison pen. Instead, however, he came to America to seek his fortune after his Polish interregnum, and when the outbreak of the Revolution put an unexpected premium upon his military ability, he was living on a Virginia plantation.

Before accepting a commission as major general in the Continental army, Lee drove a bargain with Congress which protected him against any financial loss as a result of changing sides. Claiming that large sums were owing him in England, he persuaded Congress to make them good, besides granting him a loan to pay off the mortgage on his Virginia plantation. In October 1776, despite the desperate military situation, he took time out from the war to make a trip to Philadelphia to press his claims upon Congress. All told, it cost Congress eleven thousand pounds sterling to secure Lee's services.

Lee particularly endeared himself to the patriots by casting scorn upon the valor and prowess of the British army. Coming from a military man of Lee's standing, his strictures carried authority. He assured Americans that the much-vaunted British army was composed of cowards, jailbirds, and weaklings; the officers, he said, were more suited to make conquests in the boudoir than on the field of battle. While American womanhood might tremble at their approach, the men had nothing to fear — unless it was for their women. Perhaps resentment, bred by his comparatively slow advancement in the British army, had something to do with Lee's low opinion of his late associates; but it is certain that his views, delivered with a crushing air of authority, helped many Americans overcome their reluctance to take the field against the hitherto dreaded redcoats. No one did more to convince the colonists that they were a match, if not an overmatch, for the mother country.

Few generals, excepting perhaps U. S. Grant, made a more unmilitary appearance than did Charles Lee. In a stained and threadbare uniform, he slouched along, accompanied always by his retinue of dogs, with which, in the matter of personal hygiene, he was sometimes compared — to the disadvantage of the master. Certainly, even his best friends admitted — if they did not tell Lee — that there was a strong aroma of the kennel about the general. Over six feet tall, cadaverous, and hawk-nosed, he would have been conspicuous in his own right; but surrounded as he was by a dozen yapping hounds, no man could fail to heed the presence of this hotspur. Lee was so eccentric, indeed, that many Americans somewhat rashly concluded that he must be a genius. He was, it was admitted, an exceedingly "odd fish," "a strange animal"; but, as John Adams said, "we must put up with ten thousand oddities in him on account of his abilities and his attachment to the rights of humanity." To Mrs. John Adams, he was "a careless hardy veteran," much like Charles XII of Sweden, the Madman of the North. It was observed of Lee, however, that he was fond of his

own opinion beyond most generals, and even beyond literary men. "Every idea of his must be right, and, of course, every contrary idea in every other person must be wrong," remarked a patriot after being briefly in his company.

Lee was appointed to high rank to compensate for Washington's lack of experience. A trained officer was deemed necessary to bolster the commander-in-chief in the field, and Lee, a major general of six years' standing in the Polish army, and a former lieutenant colonel in the British army, was expected to be an admirable mentor to Washington. Lee enthusiastically entered into this role – he would take Washington in hand and, while teaching him the rudiments of military science, lead the American army to victory. From the beginning of their relationship, Lee keenly felt the indignity of serving under a Virginia tobacco grower, as he was pleased to regard Washington. Far from accepting Washington as the savior of the American cause, he believed that that honor was reserved for himself alone. He was as conscious of Washington's faults as he was blind to his own.

Lee, however, saw as clearly as did Washington the necessity of injecting discipline into the army. The two generals were on the lines every day, inspecting the troops and issuing orders. "The strictest government is taking place," wrote a soldier, "and great distinction is made between officers and soldiers. Every one is made to know his place and keep it, or be tied up and receive thirty or forty lashes according to his crime." Congress was urged to raise the pay of officers while maintaining the prevailing wage of the privates; and well-tailored uniforms were declared to be a requisite for the officers.

Yet, although Washington succeeded in remedying the worst abuses, he failed at this time to make much impression on the civilian and democratic character of the army; discipline and subordination were the last things learned by American soldiers. Soldiers and officers went a.w.o.l. as the inclination struck them; they bathed in the Charles River at Cambridge and ran naked about the bridge to the horror of "Ladies of the first fashion" who happened to be passing by. Officers contended bitterly for rank; two disgruntled generals walked out of camp without so much as telling the commander-in-chief that they were leaving. Vainly Washington pointed out that in the cause of freedom any post of service was honorable; the officers nursed their outraged honor. Finally, in September 1775, weary of the "discord and confusion" that had sprung up on every hand, Washington asked Congress either to move nearer Boston or to send a committee with whom he could discuss the problems with which he was beset. Congress obliged by sending a committee to the harassed general to determine "the most effectual method of continuing, supporting, and regulating a continental army."

The vexations of the commander-in-chief came, however, not merely

from New England democrats: the democrats from the Southern frontier were quite as troublesome as their Yankee counterparts. Indeed, Washington might well have wondered if Americans were not too democratic a people to fight effectively the battles of democracy.

In taking up arms against the mother country, Americans believed that they had in the rifle a secret weapon capable of winning the war. Although originated in Switzerland, the rifle had undergone such radical development in America as to become essentially a new weapon of — to eighteenth-century warfare — terrifying potentialities. Widely used by frontiersmen from Pennsylvania to Georgia, it had evolved into a long, small-bore, highly accurate, custom-made weapon. The marksmanship of the frontiersmen quickly became legendary; some of these rangy, hard-bitten Westerners were reputed to specialize in clipping toothpicks at a hundred yards.

Not the least terrifying aspect of the riflemen was their appearance. Painted like Indians, armed with tomahawks and rifles and dressed in hunting shirts and moccasins, they looked like a particularly bloodthirsty tribe of savages. Believing that this regalia would strike terror among the British, Washington wished to see all his troops outfitted like frontiersmen; certainly, in that case, they would have been far more fearsome than were the three major generals.

With the outbreak of hostilities, large numbers of riflemen had come down from the hills and had been embodied in regiments by Pennsylvania and the colonies to the south. Shortly after the battle of Bunker Hill, several of these regiments of marksmen were ordered by the Continental Congress to join Washington at Cambridge.

On their march to Boston, the riflemen attracted almost as much attention as would a Wild West circus; droves of citizens turned out to see these tall, stalwart men from the Far West, of which Pittsburgh was then the terminus. Giving frequent public demonstrations of their marksmanship, they found themselves hailed as heroes: one thousand riflemen in the forests of America, it was confidently predicted, could defeat any regular army in the world. As a result of this adulation, the riflemen arrived in Boston nursing a bad case of conceit; in their own opinion, they were the elite corps of the army and deserved to be treated as nothing less.

At first, the exploits of the riflemen sent chills down the spines of British soldiers. They sniped at sentries, picked off officers (one officer was shot from his horse at a distance of two hundred and fifty yards), and kept the whole camp in terror of sudden death at the hands of an unseen foe. They observed none of the rules of warfare: when, in July 1775, the British sent out a flag of truce to ask for a suspension of arms for three days in which to bury their dead, a rifleman neatly cut off the flag just above the bearer's hand. "Between sunset and dark," they boasted, "our people killed fourteen of the Regulars which came out in search of their dead." Officers were of course their favorite target and they soon became expert in singling out the gold braid and epaulets among the redcoats. Mrs. William Howe's spirits rose wonderfully when she learned that her husband had been made commander-in-chief, for, as she said, he would not be obliged to go into the front lines and run the risk of being shot by a rebel rifleman.

Heavy losses taught the British to stay close to their entrenchments and to expose themselves as little as possible to the murderous fire of the riflemen. As a result, the riflemen soon found themselves with nothing to shoot at: not an enemy soldier or officer poked his head above the parapets. On the other hand, the British, snug behind their entrenchments, began to pick off the riflemen; in September 1775, General Gage declared that "their Indians and Rifle Men have been Firing above Six Weeks and have hit one poor Marine, for which they have Paid ten fold."

Nevertheless, the riflemen continued to blaze away at the British lines until Washington began to fear that all his slender supply of powder would go up in smoke. They felled few British in proportion to the vast amount of powder and shot they expended; and when they were not sniping at the British entrenchments they were hard at work in camp at target practice. Given an unlimited powder supply, Washington would no doubt have rejoiced at the zeal of his riflemen; but he was already scraping the bottom of his powder barrel, and unless the riflemen's furious fusillade were stopped, he could not hope to hold off a British attack. Therefore, the riflemen were forbidden to fire upon the enemy except when given special permission by the commander-in-chief.

Rugged individualists as they were, the riflemen did not take well to discipline. Time hung heavy on their hands; lounging around camp, inactive, and bored by the siege tactics which Washington had adopted, they soon began to make almost as much trouble for Washington as they had for Sir William Howe. Although they were given special privileges such as exemption from camp duty, higher pay than the common soldiers, and practically the run of the camp, they responded to this treatment by refusing to obey orders from their officers. When one rifleman was put under arrest for refusal to obey orders, a whole company attempted to rescue him by storming the jail; to put down the uprising, Washington was compelled to call out the infantry. To the riflemen, mutiny was a small matter: subordination and discipline were not for free Americans who did what they pleased when they pleased.

If the riflemen were permitted to ride roughshod over the officers, it was apparent to Washington that all hope of disciplining the army was at an end. The common soldiers, jealous of the special status of the riflemen, clamored for equal rights — and when these were denied, went home in disgust. As for the riflemen, shorn of their privileges many headed for the backwoods, breaking camp without leaving a forwarding address, while others deserted to the enemy in Boston. To prevent them from running off, it was necessary to station them in Cambridge – they could no longer be trusted in the front lines lest they desert to the British.

So unmanageable, in short, became the riflemen that Washington began to regret that he had ever laid eyes on them; he devoutly wished them in the backwoods distressing the Indians, instead of setting his army at sixes and sevens. General Lee "damned them all and wished them all in Boston"; in his opinion, there was no better way of making the British sick of the war than to present them with a couple of regiments of unruly riflemen.

⌒   ⌒   ⌒

After Bunker Hill, both armies began to dig in. Boston, situated on an isthmus connected with the mainland by a narrow strip of land known as the Neck, was easily fortified; and by means of entrenchments, redoubts, and artillery, the British also made Bunker Hill well-nigh impregnable. For their part, the Americans threw up a wide arc of fortifications, eight or nine miles in length, designed to prevent the British from breaking out of the city.

The British enjoyed the advantage of holding interior lines; and the American entrenchments were too extended to admit of being adequately manned. As a result, Washington lived in constant anxiety lest the British discover the weakness of his army and launch an all-out attack upon his lines. The patriots swore that it would be "the most bloody Engagement our American World ever knew," but Washington's fears grew as he watched his supply of powder and arms steadily diminishing. In lieu of muskets and bayonets, several thousand pikes with twelve-foot handles were distributed among the men. Yet Washington's alarm proved needless: the British were in no position to assume the offensive. Grown cautious since Bunker Hill, they suspected that the apparent shortage of arms and ammunition in the American army was a ruse to draw them from their entrenchments. Even though the rebels were reported to be "wretchedly clothed, and as dirty a set of mortals as ever disgraced the name of a soldier," dying by hundreds of fever, and deserting Washington by shoals, the British did not venture beyond their fortifications to learn at first hand whether the Yankees could still fight.

Thus the war became a stalemate. "We cannot get at them," lamented General Greene, "and they are determined not to come to us." The outcome seemed destined to be decided by the powers of endurance of the two armies: whether the British could hold out in Boston longer than the Americans could maintain their positions around the besieged city.

Unable to come to grips at close quarters, both sides settled down to an artillery duel. American artillery was hampered by lack of powder, balls, and gunners, and the fire was very inaccurate. A large number of American gunners were killed or wounded when their guns burst; probably American artillery killed almost as many patriots as British. For, despite all the balls and shells they directed against the British lines, it was not until the middle of September, 1775 — three months after Bunker Hill — that they succeeded in wounding a British soldier. At best, cannon fire was effective only up to twelve hundred yards, but the Americans were so wild that they seldom hit their objective beyond four hundred yards.

The British artillery was only slightly more effective. Once the Americans were accustomed to fire, British cannon balls were hardly more troublesome than hailstones. Americans discovered that withstanding cannon fire was the "most harmless sport in life; indeed," said a soldier, "I have seen more mischief done by throwing the same number of snowballs." A Connecticut officer remarked that exchanging a few cannon shots with the enemy did more to exhilarate the spirits of our people than 200 gallons of New England rum." True, the British succeeded in destroying Roxbury with their artillery and reached as far as Cambridge with mortar shells, but the shells were poor and most of them burst harmlessly in the air or proved to be duds. On one occasion, the British fired eighty-two cannon at the American lines, killing two cows and wounding a private. On another occasion they fired over one hundred cannon balls at the American lines at short range "and did what?" asked General Knox. "Why, scratched a man's face with the splinters of a rail fence! . . . Nor am I afraid they will hit me," he added, "unless directed by the hand of Providence." Familiarity with British cannon fire bred contempt. "One night a ball passed thro' my apartment in the barracks a few feet over me as I lay in my berth," recounted an American soldier, "but such things having become so common we thought little of them." Indeed, American soldiers often scrambled for possession of spent British cannon balls — it was diverting, said an American soldier, "to see our people contending for the balls as they roll along," the fortunate men carrying them to the sutlers who paid them liberally in rum. In this way, many of the British cannon balls were fired right back at them and sped on their way with the aid of a stiff swig of rum.

The siege was enlivened by skirmishes over hay, sheep, fowl, and the like on the islands in Boston Harbor. In one of these heroic actions, the British captured "8 Cows and Bullocks strayed from the Rebels"; and the first exploit of the newly formed Continental army was the burning of a barn on Noodles Island on June 10, 1775. But, in general, it was a dull business, and to sharpen the discomfort of inactivity, the army began to feel the pinch of shortages of money and provisions. The men grumbled because they were not paid promptly and because they were put on short rations of food and liquor. In September 1775, Washington predicted a mutiny unless the men were paid more regularly and were better fed. Joseph Trumbull, the Commissary General, likened his position to that of a man who, "with twenty thousand gaping mouths open full upon him, and nothing to stop them with, must depend on being devoured himself." Compared with the later sufferings of the army, however, these were the days of plenty. At few times during the war did the Continental army fare better than during the siege of Boston, and those who underwent the rigors of Valley Forge and Morristown looked back upon 1775 and 1776 as the golden age of abundance.

The British army that was to have herded the rebels like sheep was shut up in Boston, short of food, almost cut off from aid by American cruisers, and fearful of being overwhelmed by Washington's army. Such a situation was unbearably "dishonourable and humiliating to British troops, that have been a terror to Europe"; few wars had opened more unprosperously for Great Britain. Although they tore down many buildings for fuel, among them the Old North Church, firewood remained so scarce that food sometimes had to be eaten uncooked. British officers cultivated their victory gardens to eke out a meager supply of fresh vegetables, but the soldiers sickened and lost their wonted spirit upon a diet of salt pork. Moreover, the army began to feel the effects of the corruption and mismanagement in the quartermaster and commissary departments, which, said Burgoyne, would "counteract and disappoint the ablest counsels in the world."

To while away the tedium of standing siege, the British enlivened the City of the Saints by converting the Old South Meeting House into a riding academy. It was also found that pews made excellent pigsties; and a fat porker was certainly more lovely in the eyes of British soldiers than a "greasy rebel." Faneuil Hall was turned into a playhouse — hitherto banned in Boston: where Adams and Otis had thundered against British tyranny, now were heard the witticisms and flourishes of British dramatists, including Sir John Burgoyne, who wrote the prologue and epilogue to the tragedy of *Zeus* and delayed his passage home in order to attend the opening night. Early in January, 1776, the British officers staged a play entitled *The Blockade of Boston*, a burlesque on Washington and his tatterdemalion army. Copies of the playbill were sent to the American general and he was cordially invited to attend — and be hanged. Although fond of the theater, Washington wisely refrained from accepting, but he broke up the play on the opening night by conducting a raid on Bunker Hill. The British officers were in the midst of making up as women and Negroes when the alarm sounded; instantly, pandemonium broke out, women fainted in the aisles, and officers rushed to their posts in petticoats or with their faces blackened.

The British did not lack for polite company in Boston, for many of the "best people" in New England had taken refuge in the metropolis from patriot mobs. Never before had Boston contained such a large number of the genteel; and thanks to the British army and navy, the society of the city was graced with the presence of an uncommonly select company of earls, lords, and baronets. Indeed, Boston was prepared for a brilliant social season — had it not been for the presence of twenty thousand rebels outside the gates. But the soldiers could not forget that they had come to New England for purposes other than cutting a brilliant figure at balls and being lionized by provincial social climbers. The officers chafed at inactivity, gambled heavily, and fought frequent duels, while the common soldiers, finding that they could get dead drunk on New England rum for a copper or two, took that way of breaking the monotony of garrison life.

For the British, the New England countryside with its hills, forests, and stone walls was not terrain to their liking. As far as they could see, natural or man-made obstacles met the eye; even if they were driven from one hill, the rebels would entrench themselves on the next hill and exact a heavy toll for each foot of ground they yielded. Rather than risk another engagement in a country that seemed to be "the most favorable spot in the world for irregular, undisciplined troops of the rebels," the British generals began to look for new worlds to conquer.

The existence of the British army in Boston depended upon the ability of the British navy to hold open the sea lanes. But the navy, unhappily for Great Britain, was unprepared for the tasks thus thrust upon it. It is hardly too much to say that the American rebellion caught the British navy with its sails down. This state of unreadiness can be ascribed largely to one man: Lord Sandwich, the First Lord of the Admiralty.

At best, the position of the British navy would have been critical during the American Revolution. In previous wars, Great Britain had drawn heavily upon the seamen of the colonies to help man its navy and merchant marine; now it was not only deprived of their services but obliged to face them as enemies. Moreover, as a source of naval stores, America was lost to Great Britain — with the result that by 1778 the navy was suffering from a serious shortage of masts. In few wars has the British navy sustained at the beginning a blow comparable to the loss of the American colonies. The utmost wisdom and courage were required to see England through this crisis; but in the Admiralty, wisdom was definitely a scarce commodity.

Lord Sandwich, to whose hands the naval destinies of Great Britain were entrusted, was a member of the "Bedford Gang" of Whig politicians whose greed for the spoils of office made them notorious even in eighteenth-century British politics. To the office of First Lord of the Admiralty to which he was appointed in 1770, Sandwich brought a thirst for money, a talent for corruption, and a skill in defrauding the public that would have ruined a country less rich and powerful than Great Britain. As a "distinguished Votary of Wit, Conviviality, and Pleasure," he had hardly a peer in Great Britain; John Wilkes, who had shared his revels, called Sandwich "the most abandoned man of the Age." At the Admiralty he lived openly with an actress by whom he had nine children. In 1779 she was murdered by a frustrated clergyman who had been driven to distraction by her charms (she was then in her forties). The news of her death was received "by her noble admirer with the utmost concern; he wept exceedingly and spoke touchingly of the seventeen years of unmarried felicity they had enjoyed together."

Under Lord Sandwich, the royal dockyards became a scene of unexampled larceny, swindling, and embezzlement. Parliament voted vast sums for the construction and repair of ships, but got precious little for its money. Ships built of green timber, ships with bottoms so rotten that no crew would put to sea in them, ships that capsized and foundered — these were Lord Sandwich's contribution to British security. From 1771 to 1775, Parliament annually appropriated money for the repair of H.M.S. *Dragon,* yet that vessel remained during those years untouched in its dock at Portsmouth, its bottom rotting away. It was charged that naval commanders who were sent to distant stations where rich rewards could be expected from captures were obliged to divide with Sandwich a part of their loot. Sandwich and his favored contractors prospered at the expense of the country, but the people bore with good humor the tribute exacted from them by the noble lord and his henchmen. Sandwich once said in Parliament that he spoke as an honest man; whereupon the whole House burst out in laughter. Yet he remained First Lord of the Admiralty for twelve years, during seven of which England was engaged in one of the greatest wars of its history.

The results of Lord Sandwich's administration appeared early in the war and grew progressively more apparent. Within five years of assuming office, he had brought England almost to the position of a second-rate naval power. Although its navy was still formidable on paper (in Sandwich's reports rotting hulks, ships under construction, and overage vessels figured as part of the active fleet) there were too few seaworthy ships, too few seamen, too few supplies of every kind — for Lord Sandwich and the contractors had been served first. A British admiral complained in 1779 that during an action with the French, his cannon balls could scarcely penetrate the sides of the enemy vessels, whereas enemy balls of the same weight ripped through British hulls. Such incidents so shook the confidence of British naval officers in their own ships and men that the Earl of Bristol declared that "God forbid that he should set his foot in the ship which had been assigned him, so wretchedly as it was at present manned," and Lord Chatham charged in 1777 that there were not more than twenty ships of the line in the entire British navy on which a naval officer of any rank would stake his credit.

Sandwich made the Admiralty a private preserve in which no other ministers, not even the Prime Minister, were permitted to interfere. He had only contempt for Lord North, toward whom he assumed a patronizing air, treating the Prime Minister's opinions much as he would those of a not too bright schoolboy. He was the real ruler of the King's Navee; peevish, obstinate, and intractable, he disdained to work in harness with his colleagues even when the outcome of the campaign depended upon combined operations of the army and navy. Germain complained that "if Lord Sandwich proposed or fully approves of any plan, we seldom want resources; on the other hand, if he does not heartily adopt what other ministers think right, official difficulties occur, and the state of our fleet is such that no new measure can be pursued."

Always a vast consumer of manpower — in the Seven Years' War, out of the 185,000 men who served in the navy, over 100,000 are estimated to have died of disease, and most of these by scurvy — the navy was hard pressed, during the War of American Independence, to man its ships. English sailors received higher pay and better working conditions aboard merchant ships or privateers than in His Majesty's navy; and the cat-o'-nine-tails, having laid bare many a sailor's back, had given the navy a bad repute among men who went down to the sea in ships. Press gangs ranged the ports and even far inland for men, and extraordinary measures such as the suspension of the writ of habeas corpus for impressed seamen were resorted to, but still the omnivorous men-of-war remained unsatisfied. In some ships, the crews were tumbled aboard without prior training; on several occasions ships were so hastily manned that not a single sailor at some of the guns had ever fired a cannon. Despite these desperate measures, in May 1782 England had ten ships of the line with hardly a man to sail them.

Admiral Graves, in command of the fleet at Boston, not knowing whether the British government intended peace or war, kept his fleet in harbor while American privateers, cruising freely in Massachusetts Bay, seized ships carrying food, munitions, and arms to the beleaguered British army. True, the Admiralty was at fault in sending out store ships unprotected, but the admiral did nothing to repair this error. The rebels even shipped aboard whaleboats and plundered the islands in Boston Harbor and burned the lighthouse under the muzzles of the guns of the men-of-war. Three prizes, loaded with arms and provisions, were captured by the Americans with the loss of only one man. Every river seemed to harbor a privateer or naval vessel: the citizens of Cohasset, Massachusetts, observing a ship coming up the bay, armed themselves, leaped into whaleboats, and captured the ship, which proved to be a British merchantman loaded with rum and sugar for Howe's army.

To observe the movements of the British and to capture their shipping, Washington created a navy out of small craft and former seamen serving in his army. Some of his officers held commands in both army and navy, and Washington himself directed the operations of the land and sea forces of the United States.

When the Admiralty finally got round to ordering Graves to take action against the rebels, it was found impossible for his few cruisers to carry out such diverse orders as rescuing royal governors, convoying transports, destroying American privateers and merchant shipping, and visiting "every harbour in the said colonies to disable ships fitting out." Graves destroyed only one American harbor — Falmouth, Massachusetts (now Portland, Maine) — and, although he achieved little of military value, he gave American propagandists an opportunity to exclaim that Great Britain was seeking "with fire and sword, to butcher and destroy, beggar and enslave, the whole *American* people."

The navy's remissness brought upon it the wrath of the hungry British soldiers in Boston who sorely needed the food and munitions captured by the rebels at sea. In the officers' mess, the navy was bitterly blamed for the inactivity, disgrace, and distress of the army. Some accused the admiral of operating a black market on the side — "miserable lean mutton may now and then be bought in Boston at eighteen-pence a pound," it was said, "and slander does not scruple to hint at the Admiral as the seller." The admiral was even accused of appropriating for his own table some turtles and pineapples sent to British officers in Boston by friends in the West Indies; whereupon some excitable army officers swore that the admiral ought to be strung from his own yardarm. The admiral and the general openly quarreled; and the bad blood extended downward to the rank and file of the services — a state of affairs which was to grow steadily worse during the War of American Independence. The real culprit, however, was resting comfortably in his quarters at the Admiralty.

෨ ෨ ෨

Washington's immediate objective was to confine the British army in Boston; and with this defensive strategy his generals agreed. Gates declared that "the American Gibraltar will cost a sweet sum. Boston Dirt will be a Dollar a Bushel to the English Treasury" — an expense certain to convince the British of the futility of continuing the war. As the siege wore on and inactivity began to pall upon his men, however, Washington became eager to attack Boston. He could not easily forget that his army might disband in the middle of the campaign; in his situation, perhaps it was best to make war today, for tomorrow the army might go home. But his generals strenuously objected to risking the American cause upon such a forlorn hope, and Washington reluctantly permitted himself to be overridden by their advice.

Although Congress had been brought to see the necessity of assuming control of the army, it failed to recognize the necessity of making the army permanent. The war itself was expected to be of short duration; reconciliation with Great Britain seemed to lie just around the corner;

long enlistments were regarded as "a state of slavery" abhorrent to the temper of American freemen; and it was feared that an army of long-term volunteers might be transformed into the standing army of which American patriots lived in dread. For these reasons, the Continental army created by Congress in 1775 was composed of soldiers pledged to serve only to the end of the year.

The hope of reconciliation helped to obstruct the enlistment of a long-term army; but the strongest opposition came from New England, where the hankering for reunion with Great Britain was least influential. John Adams declared that only "the meanest, idlest, most intemperate and worthless" New Englanders — of whom, of course, there were very few in the land of sobriety and steady habits — would enlist in the army for the duration of the war; but, he pointed out, in the Middle states, where convicts and indentured servants were common, many recruits might be obtained. New Englanders joined Adams in insisting that soldiers ought not to be enlisted for longer than one year and ought to have the privilege of electing their own officers. A Pennsylvania member likewise warned Congress that in his state even "the most desperate of imported laborers" would not enlist for the war — and certainly all above this level would refuse such extended service. In short, the opposition contended that to create a long-term army would be to fill the ranks with the scourings of the states rather than with those freeholders who constituted the chief hope of the republic.

Granted a short term of enlistment, few doubted that in this war for liberty and independence the army would be filled with zealous volunteers. It was deemed an insult to freemen to offer them bounties or high pay or, indeed, to solicit them to do their duty. "I saw a recruiting sergeant and 6 men beating up for soldiers about the streets as the regulars used to do," said a New York patriot in 1775, "which appeared to me ridiculous and disagreeable among American freemen, where I expect the poor would cheerfully offer to join and not wait for the importunity of a recruiting chattering sergeant."

In conformity with this point of view, low pay and no bounties for enlistment became the rule in 1775 for the Continental army. Privates were given about six dollars a month; even major generals received only one hundred and sixty-six dollars; and the pay of subalterns was little more than that of the privates. As for offering a bounty to recruits, Congress swore that "before they would give a bounty they would give up the dispute."

The low pay for officers and men of the armed forces accorded with Congress's strong bent towards keeping down expenses. It was sometimes objected that congressmen were in danger of losing the war out of fondness for pinching pennies; true it is that in many matters Congress displayed a parsimony that often reacted disastrously upon the army. No expense escaped the vigilance of the economizers, although their attention was often centered upon trivialities. For example, when Esek Hopkins was appointed to command the American fleet, it was hotly debated whether his pay of one hundred and twenty-five dollars a month ought to be supplemented by an allowance to be made "to the Admiral for Table Expences" — and the motion was defeated.

Recognizing the strength of this prejudice against a long-term army, hopeful that idealism would prove sufficient to induce Americans to enter the army, Washington at first supported Congress in its stand for short enlistments and its opposition to bounties. The first trial of this faith in patriotism came late in 1775. The troops besieging Boston were committed to serve not later than December 31, 1775; then, unless they re-enlisted, they were free to go home, leaving Washington to find another army if he could. With the existence of the army at stake, Washington spared no effort to induce the men to re-enlist: he appealed to their patriotism, plied them with extra rations of rum, and dwelt upon the ruin that would follow upon the disbandment of the army, but all to little purpose. In general, the soldiers abided by the letter of their contract: they would serve as long as they had promised — but no overtime. When their period of enlistment was up, the war was over for them: let others take their places, they had done their bit. This was the system they had become accustomed to in the French and Indian War, and they failed to see that this war was any different from other wars. Moreover, they were disgusted with the hardships of camp life, the low pay, and the government's failure to offer bounties for re-enlistment.

General Charles Lee tried the effects of plain speaking upon the soldiers. "Men," he told the Connecticut troops who were on the point of breaking up camp, "I do not know what to call you, you are the worst of all creatures"; and in the words of a Connecticut soldier, he "flung and curst and swore at us, and said if we would not stay he would order us to go to Bunker Hill and if we would not go he would order the riflemen to fire at us." But the troops merely laughed at the irate general: a notice was posted on his door to the effect that "General Lee was a fool," and the day their enlistments expired, the Connecticut troops rushed out of camp, burning up the road to Hartford.

Since Congress had ordered every recruit to furnish his own gun, they took their guns with them, although Washington was already short of arms. Finally, to save himself from being completely stripped of weapons, Washington refused to permit soldiers to take their guns out of camp, and thereby incurred the resentment of many of the men for invading the rights of private property.

And so, with a hostile army a few miles away, Washington watched his own army pick up and go home. On December 31, 1775, the American camp looked like moving day: soldiers packing their kits, folding their tents, and celebrating their return to civilian life. The highways were jammed with soldiers moving away from the scene of action; a spectator might have supposed that the war was over and that the colonists had so soundly trounced the British army that they no longer had anything to fear from that quarter.

"Such a dearth of public spirit, and such want of virtue," Washington had not foreseen; he had expected to lead freemen fighting for liberty, not men who calculated patriotism in dollars and cents and who coolly deserted him in the hour of danger. In his disillusionment, Washington regretted that he had accepted the command; he wished that he had gone west and lived in a wigwam and that he had never heard of the Continental army. He repented that he had not attacked Boston in the summer — "all the generals upon earth," he now declared, could not have diverted him from an assault in force had he known that his army would melt away before his eyes.

Washington would have been left virtually without support had not the New England militia and minutemen turned out to fill the ranks during the critical period between the dissolution of the old army and the enlistment of a new. In these irregulars Washington placed little confidence, but they at least served to screen from the British in Boston the disorganization and weakness that prevailed in the American camp, the militia and Continental troops being hardly distinguishable since neither had uniforms and both were equally "rabble" to the British. This period of transition from one army to another gave Washington some of the worst moments he was to experience during the war: by the middle of January, 1776, he had only half as many men as he needed to hold his lines — and this despite the fact that standards were virtually abandoned and recruits without guns were handed spears. Nations at war have often changed generals in midstream, but it remained for the Americans to change armies.

And, perhaps worst of all, Washington was obliged to look forward to repeating the experience on December 31, 1776. The army that he finally succeeded in recruiting at the expense of much worry and toil was enlisted for only one year. Washington could only pray that the war would be over by that time.

Procuring recruits for the army was only part of Washington's problem: had he possessed thousands of willing soldiers, he had few guns and little ammunition to place in their hands. At times during the siege of Boston, the magazines were so depleted that Washington doubted whether his army could cope with a British attack. To conserve powder, strict orders were issued against firing at geese or other game, and violators were made subject to court-martial. In November 1775, with the troops down to five rounds of powder a man, the firing of the morning and evening gun was eliminated and the artillery was ordered not to reply to British fire. Lest the British learn of the plight of the rebel army, the American soldiers were not informed of this critical shortage, although they might have guessed the true state of affairs from the frequent injunctions given them to hoard every cartridge.

But by the early spring of 1776, the American army, having weathered the crisis of disbandment and re-enlistment and having received fresh supplies of powder, was ready for offensive action. And, thanks to General Henry Knox, it had a large train of artillery.[4] During the winter, Knox had labored to bring down to Boston many of the two hundred and forty brass and iron cannon captured from the British at Ticonderoga. It was a herculean task: the cannon had to be carried upon sleds drawn by oxen over mountains and frozen lakes and rivers. But when they finally reached Washington's camp, the position of the British in Boston became desperate. For with these cannon in his possession, Washington was at last ready to move against Dorchester Heights.

There were two keys to Boston, and the British held only one. Two hills commanded the city — Bunker Hill and Dorchester Heights — and until both were firmly in British possession, His Majesty's fleet and army were in danger of waking some morning to find cannon balls and mortar shells raining down upon them from American batteries on the heights, Since Bunker Hill already was in British hands, Dorchester Heights was the focal point of danger to the King's forces.

Aware of their peril, the British could do nothing to avert disaster. Although plans were drawn up for a surprise move upon Dorchester Heights, always the shortage of manpower dissuaded Howe from making the attempt. With his army already divided between Bunker Hill and Boston he could not risk spreading it thinner, as the seizure of those heights would have necessitated. Ironically, the Americans were in the same position: Washington recognized the vital importance of Dorchester Heights but he did not feel strong enough to hold it against a British attack. So Dorchester Heights became, like Bunker Hill before it, a no man's land watched narrowly by both antagonists.[5]

On March 2, aided by the cannon brought down from Ticonderoga, the Americans opened a heavy bombardment, galling the British in Boston with a steady drumfire. "Our cannon balls went Bang, every shot through the houses," exclaimed an awed spectator of this action. After two days

---

[4] General Henry Knox was described by the Marquis de Chastellux, a French nobleman who visited the United States during the Revolutionary War, as a young man "very fat, but very active, and of a gay and amiable character." As a bookseller in Boston he had developed the habit of reading military books in his shop.

[5] As early as June 1775, Clinton told Howe that if the British "were ever forced to evacuate Boston it would be owing to the rebels getting possession of Dorchester Heights." But it would appear from Clinton's account that Howe was not greatly concerned over the danger from Dorchester: he told Clinton that the rebels never would attempt to burn Boston from the side of Dorchester because "they never would risk their Mortars."

of almost incessant firing, the Americans moved at night to Dorchester Heights. But this time there was none of the haphazard, irresponsible conduct of affairs that had marked the Americans' occupation of Bunker Hill: three hundred teams were on hand to carry supplies to the troops on the heights and at three o'clock in the morning they were relieved by three thousand fresh troops. Strong defenses were erected on the summit of the heights; and hundreds of casks, filled with sand, were placed in such a position that a slight touch would send them rolling down the hill upon an advancing enemy. Near the water, riflemen lay in ambush ready to annihilate British landing parties. At the same time, boats and floating batteries were held in readiness to embark four thousand men under "the great and brave General Putnam" against Boston the moment the British made a move to attack Dorchester Heights. In the careful planning and execution of this enterprise was demonstrated how far the American army had come since Bunker Hill.

By eight o'clock on the morning of March 4, the Americans on Dorchester Heights were ready to receive visitors. When the British in Boston looked upon the hill, they swore that it was something out of *The Arabian Nights;* Howe said that not less than twelve thousand men must have labored all night to have erected fortifications of such strength. But the British had little time to devote to speculating how .the Americans had wrought this wonder: Howe knew that unless he dislodged the rebels from Dorchester Heights, Boston would shortly be untenable by the British fleet and army. So critical was the danger that he determined to storm Dorchester Heights by means of a night attack with bayonets despite the strong American defenses. The expedition, however, could not leave Boston because of a heavy storm — to the acute disappointment of the Americans, who had promised themselves another Bunker Hill.

His last hope of driving the Americans off the heights gone, nothing remained for Howe but to evacuate Boston — if he could. American artillery on Dorchester Heights was in a position to knock the town about the heads of the British troops and to drive the British fleet out to sea. In short, if Washington chose to spring the trap, it was improbable that the British enemy would ever get away.

Washington had been authorized by Congress to destroy Boston if military necessity so dictated. Now the town, crowded with civilians and British troops, lay at his mercy; the guns were trained against the city, and the commander-in-chief had only to give the order to fire to destroy the city and perhaps most of the human life within it. But Washington did not give the order; instead, he permitted the British to go in safety in their ships.

The British threatened to destroy Boston unless they were permitted to leave without interference, and apparently it was this menace that decided Washington to let them go in peace. An informal understanding was reached between the American and British commanders that, in exchange for the safety of the city, the Americans would hold their fire until the British had evacuated Boston.

Howe was reconciled to leaving Boston; he had long wished to withdraw from this unpromising post. In November 1775 he had received orders from the government to evacuate the city, but the lateness of the season, the shortage of transports, and the fact that there was no place to go kept Howe at his post. It ill accorded with Howe's plans, however, to quit Boston in March 1776.[6] Lacking reinforcements and provisions — the army was forced to draw from the naval stores, and the sailors were on short rations — he was debarred from sailing directly to New York as he had planned, and was obliged to make a long detour to Halifax and there await the arrival of fresh troops and provisions from Great Britain.

Howe was in no position to do other than to make the best of this unsatisfactory state of affairs. On March 17, 1776, the evacuation began, the British soldiers blackly swearing that they would one day return to Boston and have their revenge upon the rebels. It was indeed a sorry pass when the British army had no other means of saving itself than the threat of burning a defenseless town. It did not usually purchase immunity by such means, and the humiliation was doubly bitter inasmuch as it had been inflicted by despised "peasants."

The evacuation of Boston, it was remarked, "resembled more the emigration of a nation, than the breaking up of a camp." The Loyalists who had flocked to Boston for protection could not be left to the mercy of the patriots; over fifteen hundred chose exile rather than to take their chances with the victorious rebels. This was the first of the great Tory emigrations which ultimately sent over one hundred thousand of these champions of King and country to Hell, Hull, and Halifax.

Since English newspapers had pictured the King's troops living at their ease in Boston, "drinking their punch and warming their feet, whilst the insurgents were dying of cold and hunger," the government was hard pressed to explain the evacuation of Boston to the English people and to the watchful and waiting French. Edward Gibbon, for instance, had assumed that the Americans, unless they were actuated by a fanaticism of which he doubted they were capable, would abandon the siege of Boston and go home to take care of their crops. It was now said that the abandonment of Boston was a ruse ordered by the British command — a retreat to previously prepared position — but no one was deceived, and least of all the French, by this attempt at face-saving.

With the fall of Boston, the British army lost its last foothold in the thirteen rebellious colonies. Except for weakly held posts in Florida, only

[6] Embellished by frequent telling, the story soon spread abroad that Howe was in such haste to get away from Boston that he fell into his boat.

Halifax remained as a base of operations. The conquest of the colonies seemed farther away than ever — a year after Lexington, Great Britain could not claim possession of an acre of ground in the provinces that had joined the revolt. To establish a bridgehead and conquer a hostile continent — this was now the task of the British army and navy.

To temper Americans' exultation over their victory at Boston it was
necessary merely to look at the progress of the war in Canada. There
the prospect for American arms was as gloomy as it was bright in New
England, and many patriots were beginning to regret that they had
allowed themselves to be drawn into an adventure in the North. Late in
1775, the high drama of war had shifted to Montreal and Quebec, where
a heroic band of Americans were besieging a no less courageous army of
Englishmen and Canadians. The decisive battle in the hundred years'
struggle of the British and French for mastery of the North American
continent had been fought upon the Plains of Abraham, and now Americans and Englishmen were meeting on the same battlefield and contending
for equally high stakes.

American patriots could have given convincing reasons for their decision to invade Canada, but the causes of their failure to conquer that
British colony were not to them equally manifest. It is clear that from the
beginning there was a powerful expansive ideology in the American Revolution. As has been said, Americans expected ultimately to revolutionize
the world; but that, they candidly admitted, would take some doing. In
the meantime, they proposed to incorporate within the American union
all British territory upon the North American continent and even some
of the Atlantic islands belonging to England. Americans spoke of bringing
freedom to oppressed peoples, but the compelling and immediate motive
for carrying the war into Canada was the necessity of making their frontiers secure. It was expansionism in the interests of security.

Nova Scotia, for example, early caught the eye of American expansionists. Settled partly by immigrants from New England, Nova Scotia seemed
likely to follow the leadership of Boston rather than that of London; but

the proximity of the British fleet and the vigorous efforts of the government preserved this colony for the Crown.[1]

Nor did the expansionists fare better in Bermuda. At the beginning of the rebellion, the patriots had recognized the strategic importance of these Atlantic islands as outposts of defense against a sea-borne attack upon the United States. Bermudians were for the most part eager to join the confederation: bound by close commercial ties to the North American continent, it was difficult for the islands to prosper, or indeed to survive, should that connection be severed. The American Revolution threatened the Bermudians with famine because almost their entire food supply came from the colonies. Observing the friendly disposition of the islanders and the vital importance of possessing this bastion in the Atlantic, Silas Deane urged Congress in 1776 to seize the islands. Nothing came of this suggestion: as long as the British controlled the sea, Bermuda was effectively out of reach.[2]

No part of the British Empire was more vital to American security than was Canada — the key to Great Britain's control of the thirteen revolted colonies. As long as Canada could be made to serve as a base for British and Indian attacks upon the rebellious colonies, the cause of freedom would labor under grievous difficulties. The power that dominated Canada controlled the Indians, and with the Indians the fur trade.

In 1775, there seemed every likelihood that the British would shortly assemble a huge armament in Canada for the purpose of sweeping the rebels into the sea — where presumably the British navy would be waiting for them. Lord George Germain, for whom this strategy held great attractions, remarked that the Canadians would make particularly valuable allies inasmuch as they fought "behind walls and trees at least as well as the Bostonians and," he added, "I believe the Canadians would be very ready to chastise their neighbours under the sanction of Government." As Germain well knew, the Canadians were Roman Catholics reputedly imbued with hatred of the heretics to the south.

Thoroughly aware of this danger, Americans called for an immediate attack upon Canada. Offensive war had no place in their philosophy; yet, as Edmund Burke said, "there was no natural law . . . by which a person was to be a simple and inactive looker-on, while his enemy was loading a gun for his destruction." Canada was being primed for that very purpose.[3]

---

[1] By 1784, about thirty thousand Loyalists had been settled in the province. From a doubtful, half-rebellious colony, Nova Scotia became one of the most loyal of His Britannic Majesty's possessions in the New World.

[2] It was not until 1781, however, that Congress, hopeful almost to the last that Bermuda would be ours, declared Bermudian vessels lawful prize for American privateers.

[3] The province of Canada in 1775 included only Quebec. Nova Scotia, New Brunswick, and Newfoundland were separate provinces. However, by the Quebec Act of 1774, the borders of Quebec were extended south to the Ohio and west to the Mississippi.

Americans firmly expected to be welcomed by the Canadians — did they not come bearing the inestimable gift of liberty? It was intended that as soon as the British had been driven from Canada, a free government should be established and representatives admitted to the Continental Congress in full equality with the other colonies. Few doubted that the Canadians were smarting under the whiplash of British tyranny. By the Quebec Act of 1774, the British government, after having given the Canadian peasants ten years of freedom from priestcraft and feudalism, had restored the privileged position of the Roman Catholic Church and the seigneurs. By Americans' reckoning, the Canadians ought to be so resentful of this attempt to turn back the clock that they would join heartily in the work of driving out the British. That they would look upon Americans as friends and liberators was scarcely questioned; as Washington said, "The cause of America and of liberty is the cause of every virtuous American Citizen Whatever may be his Religion or his descent."

For this adventure all the auspices seemed favorable. The province was weakly defended; most of the British army in North America was out of action in Boston — cooped up, as the British themselves admitted, like "a parcel of Chickens" — and no British reinforcements could arrive before the spring of 1776, when, presumably, the province would be securely in American hands. There were only about seven hundred regulars in Canada and they were so widely scattered that the British could not concentrate more than a regiment at any point. Weak as the Americans were, the British seemed to be weaker still. Washington believed that a bold push into Canada would overwhelm the enemy; and Ethan Allen, the redoubtable leader of the Green Mountain Boys, roundly declared: "I will lay my life on it, that with fifteen hundred men, and a proper train of artillery, I will take Montreal." Benedict Arnold said that with two thousand men *he* could conquer all Canada — but, he added, "no *Green Mountain* Boys" were wanted on the expedition. Certainly there was to be no lack of conquerors of Canada; on the contrary, the northward-bound traffic promised to be stupendous.

Moreover, the Americans already possessed in Ticonderoga an excellent jumping-off place for the invasion of Canada. This fortress guarding the approaches to Lake Champlain had been captured by Ethan Allen and Benedict Arnold in May 1775, when they surprised the small garrison of British soldiers, their wives and children. Allen is reputed to have demanded surrender from the dumfounded British commander in the name of "the Great Jehovah and the Continental Congress" — and whether it was owing to this invocation or to the sight of several hundred New England musketmen, the British surrendered without firing a shot.

The capture of Ticonderoga was wholly a state enterprise — Arnold bearing a commission from Connecticut, and Allen from Massachusetts.[4] The two leaders fell out over the question of who was to command the captured fort; Allen was prepared to assert his claims by force, and one night Arnold awoke to find the Green Mountain Boy brandishing a sword, and behind him, his men pointing their guns at Arnold's head. Arnold succeeded in placating the Green Mountain leader, but the incident served to reveal the necessity of control of Ticonderoga by the Continental Congress before Americans began fighting each other over the spoils of victory.

Yet Congress in May 1775 was not at first disposed to accept the gift of a British fort from these impetuous New Englanders. Although the British were being besieged in Boston by the Yankees, Congress wanted if possible to avoid a shooting war; it much preferred petitions and remonstrances to bullets. And the seizure of a British fort ill accorded with the position of Congress that defensive war alone was proper for Americans. But, together with the fort itself, Congress found dumped in its lap a large number of cannon which made the gift the harder to turn down. So, on the strength of the argument that if given the opportunity, Great Britain would use Ticonderoga against the colonists, Congress decided to hold the fort and cannon pending settlement of the dispute with the mother country.

The decision to invade Canada was made by the Continental Congress in September 1775, just before the onset of the Canadian winter. "God is with us indeed!" exclaimed Richard Montgomery, "a winter Campaign in Canada! Posterity won't believe it." Moreover, the invasion was undertaken without adequate supplies, without cash and without transport. To overcome these disadvantages, the American soldiers had only courage and enthusiasm — qualities which, Congress fondly hoped, would triumph over all. John Adams admitted that the army was not well armed or disciplined, "but," he added, "they are filled with that spirit and Confidence that so universally prevails through-out America, the best Substitute for Discipline." Audacity and impetuosity were to carry all before them; if faith could move mountains, it could certainly conquer Canada.

As a result, the American invasion of Canada was more like a rush to the gold fields than an organized attack by a regular army. It is true that two armies converged upon Canada by different routes, but there was little plan or co-ordination in their movements. The main assault was to be delivered by a force under Richard Montgomery — a former British officer who had come to reside in New York — moving up the Champlain waterway to Montreal; a secondary attack was to be made by Benedict Arnold against Quebec via the Maine wilderness. But there was so little over-all planning in this campaign that Washington directed Arnold to

[4] Vermont had not achieved the status of a separate colony.

march to Quebec without securing authorization from Congress, although that body was presumably directing the invasion of Canada and had already ordered Montgomery to move against Montreal.

Canada was familiar ground to Benedict Arnold, who had bought horses in that province during his varied career as a horse trader — which stamped him among British officers as a low fellow, a "Horse Jockey." Nevertheless, want of good ancestry could never be alleged against Arnold: he was descended from one of the best families in New England, even though he proved to be one of the blackest sheep ever to emerge from that shrine of the "old families."

He was described as "a short handsome man, of a florid complexion, stoutly made"; an English lord later declared him to be "a lively little man . . . more like a Gentleman (whatever he may have been) than nine out of ten General Officers." His pride and hot temper alienated many of his fellow officers: he seemed a man consumed by ambition; ruthless, headstrong, and inexorable. Richard Montgomery, with whom he was to serve brilliantly in Canada, distrusted Arnold's overweening ambition and insisted he be given complete control over the Connecticut colonel. Arnold's subordinates were well advised to treat him with circumspection. At Crown Point, when a colonel intruded upon Arnold and spoke brashly to him, Arnold reported the incident in this succinct fashion: "I took the liberty of breaking his head, and on his refusing to draw like a gentleman, he having a hangar by his side, and case of loaded Pistols in his pocket, I kicked him very heartily, and ordered him from the point immediately." He was the stormy petrel of the Continental army, always in the thick of danger, ready to match his luck against fate, the first to stake his life upon some forlorn hope. It was the fatal flaw of his character that he believed only in himself — in his own strength and courage.

Arnold set out for Quebec with an army of fourteen companies of musketmen and riflemen, hard-bitten frontiersmen dressed in Indian fashion with hunting shirts, leggings, and moccasins, and carrying tomahawks and scalping knives. Battle-hardened by the fighting around Boston, they were the pick of the army — "pretty young men," Richard Montgomery called them in admiration. After toiling for eight weeks through an unbroken wilderness of forests, swamps, and rivers, they were perhaps not very pretty. In water much of the time, the men struggled upstream hauling their boats or carrying them over portages — backbreaking toil that took the heart out of the strongest among them. Provisions became so scarce that roasted dog (including skin, feet, and entrails) was a delicacy to be fought for; some famished soldiers even ate their leather shot-pouches and breeches. "No one can imagine," wrote one of Arnold's men, "who hath not experienced it, the sweetness of a roasted shot-pouch to the famished appetite." Many turned back, but

Arnold, with unshakable fortitude, led most of his men through the wilderness to the promised land of Canada.

Reaching the St. Lawrence, Arnold crossed the river in canoes and ascended to the Heights of Abraham by the same path that Wolfe had used fifteen years before. But he failed to take the defenders by surprise and the walls of Quebec were too thick to be breached by the light American artillery. The garrison, moreover, was in no mood to discuss surrender; when Arnold sent a surrender ultimatum under a flag of truce, the flag was fired upon by the British defenders of the city. Fearing a British sortie against his exhausted men and finding that much of his powder had been spoiled, Arnold withdrew about eight miles from Quebec to wait the arrival of reinforcements. This delay proved costly to the Americans: the enemy were given an opportunity to bring up fresh forces, and Carleton, the British governor, was enabled to slip into Quebec to direct the defense of the city.

Unlike Arnold, Montgomery was obliged to fight his way into Canada. Across his path lay the fortress of St. John where Governor Carleton, in command of the British forces, intended to delay the American advance while he strengthened the defenses of Lower Canada. This plan came to grief when St. John's fell to the overwhelming superiority of the invaders; and with it they came into possession of a rich store of cannon, howitzers, mortars, military stores, clothing, and provisions. The way was now cleared to Montreal; moreover, for the first time, the American army had adequate supplies of guns, ammunition, and clothing.[5]

Although Ethan Allen, acting without orders, attempted to capture Montreal by a wild dash upon the city and was taken prisoner together with all his men — a mishap that Washington hoped would "teach a lesson of prudence and subordination to others who may be ambitious to outshine their general officers" — the city fell a few days later to Montgomery and the main army. Disguised as a Canadian peasant, Carleton escaped from the city just before the Americans moved in. Chased by the rebels over a large part of Lower Canada, he finally turned up at Quebec, having wormed his way through the dragnet. Americans were soon given good cause to rue the day that they had let Carleton slip through their fingers: to the British cause, he was worth several regiments of crack regulars.

It had by this time been revealed to Montgomery that to conquer he must be a politician as well as a soldier. The support of the Canadians was vital to the success of the American invasion, yet the *habitants* failed to

[5] During the early period of the war, Congress insisted that every American soldier furnish his uniform. This policy was not relaxed even in the case of invading Canada in the dead of winter. From this it can be understood with what joy the Americans discovered warm British uniforms among the booty of St. John's.

welcome their deliverers with unmixed joy. They were by no means transplanted Frenchmen, ready to fight an Englishman at the drop of a hat. Neither did they call themselves French nor behave like French. "They are austere rather than volatile or lively," it was remarked, "and have lost much of the vivacity of their ancestors." Then as now, the French-Canadians were a stubbornly independent people, inflexibly set in their ways, provincial to the core, and serving no masters overseas, whether French or British. Englishmen found that the Canadians, exposed to a measure of English liberty, quickly caught the spirit of Englishmen. "They are become insolent and overbearing, easily offended," reported a traveler, and when they fancied themselves oppressed, they insisted as peremptorily as did Englishmen upon redress of grievances.

To the amazement and chagrin of the invaders, the Canadians had no particular quarrel with the British government. Indeed, relations between the people and the home government had never run more smoothly, for the Quebec Act of 1774 had proved popular in the province. To Canadians, this law had the saving grace of restoring the old landmarks and institutions swept away by the British victors in 1763. Above all, the Quebec Act conciliated the *noblesse* and clergy of Canada, who in this crisis of Britain's fortunes threw their weight into the scale against the rebels. Thus, the same British Ministry that lost the thirteen colonies helped to save Canada by a policy of forbearance and conciliation. Unfortunately for the empire, the Ministry exhausted its somewhat slender store of wisdom upon Canada and had none to spare for the thirteen English-speaking colonies to the south.

At first, the *habitants* were not unfriendly toward the invaders; they wished above all to be on the winning side, and when victory inclined to the Americans, they were prepared to aid them with supplies and labor. To the invaders, critically short of transport, this assistance was invaluable; without the good will of the Canadians, Americans could hardly have maintained themselves for a month in the province. This state of benevolent neutrality was short-lived; when they saw that only a few thousand Americans had been sent to conquer the province, the Canadians began to doubt eventual American victory. "Our feebleness has intimidated the Canadians from embarking in so uncertain an adventure," reported General Montgomery. Although both Congress and General Montgomery promised the Canadians that they would never be abandoned to the vengeance of the British, Montgomery confided to his friends, "Should things not go well, I tremble for the fate of the poor *Canadians*, who have ventured so much." Throughout the American occupation, the influence of the seigneurs and priests was steadily exerted against the invaders, the priests even refusing absolution to those who aided the infidel enemy. At no time did Montgomery feel himself strong enough to take punitive action against the clergy.

Although a few hundred Canadians joined the American army, in general they could not be depended upon for military aid. "They are a People by education averse to resistance of the commands of their Sovereign be they just or unjust," sorrowfully said an American officer; Benedict Arnold found them "too ignorant to put a just estimate on the value of freedom." Although Congress hired a French printer to go to Canada and set up a free press, the *habitants* seemingly remained indifferent to the patriots' propaganda.

At the same time that Montgomery was learning something of the character of the people to whom he sought to bring the message of liberty, he was rapidly filling in the gaps of his knowledge of the American soldier. As a former British officer, Montgomery was a disciplinarian whom fate had placed in command of soldiers to whom discipline was merely another name for tyranny. "At the head of troops who carry the spirit of freedom into the field and think for themselves," he declared, he was faced with "the disagreeable necessity of acting eternally out of character, to wheedle, flatter and lie." He was compelled to cope, for example, with such turbulent spirits as Captain John Lamb, late leader of the New York mob, who could not forget that he was a Son of Liberty even after he had donned the uniform of an artillery officer. Captain Lamb, at a critical point in the campaign, declared that he would go home — "he says the pay is such a trifle that he is consuming his own property to maintain himself, & that by & by his family must starve at home." At the same time, Lamb harangued his men in the strident tones of a mob orator, telling them that as freeborn Americans they ought to stand up for their rights rather than submit to the tyranny of their officers. The culminating discomfiture from Montgomery's point of view was that this mutinous officer was almost the only experienced artilleryman in the army: if he went home, the rest of the troops might as well follow; yet if he remained, he seemed likely to break up the army. Montgomery persuaded him to stay, but the harassed general swore that as soon as his honor would permit, he would resign his command and go back to his farm and try to forget the mortifications he had suffered at the hands of American soldiers.

For Montgomery, that moment never came; and unhappily for his peace of mind, Captain Lamb's eagerness to go home in the middle of the campaign was shared by many other officers and enlisted men. To hold his army together until Montreal was captured, Montgomery was obliged to promise his men freedom to return if they would consent to stay until the city was in American hands. Many took him at his word and after the capture of Montreal struck for home. Some of these pleaded ill health as an excuse to return, but it was observed that after receiving their discharges they "slung their heavy packs . . . and undertook a march of two hundred miles with the greatest good will and alacrity." Invalids were often "the foremost in the flight, and carried off such burdens on their backs as hearty and stout men would labor under." Among the wounded and sick, an American general discovered "upwards of a hundred damned rascals crowded amongst them fit for duty." Most of those whose terms of service expired during the campaign (and there were many enlisted for as short a period as three months) could not be persuaded to re-enlist, with the result that Montgomery's seasoned troops steadily melted away. Thus, sarcastically remarked this long-suffering officer, he sent "the lame, the blind, the halt, the lazy and the lads who are homesick and of too delicate a Texture to encounter more Hardships and this frigid Climate, to the *Mammies* and *Daddies* and *Wives* and *pumkin Pies.*"

The invasion of Canada was a record of heroism, desperate adventure, and glory colored over by weakness and human frailty. While some were freely sacrificing themselves for the cause, others were turning the war into an opportunity for graft. It was not uncommon for officers, taking advantage of the failure of Congress to appoint regimental paymasters, to cheat the men of their pay, drawing double pay themselves and going home without rendering an account. There were ruinous waste and embezzlement at the same time that the troops were suffering acute want.

Montgomery had captured Montreal without difficulty, but the key to Canada was Quebec, where Carleton still held out against Arnold. Thus the fortunes of war decreed that the decisive battle of the invasion would be fought for possession of Quebec.

To defend the city, Carleton could muster about twelve hundred men — a motley group of British regulars, militia, seamen, and civilians — far too few to guard the walls in their entire circumference. The fortifications were in a bad state of repair; and although the town was well stocked with provisions, it was doubtful whether it could endure a long siege. Carleton put on a bold front to the Americans, refusing to discuss surrender and firing upon their flags of truce, but he wrote to his home government that there was little hope that Quebec could hold out until spring.

Carleton did not imitate Montcalm by sallying out of the walled city and meeting the enemy in pitched battle upon the Plains of Abraham. Montcalm's fate furnished effective warning against such rashness. And so Carleton remained within his walls — a strategy not welcomed by the Americans, who were well aware of the hazard of attempting to carry Quebec by assault. Montgomery would have preferred to besiege the city until hunger had forced its surrender, but an immediate assault was virtually forced upon the American commander. Only by means of a quick and decisive victory could the Canadians be brought to join the Americans; and a large part of the American army was due to go home after the first of the year when its term of service expired. Montgomery at Quebec and Washington at Boston faced the same problem. Unlike Washington, Montgomery decided to attack before his troops abandoned him; when the first northwester would give concealment to the troops, he planned to launch three simultaneous attacks upon the city.

Against Quebec, Montgomery and Arnold could bring to bear about eight hundred men fit for duty, plus a few hundred Canadians. Their artillery could make little impression on the walls; indeed, most of the American cannon had been put out of action by well-directed fire from the defenders of Quebec. Montgomery was not discouraged by this loss; he had never expected, he said, that his artillery would do more than mislead the enemy as to his real plans of attack. According to his plans, it was to be an infantryman's show, with the attackers outnumbered by the defenders and the assault directed against powerful walls protecting easily defended streets and houses. This might seem a forlorn hope, but Americans had come far by taking desperate chances, and Arnold and Montgomery were again ready to match their skill and courage against heavy odds. The walls of the city were weakly defended — not knowing where the blow would fall, the British might be undone by a feint. Arnold and Montgomery felt safe in trusting to surprise and darkness to offset British superiority in artillery and numbers.

While the American army waited for a favorable night to launch its attack, mutiny broke out in Arnold's corps. Arnold's unbridled temper had made numerous enemies among his officers, some of whom now swore that they would not follow him into battle, although they offered to serve under Montgomery. Three entire companies sided with their officers against Arnold, and for a time it seemed that the army would break up and go home without striking a blow for Quebec.

Through painful experience, Montgomery had learned to run his army along the lines of a New England town meeting, so he made a short speech to the men, assuring them that the capture of Quebec would probably put an end to the war and that they could all go home filled with glory. He then conducted a poll of the officers and men to determine their wishes regarding an attack upon the town. If they did not agree to the enterprise, said Montgomery, "I shall not press it upon them, well knowing the Impossibility of making Troops act with Necessary Vigour on such an Occasion if their Minds are possessed with Imaginary Fears." The men voted to attack; and sustained by this vote of confidence, Montgomery prepared for the assault.

Having decided to attack the Lower Town while a feint was being made against the Upper Town, Montgomery, on the night of December 31, 1775, in a raging snowstorm with the snow over four feet deep, led his men against the city. On their caps, the Americans had pinned slips of paper on which was written "Liberty or Death." After marching for four miles through the blizzard they reached the city walls, but the British were waiting for them in force. In the first fire, Montgomery fell mortally wounded and his men were forced to retreat from the Lower Town after they had passed the first barrier.

Arnold, leading the attack upon another part of the Lower Town, at first met with considerable success. Captain Lamb and his artillery, including two fieldpieces mounted on sleighs, blazed away at the British to such good purpose that the forward British batteries were silenced and the wall was breached. But just as Arnold was scrambling over the last barrier he was shot in the leg; he was not dangerously wounded and insisted on remaining at the scene even though he was losing much blood. With Arnold out of combat, the Americans lost their way in the winding narrow streets of the Lower Town, and while they milled about, they were mercilessly galled by the enemy. The British fired from houses and barricades, raking the American ranks with withering volleys. Outnumbered, and with their retreat cut off, the Americans were forced to surrender.

A large part of the American army was killed, wounded, or captured; Captain Lamb's artillery regiment, together with most of the cannon and mortars, fell into the hands of the enemy. For the British, the cost of this victory was five men killed and thirteen wounded.

In the American army, the survivors were in such a state of panic that over four hundred officers and men set off incontinently for Montreal, leaving Arnold with only a few hundred troops fit for action. Suffering from hunger and exposure, his army melting away and his powder almost gone, Arnold could hardly have been blamed had he raised the siege and sought safety in Montreal. Quebec seemed destined to be a deathtrap for any Americans so foolhardy as to remain.

Yet when it was suggested to Arnold that he permit himself to be removed to a place of safety, "he would neither be removed, nor suffer a man from the Hospital to retreat. He ordered his pistols loaded, with a sword on his bed, &c. adding that he was determined to kill as many as possible if they came into the room." Arnold had suffered torments to conquer Canada and he was prepared to give his life for Quebec. "I have no thoughts of leaving this proud town," he declared, "until I first enter it in triumph." Give him five thousand men, he cried, and he would guarantee to drive the last British soldier from Canada.

The repulse at Quebec did not dampen the zeal of the Continental Congress to make Canada the fourteenth colony. New generals were appointed to command the army; a committee of three members of Congress, accompanied by a Roman Catholic priest, were dispatched to Canada; a frantic effort was made to scrape together enough hard money and military stores to enable the army to keep the field; and resolves were passed by Congress which, had they been executed six months earlier, might have won Canada for the union. Orders were sent to Washington to dispatch reinforcements from his army to the North, and a new army was recruited with the aid of bounties; blankets for the troops were collected in a house-to-house canvass of Philadelphia; and the Canadians were promised an opportunity to establish "such a form of government, as will be most likely, in their judgment, to produce their happiness." Despite these exertions, fortune had forsaken the Americans in Canada, and Congress failed to avert disaster. The initial mistake — an invasion without plan or preparation — now began to yield its fruit in the form of starvation, disease, and utter rout.

Meanwhile, in Great Britain, a relief expedition was preparing to sail for Canada. At one time, the Ministry had been prepared to write off the colony; and at the last news, only Quebec had remained in British possession and it seemed on the point of falling to the rebels. Anguished Englishmen could only exclaim against the rebels for this "lawless invasion of the unoffending Canadians, merely because they preserved their allegiance, and would not join in their unnatural rebellion"; but if the invasion of Canada was proof of the rebels' iniquity it was also melancholy evidence of the weakness and unpreparedness of the mother country. Although little hope of saving Canada remained, a fleet and army were dispatched in the spring of 1776 to Quebec; if the Americans had conquered Canada, they would certainly be made to fight to hold it.

With the coming of spring in the North, transport suffered a breakdown which almost completely cut off the invading army from supplies of food and ammunition. Wagons and boats could not be procured; yet, at the same time, over seven thousand American troops were pouring into Canada. As a result, they starved miserably, their powder ran low, and the officers began to quarrel among themselves over the responsibility for the wretched state of affairs. General Wooster, a New Englander who had been appointed to succeed Montgomery, quarreled with General Schuyler, a New Yorker, in charge of transporting supplies to the army in Canada. Schuyler claimed that Wooster had failed to treat him with the respect due a gentleman; to which Wooster replied that the New Yorker had deliberately insulted him. Both of the aggrieved generals appealed to Congress, and their quarrel spread through the army from the officers to the privates — Yorkers and New Englanders eying each other balefully, as was their unhappy custom.

With the weakness of the invaders becoming daily more apparent, the Canadians began to grow perceptibly cooler toward these unwelcome visitors. They refused to touch American paper money, and the rebels, in retaliation, began to seize supplies from the *habitants*, a method of which Arnold, for one, heartily approved: the only way to give currency to Continental paper money in Canada, he said, was to brand as enemies all who refused to accept it. Arnold yearned to make examples of the citizens of Montreal, most of whom, he declared, were bitter enemies of the rebellion. In face of this treatment, the Canadians sullenly bided their time, waiting for the British to deliver them from the tyranny of their would-be benefactors. Some Canadians, particularly hostile to the Americans, were sent out of the country as prisoners, but nothing short of force could induce the people to accept paper money. As a result, the troops began to look upon the Canadians as enemies. Soldiers ran off without paying their debts (one soldier killed his host when presented with a bill); and, to an ever-increasing degree, American rule in Canada came to be based upon force.

If the American invasion of Canada had resembled a gold rush, the retreat from Canada was like a flight from the plague. When, in May 1776, the British fleet and army reached Quebec, little fight remained in the Americans. The besiegers of Quebec broke in panic, leaving their sick behind as they took to the woods — "a flight perhaps the most precipitate ever heard of," said a British officer, "for they left not only their undischarged Cannon, ammunition, scaling ladders, entrenching tools, and provisions, but even many of them their Muskets." Although the British set off in pursuit of this "panick struck Multitude," the Americans ran well and soon reached shelter in Montreal.

But there was no safety here: the British were hot on their trail and the American army was in no condition to stand and fight. Even Benedict Arnold was ready to abandon Canada: what could the Americans do, "sick, divided, ragged, undisciplined, and unofficered" as they were, against a British army of ten thousand men? "Let us quit them & Serve our own Country before it is too late," he urged; "there will be more honour in making a Safe retreat, than hazarding a Battle, against such Superiority." The soldiers needed no urging; they bolted for the border, a mob of exhausted, panic-stricken men subsisting on plunder from the countryside. It was either steal or starve — and the troops seized what they could, leaving behind a legacy of hatred. Of the seven thousand men who had marched into Canada in 1775 and 1776, five thousand were sick; and most of them, sick or well, were without blankets, shoes, or warm clothing and were "Lousey as the Devil for want of soap." Men struggled up to their armpits in water, pushing boats laden with sick, baggage, and stores; some regiments did not have enough men on their feet to transport them down the lakes. Frenzied, famished, and plague-stricken, the men were "Daily Dropping off Like the Israelites before the Destroying angel." From May to July, 1776, the American army in its retreat from Canada suffered five thousand casualties by death, wounds, disease, and desertion.

To multiply the Americans' woes, a new enemy sprang up to harass their retreat. During the invasion of Canada, the Americans had enjoyed the benevolent neutrality of the Indians; even the Six Nations, traditionally leagued with the British, were content to wait the outcome and join the stronger side. On his march to Quebec, Arnold had been joined by about forty braves. But when disaster began to overtake the invaders, the Indians showed their hand: they fell upon the retreating Americans, cutting off stragglers and ambushing small parties in the forests. Instead of fighting for every inch of ground as Congress ordered, the American army fled in utter rout: at the Cedars, a strong garrison surrendered to a small force after one American had been wounded in an exchange of gun-fire.

As if this did not fill the cup of misfortune to the brim, the Americans encountered a foe "ten times more terrible than Britons, Canadians and Indians together" — smallpox. In some colonies, particularly New England, this scourge had been brought under control by means of vaccination; but elsewhere there was such a strong prejudice against this preventive that some colonies prohibited vaccination by law. Southerners were particularly susceptible to the disease and hundreds fell victim in Canada, Morgan's riflemen, in particular, being almost wiped out. Others lived in such terror of the plague that they were said to be "frighten'd at their own Shadows," and deserted by scores to escape contagion.

By the middle of June, 1776, so swiftly had the British overrun Canada that General Burgoyne, who had arrived with the first contingents of the relief expedition, declared that it was difficult to believe that Great Britain had ever had an enemy in the province. "All is joy," he reported; so eager were the people to assist the troops in completing the destruction of the invader that the British could hardly supply them with sufficient arms and ammunition. The Canadians, he noted with satisfaction, knew that their interest lay in supporting the stronger side: they had successively joined hands with the French, Americans, and British — and, he added, "they would be the same to the Emperor of Morocco" could they be persuaded that he possessed the strongest legions.

The Americans' flight from Canada did not stop short of Ticonderoga — even Crown Point was abandoned in the panic of the rout. So completely had the tables been turned that it was now doubtful whether the Americans could withstand a British invasion from Canada. Ticonderoga — the last bastion between Canada and the Hudson River — was still, it is true, in the Americans' hands, but Lake Champlain no longer seemed to them a pleasant and easy water route to Canada but a dagger pointed at a vital part of the United States which, in British hands, might be used to cut the union in two.

In this disaster in Canada, some congressmen detected cowardice, incompetence, or drunkenness on the part of high-ranking officers in the Continental army, but John Adams asserted that the blame ought to be laid upon Congress for "embarrassing and starving the war in Canada" — an opinion in which most army officers concurred. When shortages first began to disrupt the operations of the army, they had railed at Congress and at the Tories, whose "Machinations in & out of Congress," Montgomery believed, were the cause of "the Hardships we have endured and are further to undergo." Short enlistments had effectively blasted American chances of victory in Canada; the lesson of the defeat, a congressional committee reported, was that "no duty must be expected from soldiers whose times are out, let their country stand ever so much in need of their services."

Congress was unable to share Washington's philosophical resignation to defeat in Canada or to learn from that disaster that "the events of War are exceedingly doubtfull, and that Capricious fortune often blasts our most flattering hopes." In June 1776, although the news was so bad that Congress dreaded the sight of an express from Canada, the statesmen in Philadelphia were briskly engaged in drawing up plans for the next expedition to the North under General Gates. Gates was given "the powers of a Roman Dictator" in Canada, but before exercising this sweeping authority he had to fight his way back into the country — in itself no mean undertaking. Unfortunately for these hopes of conquest, Canada had become a name of ill omen to American soldiers: even large bounties failed to tempt them to enlist for service in that inhospitable land. The disaster of the North planted a "damned notion . . . that one in three must die of the Fever and ague" in the army. The British were welcome to keep such a pestilential land: they deserved no better.

CHAPTER VII

Supply

THE American colonies embarked upon what proved to be a seven years' war deficient in every necessity for carrying on a prolonged struggle — guns, ammunition, flints, artillery, steel for bayonets, clothing and blankets, to name only a few of the more conspicuous shortages. Lacking tents, soldiers were obliged to endure exposure to wind and weather; nails were often unobtainable; anchors could not be cast for want of coal; and so acute was the shortage of cartridge paper that General Gates instructed his troops upon one occasion to tear up old books for that purpose. Americans outdid even the British in jumping into war ungirded and unready, armed chiefly with a sense of righteousness and illimitable self-confidence. At the time of the battle of Lexington, for example, there were only ten tons of gunpowder in the entire colony of Rhode Island; and by June 1775, one hundred pounds of powder could not be purchased in New York City at any price.

It was a question whether the rebellion would first collapse because of lack of powder or because of lack of guns. The cry "Oh, that we had plenty of powder!" was closely followed by the plea "For God's sake, let us have arms!" But Heaven remained noncommittal to these appeals. In February 1776, with two thousand men in his army lacking guns, Washington besought his generals to collect every available musket and send it to Boston; but in truth the generals had not enough guns for their own needs. In 1776, the New York Convention ordered one thousand guns for its troops: it received less than twenty-five. General Sullivan asked for one thousand muskets: he found only one solitary musket in the magazines. It was vain to appeal to Congress: in August 1775, Benjamin Franklin had watched the last wagonload of powder in the possession of the Continental Congress leave Philadelphia for General Schuyler's army, then on the point of invading Canada.

Frantic efforts were made to overcome these deficiencies: instructions for the household manufacture of saltpeter were broadcast and the mountains were scoured for saltpeter caves. Less venturesome patriots confined their explorations to old cellars. "If every planter and farmer," said the Charleston Council of Safety, "would devote a very little of the time and labor of his servants to the manufacture of that article [saltpeter] America would not require supplies of gunpowder from abroad." Two French experts were brought to this country by Congress to superintend the manufacture of saltpeter and gunpowder and to train American workmen in the art; and American diplomats in Europe were instructed by Congress to send across the Atlantic as many skilled gunmakers as they could engage.

In the meantime, to cope with the critical shortage of arms, it was suggested that the soldiers be armed with pikes and staves. Franklin favored bows and arrows, although, it must be acknowledged, it was rather late in the history of warfare to expect another Crécy and Agincourt. Franklin, however, succeeded in making out a surprisingly strong case for bows and arrows: an archer, he reminded Congress, could send four arrows at the target in the same time that it took a musketman to load and fire one bullet. Although Franklin's views were never put into practice by the army, many soldiers, particularly during the early part of the war, carried nothing more lethal than spears and tomahawks; at Long Island, for example, some soldiers complained that they had "nothing but damn'd *Tomahawks*." As has been seen, some of the troops besieging Boston were armed with spears. Washington complained that those used by the New Hampshire contingent were "ridiculously short and light, and can answer no sort of purpose."

For this state of affairs, Americans had themselves at least partly to blame. During the period covered by the events just narrated, the American colonies had been living in a state of self-imposed blockade. To a great degree, they were attempting to wage war at the same time that they denied themselves the means of effectively carrying on the struggle.

In 1774, the Continental Congress had adopted the so-called "Continental Association" by which Americans pledged themselves not to import or buy British merchandise and to keep at home the tobacco, indigo, rice, and other products which they normally exported to the British Isles. By this means, it was intended to present the mother country with a choice between economic ruin and agreeing to the demands of the colonies. The Continental Association proved in practice, however, to be a two-edged sword: at the same time that it deprived the British of valuable markets and trade (which failed to bring them to their knees) it cut off the American insurgents from supplies of arms and ammunition which were essential to victory. The Continental Congress rightly called it "the last peaceable admonition that our attachment to no nation upon earth should supplant our attachment to liberty."

So incompatible with the needs of the colonies were the provisions of the Continental Association that Congress in 1775 removed some of the most onerous self-denying features of the embargo. Because it was depriving thirsty Americans of wine, John Hancock moved in Congress that Madeira wine be excepted from the association — and thereby won the undying gratitude of the winebibbers. More significantly, in July 1775 the colonies were advised by Congress to export provisions to countries other than Great Britain and to accept in exchange arms and ammunition; and in September 1775, Congress created the Secret Committee to supervise exports and imports of vital materials. Licenses to leave port were given shipmasters on condition that they return with military stores. Under this dispensation, American ships set out for Europe, Africa, and the West Indies in search of powder and arms.[1]

Not content with having opened these loopholes in the Continental Association, many merchants endeavored to remove it altogether and to establish free trade with the world. Under the boycott, ships were tied up, merchants' shelves were empty, and business was at a standstill. As early as July 1775, Benjamin Franklin advocated opening American ports to every state in Europe that would admit and protect American ships, but for most members of Congress this step was too long a stride in the direction of independence. It was not until April 1776 that the Continental Association was finally relinquished, ports were opened to all nations, and American merchants were permitted to trade freely where they pleased — British cruisers and men-of-war willing.

Congress cast off these restraints upon trade with considerable searching of conscience. Its action meant, of course, that the final break with Great Britain was brought much nearer; but it also gave a freedom and scope to American businessmen that many patriots were unwilling to concede. In some quarters, American merchants were under suspicion as men prone to put profits above patriotism. The conduct of the merchants during the Nonimportation Agreement of 1768–1770 had aroused distrust of their good faith, and now, in 1775–1776, some patriots feared that these businessmen, if permitted to break through the barriers of the Continental Association, would betray the patriot cause by carrying American products to Great Britain and importing British merchandise into the colonies. "The merchants," exclaimed General Nathanael Greene, "are generally a people whose good is gain, and their whole plan of policy

[1] Africa was an important source of supply because off the coast of Sierra Leone were to be found European ships engaged in the slave trade, and from them powder was procured in considerable quantities.

is to bring publick measures to square with their private interest." John Adams declared that the spirit of business was "incompatible with that purity of Heart and Greatness of Soul which is necessary for an happy Republic. . . . Honour, Power and Glory must be established in the Minds of the People, or there can be no Republican Government, nor any real Liberty: and this Passion must be Superiour to all private Passions."

Rather than make private profit the polestar of the republic, some patriots proposed that the states themselves manufacture powder and implements of war. State enterprise played a part in the War of American Independence, although its achievements fell far short of the expectations of its advocates. At the recommendation of the Continental Congress, the states engaged in the export of provisions and the import of war supplies, and even undertook to manufacture powder and saltpeter. Several states, notably Pennsylvania and Virginia, operated their own armament factories; and Congress itself established foundries for the manufacture of brass cannon in Pennsylvania and Connecticut. North Carolina bought ore lands, and erected furnaces and slitting mills which supplied the army with guns and bullets; and this state also took occasion to proclaim the principle that these enterprises, in every well-founded commonwealth, ought to be owned and operated by the people.[2]

Businessmen, then as now, denounced state enterprise as an invasion of the rights of property and as the intervention of government in a field outside its proper sphere. Certainly this was not the liberty they had been seeking when they rebelled against Great Britain; from their point of view, government in business was worse than British tyranny. Many had joined the insurrection in the hope of attaining freedom of trade with the world; yet now they found themselves confronted with the threat of the competition of government in commerce and manufacturing. John Jay, a spokesman for the businessmen of the United States, declared in Congress: "We have more to expect from the enterprise, activity and industry of private adventurers, than from the lukewarmness of assemblies. . . . Public virtue is not so active as private love of gain. Shall we shut the door against private enterprise?"

Businessmen might take comfort in the fact that the Continental Congress and the new-fledged state governments were too weak and insecure to meet the demands laid upon them by friends of state ownership. The merchants proved to be indispensable to the success of the American Revolution. Congress and the states leaned upon them, and because of their financial resources, commercial connections in foreign countries, and

---

[2] In 1779 a committee of Congress recommended a plan that would have taken foreign trade almost wholly out of the hands of the merchants: five million dollars' worth of European merchandise was to be purchased by Congress, carried across the Atlantic by ships of the United States navy, and sold at public auction — all profits from the transaction being retained by the government.

experience in trade, they had little difficulty in meeting the challenge of government-in-business. Called upon to provide the sinews of war — provisions, arms, powder, and clothing for the troops — they accounted for the great bulk of the supplies brought into the United States during the war.

It must be admitted, however, that some businessmen, after a taste of carrying on business during the war, were eager to have the state take over. For example, Robert Livingston, operator of an iron mill in New York, said in 1778 that he was sick of business, having been plagued, he wrote, with "numberless difficulties and Vexations in Every branch. I have been expos'd to immoderate exactions; Cartage of Ore . . . which was formerly Eight pence a mile for a Tun, is now risen to Six and Eight Shillings; workmen and labourers of every Class, contented with no Indulgence, and bound by no Contract, desert my service at their pleasure." And, to top it all, he was accused of being a profiteer! Thoroughly disheartened, he asked the state of New York to assume control of his business.

On the other hand, merchants like Robert Morris of the firm of Willing and Morris made huge fortunes out of the war. In 1775, for instance, Morris made a contract with Congress to supply powder to the government, and by its terms ensured a clear profit of sixty thousand dollars for his firm without risk of loss. Whether the powder reached the United States safely or not, Congress was obliged to pay a flat price of fourteen dollars a barrel. It was an arrangement by which Morris and his associates could not fail to prosper; but such deals merely sharpened the suspicions of the radical patriots that businessmen were untrustworthy.

Whether state or privately owned, American manufacturing resources proved insufficient to the demand imposed by war. In 1776, the American colonists were an agricultural rather than an industrial people. Over 90 per cent of the population lived on farms; such towns as the country boasted were commercial rather than manufacturing centers. As a result, the American businessman of the eighteenth century was generally a merchant — a shipowner, importer, or retailer, rather than a manufacturer. The manufacturing carried on in British America was largely of the household variety.

The most notable exception to this rule was Philadelphia, the manufacturing center of the colonies and the largest city in British America. Long before the Revolution, it was remarked that Pennsylvanians were "by far the most enterprising people upon the continent." The beaver hats, cordage, candles, shoes, soap, earthenware, stockings, and guns produced in Philadelphia alarmed Englishmen who wished to see the mother country enjoy a monopoly of manufacturing for the empire. In the winter of 1775–1776, Pennsylvania manufactured over four thousand stand of arms; and there were six powder mills in the state which produced several thousand pounds of powder a week. Late in the war, the first spinning jenny in the United States was set up in Philadelphia.

Everywhere, the shortage of labor blighted American enterprise. In Connecticut, Sudbury Furnace, which had been converted into a cannon foundry at the beginning of the war, had by 1778 almost ceased to operate. The lead mines of Virginia were abandoned comparatively early in the war; and the foundry established in Philadelphia for casting brass cannon soon wound up its affairs. Cannon produced in the United States were generally inferior to those manufactured abroad, and Americans came to depend upon the brass and iron cannon imported from France or captured from the British to see them through the war. The Department of Military Stores at Springfield, Massachusetts — the most important arsenal in the United States — was so inefficiently managed that the Board of War recommended in 1780 that the post be abandoned rather than continued under its directors. In the field of powder manufacture progress was achieved, yet American powder was accounted inferior to that imported from abroad. Although American gunsmiths carried their work to a high degree of perfection, it cannot be said that, in the War of Independence, Americans revealed the inventive and scientific bent or the genius for laborsaving devices that carried them to victory in their later wars.

Spurred by the pinch of necessity, Americans scoured the islands of the sea in search of arms and ammunition. A large supply was seized in Bermuda; and early in 1776 the American navy, under the command of Commodore Esek Hopkins, raided the Bahama Islands. The garrison having been withdrawn to the continent, the islands were almost defenseless, and most of the inhabitants refused to fight against the Americans, deserting the governor and his friends when they attempted to make a stand. Hopkins loaded all the cannon, mortars, and artillery stores, together with the governor, aboard his ships and sailed back to the United States in triumph.

At the same time, the royal arsenals in the colonies were captured, turning against the British troops the powder and shot belonging to the Crown. The artillery and stores in New York City were pounced upon early in 1776; a large supply of powder intended for the Indians was confiscated by the rebels in Savannah, Georgia; and the fort at Ticonderoga yielded a rich store of powder, artillery, and lead. In this quest, nothing was overlooked: in New York, the lead statue of George III representing the King mounted on a charger, both figures covered with gold leaf, was pulled down by the citizens in July 1776 and converted into musket balls. Window and clock weights, church bells, and kitchen utensils went into the same pot with "melted majesty."

⌢ ⌢ ⌢

In the business of bartering American farm and plantation products for guns, cannon, powder, and other essentials of war, the French, Spanish, and Dutch islands in the West Indies became the most important centers of trade in the hemisphere. St. Eustatius, Martinique, Hispaniola, Guadeloupe, Havana, Cap François, Port-au-Prince — these were the ports of call of hundreds of American ships. It was much less hazardous to run down to the West Indies for a load of war supplies than to cross the Atlantic to Europe where, particularly off the coasts of France and Portugal, British cruisers lurked. Fast pilot boats out of Philadelphia and Baltimore regularly made the run to the French and Dutch West Indies, where munitions were transshipped from European merchantmen. Huge profits were thus made: a cargo worth ninety thousand dollars at Nantes, France, sold for two hundred and forty thousand dollars in Boston.

That the West Indies became a great emporium of powder and arms was largely owing to the enterprise of Dutch and French merchants who saw in the dissensions of the British Empire an opportunity to glean substantial profits. It is true that the French government itself quickly took a hand in this traffic in arms; but the necessities of the rebels were relieved during the early period of the war, when the scarcity was most acute, by the exertions of individual merchants rather than by the interventionist policies of foreign governments.

In 1775, these merchants began to rush shipments of arms and munitions across the Atlantic. One Bordeaux firm was reported to have sent over twenty-eight hundred barrels of gunpowder to Martinique and to have netted a handsome profit by exchanging them for American tobacco. By June 1776, thanks to Dutch and French merchants, the powder crisis in the colonies had definitely passed; never again during the war were Americans brought to the verge of defeat because of a shortage of powder.[3]

A commodity almost as essential as powder to the war effort — and almost as scarce in the United States — was salt. Without salt, meat could not be preserved, the New England fisheries could not operate, and the Continental army could not be fed. Subsisting in large part on salt provisions, New Englanders might be starved into submission by depriving them of salt. Loyalists assured the British government that if the supply could be cut off the rebellion would receive "a deadly wound if not a fatal stab." This promised to be a comparatively easy matter: the colonists' supply of salt came chiefly from Turks Island in the West Indies, a British possession which early in the war was closed to American shipping.

[3] It is true, however, that the scarcity of military supplies continued to give Washington concern and, in several instances, to upset his plans. For instance, the failure of gunpowder to arrive from the West Indies disorganized the campaign of 1779. Congress complained that the supply of arms, ammunition, and clothing from France had been "irregular, fortuitous and scanty" and that unless more regular shipments arrived, the United States could make little contribution to the war.

In consequence, salt became critically short during the war. Mobs rioted for salt: it had only to be whispered that salt was stored in a warehouse to raise a mob of housewives. Despite attempts to regulate its price, it soon rose to prohibitive levels; easily hoarded, it fell into the hands of profiteers who gouged the public mercilessly. British men-of-war also did a thriving business along the American coast trading salt for fresh provisions; so profitable was this traffic that sometimes British ships carried salt as ballast. The army, as usual, was the worst sufferer. The lack of salt often made it impossible to store adequate supplies of meat for the troops; no magazines could be formed; and the army was obliged to live from hand to mouth.

This crisis was met by running cargoes of salt from Bermuda and the West Indies and by establishing salt factories along the seacoast. Benjamin Franklin drew up instructions for producing salt from sea water and soon the coast hummed with activity; in August 1777, John Adams remarked that "all the old women and children are gone down to the Jersey shore to make salt. Salt water is boiling all around the coast." But saltworks were highly vulnerable to raiding parties from British men-of-war, and British commanders seldom overlooked an opportunity to wreck these installations. In 1778, Clinton raided the New Jersey coast "where," he said, "the enemy had a number of privateers and prizes, and, what was still more interesting, some very considerable salt-works." "We have lately made a prize that must distress them exceedingly," wrote a British officer in New England, "no less than a church full of salt; so that the poor Yankies, literally won't have salt to their porridge." In 1781, during his raid in Virginia, Benedict Arnold never failed to blow up a powder mill or a saltworks within his reach.

⌢ ⌢ ⌢

Almost a year before the colonies declared their independence of Great Britain, they had begun to seize upon the high seas ships carrying the British flag. In 1775, both the mother country and the colonies issued letters of marque and reprisal — the credentials which distinguished a privateer from his near relative, the pirate. By virtue of these credentials, it was made lawful to prey upon the shipping of the enemy and to conduct what was essentially war for private profit.

Americans were skilled in privateering; as British subjects they had learned the trade at the expense of the French and Spaniards: during the Seven Years' War, for example, New York alone had over four thousand men engaged in privateering. Americans were well equipped for this kind of enterprise. The schooner, an American contribution to navigation, was a fast, long, low vessel with raking masts, capable of great speed and maneuverability, which, converted into a privateersman, gave the colonists at sea much the same advantages which the rifle gave them on land.

For a time, privateering was the brightest spot in the American war effort. British shipping, unconvoyed at the beginning of the war, was vulnerable to the privateers: the entire Quebec fleet, worth more than five hundred thousand dollars, was captured early in the struggle, and over half the Jamaica fleet was taken in 1776. Exclusive of transports and government store ships, the British loss during 1776 in captures was considerably more than one million pounds sterling; and large quantities of guns, ammunition, clothing, and other military supplies intended for the British army ended in the possession of the rebels. Thanks to the depredations of the privateers, Americans could boast that during the first two years of war, the struggle was carried on largely at British expense. In 1777, Benjamin Franklin declared that the United States was "enriching itself by Prizes made upon the British Commerce, more than it ever did by any Commerce of its own, under the Restraints of a British Monopoly." All told, during the war, the British lost almost two thousand ships to American privateers and naval craft, and over sixteen thousand British seamen were made prisoners of war, most of whom were given their paroles and set at liberty or enlisted on board American privateers. Indeed, the privateersmen switched their allegiance without great searching of conscience; having entered the profession for profit, they were little concerned on which side they fought.

There was, however, another side to this picture. During the war, over two thousand British privateers scoured the seas for enemy shipping, and Americans lost heavily to both the privateers and the navy of the enemy. As an Englishman said in 1778, captures of American vessels by British ships "probably much overbalanced the losses which we sustained from their privateers. But," he added, "it was, to a thinking mind, melancholy that we had a computation of that kind to make."

The partition between a privateer and a pirate — at best thin and unsubstantial — was frequently broken through by American privateers; a prize was a prize, no matter what its flag, was the sentiment of some of the more unscrupulous members of the fraternity. Portuguese ships, because of the unfriendly action of the government of Portugal in excluding American ships from its ports, were deemed fair game by the privateers; but even French ships were not wholly secure from spoliation. The French farmers-general were obliged to ask Franklin for protection for their ships against American privateers. Dutch and Spanish ships likewise were scooped up in the Americans' net — all of which gave color to the British charge that these privateers were no better than pirates sailing under the Jolly Roger, and ought, when caught, to be swung from the yardarm.

In New England, where the fishing and carrying trade had been ruined by the war, leaving hundreds of ships and thousands of seamen idle, privateering flourished. Some New England towns were almost deserted by the men, leaving the women to get in the harvests. The arrival of a rich prize became a frequent occurrence in New England ports; well over one thousand captures were made by Massachusetts privateers alone during the war.

The New Jersey coast afforded numerous hide-outs for the privateers which hunted in the waters off New York Harbor. Little Egg Harbor — "a seminary for little rascally privateers" — boasted thirty of these marauders; what with saltworks and privateering, the New Jersey coast enjoyed a boom unequaled until the coming of summer tourists.

⌒　⌒　⌒

Dependent almost wholly upon outside aid for munitions and implements of war, the American revolutionaries had everything to fear from the British navy, which, by blockading their ports and sweeping their shipping from the sea, could sever the lifelines of the rebellion. At the outbreak of the war, however, the British had few ships in North American waters. Two or three cruisers stationed off the Chesapeake and Delaware would have effectually bottled up those estuaries and kept the gun-runners at bay, but the fleet in Boston could spare only one sloop for such service.

In 1776, as part of the Ministry's plan for ending the war in a single campaign, a huge fleet under the command of Lord Howe was sent to North America. But because Howe adopted the policy of employing the fleet almost wholly in joint operations with the army, the British men-of-war were tied up in New York Harbor during most of the campaign. Howe, moreover, built up a fleet of large warships rather than of fast cruisers and sloops; and Americans soon found that their smaller and speedier ships could run circles around these great ships of the line. Thus the door was left open for Americans to bring in vitally needed war supplies. They took full advantage of the preoccupation of the British navy; Philadelphians, for example, were seized with such a craze for making their fortunes by running guns and powder that it was said that the whole town seemed about to put to sea. Not until 1778 did the British navy go into action in earnest against American privateers and merchant ships, but by that time the best opportunity of smothering the rebellion by an airtight blockade had passed.

As for burning American seaports — to Germain and Sandwich proper punishment for rebels — Lord Howe refused to soil his hands with such warfare. He had come to make peace as well as to wage war, and he believed that his chances of making an enduring peace depended largely upon the manner in which he waged war. Therefore, instead of carrying fire and sword to American seaports, he deliberately permitted them to enjoy

uninterrupted trade. This policy, he told Germain, was sound statesmanship: he avoided troubling the rebel ports in order "that the People might
not be forced to take arms for a subsistence. . . . Every precaution should
be taken to detach the lower Class of people from their dependence on
their Leaders."

The Ministry was dismayed when it learned that Lord Howe was permitting American privateers and merchantmen to pass almost without
interruption. Had the British fleet been sent to coddle the rebellion? demanded Lord Sandwich. "These kind of indulgences," he exclaimed, "are
more likely to protract than hasten the conclusion of this unnatural contest." Since British admirals on active duty received an eighth part of the
proceeds realized from the sale of prizes captured by ships under their
flag, Lord Howe, it is clear, was overlooking an opportunity to make a
sizable fortune for himself. To Lord Sandwich such conduct was inexplicable.

In keeping the sea lanes open to American shipping, little help could be
expected from the Continental navy, which was crippled by manpower
shortages and kept weak by reason of the determination of the individual
states to maintain navies of their own. Created in 1775, the navy consisted
of about a dozen frigates together with a few smaller vessels; the flag carried by these ships depicted a snake with thirteen rattles, in the posture of
striking, with the motto "Don't tread on me!" With the exception of
John Paul Jones and a few other resourceful officers, American naval commanders were seldom able to make good this threat. Seamen shipped
aboard privateers in such numbers that the navy was sometimes forced to
draw its crews from captured British sailors and deserters; many of its
ships remained tied up in port for much of the war, and when they did
put to sea, they confined themselves to convoying merchantmen and
supplementing the raids of privateers upon enemy shipping rather than
challenging the British fleet to combat.

The first commander of the navy was Esek Hopkins, a grizzled old sea
dog who was serving as a brigadier general in command of Rhode Island
troops when the Continental Congress drafted him as "Commander in
Chief of the Fleet of the United Colonies." "An antiquated figure," General Henry Knox called him, adding optimistically that he brought to
mind Tromp, the redoubtable Dutch admiral of the previous century.
Knox was so overcome by the sight of this ancient mariner that he declared that he "should have taken him for an angel, only he swore now
and then." This resemblance to Tromp as well as to an angel seems to have
been wholly coincidental: in any event, Hopkins did not succeed in making the United States navy (as Tromp had threatened to make the Dutch
navy) a broom with which to sweep the seas clear of the English.

CHAPTER VIII

※

The Battle of Long Island

WHILE immured in Boston, Howe had given much thought to the campaign of 1776; he had ample time for meditation and, indeed, took more satisfaction in contemplating the future than the painful present. The more he considered the matter, the less disposed was he to underestimate the American army, which had in it, as he said, "many European soldiers, and all or most of the young men of spirit in the country, who are exceedingly diligent and attentive to their military profession." To destroy this force would require, he decided, at least twelve thousand men; but he soon raised his estimate to nineteen thousand — and he added, if Great Britain was unable to send that many men across the Atlantic, it would be "better policy to withdraw the troops entirely from the delinquent provinces, and leave the colonists to war with each other for sovereignty." Disquieting news to Englishmen who had spoken airily of marching five thousand regulars armed with horsewhips the length and breadth of the colonies!

As to the strategy of the campaign of 1776, Howe advocated an attack upon New York City, a dash up the Hudson River to join forces with a British army operating out of Canada, and the capture of Newport, Rhode Island. He hoped to put New England out of the war not by direct attack — his experiences in Boston forbade such ambitious schemes — but by isolating the Northern provinces from the rest of the colonies.

Howe was by this time well aware of the difficulties of conquering a continent and overcoming a foe that, he had begun to fear, could not be brought to risk a decisive battle. Duly appreciative of Washington's resourcefulness, Howe suspected that he would be obliged to pursue the rebel army over half the continent before it could be brought to earth. As a fox hunter, Howe was familiar with foxes who by virtue of their speed and slipperiness led the pack a merry chase, and he was rapidly coming to the conclusion that in General Washington he was dealing with a fox of this breed.

Howe's frame of mind was anything but that of a conqueror to whom failure was a thing impossible and unknown. On the contrary, he was becoming increasingly disposed to look for the dark clouds and to ignore any silver linings that might appear upon the horizon. Thus the man who had fought recklessly with Wolfe on the Heights of Abraham and had flung his men improvidently into the slaughter on Bunker Hill began to think largely in terms of avoiding risks. To play the war safe, to brood over the rebellion as though time were working in his favor, and to squander his opportunities prodigally — these became the dominant characteristics of Sir William Howe. In his military lexicon, prudence was exalted into a cardinal virtue, and the result was indecision, delay, and half measures.

By forcing the British to evacuate Boston before they were ready to move against New York, Washington completely disrupted the British timetable for the campaign of 1776. The long voyage to Nova Scotia, the interminable delay in the arrival of supplies at Halifax, the necessity of assembling a convoy hundreds of miles from the British objective — these unforeseen events postponed the opening of the campaign against New York until midsummer and thereby gave the Americans time to prepare their defenses. The British commander fretted at this delay; he had urged the Ministry to open the campaign early in the spring before the rebels could fortify the city. Delay was to become characteristic of Howe's operations; but here, at least, was one delay for which he was not responsible.

Because Howe was held up at Halifax, the first blow of the campaign of 1776 fell not upon New York but upon Charleston, South Carolina. General Clinton, in command of the expedition against the Southern colonies, sailed from Boston in January 1776, stopped off in New York, and obligingly communicated his plans to the Americans. His destination, he announced, was North Carolina and he waited only for reinforcements from Ireland before proceeding to reclaim that colony for the King. But these reinforcements were slow in coming, and Clinton, like Howe, was far behind schedule when the expedition finally got under way.

In North Carolina, the British had been led to believe, there were a large number of Loyalists, among them many Scotch Highlanders, ready to rise up against the rebels the moment British troops appeared. Although the royal governor of the colony had been forced to take refuge on board a man-of-war, he continued to urge the government to send military aid to the Loyalists, most of whom were in the back country and cut off by the rebels from communication with the coast. It was these staunch friends of Britain that Sir Henry Clinton expected to assist in regaining North Carolina for the Crown.

However, when Clinton reached the scene, he found that the Loyalists had risen prematurely and had been routed by the patriots at the battle of Moore's Creek Bridge. The leaders were in jail, the rank and file had scattered to the winds, and the patriots were securely in control of the colony. Deprived of his allies, Clinton did not choose to risk a landing upon this inhospitable coast; instead he turned his armament against Charleston, South Carolina. The Ministry had expected that after the conquest of North Carolina, Clinton would return to New York to join his force to that of Sir William Howe; but Clinton was eager to atone for his failure in North Carolina by a brilliant victory farther south.

Congress meanwhile had countered the British threat to the Southern provinces by sending General Charles Lee to take command of the American forces in that region. Lee, at one time ordered to Canada (fast becoming the graveyard of reputations of American generals), had luckily escaped that assignment and now, in the height of his reputation as a "military genius," went south to balk the British plans of conquest.

Charleston was undoubtedly a prize worthy of Clinton's attention: a notable base of privateers, and the largest port and commercial emporium of the South, it exported rice, indigo and naval stores to Europe, receiving in exchange manufactures and military supplies. But it was also one of the most strongly defended seaports in the South; its harbor was protected by a fort (later called Fort Moultrie) on Sullivan's Island which must be reduced before the city itself could be attacked. General Lee, however, had no confidence that the South Carolinians could hold Fort Moultrie and he urged its evacuation on the ground that there being no way of retreat from the island, its defenders would be annihilated by the British fleet and army. Colonel Moultrie, in command of the fort, refused to abandon his position; whereupon Lee demanded the colonel's removal from command. No doubt, Moultrie was none too strong on the score of discipline and military book-learning, but he was a brave officer and it was fortunate for the American cause that he remained at Fort Moultrie over Lee's protests.

Yet, when the British fleet sailed into Charleston Harbor and began to disembark troops on Long Island, near Fort Moultrie, preparatory to a combined sea and land attack upon that stronghold, many began to fear that Lee was right and that Americans could not stand against such overwhelming naval and military power. With two thousand men and a squadron of eight frigates under the command of Sir Peter Parker, Clinton was supremely confident of success. But he had not taken into account the virulence of the Carolina mosquitoes, the strength of Fort Moultrie, or the courage of its defenders. The British troops on Long Island were attacked by "millions of musketoes, a greater plague than there can be in Hell itself"; the palmetto logs of which Fort Moultrie was constructed were impregnable to British cannon balls; and the channel between Long Island and Sullivan's Island, on which Fort Moultrie stood, was too deep to admit of passage by the British troops. As a result, when the fleet opened fire on Fort Moultrie, the troops on Long Island, deprived of aid from the navy, were completely out of the action. After twelve hours of bombardment, the British fleet withdrew and Fort Moultrie — and with it, the city of Charleston — was saved. The South Carolinians had behaved "like Romans in the third century"; although less than a dozen had been killed by all the balls and shells hurled at them by the British, they had inflicted heavy losses upon the British both in ships and men. Seldom had the navy of Great Britain suffered so rude a rebuff. The admiral, Sir Peter Parker, "Receiv'd a wound which Ruined his Britches" — they were, indeed, quite "torn off, his backside laid bare, his thigh and knee wounded." Smarting under this defeat, the British fleet and army gave up their efforts to capture Charleston and sailed away to New York to aid Howe in his attack upon New York.[1]

That the main British blow would fall upon New York was no secret to the Americans — indeed, the British, disdaining subterfuge, boasted freely of their plans. Thus forewarned, the American command was confronted by one of the most crucial questions of the war: Ought an attempt be made to defend New York against the combined strength of the British fleet and army; or ought the city, perilously situated upon an island, be surrendered with little more than token resistance?

Before going to South Carolina, General Charles Lee derided as fainthearted those who favored abandoning the city. The British were not so terrible, he said, that Americans should run at their approach; on the contrary, let the Americans but stand their ground and it would be the British who would run. Washington, too, wished to put New York to the hazard. Strategically the city was of such importance that he was ready to risk his army in its defense. To surrender New York tamely would, he feared, have disastrous effect upon patriot morale. Moreover, he was confident that if the American soldiers fought like freemen, the British would "have to wade thro' much Blood and Slaughter before they can carry any part of our Works, if they carry them at all; and at best be in possession of a Melancholly and Mournfull Victory" — in other words, another

---

[1] Clinton later gave this explanation of the strategy of the British commanders at Charleston: "The Idea of landing on Sullivan's Island during the attack of the fleet had long been given up; it was positively understood that when the Commodore should make his attack, 700 of the army were to land on the main to cooperate with three frigates the Commanders intended sailing to the westward — these frigates got aground and nothing could be done. . . . The short fact is, the Commodore expected to succeed without the army, and perhaps, if he had placed his ships as near as he might have done, he would have succeeded, but at 800 yards distance, it was merely a cannonade. The army could do nothing."

Bunker Hill. He urged his troops to remember how the enemy had been repulsed "on various occasions, by a few brave Americans: Their Cause is bad: their men are conscious of it, and if opposed with firmness and coolness, at their first onset, with our advantage of Works, and Knowledge of the Ground; Victory is most assuredly ours."

Congress was likewise resolved to hold New York at all costs. In January 1776, Congress sent a committee to New York to supervise the construction of the defenses of the city; and to make sure that the will of Congress was respected, this committee was made superior to the military authorities. "The gentry at Philadelphia," said General Mifflin, "loved fighting, and, in their passion for brilliant actions with raw troops, wished to see matters put to the hazard." Their optimism — little shaken by defeats in Canada — encouraged them to believe that the enemy would suffer a bloody repulse on the beaches of Manhattan Island. "Let us drubb Howe, and then We shall do very well," was John Adams's advice to American generals; but with all his rare perception of the military necessities of the hour, Adams failed to point out how this notable deed of arms was to be accomplished. Even after the defeat at Long Island, Congress refused to permit the American army to burn New York because it felt certain that the city could still be held against the enemy.

Ten thousand men labored upon the fortifications of New York during the spring and summer of 1776. The soldiers were kept so busy digging trenches, redoubts, flèches, abatis, and constructing artillery emplacements, that they had little time or energy to devote to maneuvering, drill, or the fundamentals of military training. To get a sizable pile of the good earth between himself and the redcoats seemed to be the goal of every rebel; the British, when they reached New York, could hardly see them for dirt.

The American command depended upon guns and fortifications to neutralize British command of the sea. General Lee — always ready to disparage the nation in whose army he had lately served — flatly declared that shore batteries could keep the British warships at a safe distance; and under his direction, guns were set up on the islands in the harbor and in the city itself. "If he [Howe] comes up like a man and brings his Ships too before our Batteries," said General Henry Knox, "there must be the finest fight ensue that ever was seen — we shall in that Case be able to bring a great number of cannon and mortars to bear on the Ships at once, plenty of ammunition, and every kind of Obstruction." Even if the British effected a landing, they would find New York City turned into a fortified camp: redoubts, forts, and artillery emplacements sprouted everywhere; every street leading from the water was barricaded; and the coast of Manhattan Island from Hell Gate round to Bloomingdale was fortified at every accessible point. Almost all considerable hills on the island boasted a redoubt and battery; on Bayard's Hill stood a fort hopefully named Bunker Hill. Obstructions were placed in the channel of the Hudson River to keep British ships from ascending, and batteries were erected on Long Island to close the East River. If salvation was to be found in fortifications, then the Americans at New York assuredly had nothing to fear.

Washington had such implicit confidence in these defenses that he divided his army among the islands in New York Harbor, seeking to guard every vulnerable point against attack. In accordance with this strategy, the American army was dispersed over Manhattan Island, the Jersey shore, Long Island, Governor's Island, and Bedloe's Island. Thus, practically the entire army was stationed on islands where its retreat might be cut off by the British fleet if the American guns failed to keep the men-of-war at bay. American resources were almost wholly pledged to the hazardous and dubious defense of New York City. In trying to save all, Washington risked losing all — and under circumstances extremely unfavorable to the defense. Singular conduct from a man who was later to be hailed as the American Fabius! [2]

On July 2, the British landed without opposition on Staten Island — the first of many unopposed landings they were to make upon American soil. The rebels vacated the island the day before the British moved in; and the inhabitants, largely Loyalist in sympathy, warmly welcomed the red-coats and took the oath of allegiance to George III. Over two hundred Staten Islanders volunteered to serve with the British in subjugating the rebels.

With Staten Island secured, British ships carrying troops, armament, and supplies continued to drop anchor in New York Harbor until the roadstead was filled with merchantmen and men-of-war. "The whole world seems leagued against us," exclaimed a dismayed patriot. "Enemies on every side, and no new friends arrive." Nevertheless, on July 18, 1776, in full sight of the British fleet, independence was boldly proclaimed in New York and the King's Arms were torn down and trampled under foot by the patriots.

Washington received unmistakable warning of the danger of his position when, early in July, the British men-of-war sailed up the Hudson River past the American batteries on Red Hook, Governor's Island, and the Battery, without suffering more than slight damage. On one ship, supposing that the last battery had been passed, "the captain ordered a bowl of punch and a bottle of claret; but whilst we were refreshing ourselves," recounted one of the officers, "we were accosted by the last shot, which . . . went through the captain's cot." But the British sailed on and drank their claret in peace in the reaches of the Hudson above New York. By this move, they threatened to cut Washington's communications with New Jersey and Albany and exposed the rear of the American army to attack. After this demonstration of naval might, Americans could hardly

[2] Fabius was the Roman general whose delaying and harassing tactics had ultimately defeated Hannibal's invasion of Italy.

hope that their much-vaunted batteries could hold the British fleet at bay.

As the peril of the beleaguered city mounted, it is not surprising that the patriots should have raised the cry that Loyalists were plotting an uprising in favor of the enemy. Although many enemy sympathizers had been rounded up, the place was still believed to be swarming with secret and avowed friends of the British. Certainly, Toryism was strong in New York City and environs: "The sharpest eye must be unremittedly kept on the people of New York," warned Major Hawley; "their manoeuvres and tergiversations exceed the depths of satan." Even mobs which made "a number of them ride upon sharp Rails, up and down the City, to the great detriment & injury of their lower Regions," failed to cow the sturdy upholders of the British cause.

And so, when it was ascertained that a few Loyalists were conspiring with the enemy, hysteria broke loose. The excited patriots claimed to have unearthed "the most Hellish and Diabolical Plott that ever hath been planned since the Powder Plott" to murder Washington and his staff, burn the city, blow up the powder magazines, and destroy the American army — certainly quite an undertaking for a handful of conspirators. Although their complicity was not proved, the mayor and many prominent citizens were thrown into jail. In fact, a Tory witch hunt was begun not only in New York but all over the country as a result of the New York "Powder Plot."

For Howe, the repulse suffered by Clinton at Charleston had a compensating mercy: British strength was now concentrated at one point. The initiative rested wholly with Howe; nevertheless, he remained inactive upon Staten Island for two months, biding his time while the best part of the campaigning season slipped away. He made no move until he had under his command thirty thousand men, one of the largest expeditionary forces ever sent out by Great Britain. By his own calculations, Howe ought to have had a safe margin of victory — he reckoned that one British soldier was the equal of two Americans. Nevertheless, he still postponed the attack, waiting the arrival from England of camp equipment for the army.

Washington was baffled by Howe's dilatoriness — what the British general was waiting for, unless to weary the Americans into going home, he could not imagine. It was past the middle of August, yet the British were only in possession of Staten Island — which, remarked Washington, "is but a small step towards the Conquest of this Continent." But he was not disposed to complain if Howe chose to fritter away the summer: every day his army was growing stronger and his fortifications more formidable. During the final weeks of this unlooked-for respite, almost ten thousand additional men joined Washington's army. Nevertheless, the American army remained seven or eight thousand below the strength of the force Howe had assembled, and Washington made no promises of victory. "I can only say," he wrote, "that the Men appear to be in good Spirits, and if they will stand by me the place shall not be carried without some loss."

Howe's immediate objective was to bring the rebels to battle upon ground favorable to the British army. Although eager to fight Washington, the British general was not willing to attack the rebels when they enjoyed the advantage of strong entrenchments on a hill — Bunker Hill was not so easily forgotten. Given a fair field, however, Howe was reasonably confident that the rebellion could be wound up without further delay.

Another circumstance which profoundly influenced Howe's strategy at this juncture was the necessity of obtaining winter quarters for the army. If the troops were to have shelter, New York City must be captured intact. This debarred a direct attack upon the city: in that event, the Americans would burn the town before escaping to the mainland.

Moreover, even though Howe succeeded in occupying New York before the rebels put it to the torch, the American artillery on Brooklyn Heights was in a position to make the city untenable by the British. Brooklyn Heights on Long Island were to New York what Bunker Hill and Dorchester Heights were to Boston: they commanded the city and, in the possession of the enemy, might lead to its destruction.

These considerations required that Howe eliminate the Americans on Long Island before moving against New York. This step was made the easier for the British commander by reports that Long Island was swarming with Loyalists who would give the King's troops every aid and comfort, and that the island was so fertile that it could support the British army in plenty.

Of their intentions to defend Long Island, the Americans left no doubt. In Washington's opinion, the island was of such paramount importance that he had moved over one third of his army across the East River; could he hold Long Island, the American commander believed that it was within his power to starve the enemy out of the country.

To oppose a British landing on Long Island was not Washington's strategy; not a rebel was in sight when the British came ashore. Americans had conceived a healthy respect for British naval guns. "The Soldiers & Sailors seemed as merry as in a Holiday," said an eyewitness to the landing. ". . . It was really diverting to see Sailors & Apples tumbling from the Trees together." The chief hazard was not rebel bullets so much as green-apple colic; but British digestions proved equal to the occasion and the troops quickly moved inland to ferret out the "skulking rebels."

On Long Island the Americans had set the stage for another Bunker Hill. Confiding in the obtuseness of the British high command, they expected the redcoats to fall into the trap that had cost them dearly at Bunker Hill. Having taken their position on a hill, it was assumed by the Americans that the redcoats would make a frontal attack and permit themselves to be mowed down by the entrenched sharpshooters.

But from the beginning, misfortune dogged the Americans on Long Island. Nathanael Greene, one of the ablest generals in the army, under whose direction the defenses of Brooklyn Heights had been constructed, fell ill on the eve of the battle and was replaced by General Putnam, a lionhearted but unreliable commander. Moreover, the fortifications on Brooklyn Heights were not yet complete. And as Washington later admitted, he was caught off guard by Howe's strategy: an attack upon New York City was expected, and it was not until after the battle of August 27 that Washington ceased to regard the operations on Long Island as a diversion to cover the main British attack on the city itself. It was for this reason that Washington remained in New York during most of the fighting on Long Island, coming to Brooklyn Heights only in time to evacuate the army.

Worst of all for the Americans, the British had divined Washington's strategy; they were well aware that the rebels "fondly imagined the troops would always rush on headlong to their works, as in the *Bunker's Hill* affair." Sir William Howe was no longer disposed to demonstrate British superiority by giving the American rebels weight and then beating them hands down. Howe had learned caution — indeed, as he was soon to show, he had learned timidity.

Americans as yet knew nothing of the change that had come over Sir William, nor did they know the danger to which negligence had exposed them. Owing to the mistake of a subordinate officer, the back roads leading to Brooklyn Heights were left unguarded.[3] The British, instead of advancing up the main road and obligingly falling into the trap prepared for them, went round by the unguarded secondary highways and took the American advance parties under Lord Stirling and General John Sullivan from the rear. By this maneuver, they scored such a complete surprise that the Americans, upon seeing the British and Hessians approaching, assumed them to be American soldiers. It was not until the enemy opened fire at a distance of fifty yards that the rebels learned their error.

In the woods guarding the approaches to their works on Brooklyn Heights, the Americans had posted strong parties of riflemen. Here the riflemen were expected to take a heavy toll of the British regulars, for the riflemen were at their deadliest in the forest, where they climbed trees to fire upon the unwary enemy below, wriggled through underbrush on their bellies, and camouflaged themselves with boughs and leaves. But,

[3] General Sullivan had warned Putnam and Lord Stirling of the danger of leaving these roads unguarded and had at one time posted horsemen to give warning of the enemy's approach; but Putnam and Stirling were so certain that the British were coming by the main road that the cavalry were withdrawn. Lord Stirling (William Alexander) was claimant to a Scottish baronetcy, but his title was not recognized in Great Britain.

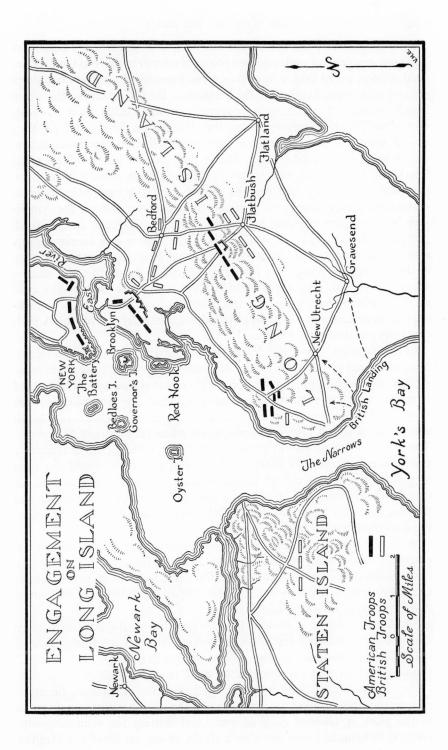

ENGAGEMENT
ON
LONG ISLAND

LONG ISLAND

NEW YORK
The Battery
Bedloes I.
Governor's I.
Red Nook
Oyster I.
Brooklyn
East River
Bedford
Flatbush
Flatland
Gravesend
New Utrecht
British Landing
The Narrows
York's Bay
Newark
Newark Bay
STATEN ISLAND

American Troops
British Troops
Scale of Miles
1   0   1   2

caught off guard by the British, the riflemen were thrown into confusion. The shortcomings of undisciplined troops were never more evident. They fired wildly; every man sought safety for himself; and officers could not control their men. Meanwhile the Hessians — for the attacking force was largely composed of German mercenaries — were using their bayonets with dreadful effectiveness: giving the riflemen no time to reload, they rushed upon the rebel marksmen and pinned them to the trees behind which they tried to take cover. Howe had ordered his troops to adopt this tactic of drawing the riflemen's fire and then rushing them with bayonets before they had time to reload — and the method worked to perfection. Never having encountered this maneuver before, the Americans had no defense against it, and they were quickly cut up into small groups in the swamps and woods where the British and Hessians made short work of them. One panic-stricken group of soldiers burned a bridge in their retreat, leaving their comrades behind to fall before the enemy. Many individuals, however, fought bravely to the last and thereby held up the British advance; the time and casualties lost by the British in rooting the Americans out of the swamps helped materially to save the American army on Brooklyn Heights.

In this fighting, "the English gave little quarter," said a Hessian officer, "and encouraged our men to do the same thing." On their part, some Americans refused to surrender because they feared they would be hanged if taken alive; and some tried to trap the enemy by pretending to surrender and then opening fire at close range — a trick which led the British and Hessians to kill rebels on sight, even when they begged for mercy. The officers made no effort to restrain their men, who, fearful of treachery and resolved to give the rebels a blood bath that they would not soon forget, took a heavy toll of the disorganized Americans. Hundreds of fleeing soldiers were killed; almost a year after the battle, a traveler said that his nose was "now and then regaled with the stink of dead Rebels, some of them having lain unburied since last August."

With the American forward positions overrun, the British moved impetuously to the main position on Brooklyn Heights. American resistance had crumbled; the British army was rolling as it had seldom rolled before; and everything seemed to point to the speedy annihilation of the entire American army on Long Island.

Sir William Howe, it is clear, held a mortgage on the American army which it remained only for him to foreclose. And yet the British general hesitated, pondered, and finally ordered the attack halted — "the Troops," he said, "had for that day done handsomely enough."

Had Howe known how utterly routed were the Americans, he probably would have ordered his men to storm the rebel positions. In response to the pleas of General Sullivan and Lord Stirling for reinforcements, General Putnam had sent out almost all the troops on Brooklyn Heights.

Less than five hundred men were left to man the defenses, and although they were being reinforced by the troops fleeing before the advancing British, the plight of the American army, now commanded by General Washington in person, was as perilous as a British commander could have wished.

Furthermore, so eager were the British troops for battle that it required repeated orders to stop their advance. Having come within three hundred yards of the enemy lines and observed the terror of the rebels, it was hard to make them see why they should turn back before "Mr. Washington and his dirty pack of New England long-faces . . . a vagabond army of ragamuffins."

Howe stopped the British advance because he feared being drawn into another Bunker Hill. The American entrenchments on Brooklyn Heights looked formidable to his eyes; whenever, in fact, he saw the rebels on a hill, he seems to have been reminded of Bunker Hill. He did not doubt that he could carry the American positions, but he feared that the price would be excessive. A large casualty list would cripple him for the rest of the campaign; the loss of fifteen hundred men, he pointed out, would be a heavier loss to the British than the sacrifice of double that number for the Americans. Situated as he was, three thousand miles from his base of supplies and reinforcements, he could not, he declared, commit such "an act of desperate rashness" as to attack the rebels in a strongly entrenched position without first bringing up artillery, scaling ladders, and other equipment necessary for a siege. Moreover, since the rebels were securely caught in a trap, it was not necessary to risk heavy losses by storming their last defenses: they could be devoured at leisure and by regular siege approaches which would keep British casualties at a minimum. In short, the battle was won and the Americans were doomed; it remained now only to draw the noose around their necks.

Howe always insisted that any prudent commander would have adopted this course of action. No general, he declared, ought to expose his troops to avoidable dangers, particularly when the objective could be gained without risk. "In this instance," Howe said, "from the certainty of being in possession of the lines in a very few days, by breaking ground, to have permitted the attack in question, would have been inconsiderate and even criminal." [4] That the Americans would slip out of the trap by escaping

---

[4] Certainly Howe did not lack personal bravery: *vide* Germain's letter to Howe, dated October 18, 1776, commenting upon the battle of Long Island. "It is the first Military Operation with which no fault could be found in the planning of it, nor in the Conduct of any Officer to whom you entrusted the Command," wrote Germain. "The King, indeed, made One Remark, I fear with too much Justice, that the Commander-in-Chief was too fond of exposing his Person, which he said was wrong in a Man who had upon so many Occasions shewn his Personal Bravery, and who ought now to consider how much the Publick would suffer by the loss of a General, who had gained the Affection of the Troops, and the Confidence of his Country."

to New York he did not seriously consider: the British fleet was near by and might be counted upon to keep Washington's army prisoner on Long Island. Strategy had already proved its worth against the Americans on Long Island and Howe was disposed to rely upon strategy to bring the remainder of the rebel army into his hands.

Had Howe gone on to capture the "trapped" Americans on Brooklyn Heights, his countrymen would have applauded his strategy. Yet actually, he could hardly have been more bitterly criticized had he lost the battle. For, thanks to Howe's decision to finish off the Americans at his leisure, Washington was given an unexpected reprieve. Washington was always at his greatest in adversity — and certainly during the Revolutionary War he was given frequent opportunity to show his mettle in the face of disaster. Extricating himself from impossible situations, striking back when his army was disintegrating, holding the troops together when the Revolution was collapsing about his head — to Washington, these became almost commonplace. Yet never was he in a more desperate situation than on Long Island with a British army champing at the bit and the British fleet riding at anchor a few miles away.

Fortunately for Washington, the winds, tides, and Sir William Howe worked in his favor. On the night of August 29, with the British lines only six hundred yards from their positions, the Americans began to break up camp, leaving their fires burning to deceive the overconfident enemy. Owing to a strong northwest wind, the British fleet could not enter the East River, so the passage between New York and Brooklyn remained open to Washington's army. The Americans' good fortune did not end here: on the morning of the retreat, a heavy fog screened their movements from the British warships. It was not until daylight that Sir William Howe realized what was going on, but by the time his troops were ready for action, the American rear guard was pushing off for New York.

This retreat from Long Island was so masterly that, in history at least, it overshadowed the American defeat on Long Island just as Dunkirk stood out over the British defeat in the Low Countries in 1940. At the time, however, Washington took little pride in this achievement: his chagrin over the loss of Long Island was too acute and the state of his army was still too precarious to admit of much self-congratulation upon his escape. The troops that had made good their retreat from Long Island were more like a mob of refugees than an organized army. Having scarcely slept for three nights, their faces covered with a stubble of beard (those that were old enough to grow whiskers), they "looked sickly, emaciated, cast down," observed a New Yorker; "the wet clothes, tents — as many as they had brought away — and other things, were laying about before the houses and in the streets to dry; in general everything seemed to be in confusion." Many soldiers, visibly shaken by their harrowing experiences on Long Island, struck for home without tarrying for discharges or leaves, their only thought being to put as many miles as possible between themselves and the dreaded British. "The fiery Sons of Carolina," it was remarked, "who were so apprehensive there would be an Action before they came, have taken wing." The Connecticut militia which before the battle had been eight thousand strong was soon down to two thousand men, and most of the departing warriors carried their guns and ammunition away with them. "The impulse for going home was so irresistible it answered no purpose to oppose it," said Washington, and he had no money with which to tempt the soldiers to remain; so the American commander-in-chief found himself in the familiar position of being "left by Troops just when they begin to deserve the Name, or perhaps at a Moment when an important blow is expected."

The battle of Long Island served notice upon the Americans that the British were not to be caught twice in the same trap, that they did not always march their men to be slaughtered by well-entrenched marksmen. It also gave a rude shock to Americans' remaining faith in the rifle. Instead of being objects of terror, the riflemen were now contemptible in the eyes of British and Hessian soldiers. "These frightful people," remarked a German officer, "deserve pity rather than fear." Although riflemen continued to be important in border fighting and in the war in the Southern states, after 1776 their popularity steadily waned in the North; in July 1778, Morgan's corps of riflemen was disbanded. The irremediable weakness of the rifle was that it had no bayonet and was slow in firing, thereby leaving the riflemen almost defenseless against British bayonet charges. Morgan admitted that his riflemen could be used effectively only if they were supported by musketmen with bayonets.

Disillusioned in the rifle, American officers now urged Congress to purchase muskets at least two inches longer than those used in the British army, in order that Americans might have the advantage in bayonet fighting. In brief, there was no short cut to victory: Britain must be conquered by its own weapons. This was the unhappy lesson of Long Island.

In escaping from Long Island, Washington had averted immediate disaster, but as long as the Americans remained on Manhattan Island encompassed by the British fleet and army, Sir William Howe still held his mortgage on the American army, and it could hardly be expected that the British commander would fail a second time to foreclose. Nevertheless, he again held his hand and Washington was given another chance to stave off disaster. Once more, the tides and the plans of the Howe brothers, Sir William and Lord Howe, came to his aid. The tides were not favorable for a sea-borne attack upon Manhattan Island, and while waiting for a propitious moment for making war, the Howe brothers were resolved to try their hand at peacemaking.

Like his brother, Lord Howe suffered from what George III could only regard as a malady of the English aristocracy — Whiggery. Lord Howe had repeatedly crossed the King in politics but, again like his brother, he was regarded as the ranking man in his profession. Much to the exasperation of the King and Lord George Germain, the admiral refused to take command of the British fleet unless he was empowered to make peace with the colonists. Germain demanded nothing less than unconditional surrender, but Howe resolutely held out for terms. Finally the King and his minister gave way, but only in form: although Lord Howe and Sir William Howe were appointed peace commissioners, they were authorized to offer nothing more than a promise of pardon. Americans were in effect to be told: submit and trust to the benevolence of the mother country.

This delay blighted Lord Howe's chances of restoring peace to the empire. While the King and Lord Howe argued over the concessions to be offered the rebels, the Americans had taken matters into their own hands and walked out of the empire. It was difficult to believe that they would ever walk back again.

CHAPTER IX

The American Crisis

WITH the Declaration of Independence, Americans put an end to the anomaly of waging war against a sovereign to whom they professed allegiance and against a country they called "mother." The course was now clear and unmistakable: to conquer or to be conquered, to achieve complete independence or suffer the fate of rebels.

The Declaration of Independence might have discouraged even the most zealous peacemakers, yet the Howes, nothing daunted, began to explore the possibilities of a peaceful settlement of the dispute immediately after the battle of Long Island. This, they held, was the proper time to send out peace feelers: "no decisive blow was struck, and neither party could say they were compelled to enter into the agreement." A captured American general, Sullivan, was released on parole to go to Philadelphia to inform Congress that the British general and admiral would be pleased to receive a deputation from Congress, but strictly as private gentlemen, for the Howes "could not own any such a body as Congress."

Similarly, the Howes could not recognize Washington by his title of general. In their eyes, he was the leader of a crew of outlaws; therefore "Mr." Washington was good enough for him. On the other hand, Lord Howe was eager to have Washington sit in on the peace conference; but how was he to address the rebel commander without giving him a military title that might convey a recognition of the legality of the rebellion? Howe first tried writing to Washington under the name of "George Washington, Esq." When that was refused on the ground that there was no such person in the American camp — did Lord Howe mean General George Washington? he was asked — Howe wrote another letter to "George Washington, Esq., etc. etc.," pointing out that "the etc. etc., implied everything." "It does so," drily replied Washington when he received the letter, "and anything." Washington held out for an explicit recognition of his title, and when it was not forthcoming, declined to hold any correspondence with the Howes.

Lord Howe entertained the kindliest feelings toward the Americans and would gladly have offered them everything they had asked in 1775. To General Sullivan, Howe declared that "he was ever against taxing of us . . . and that he was very sure America could not be conquered, and that it was a great pity so brave a nation should be cutting one another to pieces." While sympathizing with Americans' reluctance to discuss peace with a Tory government, he expected that they would listen appreciatively to an English Whig exuding benevolence toward the colonies and resolved to do them justice. Under this persuasion, he expected peace would be made within a few days of his arrival in America.

Had the Howes been given extensive peacemaking powers, the American people might have gladly opened their arms to them and even have returned to their allegiance to George III, after first making sure, however, that the King and Parliament had no real authority over them. Therefore, lest public opinion turn against Congress as a warmongering body which flatly turned down all compromise, some congressmen argued that it was necessary to send a deputation to the Howes and so satisfy the people "that we are always ready to hear anything that will restore peace to the country." Although few of these congressmen had any hope that good would come of such a meeting, they recognized that the majority of their countrymen, to whom independence was merely a disagreeable necessity, had still to be shown that there was no hope whatever that they could live happily under the same roof with Englishmen.

For the radicals, the Howes' peace overtures raised the specter of reconciliation. They had hoped that the Declaration of Independence would put an end to all thoughts of going back — America had made her decision, now let her adhere to it. Washington declared that instead of "feeding themselves upon the dainty food of reconciliation," his countrymen ought to be savoring the sweets of independence and preparing themselves for the rigors of the field. Americans ought to remember that they were now an independent people engaged in a life-and-death struggle for liberty in which there could be no compromise.

To the consternation of the radicals, many members of Congress seemed disposed to help wheel in the Trojan horse if, indeed, the Howes could be regarded in that invidious light. Apparently, some patriots supposed that they had left the British Empire only in order to get back on better terms. The Ministry — so ran the story — was now at its wits' end to prevent an uprising in Great Britain itself in favor of the Americans: mobs of honest Britons were preparing to storm Parliament and the King's palace to protest against war with the colonies. Therefore, Lord North had been driven to make peace — or to lose his head. The Howes had come prepared to yield everything in dispute; in fact, Americans were now in a position to write their own terms for returning to the empire. Here, then, was an opportunity to exchange the doubtful blessings of independence for the solid advantages of reconstructing the British Empire in accord with American ideas; in short, to go back to first principles and make the empire a league of free commonwealths.

All were agreed, however, that if the Howes had nothing more to offer than pardons and good wishes for Anglo-American amity, the war must go on. In that event, independence would stand upon firmer ground than before as the only alternative to "slavery and wretchedness," and Americans would be more firmly united in their determination to win independence and liberty.

Accordingly, early in September 1776, Congress appointed a committee of three — John Adams, Benjamin Franklin, and Edward Rutledge — to attend the Howes, not as private gentlemen but as representatives of the sovereign Congress. On the road to New York, the American delegates encountered so many stragglers from the army roistering in the taverns that they could find lodgings only with great difficulty. At Brunswick, John Adams and Franklin were obliged to share a bed in a room only a little larger than the bed itself. Here Adams was treated to a disquisition by Franklin on the importance of fresh air as a preventive of colds, but Adams dropped off to sleep in the middle of this lecture. It was perhaps well that he did — for, some years later, Franklin fell a victim to his own theory: he insisted on sleeping with the windows open and, said Adams, caught his death of cold.

The spectacle of the highways filled with deserters from Washington's army, the recent defeats in Canada and on Long Island, the great British armament poised to invade the United States both from New York and Lake Champlain, reminded the delegates that they were not in a strong bargaining position as they sat down to a cold collation consisting, they noted, of "good claret, good bread, cold ham, tongues, and mutton" on board Lord Howe's flagship in New York Harbor and waited for the admiral to open the conference. None of them expected, however, that Howe would whip a satisfactory peace plan out of his pocket and that the American Revolution would be wound up then and there. They expected, on the contrary, what they received: an offer of pardon, lofty sentiments, assurances of good will, and vague promises that all would be well if the colonies would trust to Britain's mercy and justice. Lord Howe was compelled to admit that he had power to "converse and confer" but could commit his government to nothing; he could not even promise that Parliament would renounce the right of taxing the colonies. Only after the colonists had returned to their allegiance would the mother country consent to talk peace terms — in short, unconditional surrender, which to the patriots was no better than thrusting their heads "into the devouring jaws of hellish tyrants."

The interview, indeed, cruelly strained Lord Howe's affection for the Americans. When he remarked that he could not receive the delegates as members of Congress, a body of which his sovereign had no cognizance, John Adams answered that he perfectly understood the noble lord's delicacy, and that he and his colleagues were perfectly willing to be received "in any Capacity his Lordship pleased, except in that of *British Subjects*." When Lord Howe tried to express his affection for America by observing that "he felt for America as a brother, and, if America should fall, he should feel and lament it like the loss of a brother," Benjamin Franklin spoke up. "My Lord," he said, "we will do our utmost endeavors to save your lordship that mortification." It was apparent that in this encounter between the British nobility and American commoners, the nobility was coming off a bad second-best.

Upon that note, the meeting broke up. The gentlemen had talked peace but actually they had cleared the decks for war: it could no longer be doubted that the rebels must be made to feel the wrath of Great Britain, rather than its benevolence, before they would be brought to return to their allegiance. "Nothing remains," said Lord Howe's secretary, "but to fight it out against a Set of the most determined Hypocrites & Demagogues, compiled of the Refuse of the Colonies, that ever were permitted by Providence to be the Scourge of a Country."

The radicals in Congress were of course overjoyed by the collapse of the peace conference; surely now the American people would see, if they had not seen before, that it was futile to attempt to patch up the rotten hulk of empire. Congress immediately rushed into print an account of the meeting in order to "strike the Tories dumb," dispel the doubts of the hesitant, steel the zealous in the cause, and lay forever the specter of reconciliation. The utmost that the mother country offered was a pardon — and "to receive a Pardon," said Congress, "was to acknowledge that asserting the essential Rights of Freemen was criminal; and to promise never to assert them any more."

Thus Great Britain permitted to slip through its fingers another opportunity of reconstituting the empire by means of timely concessions. A generous peace offer in September 1776, affording permanent security to colonial liberty under British sovereignty, might have turned the scales toward reunion with the mother country. The abortive mission of the Howes proved to be a triumph for the irreconcilables on both sides; and England reposed in military conquest its sole hope of saving the empire.

Although it was true that Lord Howe had little to offer Americans by way of peace terms, he and his brother had much to offer them if they persisted in war. The peace negotiations had not halted British preparations to capture New York: Sir William Howe was ready to land above Washington's position on Manhattan Island and he waited only for favorable tides before beginning the amphibious operations expected to trap the entire American army.

From August 29 to September 15, 1776, however, the British army remained inactive. Having no hope of a favorable result from the peace talks, Washington spent this breathing spell in strengthening his fortifications on Manhattan Island and in Westchester County.

With the British in possession of Long Island and their ships patrolling the Hudson and the East River, American efforts to hold New York City and Manhattan Island might well seem hopeless. Washington was in a state of agonizing uncertainty: whether to try to defend New York, in conformity with the wishes of Congress, or to abandon the city, in accord with the dictates of military prudence. As was his custom in such emergencies, he called a council of general officers on September 7, 1776, to decide upon a course of action. He did not find here the assurance that he sought: the officers were evenly divided between evacuating and defending the city. Washington's own opinion was that New York could not be retained; the city was at the Howes' mercy, he said, and "nothing seems to remain but to determine the time of their taking possession." Yet there was in the American general a streak of stubbornness which made it difficult for him to give up New York without hazarding another battle. Therefore, he adopted a compromise whereby the army was divided between Manhattan Island and the mainland: five thousand troops were allocated for the defense of New York, nine thousand were sent to the fortified camp at Kingsbridge, and the remainder were strung out to hold the intervening territory and to act as reserves for the two main divisions of the army.

After having so narrowly escaped disaster upon Long Island, it might be supposed that Washington would have learned the danger of risking his army upon islands in the face of British military and naval superiority. Certainly had he been the Fabius that history has acclaimed him, he would not have gambled the fate of the Revolution upon such long chances. He trusted to fortune and to the dilatoriness of Sir William Howe — and, fortunately for the American Revolution, neither failed him.

With the peace conference out of the way and the tides running in his favor, Sir William Howe turned his attention to the problem of how the Americans could be attacked to the best advantage. A direct assault upon New York City was ruled out because of the risk of destroying the town. Sir Henry Clinton urged that a blow be struck against the American positions at Kingsbridge, thereby cutting off the American detachments on Manhattan Island; but Sir William Howe was disposed to attack at some less strongly fortified point on Manhattan Island itself in the hope that the Americans might risk a general engagement. As usual, it was Howe's strategy that was adopted; and on September 16 the British fleet began to bombard the American positions at Kipp's Bay while the British troops were brought ashore in flat-bottomed landing boats with bows equipped with ramps for the speedy disembarkation of the troops.

Howe had indeed chosen a weak spot in the American defenses. The few American troops at Kipp's Bay were green recruits among whom the "horrid din" of the British naval guns struck panic. When they saw the enemy landing by hundreds on the beaches, their courage utterly vanished: bouncing out of their trenches, they scurried to the rear, conveying their terror to other units, many of which threw away their guns in their haste to get out of harm's way. Officers as well as privates joined the flight; many officers, in fact, outstripped their men. Two brigades of New England troops ran away from about fifty British regulars, leaving Washington to shift for himself within eighty yards of the onrushing enemy. "Nothing appeared," wrote a spectator, "but fright, disgrace, and confusion. . . . I could wish the transactions of this day blotted out of the annals of *America*."

It was Washington who finally rallied the disorganized troops. Freely using his cane upon these "dastardly sons of Cowardice," he swore that he "would Run thro the Body the first man who ran from his Post." He led his men, many of whom were without officers, into action and exposed himself to enemy bullets as he had done twenty years before at Braddock's defeat. Washington, said General Greene, was "so vexed at the infamous conduct of the troops, that he sought death rather than life." Fortunately for the Americans, the British were no marksmen; had they hit Washington it would have been a minor miracle. Spared by the ineptitude of his foes, Washington rallied his men and stopped the British so abruptly that some of their advance parties were thrown back. In good order, the Americans then retreated to their positions on Harlem Heights.

The rout at Kipp's Bay put it in the power of the British to sweep across the island to the Hudson River side of Manhattan, thereby cutting off the American troops that still remained in New York City.[1] Most of the Americans, it is true, were safely north of the British landing, but Howe made little effort to capitalize upon his opportunity of trapping those who had incautiously stayed in the city. The story that Howe and his staff dallied over their teacups and surrendered themselves to the charms of an American lady who deliberately immobilized the British command during the critical hours of the afternoon is, unfortunately,

[1] Three days before the British landed at Kipp's Bay the American command had decided to evacuate New York City lest the defenders be cut off by a British drive across Manhattan Island. When the British struck at Kipp's Bay, however, there still remained a force in New York City.

without foundation; unfortunately, that is, for Howe's reputation, for it would at least have been then understandable why he permitted the Americans to get away. But he did not have even this excuse for his immobility: he was simply looking for comfortable quarters for himself and his staff. When one of his officers urged that he make haste, he grew angry and swore that he would not be hurried. Howe loved to take his ease and he was determined not to permit the rebels to deprive him of the comforts to which he was accustomed.

While escaping entrapment, the Americans lost New York City, the prize for which they had risked so much. Before evening of the day they landed at Kipp's Bay, the British entered New York City and took possession without firing a shot. The entire southern end of the island, including New York City, had been won at a cost of about two British casualties. "Thus," said an Englishman, "this Town and its Environs wch. these blustering Gentlemen had taken such wonderful Pains to fortify, were given up in two or three Hours without any Defense, or the least appearance of a manly Resistance."

The British gaped at the network of defenses constructed by the rebels in New York with much the same amazement that present-day travelers inspect the Pyramids and speculate upon the vast amount of human labor that went into their construction. "The infinite Pains and Labor," remarked an Englishman, "which they must have bestowed one would thought from Regret alone, would have inclined them to make some kind of stand." But perhaps the most astonishing thing about these works was the haste with which they had been abandoned by the rebels: as long as the fortifications remained, it was predicted, they would "serve as striking Monuments of their Cowardice and Folly."

The British were given a warm welcome in New York by the few inhabitants who still remained. When they marched down Broadway, it was observed that "joy and gladness seemed to appear in all coun-tenances"; the officers were hoisted upon the townspeople's shoulders and carried in triumph about the city. Women as well as men "behaved like overjoyed Bedlamites": two women pulled down the American flag from the fort and, after trampling it under foot, hoisted the Union Jack in its stead.

Having captured New York undamaged, Sir William Howe congrat-ulated himself upon having acquired excellent winter quarters for his troops. Although some American generals, notably Nathanael Greene, had urged that the city be burned before evacuation, Congress, which had been willing to burn Boston about the heads of the British, could not bring itself to sanction the destruction of New York. Yet hardly had the conquerors settled themselves in the city before a destructive fire, set by Americans who had hidden themselves in the town after the Brit-ish occupation, broke out simultaneously in three different places. The fire gained great headway because the fire company had been disbanded, the fire engines were out of order, and all the church bells had been removed by Washington, ostensibly to be cast into cannon, but actually, the British now suspected, to prevent an alarm being given. The conflagration was finally stopped at Broadway by a change in the wind and by the quick work of the British seamen and soldiers in pulling down houses in its path, but almost a third of the town was destroyed, including Trinity Church, the oldest and largest of the Episcopalian churches. However, the ship docks, warehouses, and the business section were saved, and enough of the residential district was intact to permit the British army to make the city its headquarters for the remainder of the war. After the fire of 1776, however, New York no longer afforded the pleasant quarters to which the British had looked forward: they were forced to crowd into the remaining houses "like herrings in a barrel," and so many of the citizens suffered from the "Itch, Pox, Fever, and Flux," said a Tory, "that altogether there is a complication of stinks enough to drive a person whose sense of smelling was very delicate and his lungs of the finest contexture, into consumption in the space of twenty-four hours."

Even though New York City was lost, Washington refused to concede Manhattan Island to the British; he was determined to make them fight for every foot of American soil. At Harlem Heights on Manhattan Island he regrouped his army and waited the British attack. Here again were the makings of another Bunker Hill provided the British were willing to march boldly against the American defenses; but after a brief battle they withdrew and left Washington on his mountain while they probed for a weak spot that would enable them to take the Americans from the rear. It was to prevent the British from cutting off his retreat to the mainland that Washington abandoned his impregnable defenses on Harlem Heights and retreated to Kingsbridge on the mainland — a position so strong that Washington believed that he could repel twice the number of troops Howe was able to bring against him. Thus Washington continued his island-hopping in the teeth of British sea power.

Howe declined to seek out Washington in his stronghold at Kingsbridge. He preferred to come upon the rebels from the rear, but when he landed north of the American lines in Westchester County his movements were so leisurely that Washington had ample time to pull back to White Plains. Here the situation was the familiar one of Washington atop a hill, and Howe at the bottom daring him to come down and fight. This Washington refused to do. "It would be presumption," he remarked, "to draw out our Young Troops into open ground, against their Superiors both in number and Discipline." When the British attempted to go up the mountain after Washington, the Americans merely retreated to a higher and stronger position where Sir William did not dare to pursue them.

Obviously, Washington's strategy was to avoid battle except upon the most advantageous terms. He had sound reason for so doing: the American army could not afford another defeat; the country was panic-stricken after the calamity on Long Island; and only fourteen thousand effectives could be put in the field against Howe's twenty-five thousand. " 'Tis our business to study to avoid any considerable misfortunes," said General Greene, "and to take post where the enemy will be obliged to fight us, and not we them." Americans' best hope seemed to be to delay the British advance; nothing, except defeat, was more pernicious to Howe than to be forced to fritter away his strength in small actions which inured Americans to the smell of gunpowder and cost the British men that could not be easily replaced.

It was not merely British superiority in numbers and matériel that accounted for Washington's reluctance to risk battle. He might have fought the British despite these unequal terms had he trusted his men more fully. The real source of his weakness, he had found, was that American troops could not be relied upon to fight well in a pitched battle. No one was more eager than he to challenge the British army could he be sure that his men would show courage, discipline, and tenacity — but this, he said, "experience, to my extreme affliction, has convinced me . . . is rather to be wished for than expected." Behind entrenchments and in a strong defensive position, the American soldiers sometimes fought skillfully, but put them in the open against British regulars and they were almost certain to wilt. Many of his troops were militia who, Washington said, "were continually coming and going without rendering the least Earthly Service." His perennial complaint, however, was the poor quality of his officers — all his misfortunes, he exclaimed, arose from their deficiencies. Most of them were "Beardless Boys" and few were gentlemen by Washington's standards. General Knox declared that no army was ever worse served by its officers than was the Continental army: when they did not decamp before a battle, they generally "most manfully turned their backs and run away, officers and men, like sturdy fellows." Most of the officers, he swore, were "a parcel of ignorant, stupid men, who might make tolerable soldiers but who are bad officers. . . . As the army now stands, it is only a receptacle for ragamuffins."

Sir William Howe, it has been seen, spared no efforts to make Washington fight. He followed the usual procedure of an invader, attempting to bring the enemy to a general action and to avoid skirmishing, but Washington rejected these invitations to battle. Howe confessed that he found the motions of the Americans "very extraordinary . . . and not a little perplexing." An adversary who refused every challenge to fight was something new in his experience, although he had expected as much when he drew up his plans for the campaign of 1776.

Sir William Howe, it will be observed, was now paying Washington the compliment of feinting and maneuvering as though he regarded "Mr." Washington as a foe worthy of his steel. The American war was becoming more and more like conventional eighteenth-century warfare with each side attempting to outmaneuver the other. The British general would not risk another Bunker Hill, and Washington would not risk a battle on ground where the two armies were relatively equal. The result was a stalemate; the war reposed on dead center. While the Americans roosted on the heights at White Plains, everything was as quiet, said Washington's aide-de-camp, "as if the Enemy were 100 Miles Distant from us."

Obviously, this game of hide-and-seek could go on all winter without profiting the British in the least. The country north of New York favored the defense: mountainous and rocky, abounding in stone walls and interspersed with forests, it was terrain not to Howe's liking. Moreover, the farther Washington retreated, the more rugged and inaccessible the country became and the more elbowroom for maneuvering he gained between the Hudson River and Long Island Sound. It was a forlorn hope that Howe could corner Washington and force him to fight a battle on equal terms in this unpromising country.

From this unprofitable shadowboxing, Sir William Howe yearned to escape. His opportunity came early in November when an American deserter gave the British the plans of Fort Washington on Manhattan Island. Here was unexpectedly presented to Howe a chance of breaking the deadlock that had settled down upon the war, and an opportunity of eliminating a thorn that had been sticking in his flesh ever since he forced Washington to retire from Harlem Heights. Therefore, on November 5, the British abruptly left their camp at White Plains and began to retrace their steps to New York.

Fort Washington was a natural fortification, a steep rocky hill which the Americans had strengthened by redoubts and entrenchments. The ascent was extremely difficult; large quantities of stores and provisions had been thrown into the fort, and the garrison consisted of over two thousand men. A British officer, viewing the fort after its capture, declared that he would have undertaken with eight hundred men to hold it against ten thousand.

Originally, Fort Washington and Fort Lee on the New Jersey side of the Hudson were intended to prevent the passage of British ships up the river. This purpose they had failed to accomplish: by keeping to the middle of the channel, the British men-of-war had run freely past the American batteries. As a result, both forts had lost most of their strategic value, but Fort Washington had gained new importance as a threat to the British position on Manhattan Island. By-passed by the British when they cleared the rest of the island of rebels, it remained an American hedgehog, far behind the fighting front. Supplies were ferried across the river at night from Fort Lee until the Americans' foot-hold on Manhattan Island had been rendered dangerous to the enemy. As long as the rebels held Fort Washington, the British lines of com-munication were in danger and their winter quarters in New York City exposed to hit-and-run raids. The importance of Fort Washington was revealed early in the campaign: when Howe moved his army into West-chester County, he was obliged to leave behind on Manhattan a strong force to pin down the garrison in Fort Washington.

Despite its great natural strength, Fort Washington was vulnerable to siege tactics — the garrison could easily be isolated from supplies and reinforcements. Furthermore, the British could bring to bear against the fort many thousands of men. All told, the position of the garrison would be desperate if the British moved against the fort in force.

Washington saw the hazard of trying to hold Fort Washington. His keen military sense told him that it was doomed and that the garrison and stores ought to be removed without delay. But, prone to listen to advice, Washington found that his advisers disagreed with his views. General Mifflin recommended that Fort Washington be kept as winter quarters for the American army; and General Nathanael Greene, to whose opinion Washington attached great weight, supported this plan. Greene, who had been among the first to advise the evacuation of New York City and Manhattan Island, had suffered a change of heart: he now advocated bold measures in order to confine the British army to Manhattan Island for the rest of the campaign. And in October 1776, Congress had passed a resolve requesting Washington to block the Hudson at Fort Washington to British warships. It was this, Washington said later, which "caused that warfare in my mind and hesitation which ended in the loss of the Garrison."

Certainly, as he admitted, Washington was guilty of irresolution. Caught in a web of perplexities and uncertainties, even after he made up his mind that the fort must be abandoned he could not bring himself to send the order to General Greene. Rather, he simply indicated to Greene his own opinion that Fort Washington was untenable, leaving the decision to evacuate or to stand his ground entirely to Greene. And that general, carried away by an unaccountable accession of optimism, resolved to hold Fort Washington to the last.

Washington's anxiety for the fate of the fort and its garrison would not down: driven by worry and foreboding, he left White Plains to make a personal inspection of the defenses of Fort Washington. But he had vacillated too long; just as he was stepping into the boat that was to carry him to the fort, the British opened their attack. Standing helplessly on the shore, Washington watched the battle from beginning to end. It could at least be said of the engagement that it did not detain him long.

The reduction of Fort Washington was entrusted to the Hessians and Highlanders, who, eager for honor and booty, launched a furious assault upon the stronghold. A heavy cannonade ripped through the American positions; a feigned attack threw the garrison off balance; and finally the Hessians, climbing the steep and rocky escarpment, charged the riflemen with drawn bayonets. As at Long Island, the bayonet proved superior to the rifle; the rebels fled to the central redoubt for protection, where, miserably huddled together, they ingloriously capitulated. "Fortunately for us," said a British officer, "the Americans behaved as dastardly as usual." Over two thousand men surrendered; only about twenty-five of the defenders were killed or wounded.

The loss of Fort Washington, its garrison and stores, put a new complexion upon the war. Two thousand Continental troops, together with some of the best cannon and small arms the Americans possessed, fell into the enemy's hands — a heavier loss than that suffered on Long Island. Even more noteworthy was the effect this victory had upon British strategy. The way was now open for the British to invade New Jersey where on level ground their immense superiority in men and matériel might be fully realized.

Until the loss of Fort Washington, the war had not gone badly for the Americans. Despite their vast military and naval strength, the British had conquered only two sizable islands — Long Island and Manhattan; they had secured hardly more than a foothold upon the mainland, and had not ventured more than a dozen miles from their ships. True, they had defeated the American army and had forced it to retreat whenever they had caught up with it, yet that army was still intact. At most, the British had secured snug winter quarters and a jumping-off place for the next campaign. In many skirmishes, Americans had inflicted heavier casualties than they had received; and as they acquired experience, they promised to give a better account of themselves in future fighting. The loss of New York was neither overwhelming nor unexpected; it had often been said that Americans must reconcile themselves to seeing their seaports fall to the enemy.

These triumphs hardly repaid Great Britain for maintaining one of the largest fleets and armies ever sent abroad; and at this rate, the conquest of the United States might well bankrupt the mother country. Howe's dispatches had begun to reflect his gloomy foreboding that suppressing the American rebellion was to be a slow, bloody, and costly business; he advised the home government to give up all hopes of quick victory and to prepare for another year of hard fighting. As for the Americans, their hopes soared as Howe's sense of bafflement grew. "I begin to think my friend Howe has lost the Campaign," said General Lee early in November, 1776, "and that his most Gracious Majesty must request a Body of Russians to reestablish order tranquillity happiness and good government amongst his deluded subjects of America."

Howe had opened the campaign with the expectation of accomplishing no more than the capture of New York City and Newport, Rhode Island; the lateness of the season, he wrote Germain in August 1776, would preclude more extensive triumphs. But now, with the fall of Fort Washington, these modest plans were shelved in favor of a more ambitious scheme of conquest. Everything conspired to draw the British on: New Jersey and Philadelphia were almost undefended, and the weather remained remarkably clement — it was, said a British officer, "the finest Weather for the Season ever known, and such a Fall as no Man can recollect; the Weather has been as favorable for our Operations since we took the field as it possibly could be."

Thus began a campaign which many expected would prove to be a triumphant Grand Tour of the American colonies. "Every Thing seems to be over with Them," said Lord Percy, "& I flatter myself now that this Campaign will put a total End to the War."

The immediate obstacle confronting the British in New Jersey was Fort Lee, situated opposite Fort Washington on the Hudson River. Against this fortification, Cornwallis launched a surprise attack; and although the garrison made good its escape, the margin of safety was so narrow that the British found the kettles boiling over the campfires and the rebels' tents still standing. They took only about one hundred prisoners, most of whom were said to be "a set of rascals that skulked out of the way for fear of fighting," but they captured rich stores of provisions and cannon. For the British, this was becoming a self-sustaining war.

Howe's decision to direct his strength against New Jersey caught Washington unawares. The American commander-in-chief had assumed that Howe intended to move northward up the Hudson to effect a junction with the army under General Carleton which from its base in Canada had penetrated deep into the United States. This, indeed, was one of the objectives Howe had set for his army in drawing up plans for the campaign of 1776 and it was confidently expected by the English Ministry that two British armies would join hands somewhere in New York and forge a steel wall between New England and the rest of the revolted colonies. Never doubting that the enemy was pursuing this strategy, Washington had feared as he retreated northward in the autumn of 1776 that he would be caught in a vise between two converging British armies. Howe's about-face at White Plains relieved him at least of this apprehension but left him almost helpless to stop the British sweep into New Jersey.

Washington rushed part of his army across the Hudson to meet this new peril, but his worst fears were realized in the level country of New Jersey: his troops, outnumbered and exhausted, were steadily pushed back to the Delaware. The American army was in utter rout, and it disintegrated as rapidly as it retreated. "No lads ever shewed greater activity in retreating than we," said an American soldier. ". . . Our Soldiers are the best fellows in the World at this Business." True, it was a flight before a vastly superior enemy. "About 2,000 of us," said the veterans of this retreat, "have been obliged to run damn'd hard before abt. 10,000 of the Enemy." Their cannon, ordnance stores, and supplies were left behind; the course of their flight could be traced by abandoned equipment. In such a retreat, tents, blankets, and even guns became excess baggage.

Yet it must be acknowledged that the British pursuit of the disorganized Americans across New Jersey was hardly worthy of experienced fox hunters: it took them nineteen days to cover seventy-four miles against an army incapable of effective resistance. Hardly surprising, therefore, that the fox escaped. It was not merely Howe's constitutional sloth that was responsible for this slow progress; bad roads, rain, and the Americans' work in destroying bridges as they retreated held up the British advance. Washington repeatedly deceived the British into believing that he was planning to make a stand, and the British consequently were "very Cautious & doubtfull in pursuing." So excessive was their wariness that, for the most part, they proceeded no faster than their heavy cannon could be brought up; and they scoured woods and stone walls with heavy artillery fire before they approached. The bushes were generally empty of rebels, but the British were taking no chances of being ambushed. Furthermore, lack of transport slowed British progress once the army had lost contact with the fleet.

It was Lord Cornwallis who led the pursuit of Washington and the broken remnant of the American army.[2] Howe remained chiefly in New York, admiring the "romantic Landscape" around the city, which he pronounced superior to anything he had seen in Italy. But the war, too, occupied his attention: while Cornwallis was in full cry after Washington, Howe seems suddenly to have remembered that his plan of campaign called for an attack upon Rhode Island.[3] Thereupon he

[2] In one dash Cornwallis, seeking to overtake Washington at Brunswick, covered twenty miles in a single day. But Howe had strictly ordered Cornwallis not to pass the Raritan and therefore Cornwallis was obliged to wait at Brunswick for five days while Howe came down from New York to inspect personally the situation. Whatever chance there had been of catching Washington was lost by this delay.

[3] "When the expedition was dispatched to Rhode Island, Sir Henry Clinton strongly urged that he might rather be permitted to conduct it to the Delaware or be landed at Amboy to have cooperated with Lord Cornwallis or embarked on board Lord Howe's fleet, landed in Delaware and taken possession of Philadelphia." But to none of these suggestions would Howe listen.

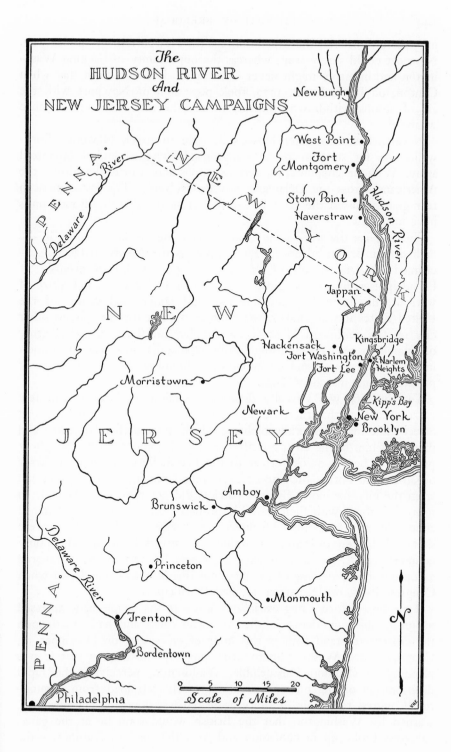

The
HUDSON RIVER
And
NEW JERSEY CAMPAIGNS

PENNA.

Delaware River

N E W

NEW JERSEY

Morristown

Newark

Brunswick

Amboy

Princeton

Monmouth

Delaware River

PENNA.

Trenton

Bordentown

Philadelphia

Newburgh

West Point

Fort Montgomery

Stony Point

Haverstraw

Hudson River

Tappan

N E W Y O R K

Hackensack

Kingsbridge

Fort Washington

Fort Lee

Harlem Heights

Kipp's Bay

New York

Brooklyn

0   5   10   15   20
Scale of Miles

N

immediately ordered the expedition against Newport to get under way. Newport could surely wait, whereas the opportunity of bagging Washington and his army might never come again. It is significant that when Clinton, on December 8, 1776, took possession of Newport with the aid of troops withdrawn from Cornwallis, he met with no resistance whatever.

Nevertheless, even after Howe's decision to attack Newport, Cornwallis was far superior to Washington's bedraggled and disorganized army. Without encountering serious opposition, Cornwallis drove the Americans across the Delaware into Pennsylvania. The last American rear guard crossed the river to safety just as the British advance units hove into view.

Philadelphia, the seat of the Continental Congress, lay squarely in the path of the British advance. "Philadelphia is the American Diana," exclaimed the alarmed patriots, "she must be preserved at all events"; "if Philadelphia is lost, all is ruined." Certainly the city was a rich prize of war: as the financial, manufacturing, and commercial center of the United States it was vital to the country's war effort as was no other city on the continent. Most of the supplies for the Continental army originated in or passed through Philadelphia; its port was the busiest in the United States, and its shipbuilding industry turned out scores of privateers and merchant ships.

Yet the city was virtually defenseless against an invader, and few citizens doubted that the redcoats would soon be marching down Broad Street. The mayor of Philadelphia cordially invited them to come and dine with him in the city; but after issuing this invitation he thought it prudent to beat a quick retreat to the British lines. A reign of terror began for the Tories: their houses were plundered and many were driven from the city by mobs. But the patriots did not remain far behind: so many left town with their movable property that Philadelphia "seemed almost deserted & resembled a Sunday in service time." The shops were shut and the few citizens who walked the streets bore "d——d gloomy countenances . . . except among the soldiers." A few die-hards favored a house-to-house defense of the city, but this plan was abandoned when Congress itself, on December 12, fled Philadelphia.

Two days before, Congress in an address to the people had expressed its unshakable confidence in the American cause and had called upon the citizens to stand firm in this hour of crisis; and on December 11, Congress asked Washington to deny publicly the rumors that it was planning to abandon Philadelphia. Washington, perceiving the rapid deterioration of the military situation, wisely refrained from committing Congress to remain in a city he feared was doomed. The next day, warned by Washington that the British would soon be at the gates, Congress broke up in confusion and took the road to Baltimore — the first of several forced exoduses that Congress was to make from the City of Brotherly Love.

The loss of a city, even though it was the largest on the continent, was relatively unimportant in Washington's mind, compared with the effect such a reverse would have upon American morale. Already there was unmistakable evidence that the patriots' resolution was weakening — the times that tried men's souls found many Americans' souls wanting. More ominous in Washington's eyes than the victories of the British army was the defection of New York, New Jersey, and Pennsylvania from the patriot cause. Although he called upon New Jersey farmers to scorch the earth before the invader, they turned out to welcome the British as deliverers. "A large part of the Jerseys," said Washington, "have given every proof of disaffection that they can do."

Sir William Howe was ill prepared to make the most of good fortune: the very completeness of his triumph in New Jersey seemed to render him more cautious and irresolute. Before him, on the other side of the Delaware, lay Philadelphia and "the vitals of the continent." Yet Howe hesitated. Should he cross the Delaware, push on to Philadelphia, and make that city his winter quarters; or should he content himself with the victories already won, settle down to digest his conquests, and wait for the rebellion to collapse of its own accord? Upon the answer to these questions hung the outcome of the war; and so, when Howe set out to reconnoiter the Delaware crossing at Trenton, to decide whether to attempt the passage of the river, the fate of the Revolution trembled in the balance.

Before fleeing across the Delaware, the rebels had carried off or burned all the boats for a distance of seventy-five miles along the lower reaches of the river. They had also mounted artillery on the south bank and fired briskly whenever the enemy showed himself. Therefore, when Sir William Howe and his party appeared on the Delaware they were treated to particularly heavy fire from thirty-seven guns; and this show of strength, together with the lack of boats, led Howe to a momentous decision: the rebels were still too strong and the season too far advanced to risk an invasion of Pennsylvania. The campaign, he declared, was officially closed: the British would rest upon their arms until next year, when the final knockout blow would be administered the rebellion.

Accordingly, Sir William Howe returned to New York, his mistress, his wine, and the provincial gaieties that the place afforded. He proposed to spend a quiet winter: the warrior had returned and his laurels were still fresh. As for "Mr. Washington" and his tatterdemalions, they might freeze and starve, but they could neither disturb the repose nor interrupt the pleasures of the British commander-in-chief.

It is probable that a general of greater resolution and of less sympathy with the Americans — Clive of India, for example — would have forced a passage of the Delaware and captured Philadelphia. True, the rebels had commandeered all the boats on the river, but in New York there were knocked-down craft shipped from England for just such an emergency as this. Had Howe been determined to cross the Delaware, he could have accomplished his purpose: it was manifestly impossible for Washington with a few thousand men at his disposal to hold a river over a hundred miles long against an army as powerful as that commanded by Howe. The Delaware was no impassable barrier; and the British army was straining at the leash to leap this obstacle and be at the rebels. "It seems to be the Study of every Officer & Man amongst them to be as distinguishable for Discipline, Spirit, & Conduct," said Lord Percy. "Nothing is a difficulty with them. Whatever they are directed to do, they do with chearfullness & Pleasure." And, on the other hand, the state of the rebel army was well known to the British command: some of Washington's letters describing the wretched condition of his troops had been intercepted by the British and published in the Loyalist newspapers.

Howe's decision to call a halt at the Delaware and to defer all military operations until 1777 was one of the most important steps of the war. If there was any energy left in Washington's army, Howe gave it scope; by allowing Washington a respite he made it possible for the Americans to form a new army beyond the river — an army which within three months was to reconquer virtually all New Jersey.

CHAPTER X

Trenton

THE troops that accompanied Washington across the Delaware were dazed by their harrowing experiences in New Jersey; they were, said Thomas Paine, "surprised how they got through; and at a loss to account for those powers of mind, and springs of animation, by which they withstood the forces of accumulated misfortune." At the limit of their powers of endurance, they could have offered little resistance had the British continued the pursuit beyond the Delaware. Blaming the cowardice of their countrymen for their misfortunes, they swore that they would "fall a Sacrafice to the British Savages"; exhausted, barefooted and ragged, without medicine or hospitals, they suffered and died by hundreds. Sickness, death, and desertion had cost the army more men than a severe battle.

To Washington, Howe's decision to terminate the campaign at the Delaware came almost like a reprieve to a condemned man. He had had no doubt that Howe intended to proceed to Philadelphia; ravaging New Jersey, he pointed out, was "playing no more than a small game"; Howe must take Philadelphia if for no other reason than to save his reputation — "for what has he done as yet, with his great Army?" The American commander had little hope of stopping Howe; once across the Delaware, the British could march into Philadelphia without interference from Washington's command, now numbering scarcely more than two thousand fighting men.

The campaign in New Jersey had erased almost the last doubt from the minds of British officers that the Americans were a pack of cowardly rascals who fought only when up to their eyes in entrenchments. Even many of the officers who at Boston had learned to respect Americans were now among the loudest in depreciating their courage. They derided the unmilitary appearance of American soldiers: "No nation ever saw such a set of Tatterde-mallions. . . . There are few coats among them but what are out at elbows, and in a whole regiment there is scarce a pair of breeches." Some Englishmen indeed were weary of waging war against a foe so lost to honor and the military virtues.

On the strength of these victories, many English officers concluded that "the most dangerous & unprovoked Rebellion that ever existed" was completely smashed. "This Business is pretty near over," said Lord Percy; it only remained to mop up the last pockets of resistance. In the officers' mess it was freely predicted that peace would be restored by Christmas; New England might hold out longer, but that, observed an Englishman, was "so much the better for Indemnifications & the Punishment of Evil-Doers." Lord Cornwallis, who had been of opinion ever since the battle of Long Island that the rebel army was incapable of further resistance, now prepared to return to England. For high-spirited young men like Cornwallis, America offered little further prospect of glory and promotion. It was, he believed, largely a matter of receiving the subjection of the beaten rebels – a business which ought not to detain him in America.

In his distress, Washington found little comfort in the home front. Most of the state of Pennsylvania seemed ready to go over to the enemy; Philadelphia was almost depopulated; and Continental paper money scarcely circulated in many parts of Pennsylvania because the people expected that Sir William Howe would soon make it worthless.

With resistance crumbling on every hand and American morale sinking under repeated blows, Washington was obliged to recruit a new army. The terms of service of the soldiers of the Continental army expired at the end of 1776, for Congress, it will be remembered, had refused in 1775 to create an army for the duration of the war. Washington's difficulties were now much greater than when he enlisted a new army during the siege of Boston. Seldom has an army had less to offer, except perhaps a hero's death, than had the American army in the winter of 1776. Congress was penitent for having clung to the "d——d foolish scheme" of enlisting troops for twelve months only; and just before decamping to Baltimore, it publicly ascribed American defeats to short enlistments rather than to any superiority in the British army, but this hardly eased Washington's task of raising a new army. On every side, his army was breaking to pieces. He appealed to the Massachusetts militia to remain with him until March 1777, but they could not be dissuaded from going home. At Brunswick, New Jersey, several brigades struck for home with the enemy less than two hours away.

Washington was in much the same position as Montgomery at Quebec: he must attack before his army packed up and went home. After the first of January, 1777, unless providentially reinforced, Washington would retain only a few Southern regiments, weakened by sickness and fatigue — in all about twelve hundred men — with which to oppose the fourteen thousand troops in New Jersey under Howe. Except for these troops — "the poor remains of our debilitated Army" — the term of service of the soldiers expired on January 1, and Washington dared not hope that they would re-enlist, be the emergency ever so pressing.

Before setting out on its travels, Congress invested Washington with sweeping authority over the army and the conduct of the war. Recognizing that temporarily at least it was not in a position to direct the war and to exercise close supervision over the army, Congress gave the commander-in-chief power to appoint the officers of the army it hoped to raise, to seize supplies, and to proclaim martial law. Only the last extremity could have wrung from these civilians such extensive powers for a Continental general, but the victories of Sir William Howe had brought Congress to this unhappy pass.

Congress also yielded to the long-apparent necessity of offering bounties to recruits and enlisting men for a period longer than one year. In the summer of 1776, a bounty of ten dollars was paid volunteers who enlisted for three years or more; and when this proved insufficient, land and a suit of clothes were added. Unfortunately for the American cause, however, it did not follow that because Congress had been finally persuaded of the need of a long-term army such an army was to be created at the stroke of a pen. More than a resolve of Congress was required to call into being an effective fighting force; and the British were hardly likely to be awed by the vast armies conjured up on paper by the statesmen in Philadelphia.

From the way recruiting was progressing late in 1776, however, it was doubtful whether Washington could again work the miracle of raising an army in the teeth of the enemy. In Virginia, for example, recruiting officers, even with the aid of a high bounty, met with much difficulty in procuring men. "None will enlist that can avoid it," reported an officer. "They get some servants and convicts which are purchased from their Masters; these will desert [at] the first opportunity." And yet, if a new army was not quickly put in the field, Washington recognized that "the game is pretty near up."

The outlook was as bleak as any faced by Washington; yet there was one small ray of hope to encourage him to fight on. The British expeditionary force which, under the command of General Carleton, had set out from Canada in the summer of 1776 to capture Albany and join forces with Howe's army on the Hudson had failed to reach its objective.

The route followed by General Carleton in his invasion of the United States was the same as that taken by the Americans when they burst into Canada: the Lake Champlain-St. John River waterway. American defenses were pitifully weak: all that remained to stop the enemy advance was the wreck of the army that had invaded Canada. The British force, on the other hand, was powerful, well equipped, and eager to come to grips with the American army in the North. Immense labor had been expended upon this campaign: supplies were rushed across the Atlantic, military roads constructed by the Canadians, and several ships brought from Great Britain knocked down for assemblage on Lake Champlain. All told, twenty gunboats, several small frigates, and a large number of flatboats to transport the army and its supplies, together with seven hundred sailors to man the ships, sailed down Lake Champlain to attack the American positions at Crown Point and Ticonderoga, the principal fortresses guarding the passage to Albany.

America's best — and perhaps only — chance of halting the British before Albany was to fight them on Lake Champlain. In the disorganized state of the American army in the North, it seemed a forlorn hope that the progress of Carleton's host could be stopped on land.

Even before Carleton reached Lake Champlain, Gates and Schuyler, the American generals commanding in the North, decided to abandon Crown Point, despite Washington's adjurations that the fort be held to the last. Smallpox had reduced the garrison of Crown Point to little more than a handful of convalescents; and the American commanders lost no time in abandoning it — smallpox and all — to the British.

It was fortunate for the American cause that in Benedict Arnold it had a man ready for any adventure, however desperate. Danger was his element and he rejoiced in attempting the impossible. Luckily, too, his talents were amphibious; having followed the sea at one point in his career, he was ready to take command of the American fleet on Lake Champlain. He supervised the construction of the ships with which he fought; New England carpenters were brought up to the lake; ship timber was procured from the near-by forests; and in an amazingly short time a fleet — somewhat jerry-built it is true, and not such as many naval officers would have trusted themselves to — rode the waters of Lake Champlain, with Arnold as admiral.

Arnold sailed boldly to the attack, although badly outnumbered and outgunned by the British. The ensuing battle proved to be a wild melee, fought at musket range, the Americans and British pouring shot and shell at each other while the Indians, who accompanied the British army, fired upon the rebel ships from the shore. Arnold himself aimed the guns of the *Congress*, refusing to abandon his flagship until it was riddled with shot and in flames. But no amount of heroism could long deprive the British of their victory; the American ships, built of green timber, were sluggish and too weak to withstand the force of heavy guns and howitzers, whereas the British gunboats, many of which were constructed of seasoned timber brought from Great Britain, enjoyed the advantage of greater buoyancy and strength. In the end, this superiority proved decisive. Six ships, all that was left of the American flotilla, limped back to Crown Point, where they were burned by their crews, while Arnold and his men took to the woods and made their way back to Ticonderoga. Lake Champlain was ruled by the British.

This action cost only about one hundred lives on both sides, yet its consequences were more portentous than many larger battles of the Revolutionary War. Carleton's army was now in position to attack Ticonderoga and, if that fortress fell, to push on to Albany where, presumably, Howe was also headed. Thus Washington, already hard pressed by Howe, would be caught between the pincers. "Fortune," mused Anthony Wayne, "has heretofore been a fickle Goddess to us — and like some other females changed for the first new face she saw." Was General Carleton, the Americans asked themselves, to be the lucky man?

Certainly Ticonderoga seemed likely to offer no serious opposition to the victors of the battle of Lake Champlain. Weakly garrisoned (many of the troops were down with smallpox) and so poorly supplied with provisions that it could hardly have withstood a week's siege, Ticonderoga seemed to be within Carleton's grasp. Nevertheless, the British commander declined to be enticed by the smiles of the "fickle goddess": judging that the lateness of the season (October) made further military operations impracticable, he turned around and went back to Canada without even feeling out the defenses of Ticonderoga, thus proving, said Anthony Wayne, that he and his army "were afraid the Americans *would fight*, and that they themselves were not so fond of it."

Thus, by fighting a delaying action on Lake Champlain, Arnold had helped to save the Americans from what might have proved a disastrous defeat in the North. Had Carleton captured Ticonderoga and held it throughout the winter, Burgoyne would have had a jumping-off place for the campaign of 1777 that probably would have carried him to Albany. As it was, Burgoyne had no forward base when he undertook his invasion of the United States in 1777 — for which he might thank Carleton's caution and Arnold's resourcefulness. Arnold's services to the Revolution were far more important than his betrayal of the cause: the good outweighed — although it has not outlived — the evil he wrought. At Lake Champlain, he gave the Revolutionary War its closest approximation to Thermopylae.

Carleton's retreat relieved the pressure upon the Americans from the North; and it was now open to Washington, hard pressed for men after the disaster in New Jersey, to draw reinforcements from the troops guarding the Hudson River. But at this critical juncture, division in the American command threatened to complete the work of Sir William Howe in bringing ruin upon Washington's army.

In November 1776, General Charles Lee was in command of about two thousand Continental troops near Poughkeepsie, barring the advance of the enemy up the Hudson. Washington desperately needed these troops to reinforce his army in New Jersey; but when he summoned Lee to join him in New Jersey he met only with evasions and delay. Lee declined to move until he had spent several weeks in desultory correspondence with the commander-in-chief. In professional matters, he could not bear to submit to the orders of an amateur like Washington, particularly when Washington seemed to be on his way out. At first Lee simply ignored Washington's letters; then, after a period spent in expostulating with the commander-in-chief, he finally consented grudgingly to obey orders. "I really think our Chief will do better with me than without me," he said by way of explanation for his decision to yield to his superior. But even after crossing the Hudson, Lee made no effort to join Washington; instead, he remained near Morristown, hanging upon the enemy's rear, determined, he said, "by the help of God to unnest 'em even in the dead of winter." When Washington ordered Lee to join him in saving Philadelphia from the British, Lee answered that the British would not attack Philadelphia – in his opinion, they planned to turn against New England and he must be on hand to thwart their designs.

Although Lee had done little in a military way, he had kept up his correspondence diligently. An indefatigable letter writer, he gave to literary activity talents which might or might not have been meant for war.

One afternoon early in December, Lee was at a tavern in northern New Jersey, far from Washington's camp near the Delaware, busily engaged in his correspondence. Although he was four miles from his troops, he had taken no precautions against surprise; the countryside seemed quiet and there were no reports of British units in the vicinity. And so Lee felt that he might safely settle down to an afternoon of letter writing. He was in rare form – seldom had his pen reeled off sarcasm, invective, and malice more copiously. Perhaps that was because he was writing about Washington, the man whom, above all others, he delighted to slander. No time ought to be lost, said Lee, in remanding the commander-in-chief to the tobacco plantation he was so eminently fitted to oversee, and to elevate Charles Lee to the vacant post. The country could no longer bear Washington's incompetence – it was sinking under the weight of his blunders and irresolution.

In the midst of this cataloguing of Washington's shortcomings, Lee was startled by the clatter of hoofs in the roadway, and before he knew what had happened, he found himself a prisoner. Tipped off by a Tory as to Lee's whereabouts, Lieutenant Colonel Harcourt and thirty dragoons had swooped down upon the unsuspecting general. Had it happened to

Washington, Lee would not have been surprised; but that he, a veteran of thirty years' experience, should be taken in this way was unthinkable. He had to be told several times that he was really a prisoner.

The news that General Lee had been captured was broken gently to the American soldiers lest their morale be shaken by the untoward fate of their hero. Congress took the news hard. "Oh!" exclaimed a dismayed congressman, "what a damned sneaking way of being kidnapped. I can't bear to think of it." The Tories were blamed for Lee's misadventure and threats were made in Congress that "the damn'd Tories" would be wiped from the earth in retaliation. Americans, already in desperate straits from reverses in the field, could ill bear to lose the services of a man whom many regarded as the white hope of the American cause. In Philadelphia it was frequently said that "there was no prospect that America could make any further exertions" now that Lee was gone.

Yet the truth is that the capture of Charles Lee was a misfortune for no one except the British who took him prisoner. Washington was relieved of an insubordinate, temperamental, and unreliable commander who, in his anxiety to thrust himself into the post of commander-in-chief, might well have brought disaster upon the American cause. With Lee in British hands, Lee's second-in-command, General Sullivan, brought his troops safely across New Jersey and, on December 20, 1776, made contact with Washington's army. With almost six thousand men fit for duty, Washington's prospects began to improve decidedly.

The rout of the Continental army in New Jersey left the fate of the Revolution largely in the hands of Pennsylvania — a state not hitherto distinguished by its exertions in the cause of American independence. However unpropitious the prospects, Washington was obliged to lean upon this state for reinforcements and supplies with which to win the victory he desperately needed; if Pennsylvania failed him, the future would be dark indeed. To awaken the state to its danger and persuade the militia to rally round Washington on the Delaware, General Thomas Mifflin, a popular Pennsylvania politician, at Washington's order, made a whirlwind tour of the state. It was probably one of the most important missions of the war.

Mifflin's oratory, eloquent as it was, succeeded in inducing few Pennsylvanians outside Philadelphia to come to the rescue of the hard-pressed Continental army. But the Philadelphia militia turned out fifteen hundred strong and, well armed with guns recently brought from Europe, marched to Washington's camp. Never, during the course of this long and grueling war when Washington was chronically shorthanded, were troops more welcome. For it was these Philadelphians, together with the reinforcements brought by Sullivan, who made possible Washington's comeback at Trenton and saved the Revolution from ignominious defeat.

It was obvious to Washington that he could not hope to enlist men in the Continental army unless something was done to give patriot morale a shot in the arm. Specifically, he needed a victory with which to convince Americans that their cause was not hopeless. If, on the other hand, the war continued to go against him, there was nothing left for Washington but to head west and hope that the British could not track him down and hang him for a rebel.

Despite Howe's announcement that the campaign was over for the winter, the American commander was little disposed to trust Sir William's well-known lethargy — the British, he believed, would cross the Delaware when the ice was solid. There was only one way of saving Philadelphia and with it the American cause: to strike the British before they forced a passage of the river — to upset Howe's timetable by carrying the war to the enemy's country. "The Enemy," said the American commander-in-chief, "are daily gathering strength from the disaffected; this Strength is like a Snow Ball rolling, will Increase, unless some means can be devised to check, effectually, the progress of the Enemy's Arms."

It was characteristic of Washington that with the struggle going steadily against him, he thought not of avoiding risks but of devising means of striking back at the enemy. It was proof of his genius that he discerned an opportunity of turning the tables upon the conquerors of New Jersey.

By posting troops along the Delaware, the British had placed several garrisons temptingly within Washington's reach. "A luckly Blow in this Quarter," the American commander observed, "would be Fatal to them, and would most certainly raise the Spirits of the People, which are quite sunk by our late misfortunes." All Washington needed was an army — and luck.

Sir William Howe's victories had not lessened his strong sense of caution: at the time when many British officers were celebrating the end of the rebellion and preparing to go home, the commander-in-chief was asking for fifteen thousand more troops and laying extensive plans for the campaign of 1777. The extent of his conquests almost disconcerted Howe: he had not expected fortune to prove so kind and he hardly knew what to do with the bounty that had been cast into his lap. It was not Howe's intention merely to conquer territory — the destruction of Washington's army had been his chief objective — yet now he found himself embarrassed by the possession of an entire province peopled by thousands of Loyalists clamoring for his protection. And although badly beaten, there was still a rebel fighting force on the right bank of the Delaware.

Having made his decision not to advance beyond the Delaware, Howe was inclined to pull his troops back to New Brunswick, where they would be less exposed to enemy raiding parties and where his lines of communication would be safe from attack. General Clinton advised this withdrawal lest the Americans cut up piecemeal British garrisons along the Delaware, but Cornwallis, more impetuous and more contemptuous of the rebels than either of his senior officers, urged that the Delaware line be held. Howe's misgivings were by no means overcome by Cornwallis's arguments, yet the British commander recognized that a withdrawal from the Delaware would be construed as British weakness and would leave exposed to the rebels the large number of Loyalists in southern New Jersey who had taken the oath of allegiance and accepted British protection.

Although his military instincts counseled retreat, Howe could not bring himself to leave these supporters of British sovereignty in the lurch, for if he did so, how could any Americans ever feel safe in taking the British side? Garrisons were posted, therefore, at Trenton and Bordentown, with only the river separating them from the Americans.

Trenton was garrisoned by Hessian mercenaries under the command of Colonel Rahl, an officer who had distinguished himself for gallantry at White Plains and Fort Washington. His brigade was one of the best in the British service; after the battle of Trenton, General Grant of the British army declared that he for one had not believed that "all the rebels in America would have taken that brigade prisoners." But, bravery apart, there was good reason for not putting Colonel Rahl in command of such an outpost as Trenton: he was truculent and cocksure, he did not speak English, and he was a confirmed drunkard.

Trenton may have been a post of honor but there its desirability ended. A village consisting of only about one hundred houses, the Hessians could hardly have been accommodated had not most of the inhabitants fled their homes. There were no attractions here for war-weary veterans seeking relaxation from the rigors of the campaign just ended.

Against the Hessians in Trenton, the patriots waged a war of nerves. There were constant alarms and excursions; American guns on the opposite side of the river cannonaded the garrison; and, occasionally, small American parties crossed the Delaware at night, beat up the Hessian outposts, and were gone before the troops could buckle on their service belts. As a result, the Germans were obliged to lay on their arms every night; and their sleep was often broken by the crackle of musketry and the yells of rebels in the woods. It was a depressing spot to spend a winter, and only a copious supply of liquor reconciled the Hessians to their situation.

To all this uproar, Colonel Rahl, the commander at Trenton, was happily oblivious: after the labors of the campaign, the colonel celebrated by getting gloriously drunk — and staying that way. For Colonel Rahl the war was over, the rebels utterly beaten; and he sought relaxation where he habitually found it: in a bottle. His revels lasted far into the night; he rose late and began another day of drinking. "When we would go to his quarters between 10 and 11 o'clock for the parade," reported one of his officers, "he would sometimes still be in his bath . . . and on that account the guard had to march up sometimes half an hour later and stand waiting for him."

Colonel Rahl was vastly more concerned about his supply of liquor than with preparing Trenton against a surprise attack. Ignoring Howe's orders, he threw up no defenses; no scouting parties were sent out; sentries were rarely posted; and he placed his artillery before his headquarters where, although it made an impressive show, it was of no use whatever against an attack. The truth is, Colonel Rahl did not believe that the rebels would dare assail his position; and even if the rebels did venture to cross the river, he had no doubt that they would never live to recross it. When warned that the Americans might attack, he spluttered that his Hessians would wipe out these "country clowns."

Nor were the British themselves alarmed by signs of reviving patriot activity. General Grant, commanding the British forces in New Jersey, swore that he could hold the state with a corporal's guard: these "skulking peasants" were not foemen worthy of an English gentleman's steel. Grant even rebuked Colonel Rahl for "making much more of the rebels than they deserve," and he made no effort to visit the posts under his command or to see that Howe's orders had been executed.

That the Americans intended to attack Trenton was no secret to the British: from American deserters they had learned the day, the hour, and the place where Washington intended to strike. What they did not know was that Washington intended to command in person, and that it was to be a large-scale operation. General Grant warned Colonel Rahl to expect an attack on the morning of December 26, but there was nothing in his letter to lead Rahl to believe that it was to be much more than one of those hit-and-run forays launched from the other side of the Delaware that he had withstood so many times before. At least, it did not induce the colonel to take any special precautions, unless taking on a particularly heavy load of liquor can be regarded as a means of instilling courage for battle.

An accident served to undo whatever good effects this warning might have had, and to mislead further the Hessians at Trenton. It happened that early on December 25, an American scouting party, returning from New Jersey to Pennsylvania, fell in with a British detachment near Trenton. A brief but sharp exchange of fire ensued before the rebels made good their retreat. This scouting party, the Hessians reasoned, was the American force against which they had been put on their guard by General Grant; the danger was now over and they could settle down to some serious — and they fervently hoped, undisturbed — drinking. To add to their sense of security, the ice was running in the river, apparently rendering it impassable to hostile troops.

Washington intended that three armies should cross the Delaware on the night of December 25 and fall upon the Hessian garrisons at Trenton and Bordentown. The force at Trenton consisted of about twelve hundred men; that at Bordentown of about two thousand. After disposing of these troops, the three American armies were to join forces and fall upon the British cantonments in New Jersey, thus beating the enemy in detail.

At Brunswick, less than thirty miles away, lay the British stores and military chest of seventy thousand pounds, guarded only by a small garrison. Washington was eager to make a dash for this prize and, as he said, "put an end to the war."

Christmas Day, 1776, was a miserably wet and uncomfortable day: rain and hail streaked down, the wind was piercingly cold, and the roads were quagmires. By evening it turned much colder; ice formed on the river, and snow began to fall. It was a most wild and blustery night for General Washington to deliver his Christmas present to Colonel Rahl.

Christmas night in Trenton almost all the Hessians were drunk, Colonel Rahl having slipped under the table early in the evening and been carried off to his quarters, where he was now snoring peacefully. The village of Trenton had rocked to the revels of the Hessians: probably never in the history of that respectable settlement had so much liquor been consumed. But now all was quiet; the peace of prostration had descended upon the merrymakers.

On Christmas night — "one of those dark and dismal nights, which the greatest masters in the art of war recommend for an enterprise of this kind" — Washington pushed off from the right bank of the Delaware with twenty-four hundred men, mostly Continentals, and twenty pieces of artillery. The boats were hampered by the floating ice, but the wind, which was now blowing violently, was at the backs of the raiders, affording them a comparatively easy passage across the river. The countersign, chosen by Washington, was "Victory or Death," and the attack was scheduled to take place an hour before daybreak. But it was not until eight o'clock in the morning of December 26 that the Americans were in a position to close in on the enemy. Then, in the sharp crash of musketry and cannon, the astonished Hessians learned that there was still a rebel army.

No "morning after" Colonel Rahl had ever experienced was quite so harrowing as the one to which he awakened on that black day at Trenton. A man of many hang-overs, he was familiar with them in all their variegated and most horrendous forms; but what he saw on the morning of December 26 transcended his wildest alcoholic visions. When his orderly finally succeeded in awakening the Hessian commander, the guns had begun to pop all over Trenton. Roused at last, Rahl showed

himself to be a brave if somewhat befuddled man. It is doubtful, however, that even if he had been in full possession of his faculties he could
have saved the day: the surprise was as complete as though the Americans had dropped from the sky. Rahl tried to rally his men, but a deadly
fire from American riflemen quickly broke the Hessian ranks. They
tried to escape from the town but the roads were blocked by American artillery and musketmen. They ran into houses only to find themselves pursued by the rebels. They sought refuge in the streets, but
every street was commanded by cannon and howitzers. A whiff of
grape into their ranks took the fight out of the bravest.

After forty-five minutes of this kind of fighting, the Hessians had
enough: herded into a small area outside the town and hemmed in on
all sides by Americans, they hoisted the white flag. About nine hundred officers and men laid down their arms; not more than thirty of
the enemy had been killed against five American casualties. Among the
slain was Colonel Rahl. He died as he lived — brave and drunk.

Trenton ended once and for all the myth of the Hessians' invincibility. These terrible warriors, the supermen of Long Island and Fort
Washington, now stripped of their flaming brass helmets and sharp bayonets, were seen to be merely confused and almost helpless men.

At Washington's orders, the captive Hessians were marched through
the streets of Philadelphia to exhibit their weakness to the citizens, but
this maneuver almost precipitated a riot. "The old women howled dread-
fully, and wanted to throttle us all," wrote a Hessian who participated
in this march, "because we had come to America to rob them of their
freedom." It was with great difficulty that the guards prevented the
populace from murdering the Hessians in the streets of Philadelphia.

Washington's elation over his victory at Trenton was considerably
tempered by the news that the other raiding parties had failed to cross
the Delaware because of the ice, and that, in consequence, the Hessian
garrison at Bordentown was still intact. Unsupported by the reinforcements he had counted upon, Washington was in danger of being overwhelmed by the British seeking revenge for Trenton; moreover, the
large quantity of liquor found at Trenton proved more deadly to the
American troops than did the Hessians — they soon drank "too freely
to admit of Discipline or Defence in Case of Attack."

And so there was nothing for Washington to do but to retreat across
the Delaware after rounding up his prisoners and destroying all the
stores he could not carry off. Although it probably broke some soldiers'
hearts, about forty hogsheads of rum, taken among the booty, were stove
in by Washington's orders.

If the attack upon Trenton seemed a desperate trial of fortune, it
was perhaps even more hazardous for Washington to cross the river
again four days after his victory and challenge the British to do battle

for the entire state of New Jersey. He no longer enjoyed the advantage of surprise: the British were on the alert and thousands of troops were pouring across the state towards the Delaware.

But as Washington well knew, the weaker side could not wait. Had he remained in Pennsylvania, the British would soon be across the Delaware. They would not again make the mistake of failing to annihilate the Continental army. Moreover, Washington had to prove to his countrymen that Trenton was not merely a stroke of luck; only by carrying the war into the enemy's country could he demonstrate that the tide had really turned. Finally, for the first time in several months, Washington was in possession of an army and, remembering his former experience, he was eager to put it to use before it vanished utterly from sight. The victories in New Jersey so inspired the troops that many were prevailed upon to remain six weeks longer than their terms of service required; and by offering a special bounty of ten dollars, Washington induced others to sign up for a new tour of duty. True, Washington had no authority to make this offer, but, as he told Congress, he had no alternative: "the troops feel their importance and would have their price. Indeed, as their aid is so essential . . . it is to be wondered, they have not estimated it at a higher rate."

Thrusting his head into the lion's mouth was no new experience for Washington, but this time he seemed to have overreached himself. Galled by the wounds inflicted by the rebels at Trenton, the British were out for blood. A large force under Cornwallis marched upon Trenton; the American outposts were driven back in disorder; and everywhere the fight went against the Americans. Trenton promised to be the grave, as it had been the birthplace, of Washington's reputation as a great general. Fortunately, however, for the American commander-in-chief, the village of Trenton was bisected by a creek, which temporarily delayed the British advance. The Americans held one side of the creek, and the British were massed on the other side. Cornwallis could no doubt have forced a passage, but night was coming on and the British commander saw no reason to press matters to a conclusion that day. All his preparations were made for crossing the creek in the morning, and against his overwhelming strength the outlook for the American army seemed hopeless.

Retreat for Washington was impossible: the Delaware was filling fast with large blocks of ice, and the main highway leading out of Trenton was blocked by British artillery. Audacity had brought Washington into this plight; and it was clear that only audacity could get him out again. The last place the British would expect Washington to march was into New Jersey, so it was there that Washington decided to go. Leaving his campfires burning to deceive the enemy, he took his stores, baggage, and artillery, and stole away towards Princeton by an unguarded road. The first units of the British army crossed the creek about an hour after the last Americans had left Trenton. It was Long Island all over again: despite his reputation as a dashing and vigilant officer, Cornwallis had fared no better than had Sir William Howe. Both generals had the unhappy experience of waking to find the bird flown.

Washington's escape from Trenton opened up a campaign of fast and furious action — a war of movement in which the British, for the first time since they reached New York, did the running. Sir William Howe lost southern New Jersey faster than he had conquered it; and if Howe had been surprised by the ease of conquest, he was dumfounded by the breath-taking swiftness with which he was evicted. Like a pack of wolves worrying a mammoth, the Americans dodged in and out of the British defenses, cutting off foraging parties, shooting up the enemy's encampments in Wild West style, and generally leaving the British in the unhappy state of not knowing where they were — and of being somewhere else before they found out.

Washington first raced to Princeton where, a few miles from the town, he fell in with a body of British troops which, after stubborn resistance, was put to flight. Brunswick was his next objective and the road was clear ahead. Whoever controlled the vital north-south highway controlled New Jersey. The main road from New York to Philadelphia ran through Trenton, Princeton, Brunswick, and Amboy; could Washington possess himself of Brunswick, he would cut off all the British forces in the southern part of the state.

Yet Washington failed to accomplish this stroke of war in comparison with which his exploits at Trenton would have seemed paltry. His troops were simply too fatigued to march the seventeen miles to Brunswick in time to take the British by surprise. Thus was lost one of the great opportunities of the war. "If we could have secured one thousand fresh men at Princeton to have pushed for Brunswick," said Henry Knox, "we should have struck one of the most brilliant strokes in all history." At least it can be said of Washington that he saw his opportunity — a perception that was often denied Sir William Howe.

Moreover, there could be little doubt that Washington had badly outgeneraled the British commander: with an army one sixth the size of Howe's, he had thoroughly bewildered his opponent and forced him to pull his forces back to Brunswick. When the campaign opened, the British stood poised on the threshold of Pennsylvania, with Philadelphia only nineteen miles away; now they were sixty miles from their objective and on the defensive. "We have been boxed about in Jersey, as if we had no feelings," lamented a British officer.

These victories led Washington to hope that the British could be cleared entirely from New Jersey before the campaign was over. He trusted to harassing actions to make the state untenable by the enemy:

their supplies cut off by American hit-and-run raiders and guerrilla fighters, they would be literally starved out of the territory they had lately conquered. Wagers were being laid by the American troops, in the middle of January, 1777, that they would be in possession of all New Jersey within ten days. "Howe himself is Panic Struck at the Masterly Strokes of Genl. Washington," it was said on all hands; and Thomas Paine declared that the British general was fleeing "with the precipitation of a pursued thief."

This war of forced marches, surprise attacks, and hard infighting was exhausting for the Americans as well as for the British. It was, moreover, the dead of winter, the season when Howe had believed that no military operations were possible. Under these conditions, American soldiers experienced hardships which, however valuable as preparation for the greater ordeals yet to come, left them too exhausted long to continue this war of movement. Charles Willson Peale, the American painter, while serving with Washington in New Jersey, reported that one night he lay down in the straw "and thought myself happy, though the room was as full of Smoke as if to cure bacon." The next night he slept on rocks.

And so Washington took up his headquarters at Morristown, where for the next six months he remained, within twenty-five miles of Howe's army. He was in little danger, however, of receiving any unwelcome visits from Sir William: the position of the American army was accessible only through several strongly protected mountain passes into which the British commander had no intention of venturing.

These events drove from the minds of British officers all thoughts of returning home and served notice upon the Tories that they, too, were not likely soon to have the gratification of lording it over the beaten rebels. Lord George Germain ascribed the disaster to the mistake of coddling the rebels; nothing would come right, he said, until the rebels had been made to feel the full horrors of war, "so that through a lively experience of losses and sufferings they may be brought as soon as possible to a proper sense of their duty." It was a sour note upon which to end a campaign which Germain had firmly expected would terminate the rebellion.

Washington's military reputation, in eclipse since the debacle in New Jersey, was now again ascendant. Even many of his former critics joined in the chorus of acclaim. It could not be denied that this whirlwind campaign in New Jersey was more than most Americans had expected from this silent, heavy man who had hitherto seemed to be distinguished chiefly by his capacity for suffering the slings and arrows of fortune in stony-faced taciturnity.

The American army had dwindled away in the face of defeat; now, with victory on its banners, it began to go the way of all Washington's armies — homeward. Adversity and prosperity seemed to have the same effect: the troops grew homesick, deserted, or went home when their term of service expired, leaving Washington to continue the fight as best he could. Two entire companies ran off, leaving only a lieutenant, a sergeant, and a drummer boy behind. The Delaware militia spent nearly three weeks in marching to Washington's headquarters, remained about one week, and then left for home "without Rendering a Single Copperworth of Service to the Public." Since his chief dependence was upon militia, until a new army of regulars could be recruited, this aversion to service on the part of citizens damped Washington's hopes of ever again taking the field against the enemy, who had at least three times his numbers. In the height of the campaign (January 1777) he was obliged to order many officers to go on recruiting service; still, so few reinforcements arrived that he began to fear his army would melt away before aid arrived. The people, he lamented, "are so extremely averse to turning out of comfortable Quarters, that I cannot get a Man to come near me." By the beginning of April, 1777, only a few hundred men of the new Continental army had joined him.

As long as his army, like an insubstantial pageant, seemed to melt away at his touch, Washington could take little satisfaction in his victories or regard the future with anything but alarm and foreboding. "How we shall be able to rub along till the new army is raised, I know not," he said. "Providence has heretofore saved us in a remarkable manner, and on this we must principally rely." More and more, he looked to Providence for salvation.

CHAPTER XI

Propaganda

THE British defeat in New Jersey was not wholly owing to Washington's strategy: by their conduct as conquerors the British had helped materially to undermine their position in the state. Voltaire once said that a great conqueror must be a great politician. Certain it is that the political ineptitude of the British was one of the chief causes of their failure to master the rebellion.

Sir William and Lord Howe had been magnanimous in victory: never forgetting that their chief purpose was to restore the empire, they offered, in November 1776, a free pardon to all persons in arms against the mother country who took within sixty days an oath of allegiance to the King. To them were given "protections" designed to guard them against molestation by British troops. Thus the Howes made use of every weapon, psychological as well as military, in waging war and were repaid by seeing thousands of Americans affirm their loyalty to the British Crown. The patriot cause suffered a blow almost as severe as a major military defeat: farmers supplied the British army liberally with provisions; Loyalists volunteered to serve with the British army; and hundreds of rebels gave up the dubious struggle and made their peace with the conquerors.

The importance of this experiment could not easily be exaggerated: the fate of the American Revolution depended in a large measure upon what occurred in New Jersey. Had the British been able to conciliate the inhabitants, establish just and orderly government, and promise absolution from taxes imposed by the British Parliament, the Revolution would have suffered a severe setback. In this event, perhaps all the Middle colonies would have renounced the rebellion and returned to the empire.

During the entire war, the British never had a fairer opportunity of redeeming a colony than in New Jersey in 1776. Everything favored the success of Howe's experiment: the people were predominantly loyal, they rejoiced in British victories, and were eager to return to their allegiance. The reconstruction of New Jersey was, in the main, a matter of building upon the solid foundation of New Jersey Loyalism. Yet, instead of grasping this opportunity, the British turned the province into a hotbed of patriotism.

The work of reconciliation was largely undone by the conduct of British and Hessian troops in the conquered territory. They plundered remorselessly: instead of coming as deliverers intent upon restoring peace and order, they descended upon the countryside like a swarm of locusts. Beginning by confiscating the livestock and horses of the rebels, they graduated to the higher forms of larceny, devoting their attention to silver plate, furniture, clothing, wines, bric-a-brac and, indeed, everything of value that could be carried away. Even Loyalists armed with "protections" were not exempt from their rapacity: whatever the soldiery wanted they declared to be rebel property, and under this convenient fiction robbed friends as well as foes. "Thus," lamented a British officer, "we went on persuading to enmity those minds already undecided, and inducing our very Friends to fly to the opposite party for protection." [1]

Taught to hate Americans as rebels, the British soldiers were anything but good-will ambassadors; toward them they practised cruelties that they would have scorned to employ against a foe whom they respected. This was a struggle in which the common Englishman was deeply moved by the passions of war: in his eyes, colonists were attempting to destroy the empire and to set themselves up as rivals of the mother country. It was inevitable, therefore, that they should have regarded Americans as treacherous parricides — "desperadoes and profligates, who have risen up against law and order in general" and who had thereby placed themselves outside the law.

As a result, what to the Americans were atrocities were sometimes to the British merely proper and wholesome chastisement. As rebels, Americans were not merely enemies of the mother country but its children who had plunged the knife into its back without provocation. Therefore, their punishment must be more severe than that meted out to foreign enemies; rebellion was an atrocity and ought to be fought with atrocities. "I think we should (whenever we get further into the country)," said Lord Rawdon in 1776, "give free liberty to the soldiers to

---

[1] No doubt, the worst offenders were the women who followed the army in swarms. These harpies even stripped children of their clothing, so thorough was their pilfering.

ravage it at will, that these infatuated wretches may feel what a calamity war is."

The German mercenaries plundered less from hatred than from a desire to make their fortunes while the war lasted. Having come to America to pillage as well as to fight, they were apt to make no distinction between friend and foe — booty was booty whether belonging to patriots or Loyalists. "It is a misfortune," exclaimed an Englishman who saw them at their chosen work, "we ever had such a dirty, cowardly Set of contemptible miscreants. The Hessians are more infamous & cruel than any." They displayed typical German thoroughness in their pillaging. The roads were crowded with their wagons carrying loads of plunder to the rear; after they had passed through the country, precious little remained in the form of movable property.

It was, however, the sex crimes of which the invaders were accused that cast the most lurid light upon their proceedings in New Jersey. "Deflowering virgins," together with bayoneting wounded prisoners, was, according to the patriot newspapers, the art of war as practised by the British army. Fleeing women were said to be herded together and brought to camp for the sport of the soldiery; "men slaughtered, women ravished, and houses plundered, little girls not ten years old ravished, mothers and daughters ravished in the presence of the husbands and sons who were obliged to be spectators to their brutal conduct." For virgins, there had been nothing like it since the Goths sacked Rome. "These damn'd Invaders," exclaimed a patriot, "play the very Devil with the Girls and even old Women. . . . There is Scarcely a Virgin to be found in the part of the Country that they have pass'd thro!"

Probably the British army was neither as black as it was painted nor as guiltless as it professed to be. Howe showed much concern over the behavior of his troops and issued frequent orders against plundering. Despite all that he could do, the troops occasionally got completely out of hand. Officers who attempted to restrain them were threatened by their men as the army joined in a mad scramble for loot.[2] The Loyalists and even the British themselves admitted that the conduct of the army had been disgraceful — where Congress had made one patriot, it was said, the British army had made ten. And as for sex crimes, Lord Rawdon has left this description of the activity of the British army on Staten Island: "The fair nymphs of this isle were in wonderful tribulation, as the fresh meat our men have got here has made them riotous as satyrs. A girl can-

---

[2] At this time, there was a serious shortage of officers in the army. Howe declared that in some companies there were only two officers to three hundred men "and altho' the Men behave with great Spirit, yet, the Temptations for Plunder are so great, that it is not in the power of a few Officers to keep the Men under proper Restraint." Howe to Germain, November 30, 1776. Germain MSS., Clements Library.

not step into the bushes to pluck a rose without running the most imminent risk of being ravished, and they are so little accustomed to these vigorous methods that they don't bear them with the proper resignation, and of consequence we have most entertaining court-martials every day."

Shortsightedly, the British also played into the hands of propagandists by mistreating American prisoners of war.[3] The spectacle of emaciated, haggard survivors of British jails and prison ships dragging themselves along country roads was more effective propaganda than even Thomas Paine could have coined. One look at these "poor miserable starved objects" completely disproved the claim of British generals that the atrocity stories were "a parcel of damned lies."

On board the prison ships in New York Harbor, hundreds of Americans paid the full measure of devotion to the cause of freedom. Crammed into the holds of the ships, they were confined in "a most nasty stinking Place" sometimes compared to the Black Hole of Calcutta. But the torture at Calcutta lasted only one night; aboard the prison ships it was protracted for years. Here were to be found worse horrors than those of the battlefield: hundreds of men fighting for food and air "some swearing and blaspheming, some crying, praying and wringing their hands, and stalking about like ghosts and apparitions; others delirious . . . raving and storming; some groaning and dying — all panting for breath; some dead and corrupting." "The air was so foul at times," said a prisoner, "that a lamp could not be kept burning, by reason of which three boys were not missed until they had been dead ten days." Although the Americans sent provisions to the prisoners in New York, it was charged that the British appropriated most of the foodstuffs to their own use.

It cannot be said that the sufferings of the American prisoners in New York excited pity from the British or the Loyalists. No charity was extended these unfortunates; indeed, the Loyalists protested against the leniency shown some American officers by the British in permitting them to wear their uniforms and to walk the streets of the city after giving their parole. Some Loyalists expressed their regret that the American prisoners had not been put to death — in that event, they predicted,

---

[3] In pursuance of the King's proclamation of August 1775, which declared Americans in arms to be traitors to the Crown, the British Ministry began by treating American prisoners as common malefactors and outlaws. They were thrown into jail and preparations were made to bring them to trial for treason. Lord George Germain and Lord Sandwich were eager to decorate Tyburn with American rebels; and many of the wounded prisoners taken by the British at Bunker Hill confidently expected to be hanged. Some Americans captured at Quebec were actually transported to England and imprisoned in Pendennis Castle as traitors. But the Ministry declined to take the next step: treason trials and executions. No American prisoners were put on trial for treason, and although many were badly mistreated, in general they were accorded the rights of belligerents. Yet it was not until 1782 that, by act of Parliament, they were officially recognized as prisoners of war rather than traitors.

it would have struck "such a panic through the Continent, as would have prevented the Congress from ever being able to raise another Army."

And yet the way was open for American prisoners to gain a speedy release from these horrors by signifying their willingness to enlist in the services of the British Crown. In fact, the ordeal of the prison ships was in part deliberately contrived to induce Americans to desert their cause and go over to the British side. During the early part of the war, some British commanders made a practice of keeping American prisoners, when first captured, without food for three or four days, as a means of overcoming their reluctance to taking up arms for the King.[4]

Nevertheless, for the most part, American prisoners refused to take this easy way out of their misery. There were three hundred American prisoners at Halifax dying of jail distemper and smallpox; "yet," acknowledged Admiral Arbuthnot, "surrounded as they are by distress, they are deaf to every solicitude of taking the oath of allegiance or subscribing to any Act whereby they may be liberated." Over twelve hundred American prisoners in England stood steadfast through privation and ill treatment, refusing to the end to bear arms against their fellow Americans. Benjamin Franklin said that Englishmen "ought to glory in descendants of such virtue"; and the English Whigs, in this spirit, opened a public subscription for the relief of American prisoners in Great Britain. Edmund Burke declared that in the treatment of prisoners "the Turk, the savage Arab, the cruel Tartar, or the piratical Algerine, when compared to our ministers, might be thought humans." To the Tories, however, the courage and endurance of these American prisoners brought no rejoicing; it was apparent that men of such stern fiber were not easily conquered.

Many patriots exulted in these atrocities as an effective means of weaning Americans from their love of the mother country. It was believed that if the struggle ended with Americans still harboring the least spark of affection for Great Britain, their independence would be in jeopardy: the price of liberty seemed to be eternal vigilance against the wiles of John Bull. Although the patriots told themselves that for John Bull to seek to restore himself in the graces of Americans was "like a foolish old dotard taking to his arms the bride that despises him," nevertheless they feared the charms of this old reprobate. Therefore they

---

[4] Particularly in the later stages of the war, it was not necessary to resort to cruelties to induce American prisoners to enlist in the British service: the promise of higher pay and bounties sufficed. After the fall of Charleston in 1780, for example, several hundred American prisoners joined the British army and were sent to the West Indies. General Clinton was delighted with these recruits. "Such has been the Mortality from Sickness among the Troops there," he remarked, "that I do not see any other Means of recruiting them." The Continental Congress was moved to protest, alleging that these prisoners had enlisted under duress. But when it was proved that they had joined the British army voluntarily, the case was dropped.

piled on atrocities with good will, persuaded that in so doing they did a holy work. "Let us cherish our resentments," they exclaimed. "Let us instil them into the minds of our children: and let the first lessons we teach them be, that to love liberty and to hate Englishmen is one and the same thing."

Benjamin Franklin who, had he not won greater fame as a scientist, philosopher, statesman, and man of letters, would have deserved imperishable renown on the strength of his talents as a propagandist, skillfully dressed these atrocity stories in the guise of fact. In France, he set out to compile a "School Book" of choice atrocity stories, profusely illustrated, "in order to impress the minds of Children and Posterity with a deep sense of [British] bloody and insatiable Malice and Wickedness." On his press at Passy he printed a fictitious newspaper purporting to be a copy of the Boston *Independent Chronicle* containing an account of the cruelties perpetrated by the Indians at the orders of the British. Scalps of soldiers, farmers, women, and children — some of whom "were ript of their Mother's Bellies" — were sent to George III in order "that he may regard them and be refreshed; and that he may see our [the Indians'] faithfulness in destroying his Enemies, and be convinced that his Presents have not been made to an ungrateful People." This fabrication, widely circulated over Europe, was regarded as a genuine document. Franklin later denied that he had done injustice either to the Indians or to George III — a man who, he said, loved blood and hated Americans.

Washington took satisfaction in giving wide publicity to tales of British cruelty: they served the salutary purpose of discouraging desertion to the enemy. Upon a report being circulated that the East India Company purchased all American deserters from the Crown and sent them to the East Indies as slaves, Washington urged his friends to spread the tale, instructing them at the same time in the fine art of propaganda. It should be done, he directed, "seemingly with indifference, drop it at table before the Servants," and let the story filter down to the men.

Washington was the more inclined to make use of atrocity stories because they had the gratifying result of inducing Americans, hitherto indifferent to the patriot cause, to reach for their muskets resolved to send "the more than savage Britons . . . to Hell in the midst of their iniquities." The New Jersey farmers who had joyfully welcomed the British in 1776 were a few months later in arms against the invaders. Viewing this phenomenon, a patriot expressed the wish that the enemy would march the length and breadth of the United States. "America," he observed, "acquires strength by the progress of Howe's army — for wherever he goes he confirms the timid and the neutral characters ir the cause of America, and at the same time, like a good scavenger, carries away all the Tory filth with him that lies in his way."

After the surrender of Burgoyne's army in 1777, the condition of Americans held prisoner by the British rapidly improved: the fear of wholesale retaliation and the growing recognition that fortune might not incline to the British side stimulated humanitarianism. Washington admitted that he had nothing to complain of as far as the treatment of American soldiers was concerned; but he did not fail to observe that the plight of American seamen captured by the British was becoming worse. After 1776, the prison ships were seldom used for American soldiers captured by the British, but sailors continued to be cast into those pestilential holes by the hundreds. Other captured sailors were sent to the East Indies, condemned to serve at hard labor at the British post in Senegal, or kept in close confinement in Great Britain for the duration of the war.

The danger of mistreating American prisoners of war was vividly illustrated in the case of General Prescott of the British army. Prescott captured Ethan Allen in Canada, loaded him with chains, and sent him to England to be tried as a traitor.[5] A short time later, however, Prescott was himself taken prisoner by the Americans; whereupon Washington proceeded to treat Prescott as the British general had himself dealt with Ethan Allen. Prescott spent sixteen weeks in close confinement, and at the time of his release was languishing in jail in the company of "common Malefactors, and the most notorious Villains." After being rescued from this duress, the unfortunate general was captured a second time — being taken, upon this occasion, "in bed with a Farmer's Daughter near Newport."

The Continental Congress threatened to retaliate upon British prisoners of war for the "enormities" committed against American prisoners, "at the mention of which," said Congress, "decency and humanity will ever blush." If violence was the only language Englishmen understood, Congress was prepared to conduct a war of frightfulness. In this spirit, the Americans established prison ships where British captives died by hundreds from privation and disease. In 1779, Congress ordered the imprisonment on board prison ships of all British seamen captured by Americans, and directed that they be subjected to the same treatment as that meted out to American sailors taken prisoner by the enemy. "There was not a post that arrived from America," said Lord George Germain, "which did not bring him letters filled with complaints of the barbarity experienced by prisoners at the hands of the Americans."

On both sides, prisoners of war, especially officers, were released on parole. When giving their parole, Englishmen did not always feel them-

[5] Ethan Allen expected to be made a martyr. "I thought to have enrolled my name in the list of illustrious *American* heroes," he said, "but was nipped in the bud." Instead of being hanged when he arrived in England, he was sent back to the United States and exchanged for a British officer held prisoner by the Americans.

selves obliged to keep faith with rebels: in their eyes, they were no more bound to keep their word than "to perform acts of common gratitude & generosity with rebels." British officers on parole were known to pay their American creditors with bills drawn on their bankers in London, and then, when given their freedom in an exchange of prisoners, to stop payment on such bills. Moreover, they frequently broke their paroles by escaping to the British lines. Over five hundred Britons captured on the high seas by John Paul Jones were given their liberty in exchange for a promise to procure the release of American prisoners in Great Britain; and yet, Franklin pointed out, not one of them carried out his promise — "so little Faith and Honour remain in that corrupted Nation." But it cannot be said that Americans showed more scruple in keeping their word.

British and German prisoners were used as farm laborers, employed in the saltworks, or, if skilled workers, sent to the gun factories. In general, the Germans were shown better treatment than were the British prisoners of war. They were given greater freedom of movement and encouraged to settle down as farmers or artisans. Frequently they were swallowed up in the country, particularly in the German-speaking sections of Pennsylvania. Sometimes they were even lionized by local society, although this privilege was usually reserved for British officers. In Fredericksburg, Virginia, for example, the Germans were made much of by the local gentry, their musical talents especially being admired. "In Europe," said one of the German officers, "we should not have got much honor by our music, but here we passed for masters. We were so overwhelmed with praise that we were really ashamed. Some of the American young gentlemen were jealous."

⌒   ⌒   ⌒

It was a favorite plan of Benjamin Franklin's to burn several English and Scottish cities in retaliation for the destruction wrought in the United States by the British army. Setting the torch to Liverpool and Glasgow, said his colleague, Silas Deane, "would be a most glorious Revenge"; and Franklin expressed the hope that when the French landed they would make the English "feel a little more of that kind of Distress they have so wantonly caused in America." In May 1777, he and Deane urged Congress to send frigates to European waters and to strike a blow "that would alarm and shake Great Britain, and its credit, to the center"; "the burning or plundering of Liverpool or Glasgow," the American diplomats pointed out, "would do us more essential service than a million of treasure and much blood spent on the continent." But Franklin, however great his zeal, could hardly apply the torch to English cities, although it was age and infirmity rather than lack of inclination that kept him from this work. The Continental Congress, falling in with Franklin's idea, authorized attempts to burn London and other British seats, directing the firebrands to give particular attention to the royal palace. But no arsonist appeared to rout the King and his household from St. James's.

In John Paul Jones, Franklin found a man capable of executing his bold plan. Like Poor Richard, Jones had been deeply stirred by what he regarded as British inhumanity. "The late brutalities of the Britons in America fill me with horror and indignation," he wrote. "They forget that they are men; and I believe nothing will bring them to their senses but the most exemplary retaliation." In coming to France, his chief purpose was to secure the release of Americans confined in British prisons as traitors and "to put a stop to the savage burnings and wanton cruelties of the enemy on this continent." It cannot be said that Jones succeeded in achieving either objective, yet he wrote his name indelibly upon the naval history of the war.

John Paul Jones was a Scotchman of a philosophical and poetic cast of mind who was attracted to the cause of the colonies by his ardent conviction that Americans were upholding the rights of man against reactionary elements in Great Britain. Like many British liberals, he believed that the future lay with American republicans rather than with British imperialists; but, going beyond the English Whigs, he joined the American rebels with his sword. It must be acknowledged, however, that Jones had already shaken the dust of Britain from his feet. As John Paul — the Jones was a later addition — he had knocked about the world, serving as cabin boy, ship's mate, and actor in the West Indies. Accused of murder, he experienced great difficulty in clearing himself, although his innocence seems well established. No sooner had he put this unsavory incident behind him than his crew mutinied in the West Indies and charges of highhanded and cruel treatment were brought against him by his crew in the admiralty courts. All this served to persuade John Paul, in 1772, that it would be wise to change his name, bury the past, and settle down in Virginia. It was here that the outbreak of the Revolution found him.

Had the French and Spaniards shown the spirit, fighting skill, and audacity of John Paul Jones, the event might have been very different for the British. While most of the ships of the United States navy remained in port, John Paul Jones carried the American flag to the shores of the British Isles, falling like a scourge upon the shipping and coastal towns of the enemy. "If you can take 'Paul Jones,'" exclaimed Lord Sandwich in 1779 to a British admiral, "you will be as high in the estimation of the public as if you had beat the combined fleets [of France and Spain]." And Lord North promised himself that as soon as England was free from the danger of invasion, he would send "a squadron, or perhaps two, to look for Paul Jones and prevent the mischief he intends against the coasts of Great Britain and Ireland."

In command of the *Ranger*, with a crew of thirty men, Jones in 1778 attacked the English town of Whitehaven intending to burn the town and the shipping in its harbor, but a traitor in his crew prevented the success of his plan. Yet he braved the might of England by landing upon English soil and burning British ships in port; and to prove that this was not a mere fluke of luck, he went ashore the next day in Scotland in order to take a British nobleman as hostage for the good treatment and exchange of American prisoners of war in Great Britain. Fortunately for his own safety and comfort, the Earl of Selkirk was not at home when Jones and his crew paid their call. The family plate, however, was available, and in order to quiet his crew, Jones was obliged to make off with it. However, there was nothing of the pirate in Jones's make-up: he bought the plate and returned it with his compliments to the Countess of Selkirk. "Tho' I have drawn my sword in the present generous struggle for the rights of men," wrote Jones, "yet I am not in arms as an American, nor am I in pursuit of riches. . . . I profess myself a citizen of the world, totally unfettered by the little mean distinctions of climate or of country, which diminish the benevolence of the heart, and set bounds to philanthropy."

The British were impressed by neither the philanthropy nor the benevolence of John Paul Jones. In 1779, openly flouting the maritime might of Britain, he intercepted the Baltic fleet, capturing the *Serapis* and the *Countess of Scarborough* off the coast of Scotland. Not until the War of 1812, when a few "fir-built frigates, manned by bastards and outlaws" began to send British shipping to the bottom with disquieting frequency, was England's pride made to suffer as it did at the hands of John Paul Jones.

CHAPTER XII

The Turning Point

MEANWHILE in England, before the black news of Trenton had crossed the Atlantic, Sir William Howe was being acclaimed as the conqueror of America. He was made a Knight of the Bath, and it was said that before the campaign was over, the King would exhaust all the honors of the peerage in rewarding Howe for his victories. The King's policy of laying on the rod seemed to be triumphantly vindicated. The friends of colonial liberty were downcast. "Reason and liberty are ill received in this world," mourned Voltaire.

Therefore, the news of Trenton and the war of movement it touched off in New Jersey struck England like a thunderclap. Still, crestfallen as they were, Englishmen could look forward to the glorious triumphs promised them by the government in the coming campaign. Sir William's plans for 1777 were exceedingly ambitious, having been drawn up in the flush of victory in November 1776, and in the expectation that heavy reinforcements would soon be pouring across the Atlantic. He proposed to attack Boston, to effect a junction on the Hudson River with an army invading the United States from Canada, to attack Philadelphia, and to overrun South Carolina and Georgia. A very large order, perhaps — but Howe intended no further temporizing with the rebellion.

Lord George Germain was overjoyed to see Howe displaying so much vigor, even if only on paper. Nonetheless, the Colonial Secretary was staggered by Howe's demands for reinforcements and supplies. Germain habitually acted upon the assumption that he knew better than did the generals in the field the wants of the British army. He pruned ruthlessly Howe's estimates of men, horses, and supplies required for the campaign: where the general asked for ten thousand men, he was fortunate to get three thousand; where he asked for five hundred horses,

Germain sent one hundred. And he accompanied these reductions with a tart lecture on the importance of living off American resources as much as possible. The Colonial Secretary aspired to fight a largely self-sufficient war: the army ought to draw its supplies from the country and its reinforcements from the Loyalist population of the colonies. According to Germain's plans, the war was to be won by a comparatively small British army, aided by thousands of American Loyalists whose duty it was to preserve order in the districts conquered by the red-coats. Obviously, it was cheaper and more expeditious to engage the Loyalists than to transport thousands of men across the Atlantic; yet British generals, he complained, seemed intent upon depopulating Great Britain and Germany. Already the reserves of the British army were dangerously depleted: insufficient men remained in the British Isles to defend the homeland from foreign aggression.

To Germain, there seemed to be something in the atmosphere of America that sapped the courage and resourcefulness of British generals. Generals who, when they left England, were full of confidence of speedy victory no sooner arrived on the opposite side of the Atlantic than they began to magnify the difficulties of their task and to spend their time writing home for reinforcements and supplies. And General Howe was the worst offender!

Germain was the less inclined to give Howe these reinforcements because he had conceived a plan of his own upon which he lavished the resources of the country. This plan called for an attack upon the United States by a powerful army which, advancing from Canada, was to follow the route opened by General Carleton in 1776 and cut the United States in two.

General Carleton's lenity toward American prisoners of war, his reluctance to use Indians against the rebels, and his failure to take Ticonderoga in 1776 had cost him the favor of Lord George Germain. Therefore, when Burgoyne reached England late in 1776, he found that the Colonial Secretary had already made up his mind to seek a more enterprising commander for the Northern army; and Burgoyne was not slow to press upon Germain his own qualifications for the post. "Gentleman Johnny's" suit was received with favor, and in 1777 he returned to Canada as commander of the expeditionary force that was to invade the United States, while Carleton was given the consolation prize of commanding the British army in Canada.

The purpose of Burgoyne's expedition was to cut off New England from the rest of the union by holding the Lake Champlain-Hudson River line.[1] The mother country had long aimed by political means to divide

---

[1] The absence of any specific mention of this objective in the correspondence between Germain and Howe has led some historians to conclude that the government had some other purpose in mind. But I am of opinion that the idea of isolating New

the colonies and, in particular, to isolate New England; now Germain intended to achieve this purpose by military force. Strategically, no other policy offered better prospect of quick victory over the rebellion: New England furnished thousands of men to the Continental army, the beef of Connecticut was essential to the sustenance of Washington's army, and New England's ports swarmed with privateers.

Burgoyne had served in America and had seen something of the country his army was to traverse; Germain, on the other hand, had no first-hand knowledge of the physical obstacles the expedition might expect to encounter. It is surprising, therefore, to find Germain exerting a re-straining influence upon Burgoyne and pointing out to him the difficulties in his path. The general was supremely confident of success; in the genial atmosphere of the Colonial Secretary's office his optimism and self-confidence burgeoned astonishingly. He asked to march his army through the heart of Yankeeland, cutting a wide swath of destruction from Lake Champlain to the sea. That a man who had seen New Englanders in arms around Boston, and had experienced personally the "fanaticism" of which they were capable, should have believed that with ten thousand men he could conquer half a million New Englanders shows that Burgoyne had not yet learned to place a high value upon Americans as fighting men.

Dear to the hearts of the King and Lord George Germain was the idea of wreaking vengeance upon Boston — in their eyes, the very hub of the rebellion. Judging that Boston was to Britain what Carthage was to Rome, Germain ruled that it must be destroyed as a plague spot in the British Empire. It was a "Volcano of Rebellion" that had spewed re-publicanism and revolution over the thirteen colonies and, unless speed-ily extinguished, might engulf the whole empire. He was eager, there-fore, to make Bostonians feel the aggravated horrors of the war "which their detestable Principles have occasioned, encouraged, and supported. The other Colonys are more to be pitied," he went on, "as they have been gradually seduced into Rebellion by those Independants, under the specious Pretext of struggling for their Liberty."

Despite his yearning to fall upon New England with fire and sword, Germain denied himself this pleasure in the interests of military strategy. New England's turn would come next; in the meantime, Burgoyne must march directly to Albany and place himself under the command of General Howe. Then, with New England severed from the rest of the union, the score could be settled with the Yankees.

Therefore, Germain begrudged no expense to attain this coveted objective. The British troops under Burgoyne's command were the

England was so generally understood that it was not thought necessary to dwell upon it specifically. Moreover, in May 1777, Germain promised the House of Commons that New England would soon be cut off and the rebellion ended.

crack light corps of the army, composed of men picked from all the regiments; and the Germans were the best mercenaries that money could buy. The troops were equipped with every necessity, under the command of able officers, and provided with abundant heavy artillery to blast the rebels out of their blockhouses. Because it was an amphibious operation, the frames of six sloops and over eight hundred smaller craft were sent knocked down from Great Britain to be assembled on the lakes. To each regiment were assigned twenty-five boats, and the men were taught to sail in line by companies.

Only in one respect was the expedition deficient — and that was in the all-important field of transport. The British supply service never adequately solved the problem of transporting and provisioning a large army across hundreds of miles of wilderness. In the case of Burgoyne's expedition it was the failure of transport which, together with American resistance, largely accounted for the final catastrophe.

The element of surprise was conspicuously absent in Burgoyne's expedition: his plans were almost as well known to the enemy as they were to himself, and the Americans were given months of warning in which to prepare their defenses. Before Burgoyne left Montreal, he was startled to read in a newspaper the whole plan of his campaign as accurately transcribed, he exclaimed, "as if it had been copied from the Secretary of State's letter." The rebels knew the route he expected to follow, the strength of his army — everything, in short, that it was to his interest to conceal. Sir William Howe succeeded in deceiving and confusing the Americans, but Burgoyne enjoyed no such advantage — he deceived no one unless it was himself.

Nevertheless, the campaign opened auspiciously for the British with a spectacular victory at Ticonderoga. The British expected to meet with determined resistance; indeed, it seemed probable that the decisive battle of the campaign would be fought here. Yet, despite all the warnings the Americans received of Burgoyne's advance, they were unprepared to give battle. Ten thousand men were needed effectively to defend Ticonderoga, but St. Clair, the American general in command, had less than half that number. Moreover, his stock of provisions was so scanty that he could not handle more recruits. "Should they come in fast, which I believe they would," he remarked, "they might eat us out before either the arrival of the enemy or the supplies." Only a miracle, "which we sinners have no right to expect," would save him, declared the anguished general. He might well envy General Schuyler who, confined to a sickbed at Albany, had been unable to assume personal command of the army at Ticonderoga.

However, the real weakness of Ticonderoga lay not in the unfinished state of its fortifications or the shortage of men and supplies but in the fact that it was commanded by a near-by eminence known as Sugar-

Loaf Hill. If an enemy was able to move cannon to the summit of Sugar-Loaf the fortress of Ticonderoga would be brought under a destructive fire. Although Kosciusko, the Polish engineer, General Gates, and other officers had pointed out the importance of fortifying Sugar-Loaf Hill, nothing had been done toward rendering it inaccessible to the enemy: the supposed impossibility of dragging cannon up its steep slopes quieted the patriots' apprehensions from that quarter.

Burgoyne took advantage of this neglect by sending his engineers to scale Sugar-Loaf Hill. Hoisting cannon from tree to tree, the British soon had Ticonderoga under range. It proved unnecessary to fire a shot — the Americans hardly paused to take a second look at the British on Sugar-Loaf Hill: they knew that the fortress was doomed and that to remain was to face death or capture. There was no time to save the artillery and stores; St. Clair ordered his troops to evacuate the fortress without even tarrying to destroy their supplies.

The rebels made good their getaway; all the British saw of the garrison was a cloud of dust kicked up by the fleeing Americans. Guns, cannon, ammunition, and provisions they found in plenty, but of rebels none except four soldiers who had been left behind to fire a large cannon at the British when they came within range. But even this suicide squad was found "dead drunk by a cask of Madeira." About twenty miles from Ticonderoga, British patrols picked up "about 20 Rebels all very much in liquor"; and as the British fanned out over the country in pursuit of the fleeing Americans, they met and defeated small parties at Skenesborough and Hubbardton. As for the rest of the garrison, their only purpose seemed to be to put as much territory as possible between themselves and the enemy. To better their chances of escape, they dispersed themselves over the countryside, some three thousand of them finding sanctuary in New England, "the Lord knows where or when to return." Scattered to the winds, disorganized by defeat and without camp equipment, tents, wagons, cannon, and ammunition, St. Clair's army seemed out of the war for the duration.

The ease with which Ticonderoga was captured swelled Burgoyne's already overweening confidence. His contempt of the rebels grew with his triumphs: with their usual futility, he remarked with blistering scorn, they had spent over a year fortifying Ticonderoga "upon the supposition that we should only attack them upon the point where they were best prepared to resist." In his opinion, little was to be feared from the courage of the Americans, but as a wily and treacherous foe he deemed them extraordinarily dangerous. At Skenesborough, for example, a body of Americans pretended to offer to surrender. With their guns clubbed, they came up to the British, but when they got within a few yards "they in an instant turned round their musquets, fired upon the grenadiers, and run as fast as they could into the woods." They sniped at the British from behind trees, ambushed them, and practised every wile of Indian warfare; but they did not stand up and fight in European fashion. That these tactics, however annoying, would prevent the British army from reaching Albany, Burgoyne had no fears.

Burgoyne was a man of letters as well as a soldier and he could not resist the temptation to celebrate his triumph at Ticonderoga with a literary flourish. Certain that final victory was in sight, he composed a proclamation to the American people which, if bombast could kill, would surely have depopulated the colonies. Dilating upon the prowess of the British army, he imperiously summoned Americans to lay down their arms and to make peace before they were obliterated from the earth. Englishmen who complained that Sir William Howe did not write enough were aghast at Burgoyne's verbose vauntings: Heaven save England from literary generals, they implored. Horace Walpole remarked that if Burgoyne ("General Swagger") had overrun ten provinces his proclamation would still appear pompous; and Benjamin Franklin mildly suggested later that Burgoyne's proclamation ought to be set beside his capitulation.

Despite the solid victory won by the British, most Loyalists seemed to regard fighting as strictly the business of the army; in any event, only about four hundred joined Burgoyne, less than half of whom were well armed. From this disappointing turnout, Burgoyne learned that he had not yet attained his Land of Tories, but he heard encouraging reports of the vast number of Loyalists in the vicinity of Albany, so he pressed on, confessing that "the great bulk of the country is undoubtedly with the Congress, in principle and zeal." Contrary to his expectations when he set out from Canada, he was to meet with "Treacherous friends, and hosts of powerful and inveterate enemies."

In Burgoyne's headquarters, the rigors of a wilderness campaign seemed far removed. Since he laid in beforehand a comfortable stock of choice liquor, the wine flowed freely as the general frolicked with his friends and, properly primed with champagne, burst into song, hitting notes probably never heard before in those forest glades. Accompanying Burgoyne were his mistress and her husband (a complaisant commissary officer in the army) — all the makings of a bedroom farce. Burgoyne often spent half the night in revelry while his officers, among them Lord Ackland, "a plain, rough man . . . almost daily intoxicated," drank themselves under the table. Dining upon such delicacies as rattlesnake soup, and drinking with such convivial companions, Burgoyne made the expedition seem like a pleasant outing; it might not have been war but it was glorious.

Burgoyne was idolized by his men; among the rank and file, he was known as the soldier's friend. A brave, hearty, bluff, forthright, and charming man, he had repeatedly risked his life in battle to animate his troops, and they responded by vowing that "they were ready to follow him to the field, and die with their arms in their hands." Despite the suffering and hardships experienced by the British soldiers under his command, there was scarcely a murmur of discontent against Burgoyne. On the contrary, it was Burgoyne's boundless confidence in the fidelity and courage of his men which led him to his doom. "The alacrity, I might almost say enthusiasm which the troops shew in the cause of Britain," he declared, "must strike with confusion the Americans. . . . No difficulty, no fatigue, no scarcity abated it."

The news from Ticonderoga started General Schuyler from his sick-bed. Gathering a handful of Continental troops around him, the gout-stricken general set out for Fort Edward in the forlorn hope of stopping the British before they reached Albany. Threatened by Burgoyne's advance, he fell back to Stillwater, where he began to construct a line of fortifications; yet he acknowledged that he might be obliged to make his stand in Albany itself. His army was being steadily depleted by deser-tion, skirmishes, sickness, and the expiration of the terms of service of the militia; and the troops were eager to go home for the harvest. Only a few old iron cannon remained, the rest of the artillery having been lost at Ticonderoga or sent south to Washington. With Schuyler remained about three thousand Continental troops "one third of which," said the discouraged general, "are negroes, boys, and men too aged for field, or indeed any other service." He doubted whether they could properly be called troops. His officers were no better; many of them, he declared, would disgrace "the most contemptible troops that were ever collected, and have so little sense of honor, that cashiering seems no punishment." It is apparent that Schuyler had lost confidence in his men as completely as they had lost confidence in him. Only large reinforcements of Conti-nental troops from Washington's army could save him, he wrote de-spairingly.

The fall of Ticonderoga and the rapid deterioration of American de-fenses in the North — "an event of Chagrine and Surprise, not appre-hended, nor within the compass of my reasoning" — shocked Washing-ton out of his complacent confidence that the British would never penetrate to Albany. In August 1777, he gave proof of his concern by dispatching Colonel Morgan and his corps of riflemen to the Northern army, these being the troops Washington could most conveniently spare and the type of reinforcement he believed would be most useful in the forest fighting against Burgoyne.

After the fall of Ticonderoga, the success or failure of the expedition depended largely upon Burgoyne's ability to avoid mistakes. The cam-paign, despite its victorious opening, was far from over: the real perils of the march to Albany lay ahead. It is significant, therefore, that imme-diately after the capture of Ticonderoga, Burgoyne began to blunder.

From Skenesborough to Fort Edward, the next objective of the British army, the easiest and most expeditious route lay by way of Lake George. This all-water highway led the British straight to Fort George at the head of the lake, from whence it was only sixteen miles by road to Fort Edward. Moreover, Lake George was open to British shipping, no American armament having been assembled for its defense. That this was the proper and natural course for Burgoyne to follow admitted of little doubt; nevertheless the British commander decided to strike overland from Skenesborough to Fort Edward, thereby abandoning the lakes, where he was invincible and where his progress was rapid and smooth, for the land, where the Americans, disorganized and beaten as they were, might yet trip up their conquerors.

Burgoyne made this decision for a reason which had little to do with military strategy: to go by water to Fort George involved a short retreat from Skenesborough over the route the British had already traversed. Burgoyne could not bring himself to turn his back upon the rebels even for a moment. The British army, he proudly declared, never retreated — a maxim which, in his eyes, apparently excluded even a strategic retreat. So Burgoyne moved ponderously forward through the wilderness with his train of six hundred wagons. He had two enemies to conquer — the wilderness and the rebels; and Burgoyne might well have believed that of the two, the wilderness was the more to be feared.

Burgoyne's decision to strike overland from Skenesborough enabled the Americans to delay his advance while they brought up reinforcements. Time was all-important in the success of the invaders; the Americans had been thrown off balance and the British commander ought to have followed up his advantage while the enemy was still reeling. But the march to Skenesborough gave the Americans what they most needed — a respite. As they retreated, they carried out a scorched-earth policy: the cornfields were laid waste, cattle were driven away, grain and forage destroyed. As a result, instead of living off the country as he had planned, Burgoyne was obliged to depend upon the supplies brought from Canada. And to crown his vexation, the Americans blocked the roads with felled trees and systematically destroyed the bridges. So effective were these tactics in slowing Burgoyne's progress that at one point on the march to Fort Edward he covered only twenty miles in twenty days, being compelled to construct more than forty bridges, one almost two miles long across a morass.

The slow progress made by the army after leaving its boats at Skenesborough told heavily upon Burgoyne's supplies. The army was soon living from hand to mouth; hardly a day's supply remained in the provision wagons. A British officer said of Burgoyne that "for one hour that he can devote in contemplating how to fight his army, he must allot twenty to contrive how to feed it." There were not enough wagons or drivers, and there were too few men to repair roads and to transport supplies by water. On many occasions, supplies had to be carried on men's backs when other means of transport failed. After the army had advanced a few miles, it was sometimes necessary to wait eight or ten days for the supplies to be brought up. Liquor and food ran short. "Pork at noon, pork at night, pork cold, pork hot," grumbled the soldiers; but even worse was to come — no pork at all.

Despite all obstacles, the British reached Fort Edward by the end of July and a few days later established themselves on the east bank of the Hudson opposite Saratoga. On August 14, a bridge of boats was thrown across the river; six weeks after the fall of Ticonderoga the British were almost ready for the final push to Albany. But, precariously low in supplies, Burgoyne did not dare to cross the Hudson until he had replenished his stores. Yet, to wait the arrival of supplies from Canada promised to delay his passage for many weeks. Therefore Burgoyne began to consider how he could seize from the rebels the supplies that were essential to the further progress of his army.

In this emergency, fortune seemed to be with Burgoyne: it was learned that the rebels had collected a large store of corn, flour, and cattle at Bennington, guarded, so rumor had it, by only a few militia. Bennington was off Burgoyne's line of march and the whole army could hardly move toward the place without giving the Americans time to remove the stores. On the other hand, to send a detachment to Bennington from the main army would give the Americans an opportunity of beating the British in detail — a danger run by every commander who divides his army in the face of an enemy. Nevertheless, Burgoyne decided to take this risk — if risk it could be termed, considering the weakened state of the rebels and the cowardice that had apparently seized them. Placing a motley corps of Germans, British, Indians, and Canadians, numbering all told five hundred men, under the command of Colonel Baum, a German mercenary, Burgoyne ordered a surprise attack upon Bennington. To reinforce this corps, five hundred Germans under Colonel Breyman were directed to hold themselves in readiness to march.

Burgoyne, it can readily be seen, displayed commendable caution in preparing this blow at Bennington: despite his contempt of the rebels and his conviction that they could not stand up to regular troops, he assigned about one thousand men to the expedition.

Burgoyne aimed to take the Americans at Bennington by surprise; but the German heavy infantry, crashing through the forest, gave the expedition about as much secrecy as would a herd of elephants. At best, the Germans who composed the bulk of the raiding party were ill equipped and poorly trained for such an enterprise. They were heavy, slow-moving foot soldiers and dismounted dragoons who were expected to pick up horses for themselves at Bennington. The skirts of their coats trailed about their knees; they carried huge swords and wore heavy brass helmets that made them conspicuous targets for American marksmen. Accompanying them were Indians and Canadians, experienced forest fighters, but the expedition could move no faster and no more stealthily than the German mercenaries. As a result, the Americans were ready and waiting for the enemy: at Bennington were gathered not the four or five hundred men that Burgoyne had expected to deal with, but eighteen hundred Green Mountain Boys and Continental troops under the command of General Stark.

Nothing daunted by the unexpected strength of the rebels, Colonel Baum established his camp and sat down to wait the arrival of the swarms of Loyalists which, he supposed, were eager to join the British. And the Loyalists, or at least men professing to be such, came into camp in numbers highly gratifying to the colonel. He was so pleased, in fact, that he did not think it significant that all these lovers of King and country demanded arms from the British; they were permitted to help themselves from the British stores, and Colonel Baum congratulated himself upon having procured allies who were so eager to shed blood.

No doubt, Colonel Baum had heard of the Trojan horse, but apparently he did not credit Americans with knowledge of that classic trick of warfare. When a body of Americans were reported approaching the British camp, Colonel Baum decided that they must be Loyalists come to tender their services to the Crown; and lest they be frightened away, he gave orders to the outposts to allow them to pass without interference. Before the commander knew what had happened, these "Loyalists" threw off their disguise and the British camp was surrounded by rebels who poured a withering fire upon the unprepared and disorganized troops. The fact that many of the guns which mowed down his men had been distributed by him among the rebels did not sweeten the last hours of the unfortunate commander. The manner in which the Americans fought was hardly less shocking to Colonel Baum: without entrenchments or artillery, the Vermont militia, supported by only a few Continental troops, rushed the British lines, in some cases coming within "eight paces of the cannon loaded with grape-shot in order that they might shoot down the artillerymen the more surely." Outnumbered by the Americans, most of the British force was killed or captured; only a few of the Indians, Canadians, and Tories succeeded in fighting their way through the rebel lines. And, to complete the misfortunes of the British, Colonel Breyman, struggling to come to the aid of Baum, was ambushed in the woods and driven back to the main army.

Bennington gave Burgoyne a faint glimmering of what lay in store for the main army. As he penetrated deeper into the country, armies seemingly sprang fully armed from the earth. The Continental army he had routed at Ticonderoga, yet now he was confronted with a militia more like an underground than a regular army. "Wherever the King's forces point," Burgoyne now found, "militia, to the amount of three or four thousand, assemble in twenty-four hours: they bring with them their subsistence &c, and, the alarm over, they return to their homes." How was he to cope with such a foe? Vermont, he said, "abounds in the most active and rebellious race of the continent, and hangs like a gathering storm upon my left." Yet the Green Mountain Boys were beyond his reach; he could not spare enough men to conquer that state while he marched to Albany. The wilderness alone had been bad enough; but now that it had begun to sprout rebels on every side, Burgoyne found his troubles had begun in earnest.

Accompanying Burgoyne were thousands of Indians. To harry the rebels with savages was a project dear to Germain's heart. Burgoyne was instructed to bring as many Indians as possible on his expedition, and Germain anticipated the most salutary results from their hatchets and scalping knives. The Six Nations, one of the most formidable bodies of Indians in North America, assembled in May 1777, and all the tribes except the Oneidas declared themselves ready to take up the hatchet for the King. Burgoyne gladly accepted their aid, specifying, however, that they submit to the strict control of British officers. He was resolved, he asserted, "to be the soldier, not the executioner of the state."

At first, Burgoyne was charmed by the Indians, who "spread terror without barbarity" and behaved with "European humanity" towards prisoners. Under the command of English and Canadian officers, they were instructed to kill only those opposed to them in arms — women and children were to be spared; and although paid for prisoners, they were called to account for every scalp taken. Burgoyne rejoiced in his tawny allies. "I have but to give stretch to the Indian forces under my direction," he boasted, "and they amount to thousands, to overtake the hardened enemies of Great Britain and America."

It could not be denied that the Indians, while reconciling few Americans to British sovereignty, fulfilled all Germain's expectations in spreading terror. As a means of waging a war of nerves they were unequaled: scouting parties disappeared never to be heard from again; scalped and maimed victims of their savagery were found where they had fallen in ambush; and the troops quailed to hear "the Cursed War hoop, which makes the Woods ring for Miles." "One Hundred Indians in the Woods do us more Harm than 1000 British Troops," said an American soldier. "They have been the Death of many brave Fellows."

Despite his prepossession toward his Indian allies, Burgoyne soon suffered a change of heart: as an English gentleman he was horrified by the bloodthirstiness and rapacity they exhibited when warmed to their work. Their uncontrollable fierceness threatened to turn the expedition into a massacre, directed against Loyalists and rebels alike. As scouts and skirmishers they were of great aid to the expedition and Burgoyne could ill dispense with their services; yet when it became clear that they could be retained only by allowing them to wage war in their own way, Burgoyne refused to yield. His humanitarianism cost him practically all of his Indian allies: disgusted by the restraints laid upon them by the British general and by the unhappy outcome of the expedition against Bennington, they walked out of camp. They had come along largely for the plunder, and this expedition promised, in that respect, to be a total loss.

The Canadians were next. Feeling no strong impulse to risk their lives fighting England's battles, they went home when the going became rough, leaving Burgoyne with only his British and German troops, ill equipped for wilderness warfare.

Following upon the heels of these setbacks came news of another reverse that might well have persuaded a commander of less bulldog tenacity than Burgoyne that it was high time to call a halt, if not a retreat, before the expedition was engulfed by the rebel army.

While Burgoyne moved along the Lake Champlain-Hudson River route to Albany, a second expeditionary force under the command of Colonel St. Leger was to march down the Mohawk Valley from Oswego to the Hudson — a diversion for Burgoyne's march upon Albany. But St. Leger encountered unexpectedly stiff resistance in the Mohawk Valley. Although he had seventeen hundred men under his command, including a large contingent of Indians, the Loyalists upon whom he relied for reinforcements failed to rally to the King's standard: instead of the throngs of volunteers that were expected, only a few suspicious-looking individuals drifted into the British camp. At Fort Stanwix, the chief barrier in St. Leger's path, the Americans resisted stubbornly, and the British commander did not dare to by-pass the fort, leaving the garrison in his rear. The New York militia under General Nicholas Herkimer fought to the death at the fiercely contested battle of Oriskany; and the Indians, who bore the brunt of these assaults, suffered such heavy casualties that they lost all stomach for further fighting. Finally, learning that Benedict Arnold was advancing up the Mohawk Valley to the relief of Fort Stanwix, St. Leger precipitately abandoned the siege and fell back to Oswego. The diversion had failed and the Americans were now free to concentrate their entire strength against Burgoyne.

Burgoyne's wings were clipped at Bennington and Fort Stanwix; and yet, although the expedition had now all the vulnerability of a sitting duck, Burgoyne resolved to struggle on to Albany. The Hudson River, as he well knew, was his Rubicon; from the hour he passed the river, his communications with Canada would be cut by the rebels, and there would be little chance of making a successful retreat. But "Gentleman Johnny" Burgoyne was a brave and stubborn man who preferred to endure any perils and hardships rather than retreat before rebels.

Up to this time, one of Burgoyne's most potent allies had been the jealousy and suspicion entertained by Americans toward their countrymen from other parts of the union. Sectional ill will had immeasurably aided Burgoyne's advance: at one time it seemed probable that he would march to Albany almost unopposed simply because New Englanders and New Yorkers could not lay aside their mutual dislike long enough to make a stand against the invader. The colonies were still at best a league of nations, the jarring and antagonistic elements of which constantly broke through the thin crust of nationalism. Without tolerance and understanding of one another, Americans were lost; but to conquer their prejudices and to submerge local attachments in unconstrained affection for the nation proved almost as difficult as conquering the enemy.

Americans were prone to appropriate to their own states the glory of victory, to cast upon other states the opprobrium of defeat. John Adams, for example, confided to his wife his opinion that "New England must produce the heroes, the statesmen, the philosophers, or America will make no great figure for some time." On the other hand, John Taylor of Virginia exclaimed: "I wish from my soul we had more Virginians than one, but as we have not, the honor of preserving America must be acquired by one alone." Benjamin Rush of Pennsylvania had no hesitation in claiming "the palm of military glory" for his state.

There was no lack of incidents during the war to lend a specious sanction to the low esteem in which Americans held each other. In an action near Crown Point in 1776, a New Yorker declared that he and his men attempted "with fixt Bayonets to stop the New England Men in their Flight, but in Vain, for they made their Way Thro' the Water up to their Waists" and the "fugitive Rascals" did not pause for breath until out of earshot of the enemy's cannon. The panic that struck the Connecticut troops on Manhattan Island in September 1776 reflected upon the courage of all New Englanders. "Our light Corps will soon be *very light indeed*," exclaimed a Pennsylvania officer, "by the Constant desertion of these *fine fellows the Yankees*," for whom home cooking and feather beds had irresistible attractions — particularly when danger threatened. If only New Englanders would fight with as much spirit as Southern troops, it was often said, the United States would certainly give the British "a genteel drubbing." "My heart bleeds for poor *Washington*," said Anthony Wayne in 1776; "had he but Southern [i.e. Pennsylvanians] troops he would not be necessitated so often to fly before the enemy." Sneering at the Yankees became common in the army. When Fort Washington surrendered to the Hessians in 1776, New Englanders breathed a sigh of relief that a Southern officer had been in command of the ill-fated fort: if a New Englander had occupied that post, they feared that they would never have heard the last of it.

The equality practised by New Englanders was to their critics their most offensive characteristic — it was bad enough to proclaim the equality of all men without practising it, as New Englanders seemed bent upon doing. New Englanders were regarded as a canting tribe, but in this matter of equalitarianism it was their performance rather than their cant which conservatives found most disturbing. When conservatives were trying to persuade Americans to hate only kings, they seemed to hate aristocrats and kings with equal intensity. "I dread their low Cunning," exclaimed a South Carolinian, "and those levelling Principles which Men without Character and without Fortune in General possess, which are so captivating to the lower class of Mankind."

In 1776, the garrison at Ticonderoga was composed of Pennsylvania and New England troops. Tension began to mount alarmingly as the men from the two sections looked each other over with a cold and critical stare. First impressions were decidedly unfavorable. New Englanders, said a Pennsylvanian, "are a set of low, dirty, griping, cowardly rascals. . . . The miserable appearance, and what is worse the miserable behaviour of the Yankees, is sufficient to make one sick of the service. . . . Among them there is the strangest mixture of Negroes, Indians, and Whites, with old men and mere children, which together with a nasty lousy appearance make a most shocking spectacle." Another Pennsylvanian curtly summed up his opinion of the Yankees: "The more I am acquainted with them the worse I like them." But, at least, the old wives' tale that New Englanders would conquer the union was effectively scotched by this opportunity to observe the Yankees at close quarters; ten thousand Pennsylvanians, it was said in the officers' mess, would be a match for these craven, puling "Saints."

The inevitable outbreak occurred when a Massachusetts colonel who shared his quarters with a shoemaker was rebuked by a Pennsylvania officer for thus degrading his rank. To lend emphasis to his remarks, the Pennsylvanian upset the shoemaker's bench and knocked down the Massachusetts colonel. Instantly the garrison was in an uproar: the Pennsylvanians rushed for their arms and drove the Yankees out of their huts and barracks, wounding several in the melee. But order was restored by the officers, and the Massachusetts colonel and his late antagonist shook hands and sat down in good fellowship to a dinner of bear meat.

Like these two officers, Washington learned at Boston the folly of acting upon prejudices born of first impressions. After his experiences at Boston, he resolved to suppress all evidences of sectional bias either in himself or in the army. Deliberately he avoided showing favor to Virginians; and in his anxiety to prove that he was without partiality to his "countrymen," he gave them less than their due. Among the troops of the Continental army he strove "to discourage all kinds of local attachments, and distinctions of Country, denominating the whole by the greater name of American"; and he refused to detach any part of the Continental army on state service, insisting that its operations be conducted "on a General and impartial Scale, so as to exclude any first cause of Complaint and Jealousy." He repeatedly told his men that they were "the same people engaged in the same noble struggle" and had "one common and general interest to defend." They were "one patriotic band of brothers"; to give way to prejudice was to play the enemy's game: the only way the British could hope to conquer was to divide Americans.

But sectionalism could not be talked down. Washington's proclamations and even the punishment meted out to offenders were unavailing. It was necessary for Americans to learn from experience that sectional prejudice was the product of error and ignorance and that only by standing shoulder to shoulder could they win victory.

Between New Englanders and New Yorkers there existed a peculiarly virulent dislike which took its origin in the rivalry and nationalistic animosities of the Puritan and Dutch settlers. This prejudice cropped up repeatedly: the father of Gouverneur Morris, for example, a staunch New Yorker, forbade his son to go to Connecticut for his education "lest he should imbibe in his youth that low craft and cunning so incidental to the people of that country." Dutch influence was still strong in many parts of New York, Albany being in many respects a Dutch town where the people clung tenaciously to the traits their ancestors had brought from the Netherlands. "Their Houses," observed a traveler, "resemble a welchman's Breeches, void of all form and Comeliness. . . . Their women are continually employ'd in scowering their floors, one drop of Ink in a house will breed a Riot, till it is eraz'd by soap & sand, & Dishclouts." A less innocent custom was the practice of the Dutch traders in keeping the Indians supplied with arms and ammunition, which New Englanders believed were used to ravage the New England frontier, with the Albany merchants acting as receivers of the pillaged goods.

The American commander in the sector immediately threatened by Burgoyne was Philip Schuyler, a New York patroon, distinguished even among the Dutch-descended aristocracy of New York by his lofty manners and pride of family. As one of the greatest landowners in New York, he possessed a numerous tenantry; upon his patrimonial estates he moved among his retainers almost like a feudal seigneur. It might seem the part of wisdom to entrust the defense of this region to one of its greatest landowners; led by this aristocrat, the common people would presumably be the more willing to take the field. Perhaps this was true of New York, but unfortunately for the American army, Schuyler's popularity ended with his own bailiwick. The very circumstances which made him popular and respected in New York rendered him anathema among New Englanders. East of the Hudson he was not a great and admired patrician but "a damned Dutchman," of a particularly obnoxious kind.

Schuyler's insistence upon discipline in the army rendered him downright hateful to New England democrats, in whose eyes discipline was merely another name for tyranny. Schuyler demanded that his troops make a smart military appearance, obey the commands of their officers without hesitation, and subordinate themselves completely to his authority. Anyone looking for such qualities among American soldiers was certain to be grievously disappointed; it was not in the nature of the patriots to suffer gladly military authority in any form. Schuyler further outraged their democratic predilections by attempting to carry over into military life the grand manner and sweeping authority that pertained to him as a patroon. Even in the army, he never ceased to draw the class line. When a New England soldier, a blacksmith in civilian life, approached Schuyler and, without the formal deference that the New Yorker expected as his due, attempted to give him some information, Schuyler looked him over witheringly and then "spake very sharply to the poor man and bade him begone." It was not until it had been explained to Schuyler that the man was of good family, but had suffered reverses, that the general could be persuaded to listen.

Such high and mighty airs persuaded New Englanders that Schuyler was no better than the Tories and other "vermin" that menaced the success of the Revolution. In their eyes, it was impossible for Schuyler to do good; even his patriotism was suspect, and stories that he had turned traitor and, in league with the Tories and Indians, was preparing to drench the frontier in blood were eagerly credited. The Green Mountain Boys stood ready to seize Schuyler at his first untoward move — and this at a time when Schuyler was actually bending every effort in New York to suppress the Tories!

New Englanders carried their distrust of Schuyler to the point of staging a sit-down strike against him; rather than serve under his command, they remained obstinately at home while Burgoyne lumbered on towards Albany. Schuyler wrote repeatedly to the Massachusetts Legislature begging for men, but he did not receive so much as a reply, much less the men he asked for.

Schuyler, incapacitated by multitudinous ailments, any one of which would have laid low an ordinary man, fought his campaigns mostly from his headquarters at Albany. He was assailed, he said, by "a barbarous complication of disorders" from which the British enemy might have seemed a welcome relief: gout claimed him at an early age and held him fast in its piercing grip; and he was afflicted with "a copious scorbutic eruption" which, he consoled himself, "threw off some other more disagreeable disorder." Ill health coupled with ceaseless vexations and disappointments left its imprint upon Schuyler's nerves: he was in neither a mental nor a physical state to undergo the rigors of active war. He pitied himself as one of the most unfortunate generals in history; he had not, it is true, lost a battle, but merely to command such loutish and troublesome troops as fell to his lot was in itself a torture almost beyond bearing. "If Job had been a general in my situation," exclaimed the agonized commander, "his memory had not been so famous for patience."

As successor to Schuyler — although that general showed no disposition to relinquish his command of the Northern army — New Englanders put forward one of their favorite generals, Horatio Gates.

After long service in the British army, in which he had seen active duty in America, Horatio Gates had risen to the rank of major when in 1773 he decided to abandon the army and turn planter in Virginia, to the despair of his friends who urged him not to venture among people who "to say no worse of them, are not the politest kind of people." With the outbreak of war in 1775, Gates resumed his military career — but now against the King and army he had hitherto served. Joining the rebels, in 1775 he was appointed adjutant general of the Continental army — a post which was expected to give scope to his talents as an organizer and disciplinarian. In June 1776, he became a major general and was placed in command of the already beaten army in Canada — a dubious honor from which he was fortunate to escape without loss of reputation.

Gates's following in the Continental Congress — for every general enjoyed a greater or less degree of political backing — came largely from New England. He fully reciprocated this affection. One evening during the siege of Boston, the officers fell to discussing what nation made the best soldiers. General Charles Lee plumped for the Portuguese "if they were well disciplined, but," he added, "the Turks of Asia Minor were the stoutest Men in the world." Gates, however, awarded the palm to New Englanders — "he never desired to see better soldiers than the New-England men made." He liked their political ideals as much as he did their fighting qualities; these "zealous republicans" seemed to him to be the best hope of democracy in the United States.

It is hardly surprising, therefore, that New Englanders enthusiastically supported Gates's aspirations to succeed the discredited Schuyler. By virtue of his appointment as commander of the American forces in Canada, Gates early in 1776 claimed the right to head the troops at Ticonderoga, but Schuyler, as commander of the Northern army, refused to yield this post to a junior officer. Beset by the conflicting claims, Congress juggled the command of the troops at Ticonderoga between the rival generals, giving the honor first to the one and then to the other. Finally, however, by dint of superior influence in Congress, Schuyler carried off the honor. Gates, the unsuccessful candidate, was left without an army. "Discomposed, chagreened and angry," Gates stormed down to Philadelphia to do a little personal lobbying in Congress.

Thus Gates and Schuyler struggled for command of the Northern army as though the general who had the misfortune to lead it were not likely to go down to disastrous defeat. Schuyler followed Gates in abandoning his post and hurrying to Philadelphia to plead his cause before Congress: while the Goths thundered at the gates, the generals turned politicians. Marshaling their forces on the floor of Congress, they left Burgoyne a clear field to Albany. Bitterly they contended for the honor of saving the state; but Gates, who permitted his temper to run away with him, did his cause little good, whereas Schuyler, aided by the New York delegation, strengthened his hold upon the post of commander of the Northern army. Then, like a thunderclap, came the news of the fall of Ticonderoga and the virtual collapse of organized opposition to Burgoyne's advance. Schuyler found the ground cut from beneath his feet; although not in active command at Ticonderoga, he was blamed for the disaster. Drunkenness or cowardice, Sam Adams's usual explanation for American defeats, seemed inadequate to explain such a staggering blow; surely treason was at the bottom of the disaster. The story was told that Schuyler and St. Clair had turned traitor and had received as pay for surrendering Ticonderoga silver balls shot from Burgoyne's guns into the American camp. John Adams demanded that some general be shot, although he did not specify who was to be the victim. "We must trifle no more," he declared. "We have suffered too many disgraces to pass unexpiated. Every disgrace must be wiped off." Gates's friends capitalized upon the misfortunes of the New York general, and in August 1777 their hero was invested by Congress with the command.

With Gates, "the darling of the New Englanders" in command, the Yankees no longer sulked in their tents. The Americans had changed horses in midstream, neatly executing this difficult trick without more than wetting their feet. Decidedly, it was bad news for the British, who hitherto had profited from the dissensions among American generals. "We can eat them up at a Meal," vowed thousands of New England farmers as they took down their muskets and headed west.

As if to seal his fate, Burgoyne about this time began to spread the report that his army was on its way to Boston, there to link up with the British forces operating from Rhode Island. Burgoyne's purpose was to deceive the enemy, but it was not the kind of deception likely to keep New Englanders dozing by their firesides while the British uninterruptedly marched down to Albany.

Balked in his efforts to seize supplies from the rebels, Burgoyne was obliged to depend upon his own inadequate transport to bring up provisions. This consumed precious time: not until September 13, a month after the bridgehead had been established on the west bank of the Hudson, was he prepared to cross the river with his army.

Before taking this decisive step, Burgoyne attempted to get in touch with the British commander in New York. That his progress to Albany would be a triumphant victory march, Burgoyne no longer supposed: a long, dark, and bloody road lay ahead, filled with unknown perils. Reluctantly, Burgoyne was compelled to admit that his army might soon urgently require aid and reinforcements from New York.

But where, in this emergency, were Sir William Howe and his army which alone could save the British expeditionary forces from disaster? The answer — hardly comforting to Burgoyne — was: Deep in the heart of Pennsylvania.

That Sir William Howe sailed away from New York in July 1777, leaving Burgoyne to meet his fate at Saratoga, is often pictured as a consummate piece of British blundering. Actually, however, it was carefully conceived strategy which, although it went awry, was based upon sound military maxims. Howe made one cardinal error — he forgot that he was fighting not an army but a people in arms. To that oversight may be ascribed all the disasters that overtook British arms in 1777.

Disappointed in his request for reinforcements, Howe began early in 1777 to scale down his projects for the campaign. The first to go was the expedition against Boston; shortly afterward South Carolina and Georgia were eliminated. There remained only his proposed junction with the Northern army and the attack upon Philadelphia; but gradually Sir William began to disregard the former until he had little left except the invasion of Pennsylvania. Upon this expedition, Howe placed all his hopes of ending the war in 1777.

Howe had never thought highly of an attack from Canada upon the United States: he preferred to strike a blow from New York at the heart of the rebellion rather than to assail it from the periphery. He was particularly chilly toward Burgoyne's expedition because he believed that it had deprived him of the reinforcements he had requested for the campaign of 1777. But pique was far from being the principal reason for Howe's decision to abandon his plans of a junction on the Hudson with Burgoyne.

In the first place, all reports pictured Pennsylvania as a stronghold of Loyalism; the people, restless under the rule of Congress and the patriot committees, were said to be ready to welcome the British army as deliverers. Moreover, from its key position in the union, the reduction of Pennsylvania by the British would split the rebellion in twain; and all the Middle states might be swept into Howe's net. Casting off his habitual pessimism, Howe now permitted himself the hope that the Loyalists living around Philadelphia would "be found so numerous and so ready to give every aid and assistance in their power, that it will prove no difficult task to reduce the more rebellious parts of the province."

In this opinion, the patriots themselves concurred: Pennsylvania was called "the enemy's country" and it was predicted that if the state were relieved of the pressure of New England on the north and Virginia on the south, it would soon gravitate to the British side. Pennsylvania, exclaimed a patriot in 1777, "is at present a dead weight on us . . . their Council & Executive are puerile weak & Inanimate. they deserve to be D——." In regarding Pennsylvania as one of the weakest spots in the American armor, the patriots and Sir William Howe were agreed.

It would be wrong to suppose, however, that the British commander was merely seeking to conquer territory; he correctly perceived that his major objective was to destroy Washington's army, the conquest of provinces and cities being secondary to the task of eliminating the hard core of American resistance — the Continental army.

The American comeback in New Jersey which began at Trenton had ended, it will be recalled, with Washington encamped in a strong position at Morristown and the British established at Brunswick. Americans now swelled with a confidence which they had not felt since Howe landed on Long Island. John Hancock, with a flourish of his goose quill, declared that "we must give these fellows a trimming. . . . I believe they will soon be tir'd of their Game. We have got the troops"; and John Adams advised all military men to take "CONQUER or DIE" as their motto. John Adams, indeed, felt martial ardor stirring within him so strongly that he yearned to take the field himself against the "barbarian Britons."

Although inspirited by Washington's victories in New Jersey, few Americans were carried by patriotic zeal to the length of enlisting in the Continental army. In his camp at Morristown, Washington would never have known from the thin trickle of recruits that came his way that he had just wrested a province from Sir William Howe. On the contrary, the country seemed "lulled into ease and Security"; instead of stimulating his countrymen to arms, Washington appeared to have convinced them that they could now safely enjoy the sweets of victory. In the spring of 1777, a few weeks after the battles of Trenton and Princeton, Washington feared that he would have no army whatever with which to face Howe in the next campaign. The states were laggard in filling their lines, and desertion almost kept pace with enlistments in the army. In March 1777, he had only about three thousand men under his command in New Jersey, less than one thousand of whom were regulars, the rest being militia engaged to serve only until the end of the month. And these troops were strung out over the state in small posts, thus giving Howe an opportunity of destroying the army in detail.

However bitterly Washington might lament his countrymen's lethargy, he could only applaud the lethargy of Sir William Howe. Fortunately for Washington, Howe was inclined to concentrate his attention upon his own difficulties rather than upon those of his opponent, and to move when it was convenient for the enemy. Howe's apparent sluggishness was owing in part to the failure of fodder for the draft horses of the army to arrive from England, but his delay in opening the campaign tided Washington over the crisis: when the British were ready to open the action, there was gathered at Washington's new headquarters at Middlebrook what Henry Knox called "the most respectable body of continental troops that America ever had, no going home to such — hardy, brave fellows, who are as willing to go to heaven by the way of a bayonet or sword as any other mode."

Howe's aim was to draw Washington into battle by marching down the road to Philadelphia as though he intended to take up where he had left off in the winter of 1776. His objective was the Continental army rather than the Continental Congress and the city which gave it shelter. Sir William might be overcautious, but he seldom lost sight of the importance of destroying Washington's army. To bring this about, it was first necessary to entice Washington to descend from his mountain and fight on the level ground where British troops and artillery might be deployed to best advantage.

Therefore Howe marched his army bravely down the road to Philadelphia carrying pontoons, bridges, knocked-down boats, and other paraphernalia necessary for crossing the Delaware in force. Approaching Washington's camp, he marched and countermarched, flaunting his flag before the rebels and exhausting every trick at his command to persuade them to come down and fight. Not for a moment, however, did Howe lose his customary caution; everywhere he surrounded himself with entrenchments that probably would have discouraged even the most reckless enemy from attacking. In fact, Sir William displayed such healthy appreciation of his opponent that he camped only in well-nigh invulnerable positions. He challenged Washington to battle, it is true, but he took the precaution of making sure that the advantage of terrain would all be on his side. It was now the British troops who wielded the spade and pickaxe and who did not seem to consider themselves safe unless they were up to their eyes in dirt.

Naturally, Washington declined Howe's invitations to do battle upon these terms; the American general was not so poor a fly as to be caught in such a clumsily woven web. Washington did not believe that Howe would attempt to march to Philadelphia leaving an army in his rear to play havoc with his supply lines. The position of the American army was virtually unassailable; the surrounding region was rich in cattle, horses, and provisions; and from his vantage point Washington could march in any direction necessity dictated. To risk a battle was to put at hazard the fate of the American cause; by playing a waiting game, he might force the British to waste the greater part of the campaign in fruitless maneuvers. For the moment, Fabius was in favor at Washington's headquarters.

But the British were by no means allowed a free hand in New Jersey. Howe's detachments and foraging parties were attacked; sniping, bush fighting, and skirmishing met the British wherever they turned; and food, horses, and cattle were whisked away to safety before they could seize them. Howe was made to feel that he had walked into a hornets' nest: on every side, the militia rose against him and fought with an inveteracy that startled the Englishmen who, six months before, had been welcomed as deliverers.

Despairing of bringing Washington to action and fearful that his army would melt away in skirmishing, sniping, and ambuscades, Sir William Howe brought his army back to Brunswick. Yet, before abandoning all hope that the decisive battle of the war would be fought in New Jersey, he tried one last trick. Ordering his army to retreat to New York, he deliberately exposed his troops while he prepared to hurl his entire army upon the Americans if they rose to the bait. On this trial, Sir William almost landed his game: the American army, seeing the British in retreat, left its mountain hideaway to give a parting blow to the British rear guard. In the nick of time, Washington saw the trap and drew back before Howe could bring up his main army. Much chagrined, Howe went on to New York, leaving the rebels in possession of virtually the entire state of New Jersey.

The retreat from New Jersey was an inauspicious beginning to a campaign that was expected to end the rebellion: a British army had abandoned an entire province to the rebels and had taken refuge in New York from an enemy inferior in numbers. To crown the discomfiture of the redcoats, Americans boasted that it was the New Jersey militia that had cleared the state of invaders; when they saw the militia rising up in wrath, the Britons' hearts "sank within them," said John Adams, "and they sneaked away in a Panic." The self-confidence with which Americans had begun the war was renewed by the spectacle of the British army in full retreat; John Hancock declared that the enemy had made an "explicit declaration to the whole world, that the conquest of America is . . . an unattainable object."

Having failed to run Washington to earth in New Jersey, Howe was obliged to make one of the most momentous decisions of the war: whether to advance up the Hudson River and join hands with Burgoyne in Albany or to proceed to Pennsylvania, there to resume the struggle with Washington.

If he chose to make the Hudson a scene of operations, Howe expected that Washington would throw his army into the Highland forts near Haverstraw and in that strongly defended position defy the British to dislodge him. If this occurred, Sir William would gain nothing by his maneuver: it would still be the familiar situation of Washington on top of a hill and the British in the valley. For this reason, the Hudson River possessed few attractions for a commander who, like Howe, was in search of flat country on which to meet his adversary in battle. Pennsylvania, on the other hand, was much to his liking.

In these calculations, Howe was not unmindful of Burgoyne. Later the charge was to be made that Sir William, in order to spite his rival for top honors in the war, deliberately abandoned Burgoyne; but calumny is the lot of unfortunate generals. Howe's mistakes, it is now clear, were the result not of malice or jealousy but of underestimation of the strength of the enemy. Not doubting that all Burgoyne had to fear on his march to Albany was an attack by Washington's army, Howe reasoned that if he could divert Washington's attention to the southward, Burgoyne's progress to Albany would be hardly more than a pleasant tour of upper New York.

And thus, by gradual yet logical stages, Howe's reasoning brought him to the conclusion that the best way to aid Burgoyne was to march not toward but away from him. Far from leaving Burgoyne in the lurch, Howe believed that he was ensuring the success of the Northern expedition: the Pennsylvania campaign might be regarded as a large-scale diversion in Burgoyne's favor.

In all that he did during the spring and summer of 1777, Howe was thinking of the impending showdown with Washington and the Continental army. He sought to draw Washington to Pennsylvania, but if the American general chose instead to march against Burgoyne, Howe intended to lose no time in camping on his trail. If Washington would not follow him, said Howe, he would follow Washington. When he sailed for the Chesapeake, in July 1777, he left in New York what he deemed to be a sufficient number of men to cope with Washington until the rest of the British army could be brought into action. Howe firmly intended to be on hand, whether in Pennsylvania or New York, for the final reckoning with the rebel army.

As matters stood in July 1777, Howe's strategy seemed judicious; moreover, to a point, it worked. Yet, as has been said, Sir William forgot that he was fighting a people capable, on occasion, of heroic efforts, and he did not realize that, thanks to French secret aid in guns and ammunition, a new army was being formed in New England to contest Burgoyne's advance. As Howe was to learn, American armies might come and go, but as long as the people had guns in their hands, there was no security for the British.

The struggle in America was not like European wars where armies were composed of professional soldiers, limited in number, whose strength was usually known to their adversaries. As Howe ought to have learned from his experience in Boston in 1775, the strength of the Americans was incalculable and held in reserve for emergencies such as that created by Burgoyne's invasion. In such a war, the balance of military power might be upset in the span of a few weeks.

There was the less justification for this oversight inasmuch as the danger was pointed out to Howe by several of his officers. In fact, with the exception of Howe and Cornwallis, few high-ranking officers in the army approved the voyage to Pennsylvania. Sir Henry Clinton, in particular, was not backward in enlarging upon the fallacies of the commander-in-chief's strategy: as soon as Howe put to sea, Clinton predicted, Washington would attack New York or march against Burgoyne. In either event, he saw disaster to British arms. Mincing no words, Clinton told Howe that "Philadelphia had better close than open the campaign, as it required an army to defend it." Clinton failed to share Howe's confidence that Burgoyne could safely be left to make his own way to Albany: to face "the most power, the most inveterate and numerous colonies," alone and unaided, was to invite calamity.

Howe's plans, now stripped to an invasion of Pennsylvania and an ambiguous promise of support to Burgoyne, were approved by the government, although the King took it hard that there was to be no attack upon New England. Lord George Germain, who was as eager as his sovereign to chastise New Englanders, continued to urge Howe to attack Boston as a diversion for Burgoyne. Threatened from the sea, he pointed out, the Yankees' chief strength would be pinned down at home while Burgoyne pursued his way uninterruptedly to Albany. But Howe declined to be talked into an attack upon New England; by his reckoning, the decisive battles of the war were to be fought in Pennsylvania and every available British soldier was needed in that state.

It was characteristic of Germain that he enthusiastically approved Howe's plans for an attack upon Philadelphia although he did not quite understand them. He took it for granted that Howe knew what he was about; Sir William had been informed that Burgoyne was on his way to Albany and that he was expected to "co-operate" with the Northern army. Although a bit bewildered by Howe's decision to concentrate virtually all of his army in Pennsylvania, Germain did not believe that this step would work any hardship upon Burgoyne. In fact, he expected Howe to return from his jaunt into Pennsylvania in time to meet Burgoyne on the Hudson. In Germain's mind, "co-operation" meant an actual joining of forces by Howe and Burgoyne; and he believed that Sir William had pledged himself to effect this junction. That Howe would spend the summer and autumn in Pennsylvania, leaving Burgoyne to fight his own way, was apparently not envisaged by the Colonial Secretary.[2]

---

[2] There is ample evidence in Germain's correspondence to substantiate the statement that he expected Howe actually to move up the Hudson to meet Burgoyne in the vicinity of Albany. As late as the end of June, 1777, he believed that Howe was already beyond that city. In May 1777, he informed the House of Commons that victory would be certain after the army based in Canada had united with Howe's army, "adding 12,000 men to it, besides Canadians."

Everything that Howe had said up to this time indicated that he intended to effect an actual junction on the Hudson between his own army and that marching down from Canada. In May 1776, he had outlined this strategy to the home government and had even worked out a plan for sharing the command with General Carleton, the commander of the Northern army, when the two armies should join. At that time,

It was the easier for Germain to fall in with Howe's views because, as a cabinet member, he had long pressed for an attack upon Philadelphia — the wounded pride of Britain could not be fully assuaged, he believed, until the flag had been planted upon Independence Hall. The British Colonial Secretary did not hesitate to make his ideas known to Sir William Howe. "The punishing that Seat of Congress," he told Howe, "would be a proper Example to the rest of the Colonys," and would give as much joy to the King as it would strike terror among the rebels. With New York and Philadelphia firmly in his grasp, there were no honors for which Howe might not ask.

Moreover, any objections that Germain might have raised to Howe's proposed excursion to Philadelphia were silenced by the fact that the British general intended to seek out the Loyalists. There was nothing dearer to Germain's heart than attaining the Land of Tories; and any project that seemed likely to reach that end was certain to be eagerly embraced by him. At the very mention of the word "Loyalist" his imagination took flight: he saw thousands of Pennsylvania Tories rushing to Howe's aid, trampling the rebels under foot, and holding the province for their King and country while the British army marched off to conquer new provinces.

Thus it can be seen that the strategy of 1777 was partly the Ministry's and partly Sir William Howe's — but never did the twain meet.

From Burgoyne's invasion, Washington believed he had little to fear: Burgoyne's army was hemmed in between New Englanders and New Yorkers, and Washington did not anticipate that it would reach Albany. The physical obstacles in the path of the British army, the difficulty of transporting supplies, the necessity of leaving garrisons behind, and the consequent slowness of Burgoyne's advance — all this served to persuade Washington that he could safely mass the Continental army against Howe while the Northern states disposed of the invaders from Canada. "It is pretty obvious," he said, "that if General Howe can be completely kept at bay, and prevented from effecting his principal purposes, the Successes of Mr. Burgoyne, whatever they may be, must be partial and temporary." In short, both Howe and Washington were agreed that their proper objective was to seek out and destroy each

---

at least, Howe did not mean to leave the Northern army to its fate while he went off in search of new worlds to conquer. As late as November 1776, he continued to speak of the "Junction of the Northern and Southern Armies," leaving no doubt in Germain's mind that Howe's army would move up the Hudson to join forces with the army coming down from Canada.

In one of his letters to Germain, Howe had remarked that it probably would be the middle of September before Burgoyne would reach Albany, implying to Germain, at least, that Howe expected to wind up his Pennsylvania campaign before that date and be back in New York ready to link up with Burgoyne. Of course, this necessitated dashing about the country in a manner wholly foreign to Howe's methodical and ponderous manner.

other and that they must not be distracted from this purpose by diversionary attacks from any quarter.

What the American commander most feared was that Howe would strike up the Hudson to join forces with Burgoyne. It was an easy and natural course for the British general to follow: once the American forts on the Hudson near Haverstraw had been reduced, he would have clear sailing up the Hudson to Albany. And while the British traveled comfortably and swiftly by water, Washington would be obliged to lead his army on a backbreaking march overland across some of the most difficult terrain in the Northern states. As Washington knew, the loss of the Hudson River, and the consequent severing of communication between New England and the rest of the union, might well prove the deathblow of the Revolution. It was difficult for him to believe that Howe would not seek to deliver it.

Having seen Howe in action, Americans found some ground to hope that he would do the wrong thing. Howe, said Henry Knox, would try to join forces with Burgoyne "if he is not a fool" — and many Americans took comfort in the belief that he was just that; Hamilton declared that Howe was "fool enough to meditate a southern expedition"; John Adams pronounced him to be "a wild General" given to unaccountable vagaries; and Thomas Paine, never a respecter of the British military mind, was certain that Howe could be trusted to bungle. "They suppose Philadelphia to be rich with stores," observed Paine, "and as they think to get more by robbing a town than by attacking an army, their movement toward this city is probable. We are not now contending against an army of soldiers, but against a band of thieves, who had rather plunder than fight, and have no other hope of conquest than by cruelty."

These happy expectations that Howe would ignore all the signposts and take the wrong turning because it was his nature to be perverse were dispelled by the fall of Ticonderoga. This event left little doubt that the next act in the war would bring forth a dash by Howe up the Hudson to Albany, the union of the two armies, and the isolation of New England.

Upon Howe, however, the fall of Ticonderoga had precisely the opposite effect: instead of deducing from that event that he ought to go up the Hudson, it settled his conviction that Philadelphia was his proper destination. Burgoyne, he reasoned, had solidly improved his fortunes and could be trusted to find his own way to Albany; the strongest obstacle in his path had been cleared away, and in a manner which seemed to indicate that there would be little further resistance on the part of the rebels.

In New Jersey, Howe had learned the hazard of attempting to march overland to Philadelphia leaving his line of communications exposed to the rebels. Rather than risk another Trenton, he decided to take his army by sea to Pennsylvania. By this maneuver, he expected to safeguard his communications, take the Americans by surprise, and give his troops the benefit of a healthful sea voyage during the hottest season of the year.

Delay, as usual, upset Howe's timetable. In this case, the delay was owing to Howe's reluctance to leave New York before he had news of Burgoyne's progress and Sir Henry Clinton's arrival from England. In the meantime, however, the troops were embarked; and lying off Staten Island in sweltering heat, they consumed a large part of the fresh provisions intended for the voyage. On July 5, Clinton reached New York; on July 15, news of the capture of Ticonderoga was brought to Howe; and a few days later the fleet finally sailed from Sandy Hook. By that time, the season for active campaigning was well advanced and the troops aboard the transports were already complaining of the hardships of their cramped quarters.

After he had finally got under way, everything seemed to conspire to retard Howe. Seldom has a man been better formed for loitering or had more assistance from nature in confirming his sluggishness. At sea, Howe encountered head winds which slowed down his progress to a snail's pace: twenty-four days were required for the fleet to cover three hundred and fifty miles — with a favorable breeze, he might have gone to Europe in less time. Even as a rest cure, the voyage was not a success: "condemned to broil in that Cursed Climate," the soldiers wilted in a heat which veterans of Africa and the West Indies pronounced worse than anything they had experienced. Over three hundred horses — sorely needed in the coming campaign — died at sea and those that survived were "mere Carrion" by the time the fleet reached its destination. Most important of all, six weeks of the summer, while Burgoyne's doom was being prepared in New England, were spent by the British army completely out of action on the Atlantic.

Howe disappeared into the Atlantic, and so completely did the British dominate the sea that no American ship dared put out to keep an eye upon the armada. Washington was left completely in the dark as to Howe's movements; the army was "compelled to wander about the country like the Arabs" in search of the enemy fleet and army. As a vanishing act, Howe's maneuver was eminently successful; but it may be questioned whether his disappearance at this time was opportune.

Howe broke his voyage at the Delaware, where he stopped briefly to interrogate pilots concerning the strength of the rebel forts on the river and to ascertain the whereabouts of Washington's army. The information he thus gleaned was that the Delaware forts were powerful and that Washington had not yet marched up the Hudson. Therefore, certain that Washington meant to oppose him in Pennsylvania, and unwilling to hazard an attack upon the powerful American positions along the Delaware, Howe again put to sea and headed south for the Chesapeake. By this maneuver, he hoped to keep Washington guessing where the British fleet and army intended to strike, and to draw the American army still farther away from the Hudson and Burgoyne.

Howe's decision to go to the Chesapeake sealed Burgoyne's fate. Whatever chance there may have been of overwhelming Washington, capturing Philadelphia, and joining forces with Burgoyne was now at an end: the five weeks consumed in this leg of the sea voyage completely upset the schedule Germain supposed Howe was following.

The news that the British fleet was off the Delaware brought Washington and his army in double-quick time to Philadelphia. On the march, however, it was learned that Howe had put to sea again. This game of "now you see him, now you don't" was little to Washington's liking: since Howe had left New York the American troops had been "more harassed by Marching and Counter Marching, than by any thing that has happen'd to them in the course of the Campaign." Rumor placed Howe's whereabouts in such diverse places as Virginia, Nantucket, and the Carolinas; and, as Hamilton said, Howe was "such an unintelligible gentleman, that no rule of interpretation can possibly be found out by which to unravel his designs." In short, the British fleet and army might turn up anywhere, but if Washington were to give credence to all the reports which reached headquarters, he would find himself dragging his army over most of the continent. Sifting all the possibilities, the American commander-in-chief concluded that Howe intended to sail up the Hudson to join Burgoyne, and that his jaunt to the Delaware had merely been an elaborate ruse designed to throw the Americans off his trail. Satisfied that he had penetrated Sir William's strategy, Washington prepared to march his army northward to hold the Hudson against the expected attack. On August 21 he was awaiting only the approval of Congress to put his plan into execution, when news reached the American camp which finally unfolded to Washington the plans of Sir William Howe.

This news was that the British fleet and army were in the Chesapeake, leaving no doubt that Howe's objective was the conquest of the Middle states. What Americans had regarded as too good to be true had actually occurred: the British were making no effort to join their forces on the Hudson. There was at least a fighting chance of beating the two invading armies separately.

The British fleet sailed majestically up the Chesapeake, by far the greatest naval force that had ever been seen in those waters. Three hundred vessels, including five ships of the line, composed this armada. Had Americans been inclined, as Howe first supposed, to suffer themselves to be awed into surrender by the spectacle of the armed might of Britain in full panoply, this fleet might have accomplished the purpose. Nevertheless, as the fleet passed Annapolis, the American flag was seen flying defiantly from the rebel forts. This augured no quick break in American

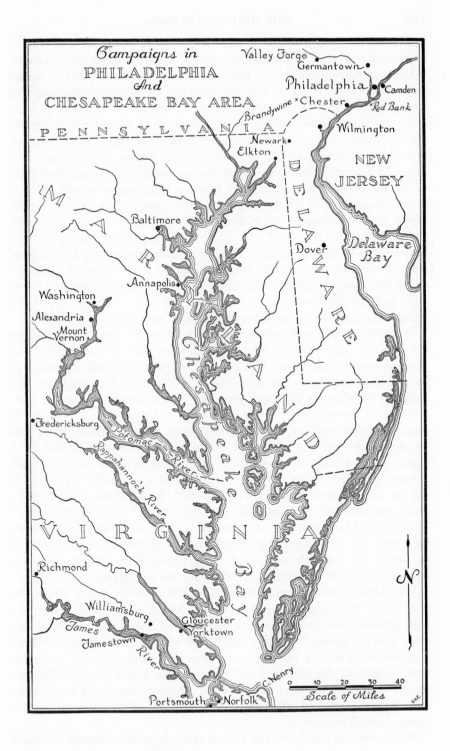

Campaigns in
PHILADELPHIA
and
CHESAPEAKE BAY AREA

Valley Forge
Germantown
Philadelphia
Camden
Brandywine ×Chester
Red Bank
PENNSYLVANIA
Newark
Wilmington
Elkton
NEW
JERSEY
MARYLAND
Baltimore
DELAWARE
Dover
Delaware
Bay
Annapolis
Washington
Alexandria
Mount
Vernon
Chesapeake
Fredericksburg
Potomac
River
Rappahannock River
VIRGINIA
Richmond
Bay
Williamsburg
Gloucester
Yorktown
James
Jamestown
River
C. Henry
Portsmouth
Norfolk
0   10   20   30   40
Scale of Miles

resistance; but, said a British officer, "as it was an object of little importance, it was looked at with contempt, and passed without firing a shot."

Without encountering more than scattered resistance, the British landed from flatboats at Head of Elk and marched to Wilmington. American strategy was not to attack the invaders before they could gain a foothold; instead, Washington chose to permit them to get a comfortable distance from their ships before he attempted to check their progress.

As Howe advanced without seeing sizable bodies of the enemy, he began to fear that the campaign in Pennsylvania was to be a repetition of his recent experiences in New Jersey — Washington would hole up in the mountains and refuse to fight even in defense of his capital. Herein Howe did his opponent an injustice: Washington was eager for battle and was prepared to give Howe everything he desired — and perhaps a little more — in that particular. Discarding Fabian strategy, Washington readied his army to meet the British in open battle. "One bold stroke," he told his troops, "will free the land from rapine, devastations and burnings, and female innocence from brutal lust and violence. . . . If we behave like men, this third Campaign will be our last."

Washington was well aware that the country expected him to drive the invaders back to their ships. Although actually he had fewer Continental troops than Howe had regulars, he was popularly supposed to have double the number of men. So persistent and widespread was this belief in Washington's invincibility that it was necessary for the government of Pennsylvania to deny reports that his army was already too numerous and that no more recruits were wanted. Washington had saved Philadelphia in 1776, and it was not doubted that he could do it again. John Adams, upon viewing the American army on its march through Philadelphia in 1777, complained that the troops did not have the air of soldiers — "they don't," he said, "hold up their heads quite erect, nor turn their toes so exactly as they ought" — yet he feared that Howe would be frightened and run back to his ships when the Americans appeared, thus depriving Washington of a decisive victory. As for the safety of Philadelphia, he felt no apprehensions. "I feel as secure here as if I was at Braintree," he said, "but not so happy."

Washington chose to make his stand on Brandywine Creek where the road from Wilmington to Philadelphia forded the stream. Here, on high ground commanding the approaches to the ford, the American army was drawn up to receive the British attack. Morale was excellent; a soldier declared that he "never saw men with Higher spirits, when the firing began on the outguard our troops fairly Liped for joy." Nevertheless Howe, by employing one of the simplest maneuvers in the military lexicon, nullified Washington's advantage of position and again worsted the American army.

While the main body of the British army kept Washington occupied at Brandywine ford, a column under Cornwallis descended the stream, crossed at an unguarded point, and switched back to attack the Americans from the flank. Washington was not caught wholly by surprise, but his intelligence was so faulty that he did not make preparations in time or in sufficient force to hold his left flank. General Sullivan, who commanded the left wing of the army, found himself in much the same position as at Long Island, and although he escaped being captured a second time, he was forced to give way. Luckily for the Americans, however, darkness fell in time to save them from pursuit; they abandoned the battlefield, but their army was still intact and ready to fight another day.

At Brandywine, it is fair to say, Washington was more outgeneraled than in any other action of war. Perhaps his choice of position was at fault: the defense of a river, frequently intersected by fords, was difficult if not impracticable. It is true, however, that he had permitted himself to be caught by the same kind of flanking movement that had brought disaster upon the American army at Long Island; and he had been slow, despite warnings, to realize his danger. On the other hand, the prompt and judicious measures he took to stop the British, once their presence on his left flank had been ascertained, helped prevent the defeat from being turned into a rout.

So little cast down was Washington by his defeat at Brandywine that a week after the battle he tried again to bring Howe to action. When the British reached Chester, Washington marched towards them; whereupon Howe fell back to Wilmington — singular conduct in a general who always professed himself eager to come to grips with the rebels. Washington continued to shadow the British and on September 19 he caught them by surprise when they were marching in three columns so far apart that they were out of reach of one another. By an immediate assault, the Americans might have won an important victory; but they insisted upon executing various maneuvers before going over to the attack, with the result that the British were given time to bring their columns together. When the final dispositions for the battle were ready, rain began to fall in torrents, giving this encounter the name of "The Battle of the Clouds." Lacking waterproof boxes, the Americans' powder was quickly spoiled; and since a battle was out of the question, Washington was forced to order a precipitate retreat lest the British attack his almost helpless army.

Washington had nearly caught the British by surprise; at Paoli, a few days later, it was the British who surprised the Americans. A corps commanded by General Anthony Wayne had been detached from the main army to attack the British rear; waiting for an opportunity to strike, Wayne had taken a position near Paoli. Without warning, the British fell upon the unsuspecting Americans at night and, using their bayonets exclusively — not a shot was fired by the regulars — almost entirely wiped out Wayne's detachment. At the cost of only three or four Britishers, several hundred Americans were killed; but Wayne escaped to have his revenge a few days later at Germantown.

Philadelphia — and with it, the Continental Congress — was again threatened by the British advance. Early in 1777, Congress had returned from Baltimore vowing never, except in case of extreme danger, to desert the Quaker City again.

Now, however, the streets of Philadelphia rang to the cry "The British are coming!" On September 18, Congress had been warned by Colonel Hamilton that the enemy was preparing to cross the Schuylkill and that the city could not be defended by the Continental army; there was not a moment to lose in evacuating Philadelphia. Congress was prepared for this eventuality, for the loss of the capital had seemed imminent ever since Washington had failed to stop Howe at the Brandywine. "If Howe comes here, I shall run away, I suppose with the rest," said John Adams. "We are too brittle ware, you know, to stand the dashing of balls and bombs." In this spirit, Congress broke up so precipitately that there was not even time for an adjournment — it was every congressman for himself and Howe take the hindmost. One congressman, it was reported, left in such haste that he did not take time to saddle his horse. At three o'clock in the morning, the streets were jammed with congressmen, public officials, and citizens scrambling to get out of harm's way. Thomas Paine, hurrying from Washington's camp to the threatened city, reported the scene. "It was a beautiful still moonlight morning," he wrote, "and the Streets as full of Men Women and Children as on a Market day." Paine attempted to persuade the citizens to raise barricades and defend their city house by house, but the patriots would not tarry. This was no time for heroics, they declared; the important thing was to live to fight another day.

Thus, said a congressman, "this plaguy fellow of an Howe" again sent Congress on its travels. Instead of going to Baltimore, now exposed to attack from the British fleet in the Chesapeake, the members struck west for York, Pennsylvania, where they hoped to find the peace and security that had been lacking in Philadelphia. John Adams pronounced this change of scene all to the good. "This tour," he declared, "has given me an opportunity of seeing many parts of this country which I never saw before." Unless Washington could stop the British army, John Adams's travels were not likely to end short of the Mississippi.

It was not, however, until a week after Congress left Philadelphia that the British entered the city. The citizens who remained warmly welcomed the conquerors — for as long as the British seemed to be winning the war, they did not lack friends and admirers.

The warmth of his reception persuaded Howe that he had at last reached the Land of Tories and that he might safely relax. In this frame of mind, Sir William settled down in Philadelphia as though he had conquered the rebel army as well as the rebel capital. Although a large part of the British troops were stationed in Germantown and exposed to attack, Howe did not deem it necessary to order the erection of defenses. The British commander seemingly alternated between moods of pessimism and moments of optimism, but of the two, the British cause had most to dread from his optimism.

When Washington learned that Howe had divided his army and relaxed his vigilance — two cardinal errors in the art of war — he lost no time in taking advantage of his opportunity. An attack was launched against the British forces at Germantown; and by dint of marching all night and falling suddenly upon the British lines in the early morning, the Americans caught the British by surprise. Bewildered and outnumbered, the regulars were driven back more than two miles and the entire British camp fell into the rebels' hands. Not since Lexington had British soldiers retreated so precipitately; but there was no rout, for the regulars maintained good order and fought back stubbornly from every house and hedge. Howe tried to rally his men, crying out, "Form! form! it is only a scouting party," but he quickly changed his mind when American bullets began whistling about his head. Meanwhile, in their zeal to be avenged for the "Paoli Massacre," Wayne's troops killed British soldiers even after they had thrown down their arms and offered to surrender. "Our Officers Exerted themselves to save many of the poor wretches who were Crying for Mercy," said Wayne, "but to little purpose. The Rage and fury of the Soldiers were not to be Restrained for some time — at least not until great numbers of the enemy fell by our Bayonets."

In the path of the onrushing Americans stood a large stone house, Cliveden, belonging to Judge Chew, into which a small party of British soldiers threw themselves and refused every ultimatum to surrender. Instead of by-passing Chew's house and leaving a force behind to contain the British garrison, General Knox ordered that this hedgehog be reduced before the main army resumed pursuit of the enemy's main body. Washington agreed with the strategy of his general of artillery; and so the Americans began to pound Cliveden with musketry, cannon, and shells. But all to no avail — its thick stone walls were proof against the heaviest artillery Americans could bring to bear. When surrender was demanded, the officer carrying the flag of truce received for answer a British bullet in his leg. Finally, recognizing the danger of wasting his strength against this seemingly impregnable house, Washington ordered his men to continue their advance while a single regiment remained behind to pin down the defenders of Cliveden.

Unfortunately for the Americans, this order came too late: while they were detained at Chew's house, the British had re-formed their ranks and brought up reinforcements. At the head of a large body of troops, Corn-wallis hurried from Philadelphia to the scene of battle, and these fresh troops turned the tide. Already the American ranks had been badly thinned by unwounded men helping the injured off the field. Frequently, from two to five hale men were seen assisting one wounded man, al-though some of these Samaritans could do no more than hold the vic-tim's coattails. In this way, the fainthearted were furnished with an ex-cellent pretext for shirking their duty; and at Germantown scores of soldiers quitted their places ostensibly to give a wounded buddy a hand. In consequence, the Americans were ill prepared to receive the British counterattack. Moreover, they were confused by the fog and smoke of battle; when the reinforced British began pouring a hot fire upon them, they either broke in panic or began firing upon their comrades, mis-taking them for the foe. Crying out that they were surrounded, hun-dreds dropped their guns and began to run for safety, and not even Wash-ington's example of exposing himself to the enemy fire inspired them to stay. "We ran from Victory," said Anthony Wayne. Washington, who at one point in the battle had believed that the way to Philadelphia was open, now found himself borne to the rear in a mob of cursing, panic-stricken soldiers.

Germantown was the last time that Howe fought Washington, and the victory was the least conclusive of all his triumphs. The British gen-eral gained few laurels at Germantown: he had been caught by surprise and saved from defeat by the mistakes of the Americans and by the bravery of the British regulars. It was the British private soldier rather than Sir William Howe who was the real victor at Germantown: his courage and discipline snatched victory from the jaws of defeat. Man for man, the British regulars were the superior of the Americans in dis-cipline and skill. The fog and smoke upon which the Americans blamed their defeat blinded the British as well as the Americans, but the regu-lars kept their heads in the confusion, and although caught off guard and forced to give ground, they recovered and came back stronger than before. The Americans, on the other hand, at both the Brandywine and Germantown, could not be rallied once they had been broken by the enemy.

After the battle of Germantown, Howe hastened to dig in at Phila-delphia. Although his aide-de-camp, Major André, swore that the Ameri-cans' courage was proof, not of the strength of the rebellion but of "the power of strong liquor," Howe was unconvinced: whether their bravery proceeded from rum or fanaticism, the rebels were not to be taken lightly. Lest Washington storm Philadelphia itself, the citizens and sol-diers were set to work constructing breastworks, trenches, and redoubts until the city was made almost invulnerable to attack.

⌢   ⌢   ⌢

Since his arrival in Pennsylvania, Sir William Howe had ceased to give much thought to Burgoyne and the Northern expedition: his own affairs occupied his attention almost to the exclusion of all other matters. From a rebel newspaper he learned that Burgoyne had been checked at Bennington, but he was not seriously alarmed; already his own difficulties had come to seem much greater than Burgoyne's. Whatever happened in the North, Howe had by now given up all thought of aiding Burgoyne. The rebel army in Pennsylvania was too strong, the Loyalists were too timid, and the British need of reinforcements was too great to permit Howe to worry about "Gentleman Johnny." In October 1777, he ordered Clinton to send to Pennsylvania a large part of the troops that had been left behind to garrison New York and to assist Burgoyne's progress towards Albany. Howe believed that he needed those troops a great deal more than did Burgoyne; and in a sense he was right. For, unknown to Howe, Burgoyne had just surrendered at Saratoga.

Burgoyne's long delay in crossing the Hudson gave time for Benedict Arnold to rejoin the main army with three thousand men after forcing St. Leger to raise the siege of Fort Stanwix. The British had learned to respect this swaggering little fellow as one of the most resourceful and hardest fighters in the American army, and his presence in the Northern army was hardly less ominous than the appointment of Horatio Gates to the command. Gates might boost the morale of New Englanders and persuade them to join the army, but Arnold was the man to watch in battle.

That Arnold was still in the field was owing largely to the intercession of Washington. Disappointed in his ambition of becoming a major general, Arnold was on the point of resigning from the army when Washington succeeded in persuading him to swallow his pride and to prove by deeds his worthiness of higher rank.[3] But for Arnold it proved a bitter draught: it was as a general of militia, not of Continental troops, that he joined the Northern army. His patriotism was equal to even this humiliation. "No Publick or private Injury or insult shall prevail on me," he declared, "to forsake the Cause of my Injur'd & oppressed Country untill I see peace & liberty restored to her, or nobly die in the Attempt." To these brave words there was to be a grim sequel.

To serve under General Gates in any capacity grated upon Arnold. Between the two men there had sprung up ill will based perhaps upon incompatibility of temperament. The slow-moving, deliberate Gates was not likely to please Arnold, impetuous and daring, always eager for battle and ready to call upon his men to do the impossible. In Arnold's eyes, Gates was an old fogy who ought to be spending his time com--

[3] Arnold's appointment had been held up in Congress because Connecticut already had its quota of major generals. Each state was allotted a certain number of generals in the Continental army, depending upon the number of men it furnished.

fortably dozing in the chimney corner; while Gates resented the airs assumed by "the pompous little fellow," and declared that it would not break his heart to give Arnold his walking papers.

To darken further Burgoyne's prospects, at almost the same time that Gates was taking command of the Northern army, news reached New England that Sir William Howe and the British fleet had been sighted off the Delaware heading south. This meant that New Englanders need no longer fear an attack upon their seacoast while they were engaged with Burgoyne on the frontier. They could now turn their undivided attention to the British invader in the West.

Moreover, Burgoyne's defeat was being prepared in the seaports as well as in the country villages of New England. During the spring and summer of 1777, French ships carrying the cannon, muskets, and ammunition procured by Beaumarchais continued to arrive at New England harbors. Beaumarchais's secret aid was now beginning to pay off: the arms and ammunition that stopped Burgoyne at Saratoga originally came from French arsenals.[4] Without this timely assistance, it is doubtful whether Americans could have recovered from the heavy losses in artillery and guns sustained at Ticonderoga.

Despite his numerical superiority, Gates chose to take a strong defensive position north of Albany and to wait Burgoyne's approach. Gates and Kosciusko selected a site on the west bank of the Hudson where a narrow pass between the river and the hills formed a bottleneck through which Burgoyne must pass on his way to Albany. Here, while the British waited a few miles upstream for supplies to arrive from Canada, the Americans constructed redoubts, trenches, and artillery emplacements. And all the while, thousands of volunteers continued to pour into Gates's camp. Burgoyne grew no stronger by delay — after the desertion of the Indians and Canadians, his force numbered barely five thousand men — whereas Gates soon had over fifteen thousand men under his command.

Recognizing how sharply the odds had turned against him, Burgoyne saw no salvation except in taking the offensive against the American army. To stand his ground meant eventual annihilation; the rebel army was growing stronger by the hour, and it behooved Burgoyne to attack before the disparity in numbers should incline even more to his disadvantage. Therefore, after crossing the Hudson, he directed his army against the American defenses at Freeman's Farm, a few miles south of Saratoga, in an attempt to break through the left flank of the American lines. Instead of remaining on the defensive, the Americans, led by

---

[4] The *Amphitrite*, which arrived at Portsmouth in April 1777, carried a cargo consisting of 58 brass cannon, tents for 10,000 men, clothing for 12,000 men, 5700 stands of arms, 10 tons of powder, and miscellaneous items. The *Mercury* brought 1000 barrels of powder and 11,000 stands of arms.

Benedict Arnold, went over to the attack, fought the British to a standstill in the woods, and inflicted heavy losses upon the enemy. Burgoyne failed to gain his objective and the attempt cost him over six hundred casualties.

The American victory was chiefly owing to Arnold and the riflemen and militia he commanded; Gates was too wedded to defensive tactics to win a spectacular triumph of this sort over the British. This incident helped precipitate an open break between the commanding general and his headstrong subordinate. Arnold complained that Gates treated him like "a Cypher in the Army," that he was "never consulted, or acquainted with one occurrence," and was "often huffed in such a manner as must mortify a Person with less Pride than I have & in my Station in the Army." Convinced that Gates would always steal from him the glory of victory and that he could expect only insult and humiliation at his hands, Arnold threw up his commission and announced his intention of joining Washington. Nevertheless, he hung about camp, unable to drag himself away from the battle that he knew impended. As a result, Arnold was on hand but without command when Burgoyne made his last effort to break out of the ring of steel the Americans were forging around him.

The battle of Freeman's Farm (September 19, 1777) was not calculated to make Burgoyne yearn for another meeting with the rebels: although he had asked for nothing more than to encounter them in fair fight, he had hardly anticipated such rough treatment. As a British officer said, "the courage and obstinacy with which the Americans fought were the astonishment of every one, and we now become fully convinced, they are not that contemptible enemy we had hitherto imagined them, incapable of standing a regular engagement, and that they would only fight behind strong and powerful works." Still, Burgoyne had no alternative — unless it were to retreat — except to make his way to Albany. Under these circumstances, it is hardly surprising that his breezy self-confidence evaporated and that, cut off from the outside world, he began to regard himself as the forgotten man of the British army. Increasingly, he turned for succor to the British forces in New York City, now his only hope of rescue.

Until fortune began to abandon him, Burgoyne had conceived of his expedition as a venture independent of the army of Sir William Howe. When he reached Albany, it is true, he was to place himself under Howe's orders; but meanwhile he held a separate command.[5] Indeed, it is probable that Burgoyne was averse to looking to Howe for aid; this was his hour on the stage and Burgoyne was resolved to make the most of it.

[5] What Howe and Burgoyne were to do after Burgoyne reached Albany, Germain never made clear; but by that time he may have expected that Washington's army would be beaten and dispersed and the rebellion virtually at an end.

Burgoyne was not left wholly in the dark as to Howe's plans. He knew that Howe intended to strike a blow at Pennsylvania, yet he offered no objections to Sir William's plans. Howe had left seven thousand troops in New York under the command of General Clinton with instructions to defend the city and, if it was necessary and compatible with the safety of the city, to aid Burgoyne by moving up the Hudson River. It was upon this force that Burgoyne's hopes were pinned.

It is indicative of Burgoyne's pride and obstinacy that it was not he but Sir Henry Clinton who first suggested that the Northern army might require direct assistance from the British forces in New York. Although Burgoyne had not specifically requested such aid, Clinton offered early in September, 1777, to attempt to penetrate the Hudson defenses; and after the battle of Freeman's Farm, Burgoyne answered that "an attempt or even the menace of an attempt would be *of use*." [6] Later, as the American noose began to tighten about his neck, Burgoyne urged Clinton to move to Albany; but Clinton, realizing his own weakness, answered that he could do little more than cover Burgoyne's retreat to Ticonderoga; to break through the Hudson River forts, penetrate to Albany, and maintain the line of communication was, he acknowledged, beyond his powers. With only about seven thousand troops, almost half of whom were provincials, few artillery, and orders from Howe to undertake no actions that might jeopardize the safety of New York, Clinton ate his heart out in vexation. "This is my hard fate," he exclaimed, "while others, my juniors, have most brilliant commands. I cannot, nor will I submit to it, let the consequence be what it will."

Despite this discouraging report from Sir Henry Clinton, Burgoyne refused to attempt a retreat to Canada — his orders, he insisted, precluded such a movement. Had he been left to his own discretion, Burgoyne later alleged, he would not have crossed the Hudson after Bennington and Fort Stanwix had revealed the hazards of his position, but Germain had left him no alternative except to advance. The expedition seems, indeed, to have been planned "by those who, writing in their closets, with a map before them, ridiculously expect the movements of an army to keep pace with their rapid ideas," and that nothing was said in Burgoyne's orders about retreating; yet it should be remembered that Burgoyne himself had helped to draw up those orders. The strictness of the injunction laid upon him to go to Albany was intended to make sure that he did not succumb to the temptation to go gallivanting into New England, not to compel him to march to his doom against his bet-

---

[6] One letter sent by Clinton to Burgoyne was enclosed in a small silver ball which the carrier, when apprehended by the Americans, promptly swallowed. He thereupon received a strong emetic "calculated to operate either way," but when he succeeded in concealing the ball again, the American commander "demanded the ball on pain of being hung up instantly and cut open to search for it. This brought it forth."

ter judgment. Burgoyne was too experienced a military man not to know that no orders are so peremptory as to leave no room for deviations if insurmountable obstacles are encountered. It is significant also that Germain, upon learning of Burgoyne's early reverses, expressed surprise that the general did not retreat; the Colonial Secretary clearly did not intend to bind Burgoyne to execute an impossible task. The fact is that, from the beginning almost to the end, Burgoyne was invincibly optimistic regarding the outcome of the expedition; failure was a possibility he refused to consider. Burgoyne's pride would not permit him to turn back; England expected him to crush the rebellion, and his troops were eager to force their way to Albany. "The English never lose ground," he exclaimed dramatically as the British troops crossed the Hudson. The British regulars died, but they never retreated. And, as he well knew, the Ministry and King showed no favor to generals who gave ground before rebels.

From the nineteenth of September to the eighth of October when the British began their final maneuvers, the two armies lay so close together that skirmishing and sniping were rarely broken off. Days and nights were filled with alarms and excursions; not for a moment could the redcoats relax. Constantly on the alert, sleeping in their clothes lest the rebels stage a night attack, the troops were worn down by fatigue and galled remorselessly by American fire.

Although his position seemed well-nigh hopeless, Burgoyne made one more effort to hew his way through the American lines. On October 7, 1777, at Bemis Heights, almost the identical battleground of the battle fought three weeks previously at Freeman's Farm, Burgoyne went over to the offensive. The battle swayed backward and forward, until Benedict Arnold, rushing unexpectedly onto the field, turned what had been intended by Gates to be a purely holding operation into a pitched battle by leading part of the American army in a headlong dash against the British lines. Arnold had no command, but his presence on the battlefield animated the American ranks and hundreds of men followed his wild charge. It is improbable that the outcome of the battle was determined by Arnold's reckless courage. Outnumbered three to one, their supplies almost exhausted, the British were driven back with heavy casualties. Burgoyne's second attempt to breach the American defenses had failed, and even the indomitable British commander now began to think of surrender.

Burgoyne was witnessing tragedy, not from a comfortable box in the theater, but amid the blood and grime of battle. The author of the farcical The Blockade of Boston was not likely to turn his talents for comedy toward writing The Blockade of Saratoga; and in the piece he was now playing, Burgoyne dreaded the cry of "Author! Author!" It was a tale of heroism against overwhelming odds; of men who had never before been beaten in battle, going down to death at the hands of an enemy they hated and despised. "Wounded officers, some upon crutches," related Burgoyne, "and others even carried upon hand-barrows by their servants, were occasionally ascending the field from the hospital tent, to take their share in the action." Meanwhile, the riflemen climbed high trees and from these vantage points picked off the officers. There was "seldom a minute's interval of smoke in any part of our line," said an officer, "without officers being taken off by single shot."

Desperately trying to keep up appearances to the end, Madame Riedesel, wife of the commander of the German troops, had invited some officers to dine with her one afternoon. But when the hour arrived, General Fraser, one of her guests, was carried in on a stretcher, mortally wounded. Her quarters were soon converted into a hospital. That night, recounted Madame Riedesel, "I could not go to sleep, as I had General Fraser and all the other gentlemen in my room, and was constantly afraid that my children would wake up and cry, and thus disturb the poor dying man, who often sent to beg my pardon for making me so much trouble." *Sic transit* the complete English gentleman.

The next day, during an incessant cannonade, General Fraser was buried on the fortifications. As the chaplain read the service he was covered with dust which the American cannon balls threw up on all sides of him. That night the British began to retreat.

The troops were too exhausted to go far; at Saratoga, a few miles from the scene of his last battle, Burgoyne came to the end of his journey. The rebels had almost completely surrounded his army; their artillery kept the British camp under constant fire; and provisions were almost exhausted. Burgoyne himself had spent sixteen days and nights without a change of clothes; his hat and waistcoat bore bullet holes; and on October 12, the day before he opened surrender negotiations, he was almost struck by a cannon ball. Nevertheless, there was still fight in this lionhearted Briton: if only the Americans would attack, he said, his men would make Gates pay dearly for having forced their backs to the wall. But Gates refused to accommodate Burgoyne by launching an attack; and Arnold, to whom the offensive was the heart and soul of war, was lying wounded in his tent.

Gates's strategy was to wear down the British by attrition rather than by sacrificing the lives of American soldiers in attack. Burgoyne, he believed, was securely trapped and sooner or later would be compelled by hunger to strike his colors. This cat-and-mouse game almost cost Gates his prey.

While Burgoyne was futilely seeking to hew his way through the enemy's cordon, the long-delayed relief expedition from New York was meeting with unexpected success. Obstructing the passage of British ships up the Hudson River were two forts, Fort Montgomery and Fort Clinton, on the same side of the Hudson. Across the river at this point were suspended a boom and chain which, together with the forts' guns, effectively blocked the river. However, the garrisons of these strong points had been so seriously weakened by Washington's withdrawal of two thousand troops as reinforcements for the main army, and by the anxiety of militiamen to go home to their families and crops, that only about six hundred soldiers, mostly militia, remained under General Putnam's command in the Highland forts when Sir Henry Clinton moved to the assault.

These defenses crumbled with surprising swiftness: within six days, Clinton had reduced all the rebel forts and the way to Albany was cleared for British men-of-war and transports. It was now possible to land troops within twenty miles of Burgoyne's position at Saratoga. The junction of the two armies — Burgoyne's last hope of escaping the trap into which he had fallen — thus became, at the eleventh hour, a distinct possibility.

The fall of the Hudson River forts struck Gates with consternation. Fearing that the British would soon be in Albany in force and his own troops squeezed between two enemy armies, Gates suspected that he, not Burgoyne, might be the victim of this defensive strategy.

From what we know today it is clear that Gates greatly exaggerated the threat to his army occasioned by Clinton's break-through on the lower Hudson. Clinton was in no position to take advantage of his good fortune. New York had been so thoroughly stripped of troops for the invasion of Pennsylvania that he could spare only two thousand men under General Vaughan for the dash up the Hudson. And no sooner had he seen Vaughan off for Albany than he received a letter from Howe asking that six thousand men be sent from New York to reinforce the army in Pennsylvania. But this order had no effect upon Clinton's operations: Burgoyne had already surrendered, and General Vaughan, upon learning Burgoyne's fate, burned Kingston and returned to New York. Even the Highland forts were abandoned to the rebels; and in his chagrin, Clinton swore that he would resign rather than serve longer under Sir William Howe.

Nevertheless, Clinton's abortive relief expedition played an important part in modifying the terms of Burgoyne's surrender. At first, Gates was disposed to demand unconditional surrender; but Burgoyne, emboldened by Clinton's initial success, swore that rather than submit to such humiliation "the British troops would rush upon the enemy, determined to give no quarter," and that he would "perish nobly, and leave his name unsullied to future ages." This threat Gates did not regard as wholly bravado: it was perfectly possible that the British general would decide "to risque all upon One Throw: he is an Old Gamester, & in his time has seen all chances."

Also, Gates's sympathies went out to Burgoyne and the brave men he led. Burgoyne he regarded as a gallant commander going down before great odds. "If courage, perseverance, and a faithful attachment to your Prince," he wrote to Burgoyne a little later, "could have prevailed, I might have been your prisoner." Gates was an Englishman who, although he had espoused the colonists' cause, had no wish to destroy Great Britain in the process of winning American independence. As an Englishman born, he still gloried in the name of England and felt keenly for it in its misfortunes; he had, he said, set out to punish his native land persuaded that "if Old England is not by this lesson taught humility, then she is an obstinate old slut, bent upon her ruin." He knew Englishmen too well to believe that the way to make them reasonable was to push them to desperation.

The upshot was that Burgoyne practically succeeded in writing his own terms of surrender. At his request, even the word "capitulation" was kept out of the instrument; instead, the surrender was officially designated as a "Treaty of Convention." Later, in Parliament, Burgoyne declared that the surrender at Saratoga was "a calamitous, it was an awful, but it was an honourable hour"; and he boasted that he had dictated terms to Gates while surrounded by an army four times as numerous as his own. If it was difficult for Englishmen to take pride in Burgoyne's military skill, they could at least praise his finesse in diplomacy.

As the British troops marched past the rebels, for the first time they had a good look at their conquerors. Few of the rebel soldiers, they noted, wore uniforms; but they were well armed with muskets, bayonets, and rifles. And they behaved like soldiers, erect and eyes straight ahead. "The people stood so still that we were greatly amazed," said a German officer. "Not one fellow made a motion as if to speak to his neighbor." There was, moreover, no sign of mockery or insult; in victory, the Americans had not ceased to respect a gallant enemy. "They seemed struck with our situation," remarked a British officer, "& dare scarce lift up their eyes to view British Troops in such a situation." Although the band struck up "Yankee Doodle" — a tune peculiarly grating to the ears of Britons — General Gates made amends for this affront by ordering his troops to remain in camp while the British piled up their arms. The American commander wished to spare the vanquished humiliation; when the time came for Burgoyne to surrender his sword, Gates generously remarked: "I shall always be ready to testify that it has not been through any fault of your excellency."

After the ceremonies, Gates and Burgoyne sat down to dinner together. The British general appeared to be in excellent humor; he ate and drank with good appetite, talked a great deal, and proposed a toast to General Washington — and Gates returned the favor by drinking a health to the King of England. Thus the two generals — the victor and the vanquished — put the war behind them and shook hands over a bottle of Madeira.

Among the prisoners taken at Saratoga were many distinguished Britons — the roster of titles made it appear that not an inconsiderable part of the British aristocracy had fallen into the rebels' hands. About a dozen members of Parliament, English and Scottish lords, knights, and ladies were among the spoils of victory; and not least among them was Sir John Burgoyne himself, who seemed to have more offices and titles "than any gentleman on this side of the Ganges." There was Lady Harriet Ackland — wife of the alcoholic peer — whom Gates declared to be "the most amiable, delicate little piece of quality you ever beheld." As for Lord Ackland, although devoted to his bottle and "a most confounded Tory," Gates pronounced him to be "one of the prettiest fellows I have seen." The American commander hoped to convert the bibulous lord to Whiggery before they parted; he said nothing, perhaps wisely, about winning him to temperance.

After the surrender formalities had been completed, Burgoyne's army marched from Saratoga to Boston, the "damned curious" Yankees lining the roads to see the fallen pride of Britain. "The greater the rank, the longer and more attentively one was looked at," remarked an officer; ". . . I almost believe our host charged admission." The inhabitants eagerly exchanged Continental paper money for English hard money: barrels of paper money were rushed to every stopping place of the British army, and the money-changers did a land-office business. Financially speaking, for the British it was another Saratoga: they were outsmarted as well as outfought by the Yankees. By the time they reached Boston, their pockets were a great deal lighter than when they had first fallen into the hands of the New Englanders.

By the provisions of the Saratoga Convention — as the instrument of surrender was called — the troops under Burgoyne's command, instead of being held as prisoners of war, were allowed to return to Great Britain under a promise not to serve again in North America. They were at perfect liberty to serve anywhere else, however, and against any enemy other than the United States; and there was nothing to prevent the British from using these troops as replacements for men sent overseas to fight against the Americans.

At first, in the joy of victory, few Americans caviled at the provisions of the Saratoga Convention; Congress, in awarding a gold medal to Gates, declared that the surrender was made "upon terms honourable and advantageous to these states." But when the Saratoga Convention came to be more closely scrutinized, it was seen that loopholes had been left through which the British might escape the worst consequences of their defeat. Henry Laurens, President of Congress, after scanning the terms of surrender, remarked that Gates had been "too polite to make the Lieutt. General [Burgoyne] and his Troops Prisoners at discretion," owing perhaps to his being "a little captivated by the flattery of a British Lieutt. General." Moreover, Americans had no binding assurance that the terms of the convention would not be broken by the enemy; it was well known that British officers had frequently declared that "there is no faith to be kept with Rebels." For this reason, some congressmen suspected that Howe did not intend to honor the convention: once Burgoyne's troops were at sea, they would be returned to New York and equipped to take the field against the Americans and, in answer to protests by Congress, Howe would reply that "everything is fair play with Rebels." It was not known until recently how right these suspicions had been — Howe actually planned to hi-jack the fleet carrying Burgoyne's troops to England and with them to reinforce the British army in New York.

Before this design could be carried out, Burgoyne himself gave the Continental Congress a pretext for breaking the convention. Declaring that public faith had been broken by the failure of the Massachusetts authorities to provide proper housing for his officers, Burgoyne found, much to his surprise, that Congress was ready to take him at his word and to pronounce the convention suspended. The embarkation of the troops was halted, and they were removed to Virginia for safekeeping.

But, as Washington said, they were "dangerous guests in the bowels of our Country," a burden to the Continental Congress and to the state upon which they were billeted. Gradually the number of Burgoyne's once powerful army was whittled down by desertion, death, and exchange until a mere remnant remained. In Virginia, for example, the officers and men fell to drinking peach brandy with spectacular effects: in the "absolute delirium" produced by this heady liquor, they attacked each other with swords, and one poor devil "fell a martyr to the dire effects of that pernicious liquor."

Burgoyne, however, was permitted to go home on parole — a liberality which worked wholly in the Americans' favor. In England, the defeated general bore eloquent witness to the fighting prowess of the Americans and became the storm center of a controversy that soon sprang up over the question of responsibility for the disaster at Saratoga. Burgoyne did his utmost to shatter that hardy myth that Americans could not fight. "The panic of the rebel troops is confined and of short duration," he told his countrymen; "their enthusiasm is extensive and permanent." Freely he confessed his error in disparaging American courage and skill in arms: the army which had brought about his downfall, he said, was "a better disciplined, more alert, and better prepared army in all essentials" than even the British army. And it was composed largely of New England militiamen!

⌒ ⌒ ⌒

Sir William Howe had again decided to seek a decisive battle with Washington and the Continental army — a battle which, in view of the untoward events in the North, was more imperative than ever before.

In particular, the British general was reluctant to conclude the campaign with a victory as dubious as that of Germantown. The American army which he had come to Pennsylvania to destroy was still in the field, and although the British were assured of comfortable winter quarters in Philadelphia, it hardly comported with the glory of a conquering army to shut itself in a city, leaving the country in possession of the enemy. Until the American army had been eliminated, Howe knew that he had achieved little; nor could he hope to persuade the Loyalists to declare themselves unequivocally in support of the King.

The American forts on the Delaware continued to bar passage to British shipping, giving Washington hope that the enemy could be starved out of Philadelphia.[7] Despite the combined attacks of the British sea and land forces, two forts — Fort Mifflin and Red Bank — stubbornly resisted. "'Twas a cursed little mud Island," said Cornwallis of Fort Mifflin, but its defense was one of the most heroic actions of the war. At Red Bank, on the Jersey side of the river, the Hessians were repulsed with heavy losses, and Count Donop, their commander, was killed. But finally, after a siege of almost two months during which they had held up the entire British fleet and part of Howe's army and denied the port of Philadelphia to British shipping, the forts were evacuated under direct fire from British floating batteries.

After the fall of the Delaware forts, the British position in Philadelphia seemed well-nigh impregnable. Nevertheless, Benedict Arnold urged an attack, on the ground that American honor required a do-or-die effort; and "Mad Anthony" Wayne advised Washington to lead his troops against the British lines lest his army be ruined by inactivity. And public opinion seemed to demand some high and desperate enterprise by the Continental army.

Washington, upon whom the mantle of Fabius rested uneasily, was spoiling for another try at Howe. His troops, having experienced the exhilarating sensation of driving British regulars before them, were eager for battle; and they swore that never again would the British get off as easily as at Germantown. "Tho' we gave away a complete victory," said an American soldier, "we have learned this valuable truth, that we are able to beat them by vigorous exertion, and that we are far supe-

---

[7] The forts were in serious need of reinforcements. As was his custom, Washington summoned a council of general officers to determine what steps ought to be taken; his own vote was for reinforcing the forts, but he was overruled by his council, much to the disgust of Anthony Wayne, who declared that these councils would be the ruin of the American cause inasmuch as they prevented Washington from "taking Advantage of the most Capital Strokes." When Washington finally determined to act against the advice of his council, it was too late.

rior in point of swiftness." Washington had other reasons, equally compelling, for seeking a return bout with Howe: shortages of clothing,
blankets, shoes, and money had begun to cripple the Continental army.
Because of his very weakness, Washington might be obliged to force
the fighting. Therefore, in November 1777, when he learned that Cornwallis had taken a large foraging party into New Jersey, Washington
began to feel out the defenses of Philadelphia, hopeful of finding a weak
spot. But he found no vulnerable point, Howe was on the alert, and
Cornwallis returned unexpectedly from New Jersey to reinforce the
garrison of Philadelphia.

After Gates's victory at Saratoga, Washington was on his mettle as
never before. The country expected him to do unto Howe as Gates
had served Burgoyne; and his troops could not bear to be outdone by
the Northern army. "They will never endure such disgrace," said Washington. It was generally supposed that Gates would march his army
southward to Pennsylvania and, joined with the main army, would drive
Howe back to his ships. Washington asked Gates for troops, sending
his aide-de-camp, Alexander Hamilton, to the headquarters of the "Saratoga Hero," but the disintegration of the Northern army after its victory at Saratoga put it beyond Gates's power to send more than a
handful of men to Pennsylvania.

As a result, Washington was compelled to choose between two courses:
"to fight the Enemy without the least Prospect of Success . . . or remain inactive & be subject to the Censures of an ignorant & impatient
populace." Although he was well aware that a menacing ground swell
of criticism had begun to manifest itself even in Congress against his
"Fabianism," Washington chose to be guided by military considerations rather than to permit himself to be high-pressured by a congressional group into a hazardous and perhaps hopeless attack upon Philadelphia. As one of his admirers remarked, "Washington was not the
man to throw caution to the winds, rush upon Philadelphia and be
catch'd like a d——d fool cooped up in the City."

Therefore, it remained for Howe to seek out Washington unless the
war was to end in stalemate. Hoping to wrest a last-minute victory from
the campaign in December 1777, Howe led his army out of Philadelphia to challenge the rebels to battle — the last time that Sir William
rode forth in the full panoply of war to ferret out the rebel leader. With
the deliberation that had become a settled habit, Howe approached
Washington's camp at Whitemarsh and sat down to study the ground.
After passing five days in this fashion, he marched back to Philadelphia.
"It was," said Thomas Paine, "a most contemptible affair. The threatening and seeming fury he set out with, and the haste and terror the army
retreated with, made it laughable." Instead of the decisive victory Howe

had hoped for, only the burning of several houses and the terrorizing of a few old women comprised the annals of his last expedition.

The Americans regretted to see Howe go: they had set their sights for another Bunker Hill, hoping that the British commander would revert to his earlier rashness. Undeniably, it was a tame ending to a promising encounter, and many of the troops were eager to pursue the enemy back to Philadelphia. But, happily, consolation (in liquid form) arrived opportunely at the American camp to ease the sting of disappointment. "We were more willing to Chase them in Rear, than meet such Sulky Dogs in Front," said a Continental soldier. "We were now remanded back with several draughts of Rum in our frozen bellies — which made us so glad we all fell a Sleep in our open huts — nor experienced the Coldness of the Night 'till we found ourselves much stiffened by it in the Morning."

Thus the campaign ended without Howe's having encompassed his objective of destroying Washington's army. The possession of comfortable winter quarters was meager compensation for having failed in his chief goal in coming to Pennsylvania. Howe did not deceive himself that the American army was whipped or that the war was over: he assured Germain that large reinforcements were necessary if the British expected to hold what they had gained. "A corps of ten thousand Russians, effective fighting men," he said, "might ensure the success of the war." Sir William was of the opinion that the Americans had just begun to fight.

CHAPTER XIII

Valley Forge

THE loss of Philadelphia was undoubtedly a heavy blow to the American cause, yet among the patriot leaders there was no sign of weakening of resolution. Indeed, in putting a good face upon this disaster, some patriots pictured the loss of Philadelphia as a positive advantage. Sam Adams exclaimed that the British were welcome to this "sink of Toryism"; and John Adams took comfort in the reflection that "this town has been a dead weight upon us. It would be a dead weight upon the enemy." These puritanical patriots found it easy to believe that the British troops would be so enervated by the soft life they led in Philadelphia that they would soon be rendered impotent for war. In this hopeful spirit, Benjamin Franklin observed that "instead of saying Sir William Howe had taken Philadelphia, it would be more proper to say, Philadelphia has taken Sir William Howe." And while British virility declined, Americans, it was expected, would become more vigorous and warlike. John Adams predicted that, bereft of Philadelphia, Americans would be cured of "their vicious and luxurious and effeminate appetites, passions, and habits, a more dangerous enemy to American liberty than Mr. Howe's army. . . . The spirit of economy would be more terrible to Great Britain than anything else, and would make us respectable in the eyes of all Europe." In any event, it seemed proper that Pennsylvanians should experience the horrors of war — "possibly Heaven permits it in vengeance for their defection," said a patriot.

After the abortive encounter at Whitemarsh the American commander was confronted with the problem of finding winter quarters for his army. Some of his generals advocated moving the troops into the interior of the country where supplies were plentiful and where there was no danger of attack from Howe. Disregarding these counsels of caution, Washington decided to take his position at Valley Forge, a small cluster of hills about twenty miles from Philadelphia.

As an encampment for the Continental army, Valley Forge was not without disadvantages. It was too near Philadelphia and the British army to be wholly secure; it was not situated in a rich farming section where forage and provisions could be easily procured; and Chester County, in which it lay, was notoriously disaffected to the American cause. Nevertheless in Washington's opinion, these unfavorable factors were outweighed by the advantages of remaining in the vicinity of Philadelphia. By taking his stand within twenty miles of Howe's army he would prove that there was still an American army in existence that did not fear to match its strength with the enemy. Moreover, he intended to hamper the British in their efforts to draw supplies from the country and to protect the Pennsylvania patriots from depredation. To withdraw the army into the interior might be construed as an abandonment of the cause; the lukewarm and the timid would go over to the enemy, and the entire eastern part of the country would be lost to Howe and the Tories.

The Continental army had seen something of the horrors of war; at Valley Forge it was to experience the miseries of inaction, attended by starvation, cold, and want of every necessity. Men were willing to fight and die for the American cause, but conditions at Valley Forge proved more than they had bargained for.

The soldiers were as ragged a group of scarecrows as ever graced a cornfield. Their baggage and knapsacks had been lost in the frequent moves made by the army; "and," added a soldier, "a great many have lost their clothes by the Whores and Rogues, that went with the Baggage." "Not one whole Shirt to a Brigade," reported Anthony Wayne from Valley Forge. "For God's sake if you can't give us anything else — give us linen that we may be Enabled to Rescue the poor Worthy fellows from the Vermin which are now Devouring them. . . . For God's sake procure a Quantity [of shirts] for me if you strip the Dutchman for them." Nine tenths of the deaths and desertions in the army were ascribed to dirt and nakedness. "Some hundreds we thought prudent to Deposit some six feet under Ground," said Wayne, "who have Died of a Disorder produced by a want of Clothing." "Covered with Rags and Crawling with Vermin," officers were no better off than privates. A French officer at Valley Forge observed men wrapped in blankets similar to those worn by patients in French hospitals; some of these men, he was informed, were generals.

It is not surprising that the British, viewing this ragged host, should have called it a "rabble in arms" and drawn the conclusion that only the scum of the country had taken up arms. Rags and tatters were the emblem of the American soldier; the most disreputable-looking member of the community might be its bravest defender. Virtually the only ill-clad white people in the United States were the soldiers; and it is safe to say that the Negro slaves on Southern plantations were no worse clothed, or housed, or fed.

Rations were so deplorably short that dinner sometimes consisted of one mouthful; and breakfast was merely a draught of cold water. Three ounces of meat and three pounds of flour were all the soldiers received for a week in March 1778. Rum and whiskey were virtually unobtainable — to the soldiers, the crowning misfortune. "Were Soldiers to have plenty of Food and Rum, I believe they would Storm Tophet," said a Continental officer; but with scant food and no liquor they languished into mere shadows of fighting men.

The country round Philadelphia was plucked clean of supplies by the two armies, Lancaster County suffering the worst depredations. Some farmers were even forced at the bayonet point to surrender the grain they had stored for seed. "I am ashamed to say it," said a famished private, "but I am tempted to steal Fowls if I could find them — or even a whole Hog — for I feel as if I could eat one." He was preserved from such wrongdoings, however, by the fact that the country had been so thoroughly ravaged that there was nothing left to steal.

Because of the shortage of teams, wagons, and drivers, transportation came to an almost complete standstill. Over fifteen hundred horses died at Valley Forge from starvation, forage being practically unobtainable. Detachments were sent out to impress wagons and teams but they usually returned empty-handed: the farmers became very skillful in concealing their property from redcoats and rebels alike. At the worst of the crisis, the teamsters went on strike: Congress had fixed their wages so low that they claimed they were losing money on every load. It was certainly true that for every thirty shillings paid by Congress, they could get fifty shillings from private employers. Furthermore, wagons, tools, and other government property had been so scattered over the country that it was said that "not an encampment, route of the army, or considerable road but abounds with wagons, left to the mercy of the weather, and the will of the inhabitants." A congressional committee later found that hundreds of wagons belonging to the government had been sent without authorization to New York and New England with flour and iron, and that private contractors made fortunes by this traffic. In consequence, there were no wagons available for the army. Pork was plentiful in New Jersey, and hundreds of barrels of flour awaited shipment on the wharves along the Susquehanna; but these desperately needed supplies never reached the starving men at Valley Forge.

For the privations it suffered, the army could blame the preoccupation of the people with their private concerns, the widespread distrust of Continental and state paper money, unwise price-fixing laws, the hard cash dispensed for provisions by the British army, the breakdown of transportation, and the resignation, because of alleged ill health, of General

Thomas Mifflin in November 1777 as quartermaster general of the Continental army.

Outside the region gleaned by the armies, life went on in the United States much as usual. Civilians declined to forgo their pleasures merely because the army was in want: at a ball at Lancaster, Pennsylvania, in January 1778, over one hundred ladies and gentlemen gathered in all their finery to enjoy a "cold collation with wine, punch, sweet cakes, &c. music, dancing, singing, &c.," which lasted until four o'clock in the morning. The music was provided by a band composed of Hessian prisoners, and among the guests was General Mifflin. A few days later, a brilliant ball was held at the home of Major Wertz of Lancaster, a gentleman who before the war had been a tailor. These civilian revels, it will be observed, took place a few miles from where the American army was encamped at Valley Forge.

The soldiers who huddled miserably in their huts could hardly fail to see that their sufferings were owing, in part at least, to the neglect and indifference of the people, who, as Anthony Wayne said, had become "so absorbed in Accumulating Wealth, that they have become totally Insensible to our Sufferings and Danger, and sunk into a torpid supineness."

A few examples will serve to illustrate why Valley Forge has become a symbol of American courage under adversity. During the winter of 1777–1778 there was ample wheat and flour in New York State, but practically all the surplus was exported to New England for civilian consumption and to Long Island for the use of the British army. The American army depended largely upon Connecticut for its meat; but Connecticut, about this time, imposed a price ceiling on beef, with the result that farmers declined to sell their cattle at fixed prices. Boston merchants refused to sell to the government clothing — of which they had ample stocks — except at prices representing a profit of 1000 to 1800 per cent, and they would not deliver the goods unless they received cash on the barrel head. As a congressman pointed out: "Though America abounds with provisions we cannot get sufficient for a few Thousand men without expending Millions in the purchase of it." And in all parts of the country, men were making fortunes by speculation, profiteering, and monopolizing. While the army experienced in the heart of Pennsylvania an ordeal that might have been visited upon a lost battalion cut off from all aid in some distant frontier outpost, the country was rolling in the prosperity begotten by easy money.

It made the blood of European officers boil to see how inconsiderately the American people treated their soldiers. To these foreigners, it seemed as though civilians accepted suffering and privation as the soldiers' lot, and with exemplary fortitude steeled themselves to endure the sight of a ragged and starving army. No other government than a republic, they remarked, would have inflicted such unnecessary suffering upon its defenders. A French officer, observing the domestic life of Americans, concluded that they spent most of their time at table; but he ascribed this fondness for food more to boredom than to appetite. "As they go out little in winter and spend whole days along side of their fires and their wives," he remarked, "without reading and without doing anything, going so often to table is a relief and a preventive of *ennui*." There was nothing like a succulent joint of mutton or roast of pork to keep up morale on the home front!

Civilian tours of Valley Forge might have shocked these complacent stay-at-home patriots into aiding the army. Lean, starving, wolfish, ragged men, living in wretched huts, the whole place "dirty & stinking" and conspicuously without sanitation — Valley Forge proved the adage more eloquently than many battlefields that war was hell. One soldier thus described his plight: "poor food — hard lodging — Cold Weather — fatigue — Nasty Cloaths — nasty Cookery — Vomit half my time — smoak'd out of my senses — the Devil's in it — I can't Endure it — Why are we sent here to starve and freeze . . . a pox on my bad luck." Anthony Wayne declared that though he did not love danger he would "chearfully agree to enter into Action every week in place of Visiting each hut of my Encampment (which is my Constant Practice) and where Objects strike my eye & ear — whose Wretched Condition beggars all Description." Indeed, Wayne said that he sometimes wished that he could neither see nor hear; and the sense of smell could hardly be regarded as a boon at Valley Forge.

It is fair to say that the state of the home front did more to undermine the morale of the soldiers than all the defeats administered by the British army. Most soldiers were confident of winning the war, but at Valley Forge they began to ask themselves the most disquieting question soldiers can ask: To what end victory? "I shall soon be no more!" exclaimed a dispirited veteran, "and all the reward I shall get will be — 'Poor Will is dead!'" But the shirkers, the profiteers, the war rich — they would be alive and would regale themselves with the fruits of the victory poor Will's sacrifice had made possible. "I know of no reason why one part of the community should sacrifice their all for the good of it, while the rest are filling their coffers," said another soldier; and it was not deemed a sufficient answer that this was the way of the world. In their letters home, the men gave vent to their longing and despair. "What sweet Felicities have I left at home," wrote one veteran; "a charming Wife — pretty Children — Good Beds — good food — good Cookery." But in the middle of these daydreams he was abruptly brought back to reality by the call to dinner, which consisted of a bowl of soup "full of burnt leaves and dirt."

Denied as they were many of the elementary necessities, American soldiers could still indulge to the full the luxury of griping. They complained bitterly, found fault with everything, and were, in their way, almost happy. They cursed the British, the Tories, and the folks at home who seemed utterly to have forgotten them — and their morale rose accordingly. Moreover, the men were learning that "nothing tends to the establishment of the firmest Friendship like Mutual Suffering" — which, from the amount of suffering in the American army, ought to have produced a thousand Damons and Pythiases.

Fortunately for the soldiers, nature proved kinder than their own countrymen. The winter was unusually mild and there was much less disease than might have been expected under the conditions prevailing in the American camp: far more men were unfit for duty because of lack of clothes and shoes than from actual sickness. There was plenty of firewood, although to get it to camp the men were obliged to hitch themselves to wagons, sloughing barelegged through mud and snow. And the men kept warm — at least on one side — by huddling around campfires.

For every man who stuck it out at Valley Forge, there were many others who, unable to endure the sufferings and privations of that testing ground of fortitude, deserted or refused to enlist when their term of service expired. In December 1777, for example, over two thousand men went home. Hundreds of officers tendered their resignations; on one day alone, fifty threw up their commissions. Resigning reached epidemical proportions, and for a time it seemed that the army would be left without officers, if, indeed, an army remained.

Rather than await the slow dissolution of his army, Washington was urged by some of his advisers to hurl his troops upon the British lines in Philadelphia in a sort of banzai charge. Washington himself was not averse to such a move if he could see the slightest prospect of success; his spectacular victories in the winter of 1776 encouraged him to think favorably of winter campaigns. To crush Howe's army before he could be reinforced — here was an opportunity, perhaps Washington's last, to turn the tables on Sir William. True, Washington needs must rely largely upon militia, and the enemy was strongly posted, but victory still seemed possible to Lafayette, who, with a keen eye for the weakness of the British army, urged that the Americans take the field "before the enemy will think of leaving the philadelphia girls, or be cured of the cruel cupid's wounds." But mighty as he knew Cupid's darts to be, Washington doubted whether, even with their aid, he could drive the invaders from Philadelphia. The American troops were too few to assume the offensive and they were shockingly lacking in arms, clothing, and provisions. Only a few thousand men were in condition to take the field — over three thousand men were reported unfit for duty because they did not have shoes or clothing. At one time during the spring of 1778 practically the whole army was immobilized because of smallpox inoculations; and frequently the troops were unable to attack British foraging parties because of fatigue and hunger.

The British invasion revealed that with good reason American patriots, long before the arrival of Sir William Howe and his army, had called the Middle states "the enemy's country." In Pennsylvania, a state containing almost three hundred thousand people, sixty-five thousand of whom were enrolled in the militia, less than three thousand militiamen joined Washington's army during the campaign of 1777. Although the Pennsylvania Line in the Continental army acquitted itself with honor, most of the citizens of the Quaker State preferred to quarrel over local politics or to wait the outcome before committing themselves in the struggle. As a whole, Pennsylvania badly let down the patriot cause. Washington declared that the people were "totally disaffected, or in a kind of Lethargy." New Englanders in Washington's army concluded that there was no hope for the American cause save in Yankees. "Such events would not have happened in New England," remarked Timothy Pickering of Massachusetts. "I rejoice that I can call *that* my country."

After the capture of Philadelphia, the near-by country seemed largely to have gone over to the British side: foraging parties went out twenty miles from the city without molestation; farmers trooped to market with supplies for the army; and the inhabitants freely took the oath of loyalty. In Delaware, where Tories and Whigs were evenly divided, the Loyalists now came to town on election day and began "drinking prosperity to king George, Damning the Whigs, and swearing there was not Rebels enough in Town to take them up." The British fleet in the Delaware was plentifully supplied with provisions by the inhabitants living along the river. As Washington said, the people were "only restrained from supplying the Enemy with Horses and every kind of necessary, thro fear of punishment"; and to that end he advocated making examples of some of the most notorious offenders. American troops patrolled the roads with orders to stop supplies from reaching the city, but they were either bribed to permit the wagons to pass or the countrypeople tipped off the British as to the whereabouts of these patrols — with the result that they were often taken by surprise and wiped out. The people were determined to sell their farm products to the British, and all Washington's horses and men could not prevent them. A committee of Congress finally recommended that Indians be used to break up this traffic, but it may be doubted if even redskins were equal to the task, although scalp-lifting might have had a salutary effect. The British appeared likely to want for nothing during their stay in Pennsylvania — at least, as long as they seemed to be winning the war and were in a position to pay cash for supplies.

It was chiefly the color of Englishmen's money that procured necessities for their armies in the United States. Rather than accept the dubious paper money of their own government, many Americans sold their products for hard cash to the British — while the patriot army went hungry. "Notwithstanding they are displeased with our Government, they are not so with our guineas," remarked an English officer in New England, "and although they are fighting for independency, they place very little dependence upon paper money; for however martial they are at present, still they have an eye to traffic and merchandize." "If any people worship money, it is the Americans," observed a German officer. The cult of the Almighty Dollar seemed already firmly established.

Despite this love of British pounds and guineas, Sir William Howe could not flatter himself that he had attained the Land of Tories. Comparatively few citizens were disposed to take up arms alongside the British troops: despite his best efforts to raise Loyalist corps, less than one thousand volunteers came forward during Howe's stay in the state. "They all prate & profess much," it was observed; "but, when you call upon them, they will *do* nothing"; and it was clear to the British commanders that "those who have neither spirit to defend rebellion, nor to oppose it, cannot be of much use to any party."

Nevertheless, during its stay in Philadelphia, the British army lived off the fat of the land and enjoyed a "frolicking winter." The winter that is memorable in the annals of the American army for heroic endurance was for the British army one of the easiest and most pleasant in its history. Flour sufficient for ten thousand men and large quantities of other provisions were brought every day to Philadelphia by the countrypeople. Indeed, a British officer complained that there were too many delicacies in the city "for the hardy deeds of a soldier."

But the war seemed far removed: gambling, drinking, balls, and gay parties flourished in the City of the Holy Experiment. The women of Philadelphia had awaited with some trepidation the arrival of the redcoats: stories of rape and violence had preceded their coming and the Philadelphia beauties knew not what to expect at their hands. These apprehensions quickly vanished; never before, said the ladies, had they seen such breeding and fine manners. The British officers devoted themselves to other conquests than those of the battlefield — and although many patriot ladies held aloof, the redcoats did not lack for female society. Rebecca Franks, one of the belles of the town, confided to a friend in the country: "You'd have an opportunity of rakeing as much as you choose either at Plays, Balls, Concerts or Assemblys. I've been but 3 evenings alone since we mov'd to town. I begin now to be almost tired."

Sir William Howe bore up well under the strain of Philadelphia night life. He lived in one of the principal mansions, drank his wine, enjoyed the favors of his mistress, and graced the balls, assemblies, and concerts with his presence. The British commander was a dull, heavy, saturnine man who, as is said to be the wont of Englishmen, took his pleasures sadly. There was hardly a glimmering of brilliance about him; "sullen gloom," it was observed, sat heavily upon him. But, in his way, Howe was not an unhappy man. General Lee said of him that "he shut his eyes, fought his battles, drank his bottle, had his little Whore"; and if this was not the sum of happiness, Howe hardly missed the so-called finer things. Compared with some of his fellow officers, Howe was an energetic and moral man. For example, General Robertson, the military governor of New York, although in his seventies, was said to be "waddling about town with a couple of young tits about twelve years of age under each arm . . . sighing, languishing, and bending at the shrine of such misses, and lavishing away the City funds upon every well-dressed little female."

By his example, it was alleged that Howe corrupted the British army. Certainly it is true that he did nothing to prevent the officers and men from finding what pleasures they could in the Quaker City. Sir William believed in letting his men enjoy themselves in the intervals between campaigns: a pleasure-loving man himself, he did not begrudge others their pleasures. Yet, to lovers of action, the spectacle of the British army taking its ease was hardly edifying. "Our officers," it was remarked, "were practising at the dice-box, or studying the chances of picquet, when they should have been storming towns, and crushing the spirit of rebellion; and the harlot's eye glistened with wanton pleasure at the general's table when the brightness of his sword should have reflected terror in the face of the rebels."

Certainly it is true that Howe permitted his sword to grow rusty in its scabbard. Despite his great superiority in manpower and matériel, he made no effort to dislodge Washington from his position. Sir William's fondness for resting upon his arms had now become settled habit and he seemed to have grown too old and heavy further to chase his quarry, now snug in his burrow at Valley Forge. As Howe knew, the Americans had transformed Valley Forge into a strongly defended camp bristling with redoubts, artillery emplacements, and trenches. At work upon these fortifications and their log huts, the American troops, said Thomas Paine, looked "like a family of beavers, every one busy; some carrying logs, others mud, and the rest plastering them together." Sir William Howe had no mind to disturb them.

Gossip ascribed Howe's lethargy to his affair with Mrs. Loring, an American lady whose complaisant husband seems to have regarded his wife's exaltation as mistress of the British commander-in-chief as a piece of unqualified good fortune. Like Antony, Howe was supposed to have surrendered himself to the charms of his Cleopatra. Yet, in actuality, Howe was rendered inactive in Philadelphia for very different reasons from the Egyptian fetters that bound Antony to the Nile.

Sir William was not in the toils of an adventuress: he was deliberately marking time until his request to be relieved of his command had been acted upon in London. To his successor, Howe intended to leave the problem of disposing of the American army, and the hardly more difficult task of getting on with Lord George Germain.

In the autumn of 1777 Howe decided that the time had come to retire from such an unpropitious struggle. He therefore asked to be relieved of his command, pointing out that because he did not enjoy the confidence and support of the government, it was impossible for him to carry on. Later he declared that he had resigned because of "a total disregard to his opinion. . . . The war had not been left to his management, and yet when he applied for instructions, he frequently could not get them." Realizing that he would be called to account for the disaster in America, Sir William was prepared to put the blame wholly upon the Ministry.

Howe's decision to come home was not unwelcome to the King and Ministry. George III complained that the British commander had failed to display the fury that ought to distinguish the British lion in attack. "To me," observed the King, "it has always appeared that there was more cruelty in protracting the war than in taking such Acts of vigour which must bring the crisis to the Shortest decision." Englishmen had been led to expect better things of their generals — were they not in command of spirited, well-equipped troops opposed by a "despicable, inconsiderable rabble," "a half-starved, half-naked, half-armed indisciplined mob"? Had not one British sergeant disarmed singlehanded a party of forty of these caitiffs and brought them back to camp in triumph? — a story which, although widely believed in Great Britain, reminded Franklin of the tale of the Irishman who captured five enemy soldiers by surrounding them.

Lord George Germain, who made the fatal mistake of believing his own propaganda about the Americans, found Howe's conduct of the war unfathomable. Even when he seemed to be winning the war, Howe's letters were stuffed with complaints and demands for more troops, and were pervaded by a pessimism which cast a pall upon Germain's spirits. The more victories Howe won, the more reinforcements he demanded and the less confident he seemed of the eventual outcome; his habit was to slur over his triumphs and to dwell at agonizing length upon his difficulties. From his letters, it was difficult to determine just who was winning the war — and every now and then a doubt seemed to intrude as to whether or not Great Britain ever could conquer the colonies. This, assuredly, said Germain, was not the strain in which a victorious general ought to write; and doubt grew upon him that Howe was the man to snuff out the American rebellion.

It is perhaps significant that there was little rejoicing in the American camp when it was learned that Howe had thrown up the command. Lafayette was saddened by the prospect of losing an enemy who had unwittingly done much service to the cause of American independence. "That gentleman," he said, "would be a great loss for america."

Sir Henry Clinton remarked that it would have been better for England if Howe had gone to the devil before he came to America, but despite his failure to crush the rebel army, Howe was more beloved by his men and officers than any other British commander during the American war except perhaps Cornwallis. Civilians, for the most part, failed to share this enthusiasm; but the men who served under Howe swore by him as an able general and withal a good fellow. Certainly, after Bunker Hill, he had never thrown away lives unnecessarily or exposed his men to undue hardship or risk. Therefore, the news that Howe had resigned his command and was going home brought sorrow to the British camp. Howe's admirers immediately resolved to give him a send-off that would vie with a Roman triumph. A fete or Mischisanza was held in Philadelphia to which seven hundred and fifty guests were invited, the ladies wearing Turkish trousers, much to the scandal of the Quakers. Fireworks, dancing, a regatta on the river, a tournament in which Knights of the White Rose jousted with Knights of the Burning Mountain to prove by dint of arms that their mistresses were the fairest in the world, a triumphal arch through which the Howe brothers passed with fifty-two ladies and officers, a banquet where Negro waiters were "fancifully habited, ranged in order, and performing the submissive Grand Salam as the Ladies passed by," a reception, and finally a ball — such was the Mischisanza with which Sir William Howe was sped on his way to England. The guests staggered home at six o'clock in the morning, vowing that it was the biggest thing that had ever hit Philadelphia.

There was only one fault with the Mischisanza — the British had nothing to celebrate. All this feasting, revelry, and playing at being knights and ladies struck a hollow note; instead of commemorating a victory, the Mischisanza proved to be the farewell appearance of the British army in Philadelphia. Orders had been sent to the British commanders to evacuate Philadelphia with all speed. A few weeks after the British officers had danced on the green and jousted for the honor of fair ladies, they were beating a retreat across New Jersey, and Philadelphia was once again the rebel capital.

⌢   ⌢   ⌢

The torments of Valley Forge proved to be the birth pangs, not the death struggles, of the Continental army. Valley Forge winnowed the grain from the chaff in the army; those who survived the threshing of that grim encampment were, said a Continental officer, "the most virtuous men living . . . brave, patient soldiers." These were the men who were willing to suffer and die for the cause in which they fervently believed — the men who hated British tyranny and who had caught a vision of the greatness that lay in store for the American republic. Nothing could equal their sufferings unless it was the fortitude with which they endured them.

To Valley Forge came General von Steuben, one of the best drill-masters the American army ever had. When the troops broke camp at Valley Forge in the spring of 1778 they were, thanks to Steuben, disciplined, organized, and trained along the lines of the most advanced military practices of the time. In fact, the American army which emerged from Valley Forge was, in point of training and discipline, almost the equal of the British army itself.

General von Steuben, whose baton wrought this reformation, was an able officer in the Prussian army who succeeded in passing himself off among Americans as a comrade in arms of Frederick the Great, the reigning military master of the day. Coloring the facts freely, he claimed to have been lieutenant general, quartermaster general, and aide-de-camp to Frederick himself; and he adroitly encouraged the rumor that he had been sent by his master to serve with the Americans. All this might seem to be the build-up for a mercenary who hoped to make a good thing out of the American Revolution; but Steuben was no ordinary military fortune hunter. He came to the United States as a volunteer and he asked for no reward until he had proved his worth to the American army. Congress had rarely encountered such modesty in a foreign officer, and the delegates were charmed by this high-ranking German who asked so little and offered so much in return. Accepting his qualifications at Steuben's own valuation, Congress appointed him adjutant general of the army and sent him to Valley Forge to begin his duties.

A quick look at the American army convinced Steuben that the task he had undertaken would baffle the great Frederick himself. He had never seen an army like Washington's, nor had he ever dealt with men like American soldiers. Ragged and hungry, crouching around their camp-fires or sprawled in their huts, the Americans bore little resemblance to the kind of soldiers Steuben was accustomed to command; and it would not have been surprising if he at first doubted whether these men could ever be made the equal of British regulars. He saw immediately that if the army was to be whipped into shape, it would be necessary to start from fundamentals — everything, he said, was wrong. Yet he recognized that undiluted Prussian methods would never do for this army: Americans were fond of British ways — they dearly wanted to be like redcoats and were not at all inclined to be Prussians. In the Prussian army, officers said to a soldier " 'Do this,' and he does it, but I," said Steuben, "I am obliged to say, 'This is the reason why you ought to do that,' and then he does it." And so he wisely refrained from introducing the Prussian system of drill, tactics, maneuvers, and discipline into the army. "I would have been pelted," he observed, "had I attempted it, and should inevitably have failed." Instead, he patiently overlooked many irregularities in the rebel army, took Americans as they were, and sought to fashion an efficient fighting machine out of the materials at hand.

Steuben was a hard-driving, irascible officer who, knowing little English, pieced out his ignorance of the language with frequent interjections of profanity. He later claimed that he owed his success to the earsplitting "God damns" he thundered at the men. On their part, the soldiers took Steuben — tantrums, broken English, curses, and all — with good humor and knuckled down to learn what he had to teach. Steuben became one of the most popular officers in the army; he was a slave driver but at the same time he was eminently a good fellow and more democratic in his ways than many American officers.

Steuben's chief criticism of Washington's handling of the army was that the troops had been taught to parade to the neglect of military fundamentals. Accordingly, Steuben taught them to march properly, to wield their bayonets, to break ranks, and to advance to the charge. He drilled the men personally, "exerting himself like a lieutenant anxious for promotion"; and he compiled a manual which was printed for the use of the army. In this way the methods of drill used in the American army were standardized and for the first time the various state lines that made up the Continental army followed uniform practices.

With the advent of spring, conditions at Valley Forge underwent marked improvement. Clothing continued scanty — as late as April 1778, Wayne declared that over one third of his men had "no kind of Shirt under Heaven" — but food became more plentiful. In March, Congress appointed General Nathanael Greene quartermaster general and undertook the reorganization of the commissary department. For the first time in many months, the officers and men began to experience some of the amenities of life. A female contingent descended upon Valley Forge: Mrs. Washington, Mrs. Nathanael Greene, Lady Stirling (wife of Lord Stirling) and her daughter Lady Kitty Alexander, Mrs. Biddle (wife of Colonel Clement Biddle of Philadelphia), and many others of less celebrity brightened considerably the scene at Valley Forge. The ladies gave frequent parties, but a strict prohibition was laid upon balls, dancing, and card playing. At first, singing was the only entertainment approved, but later a theater was opened, with officers playing both male and female roles. *Cato* was given "before a very numerous & splendid audience" and it was planned to present such favorites as *The Fair Penitent* and *The Recruiting Officer*, but these performances were called off when the British unexpectedly abandoned Philadelphia. General Steuben, who affectionately called the American troops "Sans Culottes," gave a Hard Times Party to which no one was admitted wearing a whole pair of breeches. The party was well attended — hardly the case had he insisted upon making a whole pair of breeches a passport to the affair — and the ragged, merry fellows spent half the night drinking and feasting "sumptuously on tough beef-stakes, and potatoes, with hickory nuts for dessert."

CHAPTER XIV

❊

The Conway Cabal

F OR Washington, the winter of Valley Forge was in many ways the most harrowing period of the war. From these bleak heights, he beheld his army on the point of scattering to the winds, the patriotism of the people gravely impaired, and his leadership of the army jeopardized by the intrigues of his enemies at home. It is significant that Washington was now more preoccupied and distressed by the backslidings of the home front than by the menace of the British army — a state of affairs that was to endure for the rest of the war.

In the American colonies, Englishmen's traditional dislike of regular armies had been intensified by the struggle for liberty waged with the home government. From 1765 to 1775, the colonists were in a ferment over the dread of military power with which, it was feared, the mother country intended to enforce its tyranny. In Boston, on each anniversary of the Boston Massacre, a public oration was delivered upon the iniquity of standing armies, with special reference to the British standing army that had spilled the blood of American patriots.

Americans carried over into the War of Independence much of the fear of a regular army engendered by their experiences as British subjects. It was upon an "inspired yeomanry," embodied in militia, that many patriots at first depended to defeat the British army. Even after its inadequacies had been exposed they clung to the militia as the sheet anchor of their faith that free people were the best defenders of liberty and that to create a regular army was to place in jeopardy the very liberties it was called upon to protect. The militia was often identified with democracy. "The Militia," said a patriot, "is the fundamental line of every well constituted Government." Freedom was not secure unless every citizen was a soldier and every soldier a citizen. Victory with such an army was certain. "It is impiety," exclaimed a patriot, "to believe that a freeman thus animated can ever be conquered."

In most of the colonies, the militia was established upon the English model. Theoretically this system made every able-bodied citizen a soldier; it ought, therefore, to have provided approximately a half-million Americans with basic military training. Unfortunately for the patriot cause, however, the militia had been allowed to deteriorate until, by 1774, muster days were spent chiefly in a show of parading on the village green and much drinking in the village tavern. To their grievous disappointment, those who expected to learn the art of war in the militia found that they were "left to burn powder to no purpose; to march without order; to be the spectators of an untimely feast; and to return home, without acquiring any other knowledge than that which arose from seeing the near resemblance between a general-muster and a riot." There were many thousand colonists who, contrary to the legend which makes every American a sharpshooter, did not know how to shoot and did not own a gun. Rhode Island, for example, protected by Connecticut and Massachusetts from Indian forays, had completely neglected its militia, even to the point of disposing of its weapons.

Nor did the militia necessarily consist of the freedom-loving yeomanry of the country. By law it was provided that a man called up for militia service might procure a substitute — with the result that well-to-do colonists often shirked active duty and hired someone to take their places in the ranks. This tended to make the militia a poor man's club. The Pennsylvania militia, said one of their commanders, were "some of the most rude, turbulent, impudent, lazy, dirty fellows" he had ever seen. Many officers felt that way about their men, particularly after a day spent in trying to teach them how to march and shoulder arms properly. Thus the substitute system impaired the militia in its most democratic aspect, the obligation to universal military service.

In some states, the only penalty for refusing service in the militia was a fine — which many gladly paid in preference to the hardships and dangers of active duty. There was excellent prospect, moreover, of escaping even a fine; the state governments were so weak that they hesitated to deal sternly with recalcitrant citizens. "I cannot make our Assembly sensible of the Importance of an effectual Militia Law," said the governor of New Jersey, " — or, if they be, they are so unduly influenced by the Fear of disobliging their Constituents, that they do not exert themselves with the requisite Spirit for the Exigencies of War."

With the waning of popular enthusiasm for the war, substituting became almost a recognized profession; and if substitutes could not be called professional soldiers, they at least made a profession of carrying guns on their shoulders and drawing soldiers' bounty and pay. Fighting, however, was something else again: substitutes generally made sorry soldiers. "They know if they can keep out of harm's way for a few months," it was observed of them, "they will be at liberty to retire or to renew their bargain. They know, that if called to answer for their conduct, they will be tried by laws milder than mercy and by men who judge with a gentleness incompatible with the welfare of an army." Under these circumstances, it was not unusual for a substitute to jump from bounty to bounty until, having accumulated a sizable nest egg, he was ready to go west. As the war went on, however, substitutes began to raise their prices, until the high price of substitutes became one of the grievances of American freemen — only the well-to-do, it was said, could afford to hire men to fight for them.[1]

Washington saw that this system was likely to bring ruin upon the American cause. "Every injurious distinction between the Rich and the Poor ought to be laid aside now," he declared, and service made equally obligatory upon all. By abolishing substitution, he said, "a number of idle, mercenary fellows would be thrown out of employment, precluded from their excessive wages, as substitutes for a few weeks or months; and constrained to enlist in the Continental army" — all of which would be to the advantage of the war effort. At his urging, many states resorted to drafting the militia to fill the ranks of the Continental army, but substitution continued and the wealthy were still able to dodge the draft.

Although the militia did not conspicuously exemplify the military virtues, it gave notable expression to the democratic inclinations of the colonists. Strongly disposed not to obey but to reason why, the militiamen carried democracy to such lengths that privates sometimes insisted upon judging the propriety of the orders they were given, declining to act "till the *necessity* for it *strikes* them." This was a citizens' army in which the soldiers had not surrendered the liberties of citizens.

The malady that exacted the greatest toll among militiamen was homesickness. Americans seemed to be a nation of home-lovers; certainly "that terrible disorder, the homesickness" which could be cured only by prolonged exposure to the comforts of home, played havoc with military efficiency during the Revolutionary War. Having perhaps smelled powder and seen action which, properly embellished, would make a good story at home, men were irresistibly drawn to their families.

Often it was more than homesickness that sent militiamen over the hill: the stay-at-home patriots were making money and gobbling up the busi-

---

[1] The life of the militiamen had its full share of privations and dangers. Although looked down upon by the Continental army as fair-weather soldiers, the militia sometimes had good cause for their anomalous behavior: without a commissariat, they were obliged to choose between deserting and starving; they had no shoes or clothing; and if they fled from battle, it ought to be remembered that they had slow-loading muskets without bayonets and were, therefore, easy victims of British regulars in hand-to-hand combat.

nesses of those who patriotically served the cause. There was, for example, little enthusiasm on the part of the Philadelphia militia to turn out in the autumn of 1777, because many who had taken part in the battle of Trenton and the campaign in New Jersey "found their business and customers so deranged on their return, and engrossed by those who staid at home," that they had no wish to repeat the experience.

The rapid turnover of the militia made army headquarters "a constant shifting Scene of Comers & goers": the actors tarried for only a brief moment before moving off stage to give the newcomers an opportunity to strut their hour. Always there was a vast discrepancy between the paper strength of Washington's army and the actual number of ablebodied men he could put into battle. At Valley Forge, for example, the army drew thirty-two thousand rations, whereas the most that could be mustered for duty was seventy-five hundred men, proving how conservative was General Nathanael Greene's estimate that "in all irregular armies there will be generally a third more rations drawn than is in a well-appointed one."

Amidst this swirling tide of human traffic, Washington remained at his post, although he confessed that he was "wearied almost to death with the retrograde motion of things" and that he would not undergo what he suffered for one hundred thousand dollars a year.

Washington's fortitude almost deserted him when dealing with militia; "the Vexation I have experienced from the Humours and intolerable Caprice of Militia, at a critical time," he said, made him pity any officer who had to command them. "I solemnly declare," said Washington in 1780, "I never was witness to a single instance that can countenance an opinion of Militia or raw troops being fit for the real business of fighting." Preparation for that business, he never ceased to point out, was to be attained only by constant and unremitting discipline and service. Among the militia, said a Continental officer, "there was no more regulation . . . than among a flock of Bullocks." So lax, indeed, was their discipline that Washington disliked to bring them into close contact with regular troops lest their disorder prove contagious. The militia in numerous instances ran away from the battlefield — not with any intention of fighting another day, but simply to save their skins. A general who fell from his horse during an action was taken prisoner when the militia he commanded took to its heels upon seeing his plight.

Most of their execution, it was lamented, was done at table. "They eat up the colonies," groaned an officer as he surveyed the havoc they had wrought among his stores. Some officers doubted if these recruits were worth their salt: among the militia there were numerous graybeards and young boys whose tender constitutions broke down under the fatigue of camp life and had to be invalided home. In consequence, officers sometimes found themselves obliged to act as wet nurses to these striplings and, at the same time, to minister to the endless complaints of valetudinarians.

To rely upon such untrustworthy, undisciplined, and battle-shy troops as were the militia was to Washington's mind to court disaster: they were "useless Hands and Mouths . . . who are here today, and gone tomorrow; whose ways *like the ways of Providence*, are, almost, inscrutable." Indeed, the commander-in-chief was moved to unwonted eloquence when enlarging upon the deficiencies of the militia: "They come in you cannot tell how, go, you cannot tell when, and act, you cannot tell where, consume your Provisions, exhaust your Stores, and leave you at last in a critical moment." From which he concluded that there was no salvation for Americans short of raising a regular army enlisted for the war.

Admitting these shortcomings, it is nevertheless true that Washington could not have taken the field without militia. Failing an adequate body of regular troops, he found himself dependent upon militia; the Continental army was never sufficiently strong in itself to meet the enemy. Moreover, militia were useful in mounting guard, patrolling the roads, laboring behind the lines, suppressing the Tories, and skirmishing with the enemy. A Hessian officer said that these embattled farmers were "the worst, and most dangerous spies, they betray and frustrate the actions of our spies; they attack our patrols and detachments, they keep our outposts in constant alarm and when we are gone, they harass and cruelly maltreat their neighbours, who are Loyalists." The militia were the only troops that could be drawn upon in an emergency; and particularly in the Southern states, they formed the nucleus of resistance to the enemy. General Steuben acknowledged that it was from the militia that the country was compelled to draw its strength. "Our business is," he observed, ". . . to find out the means of rendering the Militia capable to supply the want of a well regulated Standing Army, at least as much as lies in our power." And it must be confessed that however weak the militia might be, the British often succeeded in making it formidable. "The enemy never have been long in any of the States," said a patriot, "before the militia became gallant warriors, and were soon a dread and terror to them."

Battle-wise generals soon learned how to use militia effectively. It was fatal to depend upon them to bear the brunt of fighting, but they might be employed to good purpose in holding quiet sectors of the line or in absorbing the first shock of the enemy's attack. Anthony Wayne remarked that the utmost that could be expected from militia was three volleys; other generals accounted themselves fortunate if the militia fired one good volley before making tracks for home.

During the Revolutionary War, the states devoted at least as much effort to building up their militias as to strengthening the Continental army. Militiamen were under the control of the state: only when serving in conjunction with the Continental army were they compelled to obey the orders of Continental officers. Since no state was willing to entrust its defense wholly to the Continental army and some were prone to regard the militia as the state's principal defense, it is not surprising that the states began to pay higher bounties for service in the militia than for volunteering in the Continental army. In effect, this practice almost put a stop to enlistments in the Continental army, for few engaged to serve three years or for the duration of the war when by volunteering to serve in the militia for a few months they received a bigger bounty and higher pay. A French officer observed that these militia laws seemed admirably designed to destroy the American cause; "Lord North," he said, "could not have managed it better."

Keen rivalry existed between the Continental army and the militia, and each had its champions in Congress and in the state governments. Every victory won by the militia alarmed the friends of the Continental army lest reliance upon the irregulars be thereby encouraged. Trenton was in part a triumph of militiamen (the Philadelphia militia playing a particularly important part) and after the battle the proponents of militia sang its praises so loudly that fear was expressed by a French officer that the victory had done more harm than good inasmuch as it tended to foster the view that a regular army was unnecessary. He ascribed the outcome of the battle entirely to surprise — and, he observed, "Women and Children are as good in a surprise as men." Likewise, Saratoga was hailed as a victory of militiamen over regulars and inspired some patriots to exclaim that "if there was not a single regular soldier with our immortal General Washington, the substantial militia of the country are fully adequate to the defence of this country."

To these patriots, a potential dictator lurked in the uniform of every Continental general; they lived in dread lest the war "kindle the fatal ambition of some Cromwell, that would otherwise have slept guiltless of his country's ruin." In this vein, John Adams warned his countrymen that their salvation depended upon keeping "a watchful eye over the army, to see that it does not ravish from them that liberty for which all have been contending."

So deep-rooted was suspicion, that even the appeals of the soldiers for relief were sometimes looked upon askance. The Pennsylvania Council, for instance, declined to heed the requests for clothing of the officers of the Pennsylvania Line, then stationed at Valley Forge, on the ground that they aspired to lord it over civilians and strut about in "Fine beaver Hats, Gold Laced Hats, Silken Stockings, fine Cambrick, and other expensive Articles of Dress." Actually, the shivering officers would have gladly settled for a warm suit of homespun had it been offered them. Instead of supplying the needs of the officers, the Pennsylvania Council contented itself with recommending patience and frugality and with holding out the promise that steps would be taken "for covering the naked part of the Army."

Much of this fear of military tyranny was a reflection of a quite natural reluctance on the part of the civilian leaders of the Revolution to take a back seat while the generals assumed control. The American Revolution was the work of civilians; it was they who had laid the foundations of the American union, had organized resistance to British authority, and had assumed the leadership of the American people. Now, the Revolution having passed from the stage of constitutional argument to that of armed conflict, their leadership was jeopardized by the emergence of a new class of men, the military leaders. Many of these new heroes of the American people had scarcely been heard of during the earlier dispute with the mother country; nevertheless, they now threatened to cast into obscurity the "heroes of '74." "What has been often called a laudable Jealousy of military power," remarked an acute observer of the congressional scene, "if prob'd to the Bottom, would be found a real Rivalship in Fame." The same men who had made the Revolution aspired to direct the war against Great Britain — and they persuaded themselves that the liberties of the country were safe only when in their hands. Some sought to take active command in the army. Patrick Henry, although inexperienced in military matters, set his heart upon a high post. In February 1776, when Congress failed to make him a general, he resigned in a huff his commission as head of the Virginia troops; whereupon the soldiers "assembled in a tumultuous manner and demanded their discharge, and declaring their unwillingness to serve under any other commander." It required all Henry's oratory to prevent the soldiers from packing up for home.

Since it could not actively direct the operations of the army in the field, the Continental Congress insisted strenuously upon its superiority in point of authority and dignity over the army. Far from being content merely to enjoy theoretical superiority over the military power, Congress took upon itself the organization of the army and the determination of strategy. It drew up regulations for the armed forces, determined the number and terms of enlistment of the troops, appointed commanders to the various fronts, and dictated their strategy. In 1776, for example, Congress insisted upon the defense of New York; and in 1777 it ordered that a special corps be created for the defense of Philadelphia. Jealous of the power of the commissary general and quartermaster general to appoint and remove subordinates, Congress appropriated the authority; whereupon these officers resigned, leaving Congress to wrestle for years with the problem of finding able successors. Likewise, Congress arrogated the right of appointing and promoting officers in the higher ranks. It was urged that appointments be made upon the recommendation of Washington and his staff; but, except for the brief grant of dictatorial power to the commander-in-chief in 1776–1777, Congress kept this right tenaciously in its own hands. Dr. Witherspoon, President of Princeton College, who had become a delegate to the Continental Congress, drew upon his rich store of experience as a schoolmaster to clinch the case against the generals. "I once left the honors of the college over which I preside to the choice of the senior class," he recalled. "But it produced so much confusion and ill Blood, that I was obliged to resume that power again." Apparently no one dared the wrath of this don by pointing out that the generals were not Princeton seniors.

John Adams would have gone further than Dr. Witherspoon in putting the generals in their place: true democratic principles required, to Adams's way of thinking, that the generals be elected annually by Congress. By this means, he said, the army would be kept clear of deadwood, generals would be taught that they were the servants of Congress, and a "Spirit of Enterprize" would be infused into men who knew that they were shortly coming up for election. Adams even opposed giving Washington permission to appoint his own quartermaster general and commissary general because these officers ought, according to Adams, to be a check upon the authority of the commander-in-chief. Although Adams's plan failed of adoption, the debate made clear that most members were convinced of the necessity of keeping a tight rein upon the generals lest Congress find itself bound to the chariot of some Caesar.

By reserving unto itself the privilege of making appointments, Congress obliged officers to look to Philadelphia for preferment. If a general were to be secure in his post, he could hardly dispense with a following in Congress. Cultivating the good will of the legislature was a recognized form of protection. This resulted in frequent complaints that officers were promoted who had done no more than "modestly trumpet their own Praise to Congress"; a short residence in Philadelphia spent in hobnobbing with the right people was sometimes more rewarding than service in the field. The "whimsical favoritism" displayed by Congress in appointments and promotions, and particularly the "absurd prodigality of rank to foreigners," disgusted many officers. Congress, they complained, was "bullied by every petty rascal who comes armed with ostentatious pretensions of military merit and experience." General Knox ascribed this condition "to no other cause than a disinclination to say, no."

Congress sought to implement its control of the army by dispatching committees of members of Congress to headquarters. Through this system — essentially the same as that of the political commissars of Soviet Russia — the wishes of Congress regarding military strategy were conveyed to the army, the troops were inspected, and the ability and ideas of the generals were brought under scrutiny. When the committees returned from camp infected with army notions, as sometimes happened, their recommendations were unceremoniously thrown out.

Congress was extremely sensitive to any slights or aspersions cast upon its authority by the army. When, in 1776, an officer "grossly abused the President and damned Him and the Congress" he was summarily stripped of his commission and ordered to appear before Congress to answer for his words. When a captain of a Continental frigate wrote an insulting letter to the governor of Maryland, almost every member of Congress, it was observed, seemed "to feel his own State injured in this insult, and . . . determined that nothing less should do, than what would satisfy Maryland, and convince officers that they were very inferior to the magistrates of States, and must treat them with the most profound respect." Sam Adams insisted that in all patriotic toasts Congress must take precedence over the army; to drink to the army before emptying a bumper in honor of Congress was enough to bring one under suspicion of being a favorer of military dictatorship.[2]

At all times, the states dedicated themselves to shielding citizens from the exactions of the military; civilian rights were sacred and the citizen came before the soldier. Even the temporary abeyance of civil government was dreaded: behind the soldier stood the despot and, let the door be opened ever so slightly, he would force his way into the temple of liberty. Impressment of supplies — often the only means of saving the army from want — was opposed by state leaders; the troops might go hungry but civilian rights must be preserved inviolate. In 1781, for example, Pennsylvania resisted efforts by Congress to impress wagons in the state for the use of the Continental army, on the ground that the people of Pennsylvania were "sovereign, free and independent" and superior to any power upon earth.

Congress undertook to direct the army without fear — and often without military knowledge. As the war progressed, the inability of Congress to do more than exercise general supervision over the war effort became increasingly apparent. The statesmen in Philadelphia were incapable of properly attending to every detail of military business, and in attempting to do so they invited disaster. So engrossed were they in other matters — finance, diplomacy, and the like — that General Schuyler's letters were left unanswered for five months. Complaining of the silence of Congress, Anthony Wayne asked if the members "have commenced wine bibbers, & forgot that there are troops in the field and Gentlemen who

[2] The difficulties to which this fear of military power gave rise are well illustrated by the experiences encountered by a small body of Continental troops on their march through New England in 1779. "We had to combat their civil authority," reported the commander of this outfit, "which consists of their Clergy with their Selectmen & Magistrates, and so jealous were they of their rights, that they Imagine them continually infringed upon — they always insisted on Seeing the Colonel's orders, and had the Impudence to demand his private instructions from the Commander in Chief, which he prudently refused — they indeed once threatened to turn out their Militia to chastise us, but they thought proper to retract their threats, when I informed them that we had nothing to fear."

have some right to hear from them." Having few or no members who could pretend to military knowledge, Congress often ventured far beyond its depth. Nevertheless, instead of creating a War Department composed of men versed in military matters, Congress's only concession to necessity was to turn this business over to a Board of War which, until late in 1777, was made up of members of Congress.

By act of Congress, Washington was appointed commander-in-chief of all the forces raised by the United States, but it was made plain to him that he must not presume too much upon that title. In appointing Washington to the command, Congress by no means intended to relinquish the direction of the war to him or to any other military leader. Lest he seek to make himself supreme over Congress, his authority was carefully hedged; and in practice he was denied powers clearly vested in him by his commission. For instance, although the Northern Department (Canada and New York) was admitted to be under the command of Washington, Congress frequently sent orders directly to the commander of that department without consulting the commander-in-chief. Not until 1779 did Congress give Washington express authority over the army in the Northern Department.[3]

Occasionally, Washington was unwilling to exercise fully even the powers with which Congress had invested him. In seizing supplies from citizens, he acted with so much caution and forbearance that Congress rebuked him publicly for showing too much consideration for the rights of those who, in many instances, were probably Tories. Even the urgings of Congress could not make Washington confiscate supplies at the bayonet point — although, before the war was over, necessity compelled him to adopt the practice. He never ceased to regret that a system of sustaining his army so averse to the discipline and ideals he had inculcated in his men should have been forced upon him. Whatever he took he paid for, even though the money was next to worthless; and he instructed foraging parties to observe strictly the laws of the state "and a sacred regard to the property of each Individual Member as far as it can be done."

The patience and forbearance displayed by Washington in his relations with Congress are perhaps not the least of his titles to greatness; he might well be accorded rank alongside Job. Even Washington's vast fund of patience was severely taxed by the slowness and inefficiency of civil government. He was often tempted to denounce Congress as a knot of cantankerous politicians, fond beyond even the usual nature of the breed of delay and wordiness. Procrastination he could not endure. "An early decision, in many cases, though it should be against the measure

---

[3] Washington was in direct command of the Middle Department (lower New York, New Jersey, Pennsylvania, Delaware, and Maryland); the Northern and Southern Departments were under other commanders.

submitted," he declared on one occasion, "would be attended with less pernicious effects" than delay.

In May 1776, when he came to Philadelphia to confer with Congress upon a plan of campaign, he was obliged to wait for days until that body could spare time to hear him. Nor did he find it easy to open the eyes of congressmen to wisdom. "In a word," he said, "when they are at a distance, they think it is but to say Presto begone, and everything is done. They seem not to have any conception of the difficulty and perplexity attending those who are to execute." Congress, he said in 1780, was prone to occupy itself with trivial matters to the neglect of great national concerns — but, he remarked resignedly, "you might almost as Soon teach the Streams to run back to their Sources as persuade Congress out of Their Ancient Trait."

Although Washington usually deferred to the wishes of Congress and freely shared military secrets with that body, it cannot be said that Congress returned the favor; matters of state were often deliberately concealed from the commander-in-chief. For example, news of the Franco-American alliance was withheld by Congress from Washington despite the protest of Henry Laurens that it was more appropriate to inform the commander-in-chief than "the Member who lay snoring fuddled on one of the Benches while those papers were read." But the statesmen in Philadelphia loved to put the military gentlemen in their places, so Washington was denied information essential to the military strategy of the United States.

Washington keenly resented being treated like a schoolboy to whom it was not safe to confide secrets. Congress, he declared, ought to take him as unreservedly into its confidence as he had taken it into his. If he were privileged to know no more of what was going on in Congress than any other outsider, he could not be expected to fight the war successfully; and he reminded Congress that he was a "Citizen and Soldier" and had no intention of subverting the liberties of his country. The apprehensive statesmen were unconvinced: Caesar bulked too large upon their horizon to admit of trust in generals.

A small group of politicians, of whom Dr. Benjamin Rush of Pennsylvania and James Lovell of Massachusetts were the most active, agreed that if the American Revolution were to have its Caesar, the finger of destiny pointed to General Washington as the chief contender for the purple. Already they saw evidences of his approaching exaltation. To his admirers, he was the "one great Man whom no Citizen shall dare even to talk about," the "bright luminary of War." Rush complained that criticism of Washington was treated by his friends as lèse majesté — which surely portended the glorification of the commander-in-chief into a divinity specially consecrated to rule his fellow men. By reason of his boundless popularity, Washington seemed to menace republican institutions. These skittish patriots feared that he would take the place in the hearts of his countrymen lately vacated by George III, and, as George I, ascend the American throne. This fear was given added force by the fact that the American people had been free of monarchism for only a year; republicanism was still on trial and menaced on every hand. Rush estimated that it would take at least half a century to wean the people from their monarchical habits and prejudices — unless, as seemed more likely, Washington or some other popular hero became king in the meantime.

The moral seemed to be that a people ought not to look to one man for salvation. John Adams, although he took no part in the move to displace Washington, groaned to see his countrymen adulating the commander-in-chief: to his mind, republicans ought to put their trust in well-balanced governments rather than in any individual, no matter how great or worthy. "The Idea that any one Man alone can save us is too silly for any Body . . . to harbour for a Moment," said John Adams; and to emphasize his point he excluded Washington from a list of American heroes he compiled in 1778. Benjamin Rush warmly approved this excision: had he been doorkeeper, Washington would never have crashed the Hall of Fame. The safety of republican institutions, said Rush, lay in the number of its great men; for one man to stand pre-eminent above the rest endangered popular liberty. "Monarchies are illuminated by a *Sun*, but republics should be illuminated by *constellations* of great Men."

Actually the roots of republicanism had penetrated deeper than these patriots knew. The American people could have their great men without surrendering to them their liberties. They were not of the stuff of which dictator-ridden people are made; and merely because they were willing to follow an able and inspiring leader did not make them the tools of tyranny. Instead of removing the necessity for leadership, democracy had made it more essential; and in the War of Independence, Americans suffered from too little, rather than too much, leadership.

It was probably true, as Washington's enemies grumbled, that he was regarded by the people as indispensable. In supposing Washington to be a potential dictator, however, his critics utterly mistook their man. Civil liberties, in Washington's hands, were as safe as in the custody of the Continental Congress itself. Washington's chief ambition was the same as that of the private soldier: to get the war over with and go home. Throughout the struggle, he dreamed of the day when he could settle down at Mount Vernon and spend his declining years "cultivating the affections of good men, and in the practice of the domestic virtues." His only purpose in taking up arms, he frequently said, was to earn the privilege of being a private citizen in a free country — "as pure motives," he remarked, "as ever man was influenced by." The life he loved was that of a landowner, tending his estates and enjoying the society of his peers; he accounted it a misfortune that his life was not cast in quieter days. Few great men, it is clear, have cared less for personal power than did Washington: it was only his patriotism and love of liberty that placed him in the forefront of the conflict.

Nor need Congress have feared dictatorial ambitions in other American generals, who, with the possible exception of General Charles Lee and the proved exception of Benedict Arnold, were loyal to the civil government. Washington said that although criticism of Congress was frequently heard, he knew of no officers or men in the army who wished to replace it with military rule. "The most distant lisp of it," he assured the anxious congressmen, "never reached my Ears, and would have met with the severest checks if it did." The fault of Americans, if Washington diagnosed their case correctly, was not that they loved uniforms and military power too well, but that they were too fond of remaining civilians and too eager to get out of uniform once they had donned it. Certainly, they had no desire to establish military rule in the country; General Nathanael Greene spoke for thousands of men and officers when he declared that his ideal was a state in which "the Soldier is lost in the Citizen, and the Citizen ever ready to become the Soldier when the interest or safety of his Country requires it." "Nothing," he remarked in 1782, "would give me greater pleasure than to become a Citizen. If we have less power we shall have more liberty. To be with my family is what my soul longs for."

If Washington was a colossus, his feet, said his critics, were Virginia clay. It was bad enough for the American people to venerate a military leader, but the case became desperate indeed when the man they singled out for adulation was as incompetent as Washington was judged to be.

However much he might look like a Roman senator, Washington's enemies were satisfied that actually he was weak, vacillating, and unduly dependent upon his friends for advice. The jut of Washington's jaw, in effect, belied his real character.[4] It was alleged that he was so uncertain in his own mind upon matters of strategy and tactics that he was apt to believe the man who talked to him last; and, trying to avoid the necessity of decision, he called frequent councils of his officers which, by the sharp differences of opinion they exposed, confused and perplexed him the more. As Baron De Kalb said, Washington was brave and upright, but "I am convinced he would do good work if he dared to take more upon himself than he does; but he is indeed the weakest general and the most badly counselled by those who possess his confidence in the largest degree, and

---

[4] His detractors supposed that it was his false teeth which gave him the air of a master of men. Throughout the war, his teeth, which were bad, gave him excruciating pain. Lacking the services of a competent dentist, he was obliged to make his own plates.

those are so many ignorant persons if they are not traitors." And General Nathanael Greene, one of Washington's closest friends, remarked of the commander-in-chief: "Why, the General does want decision; for my part, I decide in a moment." It was reputed that Greene, together with Henry Knox and Alexander Hamilton, made Washington's decisions for him.

Furthermore, the commander-in-chief appeared so fond of Fabian strategy that, his enemies complained, he repeatedly missed his opportunities of destroying the foe. Many Americans longed for the high excitement of heroic deeds of arms and glorious acts of self-sacrifice: to stake the cause upon a single pitched battle was in their eyes the only way to achieve independence. It is significant, however, that few of these lovers of action were in the army. "I am glad to hear of fighting, even though we come off second-best," exclaimed John Adams, ". . . because I believe by delay we should lose more lives than by the sword. It sinks our spirits, disheartens our soldiers, makes them both idle and wicked. . . . Fighting will certainly answer the end, although we be beaten every time for a great while." "We have tried Fabius," exclaimed another civilian; "now let us see what Hannibal can do."

It is true that Washington was not a man to rely upon intuition; he had never, he told Congress, "presumptuously driven on under the sole guidance of my own judgment and self will." Fearful that his own inexperience might, if not corrected by the judgment of others, lead to disaster, he took frequent counsel with his fellow officers. Although resolute in the cause, he was beset by doubts and uncertainties which he sought to resolve by letting the majority voice prevail — sometimes with unhappy results. Early in 1777, therefore, Congress relieved the commander-in-chief of the obligation of consulting with the general officers, and made it his duty, regardless of the opinion of the majority, to follow his own judgment.

Washington's severest critics were civilians — men who took all military knowledge for their province and presumed to lecture generals upon the elementary principles of their profession. In his prayers, Washington might well have besought heaven to deliver him from the armchair generals — they sometimes were more troublesome than the enemy.

Dr. Benjamin Rush, an opinionated and somewhat waspish Philadelphia physician and member of Congress, was especially given to passing judgment upon American generals with crushing finality. He knew little of the art of war, and that little was self-taught, but he was not ready to admit that war, like medicine, was a science that might best be left to the experts. Cocksure, arrogant, and expert in forging quarrels, he particularly loved to dwell upon the errors and shortcomings of Washington. He declined to credit the Virginian with any talents other than perhaps a certain knack in hoeing tobacco; as a military man, Washington was so abysmally incompetent that if he won a battle it was by sheer accident. Rush dreaded Washington's victories more than his defeats — for if, by some lucky stroke, Washington succeeded in defeating the enemy it would, said Rush, "stamp a value upon ignorance & negligence which would greatly retard military knowledge & exertions among us." Washington had committed "such blunders as might have disgraced a soldier of three months' standing"; his "languor" and "slackness" and failure to impose discipline and to act with decision made him, in the opinion of Dr. Rush, the evil genius of the American cause.

Like many other civilians, Rush was inclined to hold generals solely responsible for victory or defeat: he could not see the army for the generals. Defeat he regarded as prima-facie evidence of "the ignorance, the cowardice, the idleness and the drunkenness of our major generals. . . . I believe the always unfortunate general is always a culpable one." There was scarcely an instance, he maintained, of the troops giving way until they had been abandoned by their generals. The dry rot had settled first in the top of the army and it was here that the cure must be effected. "A few able Major Generals," he predicted, "would make them a Terror to the whole power of Britain."

Rum and rebellion, in Dr. Rush's opinion, ought never be mixed; liquor promised to be the undoing of the American Revolution — for how could befuddled generals be expected to win battles, unless indeed, the enemy was even more inebriated? Rather than rely upon the drinking habits of British generals, Rush advocated curbing the evil among American generals by laws of Congress. Under the current system, he pointed out, "a general may play the coward both in the cabinet & the field, or he may raise the price of whiskey by getting drunk every day of his life, and yet it may be impossible to prove either of these things against him in a Court of Enquiry." Therefore Congress ought strictly to ration intoxicants to the higher officers. If any general drank more than one quart of whiskey or got drunk more than once in twenty-four hours, Rush urged that he be publicly reprimanded at the head of his division or brigade; and in all battles and skirmishes, it ought to be required that generals remain no more than five hundred yards in the rear of their troops, on pain of court-martial. Generals, said Rush, ought to sleep in their boots — and it would seem, if his ideas were carried out, they would die in them.

These strictures were given some color of authority by virtue of a tour of inspection of Washington's army that Rush made in the autumn of 1777. His report was calculated to blow the lid off the Continental army. He went down the line lambasting generals and privates alike: General Sullivan he pronounced to be "fond of scribbling, in the field a madman"; Stirling was "a proud, vain, lazy, ignorant drunkard"; Stevens "a sordid, boasting, cowardly sot." As for conditions in the camp, they were as might be expected from such commanders: "the troops dirty, undisciplined, & ragged, guns fired 100 a day; pickets left 5 days & sentries 24 hours without relief; bad bread; no order; universal disgust." And, to cap the misfortunes of the army, this "uniformed mob" was commanded by a man who had been "outgeneraled . . . outwitted and twice beaten," by reason of his "ignorance, idleness, and blunders." This paragon of incompetence was, of course, General Washington.

In the case of Lord Stirling, it must be admitted, there was good ground for complaint. This noble lord presented a majestic front to the enemy and possessed, it was agreed, "the most martial Appearance of any General in our Service." This martial appearance, unfortunately, was no more than skin-deep. A notorious toper, he was rarely sober by evening; fond of "the table and the bottle, full as much as becomes a Lord, but more than becomes a General," he seemed to be "the quintessence of whiskey, soul of rum." Unhappily for the Americans, he found no inspiration in liquor: drunk or sober, he was always unfortunate in action. But he was never disloyal to the cause and he died during the war full of honor and, as some of his detractors pointed out, full of good liquor.

        ⌒   ⌒   ⌒

After Gates's victory over Burgoyne, the suspicion and fear with which Washington was regarded eventuated in an effort on the part of certain members of Congress and army officers to replace Washington with General Gates, the "Saratoga Hero." Although this plot is known as "the Conway Cabal," it had little to do with Conway and was hardly worthy of being called a cabal. In itself, it was perhaps a minor interlude in the Revolutionary War, but it conveniently serves as a peg on which to hang many more important matters.

To carry the good news from Saratoga to Philadelphia, Gates sent his aide-de-camp, Colonel James Wilkinson, whom he had once pronounced to be the most promising "Military Genius" he had ever met. Although Wilkinson broke no speed records — in fact, he dallied on the way to visit his sweetheart and was for that reason so laggard in reaching Philadelphia that Sam Adams suggested that Congress ought to present him with a pair of spurs — Congress was so jubilant at the news he brought and so eager to honor Gates that it decided to appoint his protégé, Wilkinson, brigadier general.[5]

Had Wilkinson spent more time dawdling with his fiancée and less in gossiping in taverns, General Gates would have been better served. For,

[5] Wilkinson did not reach Philadelphia until twelve days after the first reports from the Albany Committee of Safety arrived in the city.

on his way to Philadelphia, he told a fellow officer, whom he encountered in a tavern, that he had looked into the correspondence of his commander and found that a certain General Conway had written derogatory remarks about Washington. "Heaven has been determined to save your Country" was Wilkinson's paraphrase of Conway's letter to Gates; "or a weak General [Washington] and bad Councillors would have ruined it."

Whether Wilkinson blurted out this information in a state of alcoholic bonhomie or whether it was deliberately imparted in the hope of furthering his own ends is not easily determined. It can at least be said that Wilkinson, who for over twenty years was a pensioner of the Spanish government at the same time that he served as a general in the American army, was a man who habitually played both sides and prospered at the game. If this was his plan, it went awry. Although he had given his information originally with the stipulation that his name was not to be mentioned and he continued to address his letters to Gates as his "beloved friend," Wilkinson was soon smoked out. Before he was through with the scrape, he had fought a duel with Gates, but his good name was not cleared merely by standing fire on the field of honor. "If he betrayed the Confidence of his Patron he may do the same by his Country," remarked a patriot – a prediction that came true in the end.

General Thomas Conway, the author of the letter from which Wilkinson quoted, was an Irish expatriate who, having joined the French army at the age of fourteen, had risen to the rank of colonel. Eager for advancement, he saw in the war in America a heaven-sent opportunity for him to rise in the French army: he would go to the United States, secure a high commission in the American army, and return to France with his prestige enhanced and, he hoped, with a substantial increase in rank. He felt little zeal for the establishment of republicanism, but he was ardent in pushing his own fortunes. Enjoying favor in high places, he came warmly recommended to Silas Deane, who promised him the rank of major general in the American army.

As an officer in the American army Conway's professional feelings were shocked by the irregularities he witnessed in camp, by the style of fighting favored by the rebels, and above all by the grievous shortcomings of General Washington. At the battle of Germantown, Conway declared that Washington was so bewildered and irresolute that he permitted a subordinate to countermand his orders. Some of Conway's admirers held him responsible for whatever success had been scored at Germantown, and it is noteworthy that Conway did not deny the report.

Conway, to give him his due, was an able officer, a strict disciplinarian and excellent drillmaster. His brigade, one of the smartest in the army, marched and deployed with a smoothness that put the rest of the army to shame. Lafayette thought so highly of Conway that at one time he planned with him to attack British India from the United States. A harebrained scheme, perhaps, but Lafayette had the greatest confidence in Conway's military capacities.

Conway basked in this hero-worship without sharing, however, any of Lafayette's esteem of the people he had come to assist. He loved to jeer at the puerilities of American officers, from Washington down; as a professional military man, he had only contempt for the American civilians who had presumed to adopt the titles and uniforms of officers. "Fools, cowards, & drunkards," he called them; and the greatest fool of all was General Washington. For General Gates, on the other hand, he entertained warm regard. Gates was a professional; he had not won his spurs in the Virginia backwoods; and he was known to be at odds with General Washington.

Having been promised the rank of major general by Deane, Conway quickly set out to force Congress to make good its contract. It cannot be alleged that his methods were delicate: he summoned Congress to stand and deliver much as he might have addressed a squad of not too bright recruits. "I commanded fifteen hundred men in France and here I command five hundred under the orders of a major general [Lord Stirling] who is not able to command one hundred although a brave man," he declared. ". . . I cannot remain under the orders of a man who will not let people do good, who cannot do it himself because he knows nothing of the matter, and if he did cannot do anything reasonable after dinner." Conway concluded this recital of his own merits and the delinquencies of his superior officer by demanding a "very speedy and categorical answer" from Congress to his request that he be made a major general.

Well aware of the contempt Conway entertained for him, Washington let it be known to a member of Congress that if this insufferable Irishman were made a major general he would regard it as a vote of no confidence and as an "insuperable difficulty" in the way of his retaining the chief command. Perhaps Congress as a whole was not informed of Washington's strong feelings towards Conway — later many members claimed that they had been kept in the dark — but that is by no means the whole story. This brash soldier of fortune succeeded in convincing Congress that he enjoyed great influence in France and that if he went home without his commission there would be important, not to say earth-shaking, international repercussions. In that event, he intimated, there would be no more loans, no secret aid, no alliance — in short, one word from him and His Christian Majesty would wipe his hands of the American rebellion. "For God's sake," exclaimed Benjamin Rush, "do not suffer him to resign. . . . He is the idol of the whole army" as well as the favorite of the King of France. Congress dared not risk the displeasure of such a tycoon: in November 1777, Conway received his commission as major general in the Continental army.

It is undeniable that some patriots, both in and out of Congress, found merit in Conway's outspoken criticism of the army and its commanders; the fact that he upbraided the generals for stupidity and cowardice was, said Benjamin Rush, "proof of his integrity, and should raise him in the opinion of every friend of America." They mistook his insubordination for spirit and resolution — qualities which they believed were all too rare among American military men. If Conway chose to castigate the commander-in-chief, it was his democratic privilege to do so.

Conway had never made any secret of his low opinion of Washington; nevertheless, by putting it in writing in a letter to Gates he was guilty of a costly indiscretion. No one cared greatly about what Conway thought, but Gates had suddenly become the most talked-of personage in the United States, and his every action and opinion were now of first-rate importance.

There was much more than Gates's victory over Burgoyne to recommend him to congressmen in search of a successor to Washington. He had always paid court to Congress, communicating directly to that body rather than through the commander-in-chief. And, unlike Washington, he was not a high-toned aristocrat, but a commoner of free and easy manners and of genuinely republican, not to say radical, principles. Without democracy, Gates said, "our Independence will expire in its Cradle" — an opinion which to some patriots made him a better leader of a republican army than the Virginia grandee, Washington.

In contrast to the commander-in-chief, Gates was fond of working with militia: he accounted them the equal, if not the superior, of regular troops. Having given much study to the vagaries of militiamen, he knew how to handle them; his system was "never to call for them, until the instant they are wanted, and to return them to their Homes as soon as the Service is performed." Against Burgoyne, he had made such effective use of militia that his admirers claimed that he had revealed "the folly and danger of standing armies in the time of peace, by conquering a body of veterans with the militia of the country."

The men leagued against Washington were all ardent believers in the militia. James Lovell held that the New Jersey militia were better than the Continental troops. "The last fight from duty," he said; "the first from a spirit of revenge." But none yielded to Benjamin Rush in exalting the militia over the regular army. He went so far as to declare that it was a mark of depravity for a man to enter the Continental army: "I should despair of our cause if our country contained 60,000 men abandoned eno' to enlist for 3 years or during the war." Convinced that "the liberties of America are safe only in the hands of the militia" and that "in every victory as yet obtained by the Americans, the militia have had the principal share," he would have forthwith liquidated the Continental army. All that the militia required was an active and enterprising commander. "Good General Officers [like Gates]," he said, "would make an army of six months' men an army of heroes. . . . The militia began, & I sincerely hope the militia will end the present war."

Even these recommendations, powerful as they were, were outweighed by the consideration that in removing Washington to make way for Gates, the principle of rotation in office — a principle dear to republicans — would be applied to the army. And the superiority of Congress over the army would be triumphantly vindicated; no longer could it be questioned who was master in the household.

Gates did not lend himself to the scheme of turning out Washington. Certainly he sent no orders to his partisans in Congress and the army to asperse the commander-in-chief, nor did he seek to produce an open rupture. Had Washington been routed in Pennsylvania, it can be surmised that Gates would have stepped forward to save the cause, but in the autumn of 1777 the military situation was not sufficiently critical, in his opinion, to warrant an effort to pull down Washington. The timing of the Conway Cabal was wrong — so wrong indeed, that it is difficult to believe that it represented a serious and well-considered effort to deprive Washington of his post. Everything points to the probability that Gates was dragged unwillingly into the affair; that he deplored it from the beginning; and that he was almost ruined by his friends.

That is not to say, however, that Gates was above finding satisfaction in the discomfiture of the commander-in-chief and in taking a few shots of his own at Washington's "incompetence." In September 1777, for example, he remarked that Washington was being badly outgeneraled by Howe. Moreover, Gates approved Conway's "judicious observations" upon the conduct and character of the commander-in-chief and urged him to stand his ground regardless of what happened. Those who knew Gates best were not sure that his wife was not egging him on. Mrs. Gates was an extremely ambitious woman and was believed to have her eye on Martha Washington's place of honor. Eager for her own and her husband's advancement, she encouraged him to take part in politics. The Saratoga Hero seems to have been a badly henpecked man. "Upon my word I pity Gates," exclaimed General Lee. "He is a honest man and has many good qualities, and that Daemoness his wife occasions him to make a very ridiculous figure."

Gates was condemned, it will be observed, not because of a letter he had written, but because of a letter he had received. It is a harsh rule that makes a man responsible for the opinions of people who write letters to him; no public man could survive an instant under such a system. Moreover, Gates had never before received a letter from Conway; it was not as though they were cronies who made a habit of mulling over the deficiencies of the commander-in-chief. Conway's letter to Gates was by way of an overture to the Saratoga Hero, a double-edged compliment designed to cast greater luster upon Gates by depreciating Washington.

To understand why Washington was ready to believe the worst of Gates, it is necessary to examine the relations of the two men over a period of years. Long before Conway wrote this fatal letter, Washington and Gates had been at odds. They had quarreled early in 1777 over the question of dividing supplies equally between the Northern and main armies. Because he expected to be engaged in a war of movement, Washington demanded "every Tent upon the Continent for the Armies to the Southward"; the Northern army, fighting from fixed positions, he argued, could build huts. To this, Gates would not agree; admitting that "Generals, are so far like parsons, they are all for Christening their own Child first," he insisted that the Northern army needed tents every whit as much as did Washington's troops. Fearing that he and the Northern army would be sacrificed to "Southern Prejudices" and that Washington would seize all the available supplies, Gates appealed to Congress to stay the hand of the commander-in-chief. This conduct on the part of a subordinate angered Washington and he began to conceive a deep and abiding distrust of General Gates.

He was soon given fresh cause for believing that Gates regarded him as a rival. Gates immediately informed Congress of his victory at Saratoga, and to his wife he wrote jubilantly that Burgoyne had surrendered "to me and my Yankees." Yet he did not see fit to send Washington a word regarding his triumph. It is true that Gates had been made responsible directly to Congress in August 1777, when he assumed command of the Northern army, but even so, good manners required him to communicate the news to the commander-in-chief. Plainly, the quarrel between Gates and Washington had passed beyond the observance of good manners: Gates longed to pay back Washington for the slights that he fancied he had received at the hands of the commander-in-chief, and he took this occasion to even the score.

Washington smarted under the insult. He regarded Gates's conduct as a calculated affront — a challenge hardly less cutting than one made with a whiplash. The ill feeling between the two men was aggravated by Gates's failure to comply with the request made by Washington after Saratoga that several thousand men be sent him from the Northern army. "Gates," it was said in Washington's camp, "is playing with his laurels at Albany and Putnam is catching oysters on the shores of the sound" — but neither made a move to come to the aid of the commander-in-chief. Although Washington assumed that Gates was withholding reinforcements in order to settle a grudge, the fact is that the Northern army, after its victory over Burgoyne, largely scattered to the winds, leaving Gates in command of only a small part of the men he had led at Saratoga. Under these circumstances, Gates was not inclined to strip himself of troops to oblige the commander-in-chief. He wished to capture Ticonderoga before the British recovered from the disaster that had befallen

Burgoyne, and he feared that Clinton might attempt another dash up the Hudson — in short, as he explained to Alexander Hamilton, whom Washington had sent to speed up the transfer of the troops, there was no reason why the Northern army should be crippled even though Washington sorely needed reinforcements. However, he offered to return to the main army Morgan's riflemen, the corps that Washington had sent north in August 1777. Hamilton was not content with this meager measure of aid; he pressed Gates for more troops until the general finally agreed to give Washington two of the three brigades he had requested. He yielded with such poor grace, however, that the suspicion was planted in Hamilton's mind that the Saratoga Hero was really inclined to make matters as difficult as possible for the commander-in-chief.

Now, in December 1777, Gates's adherents recognized that if it ever came to a direct vote in Congress between Washington and Gates, they stood very little chance of electing their man. A substantial majority in Congress would uphold the commander-in-chief; and it was generally agreed that Congress might better be employed in giving Washington the means with which to wage war than in criticizing him in time of adversity. From all direct attacks, therefore, Washington was secure; so it was necessary for the cabal to go underground. The plot thereupon took the form of an effort to humiliate Washington into throwing up the command and going back to his farm, a somewhat battered Cincinnatus, while Gates took over the direction of the army.

Meanwhile, Congress was busying itself in reconstituting the Board of War. Previously the Board — which served as the executive agent of Congress in the field of military affairs — had been composed of congressmen who, among their multitudinous duties, found little time to give to the conduct of the war. For this reason, it had long been urged by Washington and other officers that the Board of War be staffed with military experts drawn from outside Congress; running the war, they pointed out, was a full-time task requiring greater experience and knowledge than that possessed by most members of Congress. Until the autumn of 1777, however, Congress refused to call in the experts; but the military crisis that followed the loss of Philadelphia shook Congress's confidence in its omnipotence. Swamped with work and burdened with the cares of state, Congress gave up the unequal struggle and established a new Board of War composed largely of men with military backgrounds who were free to give their entire time to the needs of the army.

This was in accord with Washington's recommendations; but here Congress stopped short. In choosing the personnel of the Board of War, Congress gave high office to the men Washington regarded as his worst enemies — Gates, General Thomas Mifflin, and Conway. Gates was made president of the Board; Conway was given the post of inspector general

of the army and ex officio member of the Board; and Mifflin was designated to advise upon military concerns.

Gates and Mifflin were friends of long standing. Mifflin had warmly
backed his friend's efforts to win command of the Northern army, and
Gates had once remarked that Mifflin had an uncommon share of the
qualities that made a great general. But it was as a politician rather than
as a military leader that Mifflin specially shone. In the summer of 1777
he had incontinently dumped the responsibilities of quartermaster general
into Washington's lap and gone home to nurse his health. It would seem
that he sought his cure chiefly in playing politics; and when the movement
against Washington got under way, Mifflin was conveniently at hand
to take a hand. His health was fully restored by the high excitement of
intrigue; the alacrity with which he accepted a post with the Board of
War in the winter of 1777 when Washington seemed about to topple in
disgrace sharply contrasted with the invalidism that had prevented him
from carrying out his duties as quartermaster general during the critical
days of the campaign.[6]

Closely following this blow, Congress on December 10, 1777, reproved
Washington for failing to requisition supplies for his army from regions
likely to be overrun by the enemy: such delicacy towards citizens, Congress observed, "though highly laudable in general, may, on critical exigencies, prove destructive to the army and prejudicial to the general
liberties of America." By this resolve, Washington's critics intended to
rap "the Demigod" over the knuckles as a preliminary to a blow in a
more vital region.

As president of the Board of War, Gates was technically superior to
Washington — and he omitted no opportunity to rub in the fact. Deliberately he snubbed his rival and pointedly demonstrated that neither
Washington's advice nor his approval was necessary to the deliberations
of the Board of War. Gates and his colleagues drew up plans for an invasion of Canada without consulting or informing Washington; it was not
until Congress had approved the project that Washington's opinion was
asked for — which the commander-in-chief curtly refused to give. It was
made plain to Washington that the direction of the war, the planning and
the strategy, had passed to other hands and that he had been cast out of
the inner circle. The open partiality shown by Congress for men he regarded as his worst enemies, and his virtual exclusion from councils of
war, dispelled Washington's last doubt that a plot was on foot to remove
him from the command.

In thus giving rein to his suspicions, Washington was displaying no

---

[6] When Mifflin rejoined the army in 1778, after the winter at Valley Forge, Washington acidly remarked upon "that Gentleman's stepping in, and out, as the Sun
happens to beam forth or obscure."

extraordinary sensitivity to criticism. From his friends in Congress came reports of the strength and malignancy of the faction opposed to him; the circumstantial evidence against Gates seemed overwhelming; and the conduct of Congress bore out his worst suspicions. Washington was "slow in listening to evil reports," said Joseph Reed; ". . . being honest himself, he will not readily suspect the virtue of others." If Washington had a fault, said those who knew him best, it was "only the Excess of his amiable Qualities" — a tendency to keep his relations with his fellow men upon a ceremonious and outwardly harmonious basis. On the other hand, having once made up his mind that a man was his enemy, he was not readily persuaded otherwise.

Moreover, it should not be forgotten that in Gates's wresting of the command of the Northern army from Schuyler, Washington had recently witnessed a remarkable demonstration of the influence exerted by the Saratoga Hero over Congress. The lesson was not lost upon Washington that a general must be something of a politician; and Gates seemed to be hardly less redoubtable as a politician than as a military man.

In any event, Washington's resentment against his enemies at home overshadowed for the moment all other concerns. "I have never seen any stroke of ill fortune affect the General in the manner that this dirty underhand dealing had done," reported his secretary. Washington felt himself wronged by those from whom he had every right to expect support. "With many," he exclaimed, "it is a sufficient cause to hate and wish the ruin of a man, because he has been happy enough to be the object of his Country's favor." While he was exerting all his strength to hold the army together, his enemies, at a safe distance from the fighting, were trying to drag him down. He could not give them the lie when they claimed that his army was stronger than Howe's, lest the British learn his true weakness. "Next to being strong," said Washington, "it is best to be thought so by the Enemy," and it was chiefly to this deception that he attributed the caution and slowness of Howe.

In exalting Gates and the Board of War at the expense of Washington, there is little doubt that Benjamin Rush and his associates were grooming Gates for the chief command. James Lovell, for example, saw no hope of salvation unless Gates assumed the leadership. "The army will be totally lost," he wrote the Saratoga Hero, "unless you come down and collect the virtuous band who wish to fight under your banner."

Yet it is equally clear that most of the congressmen who voted for these measures intended only to honor Gates and to assert the supremacy of the civil over the military power rather than to humiliate Washington into resigning. It is improbable that Congress would have borne down so hard upon the commander-in-chief had there been more members present to stand up in his defense. Congress, during the winter of 1777–1778, was a mere rump — only about fifteen members were present at

York, Pennsylvania, and they, unwittingly or not, allowed Washington's enemies to take the lead.

If the loyalty of Congress to Washington was in doubt, there could be no question of the attitude of the army. Except for Mifflin and Conway, the soldiers were almost solidly behind Washington; had Congress attempted to remove him from command it would have brought upon itself the wrath of the army — a prospect which might well have given pause to the most inveterate enemy of the commander-in-chief. Already, the favoritism shown by Congress to Wilkinson and Conway had bred a mutinous spirit among the officers; the bounty of Congress, they complained, was "largely Showered on those who had Done the least" while it "treated with contempt Those Men who have Endured Every Fatigue & Despised Every Danger to Secure the Liberties of their Country." In the bitterness of their suffering at Valley Forge, the soldiers did not look kindly upon civilian intrigues against their leader. Colonel Morgan publicly inveighed against Congress "with unbounded License" for its derelictions; and the toast among the soldiers was "*Washington* or no army." His friends swore that they would challenge to a duel every asperser of the commander-in-chief: a few ounces of gunpowder would work wonders in silencing these calumniators.

To defend Washington against these slings and arrows, Thomas Paine, the ablest propagandist of the Revolution, entered the quarrel. In *The Crisis*, Paine extolled Washington, hoping, as he wrote the commander-in-chief, "by bringing your former services in view, to shame them out, or at least to convince them of their error." He became the watchdog of Washington's reputation — and surely Washington could not have asked for a better — asserting that he would "never suffer a hint of dishonor or even a deficiency of respect . . . to pass unnoticed."

The Conway Cabal diverted the attention of Congress from the plight of the army at Valley Forge; petty politics and intrigue rather than constructive measures to relieve the distress of the troops engrossed the energies of congressmen. "People are not better here than in France, and the intrigues which go on at Versailles are no worse than in the United States," said a disillusioned French officer. ". . . Sometimes, I feel quite sick when I think of all these base and shameless intrigues going on at a time of great national danger." Even Conway confessed that he never knew what a cabal really was until he visited Philadelphia.

In reconstituting the Board of War, Congress made Conway inspector general of the army — the executive officer of the Board of War whose duty it was to "reform abuses, regulate disorders and establish discipline in the army." There can be no doubt that Conway's training and experience fitted him for this post, but it was also plain that his personality and his known contempt for the commander-in-chief completely disqualified him. In view of what had gone before, Conway's appointment was virtually a slap in the face of the commander-in-chief. And the insult stung the more deeply because Washington was not asked for his opinion of Conway's suitability for the post; the commander-in-chief learned of Conway's appointment from Conway himself.

If it did nothing else, the Conway Cabal served to reveal Washington as a human being. At Valley Forge, Conway was treated to one of the most withering receptions ever accorded an officer at Washington's headquarters. The commander-in-chief gave him an icy stare that froze him in his tracks; and wherever he turned he found the same frigid looks. All the officers took their cue from Washington and cut Conway dead, and that unhappy officer reported back to his friends that the army could not even bear the sight of him.

While Conway was fretting over his unpopularity, the scheme of conquering Canada boomeranged disastrously upon General Gates and the Board of War. This hurriedly conceived project, apparently the brain child of Gates himself, was badly organized: few preparations were made, the winter was far advanced, and the American army, far from being in condition to conquer Canada, was battling for survival on the barren hills at Valley Forge. In the expectation that French officers would be warmly welcomed by the Canadians, the Board of War appointed Lafayette and Conway first and second, respectively, in command of the expedition. Lafayette, having broken completely with Conway, declared that rather than serve with a notorious enemy of General Washington he would go back to France and take with him practically all the French officers serving in the American army. Under this threat, the Board of War hastily dropped Conway and gave Lafayette another second-in-command. But Lafayette soon found that he had been sent upon a fool's errand. The Canada fever abated as suddenly as it had risen. In March 1778, Congress reluctantly called off the invasion of Canada, and Lafayette was ordered to rejoin Washington's army. Providence, Congress decided, had ordained that "the Arms of America should be employed in expelling the Enemy from her own Shores, before the liberation of a Neighbouring Province is undertaken." There were many, however, who, instead of blaming Providence for the fiasco, regarded it as a piece of folly for which General Gates was responsible.

The reaction in Washington's favor was swift in coming. Apparently, as Congress began to fill up in the early spring of 1778 and the newcomers saw what had been going on in their absence, they determined to put themselves unequivocally on the side of the commander-in-chief. Thomas Mifflin was haled before a congressional committee to give an accounting of his financial administration as quartermaster general, and Gates was given authority over the Hudson River forts, where he was under the immediate command of Washington.

Washington's authority was fully re-established. The Board of War fell into such disrepute that many officers refused to serve for the low pay and small prestige it afforded and, as a result, seats on the Board were "hawked about" in the army. And almost in spite of himself, Washington, rather than the Continental Congress, became the embodiment of resistance to Great Britain and of the nationalism to which the Revolution had given birth. As the war progressed, the authority and prestige of the Continental Congress declined, whereas Washington's reputation and popularity steadily increased.[7] Americans boasted of Washington until some Europeans were thoroughly weary of their bragging. "Their General Washington is the first of all heroes ancient and modern," remarked a French officer. ". . . If they were sure of always having Generals like him, they would soon lay down the law to the universe."

Washington emerged from this crisis stronger than before. Hardly a whisper of criticism was heard after 1778; an attack upon Washington, "be it ever so well founded or ever so ably supported," said James Wilkinson in 1781, "would excite nothing more favourable than derision & contempt, & would be esteemed a sort of impiety." Benjamin Rush acknowledged complete defeat; Washington, he said, had never been more idolized than after his enemies had shown their hand. "We derive all the blessings of our present glorious revolution from his Arm alone," he remarked sarcastically. "We say in contempt of the very genius of republicanism . . . that no man but our Commander-in-chief would have kept our Army together, and that his fall would be the extinction of our liberty." Already, Washington had mounted his pedestal, standing above the swirling party strife of lesser mortals, the indispensable man, revered by his countrymen. The attempt to destroy "the excessive influence & popularity of *One Man*" had succeeded only in increasing his influence and popularity. It was now held to be good republicanism to regard Washington as a great leader who combined "the unshaken constancy of Cato, the triumphant delay of Fabius, and *upon proper* occasions, the enterprising spirit of Hannibal."

In later years, the surest way to ruin a political opponent in the United States was to impute that he had been against Washington in '77. John Hancock, for example, tried to blast Sam Adams's reputation by accusing him of having taken part in the Conway Cabal even though Adams had not been in Congress at the time.[8] The story gained currency that there had been a vote in Congress to decide whether Gates or Washington should be commander-in-chief, and it was worth a politician's career to be charged with having voted against Washington. Every opponent of Wash-

---

[7] "It is owing entirely to his [Washington's] influence and the confidence the people have in him, and not to the authority of Congress," observed a French officer in 1779, "that the army is all it is; for without him they would not have 4000 men in the field."

[8] Adams was said to have introduced a resolution in the Massachusetts General Court to petition Congress to supersede Washington.

ington stoutly denied ever having lifted a finger against him. Thomas Mifflin swore that he had merely criticized Washington's favorites, Greene and Knox; never had he uttered a word against the commander-in-chief himself. Even when Mifflin was "pretty merry in consequence of a plentiful infusion of the juice of Grape," he was sufficiently circumspect to say that he "dearly loved & greatly admired" Washington; and it was observed that when pressed about his part in the Conway Cabal, "tipsy as he was, he was evasive."

Conway invoked freedom of speech — one of the freedoms for which Americans were fighting — to justify his habit of making free with the character of his commander. Every officer, he said, ought to enjoy the liberty of passing judgment upon the ability of his superiors; in France, he said, it was an established custom and he saw no reason why it should not be so in America.

Gates insisted that Wilkinson's version of Conway's letter was a "diabolical calumny," but he declined to produce the original, justifying his refusal on the ground that it contained strictures upon the abilities of some American officers other than Washington which, if brought to light, might throw the army into turmoil. "Honour forbids it," declared Gates, " — and Patriotism demands that I should return the letter into the Hands of the Writer." Henry Laurens, later President of Congress, who saw the letter, had a different explanation for Gates's reluctance to show Washington the original — it was "ten times worse in every view" than anything Wilkinson had quoted. In any event, Washington was left to draw his own conclusions, which, as was natural under the circumstances, were the worst.

Gates tried hard to make up the quarrel, but Washington rejected his overtures with the frosty politeness that sometimes stung his enemies more than did outright anger. He persisted in regarding Gates as his "inveterate enemy," and in believing that it was Gates's "ambition and great desire of being puffed off as one of the first Officers of the Age" that had been at the bottom of the mischief. The Conway Cabal also permanently poisoned relations between their respective partisans. Hamilton inveighed against the "impudence, folly and rascality" of Gates; and Washington even treated Kosciusko coolly because of the close relationship existing between the Polish engineer and Gates. Gates was held to be a man consumed by "Pride and ambition" and ready to stoop to any intrigue to gain his ends — and as such he has gone down in history. On the other hand, the supporters of Gates exclaimed that Washington was "a most malignant and revengeful Genius." Had their hero committed "an unpardonable Sin by the Triumph at Saratoga," they asked, that he should be persecuted the rest of his days? His friends advised him to resign his commission in the army. "You cannot serve with safety," they said; " — a mine is under your feet — the materials for your destruction are heap'd up and prepar'd, and the least error . . . blows you up" — a warning which Gates had occasion to remember after his defeat at Camden in 1780.

For several years after the Conway Cabal, little use was made of Gates's abilities. Shunted off to such inactive theaters of war as the Hudson River posts and New England, he seemed likely, by reason of Washington's continuing ill will, to rest upon his laurels for the duration of the war. When he asked to command the attack upon Rhode Island in 1778, Washington declined to "gratify . . . a doubtful friend." In Congress, Gates's supporters complained that he was hounded by "a Pack of cursed Rascals" at Washington's beck and call. Sam Adams and Richard Henry Lee stoutly upheld Gates's cause but they confessed that they could not oppose the torrent. Not until 1780 was Gates given an important command — with fatal results to his fame.

Conway, who gave his name to the cabal, in the end made an abject apology to Washington. Believing himself at death's door as the result of a wound sustained in a duel, Conway wrote the commander-in-chief begging forgiveness for having caused him any distress. "You are in my eyes the great and good man," he told Washington. It was almost an anticlimax when Conway recovered from his wounds — and, it is to be feared, from his contrition — and lived to return to France.

CHAPTER XV

The French Alliance

GREAT BRITAIN embarked upon war with its colonies little apprehending that France would make itself a party to the dispute. It was expected to be a short, decisive struggle — a brief interlude of domestic dissension which would afford the Bourbons no opportunity to make trouble. Louis XVI, said Germain in 1774, "will have enough to do at home for his amusement, and if he will not make war with us till he has established economy in the different branches of Government, and has taught morality to the bishops and the people, I shall hope for peace in my time." The British government made two costly errors in believing that the Americans would not fight and that the French would not aid them.

Decisive victory over the rebels eluded the British and by 1776, the government and people could hardly fail to see that storm clouds were piling up on the other side of the Channel. The ministers attempted to allay alarm by frequent assurances that France harbored no warlike intentions, but French military and naval preparations gave them the lie. Early in 1776, for example, Lord North told Parliament that England and France had reached a perfect understanding and that this understanding was more necessary to France than to Britain; whereupon "the whole Parliament had the common sense to laugh in his face." In fact, the government betrayed its own uneasiness by its eagerness to persuade France that peace was its best policy.

The English Whigs, far from being taken in by the government's soothing reports on Anglo-French relations, urged the government to make peace with America before France struck. An alliance with America, "let the price of it be what it will," said Burke, was preferable to driving the colonists into an alliance with France. The loss of America, he declared, was not the worst evil that could befall Great Britain: "the question of the Americans being our friends, or being in confirmed enmity, and in compact with our natural enemies, went perhaps second to that of our existence as a state."

As well-informed Englishmen knew, Great Britain had too deeply humiliated France to expect that the Bourbons would let slip an opportunity for revenge. The British ambassador at Versailles was convinced that "France will always wish, if she does not Meditate Revenge": there were ancient grudges to settle, a bitter rivalry for world domination to be resolved. And, to resolve beyond question the course of action to be pursued by France in this crisis, for the first time in many years His Most Christian Majesty was prepared to take full advantage of any opportunities to bring their empire down in ruins about the heads of Englishmen.

In the Seven Years' War, France had suffered crushing defeat at the hands of Great Britain. The ink was hardly dry upon the treaty of peace before France began to prepare for a war of revenge. Choiseul, the head of the French Ministry, reorganized the army, improved the state-owned armament industry, and strengthened the alliance with Spain in preparation for the day France should smite perfidious Albion. But his greatest service toward restoring France to the status of a first-rate power and a formidable rival of Great Britain was the rebuilding of the French navy.

France had lost its colonial empire largely because of the want of a fleet capable of contesting Great Britain's command of the sea; while the Bourbons expended their strength in unrewarding struggles upon the European continent, Great Britain appropriated the French colonies. The lesson learned by the French from their wars with England was that naval power was the key to empire. If France was again to figure as a world power, the trident must be wrested from John Bull and that beef-eating gentleman be impaled upon his own weapon. The decisive battles of the next war with Great Britain, it was generally believed, would be fought at sea; and if all went well for France, the Bourbon fleet would ride victorious in the English Channel and the fleur-de-lis would be planted upon the soil of the "eternal enemy."

Choiseul expected that the first cracks in the British Empire would appear in North America where the British, by taking Canada from France, had flung away one of the principal bonds of empire — the fear felt by the American colonists of the French and Indians in Canada. From the beginning of the disturbances in North America, therefore, the French government kept a watchful eye upon the activities of American Sons of Liberty. In 1768, a French observer was sent to the British colonies to determine whether the patriots were favorably inclined to French aid. His report dashed Choiseul's hopes: the struggle between the colonists and the mother country, he declared, was strictly a family quarrel in which any interference by an outsider seemed likely to unite the household against him. Choiseul began to fear that the luck of the British would hold and that his predictions of impending civil war did not make sufficient allowance for British capacity for muddling through. In this chastened spirit, when it was reported that there had been a bloody riot in London, Choiseul remarked: "I hardly dare hope that it is so. The English will never cut each other's throats to the extent that we desire."

Choiseul was too much of a jingo for the taste of Louis XV. That monarch had seen his country defeated too often to relish another war; and in 1770, when Choiseul, weary of waiting for the British Empire to fall apart of its own accord, attempted to hasten the process by precipitating war, Louis dismissed him from office. Although Choiseul sought to return to power, it was left to other men to wage the war of revenge upon Great Britain for which he had prepared his country.

Choiseul labored to uphold the prestige and influence of France, yet even his heroic efforts failed to conceal the fact that the Bourbon monarchy had entered upon a period of decline. Defeat had left its marks upon France. Stripped of most of its colonial empire and compelled to suffer the humiliation of an English commissioner stationed at Dunkirk to keep an eye upon French military activities along the Channel coast, France was clearly no longer the arbiter of Europe; it was questionable, indeed, whether the kingdom of Louis XVI could even be accounted a first-rate power.

Certainly it was true that the balance of power upon the European continent had shifted eastward since the Seven Years' War. Austria, Prussia, and Russia dominated the continent, and French influence, particularly in eastern Europe, had been superseded by that of its rivals. In 1772 Poland, an ally of France, was partitioned by Prussia, Russia, and Austria; and in 1774, France stood by helplessly while the Russians dismembered Turkey, the traditional ally of His Most Christian Majesty. The French alliance system was beginning to crack; and in every chancellery in Europe the low state of French prestige was apparent. Long accustomed to primacy in ceremonial rank at European courts, France was now obliged to yield first place to the British.

That France had failed to save its allies, the Poles and Turks, from their enemies did not augur well for the Americans who, at the distance of three thousand miles, looked to His Most Christian Majesty for succor. Yet the very fact that France had lost much of its ascendancy made it possible for it to intervene in the struggle between Great Britain and the United States without precipitating a general war upon the continent. In its decline, France was no longer an object of terror or jealousy to its neighbors as in the days of Louis XIV; rather, it was England which was now regarded by Europe with envy and apprehension. France, said Vergennes, was seeking to "deliver the universe from a rapacious tyrant who wishes to swallow up at the same time all power and all riches."

France was interested in the revolt in North America not because His Most Christian Majesty was a knight-errant who delighted in freeing people from oppression and setting up democracy — France was the home of the Enlightenment but philosophers were not yet kings — but because the country was ruled by hardheaded, practical men to whom the interests of France required the debasement of the enemy across the Channel. It is not surprising that France saw in the American Revolution its long-awaited opportunity to strike down its great rival; what requires explanation is why France waited so long before taking an active part in the struggle.

Although American patriots in 1768 had discouraged French hopes of profiting from the discords of the British Empire, seven years later they were in a very different frame of mind. Despite some Americans' brave talk of standing off all Europe on the American continent, few desired to put patriot fortitude to such a test. They well knew that unless they secured foreign aid, the British would probably win the war. For that reason, the ideas of independence and foreign alliances sprang simultaneously to their minds. Although many patriots doubted the wisdom of striking for independence without first making sure of foreign aid, Congress chose the perilous course of proclaiming American independence and then appealing to foreign powers.

Without a fair prospect of obtaining assistance abroad, it is doubtful whether Americans could have been persuaded that independence was attainable. Congress itself was confident that aid was forthcoming: in July 1775, it warned England that foreign assistance was "undoubtedly attainable," although at that time it had no assurances from any European country that anything of the kind was being considered. Nevertheless, this bluff had a gratifying effect upon American morale; the statement of Congress, it was observed, "passed like the voice of an Archangel throughout the continent, and did more to animate us to resistance than a thousand arguments." Congress had raised these hopes; now it remained for Congress to make good its promise. In November 1775, the Committee of Secret Correspondence was created and instructed to open correspondence with foreign powers. This betokened the eagerness of Americans to enlist the aid of other nations, but it was not until 1776 that they received any definite indications that a European power looked with favor upon their struggle for freedom.

In the winter of 1775–1776 there arrived in Philadelphia a French secret agent by the name of Bonvouloir. Traveling under the guise of a Flemish merchant, Bonvouloir had been sent by the French government to feel the pulse of the American patriots. Bonvouloir let it be known to Congress that he was in touch with the French government, although in an unofficial capacity; and the patriots immediately rose to bait. Franklin and other members of the Committee of Secret Correspondence arranged a meeting with Bonvouloir, so secret that each member came to the rendezvous in the dark by a different route. The first questions asked Bonvouloir by the committee were whether France would aid the rebellion and whether an American representative would be received at Versailles. The French agent was not prepared to answer such forthright questions and, taking refuge in his incognito, he told the committee that he was simply a friendly businessman who could commit the French government to nothing. Nevertheless, the report he carried back to France was calculated to banish all doubts that Americans were not in earnest — "their ardor and determination are incredible," he informed the French government. As for the radicals in Congress, they were in high spirits: no one believed that Bonvouloir was a businessman drumming up trade.

The Committee of Secret Correspondence lost no time in exploring the promising lead Bonvouloir had opened. Arthur Lee, a Virginian residing in England, was instructed to sound out foreign powers; and a Connecticut Yankee, Silas Deane, was dispatched to the court of Louis XVI to procure supplies.

Silas Deane was a lame-duck Congressman from Connecticut. He had been dropped from the Connecticut delegation in October 1775 — an act which his friends ascribed to the "cursed narrow Politicks" of that state. Instead of returning home after his defeat, Deane remained in Philadelphia, hoping to pick up a job with Congress. By thus keeping himself available, he was chosen to go to France as agent for the Committee of Secret Correspondence and the Commercial Committee of Congress. He spoke no French and he had no experience in diplomacy, yet his courage and forthrightness more than atoned for these shortcomings.

Silas Deane was singularly fortunate in his mission: even before he reached France, the French government had decided to give the Americans what Deane had come to ask — aid in war supplies and money. Indeed, France had gone beyond Deane's expectations by opening French arsenals to the Americans and by devising means of secretly transporting munitions and implements of war across the Atlantic. Happy beyond the usual lot of diplomats, he found that his work had been largely done for him when he reached his post: the high-pressure salesmanship of Beaumarchais and the quieter but more effective labors of Vergennes had ensured that Deane would not go home empty-handed.

The Count de Vergennes, Secretary of Foreign Affairs and leader of the interventionist faction in the French government, was a career diplomat who had served as ambassador to Turkey and Sweden. Unlike Choiseul, he was no hothead — on the contrary, he impressed the British ambassador as a "calm, prudent, cautious man," eminently fit for stratagems and spoils. Nevertheless, he was as firmly convinced as was Choiseul that Great Britain was the implacable and eternal enemy of France and that war must go on until one or the other had gained decisive superiority.

"The least glimmer of prosperity in France," said Vergennes, "is an insupportable grievance" to the unappeasable islanders. He recognized, moreover, that the revolt in North America was "a singular and unexpected piece of fortune for France. Here," exclaimed the French minister, "is the time marked out by Providence to deliver the universe from a greedy tyrant who is absorbing all power and all wealth. . . . Providence has marked the moment for the humiliation of England, and has struck her with the blindness which is the most certain precursor of destruction."

In the downfall of this "greedy tyrant," much advantage was expected to accrue to France. France as the successor to Great Britain as the greatest commercial and maritime power in the world — this was the vision which beckoned Vergennes and his colleagues to take the part of the British colonies. "If the maritime power of England falls," it was said at Versailles, "France naturally and inevitably takes her place — By her position alone she inherits all that England loses."

By Vergennes's reckoning, it was the wealth drawn from the American colonies by Great Britain that enabled the island kingdom to play the part of a great power. By furnishing the mother country with raw products, consuming its manufactures, and supplying it with ships and seamen, the overseas colonies had made England great — and, if independent, might in the same manner help restore to France the power and prestige lost in the course of its unsuccessful wars. So certain was Vergennes that it was the interest of France to separate Great Britain and its provinces that he declared it was worth the risk of "a somewhat disadvantageous war."

France aspired only to liquidate the British Empire; it harbored no designs of carving out a colonial empire of its own. Although most of their colonies had been lost to Great Britain, the French were singularly free of ambition to recover their lost provinces. Neither their own experience nor, for that matter, the experience of Great Britain was calculated to encourage them to essay again the role of empire builders: with civil war raging in the British Empire, the French might well congratulate themselves upon being virtually out of the business of ruling dominions containing large subject populations. Freedom of commerce with the Americans offered a surer foundation for French prosperity and naval power than did the recovery of Canada or Nova Scotia. Vergennes wanted for his country the commercial benefits without the headaches of empire. Had the English been content to remain traders and manufacturers, he believed that they would have won the good will of the world and would have made themselves invulnerable to their enemies. Fortunately for France, they had mistaken the true source of their strength and had forsaken commerce for empire.

Moreover, with England shorn of its colonies, Vergennes looked forward to his country's enjoying a relatively free hand on the European continent. It had been Great Britain with its doctrine of the balance of power that had thwarted His Most Christian Majesty's ambition of dominating Europe. "Experience has but too well proved," said Vergennes, "that they [the British] believe everything just and honourable which they regard as advantageous to their nation and destructive to their rivals." British money had helped raise up enemies upon the continent against France and denied her even the attainment of her "natural" frontiers. Nevertheless, the indifference displayed by France towards extending its colonial empire held true of its ambitions upon the European continent: it had no intention of extending its frontiers by wars of aggression, preferring instead to dominate Europe through prestige and the weight of its armaments.

The head of the French Ministry, Maurepas, was cautious and peace-loving, little inclined to embark upon adventures which might lead to war. It was one of Maurepas's favorite remarks that it was "too late" for Great Britain and the colonies to be reconciled; therefore, presumably, France could take its own time in coming to the aid of the Americans. Louis XVI was cut in the same pattern; unambitious and dull, he bore little resemblance to his militant ancestor, Louis XIV, who was always ready to plunge Europe into war for the greater glory of France. Although Americans later gave Louis XVI credit for the Franco-American alliance, had the King been left to his own devices, it is doubtful whether he would have lifted a finger to aid the Americans. He favored a policy of complete neutrality and often "expressed great displeasure at the public Partiality to the Rebels and the indecent Joy that was shown at the News of their pretended Victories." He loved to take apart clocks, not empires — not even the British Empire; and as later events proved, he had no capacity for dealing with revolutions, whether French or American. He was, in short, a King of France after Englishmen's own hearts. They noted approvingly his heavy features, his piety, and his preoccupation with mechanical problems — and predicted that "nothing great or commendable can be expected from him; and the history of his reign will be nothing more than an exact journal of his ministers' transactions."

The King, moreover, was not eager to help establish a republic in North America: even at the distance of three thousand miles from France, freedom was still too close for comfort. Louis did not believe that his fellow monarchs would thank him for raising up American republicans; in their eyes, intervention in behalf of the rebels might well seem to be a betrayal of the cause of monarchism for the sake of power politics. And, as the King knew, many Frenchmen were not without apprehensions that the United States might one day become "a great military and naval power, and will be very ambitious, and so terrible to Europe." Therefore, before pulling down the British Empire, the King wanted to be sure that he was not helping to establish an even more dangerous enemy to Europe and to the established order.

Louis XV may or may not have made the portentous remark, "After me, the deluge," but it is certain that his grandson, Louis XVI, acted as if he believed that the storm would come in his own time unless he took steps to prevent it by cutting down expenses. Louis XVI had been taught to regard extravagance as the bane of the Bourbons and the cause of all the misery that had descended upon the country; and he resolved that he would devote his reign to economizing in order to undo the evil his spendthrift predecessors had wrought. Saving money became in Louis a passion; he was "eternally repeating the word economy, economy," somewhat parrot-like, it is true, and probably with little real understanding of the problem. Nevertheless, he knew that wars cost money and that aiding the Americans was likely to involve France in enormous expense. The necessity for economy was to Louis a sound reason against becoming involved too deeply with the American rebels.

Louis carried his passion for economy so far as to reprobate the royal practice of keeping mistresses; he looked with abhorrence upon the excesses of his grandfather, Louis XV, and swore that he would never ruin his country for a Pompadour. He was as good as his word, although he might have done himself and his country a service by placing himself in the hands of some intelligent woman. A model husband to Marie Antoinette, he had little success in persuading her of the necessity of economizing. His queen shared neither his passion for cutting expenses nor his passion for tinkering with clocks; and she was too engrossed in frivolities to pay heed to the storm which the King, to give him his due, saw gathering on the horizon.

It has been seen that the first effort to supply the Americans with arms and ammunition had been made not by the French government but by profit-seeking French merchants. It is true, however, that even the arms and munitions furnished by private merchants came in large part from French arsenals and were sold by the French government in the knowledge that their ultimate destination was British North America. For example, the first sizable consignment of arms to reach the United States from France was shipped by Pliarne, Penet et Cie. This shipment consisted of some fifteen thousand muskets which Pliarne, Penet et Cie. had bought from a French merchant, who in turn had obtained them from the royal arsenals on condition that he replace them within six months.

Moreover, the fact that French merchants were able to export contraband to the Americans through the French customs was owing to the benevolent attitude taken by the government toward the rebellion. Vergennes was not content merely to fiddle while the British Empire burned: he was eager to throw fuel upon the conflagration. Therefore, orders were given by the government to port officials to wink at the exportation of munitions and implements of war to the rebels; to this trade, said Vergennes, "everyone must shut his eyes," and no official entries ought to be made which might embarrass the government if the British saw fit to protest.

The French government, had it wished to play the game safely, might have contented itself with merely conniving at the export of war supplies by French merchants to the Americans. No doubt, this would have sufficed to keep the American revolt alive (indeed, it was owing primarily to this aid that the Americans were able to fight the campaign of 1776) and, at the same time, have kept the hands of the French government relatively clear of any complicity in the business of supplying the rebels with munitions and implements of war. But Vergennes did not believe that private enterprise could provide Americans with these necessities as expeditiously as could the state; nor did he intend that the government should stand aside while businessmen reaped the glory of saving the American Revolution. The French minister hoped to rivet the Americans to France by ties of gratitude. Aiding the Americans was to Vergennes a matter of statecraft; therefore he urged the government to embark upon a policy of secret aid whereby Americans would be firmly attached to their new benefactor.

At the same time that Vergennes was arriving at this decision, a French playwright, secret agent, and man-about-town, Caron de Beaumarchais, was urging a similar course upon the French government. So vigorously and eloquently did Beaumarchais champion the policy of secret aid that it has sometimes been supposed that he was its author. It is clear, however, that Vergennes did not need to be reminded by this ebullient dramatist of the necessity of supporting the American rebels; yet the French minister found in Beaumarchais a brilliant, albeit somewhat indiscreet, ally in converting the King and Ministry to the necessity of taking action in behalf of the embattled colonists.

Beaumarchais had already carried out successfully for the French government a mission of peculiar delicacy. The Chevalier d'Eon, a French secret agent, who had played the dual role of brother and sister with equal convincingness at the court of the Empress Catherine of Russia (he even fooled Catherine, who usually knew a man when she saw one), returned to France and began to dress constantly as a woman. The chevalier was an hermaphrodite whose feminine characteristics now became uppermost. Unfortunately, he aroused the jealousy of Madame de Pompadour, who procured his banishment from court, whereupon the chevalier — or mademoiselle as he now preferred to call himself — went to England carrying with him some important state papers which, it was feared, he planned to sell to the British government. To recover these documents, Beaumarchais was sent to England. Although the undertaking was not exactly in his line, Beaumarchais played the gallant to this "woman" who "drank and smoked and swore like a German trooper," and carried off the papers in triumph. As for the chevalier, he was permitted to return to France on condition that he always dress like a woman.

In London, Beaumarchais fell in with Arthur Lee, an agent of the Continental Congress, with whom he discussed at length the prospects of the rebellion. Ever prone to optimism, Beaumarchais now leaped to the conclusion that the British Empire was at its last gasp and that France's supreme opportunity had come to apply the *coup de grâce*. So certain was he of American victory that he remarked early in 1776 that his liveliest fear was that the Americans would win the war before France could make up its mind to act in their favor.

Certainly it was true that only in the royal arsenals were to be found munitions and implements of war in sufficient quantities to equip the Americans. At least four hundred cannon belonging to the French army could be regarded as surplus, besides thousands of stands of small arms and several million pounds of powder. Yet the question remained: How were these supplies to be put into the hands of the Americans without exposing His Most Christian Majesty as a violator of the law of nations and of treaties then existing between Great Britain and France?

Beaumarchais resolved this dilemma by suggesting that he cover up for the French government by establishing a business firm. Through this mercantile house, ostensibly a private enterprise without connection with the government, the war supplies taken from the royal arsenals could be transported across the Atlantic to the hard-pressed rebels.

There was some difficulty, it is true, in palming off Beaumarchais upon the world as a businessman. Merchants do not often spring from the French theater fully armed with inexhaustible capital. Moreover, Beaumarchais's record was all against him: he was reported to be a spendthrift, to be heavily in debt, and to be prone to lavish his money upon attractive young ladies – his "nieces," as he preferred to call them.

Despite these handicaps, Beaumarchais was chosen by Vergennes to handle the business end of secret aid. The firm of Hortalez et Cie. was organized and Beaumarchais settled down to playing the role of a reputable businessman, the protégé of mysterious but certainly wealthy backers. It can at least be said of Beaumarchais that he made secret aid as entertaining as ever he had his own dramas: his talents for comedy were by no means suspended when he renounced literature for intrigue.

Although the source of Beaumarchais's wealth was not revealed to his contemporaries, there is no longer any mystery attaching to it. In May 1776, the French government proposed to Madrid a joint gift of two million livres to the Americans; Spain approved, and the Bourbon allies were launched upon a policy of secret aid to the American revolutionaries.

At his first interview with Vergennes, Silas Deane frankly stated the needs of his country: two hundred field cannon, forty thousand muskets, and clothing for twenty-five thousand men. Deane pledged Congress to pay for these war supplies or, like lend-lease aid, to replace them after the war. Instead of giving Deane a direct answer, Vergennes called in Beaumarchais, whom he introduced as a well-connected merchant who was eager to do business with the Americans. Whereupon Beaumarchais made a little speech, declaring that he was a "generous friend" of the rebels and aspired only to rescue them from tyranny. Deane was at first taken aback — Beaumarchais, he objected, was known "as a Man of more Genius, than Property" but Vergennes assured him that Beaumarchais, in addition to his other professions, was a man of business who, moreover, had influential people behind him. This was news to Deane, but when, after returning to his lodgings, he found a steady stream of visitors at his door offering to enter into contracts with Congress for clothing and other essentials, he began to revise his opinion of Beaumarchais's importance in the kingdom. Silas Deane was not a Connecticut Yankee for nothing: he immediately saw that Beaumarchais, Hortalez et Cie., and Vergennes were all of a piece and that the French government itself was playing the game of secret aid. "Everything he [Beaumarchais] says, writes, or does," Deane concluded, "is in reality the action of the ministry; for that a man should but a few months since confine himself from his creditors, and now, on this occasion, be able to advance half a million, is so extraordinary, that it ceases to be a mystery."

Meanwhile, in the United States, military reverses in the autumn of 1776 led the Continental Congress to redouble its efforts to procure aid from France. Ignorant of the success Deane had met with at Versailles, but keenly aware of the precarious position in which Howe's victories had placed the republic, Congress decided to send its ace diplomat, Benjamin Franklin, to France. This appointment precipitated in Congress one of the most far-reaching debates over foreign policy in American history.

While Howe boxed Washington about in New York and New Jersey, Congress debated whether an alliance with France accorded with the best interests of the United States. Despite the danger that British armies would shortly put an end to the republic, powerful voices were raised against an entangling alliance with France. It would be a poor recompense for the sweat and blood expended in the cause of American independence, they held, if the United States should become the satellite of a great transatlantic power. The first lesson that Americans must learn as an independent people was self-reliance — and there was no better way to learn it than by suffering the adversity of war. A foreign alliance, moreover, threatened to undo the good that Americans had striven for in breaking away from Great Britain — they would be inextricably entangled in the affairs of Europe and dragged into every war in which that blood-stained continent might engage. "Anything like a treaty of Alliance," it was said, "would make us forever the sport of the Politicks of the Cabinets of Europe."

It was John Adams who led the fight against commissioning Franklin to make an alliance with France. Asserting that he was "very unwilling they [the French] should rob us of the Glory of Vindicating our own Liberties," Adams preached the doctrine that Heaven helps those who help themselves. "It is a cowardly Spirit in our Countrymen," he said, "which makes them pant with so much longing Expectation after a French War. I have very often been ashamed to hear so many Whigs groaning and Sighing with Despondency and whining out their ears that We must be subdued unless France should step in."

As a result of John Adams's opposition, the idea of an alliance was dropped and Franklin was instructed to secure as much military aid from France as possible and to make a treaty of amity and commerce with the Bourbon government. Although there was to be no proffer of alliance, the policy of Congress was clearly to make France a belligerent on the side of the United States: Franklin was directed to "press for the immediate and explicit declaration of France in our Favour, upon a Suggestion that a Re-union with Great Britain may be the Consequence of a Delay."

Until 1774, Franklin had been regarded in America as a conservative patriot whose labors were largely directed toward bridging the widening gap between mother country and colonies. He stubbornly refused to yield his hope that some middle ground could be found by which colonial liberties could be safeguarded within the empire. In 1774 he had offered to pay out of his own pocket for the tea destroyed at Boston if the government would repeal the retaliatory acts. Indeed, Franklin worked so hard to hold the empire together that he incurred the resentment and suspicion of American radicals. He had too many friends among the British nobility and official class to enjoy the full confidence and trust of the patriots: when he was reported to be hobnobbing with Lord Hillsborough at that peer's castle in Ireland, some Americans concluded that Poor Richard was getting ready to sell out the cause and accept high office under the British Crown.

From the standpoint of the British government, however, Franklin was an "Arch Rebel" who sought to subvert the empire by stealth. He was dismissed from his post of deputy postmaster general of the colonies and loaded with contumely — treatment which, he said, proved to his satisfaction the truth of the saying: "*If you make yourself a Sheep, the Wolves will eat you.*" As for deserting the cause of colonial liberty in order to procure office under the Crown, he said: "They have done me honour by turning me out, and I will take care they shall not disgrace me by putting me in again; . . . God knows my Heart, I would not accept the least Office the King has to bestow, while such Tyrannous Measures are taken against my Country." In his writings he had tried, he remarked, to hold up a looking glass to England in which the ministers might see "their ugly Faces, & their Nation its Injustices." Despite his pains, he found that Englishmen persisted in regarding themselves as champions of right and justice; and they swore that the mirror reflected not their likeness but that of the Americans. Nevertheless, he continued to warn Englishmen of the folly of going to war with their colonies; to Charles James Fox he predicted, said Fox, "that our best blood and treasure would be squandered and thrown away to no manner of purpose; that like a holy war, while we carried ruin and destruction into America, we should impoverish and depopulate Britain." As a prophet, however, Franklin had little honor in Great Britain. Returning to America completely disillusioned as to the capacity of Englishmen to preserve the empire, he became one of the first to advocate independence, confederation, and foreign aid.

Franklin accepted the appointment as commissioner to France with little enthusiasm: he was an old man, he told Congress, and "all he could do, was to go to France, and die there in their Service." To a friend he said, "I am old and good for nothing, but as the shopkeepers say of their fragments of cloth, you may have me *for what you please*." These protestations had little effect upon his admirers: they confidently expected him to bring down the lightning upon Great Britain. Certainly, when he set sail for Europe in November 1776, France appeared to be the last hope of the sinking American republic. Sir William Howe declared that the hope of French aid alone kept the rebellion alive. "If that door were shut by any means and it were publicly known here," he told his government, "it would in my opinion put a stop to the rebellion upon the arrival of the reinforcements in the spring."

The British soon had cause to regret that Franklin had not been swallowed up by the Atlantic or been taken prisoner by the British navy. Lord Hillsborough roundly declared that Franklin was "the most hypocritical, abandoned old rascal that ever existed — a man who, if ever one goes to Hell, he will," and who ought not be permitted to run loose in France, stirring up that nest of hornets against Great Britain. He was known to be intimate with influential Frenchmen (having corresponded widely with French scientists and philosophers) and, said the British ambassador, "it is not to be doubted that He will make France the most insidious and tempting offers, and there is, I think, but too much Reason to fear that He will draw Her into the Snare." The best security against his wiles seemed to be that the French were not yet prepared for war, which left the British some small hope that Franklin's venom — "which," it was observed, "is more dangerous than that of his fellow Reptiles the Rattle Snakes" — would be expended in vain.

To offset the blow of Franklin's safe arrival in France, the British spread the report that the old philosopher, knowing that the game was up, had fled the United States for Europe after having exchanged his Continental paper money for thirty thousand pounds in gold. Lord Stormont, the British ambassador, tried to turn Franklin into an object of ridicule, observing humorously that "the Effect of his Fur Cap seems to be worn out and that . . . he is much less talked of since the Arrival of Picini, the famous Italian Composer." To Vergennes, however, the British ambassador was in deadly earnest in warning the French government not to have any dealings with Franklin or the cause he represented. Great Britain, Vergennes was given to understand, would regard Franklin's reception at Versailles as a most unfriendly act, certain to bring the two countries to the brink of war.

Nothing the British could do, however, prevented Franklin from scoring a personal, and later a diplomatic, triumph in France. To his reputation as a great scientist and homespun philosopher he joined a simpleness of manner and charm which proved, at least in France, irresistible. Here he met with the greatest social success ever experienced by any American diplomat; as a good-will ambassador he was unexcelled. No doubt the Franco-American alliance would have been consummated without Franklin's diplomacy, but both countries would have been the poorer had not Franklin gone to France. For Franklin helped make the alliance more than a mere formal agreement; he spread American principles and ideals in France and, in some degree, he was an advance agent of the French Revolution. In Franklin, France saw the natural man whose coming the philosophers of the Enlightenment had foretold; a man whose mind was free from the trammels of superstition, who exalted reason, and who practised the simple, free life that the French aristocracy had vainly sought in the pseudo-rustic cottages of Versailles. The finest flowering of the bourgeoisie, he brought a breath of fresh and wholesome air into the salons and palaces. He was the personification of democracy, the incarnation of the brave new world of the savants and philosophers. Even the French nobility, which, within a few years, was to be destroyed in the holocaust of the French Revolution, took Franklin to its heart.

During his residence in France, Franklin lived at Passy in "a fine airy House upon a Hill" with a garden where he walked every day. From the magnificence of the place, John Adams supposed that Franklin was paying an enormous rent — charging the bill, of course, to Congress — but actually the house was given him rent-free by an admirer. The French government approved this arrangement: at Passy, Franklin's movements could be more easily watched than in Paris, and British agents be kept at a safe distance. Franklin kept a chariot and three or four servants but he managed to live within his income as an American minister — perhaps because of the frequency with which he dined out. It was his custom to accept invitations for dinner six days a week — only on Sundays did he dine at home, and then usually in the company of visiting Americans. French cooking, he found, agreed with him better than English; he ate heartily, and in this he was in good company, for the French lived as well as any people on earth. "They stop, indeed," it was remarked, "and chat a good deal between the different entrees, and by that means lengthen the meal considerably, but they swallow more in proportion than any Englishman." An American traveler found Franklin in 1778 "quite fat, in good health, a fine constitution, eats very hearty and enjoys company, in general he is very reserved, but in company, and after dinner, he is free and sociable." He was, it is true, troubled by gout, but, as he said, he did not know whether the gout was a disease or a remedy for something worse. Being a philosopher, he inclined to the latter theory.

No doubt part of the explanation for Franklin's popularity in France was the affection he bore the French and the enthusiasm with which he took to French life. He found that in France Americans were treated "with a Cordiality, a Respect, and Affection they never experienc'd in England when they most deserved." Their frivolities — in some of which Franklin himself engaged — he held to be harmless: "to dress their Heads so that a Hat cannot be put on them, and then wear their Hats under their Arms, and to fill their Noses with Tobacco, may be called Follies, perhaps, but they are not Vices." Certainly, their manners were far superior, in his opinion, to those of the English. Yet there was nothing of the man of fashion about Franklin; he rebelled against the tyranny of fashion and the Parisians loved him for it and made him a new fashion. Even in the most brilliant companies, surrounded by powdered wigs and clothing of butterfly hues, Franklin was plainly dressed: he wore his thin gray hair under a fur cap which came down almost to his spectacles. Petted, acclaimed, and lionized, he became the reigning sensation of France; and, what is perhaps more remarkable, he retained his popularity undiminished during the seven years he remained in Paris. "If being treated with all the Politeness of France, and the apparent Respect and Esteem of all Ranks, from the highest to the lowest, can make a Man happy, I ought to be so," he said. Wherever he went, he was followed by "a genteel mob"; and so many paintings, busts, medals, and prints of him were scattered over the country that he remarked that his face was "almost as well known as that of the Moon." By the French Academy, he was hailed as the man who had drawn the thunderbolt from the clouds and the scepter from tyrants; but perhaps the greatest triumph of his career in France came in 1778 when, in a Paris theater, Franklin and Voltaire publicly embraced "by hugging one another in their arms, and kissing each other's cheeks."

In short, Franklin seemed to have blossomed into a "compleat courtier," paying pretty compliments to the Parisian beauties, flattering Marie Antoinette and the great ladies of the court, so that it was charged in Congress that he was becoming too Frenchified to represent the United States abroad. But at least it could not be alleged against Franklin that old age was interfering with either his pleasures or his business.

As might be expected, the atmosphere of Paris brought out Franklin's weakness for the fair sex — a weakness that had already caused him no little embarrassment and had produced an illegitimate child. The Parisian ladies, it must be acknowledged, succumbed gladly to the charm of the venerable philosopher: eagerly they presented themselves to be "embraced — that is," Franklin hastened to explain, "to have their Necks kiss'd." It was a common sight to see Franklin, in the fur cap which had become his hallmark, strolling in the Bois de Boulogne, "so fond of the fair sex, that one was not enough for him but he must have one on each side." "All the ladies both old and young," it was observed, "were ready to eat him up" — and Franklin, let it be said, was no mean dish. Had he been a younger man, his career in Paris might have been punctuated by frequent duels. Even at his age (he was seventy-one in 1777) and with his infirmities, he reveled in the life in which he had been cast; knowing that his popularity in France could not last forever — some other sensation would assuredly take his place — he asked only "to preserve, while I stay the Regard . . . of the French Ladies, for their Society and Conversation when I have time to enjoy it, is extreamly agreeable."

Franklin's only complaint was that too much work was thrown upon his aging shoulders by the Continental Congress. He was an old man, he reminded Congress, and he required peace and quiet; but it is evident that Franklin's schedule of nights out would have undermined the constitution of many a younger man. After a night spent in festivity, Franklin usually awakened to find his desk piled high with unfinished business which the old philosopher was hardly in a state to tackle. Besides his diplomatic duties, Franklin was expected to act as merchant, banker, judge of admiralty, and consul general. He made contracts for furnishing supplies to the United States, handled bills of exchange, directed the activities of United States vessels in European ports, supervised the American privateers operating out of French ports, and even settled a mutiny on board John Paul Jones's ship. Much of this business, particularly the mercantile end, went over Franklin's head: in such transactions, he said, "I am like a Man walking in the Dark. I stumble often, and frequently get my Shins broke." He was "plagu'd with all the Perversities of those who think fit to wrangle with one another"; one and all brought their troubles to him and pestered him for advice — "which," he observed, "is like calling upon a blind Man to judge of Colours." He urged Congress to establish consuls in European ports — a step which would have relieved him of much of the drudgery of mercantile and maritime affairs — but it was not until late in the war that Congress finally acted on this matter.

All Franklin's circumspection was required to thread his way safely through the pitfalls of French politics. The kingdom was divided into two camps: the party which advocated neutrality in the war between Great Britain and its colonies, and the party which clamored for immediate and unqualified intervention in the dispute. The first party was in power; the interventionists, led by the Duc de Choiseul, were in opposition. The civil war that had broken out in the British Empire was the event for which Choiseul had vainly waited during his tenure of power; now, out of office and out of favor at court, Choiseul asserted that the government had failed to take advantage of its opportunities. In 1775, he advocated open and immediate war with Great Britain, declaring that the French ministers were "Ideots for missing this golden Opportunity." Choiseul was intriguing to get back into power with the aid of the Queen and he also sought Franklin as an ally. No efforts were spared to induce the American commissioner to declare in favor of the interventionists. To have joined the Choiseul forces would have ruined Franklin's standing with the ministers in power; on the other hand, Franklin did not wish to alienate such ardent well-wishers to the American republic as the duke and his partisans. The British ambassador declared that nothing would better serve England's interests than to have Franklin become involved in the factional quarrels of French politics. Franklin, however, was equal to the occasion: his "reserved and prudent conduct" saw him safely through the maze of French party strife without costing him the support of either Vergennes or Choiseul.

While Franklin was establishing himself firmly in the hearts of the French people, the secret aid furnished by the French government was slowly beginning to move, but with such painful slowness that Beaumarchais, almost smothered by red tape and distracted by the vacillations of the men in power, was on the point of despair. He reasoned, he implored, he rose to new dramatic heights — but the supplies were not forthcoming in the quantities he deemed essential to the American cause.

Maurepas's memories of French defeats at the hands of British fleets and armies were too fresh to be easily blotted out; he required better evidence than Beaumarchais could supply that the British had at last met their match in American farmers and fir-built privateers. In his eyes, it was merely another romance concocted by the author of *The Barber of Seville*. So Beaumarchais found his arguments and prophecies held in small respect. "I am even more miserable than Cassandra, whose prophecies no one believed," he exclaimed, "because she always announced misfortunes. I only announce good things and people say that I realise the flights of my excited imagination." Although agreeing with the principle of secret aid, the head of the Ministry offered so many objections to its application that the Americans seemed likely to lose the war by default.

American defeats in 1776 demonstrated to Vergennes and Beaumarchais not that the American cause was hopeless but that war supplies must be rushed across the Atlantic on a larger scale than the government had contemplated. Despite all obstacles, they succeeded in drawing from the royal arsenals a large store of armaments; and early in 1777 these supplies were loaded aboard three French ships at Le Havre.

This was the kind of cloak-and-sword drama in which Beaumarchais reveled. Enemies lurked on every hand; a false step would plummet him to disaster; he was playing for high stakes and his wits were his only protection. Beaumarchais savored to the full the dramatic possibilities of international intrigue. "Unless a pistol shot stops me," he exclaimed with the grandiloquence of one of his stage heroes, "those who stand in my way will find their match."

As a secret agent for the French government, the playwright left something to be desired. Instead of remaining discreetly in the background, Beaumarchais, to whom publicity was the breath of life, began to play for the galleries and to take upon himself the airs of author, producer, and leading man in the drama of secret aid. For example, when he learned that Franklin was about to land at Nantes he took upon himself to instruct the American philosopher in the ways of diplomacy. Fearing that "on the arrival of that celebrated man in Paris, he should be so surrounded that some indiscretion might be committed," Beaumarchais told Deane to meet Franklin at the dock and "to lock him up and not to let him speak nor give letters to anyone" until Beaumarchais had the situation well in hand. Such drastic measures were necessary, the French dramatist believed, to keep Franklin from talking out of turn and thereby giving the game away to the British.

Moreover, to Vergennes's exasperation, Beaumarchais began to act as though he alone could save France and the United States. He pressed upon the government a program looking toward eventual war with Great Britain, urged that he be sent to Spain to bring that country into line, and even drew up a system of taxation which, he assured Maurepas, would enable France to wage war without fear of bankruptcy. It would appear that Beaumarchais aspired to take over the direction of France's foreign and domestic policy. "Why cannot I determine everything and do everything?" he asked Vergennes; and he intimated, with ingenuous candor, that only when he was in charge would matters come right.

Obviously riding for a fall, Beaumarchais journeyed to Le Havre early in 1777 to oversee the departure of the three ships carrying war supplies to the Americans. He thought of going to America himself, but a short outing on the Channel quickly drove that thought from his mind. As a disguise, he assumed the name of Durant. He was in a seventh heaven of plots and counterplots; a quick change of identity, he flattered himself, would throw the British off his trail. It happened, however, that a theatrical company at Le Havre was rehearsing his play, *The Barber of Seville;* and when he learned of this gratifying event, Beaumarchais could not resist the temptation to drop into the theater to give the actors the benefit of his personal direction. This, of course, spread the news far and wide that Beaumarchais was in Le Havre; and the British could hardly be persuaded that he had gone to that port to busy himself with stage directions and scenery. The British ambassador stormed into Vergennes's office and demanded that the sailing of Beaumarchais's ships from Le Havre be stopped immediately. There was a glint in Lord Stormont's eye that meant business. Accordingly, orders were immediately sent to hold in port the three ships chartered by Hortalez et Cie.

But not before Beaumarchais had been tipped off as to what was coming. He was given a few hours of grace in which to get his ships to sea; and probably the water front at Le Havre had never before seen such activity as when Beaumarchais went into action. Gangs of longshoremen worked all day and night loading the three ships with supplies, yet only one — the brig *Amphitrite* — got away before the deadline. Its cargo represented only a small part of the supplies Beaumarchais had gathered for the Americans, but, as has been seen, it was enough to bring about the downfall of Burgoyne.

As a result of Beaumarchais's unhappy penchant for seeing his own plays, Le Havre became too hot for the purposes of secret aid. British agents swarmed into the port, and the government could do no other than unload the ships as the British ambassador demanded. Vergennes still had a trick up his sleeve: the cargo was sent to other ports and in March 1777 ships carrying Beaumarchais's supplies put to sea. Although one ship was captured by British cruisers, the war supplies which got through were of priceless aid to the Americans.

Up to this time, Beaumarchais had flattered himself that he was pulling the wool over the eyes of the slow-witted Britons. Actually, however, the connection between Hortalez et Cie. and the French government, the amount of aid dispatched to the Americans through this channel, and the source of war supplies furnished Beaumarchais were well known to the London government. Beaumarchais's elaborately conspiratorial methods deceived no one. So closely was Beaumarchais kept under surveillance that even when he left Paris without even telling his mistress that he was going, Lord Stormont, the British ambassador, not only knew that Beaumarchais was out of town but could put his finger upon him at any moment.

Vergennes was well aware that "everything that took place in either London or in France got to be known in both places, and . . . it was slippery business in the face of the English." As Vergennes acidly remarked, it was only natural that the British should know more than he did himself since they had spies everywhere. The British spy system functioned to perfection: from every major French seaport full reports were relayed to London of the movement of French war supplies to the Americans. To escape the vigilance of the British, Beaumarchais was driven to such elaborate subterfuges as shipping a cargo of munitions to the United States in a ship "painted in black and white, with tear drops" ostensibly carrying to Poland the body of a Polish primate who had died at Marseilles. Even this ruse did not deceive the vigilant British agents.

Such efficiency deserves a word of explanation. The British owed their success in espionage largely to the fact that the War of American Independence was a civil war in which many Americans secretly or openly upheld the British side. As a result, the British government found it possible to plant spies in the very households of American diplomats in Europe. Few secrets, however closely guarded by American representatives abroad, were not known to the London government: their intimate correspondence and even their conversation were punctually reported to London.

The war began auspiciously for British hopes of inducing prominent rebels to betray their cause. In 1775, Dr. Benjamin Church, Director of Hospitals for the American army, a confidant of Sam Adams, a prolific writer of anti-British propaganda, and one of the leading New England patriots, was exposed as a spy. It happened that Church had acquired an expensive mistress and had got deeply in debt; to repair his fortunes, he entered into correspondence with the British commander in Boston, giving him — in code — information regarding the size and disposition of the American army. His mistress, through whom he sent his incriminating letters to Boston, incautiously left them with a man whom she supposed to be friendly to Church. He opened the letters, learned enough of the contents to arouse his suspicions, and rushed to headquarters with the news. Washington ordered the girl brought in, and after four hours' grilling, she confessed that Dr. Church had given her the letters. Although he stoutly protested his innocence, Church was put in prison, later dying at sea.

Church was apprehended before he could do serious injury to the American cause; there was, however, at least one American traitor who went through the entire war receiving pay from both the British and American governments but actually serving the side which paid best — in this case, the government of George III. As a spy, Dr. Edward Bancroft was one of the most resourceful and brilliant practitioners of that seamy profession.

Dr. Bancroft was no ordinary spy. Born in Springfield, Massachusetts, he had been a pupil of Silas Deane when that Connecticut Yankee was a schoolmaster. At an early age he went to England, where he won a medical degree, wrote several books, among them a novel, and distinguished himself as a propagandist during the dispute with the mother country. In London, he became a close friend of Franklin, who said of him that he was a "very intelligent sensible man." Held in high esteem by both Franklin and Deane, it was natural that they should have given him employment when he appeared in Paris in 1776 in the guise of a patriot seeking to serve his country. Bancroft became their private secretary — a position which gave him access to every state secret of the American commissioners.

Unknown to his patrons, Dr. Bancroft was no longer the flaming patriot Franklin had known in London or the bright schoolboy Deane had taught in New England. When the Americans struck for independence, Bancroft remained loyal to the mother country, but he did not find it convenient to take the world into his confidence. Instead, he began to seek means of turning to financial account the trust and confidence he enjoyed among the rebels. There was probably more love of money than love of Britain at the bottom of Bancroft's conduct; in any event, in December 1776, he went on the payroll of the British government, agreeing to deposit his information regularly in a sealed bottle in the hole of a tree near the Tuileries. Henceforth, he was under two flags and on two payrolls: he collected his pension from the British and his salary from the Americans. For Dr. Bancroft, everything was rosy — unless he made a slip.

Dr. Bancroft lived cozily with William Carmichael, a fellow secretary in the entourage of the American commissioners. They maintained in Paris, said Carmichael, "a very decent house. We have none but Ladies of the 1st Quality — I have not seen a Strumpet there 3 Weeks." Here Bancroft was in his element: his chief interest in life seemed to be women and "good eating & Drinking," at which, said a British agent, "he is not a Bad hand." Perhaps because he found the fare better — the feminine company provided by Carmichael seems to have been irreproachable — Dr. Bancroft broke up housekeeping with Carmichael and moved in with Dr. Franklin at Passy. Here, certainly, he was ideally placed to garner the information for which the British government was paying him.

To divert suspicion from himself, Dr. Bancroft did not overlook a trick, even going so far as to have himself arrested as an American agent while on a mission to England in Franklin's service. The arrest, of course, had been arranged by Bancroft with the British government, but it worked like a charm. Silas Deane did not for a moment doubt that his good friend had fallen into the hands of the merciless Britons. "This worthy Man," he lamented, "is now confined in the *Bastile* of England." If, for appearance' sake, Bancroft was in prison, he was a very unusual prisoner, drinking the best wines and eating the best food that could be provided. And much to the joy of Deane and Franklin, he soon popped up again in Paris, having quite miraculously been delivered from captivity. Later, on another journey to England, he arrived back breathlessly in Paris, declaring that he had narrowly escaped arrest again as an American spy. When his salary was not forthcoming, he threatened to leave the employ of the commissioners — certainly the last thing he intended, since it would have cut him off from the information for which the British were paying so handsomely. He even had the hardihood on one occasion to ask Franklin for a loan: he was hard up, he said, as a result of his self-sacrificing exertions for the cause of freedom. As Bancroft was well aware, Franklin was hearing this story from so many other impecunious Americans that it seemed proper for him likewise to try to touch Poor Richard.

Bancroft did not succeed in deceiving all the American diplomats in Paris: that lynx-eyed watchdog of liberty, Arthur Lee, distrusted Bancroft and warned Franklin against a "blind attachment" to his secretary. Arthur Lee saw traitors behind every bush and, considering how many people at one time or another he accused of treason, it is not surprising that he hit the mark at least once. His suspicions were originally aroused by the fact that Bancroft was a protégé of Silas Deane, whom Lee dearly hated; and when the Virginian learned that Bancroft was making surreptitious visits to the British Privy Council, he accused the traitor to his face. A duel was threatened between the two men, but Franklin and Deane finally succeeded in smoothing over the incident. (It is worth noting that Lee's personal secretary, Thornton, was a British spy and yet passed as a good patriot with Lee.) Despite Lee's suspicions and Vergennes's repeated warnings that there was a traitor in the camp of the American commissioners in Paris, Franklin and Deane continued to repose implicit confidence in Dr. Bancroft: to him they confided secrets that they withheld even from other American diplomats in Europe. It was not until the British archives were opened late in the nineteenth century that Bancroft's duplicity was finally brought to light.

That Dr. Bancroft earned his keep could hardly be questioned. Through him, the British government received advance information concerning the movements of American and French ships by which British cruisers were enabled to waylay them in the Bay of Biscay; and through him the nature and extent of French "secret" aid to the rebels was laid before the Ministry in London. He got word to England of the signing of the Franco-American alliance, supposedly a top secret, within a few hours of the event; and in 1778 he warned the British cabinet that a French fleet, without tarrying for the formality of a declaration of war, was on its way to attack the British fleet and army in the Chesapeake. There were, in short, few military and diplomatic secrets of the allies to which Dr. Bancroft was not privy; and he did not withhold information from his employers.

Bancroft's intelligence, authoritative as it was, met with skepticism in high quarters in Great Britain. George III distrusted Bancroft both as a "thorough American" and as a speculator who dabbled in stocks and spread rumors to influence the market. For this reason, Bancroft was tailed about Paris by British agents; his mail was opened by the British post office; and his information was often discounted as coming from an untrustworthy source. The King was right about Bancroft's speculations — he made thousands of dollars in cargoes of supplies sent to America and in his stock-market operations; but the royal judgment was at fault in holding Bancroft to be an American at heart: Dr. Bancroft had placed himself on the auction block and he did not permit sentimentality to stand in the way of business.

Dr. Bancroft was by no means the only spy installed by the British among the American commissioners in Paris. Captain Joseph Hynson, a Maryland ship captain who had turned privateer, regularly met the secretary of the British ambassador once a week to render a detailed account of the goings-on in American diplomatic headquarters. George Lupton, a British spy posing as an American patriot, succeeded in extracting much valuable information by keeping his ears open in Silas Deane's presence until Lupton was put out of action by venereal disease, having, as he put it, "been deceived by a Girl."

It was Captain Hynson who achieved one of the most spectacular coups of the war by stealing an entire budget of official papers sent by the American commissioners in France to the Continental Congress. In 1778, that body was anxiously awaiting word of the progress of the negotiations in France; after many months of silence on the part of the commissioners, letters arrived; but when Congress opened them they were found to consist of blank paper. Thanks to Captain Hynson's treachery, the original documents had long since been in the possession of the British government.

Together with secret aid vital to the war effort, France contributed aid which was neither secret nor, from Americans' point of view, essential. The numerous French officers and soldiers of fortune who came to the United States, attracted by reports of commissions and high pay for the asking, became to Americans a source of embarrassment and distress.

The need of engineers was acute in the American army: in 1776, Washington declared that he did not have a single engineer. Fortifications were constructed from plans found in military textbooks — a method which sometimes produced strange and wonderful results. Charles Lee, viewing some of these feats of engineering, declared that he did not believe that there was a man in the army capable of constructing an oven. As proof, he pointed out that American fortifications were left defenseless in the rear. It was lack of engineers which made it impossible for Washington in 1776 to erect proper fortifications in the vital defense zone of the Highlands. "Oh," exclaimed an American officer, "the *miserable* State of this

Country! As we are obliged to place our Dependance on such *miserable* Engineers." [1]

Therefore, in 1776, Congress instructed Silas Deane to procure the services of some experienced French engineers. Having opened the door a crack, Congress found that hundreds of officers swarmed in before it could be bolted and locked against these importunate warriors.

Because France had waged its last war only about ten years before the War of American Independence began, there were many officers in France and the West Indies, living on meager pay, to whom war spelled an opportunity to win glory, promotion, and hard cash. As reports of this "fine War" on the other side of the Atlantic began to filter into France and its colonies, these soldiers of fortune began to pack their kits, straighten out their passports, and go off to the wars. Some were fugitives from their creditors; others had been cashiered for misconduct in the French army; several were drunkards who drank themselves to death upon the cheap liquor they found in the United States. The worst of the lot seem to have come from the French West Indies, where stranded soldiers of fortune, from beachcombers up, had no difficulty in procuring letters of recommendation from the governor of Martinique; he was only too happy to be rid of such undesirable company.

In Paris, Silas Deane was beset by hundreds of officers eager to go to America and serve in defense of the republic. Had he had ten ships, Deane said, he could have loaded them to the gunwales with volunteers. Many of these officers came to him recommended by officials in the government as "Caesars, each of whom would have been an invaluable Acquisition to America"; and Deane hesitated to ignore their claims lest the French government take offense and cut off military supplies to the United States. Therefore, he accepted indiscriminately almost all who came to his door, and sent them away bearing contracts promising high commissions in the American army. After a few weeks in Paris, Franklin could sympathize with Deane's plight; never before, said the old philosopher, had he experienced such importunities or been subjected to such pressure. Even underlings at the American headquarters in Paris were "pestered and teazed" by these volunteers. The British ambassador, alarmed by the rebels' success in recruiting French officers, began to fear that the British would meet with great difficulty in conquering an American army led by French officers.

At first, Congress freely bestowed commissions upon French officers, leaving to Washington the problem of finding places for them in the army. Washington resented having these French officers dumped into his lap by Congress: he could not satisfy their claims, he pointed out, without offending American officers who looked jealously upon foreigners and

[1] The designs of the fortifications erected around New York City were taken from plans contained in Clairac's *Éléments de Fortification,* a standard treatise of the times.

felt that by seniority and merit the commissions given Frenchmen rightly belonged to themselves. When Congress gave a French major a horse to replace one shot from under him in battle, General Sullivan exclaimed that although he had lost "the best Horse in America They have not taken the Least notice of it." American officers refused to be impressed by the titles of French marquises or German barons. "We are a republic here," said General Steuben, "and Mr. Baron does not pass for a red cent more than Mr. Jacob or Mr. Peter." "It is by the zeal and activity of our own people that the cause must be supported and not by a few hungry adventurers," Washington reminded the statesmen in Philadelphia. He was "haunted and teazed to death by the importunity of some and dissatisfaction of others." All imperiously demanded high commands; none seemed content with what they were given. It took half his time, Washington complained, to "hear their pretensions, and explain to them the Reasons why it is impossible for me to gratifie them in their Wishes."

Congress soon began to look sourly upon these clamorous and insatiable warriors, eager for the emoluments and glory of war. Congressmen tried to dodge whenever they spotted them in the streets of Philadelphia — they were known to buttonhole an unwary victim and to make his life miserable until he yielded to their pertinacity. It was now clear to congressmen that there was no end of foreign officers "willing to come over & supersede such of ours as have been constantly in the field, and have borne innumerable hardships, when our poverty in Arms & Ammunition would have terrified the stoutest European who had been accustomed to Systematic Campaigns." To stop the flood, Congress in March 1777 resolved that no officers unable to understand and speak the English language were to receive commissions in the Continental army. But this proved to be of small avail; as Franklin said, "all that understood a little English would have thought themselves entitled to a commission, and the rest would have undertaken to learn it in the passage."

To some degree, the French government itself was behind this mass movement of officers across the Atlantic. The Ministry, however, preferred that relatively unknown men should go to the aid of the Americans — if prominent officers took passage there was certain to be trouble with the British, who had no intention of permitting the Americans to enjoy the benefit of French military leadership. And, as Beaumarchais remarked, men talked, whereas powder and shot told no tales. When French officers were overheard in Parisian cafés boasting that they were being sent to America by the government, Vergennes put them under arrest and assured the British ambassador that no officers would be permitted to join the Americans with the consent of the government; but he was careful to point out that "the french Nation had a Turn for adventure, and a wild Roving disposition, which it was impossible to controul."

The Prince de Broglie, one of the most powerful nobles of France and an ardent champion of the Americans, was eager to join the colonists — in the capacity of commander-in-chief of their army. This flattering offer deeply impressed Silas Deane: the Connecticut Yankee would have gladly replaced the Virginia planter with a prince of the blood. Broglie, he believed, had the power of procuring from the French government whatever supplies the Americans needed and would bring in his train a large number of noble volunteers; as Broglie's supporters claimed, the prince and his followers would "alone be worth twenty thousand men and would double the value of the American troops." Nevertheless, the Ministry could not be prevailed upon to dispatch a nobleman of Broglie's eminence to the Americans; so both the Americans and the prince were spared much embarrassment.

Among these "shoals of Frenchmen" who offered their swords in the service of the republic were some very capable and high-minded officers. Duportail, commander of the engineers in the Continental army; Armand, the cavalry leader; and Lafayette, to name only a few, were men who would have been distinguished in any army. Washington admitted that many of the French officers were "Men of Merit" genuinely eager to aid the American cause.

Of all the contracts entered into by Deane with French officers, none was more unpopular in the United States than that made with Du Coudray, a French engineer. Highly recommended by Vergennes and Beaumarchais, Du Coudray proved to be an apple of discord in the American army. By the terms of his contract, he was promised command of the American artillery — a stipulation which, if carried out, would have placed him above General Henry Knox and all other American artillery officers. Rather than suffer this humiliation, Generals Greene, Knox, and Sullivan threatened to throw up their commands; and since Du Coudray refused to budge an inch from his contract, duly signed and sealed by Silas Deane, Congress was left in a highly disconcerting position. Du Coudray assumed the airs of a *grand seigneur,* giving Congress to understand that he was on familiar terms with princes of the blood and that "it was to his ardent and pressing solicitations that they owed the help sent by France." Congress was impressed by this swagger; having seen few true French aristocrats, it was the more easily imposed upon. On the other hand, Congress could not risk breaking up the Continental army over Du Coudray. Fortunately for all concerned — except Du Coudray — he fell off a ferry near Philadelphia and was "drowned like a schoolboy." Congress, in particular, was put "very much at its ease by his death." [2]

[2] By Deane's contract, Du Coudray was promised the rank of major general and command of the artillery and engineers, subject only to the orders of Congress and the commander-in-chief. His pay was set at about seven thousand dollars a year and he was assured of a gift of six hundred thousand dollars after the war. In Deane's

Many French officers went to America with the connivance of the French court; but one who did not go with the benediction of His Most Christian Majesty was Lafayette. This young nobleman ran away from home, leaving his wife and child behind, to savor the high adventure of fighting for the cause of freedom in the United States. The French court was scandalized, not so much by Lafayette's unconventional leave-taking, as by the danger that Great Britain would construe this action on the part of a highly placed nobleman as an indication that France intended to jump into the conflict. Louis XVI exclaimed that it was highly blamable "in a Man of M. de la Fayette's Fashion and Rank to go and assist *Rebels*" and take with him fourteen officers; but the public was entranced by Lafayette's deed, calling it the *"Brillante Folie de Monsieur de La Fayette."* The Parisian ladies, it was said, railed at Lafayette's relatives "for having endeavoured to stop, so noble, and spirited an Enterprize." Lafayette, in fact, became the darling of French women from the Queen down. "I am well aware," sarcastically remarked General Steuben, "that in the queen's apartments the American Revolution has but one young hero, but you know that women must always have a little Jesus to work miracles."

By the time Lafayette and his party of young noblemen reached the United States, French officers had worn out their welcome with the Continental Congress. Lafayette was given the cold shoulder in Philadelphia, and had it not been for Washington's intervention, he probably would have been ordered out of town. Congress was resolved not to be imposed upon by any more Frenchmen claiming nobility and high rank in the American army: but fortunately for Lafayette, said one of his companions, Washington was able to "differentiate between the real gentlemen that we are and the freebooters who call themselves by that name." There were some advantages in being an aristocrat — at least they could spot their own kind.

Lafayette agreed to accept the rank of major general but without any pay or any command; and he was obliged to promise that he would never make any claim to command a division. Nevertheless, no sooner did Lafayette reach camp than Washington found himself tormented by the impetuous young Frenchman for a division. As Lafayette was not yet twenty years old and had never seen any action, Washington might be pardoned for doubting whether the young nobleman could be put to any use other than looking decorative around headquarters.

Lafayette was so overwhelmed by his first meeting with Washington that, in later years, he could scarcely mention the incident without bursting into tears. It was a case of hero-worship at first sight, and the

---

justification, it must be admitted that he was led to believe that Du Coudray was a highly influential figure at court and had it in his power to procure vast stores of supplies for the American army

reserved and austere Virginian was not a little taken aback by the warmth of the young Frenchman's adulation. However, Washington thawed visibly under the rays of Lafayette's admiration; although other American officers distrusted Lafayette's love of glory and his impetuosity, Washington found him brave and discreet beyond his years and entrusted him with important commands.[3]

⌒ ⌒ ⌒

Beaumarchais did not believe that secret aid was the last word in French policy; logically, the next step was the open participation of France in the struggle. To that end, he bombarded the King and Ministry with arguments for an alliance with the Americans, warning that France, by forever saying "It is too soon" (a favorite expression of Maurepas's) might be brought to exclaim, "Oh heavens, it is too late!" He did not doubt of overcoming by dint of eloquence the obduracy of the King; Louis, he pointed out, had sworn that he would never be vaccinated for smallpox, yet eight months later he submitted to vaccination. Was this not a good augury for the Americans?

In their zeal to champion the cause of the Americans and make war upon Great Britain, the people of France were far ahead of their government. As early as 1776, the British ambassador reported that the people talked of nothing but war and caught up "the most ridiculous Reports" of American victories. In 1777, the British ambassador left Paris for a week-end and immediately the Parisians joyfully spread the word that diplomatic relations with Great Britain had been broken. One would have imagined from the distress evinced by Frenchmen that Long Island was a French defeat; only the French ministers, reported the British ambassador, tried to conceal their chagrin. With good reason, the British feared the French people more than they did the government of Louis XVI. "The intemperate Spirit of the People of France," said a British agent in 1777, "may outweigh the cooler reasonings of the Court" and force it to act against its better judgment. The people, it was observed, seemed to love Americans "for murdering their old Enemies the English."

One of Vergennes's most insistent fears was that in the British Empire blood would prove thicker than water — that Americans and Englishmen would settle their differences and reconstitute the empire. Perhaps France stood to gain much by fishing in troubled waters; but he

[3] Lafayette was once asked by an Englishman how he could have endured to leave France for America, where he found by no means the best company and surroundings. Lafayette replied that he "might rather ask him how he could ever deliberately make up his mind to sail away from America, ever regretting afterwards, in the society of his frivolous countrymen, the loss of his rare and pleasant associations with General Washington."

was keenly aware of the danger that the waters might suddenly be stilled, leaving France high and dry and exposed to the enmity of both Americans and Englishmen.

Therefore, Vergennes demanded proof that America would be a fighting ally. "America says succor us, & we will never make peace," said Beaumarchais. "France says, prove to me that you will never make peace, & I will succor you."

On two separate occasions — August 1776 and July 1777 — Vergennes was prepared to take his country into war on the side of the United States, only to have the ground cut from beneath his feet by bad news from the fighting front. American defeats perceptibly cooled Vergennes's ardor for joining the rebels: he was so cast down by the reverses sustained by the Americans in 1776 that the British ambassador, after an interview with the French minister, reported home that "our neighbours will let us finish our own Business in our own way."

Yet Vergennes was sufficiently clear-sighted to see that France was traveling the road to war. That the British would long suffer tamely French "secret" aid to the rebels he did not believe. He knew that France had given Great Britain a mortal affront in aiding the American rebels and in building a fleet that threatened British maritime supremacy. Great Britain regarded the French fleet as a dagger pointed at its heart; and Vergennes suspected that rather than permit the French to become powerful at sea, the British would attempt to nip the Bourbon navy in the bud. Herein lay the chief source of Vergennes's alarm: would England strike without warning as in 1756 and, taking France unawares, destroy the fleet and overrun the colonies of its enemy? [4] To Vergennes, this was a very real danger: he knew that the Earl of Chatham, who had brought France to its knees in the Seven Years' War, yearned to fall again upon England's eternal enemy and to bind up the wounds of civil war in the British Empire by leading a crusade against the Bourbons.

Thus it happened that while giving the American rebels secret aid, the French Ministry lived in fear of a British surprise attack. In April 1777, the government was thrown into a ferment by the report that the five ships of the line recently launched in England would be turned against France at any moment. Even Maurepas, the least jingoist of the King's advisers, believed that England was on the verge of war with France; and he agreed to add seven more ships of the line immediately to the French navy. And, exclaimed the British ambassador, these fears and suspicions were "industriously, and maliciously propagated by Franklin, who pretends to have received undoubted Intelligence of it from England."

[4] In 1756, Great Britain had attacked the French fleet without a prior declaration of war. Likewise, in 1672, the British fleet had fallen upon the Dutch without warning.

In actuality, the British government was forced to accept assurances of friendship which it did not believe and to pocket injuries which it was too weak or preoccupied to resent. The government of Lord North had no desire to have two wars on its hands at the same time; if France was to be punished for its many breaches of neutrality, the reckoning must wait until matters had been settled with the colonies.

The Continental Congress showed scant respect for France's obligations as a neutral: the needs of the United States were uppermost in the minds of the statesmen in Philadelphia and they did not intend to lose the war because of any restrictions placed upon France by its treaties with Great Britain. Therefore, in October 1776, they coolly asked France to lend or sell them eight ships of the line, completely equipped for action against the enemy. Vergennes was staggered by the brashness of this request; he answered tartly that if the ships were available, France would find use for them herself.

Nevertheless, the American commissioners in Paris continued pertinaciously to ply Vergennes with pleas and arguments for more aid — even if France were involved thereby in the war. Armaments sent to the United States, they declared, would redound to the advantage of France by bringing Britain to "that state of weakness and humiliation which she has, by her perfidy, her insolence, and her cruelty, both in the east and the west, so justly merited." On the other hand, if Great Britain were victorious over the United States, her domination would be riveted upon the world — "and assuredly," said the commissioners, "from the natural pride and insolence of that people, a power to all the other states the most pernicious and intolerable."

To this it might have been answered that France was already doing far more for the Americans than was consistent with her duties as a neutral. French ports hummed with activity as supplies were rushed across the Atlantic to the faltering Americans. In 1777, about eighty ships cleared Bordeaux alone for the United States; many others set sail for Santo Domingo or other ports in the French West Indies from whence their cargoes were transshipped to Charleston, Boston, or Philadelphia. True, the British raised the point of ultimate destination, but Vergennes was adept in turning British wrath with soft answers. It was no doubt true, he admitted, that supplies were being sent from France to the rebels in America, but this was illicit trade carried on by merchants in the hope of profit. Even with the best will in the world, the French government could not entirely suppress smuggling. Every effort would be made, he assured the British ambassador, to prevent war supplies from reaching the Americans.

Although France opened its ports to American merchant ships, the government did not claim the right of sending war supplies directly to United States ports in French vessels. Vergennes acknowledged that if

French ships were captured under such conditions by British cruisers, France would have no redress. Nor did he insist upon the surrender by the British of French officers captured in America fighting on the side of the rebels.

Nevertheless, the patience of the British government under the injuries meted out by France was wearing thin. As Englishmen quickly discovered, the American war afforded "a mask for all the nations in the world, under American colours, to plunder the British trade." Particularly in the West Indies, French ships assumed the American flag and, under the guise of privateers, preyed upon British shipping. Martinique became in British eyes little better than "a nest of pirates"; in this port, privateers were openly outfitted, and British ships captured by the privateers were publicly sold. In St. Pierre, American ship captains "beat the Drum there for Volunteers to engage in the Service of the Rebels." Over five thousand Negro slaves, taken from British slave ships by American privateers, together with vast quantities of rum and sugar, were sold in the French West Indies.

Moreover, because American ships used the French flag to escape detection by British cruisers, the British found it necessary to board on the high seas, and sometimes in French coastal waters, ships flying the French flag. A powerful British squadron operated in the Bay of Biscay, sending scores of French ships to British prize courts; and in retaliation for these depredations, the French began to arm their merchant ships. Thus was created a state of affairs which at any moment might produce the incident that would plunge the two countries into war. No one except the Americans was wholly happy over this situation.

Simply by strengthening its navy, France materially aided the Americans, for the French fleet kept over forty ships of the line of the British navy in home waters. When Lord Howe asked for more ships for the American station, the Admiralty invariably answered that the threat of the Spanish and French navies made it impossible to weaken further the fleet at home. Before Britain could be secure, it was necessary, Lord Sandwich declared, that the home fleet be superior to the combined navies of France and Spain — a force which he gave Englishmen to believe they already possessed.

An even greater menace to peace was the protection given American privateers in French ports. These ships were hospitably welcomed by the French authorities, who permitted them to lay in supplies, arms, and ammunition and to pursue their depredations upon British commerce. Occasionally, as in the West Indies, American privateers were even outfitted in French ports and, manned largely by French crews, put to sea under the American flag.

Although few in number, the American privateers operating out of French ports seemed to the British to be a veritable armada. The coasts of England were "insulted by the American privateers," Britons lamented, "in a manner which our hardiest enemies have never ventured." Ships disappeared with alarming frequency; many British business houses, particularly those trading to the West Indies, were ruined; the English public was obliged to pay higher prices for sugar, tobacco (the price of tobacco more than trebled), and other colonial products; and insurance rates were boosted to such prohibitive heights that many British shippers began to resort to the use of French ships in order to carry on overseas trade without interference from American privateers. Thus the British merchants were "reduced to seek that protection under the colours of other nations, which the British flag used to afford to all the world." It was found necessary to establish convoys even in British home waters; the linen ships traveling from Dublin to England were protected by British cruisers and the harbor of Dublin was strongly fortified against an American attack. Already hard pressed for ships, the British Admiralty could not begin to meet the demand for convoys. "The sea is overspread with privateers on every part," exclaimed Lord Sandwich in August 1777, "and the demands for convoys and cruisers so great that we know not how to supply them." Meanwhile, American privateers continued to capture and destroy British ships, sometimes within British territorial waters; a bag of thirty ships or more was not unusual for a privateer in a single cruise. An English official gloomily admitted in 1777 that if the balance of naval power between the United States and Great Britain was to be determined by the number and value of the captures made at sea, the United States enjoyed superiority.

The havoc wreaked upon British shipping was made the easier for Americans by the fact that practically all the frigates and cruisers — the fastest sailing ships — in the British navy were in American waters, leaving only the large ships of the line for home defense. These leviathans, carrying five hundred or more men, and heavily armed, were not adapted to the work of tracking down the small, swift, and highly maneuverable American privateers: one does not fight gnats with cannon.

Yet it is true that without the free use of French ports, American privateers could not have held the seas in European waters. When an American privateer was chased by a British ship, it simply set its course for the nearest French port, ran down its anchor when it reached the haven, and figuratively thumbed its nose at the baffled British. Sometimes whole squadrons of American privateers put to sea from French ports and returned triumphantly bearing the prizes of the chase.

Under these circumstances, France's neutrality ceased to be even a polite fiction. Early in 1777, Weekes, an American privateer whose ship had been fitted out in France, seized five English vessels, carried them to the French port of Lorient, entered the vessels on the customs records as belonging to himself, and then sold them publicly to French purchasers. Soon after, the ships left Lorient as French ships manned by French crews.

Even English packet boats carrying diplomatic correspondence fell prey to the privateers.

This was more than the British could brook: the aid given the Americans through Beaumarchais was at least kept under cover, whereas the protection accorded American privateers was as open as day. Not only was England gravely injured by the depredations of these privateers but her honor was even more painfully lacerated; it was now plain to all that England suffered these humiliations because she did not dare to retaliate upon France. Secret aid could be passed over more lightly because both governments could keep up appearances by denying knowledge of its existence; but by harboring and equipping American privateers, France was forcing the hand of the British government. To Englishmen, it was intolerable that their shipping should be pillaged "by a parcel of contemptible Rascals, encouraged and protected by France."

To provoke war between France and Great Britain was the deliberate intent of the American privateers. "Our late Cruize has made a great deal of Noise & will probably soon bring on a War between France and England, which is my sincere wish," boasted the captain of an American privateer. France, however, had no intention of going to war at this time; and it certainly did not wish to be dragged into the struggle in the wake of the American privateers. Vergennes made no effort to conceal his displeasure from the American commissioners, and the French court was so angry, said an American diplomat, "that I firmly believe if it had not been for the success of the military operations in America we should have been all driven out of their kingdom."

In 1777, with the war apparently going in their favor, the British were in no mood longer to swallow insult and humiliation from the Bourbons. This period of British stiffening coincided with Burgoyne's advance upon Albany and Sir William Howe's efforts to bring Washington to a decisive engagement. Anticipating success in these operations, the British government called France to account in a manner which admitted of no equivocation on the part of the government of Louis XVI.

Stormont, the British ambassador, paid a visit to Versailles which could hardly be termed sociable. With little regard to diplomatic niceties, Stormont bluntly told Vergennes that he knew what the French were up to. At Bordeaux, Nantes, Marseilles, and Dunkirk, he said, ships were about to sail to the United States with war materials for the rebel army. In aggravation of this injury, privateers were being sheltered, equipped, armed, and manned in French ports and sent forth to prey upon British shipping. By these unneutral acts, declared the British ambassador, France was waging war upon Great Britain under the specious cover of neutrality. "It is a fact, sir," Stormont told Vergennes, "a Part of the force of this Country is directed against us, and whether under the flag of France, or not, is in my opinion a Matter of Indifference, a mere Formality." Great Britain had hitherto suffered these wrongs quietly but, said the British ambassador, "all human things have bounds beyond which they cannot go. We are now come to the utmost Verge of these Bounds."

This was strong language and Vergennes could hardly miss the point: unless France observed more strictly its duties as a neutral, war would be the consequence. Vergennes saw that his government had gone too far unless it was ready to embark upon war. Accordingly, in the autumn of 1777, orders to stop the vessels loading for America were issued; American privateers were ordered to depart from French harbors and not to return on pain of seizure; the sale of prizes in French ports was prohibited; captured British ships in French ports were restored to their owners; and the entire crew of one American privateer was imprisoned at Dunkirk.

The French government had seemingly abandoned the Americans to their fate. Gloom descended thickly upon the American commissioners in Paris: Franklin became more reserved than ever, Arthur Lee swore that he had known all along that the French would leave them in the lurch, and Deane was heard to say "it was a pitty that Great Britain did not bring about a reconciliation with the Colonies, and jointly make War against France."

Instead of railing against the French for deserting their friends, Franklin set about putting the French themselves in the anxious seat. Deliberately he flirted with the British and spread the report that he would soon leave France, presumably for England, where he would be accorded all the civilities of a peacemaker. At dinner, he complained to a French noble that there was "nothing better to do here than to drink," and went on to observe that it was hardly to be expected that a great monarchy like France would help republicans to achieve their independence from another monarchy. He "strongly reproached France with having done only just what was necessary to unite the forces of England against them."

Franklin did not content himself merely with frightening the French by talking peace: he actually met Englishmen secretly in Paris, presumably to discuss terms for ending the war. In September 1777, for example, he made an appointment with Benjamin Vaughan, later a British peace commissioner, at Les Bains de Poitevin, the large public bathhouse on the Seine opposite the Tuileries. "The People know me only by Sight as I go there often to bathe," Franklin wrote Vaughan. "Ask for an old Englishman with grey Hair."

Franklin professed little interest in a military alliance between the United States and France; in fact, he declared himself to be opposed on principle to such alliances with European powers. Poor Richard had counseled self-reliance and he was prepared to apply his maxims to nations as well as to individuals: the less dependence upon outside help, the quicker would the United States learn to stand upon its own feet before the world. "He thinks," said one of his colleagues in Paris, "we shall derive Resources from our Distresses, like the Earth-born Giant Anteus, who derived new Strength from his Falls." To incur heavy obligations to France might, he said, "bind America beyond its true Interests: by relieving the Necessities of America too liberally," France might take upon itself to "prevent their Industry, their ingenuity & the discovery of the Resources of a Country intended by Heaven for Independence in its utmost Latitude." Far from supplicating an alliance with France, Franklin gave the ministers at Versailles cause to wonder if he would accept an alliance if it were offered; and when the showdown finally came, it was the government of Louis XVI rather than Benjamin Franklin that seemed most eager for the alliance.

Franklin was of course aware that the best way to secure a French alliance was not to appear too anxious for it. Upon the French ministers, his equivocal conduct had gratifying effect, but the British ambassador, who knew him better than did the French, was not impressed by the old doctor's maneuvers. Franklin, Lord Stormont remarked, was playing his old game of "artifice & fraud"; he had bamboozled the British and now he was up to the same tricks with the French. The British ambassador set Franklin down as an inveterate republican who would never agree to any terms with the mother country short of independence. The ambassador was right, but Vergennes began to fear that he had been too harsh with the Americans and again the bogy of peace between the United States and Great Britain rose to torment him. He hastened to assure the commissioners that the restrictions imposed by the government upon American privateers were temporary and had been made only because the British were becoming particularly unpleasant; and behind the scenes he proposed that Spain join France in making up a purse of six million livres to bestow upon the Americans. Within a few months American privateers were again operating out of French ports; French shipyards were busy turning out ships for the purpose of destroying British commerce; and French war supplies were reaching the rebels. For this turn of events, Americans could thank Franklin's diplomacy and the victories won by their armies in the field.

In 1777, the British government was well aware that it must conquer the Americans in the coming campaign or suffer the consequences of French intervention. In August 1777, Lord George Germain acknowledged that a rupture with France and Spain was almost inevitable if war with the United States was protracted.

The singular silence in which Howe chose to cloak his operations was highly disturbing to Germain, who during the summer of 1777 began to suspect that all was not going well with the war. He could not understand, for example, why the commander-in-chief took such an unconscionable time in commencing operations; if Howe were to be back in New York from his Philadelphia junket in time to co-operate with Burgoyne, he could not let the grass grow under his feet. The King, too, was disturbed by the lack of news from Howe. Even the laconic Caesar had vouchsafed some information, albeit of a somewhat sketchy nature, to his anxious countrymen, but from Sir William Howe, not a syllable. In fact, Lord Howe's fleet might have gone down with all hands for all that the King and his ministers knew. The entire fleet and army were seemingly missing in action.

If the news from Howe — when it finally arrived — left much to be desired, that from Burgoyne was crushing in its finality. Word of Saratoga was brought to Lord North at midnight early in December 1777, just after he had returned from a fatiguing debate in the House. "He was," reported one of his companions, "so much hurt and agitated with it, That He threw Himself into a Chair, and did not speak a word for several Minutes . . . got up and walked about the Room for several Hours, and the next Day at the Levee His Distress was visible to all the foreign Ministers." In private, he remarked wryly that he envied Howe his snug quarters in Philadelphia — if he were only half as secure in his seat in Parliament as was the British general in the Quaker City, he would be well content.

The capture of Philadelphia was poor consolation for the loss of Burgoyne's army; and try as the Ministry would, it could not persuade Englishmen that there had been a fair exchange. Howe's victories, even when dressed up in official communiqués, were seen to be but dubious: Washington's army, although defeated, was still very much in the fight and, most alarming of all, every time the American commander was knocked down he seemed to come back stronger than before, whereas Howe was apparently growing weaker with every victory. Lord Chatham did not make the government's position easier by declaring that Washington had "proved himself three times an abler general than sir William Howe." In America it was the winter of Valley Forge and the times that tried men's souls; and it was hardly less an ordeal for Englishmen.

To the English Whigs, Saratoga was a vindication of all their prophecies, and proof that England must turn to other men and policies if she were to escape utter ruin. That the colonies could ever be conquered was, they declared, the veriest moonshine that had ever led a great empire to destruction. Burke and Fox took the ground that the Americans had already made good their independence; all that remained for Englishmen was to face the facts and salvage what they could from the wreckage of empire.

For a moment, even Edward Gibbon was shaken in his resolution to prosecute the war. "I shall scarcely give my consent," he said, "to exhaust still further the finest country in the world in the prosecution of a war from whence no reasonable man entertains any hope of success. It is better to be humbled than ruined." Nevertheless Gibbon was soon back on the ministerial benches, giving a silent yet undeviating vote in support of the war. In general, Gibbon's decision to take his stand with the administration in this crisis was typical of the English people.

Great Britain had gambled upon a decisive victory over the Americans — and had lost. Saratoga flashed a signal to England's foes that the opportunity had come to pull down the colossus that a few years before had bestridden the earth in its impregnability. It was clear to the British themselves that their period of a free hand in the American war was over. As Germain told Lord Howe, the French were preparing to strike and, he added, "the indecent Joy that was expressed in France" upon the news of British defeats "shows too plainly the Sense of the Nation in general."

The situation in Europe, it could not be denied, was all in France's favor. The continent was at peace and, what was more remarkable, wished to remain at peace. Frederick the Great still rattled his saber, but the "Prussian Hero" was now old and careworn; Austria was an ally of France, thus bringing to a temporary close the age-old rivalry of Bourbons and Hapsburgs; and Prussia, Russia, and Austria, having just committed a rape upon Poland, were leagued in crime if not in amity and were engrossed in plans to finish off the unhappy Poles.

Moreover, the revival of French naval power rendered it possible for the Bourbons to intervene decisively in the Anglo-American struggle. For the first time in many generations, France was able to contest against Great Britain the rule of the sea. It was fortunate for the Americans that the period of their revolt happened to coincide with the emergence of France as a first-rate naval power, for, had it not been for the French fleet, the British might well have worn down American resistance and reconquered the thirteen colonies while the Bourbons stood by helpless to avert the destruction of their ally.

Saratoga, together with Howe's failure to crush Washington in Pennsylvania, removed the last shred of doubt from Vergennes's mind that the American Revolution was a full-fledged revolt with which France might safely ally itself. But, more importantly, these American successes poised a new danger for France — the prospect of reconciliation between England and the United States. From Vergennes's point of view, the Americans had been too successful: they may have beaten wisdom into the British. Chastened by disaster and their eyes at last opened to the impossibility of conquering the United States, Englishmen might swallow their pride and make peace with the Americans.

Vergennes supposed that there was much more bad news in store for England which would give spur to reconciliation. Howe, he believed, was likely to suffer the same fate that had overtaken Burgoyne: although in possession of Philadelphia, the city might well prove to be the grave of his army. Unless the minds of Englishmen were irrevocably closed to wisdom, Vergennes assumed that this fresh blow to their hopes of conquering America would put them in a proper frame of mind for peace. When he went to the King to plead for the immediate recognition of

American independence, Vergennes made much of Howe's peril and the effect his surrender would have upon English public opinion.

If the British were converted to peace, "what," Vergennes asked, "have we to put in the way to prevent the Americans lending themselves to a reconciliation?" Assurances of good will and promises of aid — they would hardly suffice to keep Americans in the war if the mother country offered them magnanimous terms.

Lord North confirmed Vergennes's fear that Englishmen would learn wisdom from defeat. Although the Prime Minister had often proclaimed himself to be a man of peace, hitherto he had been given little opportunity to exercise his talents as a compromiser. His own party and, equally important, the King were set against conciliation; and his peace plan had been adopted by Parliament in 1775 with much grumbling by the Tories. Privately, however, Lord North continued to nourish hope of a negotiated peace. He waited only for British victory to present a peace plan to Parliament; magnanimity in the hour of triumph would, he believed, ensure the reconciliation of the colonies to the victorious mother country. That propitious hour had failed to arrive; indeed, by the end of 1777, it seemed farther away than ever. Nevertheless, with or without a decisive victory over the rebels, Lord North was resolved to attempt a settlement. In December 1777, shortly after receiving the news of Burgoyne's surrender, North announced to Parliament that after the Christmas recess he would present a complete and far-reaching peace plan.

The compelling reason that drove North to offer peace terms to the rebels was the fear not merely that the colonies would be lost by the empire but they would be lost to France. As the Prime Minister said: "Independency, with a cordial love between us, is one thing — with an union with our enemies fatal." At all costs — even at the cost of England's pride — a Franco-American alliance must be headed off.

Thus, in December 1777, Lord North served notice upon his countrymen and upon all interested parties, including the French, that the British government had determined to offer liberal peace terms to the United States. Vergennes could no longer doubt that he must act swiftly if the Americans were to be kept in the war. And, to intensify his anxiety, the singular behavior of Dr. Franklin seemed to augur that British peace overtures might bear fruit even before Lord North got round to submitting his peace plan to Parliament when that body reconvened in February 1778.

Lord North believed that Franklin held the key to peace and reconciliation: if a peace plan could be dispatched to the United States bearing the approval of Poor Richard, the Prime Minister did not doubt that it would be accepted by the Continental Congress. Even George III was brought to swallow his repugnance to dealing with Franklin. A more malignant enemy of Great Britain he did not believe existed; "yet," said George, "I think it so desirable to end the War with that Country [America], to be enabled with redoubled ardour to avenge the faithless and insolent conduct of France that I think it may be proper to keep open the channel of intercourse with that insidious man."

As self-appointed philosopher to the British Empire, Franklin had conspicuously failed to impress his ideas upon the masters of the empire. Englishmen were little disposed to sit at the feet of an American, even if he were a philosopher, for instruction in the art of conducting the affairs of a great empire. The English, Franklin once complained, went by opposites: whatever was right or reasonable, they were certain to reject; the polestar of their policy seemed to be error and shortsightedness. Yet it brought him real pain to see England, a country which he had once loved and for which he still felt affection, beating its head against stone walls; and he could never resist the temptation to lend a hand to those who walk in darkness.

In December 1777, British agents in Paris made an eleventh-hour attempt to avert a Franco-American alliance by tendering a generous peace to the American commissioners. Deane and Franklin were offered a safe-conduct to London, an immediate armistice in the war, and prominent places in the American nobility which the government proposed to create in the colonies. The American commissioners gave short shrift to these proposals. Franklin, in particular, left the British agents under no illusions as to his attitude toward restoring the empire. He insisted upon rehashing American grievances, and when he took up the subject of British atrocities, the old philosopher displayed unwonted fire. "The Barbarities inflicted on his Country — the Remembrance of them," he said, "roused in an old Man, constitutionally phlegmatick, the resentments of a High Mettled Youth." So intense was his agitation that he lost his breath in relating the burning of towns and the cruelties practised upon American prisoners. Americans, he said, could not make peace in the hope that "tho you now thirst for our Blood, and pursue us with Fire and Sword, you may in some future time treat us kindly. This is too much Patience to be expected of us; indeed, I think it is not in human nature." Only independence — complete and unequivocal — could induce the United States to lay down its arms.

Franklin did not, however, bar all hope of amity between the two countries. Let Britain recognize the independence of the United States, punish the ministers and generals guilty of war crimes, and give up all its possessions upon the continent of North America to the United States, and there would be excellent prospect of friendship and peace between the two countries. Moreover, divested of their colonies in the Western Hemisphere, the British could free their minds of the cares and responsibilities incidental to the possession of a great empire. He urged the British to recognize that they had no future upon the North American continent — sooner or later, their territories would pass under the sway of the

United States. By getting out bag and baggage beforehand, the British would save themselves the trouble and disgrace of being kicked out. If they found this strategic retreat to the home islands unpalatable, Dr. Franklin was on hand to sweeten the draught. "You may call it, if you please," he told them, "an Indemnification for the needless and cruel burning of their [the Americans'] towns."

Yet the English failed to see, although Dr. Franklin took great trouble to make it clear to them, that destiny had decreed that Canada, Nova Scotia, Newfoundland, and the Floridas would one day pass to the United States. Instead, they stubbornly clung to these possessions throughout the war, and although he gave his best efforts to the cause, Franklin failed to win them for the United States in the peace treaty of 1783.

Unwilling to surrender most of their empire to Dr. Franklin, the British found themselves in 1777 unable to compete with the promises held out by France. That matters were going well at Versailles for the Americans, the discouraged British emissaries could hardly doubt. Franklin, it was reported, "does nothing but fly from one part of Paris to t'other"; and he seemed in uncommonly good spirits despite this feverish activity. At a dinner held late in December, 1777, he gave as a toast "a perpetual and everlasting understanding between the House of Bourbon and the American Congress," which the British agents took to mean that the alliance was already in Poor Richard's bag.

It was characteristic of Franklin's diplomacy that although he unceremoniously rejected the British peace overtures, he gave Vergennes to understand that an Anglo-American reconciliation was imminent. Making a great show of frankness, he told the French minister that he had seen the British agents and implied that the British terms were not unacceptable to the Americans. The French were left to draw the inference that if they wished to keep the United States in the war, they could no longer delay their alliance. Deane inadvertently gave the game away, however, by assuring Vergennes that the British terms were inadmissible — an artlessness that endeared him to the French minister. Deane, Vergennes decided, was "the most decided of all in not wishing for any coalition with England," but Franklin remained an enigma.

Vergennes did not need Franklin to tell him that the American commissioners were meeting with British agents in Paris: Franklin and his colleagues were shadowed by French spies who gave the ministers detailed reports of every movement made and every visitor entertained by the commissioners. Between the British and French secret agents, American diplomats could hardly call their lives their own; spied upon by friends as well as foes, and without a spy service of their own, they labored under disadvantages that taxed even Dr. Franklin's celebrated astuteness.

Vergennes soon discovered that a new note of firmness and decision had crept into the tone of the American commissioners. The favorable turn of events in America was immediately reflected in the bearing of the commissioners; as the Spaniards sourly observed, "sought after by two Powers like France and England, it is not astonishing that they have become proud of their position." Vergennes was taken aback by this altered demeanor of the Americans; for a moment he feared that they had inherited "the pretensions and the greedy and bold character of their mother country." Certainly, they displayed little of the deference and humility that a French minister might expect from suppliants; but Vergennes could not conceal from himself that the American commissioners held all the cards. "They have in their hands," he admitted, "all that constitutes sovereign power. Our recognition will add nothing to the reality of that possession."

In Vergennes's opinion, the time had come to join the Americans or to lose them forever. "There is not a moment to lose," he exclaimed. ". . . Events have surprised us, they have marched more rapidly than we could have expected. The time lost, if any, is not entirely our fault, but there is no more to be lost. . . . They want positive facts and effective assurances," he added significantly, "capable of counterbalancing the definite offers of England."

The King remained almost the last stumbling block to the consummation of Vergennes's plans; and although Louis was not bright he was stubborn and opinionated. War ill accorded with his plans to make his reign a triumph of budget-balancing: he yearned to go down in history as Louis the Economizer but Vergennes would give him no peace. It was the unfortunate lot of this sovereign, who asked only to be let alone with his clocks, to have been cast in an age of wars and revolutions utterly foreign to his temperament and far beyond his powers of understanding. He was eminently fitted for the quiet, simple life of a middle-class suburbanite; as a small contractor or watchmaker in Paris he would have been respected as an honest, home-loving, and inoffensive man.

For the benefit of the King, Vergennes pictured the alliance with America as a supreme act of magnanimity that would eternally reflect glory upon his reign. The King was interested in glory, provided it did not cost too much; but he could not be approached upon the subject of a Franco-American alliance as a means of taking revenge upon Great Britain or of seeking commercial advantages for France by overthrowing the British Empire. Furthermore, he had to be convinced that war with Great Britain was an act of self-defense — that, sooner or later, England would attack his country unless he attacked first. With these arguments, specially framed for the royal understanding, Vergennes plied the King.

Despite these urgings, Louis was not persuaded that it would be safe to leap upon John Bull even though he were down. This healthy respect for England's fighting strength led the monarch to insist that Spain be brought into the quarrel on the side of France: with an ally, Louis felt much safer in challenging Great Britain. Moreover, he placed great store in the wisdom of his uncle, Charles III of Spain, an "enlightened monarch" conspicuously unfortunate in his handling of foreign affairs. Nevertheless, the decision of peace or war was submitted to the wisdom of His Catholic Majesty.

With good reason, Vergennes dreaded an appeal to Spain. From the beginning of the American revolt, Spain had blown hot and cold upon the patriot cause, but latterly the wind from Madrid had become almost frigid. In 1775 and 1776, Spain was so eager for war with Great Britain that France was compelled to restrain the belligerent zeal of its partner. Yet, however hostile to Great Britain, Spaniards had little affection for Americans; and their ardor for entering into combat with the British had little to do with aiding the American rebels.

During the early period of the War of American Independence, Spain was preoccupied with its plans for conquering Portugal and the Portuguese Empire in South America. Because Great Britain was an ally of Portugal and gave every indication of supporting the smaller country in its difficulties with Spain, His Catholic Majesty seriously contemplated war with England. In 1777, however, Spain settled its quarrel with Portugal — and therewith war lost much of its savor to Spaniards.

Spain, the world's largest colonial empire, could ill afford to encourage rebellion and republicanism in the Western Hemisphere. France risked little, for the greater part of its empire had passed into the possession of Great Britain; but the Spaniards had much to lose and stood in desperate fear of losing it. It was difficult for Madrid to regard American republicans other than as an enemy who, if less powerful than their British cousins, were equally hostile to Spanish interests. Perhaps more was to be feared from American than from British expansionism: certainly the existence of an independent republic in the Western Hemisphere was more dangerous as an example to Spain's own colonists than was British monarchism. "This republic has been born as it were a pigmy," said a Spaniard. ". . . But a day will come when it will be a great, a veritable awe-inspiring colossus in these regions"; and Spaniards might well dread that this colossus would rise upon the ruins of their own colonial empire.

The Madrid government preferred, therefore, to give the Americans just enough aid to keep them in the fight against Great Britain. A long, ruinous, and indecisive war between the British and the colonists that would leave both combatants exhausted — in short, a double knockout — was to Madrid a perfect solution for removing the menace of British imperialism and American republicanism. The War of Dutch Independence had contributed greatly to the decline of Spain: why should not the War of American Independence do likewise to Great Britain?

In pursuance of this policy the Spanish government sent secret aid to the Americans, although on a smaller scale than did the French, through the mercantile house of Gardoqui and Sons, the Spanish equivalent of Hortalez et Cie. As an intermediary between the Spanish government and the American rebels, Gardoqui handled the shipments of war supplies, clothing, salt, and other scarce commodities to the United States — for all of which payment was requested.

In Spanish Louisiana, Americans found a firm friend in the person of Governor Galvez. Here was one Spanish official who acted upon the principle that it was to Spain's interest to give the rebels full support. He sold them powder out of the royal stores, loaned money and supplies to Oliver Pollack, the American agent in New Orleans, and gave sanctuary to American ships at the same time that he denied harbor to British vessels. To aid the Americans, Galvez stretched his powers to the utmost and committed breaches of neutrality which, had Great Britain been in a position to take offense, could easily have brought the two countries to war.

As the Americans grew stronger and their cause prospered, Spain's readiness to assist them visibly abated. While the patriots were fighting for their lives, Spain was willing to help them in order to weaken Great Britain, but the American victories in 1777 brought sharply home to Madrid the menace of a victorious republic flushed with triumph and looking for new worlds to conquer. Only as a weak and small state was the United States tolerable to Spain; when the republic began to rise to its feet, it became a thing of terror to the government of Charles III.

For his part, Vergennes was by no means inclined to establish a powerful, aggrandizing republic in the Western Hemisphere, and he sought to soothe Spain's apprehensions on that score. He saw that if firmly united the United States might become a menace to Europe: it might build a navy that would be "an over-match for the whole Naval Power of Europe"; it might extend its power over all North and South America, and strip every European nation of its territory in the hemisphere. "All these Consequences would not, indeed, be immediate," Vergennes remarked to the British ambassador. "Neither you nor I should live to see them, but for being remote they are not less sure." France had "no interest whatever," he said, "to see America play the part of a power"; and he expected the Americans themselves, through their quarrels and sectional jealousies, to keep the United States from ever cutting a figure in the world.

Vergennes laid much stress upon the danger that Great Britain, if checked in its efforts to reconquer the thirteen revolted colonies, would strike at the colonial empires of France and Spain to find compensation for its losses. This seemed in accord with British character as understood in Versailles and Madrid, and it afforded a strong argument to Vergennes in his efforts to persuade Spain of the necessity of joining France in an alliance with the United States. As the largest and at the same time one of the weakest empires in the world, Spain might well be alarmed for the safety of its overseas possessions. Rightly aware of Spain's vulnerability, Vergennes harped upon this theme with a persistence calculated to send chills down the spines of the statesmen in Madrid.

All these arguments were wasted upon Florida Blanca, the head of the Spanish Ministry. For every reason advanced by Vergennes for joining the Americans, Florida Blanca had an answer calculated to keep the Bourbon monarchies out of war. There was, he pointed out in 1777, no danger that the rebels would make peace with the British; self-interest would continue to bind the Americans to France and Spain, and the King of Spain felt an invincible repugnance to allying his country with the United States. In short, to go to war with Great Britain was to play the game of the Americans, who from the beginning had sought to embroil Europe in their quarrel. As for the security of the Spanish Empire, Florida Blanca pointed out that there was little to fear from Great Britain, now hopelessly bogged down in .war with the Americans. Let secret aid be continued to the Americans, was the word from Madrid in December 1777, but forget this mad scheme of making an alliance with the rebels.

Spanish obstinacy was proverbial, and Vergennes had little hope of budging the Madrid government from its position. He took what comfort he could in the assurance given by the French ambassador to the court of Spain, that if France chose to act alone, Spain would almost certainly stand by its ally, albeit with bad grace. "Be quite sure, Sir," wrote the French ambassador, "that in whatever manner France is dragged into war, Spain will follow." Accordingly, a secret article was inserted in the Franco-American treaty reserving a place for Spain in case His Catholic Majesty decided to make it a triple alliance against Great Britain.

Vergennes had unwillingly consented to the delay necessitated by taking counsel with Spain; now that Madrid had made known its position, the French minister declared flatly that any further procrastination would be fatal. The British Parliament was scheduled to assemble in the middle of February — at which time, as Vergennes well knew, Lord North would unwrap his long-anticipated peace plan. British agents were still in Paris seeking to persuade the American commissioners to bring their country back into the empire. Vergennes did not know how far the British were ready to go, but he perceived that, while France and Spain debated, "the only opportunity which may perhaps happen for many centuries for putting England in its true place" might be lost. "The whole science of politics is concentrated in the two words *foresee* and *forestall*," said Vergennes. He had already foreseen British policy: it now remained for him to forestall it.

Under these circumstances, it was France rather than the United States which became the suitor for an alliance. Although the American commissioners had been instructed only to make a treaty of friendship and commerce with France, Vergennes pressed upon them a treaty of alliance: he wished to bind the United States as closely as possible to France and, above all, to ensure that they make no separate peace with Great Britain. To this, Franklin and his colleagues quickly assented.

Once France had decided to take the plunge, little difficulty was experienced in drawing up treaties with the American commissioners. In general, there was a meeting of minds: both countries agreed as to the purpose and scope of the military alliance and commercial agreement that were formulated early in 1778. The treaty of amity and commerce followed closely the "Plan of Treaties" drawn up by Congress in the summer of 1776; but this did not mean that the United States wrote its own terms and won a victory at the conference table over a reluctant ally. The victory was as much French as American; and the liberalism that distinguished this treaty was as much a reflection of French enlightenment as it was of American democracy.

The Franco-American alliance was conditional — it was to go into effect only in case of war between Great Britain and France. The American commissioners objected to this provision, asking for an actual instead of a contingent alliance, "but they were told in so firm a tone," said Vergennes, "that to insist on a change of that nature would be to break off all negotiations, that they decided to desist." On the other hand, Vergennes did not seriously doubt that war between his country and Great Britain would be an immediate consequence of the alliance. If this event occurred, by the terms of the alliance the United States was bound to engage in the defense of the French West Indies and not to make peace with Great Britain without the consent of France. On its part, France guaranteed the independence of the United States and promised to continue the war until that objective had been attained. In so far as it was possible at this time for France to do so, the independence of the United States was ensured.

In making a treaty of commerce with the United States, France did not demand an exclusive control over American commerce such as had been maintained by the British and as France itself imposed upon its own colonies. It was clear that the Americans would never consent to such an arrangement — free trade with the world was one of the watchwords of the American Revolution — but even if they had been brought to agree under pressure, France would not have served its best interests by seeking to monopolize the commerce of its ally. Vergennes was already attempting to align the naval powers of Europe against Great Britain; had France claimed a monopoly of American trade all hope of attaining this objective would have been destroyed. Instead, France would have found itself the object of the jealousy and resentment of other European powers, and would be in the same uncomfortable spot which England now occupied. Rather than incur such obloquy, France boldly announced that its purpose was to "give America to the whole world" after freeing the United States from Great Britain. Vergennes pictured France as a champion of all freedom-loving nations against their common enemy: she had not helped call a new world into being to monopolize its commerce.

For this reason, equality and reciprocity were the keynotes of the treaty of commerce made by France and the United States. The most-favored-nation principle was applied by each country to the other. France was accorded important privileges in trading with the United States, but Americans made clear that they were seeking "universal peace and friendship with the whole world" rather than exclusive ties with any part of it, and to this principle the French acceded.

Also, each nation agreed to uphold the doctrine that free ships make free goods — the charter of the freedom of the seas. Americans' devotion to this principle was not merely theoretical: it sprang from recognition of the fact that the United States, protected in its neutral rights, would become one of the great carrying nations of the world. Once their independence had been attained, Americans expected to remain neutral in Europe's wars and to sell to all belligerents impartially. That Europe would destroy itself in civil wars while the United States rose to prosperity and greatness upon the ruins of the Old World was a familiar idea to Americans of the revolutionary generation; and freedom of the seas, it was agreed, was essential to America's rise to its predestined greatness.

Likewise, the American conception of freedom of trade posed a challenge to European empires as menacing in its implications as American republicanism itself. Free trade was the antithesis of mercantilism, the system of economic nationalism upon which European imperialism was founded. Each colonizing power sought to erect an insurmountable wall around its overseas possessions and to reserve exclusively for itself the privilege of exploiting its colonies. Americans were seeking to break down these walls and to throw open the world to the trade and commerce of all nations; and they went over to the attack boldly proclaiming freedom of trade as one of the "natural rights" of man of which despotic governments had deprived him. France, by making a treaty of commerce with the United States, helped to undermine the mercantilist philosophy of a world divided into exclusive and independent parts, each tightly bound to its mother country.

By linking its fortunes with those of the United States, the French monarchy also gave sanction to the doctrine that oppressed peoples have a right to rise against tyrannous rulers. It was made plain to the French people, however, that this principle was for export only and that any attempt to apply it to France itself would not be tolerated. For example, a book written by Raynal, a French philosopher, putting forward the view that the Franco-American alliance ought expressly and without reservation to assert the right of misgoverned people everywhere to rise against their oppressors, was ordered to be burned by the hangman in 1781. Raynal thought himself fortunate to escape to Holland with the police at his heels.

The treaties were signed on February 6, 1778, but because the Spanish treasure fleets were not yet safely in port, France decided against making the treaty of alliance with the United States public — the British might retaliate by attacking Bourbon shipping. Although, on February 25, 1778, French guns returned the salute of John Paul Jones — an honor usually reserved for the ships of independent nations — the treaty was not announced until early in March when the French ambassador informed the British government of what it already knew: that France and the American commissioners had signed a treaty of alliance. On March 20, the American commissioners were formally received by Louis XVI at Versailles; and amid the magnificence and pomp of the most resplendent court in Europe, the United States of America assumed its place among the nations.

CHAPTER XVI

First Fruits of the Alliance

THE Franco-American treaties had been duly signed by the American commissioners and the French government, yet it remained to be seen whether the Continental Congress would accept alliance with France or reconciliation with Great Britain. A few weeks after the treaties were signed in Paris, Lord North laid his Conciliatory Propositions before Parliament. Thus the Prime Minister moved to bid against France for the favor of Americans.

The Conciliatory Propositions were submitted to Parliament on February 17, 1778, but on February 20, before the legislature had acted upon them, the drafts of the bills were dispatched to America accompanied by the government's promise that it would stand by these terms. Lord North was prepared to yield much to bring the Americans back into the empire. He relinquished, for example, the claim of right by Parliament to tax the colonies; indeed, North now declared that he never believed that it was practicable to draw a large revenue from the colonies, and prided himself upon the fact that as Prime Minister he had never proposed a tax upon them. He was even willing to concede that revenue raised in the colonies in the course of regulating their commerce ought to be spent in the provinces rather than carried to the account of the British Exchequer. On the score of taxation, it is clear, the Prime Minister was ready to give the Americans everything they had asked for in 1775.

Moreover, although North had once boasted that he would put America at the feet of Great Britain, he now saw fit to request a conference with the former colonies, under the conviction that there was "so much affection still left in that country towards this, that barely to enter on a discussion is more than half the business." The Prime Minister no longer indulged in the peremptory tone of a parent addressing a brattish child — so easy for British ministers to adopt; instead, he summoned sweet reason to restore Americans to the empire.

In his zeal to preserve the empire, Lord North did not go the length of offering the colonies what today is called "dominion status." While surrendering the right of taxation, he insisted upon the retention by Parliament of many of its privileges of controlling colonial manufacturing and commerce in the interests of the mother country. By his plan, Englishmen might resume the lucrative task of exploiting the resources of America and monopolizing the business of supplying the growing millions of Americans with manufactured goods. Thus, North proposed to renounce what was unobtainable and was, moreover, of little consequence — a colonial revenue — in exchange for the real benefits of empire — the control of American commerce and manufactures. As North told the King, "to give up the levying of positive taxes here is to give up in effect nothing as it is practically certain that none will for the future ever be levi'd by the British Parliament."

This was essentially the ground taken long since by the English Whigs. Seemingly, the Prime Minister was asking the Whigs to move over and make room for him on their side of the House; they were heard "publicly congratulating themselves on the excellent acquisition which they had just made in the person of Lord North." It was a peculiarity of the Tories during the War of American Independence that they ended by adopting the policies of the Whigs, but only after it was too late. By the time the Tories had been converted, the gates had swung shut and they could only join the ranks of the repentant, but unsaved, sinners. Edmund Burke ruefully observed that "the pride of men will not often suffer reason to have any scope until it can be no longer of service"; too often, it is strictly the last resort.

When Lord North disclosed to Parliament to what lengths the spirit of conciliation had moved him, the Tories sat stunned and confounded — "astonishment, dejection, and fear, overclouded the whole assembly." This was not the kind of language they had expected to hear from a British Prime Minister even in the dark hours of defeat. Was England's cause so hopeless, they asked, that the objectives of the war should be thus renounced and Englishmen told they must "crouch to the vipers and rebels in America"? The English Tories, perhaps narrow in vision but certainly stout of heart, did not quail before the prospect of fighting both France and America; rather than abase themselves before the colonists by offering terms "such as none but a conquered people . . . thought of granting," they would fight all the world besides. Not for them to be told "how happy, glorious and mighty a people we should be, did we only fall down before America, beg her pardon, and do whatever she commands us."

Some Tories began to think of replacing the Prime Minister with a more doughty champion of England's rights, while others "ran about the House as if they did not know which side to go." The discipline of the Tories and the determination of the King to support the Prime Minister saved North from serious trouble. It was said that at least three fourths of the members of the House opposed the Conciliatory Propositions; but most of these gritted their teeth and swallowed the bitter dose, declaring as they did so that this ought to prove beyond all doubt "the affection of the indulgent, injured mother, even to her most degenerate, refractory, guilty children!"

Many Whigs had begun to suspect that whereas acts of Parliament could make a rebellion, acts of Parliament could not repeal one, and certainly not when sponsored by Lord North. Burke questioned whether any peace overtures made by Lord North stood the slightest chance of acceptance: to Americans, North would always be a dragon, camouflage himself as he would with olive branches and a whole covey of doves. "To leap at once from an obstinacy of five years to a total concession of everything; to stoop so low, without hopes of being forgiven — who can understand such a transformation?" Fox told the House that it was already too late — France had anticipated Great Britain by making an alliance with the United States; and North was obliged to confess that it was only too probable. Although few Whigs expected any good from the Prime Minister's peace plan, they voted in Parliament for its acceptance — one of the few occasions when they enjoyed the satisfaction of voting with the majority.

Great Britain enjoyed one unexpected advantage over France in this rivalry for the support of the United States: North's Conciliatory Propositions reached the Continental Congress before the news of the Franco-American alliance; so the British peace plan stood upon its own merits without being compelled to bear comparison with the offer of an alliance by France.

Congress had not heard from its ministers in France for almost a year, the last packet, which had arrived in January, having consisted of blank paper. Nevertheless, not a single member of Congress spoke in favor of North's plan; unanimously, Congress rejected the peace offer and demanded as a prerequisite to negotiations the withdrawal of British armed forces from the country or the recognition of American independence. Thomas Paine could later point with pride to Americans' "unshaken fortitude" in spurning the British peace offer despite the difficulties and dangers that beset them. Nor were the proffered peace terms withheld from the American people: Congress gave them full publicity in the newspapers (together with appropriate remarks) and Washington saw that they enjoyed free circulation among the American troops. At least, Lord North could not complain that the people were kept in the dark.

Many patriots detected treachery in North's peace offer; by his very excess of liberality, perhaps, the Prime Minister laid himself open to suspicion. The Conciliatory Propositions, exclaimed Americans, were the crowning act of British duplicity, designed to lull the patriots into security while the mother country prepared to overwhelm them with another army. The Continental Congress declared that no trust could be placed in British faith: "upon the first favorable occasion," Great Britain would again display "that lust of domination which hath rent in twain the mighty empire of Britain."

Any hope that Americans might, on second thought, accept Lord North's scheme was shattered by the news of the Franco-American alliance. Victory and independence now seemed to be within Americans' grasp. Although Lord North had moved in the direction of conciliation as far as he could without forfeiting the support of Parliament, his propositions could not bear comparison with the dazzling offer from France. Here one of the greatest powers of Europe proposed to make the cause of American independence its own and pledged itself to fight side by side with the United States without exacting inadmissible concessions from its ally. The treaties with France were more favorable than Americans had hoped: instead of taking advantage of their necessities, France had treated them like equals. "France," it was said, "was noble and generous, and more disinterested than any people have ever been in any treaty since the world began. More has not been done by any nation to another." Naturally, they were "too much elevated with the glorious prospect of a rising empire, ever to think of becoming tributary to Great Britain." It was as though Americans, having almost attained the Promised Land, were asked to return to Egypt upon the Pharaoh's promise of good behavior. Even if Pharaoh had turned over a new leaf, to return meant, as Congress pointed out, to share all Britain's "debts, their wars, their luxuries, and their crimes." And there seemed little hope that any settlement would be long-lived; within twenty years, it was predicted, the British would embark upon "another wild expedition across the Atlantic" to dragoon their liberty-loving subjects.

The soldiers celebrated the Franco-American alliance by erecting Maypoles, "marching with fife & Drum and Huzzaing as they passed the poles their hats adorned with white blossoms." The two heroes of the occasion were King Louis and King Tammany.[1] The votaries of the Indian chieftain were dressed like braves; cheers and toasts to Louis XVI were accompanied by war whoops and the drinking of copious bumpers to King Tammany; and in the evening the officers gave a dance in his honor. An observer might have been somewhat at a loss to determine

---

[1] Tammany was an Indian chief renowned for his wisdom and love of liberty. When the American Loyalists founded societies bearing the names of St. George, St. Andrew, and St. David, the patriots canonized Tammany. The Sons of Liberty often called themselves the Sons of St. Tammany.

who had made an alliance with the United States — King Louis or King Tammany.

Washington and his officers celebrated the event less ebulliently but with no less thankfulness. An officers' reception was held at Valley Forge where "the wine circulated in the most genial manner" among the officers, Mrs. Washington, the Countess Stirling, Lady Kitty, and other ladies of repute and fashion. Washington himself looked happy — for the first time, it was observed, since the British had evacuated Boston.

Although the alliance with France could hardly be regarded as other than "entangling," some Americans found consolation in the fact that the United States did not guarantee the territory of France upon the European continent — and thereby, it was hoped, escaped involvement in foreign wars. France, it was said, "may be at war ten ages in that side of the Atlantic ocean, and we may know no more about it, and hear no more of it than we do of the rustling of the wind over some distant country." As for the guarantee of the French West Indies, this was regarded as essential to the defense of the United States itself; manifestly, it was to our interest that these islands be in friendly hands. If the United States went to war in defense of the French islands, Americans would be fighting to maintain the outposts of the republic from falling into the possession of its enemies.

If it had been hard for England to offer peace terms to the rebellious Americans, it was harder still to have them rejected. They had stooped to rebels and had been roundly kicked for their pains — the proper punishment, said the Tories, for having become "an humble suppliant at the feet of her Colonies." Americans had taken advantage of the mother country's abnegation to demonstrate the solidarity of the Franco-American alliance and to flaunt their partiality for France. The rebels were now thrice damned in Englishmen's eyes: rebels, republicans, and allies of France.

Before word had been received from America to indicate the fate of Lord North's Conciliatory Propositions, a royal commission, headed by Lord Carlisle, was sent to the colonies to negotiate with the rebels. Here again the government was risking a rebuff, yet Lord North saw no alternative but to shower attentions upon the Americans. Having delayed until the last possible moment, the British Ministry must strive to make up for lost time by the ardor with which it courted the rebels.

Up to the time of his appointment as head of the peace commission, the Earl of Carlisle had made his principal mark upon the world as one of the best-dressed young men in Britain. A close friend of Charles James Fox, he had made the Grand Tour in the company of that *bon vivant*. At the tender age of thirty-three he came down with gout — an affliction common among the bottle-a-day men of the British aristocracy. Both Fox and Carlisle were fashion plates, but both gambled so heavily that they almost reduced themselves to rags. Carlisle's greatest indiscretion, however, was in standing surety for Fox's gambling debts — an error which cost him so much money, when Fox failed to honor the obligation, that he was compelled to retire from London society for several years. This enforced rustication cured him of his fondness for gambling; unlike Fox, however, who became slovenly in dress, Carlisle emerged from his retirement more immaculately attired than before. It was said that "nobody had a better idea of what a gentleman should be than Carlisle"; and his friends asserted that even if one were to look at him through a keyhole while he was alone in his chambers, the noble earl would be found to be as correct and proper in every respect as though he had a hundred eyes upon him. John Wilkes suggested that this dandified peer was sent to America in order to "captivate the rude members of the Congress, and civilize the wild inhabitants of an unpolished country." No doubt the Ministry placed high hopes in Carlisle's "gentle manners, winning behaviour and soft insinuating address"; as Horace Walpole said, he was very fit to make a treaty that would never be made.

With Carlisle were joined two other commissioners — William Eden and Governor Johnstone. Of the three, Johnstone was the best-disposed towards the Americans, having refused to take any part in the war against the colonies and, in general, so stoutly upholding their rights that his fellow commissioners believed that he planned to sell his property in England and settle down in America. But, as events proved, he loved Americans best when they were at a distance; before he returned to England, he had distinguished himself as the most violently anti-American of the commissioners.

The Carlisle Commission was instructed to negotiate directly with Congress — a body which North and his colleagues had hitherto recognized only as "that vagrant Congress." This was merely the beginning of the sacrifices of pride, dignity, and prejudice which Lord North made in the cause of peace. The commissioners were given authority to order a suspension of hostilities, grant pardons, relax somewhat the Laws of Trade, restore colonial charters, pay the debt incurred by the colonies in their war with the mother country, accept colonial representatives to Parliament, and admit American independence while the terms of reconciliation were being discussed. Some of these concessions were, it is true, merely points of discussion, to be ratified or rejected as Parliament saw fit; but, except for independence, Lord North was prepared to let the Americans largely write their own terms.[2]

[2] Although Great Britain had renounced the right of taxation, the commissioners were instructed to do their best toward procuring from the colonists "some reasonable and moderate contribution towards the common defence of the empire when reunited." If the Americans proved obdurate, the British government was not disposed

Before the commissioners could leave England, the French formally informed the British government of their alliance with the United States (March 12, 1778). For a time, the Ministry seemed about to abandon the plan of sending commissioners to the colonies; but Lord North, to whom the news of the Franco-American alliance was no surprise, was not inclined to leave any stone unturned that might yield England advantage. As the Prime Minister remarked privately about this time, "he did not believe the Commissioners would have any Effect — That nothing short of Independence would do." Nevertheless he hoped, by sending the commissioners to the United States, to divide Americans and to unite Englishmen. American Loyalists would be strengthened when England's magnanimity was fully known; and if the patriots rejected these terms, the English Whigs could hardly continue to abet the rebellion. "It will then be all Britain against half America," it was predicted; and who then could doubt the outcome?

When the time came for the commissioners' departure, there was something casual, almost furtive, in Lord North's leave-taking that left Carlisle and his colleagues ill at ease. The commissioners had the distinct impression that North was holding something back. The Prime Minister, said William Eden, "finish'd all his Conferences on this Side of the Atlantic with me very much in the Stile of a common Acquaintance who is stepping from your Room to the Water-Closet & means to return in five Minutes." Since Eden believed the peace mission "more than half damn'd" from the beginning, this abrupt farewell persuaded him that North was inclined to wash his hands of the whole affair. But it was not until the commissioners reached Philadelphia that the full significance of the Prime Minister's behavior was made clear.

After a tedious passage of the Atlantic, the commissioners finally reached the Delaware. As they sailed up the river, they observed signs of military and naval activity on every hand, which they supposed presaged an attack upon the Americans at Valley Forge. They congratulated themselves upon having arrived in time to present their peace terms to Congress before the beginning of the British offensive. A stunning surprise awaited them in Philadelphia. The British fleet and army were not preparing to make war upon the Americans but to run away from them — and the orders for the evacuation of Philadelphia had been sent to Sir Henry Clinton before the commissioners left England, without their having been informed. Now the commissioners understood the reason for the shifty demeanor and hurried exit of the Prime Minister: he was concealing from them military orders which, he was well aware, had they been communicated to the commissioners, would have caused them to throw up their mission.

---

to press the point — if only Americans would come back to the household they might live rent-free.

Lord Carlisle and his colleagues had supposed that their peace offer would be strongly backed by the armed forces; certainly they had not intended to rely upon the olive branch alone to persuade the rebels of the necessity of peace and reunion with Great Britain. Above all, they had never dreamed that their arrival in America would coincide with the retreat of the British army from Pennsylvania. They had expected to find the people chastened by military reverses and living in dread of the next move of the British army; instead the rebels were exulting over its humiliation. The commissioners now recognized that they had come to America with two strikes against them: the French alliance had already been ratified by Congress, and the British army was in retreat. Well might they conclude that they had been sent upon a forlorn errand by the Ministry.

France had resolved to repay the British in their own coin: as retaliation for the surprise attack upon the French fleet in 1756, a powerful naval force under the command of the Comte d'Estaing was ordered to sail to the Delaware and cut off the British fleet and army in Philadelphia. There had been, it is true, no declaration of war between Great Britain and France, but the French paid little heed to such niceties when an opportunity was presented them of destroying a British fleet and army by a surprise blow. D'Estaing sailed from Toulon in March 1778, and reached the Delaware in June; but it was not until July 10 that France formally declared war upon Great Britain. Had D'Estaing successfully executed his mission, the British in Philadelphia would have been attacked several weeks before a state of war was proclaimed.

The British government was not caught unprepared: it had full knowledge of the sailing of D'Estaing's fleet from Toulon and its aggressive intentions. Only D'Estaing's destination was in doubt: whether he would attack the British fleet in the English Channel or in the Delaware, the Ministry could not tell. Yet the outcome of the war, as Germain said, might depend upon guessing where the blow would fall. Germain believed that the French fleet was on its way to America and urged that it be intercepted before it passed Gibraltar; Lord Sandwich, on the other hand, was equally certain that England itself was D'Estaing's objective and that therefore the naval strength of the kingdom must be kept at home. These divided counsels resulted in the inactivity of the British fleet during the critical days when D'Estaing might have been successfully cut off. Finally it was decided to send the fleet against the French; and the King, in his anxiety, went to Portsmouth to oversee the outfitting of the British squadron. The time consumed in provisioning the ships and waiting for a favorable wind delayed their departure until it was too late to stop D'Estaing. The French fleet sailed out of the Strait of Gibraltar and set its course across the Atlantic.

In a moment, the entire complexion of the war had changed; Pennsylvania now seemed likely to prove the graveyard of a British fleet and army. And the best that the home government could do was to send out "Foul Weather Jack" Byron to reinforce Lord Howe. But Byron, as his nickname implies, seemed to create his own tempests as he plowed the seas. If, as usual, he was delayed by heavy storms on this voyage, he would almost certainly arrive too late to save Lord and Sir William Howe.

In fact, there was every reason to fear that the failure of the Ministry to intercept D'Estaing in the Mediterranean doomed the entire British position in North America. Never again during the war — not even at Yorktown — did the French have a better opportunity of striking a crippling blow at the British fleet and army. Lord Howe had only five ships of the line, together with a few frigates, under his command; and he was encumbered with a large fleet of transports, provision ships, and merchantmen, loaded with supplies and refugees from Philadelphia. Against this unwieldy force, D'Estaing could throw double the number of fighting ships commanded by Lord Howe.

Fully aware of the precariousness of the British military position in North America, the Ministry, in March 1778, ordered the evacuation of Philadelphia by the British fleet and army, directing that the troops be brought to New York from Philadelphia by sea. The government had repeatedly underestimated the fighting prowess of the rebels, but it was resolved not to make the same mistake with regard to the French.

If it was humiliating for the British army to relinquish Philadelphia to the rebels, it promised to be a matter of life and death to the Tories who had fled to the city for protection against the patriots. To abandon them to the enemy seemed unthinkable, yet Sir William Howe, seeing no way that they could be evacuated with the British army, advised them to throw themselves upon the mercy of the rebels and to make the best terms they could.

Fortunately for the Pennsylvania Loyalists, Howe was at this time replaced by Sir Henry Clinton. Few British generals have assumed command of an army under more inauspicious circumstances; whatever else may be said about Sir William Howe's slowness, it must be admitted that he had resigned at the right time. As Clinton knew, to desert the Loyalists was, in a sense, to abandon the cause. How could Britain hope to triumph if its friends in the colonies — the majority of "good" Americans it expected to aid in overcoming the minority of "bad" Americans — were left unsupported against the rebels?

This consideration deeply impressed Clinton. At the same time, he feared that if his army went by sea to New York and was unlucky enough to be held up by adverse winds, Washington might take the opportunity of storming New York. For these reasons, he decided to violate his orders, which directed him to bring his army to New York by water; instead, he sent the Loyalists and their belongings by ship while the army marched overland to New York. There is every reason to believe that this decision was fortunate not merely for the Loyalists but for the British fleet and army as well. Had Clinton taken time to embark his troops on board the fleet, his departure would probably have been delayed until D'Estaing had sprung the trap and blockaded the British fleet in the Delaware.

As a result of Clinton's decision to embark the Loyalists — about three thousand sailed with the British fleet — there was an exodus from Philadelphia which, remarked an observer, had "altogether the appearance of a mighty nation emigrating to another country." When they finally reached safety in New York it brought to mind the spectacle of "the children of Israel walking through the Red Sea, and the pursuit of the Egyptians." It was not, however, to be the last time that Loyalists were harried on land and on sea, one step ahead of the pursuing rebels.

The British evacuated Philadelphia on June 16, the rear guard exchanging a few shots with the Americans who entered the town on the redcoats' heels. Except for a few officers who were "found in the houses of their tender acquaintances and taken prisoners," the British made good their escape, crossing the Delaware below the city into New Jersey.

Washington, it may be said, ought to have placed himself across the British line of march in New Jersey and contested their retreat to New York. Certainly he had ample warning of their intentions of evacuating Philadelphia to execute this maneuver; yet he did not know in what direction they would turn after leaving the Quaker City. General Charles Lee, who had rejoined the American army, insisted that they would move to the Chesapeake — a natural deduction, since he himself, as a prisoner in New York, had told them to go there. Gates, on the other hand, feared that they intended to attack New England by way of the Hudson. These conflicting views resulted in Washington's remaining at Valley Forge until the British had made plain their intentions.

The main road across New Jersey ran through the villages of Trenton, Princeton, and Brunswick. There was also a much less traveled road leading to Sandy Hook; and it was this highway that Clinton took in the expectation of meeting the British fleet at Sandy Hook and making the rest of the trip to New York by water.

The British were particularly vulnerable in their baggage train which, seven miles long, trailed the army in its retreat across New Jersey. In large part, this baggage consisted of goods belonging to the Loyalists and British merchants who had evacuated Philadelphia with the fleet. It greatly delayed the retreat of the British army: forty miles in seven days was its rate of progress. Moreover, the people of the country were inimical. "Every soul in the Jersies is a rebel," declared a British officer in 1778; it was a melancholy reflection that two years before, it had been regarded as the most loyal of the revolted colonies.

Despite the vulnerability of the enemy, the Americans were wary. In a general council of officers, it was decided not to risk a general engagement upon the flat country of New Jersey where the British regulars were most formidable. A few thousand men were assigned to harry the British flank and rear but a pitched battle, it was agreed, was to be avoided. Yet Washington was not wholly satisfied with this decision: an aggressive fighter when he saw a chance of victory, he was reluctant to let Clinton's army slip between his fingers. After all, he had almost fourteen thousand men to throw against Clinton's nine thousand. General Charles Lee, on the other hand, counseled caution: in accord with his new-found views regarding the invincibility of British regulars, he opposed hazarding a major action against Clinton's army. This opinion he freely expressed in council, leaving no doubt as to his position.

In view of the important part played by General Charles Lee in the battle toward which events were shaping, it is necessary to trace the checkered course of this singular warrior since his capture, in December 1776, by a British scouting party.

Lee had been taken under circumstances which led some patriots to suspect that he had deliberately permitted himself to fall into the enemy's hands. Although thousands of Americans regarded Lee as "the guardian angel that was to deliver America," there were already whispers that he was a fallen angel. Despite these rumors and the more convincing evidence of Lee's insubordination in New Jersey, Washington abated none of his esteem for Lee; General Nathanael Greene called Lee "a most consummate General" and Washington, whatever his personal differences with Lee, did not yet see fit to call in question the ability of his willful subordinate.

The first impulse of the British was to place an equally high value upon their prize. With the "American paladin" out of action, it was hoped that the rebellion might shortly collapse — certainly Washington had not up to this time shown any capacity for stopping the triumphant advance of the British regulars. It was assumed that such discipline and organization as the American army enjoyed was owing to General Lee: Washington was merely a front for his more experienced and able second-in-command — a view which found favor in the British army because it ascribed all that was good in the American army to a former British officer. Certainly, General Howe was of this mind: when informed of Lee's capture, he is said to have exclaimed that "the War was ended."

To Lee himself, capture might well mean an ignominious death. If judged to be in the service of His Britannic Majesty at the time he joined the rebels, Lee was guilty of treason, and presumably would pay the full penalty. The captured general perfectly understood his plight: the first inquiry he addressed to his captors was "What does Gen. Howe intend?" It was not, however, so much what General Howe intended as what

George III intended, for His Majesty took a lively interest in the case of this former British officer who had risen to the post of second-in-command of the rebel army. Needless to say, the King's concern with Lee's fate did not bode well for that unhappy officer's chances of escaping the gallows. As his friends said, Lee's plight promised to be "worse than that of the damned."

The King wished to treat Lee as a deserter and to make him an example which would discourage other British officers from joining the rebels. Howe was ordered to send Lee back to England, and the Ministry prepared to rush the captured general to trial. But Howe soon found that he could not return Lee to England without endangering the lives of high-ranking British and Hessian officers held prisoners by the rebels. Congress threatened retaliation if Lee was harmed. When it was reported that the American general was being subjected to indignities in New York, Congress ordered a captured British colonel to be thrown into a dungeon; British officers were deprived of the privilege of giving parole; and plans for an exchange of prisoners between Howe and Washington were broken off. Lee, it began to appear, was more trouble to the British as a prisoner than he had been as a general of the rebel army. Rather than risk a wholesale massacre of British prisoners, Howe conveniently found that since Lee had been struck from half pay in the British army in 1775, he could not be regarded as a deserter.

Congress left no stone unturned to bring about Lee's return to the American army. The British were offered an imposing array of captured Hessian and British officers in exchange for General Lee; but as the British held over three hundred American officers compared to fifty British and Hessian officers in the possession of the rebels, Congress was hardly in a position to bargain. The British declined to surrender Lee on any terms; whereupon Congress, its eagerness to procure his return whetted by the enemy's determination to detain him and by reports that some high-ranking American officers did not want his release lest "his enterprising disposition and Martial genius" reveal their own shortcomings, refused to permit any exchange of prisoners that did not include General Lee.

Far from languishing as his admirers supposed in a British dungeon, General Lee was living merrily in New York, feasting and drinking better than he had ever done as an American officer. He was confined in one of the most luxurious houses in New York, where, with five field officers as companions, he kept "a genteel Table." Even the company of his dogs was not lacking: after his capture, he requested that he be reunited with his dogs because, as he said, he "never stood in greater need of their Company," and his tender-hearted gaolers, unable to deny a dog-lover, brought him the whole kennel. Surrounded by his dogs, the general dozed away his days and spent his nights convivially over his bottle; he had "a good bed to sleep upon, into which he tumbled jovially mellow every night."

Even as a prisoner of war, Lee tried to steal the limelight from Washington. Because the fortunes of war had debarred Lee from leading the American army to victory in the field, he now aspired to become a peacemaker. In this role, he succeeded in convincing the Howes that he stood so high in the esteem of Congress that he could bring that body to talk peace. To Lord and Sir William Howe, peace was the word that unlocked all doors: the captive general was immediately authorized to get in touch with Congress and arrange for a committee from that body to come to New York. Accordingly Lee, early in 1777, invited two or three members of Congress to pay him a visit under safe-conduct from General Howe. He spoke cryptically of the great things that would come from this meeting, and Washington's hopes were so raised that he urged Congress to send a delegation to New York. But Congress swore that the project was merely another "sneaking trick of Howe's" and it refused to jeopardize the Americans' position in France, where the American commissioners were seeking aid, by appearing to enter into further negotiations with the British.[3]

The news that Lee was so eager to impart to Congress was truly startling: he had just reached the conclusion that Americans could never defeat the British army, particularly under such an incompetent general as George Washington, and that Congress's only hope of survival was to retire to Pittsburgh, build a strong fort, round up all the boats on the river, and summon all the old men, women, and children; then, when the British army approached — as it inevitably would — Congress and all could take boat down the Ohio and Mississippi rivers and find refuge with the Spaniards. Luckily for Lee's standing in Congress, this scheme was never communicated to that body.

Coming from General Lee, this was strange language: no man had done more than he toward persuading Americans that they had nothing to fear from the British army. During his captivity, however, Lee had experienced a great awakening regarding the prowess of British soldiers. He now pronounced them to be the best fighting men in the world and declared that their superior courage and discipline would always rout the Americans, no matter how great the odds.

Under the genial influence of wine, Lee began to give expression to other views which, had they been known in Philadelphia, would have horrified his admirers. Lee may have been seeking to save his neck from a noose or he may have experienced a genuine conversion: in any event, he began to decry the rebellion in the presence of British officers and

[3] Washington believed that the acceptance of Lee's plan was necessary to quiet the moderates who withheld support from the Revolution on the ground that all the possibilities of a peaceful settlement had not yet been exhausted.

to deplore that he had ever taken up arms against the King. For the further edification of British generals, Lee, when "rather gay with Liquor," lectured them upon their mistakes and missed opportunities, pointing out, among other things, that the British could easily have surrounded the Americans at Westchester and White Plains and thus "finished the whole Business of the Controversy at once." Finally, in March 1777, he drew up a plan of operations for the Howes which, he predicted, would infallibly break the back of the rebellion in six months. He proposed, in brief, the destruction of "Congress Government" by an attack upon Maryland, Virginia, and Pennsylvania, in the course of which the British army would march overland to Philadelphia and seize control of the Delaware and Chesapeake. Upon the success of this plan, Lee pledged his life, provided that France did not enter the war before it was put into execution.

If this was treason, Howe failed to make the most of it. The British general did not prize Lee's generalship or his trustworthiness as highly as the Continental Congress; he had already determined to capture Philadelphia, but here the resemblance between the strategies of Howe and Lee ended.

Although enjoying in prison most of the comforts of home, Lee was eager to rejoin his former comrades; but his need of the Americans was as nothing, in his opinion, to their need of him. He modestly suggested that he be exchanged for General Burgoyne, observing that he was worth far more to the Americans than was Burgoyne to the British; in fact, he was prepared to believe that the rebels could not do without him. He did not propose, however, to save the patriots by his prowess in the field so much as by his skill in negotiation. Certain the rebellion was at its last gasp, Lee conceived it to be his duty to open Americans' eyes to the hopelessness of resistance.

Whether Lee returned to his command resolved to sell out the American cause is a matter of doubt; but that he intended, and had promised the Howes, that he would bend every effort to bring about peace and reconciliation seems certain. In 1778, he returned to the American headquarters with Sir William Howe's good wishes; and Admiral Howe sent him a supply of liquor, perhaps as a consolation for the good things that Lee was renouncing in order to return to active service. Unluckily, some British soldiers broke into the cellar and drank every drop the night before Lee rejoined the Americans.

Whatever his understanding with the Howes, Charles Lee returned to his American comrades a changed man: formerly the ardent advocate of independence, he now yearned to reunite the mother country and colonies. "I feel for the Empire of Great Britain, for its Glory, Welfare & existence," he exclaimed. ". . . I always wished to see England the presiding part & seat of Empire." Here was one rebel, at least, who had repented of his errors and was ready to put on the sackcloth and ashes.

It is apparent that Lee had become more of a Fabius than Fabius himself; his strategy was now to risk nothing, to avoid a general engagement at all costs, and to trust to British leniency to make a just peace. Had Lee spoken these views in 1775 and 1776 he never would have risen to second-in-command of the American army. As Lee was to prove, defeatists do not win battles.

Upon rejoining the American army, Lee was given a welcome more suited, it might be supposed, for a conquering hero than for a returned prisoner of war. The officers and men were drawn up in two lines to receive the general while Washington and his staff rode about four miles down the Philadelphia road to escort him into camp. When Lee appeared, "General Washington dismounted & recd. Genl Lee as if he had been his Brother." Together the two men rode to Washington's headquarters where, with Mrs. Washington, they sat down to dinner. Lee was treated like a member of the household; a bedroom was given him near Mrs. Washington's sitting room. Lee repaid this hospitality by appearing the next morning looking "as dirty as if he had lain in the street all night." It was soon discovered that "he had brought a miserable dirty Huzzy with him to Philadelphia (a British sergeant's wife) and had actually taken her into his Room by a back door, and she had slept with him that night."

Under the persuasion that Lee was a genius, albeit a bit on the eccentric side, much was forgiven him. Washington swallowed this insult as he had taken all the other affronts from Lee: he kept his temper under control because he was convinced that Lee's skill and experience were vital to the American cause.

For this reason, it was Charles Lee who was chosen to lead the American troops in attacking the British army in New Jersey. By seniority, Lee was entitled to command the advanced corps of the army, but because he at first declined the honor, Lafayette was appointed to take his place. Lee, however, could not bear to see a younger man assume the post that was rightfully his; therefore, having reconsidered, he asked to be reinstated in command. Although it was clear that Lee neither wanted the position nor could endure to let anyone else have it, Washington gave Lee his way. Always himself the complete gentleman, Washington was perhaps too disposed to consider the gentlemanly feelings of others. Certainly, until the battle of Monmouth Courthouse, this was true of his relations with Charles Lee.

At Monmouth Courthouse, where the American army finally overtook Clinton, the terrain was well adapted to an offensive action. The British had just debouched from the hills onto an open plain; the American attack could therefore be made upon level ground with the hills behind serving as a refuge in case the enemy reacted too strongly. Moreover, when Lee gave the signal to attack, part of the British wagon train was still involved in the narrow defiles of the hills where it was particularly vulnerable to ambush.

Lee's objective was to attack the British rear guard and to destroy the wagon train. About five thousand men were detached for this purpose while Washington with the main elements of the army remained in readiness to come to Lee's support after the action had been fairly joined. This meant, of course, that Washington intended to bring on a general action despite the adverse opinion of the council of war; yet Lee always claimed that he had no prior knowledge of the commander-in-chief's change of mind. As Lee made no effort to conceal, he deemed his own strategy to be vastly superior to Washington's; in fact, Lee was tempted always to do the opposite of what the commander-in-chief recommended — it being to his mind a sound principle that in military matters Washington was always wrong.

The British responded sharply to the first assault of the rebels; indeed, they had no alternative but to fight or to permit a considerable part of their baggage train to fall into the enemy's hands. As a result, Lee's forward units found themselves engaged by a far superior enemy force. The American cavalry broke in confusion; whereupon the infantry and artillery quickly began to retreat to the hills, closely pursued by the British infantry. Twice the Americans attempted to hold positions on the hills against the British but each time they were driven back. Nevertheless, they preserved good order: it was a retreat rather than a rout, and the British were being drawn ever deeper into the hills where the ground favored the defense. Apparently oblivious of this danger, Clinton took his position at the head of the army and shouted "Charge, Grenadiers, never heed forming!" — whereupon the troops surged forward, although some soldiers later expressed surprise at the spectacle of the commander-in-chief "galloping like a Newmarket jockey at the head of a wing of Grenadiers." It brought back old days to the British; again they experienced the thrill of the chase as the Americans broke and fled before them.

Merely by running, the Americans killed almost as many British soldiers as though they had stayed and fought. The heat was stifling — the kind of day when any effort other than lifting a tall cool glass is unthinkable. In their heavy uniforms and laden with gear and accouterments, the British were obliged to chase the Americans through the steaming countryside. There was little water at hand; a grenadier who came across a small pool "drank to such excess as to burst and expired in the utmost torments. Two became raving mad, and the whole road, strewed with miserable wretches, wishing for death," looked as though American sharpshooters had decimated the British ranks. Over sixty soldiers died of the heat — almost half the fatalities suffered by the British army in this engagement.

Lee's chief mistake was in ordering a retreat before the action had been fairly begun. He gave his men little opportunity to fight: as soon as the British formed for action, Lee called a retreat despite Anthony Wayne's eagerness to make a stand. In general, he gave few orders, leaving his men to find such safety as they could; and although there were plenty of trees to afford cover for riflemen, he did not even put them into action. Nor did he send word to Washington of his plight; the commander-in-chief might have been a thousand miles away so little did Lee heed his presence. This, Lee seems to have reasoned, was his own show and he would give that incompetent farmer no chance to interfere.

Meanwhile Washington, at the head of the main army some distance away from the battle, was told that Lee's corps was flying before the British. For once the iron control that Washington maintained over his emotions was shattered. Those who saw him on that day never forgot the sight. "I saw for the first time what fury was," said a French officer, "because anything more appallingly terrible than the face of general Washington when he appeared on the scene and galloped toward Lee, I have never seen, nor has any one else. It was like the God of Battles intent to kill or destroy." Giving spurs to his horse, the wrathful general shot off for the field of battle and like an avenging fury fell upon General Lee.

Washington did not pause to question Lee why he had retreated; instead, he gave that hapless general a dressing down that has become famous in American military annals. " 'You're a coward,' he cried to Lee in a thunderous voice," reported a spectator of this meeting, "and then fired away a volley of oaths such as neither I nor any other human being ever heard before." When the storm had largely spent itself, Lee tried to interpose by saying that the British were too powerful for him to cope with. "And your orders, sir, what were they?" demanded Washington. "Whatever your *opinion* was, your *duty* was to obey the orders you had received!" Lee finally was able to get a word in edgewise to the effect that the attack was made against his advice in council and that the outcome of the battle proved the soundness of his objections; but Washington walked away leaving Lee in the middle of his self-vindication. Lee could wait, but the British were still advancing; and for the rest of the day Washington was busy bringing up artillery, strengthening his position, and holding his ground against the enemy. The American lines held, and that night the British broke camp and rejoined the main army in its retreat to Sandy Hook.

Lee may have bungled the battle but there is no evidence that he deliberately threw the engagement to the enemy. A commander with more faith in the prowess of his troops certainly would have offered stiffer resistance. Fundamentally, the trouble was that Lee was beaten before the battle began; it is safe to say that no general in his state of mind could win a battle against a resolute foe. Had he been honest he would have declined to accept leadership of the American attacking force, on the ground that he had lost faith both in the cause and in the men he commanded.

Washington's admirers contended that he had saved the day at Monmouth by rallying the troops after Lee's incompetence — or worse — had placed the American army in desperate peril. "He brought order out of confusion, animated his troops, and led them to success," said Alexander Hamilton. The truth is, however, that the British were in no condition to continue the pursuit: exhausted and dazed from the heat and the battle, they would soon have been obliged to halt from sheer exhaustion although their "ungovernable impetuosity," Clinton said, led them to attack the American lines with their last ounce of strength. Clinton was satisfied with the day's work and declined to be drawn any deeper into the hills where he might be surrounded and cut off by the rebels. He had gained time for his baggage train to move out of range and had checked the advance of the American army. With these results he was content.

On the other hand, Lee stoutly maintained that he had saved the American army by his prompt retreat — a "masterly manoeuvre" he called it. This opinion was endorsed by Clinton, who lamented that Lee's withdrawal had balked him of a complete victory. "Had Washington been blockhead enough to sustain Lee," said the British general, "I should have caught him between two defiles, and it is easy to see what must have happened." Lee also prided himself upon keeping his troops together despite a crowd of spectators who "galloped in so furiously upon our troops, that had they not been firm and cool, might have occasioned great trepidation, alarm and confusion." Other generals might not be so skillful, however, in emergencies of this kind, and Lee urged Congress to devise means of keeping these unwelcome visitors off the field of battle in future encounters.

A court-martial demanded by Lee to vindicate his reputation found him guilty on all counts: he had disobeyed orders in not attacking vigorously the enemy, he had conducted an unnecessary retreat, and he had behaved disrespectfully to the commander-in-chief. For these and sundry other offenses, he was sentenced to suffer suspension from the army for twelve months. Although Washington's critics in Congress raised the cry that Lee was being sacrificed for the greater glory of the "Divinity" and "Idol," Congress declined to upset the verdict of the court-martial.

Thus Monmouth Courthouse pricked Lee's bubble; his eccentricities were now believed to cover a multitude of sins rather than virtues. The myth of General Lee's invincibility had few believers after this fateful day; as Hamilton said, Lee seemed to be "either a driveler in the business of soldiership or something much worse." One by one, Washington's rivals were being eliminated, leaving only the commander-in-chief as the object of the people's affection.

Lee characteristically rushed into print to defend his name and blacken Washington's, but he succeeded only in writing himself out of the little reputation that remained to him after Monmouth. He swore that Washington's charges were "a most abominable dam'd lie" so crass that they "would make Job himself swear like a Virginia Colonel"; and he declared that he would retire to Virginia and there learn to hoe tobacco — "the best school to form a consummate *general*." Some of his most envenomed squibs were turned down by editors; whereupon Lee screamed that he was being made the victim of "democratic tyranny" that denied American citizens the right to speak their minds. "That degree of freedom of conversation that is admitted at Constantinople," he swore, "is not tolerated in Virginia, Maryland or Pennsylvania." As to Washington, Lee asserted that Americans "must inevitably be beat or rather drown'd if They depend on such a bladder of emptiness and pride." For these insults he was called out by several of Washington's friends, Anthony Wayne among them, and Lee was seriously wounded on the field of honor. Declaring that he was "tired of this rascally Planet," he finally quitted it in 1782. In his will he specified that he was not to be buried within a mile of any Presbyterian or Baptist meeting-house. "I have kept so much bad company while living," he explained, "that I do not choose to continue it when dead."

Because the British abandoned the battlefield, Monmouth was hailed as an American victory. Anthony Wayne wrote his friends to tell the Philadelphia belles that "the heavenly, sweet, pretty red Coats — the accomplished Gent'm of the Guards & Grenadiers have humbled themselves in the plains of Monmouth." He hastened to add, however, that the ladies ought not despair — the pretty boys in red coats had "resigned their Laurels to *Rebel* officers." To the victor belong the spoils, and to Anthony Wayne the girls he left behind him were the sweetest prize of victory.

Pretty girls and pretty boys aside, it is clear that the honors of the day were with the British. When an army that retreats four miles in the course of the battle claims a victory, the burden of proof rests upon it. True, the British advance had finally been stopped and they had retreated after the battle; but the fact remains that it was not Clinton's objective to fight a pitched battle with the Americans, but to bring his army intact to Sandy Hook. In this he succeeded. A few days after the battle, the British reached their destination, down to their last rations but with the army in good condition. Not a wagon had been lost in the long trek from Philadelphia. And at Sandy Hook the fleet was waiting to pick up the army and carry it to New York.

The British were already safe in New York by the time D'Estaing arrived in the United States. Yet, with a fleet as powerful as that commanded by D'Estaing, the British might be trapped in New York: and early in July, 1778, D'Estaing left the Delaware resolved to seek out the British in their stronghold. The French men-of-war lined up off Sandy Hook began to sound the channel preparatory to forcing an entrance. Lord Howe's fleet in the harbor was outnumbered and outgunned. Had the French brought on an immediate engagement, the British fleet and army might have been brought to surrender, for Washington was holding his army in readiness to co-operate with D'Estaing in attacking the city. Assailed by land and sea, the British would have found the odds heavily against them.

The British did not doubt that D'Estaing would cross the bar at Sandy Hook. "The wind could not be more favourable for such a design," observed a British officer; "the spring tides were at the highest; we consequently expected the hottest day that ever was fought between the two nations." Actually, however, not a shot was fired. D'Estaing decided that his ships carried too much draught to permit them to pass the bar; and so, after spending ten days looking at Howe's fleet, the French sailed away. Again the British were given a reprieve, and D'Estaing's naval superiority had gone for naught.

Rebuffed at New York, the French attempted, as their third and final effort of the campaign, to dislodge the British from Rhode Island. Sir Henry Clinton, it will be remembered, had seized Newport, and the island on which it stands, late in 1776 and had converted the town into a naval base strongly garrisoned by an army of four thousand men. American raiding parties had given the British some difficulty, one party having captured a British general who was caught in bed with a country wench; but no full-scale attack had been made upon the enemy position in Newport. On the other hand, the British were not sufficiently strong to undertake to penetrate into the country. Newport was a thorn in the flesh of the Yankees but it had fallen far short of British expectations as a base from which to harry the New England countryside.

Throughout the summer of 1778, the Americans had attempted to raise an army to besiege Newport without meeting with much success. When word was spread that the French fleet was coming to lend its aid, the response was very different: thousands of New England militiamen turned out for duty, and even John Hancock turned general and ran down to Rhode Island to pick up a little easy glory. General Gates was eager to command the attack against Newport, but the memory of the Conway Cabal still rankled Washington and his influence was thrown against Gates's appointment.

Instead, the command was given to General John Sullivan, hitherto chiefly remarkable for his ill luck. Now, however, fortune seemed to smile: as the first American general to conduct joint operations with the French, he was the envy of all military men. "You are the most happy man in the world," General Greene told Sullivan. "What a child of fortune."

Sullivan soon found that his bad luck still held; indeed, it had never been worse. As is so often the case when fortune strikes a particularly crushing blow, the enterprise at first went prosperously. The French fleet arrived off Newport; the American army drew up on the mainland; and the British garrison was seemingly caught in the allied vise. With the promise of four thousand men from D'Estaing's fleet to aid in the land operations, Sullivan felt confident of success.

This was a war of a coalition and subject to all the weaknesses that beset the combined operations of allies. General Sullivan, however, forgot this hazard. Without waiting for the French troops to disembark from the fleet, the American commander crossed over to the island held by the British. "This measure gave much umbrage to the French officers," remarked Colonel John Laurens. "They conceived their troops injured by our landing first, and talked like disputing precedence in a country dance, instead of men engaged in pursuing the common interest of two great nations."

While the French and Americans were arguing which nation should enjoy the honor of administering the *coup de grâce* to the enemy, the British in New York were not idle. Time was running out for the French; the naval superiority with which D'Estaing had done so little was already endangered by the British. Shortly after the French fleet left Sandy Hook, reinforcements, among them some of Byron's ships ("Foul Weather Jack," running true to form, was himself held up by storms) arrived in New York. With these ships, Lord Howe believed himself strong enough to contest with D'Estaing the command of the sea. Without loss of time, he set sail for Rhode Island to challenge the enemy to battle.

When Howe appeared off Newport, only a small number of French troops had been landed to support Sullivan's attack upon the town; the Americans were impatiently waiting the disembarkation of more troops before launching the final assault upon the British lines. That aid never came. Rather than permit themselves to be bottled up by Howe, the French commanders sailed out of Newport Harbor and gave battle to the British. The French still enjoyed a small measure of superiority in ships and guns but this advantage brought them no profit. A heavy storm blew up and the two fleets were driven far apart: badly buffeted by the seas, the French finally put in at Boston. Here it was decided to abandon altogether the Rhode Island expedition, on the ground that the storm-tossed French ships were in no condition to put to sea. The British fleet plundered Martha's Vineyard and threatened to sail into Boston Harbor itself to fight the French. No challenge, however insolent, could induce D'Estaing to leave his moorings.

The withdrawal of the French left the Americans in Rhode Island in a precarious position; deprived of the four thousand men and the naval aid promised by D'Estaing, they abandoned the attack upon Newport and beat a hasty retreat from the island lest they be cut off from the mainland by the British men-of-war which had returned to the scene of action. Although Sullivan and his men escaped, their deliverance was owing to the stoutness of their legs rather than to any aid given them by their allies.

In the bitterness of their disappointment, Americans blamed the French, who, they cried out, had deserted them "in a most Rascally manner as though the devil himself were in the French fleet." D'Estaing and his men were dubbed *"Heroes of Flight."* "If this is Gallic faith," exclaimed an American, "we have formed a sweet and hopeful alliance." General Sullivan, than whom no more frustrated commander was to be found in the American army, gave vent to his wrath in a manner that threatened to blow the whole alliance sky-high. The perfidy of the French, he swore, "has raised every voice against the French nation, revived all those ancient prejudices against the faith and sincerity of that people, and inclines them most heartily to curse the new alliance." Then, to top this outburst, a riot broke out in Boston between French and American sailors in which two French officers were badly injured when they attempted to stop the fracas.

Lest these riots and hard words alienate the French, Washington and many other influential Americans tried to pour oil upon the troubled waters of Franco-American relations. General Sullivan was persuaded to issue another statement considerably toning down his criticisms of the French. Sam Adams thundered that Whigs must not play the Tory game of making bad blood between the allies; and the newspapers were urged not to print articles critical of France. Washington directed his subordinates to spread the story that the French fleet had abandoned the attack upon Newport solely because of damage suffered in the storm and not, as some angry Americans were saying, because of want of courage to face the British; and he tried to keep from the public the full extent of the dissension between French and American officers. As for the riot in Boston, it was described as the work of British seamen serving aboard American privateers. The story was untrue but it helped to smooth a very rough spot in Franco-American relations.

In this way, tranquillity was restored; the alliance suffered no dislocation, and French charm was given an opportunity to undo the damage. Lafayette devoted himself to calming ruffled tempers; John Hancock spread himself to entertain the French officers, keeping open house for them from morning to night. D'Estaing responded gracefully to these overtures. Lafayette, who was present when Hancock gave D'Estaing a picture of General Washington, later told Washington that he "never saw a man so glad at possessing his sweetheart's picture, as the Admiral was to receive yours." D'Estaing and his officers entertained prominent Bostonians aboard ship, "where," a guest observed, "the Decency and good Manners with which they were entertained, was equal to the Splendor and Plenty of their Table." Indeed, the officers and seamen seemed to be "the most peaceable, quiet and orderly set of men in their profession" that Bostonians had ever seen. Hundreds of French seamen came ashore and mingled with the citizenry without untoward incidents. By November 1778, when the French fleet left Boston for the West Indies, there was no sign that the allies were not the best of friends.

Despite these amenities, the first fruits of the French alliance seemed to many Americans wholly sour. The French fleet had upset the balance of naval power but had wasted its chances of destroying the British fleet and army; and now, with D'Estaing's departure for the West Indies, the British were again undisputed masters of United States waters. Nevertheless, D'Estaing's voyage to America had not been as barren of results as some Americans supposed. It was the danger from the French fleet that had compelled the British to evacuate Philadelphia. By gaining even a momentary naval superiority, D'Estaing had obliged the British to draw in their cruisers, thereby opening American ports to swarms of privateers and merchant ships. And the British had been given a serious fright. During most of the summer the British army in New York, cut off from supplies from Great Britain and Ireland, had been threatened with starvation. Until D'Estaing's appearance in North American waters, the British had been able to move their troops and supplies almost at will, little concerned over the safety of their lines of communication. The entire British position in the United States depended upon naval power, and D'Estaing had proved that if the command of the sea could be wrested from them, their army, and with it their last hope of conquering the United States, would be destroyed.

With the ending of the campaign, the British were still in New York and the Americans were encamped north of the city at White Plains. The position of the two armies was almost the same as when Sir William Howe, two years before, had set out upon his conquest of America. It now began to appear that the march of the British army through the United States was to be a sight-seeing tour with no stopovers. Both Boston and Philadelphia, once firmly in the British grasp, had been hurriedly evacuated; only New York and Newport remained in their possession. British dominion in the United States was confined almost wholly to islands: Long Island, Staten Island, Manhattan, and Rhode Island. From the course of events of the last two years, it could be concluded, said

Nathanael Greene, that although Americans could not conquer the British army at once, "they cannot conquer us at all. The limits of the British government in America are their out-sentinels."

It was under these infelicitous conditions that Lord Carlisle and his fellow commissioners pressed their peace plan upon the Continental Congress. Congress would neither receive them nor entertain their propositions; and the commissioners, caught up in the rush of events that closely followed their arrival in Philadelphia, were obliged to evacuate the city with the fleet. "This is a miserable life," exclaimed Lord Carlisle, "always at sea, and plagued to death with business, from which I fear no possible good can arise." His distress was rendered more painful by the fear that the French fleet would capture the transport carrying his baggage — and then, Carlisle lugubriously remarked, "Monsr. d'Estaing will go about in my carriage, and drink all my wine." The Earl, assailed by mosquitoes "as large as sparrows," found that his knee breeches, while displaying his excellently turned legs to advantage in London drawing rooms, rendered him peculiarly vulnerable to these pests. He therefore took to wearing trousers, the dress of American "peasants." He resolutely refused to adopt the other American custom of sticking feathers in his hat — it reminded him unpleasantly, he acknowledged, of the coat of tar and feathers which he had no doubt the rebels were preparing for him.

The noble earl soon found that the American climate was little suited for a well-turned-out English gentleman. On the long and tedious passage to New York, the heat became so intense that, he declared, "we could not spare either hand, as there was occasion to wipe both our faces and necks every moment at the same time." Upon arriving in New York he found that the inhabitants spoke of the cold of winter "with much more horror than we of the heat we have endured. Whatever our sufferings may be," he concluded, "at least there will be variety in them."

Loathing the futile mission which they had undertaken, the commissioners settled down in New York, cut off by the French fleet from communicating with the home government. "We remain here no longer to negotiate, but to supplicate," declared Carlisle, although he could not bring himself to suit his action to the words. Instead, the commissioners tried to open negotiations with individual congressmen, hoping thereby to procure a hearing for their propositions. Governor Johnstone, in particular, wrote letters to prominent members of Congress offering to throw open the British Exchequer and the peerage to the lucky man who succeeded in restoring peace to the British Empire. Still, the patriots did not respond; and Johnstone's emissary in Philadelphia was seized and thrown in jail. After this second rebuff, the commissioners no longer wasted their time upon Congress; instead, they appealed over its head to the American people. This maneuver met with no more success than their other efforts; the patriots stood solidly behind Congress and the French alliance. If Lord

Carlisle and his colleagues really wished to make themselves useful, it was suggested, they ought to "solicit a treaty of peace, amity, commerce with the rising Stars of this western world" — in other words, get aboard the bandwagon with France and ride to glory with the American republic.[4]

Franklin had predicted that although Lord Carlisle and his colleagues would not heal the breach between the two countries they might very well widen it. This prediction was borne out when the commissioners, irritated and chagrined by the failure of their undertaking, issued a manifesto — "our last dying speech," Carlisle called it — threatening the American people with the horrors of burning, pillaging, and devastation. In this manifesto, the commissioners declared that hitherto Great Britain had prosecuted the war with benevolence and humanity — certainly news to Americans — but if the rebels persisted in their alliance with France, they must expect the kind of war reserved for Frenchmen, Spaniards, and other mortal enemies of the realm. Since the United States had made itself an appendage of France, it must be Great Britain's objective to render the acquisition valueless to the Bourbons by systematically laying the country waste.

From this it can be seen that the commissioners had come to the conclusion that the dogs of war were an indispensable part of the entourage of every peacemaker. Force to the utmost, they declared, was the only language rebels understood. "Gunpowder and guineas would fix the business," declared Lord Carlisle. ". . . But alas! our hands are tied behind us."

In this manner, the commissioners, having come to make peace, ended by urging a war of extermination. Far from furthering the work of reconciliation, they made England appear even more inveterate and bloodthirsty than before. Nor did they raise the prestige of English diplomacy; "to be laughed at, to return as they went, and to render our public counsels still more contemptible" — this seemed to be the sum total of Lord Carlisle's achievement. "You go a-begging with your King as with a brat," Thomas Paine told the commissioners, "or with some unsaleable commodity you are tired of; and though everybody tells you, no, still you keep hawking him about."

It is only fair to say that the commissioners' manifesto shocked the English Whigs, to whom it appeared to be "a declaration for desolating a vast continent, solely because we had not the wisdom to retain or the power to subdue it." This "accursed proclamation," they feared, would

---

[4] Governor Johnstone promised English guineas and honors to Washington and to Henry Laurens, President of Congress. His most important intrigue, however, was carried on with Mrs. Ferguson, a Tory lady, through whom he tried to get in touch with Joseph Reed, a prominent Pennsylvania patriot. Reed was promised ten thousand pounds sterling if he helped to bring about a reconciliation between the two countries. For answer, Reed declared that the King of England did not have enough gold to purchase him. Johnstone's letters were given to the newspapers by the patriots, thereby raising a storm of indignation against the British commissioner. Johnstone threw up his commission and returned to England.

lead Americans to demand the annihilation of England as a great power. In any event, it seemed likely to set back many years the work of reconciling the two great English-speaking countries which, to the Whigs, was the supreme task of British statesmanship.

It ill comported with the British military position to threaten Americans with total war; and even had the British forces been sufficiently strong to make good the threat, Sir Henry Clinton would not willingly have consented to the kind of warfare advocated by the commissioners. At no time since 1776 had the British been weaker: pinned down to New York and Newport, they were fortunate if they maintained their ground against the combined power of France and the United States. The commissioners' threat of a war without quarter was met by Americans with a promise to massacre Burgoyne's army. Two could play at a war of atrocity — and the Americans, with thousands of British prisoners of war in their possession, were in an excellent position to retaliate upon Great Britain. As an American Tory pointed out, the commissioners' manifesto was merely another in the long line of proclamations issued by the British since 1765, full of sound and fury but signifying nothing. "The American rebellion was the first (I believe) in the universe," said Judge Thomas Jones, a New York Loyalist, "attempted to be crushed . . . by proclamation."

The raid upon New Haven and the burning of Fairfield, Connecticut, which followed the proclamation of the commissioners, seemed to be the beginning of the war of frightfulness which Carlisle and his colleagues had threatened. In these expeditions, the British were accused of having outdone the horrors they had practised in New Jersey, "such as murdering old men, ravishing women & little girls, burning houses with the inhabitants in them, burning barns with the grain . . . cutting down all fruit trees, &c. &c." Although New Haven was not burned, it was plundered and Yale College was temporarily broken up. As might be expected, when the atrocities were recounted, the college boys fared much better than the virgins, upon whom, apparently, the full force of British bestiality descended. Even Loyalist women were alleged to have been assaulted, "some in the presence of their husbands, and others by great numbers successively." Some of the more attractive were said to have been carried off by the British, which, at least, was a new note in what was becoming a familiar dirge of atrocities.

The report brought back to England by Lord Carlisle gave little comfort to his countrymen. "The common people," he had concluded, "hate us in their hearts, notwithstanding all that is said of their secret attachment to the mother country"; and the power of the Continental Congress "every day, seems to be established upon a broader basis." If this were true, then indeed might Great Britain weary of the struggle, for in all quarters it was agreed that the mother country could hope for success only if its cause was supported by a powerful party in the United States.

Nevertheless, the Ministry and a large part of the people closed their eyes to this part of the commissioners' report and persisted in the belief that the majority of Americans were loyal and yearned for deliverance by the British army.[5]

Conquering Americans was now, however, only part of Englishmen's task: they must defend themselves in their own islands against invasion. The war which had begun as a conflict in the faraway regions of the earth was now on England's doorstep.

France hoped to end the war at a single blow by invading Great Britain itself. Long before the outbreak of hostilities, the French were preparing to cross the Channel in force; flat-bottomed barges were constructed, troops were moved into the Channel ports, and the French navy was readied for the engagement which was expected to give the Bourbons command of the English Channel. The weakness of the British fleet and army at home gave the French high hope of winning the war by a quick knockout. By May 1777, there was remaining in Great Britain only one battalion of artillery and there was "not a single matross left in the island."

Lord Sandwich had so frequently assured the country that Great Britain had a fleet superior to the united force of the House of Bourbon that Englishmen were unprepared for the true state of affairs which was now brought to light. There was no room for complacency: in North American waters, Lord Howe was outnumbered by the French fleet under D'Estaing; and in the English Channel, the French fleet was opposed by a handful of ships of the line. Of the fleet at Portsmouth, only six ships of the line were fit for sea; the rest were undermanned and in a bad state of disrepair. It was evident that Lord Sandwich had arrived at his comforting figures regarding England's naval strength by including everything that could float — and even some ships which could not. Ships in drydock, ships with rotten hulls, ships without rigging and without seamen, ships "on order" — these, in large part, were the "wooden walls" upon which Englishmen must now depend for salvation.

By heroic efforts, twenty-four ships of the line, in various states of seaworthiness, were assembled to hold the English Channel against the French fleet of thirty-two ships of the line. An embargo was imposed upon all merchant shipping to force men to join the navy, and six hundred soldiers were pressed into service as sailors. In command of this fleet was Lord Keppel, a Whig admiral and a member of Parliament who had consistently opposed the American war and who, when taking command of the fleet, made clear that he had not changed his sentiments regarding the struggle

[5] Lord Carlisle's subsequent career was more brilliant than its beginning augured. Continuing to enjoy the favor of Lord North, he became Lord Lieutenant of Ireland a few years after his return from America. But his more enduring reputation was made as a poet and dramatist. In 1783, Charles James Fox pronounced a tragedy written by Carlisle to have considerable merit; "if one could strike out a hundred or two of metaphors," observed Fox, "it would really be a most excellent play."

with the colonies. Upon Keppel rested the fate of England: if he lost, the French would be in a position to "sweep the British Channel cleaner than Van Tromp did the Medway" and England would lie open to invasion.

Despite his numerical inferiority, Keppel attacked the French fleet off Ushant in July 1778. Because the British admiral could not bring the French to a general engagement — the French, he said, adopted "the paltry game of fighting at a distance" — the encounter could hardly be termed a battle; no ships were taken or sunk, and after suffering minor damage to masts, yards, and rigging, both fleets sailed away to their home ports. Sandwich lamented that Keppel "had not a more spirited enemy to deal with"; yet many British officers observed that the French in this action "worked and manoeuvred their ships with a degree of seamanlike address and dexterity, which they never before perceived."

The danger of a French invasion at an end, Englishmen fell to quarreling among themselves over Keppel's failure to sweep the French fleet from the seas in the manner to which England had become accustomed. Palliser, an admiral who had been third-in-command in the action off Ushant, charged Keppel with having thrown away a victory by ordering the fleet to withdraw when the French were already in rout. Palliser was a Tory and a favorite of Lord Sandwich; Keppel was a Whig and one of the most outspoken critics of the First Lord of the Admiralty. Palliser's attack upon his superior officer precipitated a flare-up of partisan politics in the navy: twelve admirals signed a memorial protesting against Palliser's conduct; the Ministry supported Palliser; and Keppel demanded a court-martial to sift the charges of his subordinate. Keppel was triumphantly acquitted by the court-martial, and the Whig lords attending his trial at Portsmouth were as overjoyed as though they had scored a victory over a foreign foe. In London, the mob looted Palliser's house and broke all Lord North's windows (Lord North escaped by scrambling to the top of his house and there sitting out the riot). Meanwhile Charles James Fox harangued the mob to settle its score with Sandwich and Lord George Germain. The mob needed little urging; it was soon howling outside Sandwich's house, and the noble lord sprinted through the Admiralty Gardens until he found safety in the Horse Guards. To the Whigs, it gave great satisfaction to see "those who condemned the towns of America to fire and sword terrified with crackers"; it was reported of Lord Weymouth, a member of the cabinet, that he was in an absolute panic for he was known to have no spirit even when he was drunk. As for Keppel, he returned to London, where he was greeted with "much more than a Roman triumph merely for being an honest man, an able & judicious commander" — qualities which Horace Walpole regarded as rare among his contemporaries.

Palliser resigned under fire; whereupon the Whigs, heartened by their triumph, began to seek to bring down Lord Sandwich himself. Keppel swore that he would not serve in the navy as long as Sandwich remained in office; and in Parliament, Fox proposed votes of censure upon the First Lord for misconduct and neglect of duty. Fox called Sandwich "a faithful servant of the king of France," and the Duke of Richmond predicted that unless Sandwich resigned he would suffer death at the hands of the populace.

It could no longer be doubted that Lord Sandwich's presence at the Admiralty was gravely weakening the British navy; morale was seriously shaken by the Palliser-Keppel affair and many Whigs followed Keppel into voluntary retirement. As Sir George Rodney complained, officers presumed "to find fault and think when their duty is implicit obedience." In the British navy, politics raged almost as fiercely as in the British Parliament.

Nevertheless, Sandwich remained in office for the next three years, in complete enjoyment of the royal confidence, whatever the people of England or the officers and men of the Royal Navy may have thought of him. The King had the satisfaction of defeating Keppel's efforts to win a seat in Parliament by obliging the electors of Windsor to vote against the admiral and by publicly snubbing him at the royal levees. The King's triumph was procured, however, only at the price of further dividing the navy when England desperately needed its last ounce of strength.

Lord Sandwich was soon scraping the bottom of the barrel in his search for admirals. Grizzled sea dogs were brought out of long and honorable retirement to resume active stations: Sir Charles Hardy — "Old Mother Hardy" — was plucked from his retreat as Governor of Greenwich Hospital, after an absence of twenty years from the sea; and when Sir Charles died in 1780 his place was taken by Admiral Geary, a man well over seventy who had not been active for more than a decade. Within a few months of his appointment, Geary resigned, his health utterly broken. Indeed, sometimes Sandwich barely anticipated the undertaker; but when the admirals died on his hands, the First Lord of the Admiralty, undismayed, threw in another septuagenarian. A superannuated admiral was almost certain of official favor provided his political sympathies were agreeable to Sandwich.

Thus England faced her enemies, inferior in numbers to them everywhere, an entire army swallowed up in America, and her remaining troops menaced by French and Americans, her fleets spread thinly over distant theaters of war. Englishmen met this danger, as they did all others, with staunchness of spirit and unquenchable faith in ultimate victory. "Will Europe never learn," asked an Englishman, "that Storm tempest and adversity are the Nurse of all our Greatness?" Headed by Liverpool and Manchester, the principal cities of Great Britain raised battalions at their own expense, numbering altogether almost fifteen thousand men, for the

British army. The ardor for subduing the colonies "spread like a flame from north to south"; it was better, ran the cry, "to die with glory, than to live with infamy. . . . We should imitate the old Romans, who, in their greatest calamities, would never accept of terms, however equitable, from the conquerors." The Old Guard of English Tories screamed that the rebels must be made to suffer fire and sword — the British fleet and army ought to be instructed "to desolate a country which hath wantonly drawn upon itself the vengeance of Great Britain." "Britons!" they exclaimed, "wage an eternal sea war with America, rather than admit of their independence."

Scotchmen, hitherto not distinguished by their affection for the House of Hanover — indeed, they had gained the reputation in the uprising of 1745 of being "a damn'd rebellious crew" — now upheld the authority of King and Parliament over the colonies with more unanimity and vigor than did Englishmen themselves. "High and low, rich and poor," reported a contemporary, "are all roused; the clergy preach nothing but the sword of the Lord and of Gideon, and vast numbers enlist daily." Some of the Scotch volunteers signally proved their devotion by refusing to accept bounties, swearing that the satisfaction of chastising the enemy was sufficient reward for them.

⌢   ⌢   ⌢

With the entry of France into the war, the survival of Great Britain was at stake; the question was now whether Britain would be "a very great or a very little nation." It might therefore be supposed that the Franco-American alliance would have united Englishmen, Whigs and Tories alike, in defense of the threatened homeland.

In actuality, however, there was no truce in politics. The Whigs remained resolutely in opposition; the peril of the nation made more imperative, in their eyes, a change of men and measures. Giving North and his colleagues "the fullest credit for possessing more ignorance, more weakness, more folly, more absurdity than any other men in the kingdom," they declined to lash themselves to the mast while the Tory crew drove on to ruin.

Instead, the Whigs proposed to withdraw all British troops and ships from the United States and to leave Americans to the operation of their better natures, in the expectation that their innate loyalty to the mother country would ultimately triumph over their desire for separation. By this signal act of generosity and good will, Burke and Fox predicted, America would be won from the embrace of France. Rather than permit the enemy "to erect schemes of ambition and endless destruction on the ruins of her once kind and indulgent parent," the United States would join its strength with that of Great Britain.

At the same time that they urged peace with America, the Whigs preached force to the utmost against France. Let Great Britain direct its military and naval force "against that ancient enemy and rival of our greatness," they exclaimed; if we can, "by force of arms, carry compulsion to the House of Bourbon, we are yet a great people, and the first of nations." War against France, Fox told his countrymen, "is against your inveterate enemy and rival; every blow you strike in America is against yourselves, every stroke against France is of advantage to you. . . . Even your victories over America are favorable to France, from what they must cost you in men and money." "To wound America," said Lord Camden, "was to wound the right hand of Great Britain; to weaken France was to strengthen ourselves."

In offering to recognize the independence of the United States, Fox did not intend to cast the United States out of the British Empire and let it drift where it would. On the contrary, he insisted that the admission of American independence be accompanied by "conciliatory, healing, and friendly negociation" with a view toward making the republic an ally of the former mother country. Fox and other English liberals were persuaded that union with America would fix the power of Great Britain upon an unshakable foundation. The friendship of Americans was more vital to Great Britain than was sovereignty over them; it was inevitable that the United States would become one of the most powerful nations on earth, and it was to the interest of Great Britain to encourage the growth of the transatlantic republic. The day might come — and sooner than many Englishmen thought — when the aid of the United States might save Great Britain. "We have hitherto divided America, to keep her weak," said an Englishman in 1780; "let us now unite her, to make her great."

To these arguments, the King and his ministers turned a deaf ear. George pinned little faith to peace overtures: every offer of terms, he found, merely aided "the Demagogues in America in their Arts to convince the Deluded People that a little farther resistance must make the Mother Country yield." To all peace talk, therefore, the King returned answer: "We have it not at this hour in our power to make Peace. It is by steadiness and exertions that we are to get into a situation to effect it." From the point of view of the monarch and his ministers, the relinquishment of America meant the end of Great Britain as a first-rate power. "What will become of the greatness of Britain?" they asked; and gloomily answered that "like Carthage she will fall, when the commerce on which it is founded is no more." "Take away America," said Lord George Germain, "and we should sink into perfect insignificance; preserve it, and he would venture to say, it was yet the brightest jewel in the crown. . . . This nation never could exist as a great and powerful people, unless our sovereign was likewise the sovereign of America." This spirit admitted of little hope of peace between the United States and Great Britain until one or the other had suffered shattering defeat.

Moreover, the government had no confidence that if British troops were withdrawn from the United States, Americans would love England the more; on the contrary, it seemed probable that they would turn their efforts toward conquering what remained of the British Empire in North America. Canada, Nova Scotia, the Floridas, and the West Indies would be overrun, and Britons would awake from their dream of making allies of the Americans to find themselves stripped of the last shreds of empire. Then, perhaps, Americans might consent to extend their hand in friendship; but the Tories suspected it was more likely that they would kick their old mother while she was down and go blithely on their way.

Therefore, instead of renouncing the American war, the British government continued to make the United States the main theater of war, deliberately subordinating the struggle with the Bourbons in the hope of delivering a decisive blow at the United States. As Burke said, "it was but one story from the beginning to the end: it was and has been for seven years, nothing but American war, American war, American war; and it would be American war to the end of the chapter." Always the administration found reasons for prosecuting the struggle. First it had been claimed that troops must be sent to America to rescue the loyal majority from the tyranny of a handful of demagogues; then to deliver them from the oppressions of the Continental Congress; and now to save them from the French, whose alliance they did not want. "War," said John Adams in 1779, "is everlastingly so popular among them [the English people] when there is the least appearance of success, however deceitful . . . they will go on at whatever expense and hazard."

CHAPTER XVII

Radicals and Conservatives: The Ideological Conflict

THE American Revolution occurred during the heyday of eighteenth-century liberalism — indeed, it was itself a product of that liberalism. As Washington said, the United States came into existence in an auspicious period of the world's history, "an epoch when the rights of mankind were better understood and more clearly defined, than at any former period." Far from being a "gloomy age of Ignorance and Superstition," it was distinguished by "the free cultivation of Letters; the unbounded extension of Commerce; the progressive Refinement of Manners; the growing liberality of sentiment." In framing their constitutions, it was therefore open to Americans to draw upon the accumulated wisdom of the ages and to make the new governments of America the crowning achievement of the Enlightenment.

Philosophers had long found the source of all governmental authority in the people and had proclaimed them sovereign, but this was an inheritance the people had yet to enter upon. Indeed, it seemed as unlikely that the people would become sovereign as that philosophers would become kings. Upon the continent of Europe, democracy was firmly established only in Switzerland and a few other small states; elsewhere, monarchism was ascendant. After its extinction in the fall of the Greek city-states, democracy was almost a new thing in the world; it remained for the United States to revive democracy by proving that free men were capable of governing themselves.

As yet relatively untouched by the Industrial Revolution, society in the United States was simple and predominantly agrarian in character. The great majority of whites were independent freeholders or artisans and tradesmen in comfortable circumstances; most of the people had received at least a rudimentary education and there were few important vestiges of feudalism. With over 90 per cent of the people living in the country, the United States abounded in those self-reliant yeomen in whom Thomas Jefferson reposed his hopes of democracy.

Under these circumstances, it might be supposed that the United States was ideally suited to the establishment of democracy. Nevertheless, in many sections of the republic the aristocratic ideal was firmly planted. Each community had its squire or local magnate or rich man to whom the common people were accustomed to look for leadership; "men of property" set the example and the lesser fry followed in their train. In New York, the patroon system of land ownership nourished an aristocracy of descendants of the early Dutch families; along the seaboard of the Northern and Middle states, wealthy merchants and shipowners constituted a social elite.

Contemplating these evidences of aristocracy in the country, some democrats concluded that, given a few more years of British rule, the task of establishing the rights of man in the United States might have been impossible. "From the prejudices that I find prevail," said Charles Thomson, secretary to the Continental Congress, "& the notions of honour, rank and other courtly Ideas so eagerly embraced, I am fully persuaded had time been given for them to strike deep root, it would have been extremely difficult to have prepared men's minds for the good seed of liberty."

This aristocratic bias of society was particularly apparent in the Southern colonies, a region of great estates, Negro slaves and, in the western section, of small farmers discriminated against in politics, economics, and religion by the ruling clique of planters. In Virginia, the eighteenth century was pre-eminently the age of the gentleman; here, said a traveler, "one meets with the Descendants of the oldest Families in the American Dominion still possessed of the dignity & consequence enjoyed by their Ancestors, & whose Foundations rest on the respectable & Solid basis of Landed Property, as in the great Families in the Mother Country." Virginians agreed with Dr. Johnson when he defined a gentleman as "a man of ancestry." Like their counterparts in England, the planters of the Old Dominion held in contempt all who engaged in trade — "they say that these are not gentlemen, and will not associate with them." They called the residence of their governor not a "Province House" (as in Massachusetts) but a "Palace," and in their nomenclature the building in which the legislature met was not a "State House" but "the Capitol."

⌒   ⌒   ⌒

Despite these aristocratic leanings, it could hardly fail to be seen that the people of the United States loved liberty and as British subjects had enjoyed it in a greater measure than any other colonial people. The tyranny against which they rebelled was, for the most part, merely a threat of future evil. With truth, until the Declaration of Independence, Americans could say that they were contending for liberties they had possessed as British subjects; and the very fact that they had risen with slight provocation indicated that their passion for liberty could not easily be confined and that any government destined to endure in America must be founded upon the will of the people. Indeed, the temper of the people seemed incompatible with the restraints upon the individual necessary to the well-being of society. How could order be preserved among men possessed of such "an amazing zeal for Liberty"?

To such men, it was not enough to wage war against tyranny: they had to be given something to fight for. As John Adams said, "a whole government of our choice, managed by persons whom we love, revere, and can confide in has charms in it for which men will fight." Early in 1776, accordingly, the Continental Congress had called upon the states to establish permanent governments, leaving them at liberty to "adopt such government as shall, in the opinion of the representatives of the people, best conduce to the happiness and safety of their constituents in particular, and America in general." It was soon made clear that upon this momentous subject Americans held contrary views.

Conservatives were concerned with the necessity of "security, order and good government." Dreading anarchy more than they did strong government, they regarded the radicals as "furious patriots" to whom disorder was the breath of life. Although in defying British imperialism they had spoken frequently of the "state of nature," they had no wish to revert to that realm wherein all authority was dissolved. They strove to make the transition from British authority to independence smooth, easy, and without disorder. Under their guidance this critical period was bridged with a minimum of trouble. The danger of mob rule subsided; but still the question of the kind of government to be substituted for British authority remained.

The ideal of the conservatives was to retain the old colonial governments, property qualifications for voting and office-holding and all, putting in the stead of the British Crown the sovereign people themselves. Their ideal was the British Constitution, and they hoped to keep as much as possible of its aristocratic spirit when they parted company with the mother country. To their minds, the old colonial governments guaranteed all essential liberty. Representative government, trial by jury, habeas corpus — to give the people more was to risk "all the tumult and riot incident to simple Democracy." In the colonial governments, they found many salutary checks upon the power of the people and safeguards to the rights of property. Here, for example, a strong governor and council and an independent judiciary restrained the popularly elected assemblies and kept democracy under leash.

Conservative patriots had no wish to rush into democracy — a state where, they believed, only angels were fit to tread. In their eyes, mankind was too recently fallen from grace to enter regions where unselfishness, public spirit, and a high general level of intelligence were the passports. In short, they doubted whether the American people possessed the qualifications to make democracy work. John Adams, who sometimes distrusted the virtue of his countrymen, pointed out that in a democracy "men must be ready . . . to sacrifice their Private Pleasures, Passions and Interests . . . when they stand in Competition with the Rights of Society."

Although conservatives did not openly challenge the right of the people to rule, they questioned the people's ability to rule and they sought to limit the exercise of popular sovereignty. Essentially, the problem was to permit the people to reign but not to govern. Particularly must they be prevented from exercising power during those periods when freedom might degenerate into licentiousness, and the people, running mad after liberty, might commit endless crimes in its name. To guard against this evil, conservatives insisted that the power of the masses be restrained by a system of checks and balances designed to afford protection to property against "the wantonness of the Populace." The rich, it was said, must be given constitutional protection against the poor because "a Legislature of Beggars will be Thieves" and "the Poor never want Will to devour the Rich, if it can be done with Impunity."

Government by a single assembly they dreaded as a new tyranny — the mob in the saddle and demagogues spurring it on. Governors, they insisted, ought to be given the right to veto acts of the legislatures; the senates or councils ought "to consist of the most experienced, accomplished, and Virtuous Men" as an additional check upon the assemblies; and judges ought to be completely independent of the people.

To the radicals, on the other hand, the principal purpose of the Revolution was the furtherance of the cause of liberty by making men more free and more equal. This, they believed, was a duty owing to their own generation and to posterity: their decisions might determine for many decades the course of American history. Therefore, as the foundation of all government, they laid particular emphasis upon the liberty of the individual and his worth and dignity as a free man. Their objective was to establish a government which would be consecrated "not to the emolument of one man, or one class of men, but the safety, liberty, and happiness of every individual in the community," and which should prevent rich men from possessing too much property "and of consequence acquiring too much power and influence, dangerous to the liberties of the people."

The democrats of the revolutionary generation sought to bring government as closely as possible under the control of the people. The ideal, no doubt, was an assembly of the people along the lines of a New

England town meeting, but since this was impracticable in an area as large as a state, it was necessary to establish a representative form of government that would closely approximate direct rule by the people. Believing, as did Sam Adams, that "a state is never free but when each citizen is bound by no law whatever that he has not approved of, either by himself, or by his representatives," democrats regarded manhood suffrage, annual elections, rotation in office, and freedom of speech and the press as essential to the government of the people. These men saw no reason to be bound by traditional forms of government: were not Americans conducting a revolution intended to usher in a new era of freedom? A revolution could not go forward if its leaders kept their eyes fixed upon the landmarks of the past and refused to strike out on new paths.

Having adopted the principle that there ought to be no check upon the power of the people but the people themselves, the democrats wanted no strong governor or upper house invested with the right to negative legislation passed by the popular branch of the legislature. They took the stand that liberty was safe only under a unicameral legislature in which all power — legislative, executive, and judicial — was concentrated. "All power to the Assemblies" was a slogan which expressed the philosophy of these patriots. A single, all-powerful assembly, unchecked by a governor, judges, or councilors — this was the form of government in which American democracy could best give effect to the will of the people.

The veneration felt by many Americans for the British Constitution was to the radicals one of the most regrettable hang-overs from British rule. As long as the British Constitution — interpreted by Montesquieu as a system of checks and balances which ensured the protection of every class — retained its ascendancy in the minds of Americans, the radicals well knew that it would be impossible to establish in the United States the direct rule of the people. Hence the necessity for attacking the government and Constitution of Great Britain as a "confederacy against . . . the rights of man." Looking back upon the state from which they had been delivered, Americans were told that they ought to congratulate themselves upon having broken away from "so irrational, so ridiculous, and so bloody a form of government." As the Continental Congress said, Americans were "contending against a kingdom crumbling to pieces, a nation without public virtue; and a people sold to, and betrayed by, their own representatives . . . against a government equal only to plans of plunder, conflagration and murder."

The leading exponents of these conflicting points of view were Thomas Paine and John Adams and two more able and vigorous champions of their respective causes could not have been found in the republic. Paine pronounced an unicameral legislature to be the only truly democratic system, while John Adams as stoutly upheld a government of checks and balances.[1]

In 1775, the current of public opinion ran strongly with Thomas Paine rather than with John Adams: Adams could find few men who wished to retain the old form of a division of authority among governor, council, and assembly. The champions of a council or upper house were met with the cry: "What! shall the Representatives of the People be *checked* and *controuled* in their proceedings by a Council?" and it was pointed out that the Continental Congress had disdained to create an upper house as a curb upon its proceedings.

As British subjects, Americans had learned to keep a watchful eye upon those in power lest they abuse their trust by making themselves the masters rather than the servants of the people. Power, they believed, corrupted the best men; and its workings were so insidious that an honest public official could be transformed into a would-be despot before the people, unless they were ceaselessly on guard, had become aware of their peril. Therefore, Americans grudgingly doled out power to public officials and kept them under close scrutiny. In order to discourage ambitious men from making a career of office-holding, public jobs were poorly paid. Everywhere barriers were raised against the menace of one-man rule — a peril seldom absent from the minds of the revolutionary leaders.

Moreover, to John Adams's dismay, so sharp was American revulsion from British institutions, customs, and attitudes of mind that for a time it was accounted "a kind of merit to do everything the reverse of what [the British] did." A French traveler found that Americans studiously avoided referring to the "English" language; instead they said, "You speak American well; the American is not difficult to learn." Some patriots, in their zeal to break every tie with Great Britain, thought seriously of inventing a new language; and at least one New Englander championed Hebrew as a substitute for English. Under such conditions, there was little hope of persuading Americans to cleave to the British Constitution.

[1] The breach between Paine and Adams — symbolic of the differences that divided the American people — widened with the years. In 1776, the two men were still on more or less friendly terms: when Adams rallied Paine on his efforts in *Common Sense* to prove from the Old Testament that monarchy was unlawful, Paine "laughed out and said that he did not believe in the Bible." In 1787, however, when Paine visited Adams, he talked, said the New Englander, "so much like a Villain and a Blockhead as to excite me to wrath, and I called him, not jocularly, but bona fide and in sober earnest 'A Fool.'" Nor did Adams alter his opinion when Paine ardently espoused the cause of the French Revolution and began to dream of a second American Revolution along the lines of the French experiment; John Adams had little sympathy with efforts to storm the kingdom of democracy by violence and bloodshed, and to his mind one revolution in a lifetime was enough for any man. Paine now figured in John Adams's list of evildoers as "that insolent blasphemer of things sacred, and transcendent libeller of all that is good."

As a result, the constitutions generally concentrated power in popularly elected assemblies and weakened the authority of governors and councils.[2] It was apparent that in Americans' eyes, the only good governor was a weak governor. Indeed, many Americans could not endure the name "governor"; they vowed that it ought never to be heard among free men. "I prefer the word President," said a patriot, "as less liable to make the creature vain and domineering." But by whatever name he was known, the chief executive of the state was usually a mere figurehead. Denied the veto power, checked by executive councils, deprived of patronage, and elected for short terms of office, state governors enjoyed few of the trappings of authority. One governor complained that his power consisted of signing a receipt for his salary!

In these constitutions, emphasis was laid upon protecting the individual from oppression by government. The rights rather than the duties of citizens were most highly prized by the constitution makers. Government was under suspicion: what most concerned Americans was not the good government could do, but the evil it might do. This was in accord with the philosophy of John Locke, the English political thinker whose influence upon Americans of the Revolutionary period was probably more profound than that of any other writer. Locke taught that the primary purpose of the state was the protection of property. Deliberately, government was kept weak and decentralized; "nothing has been done without the approbation of the people," said George Mason of Virginia, "who have indeed outrun their leaders, so that no capital measure hath been adopted until they called loudly for it."

If freedom from strong government was a goal of American revolutionists, they attained their objective more completely than is usually granted to revolutionists. It was the individual citizen rather than the government that was exalted by the philosophy of 1776; freed to a great degree from governmental control, the citizen was now on his own. Here, then, the philosophy of the innate goodness of man was to be tested. Would he rise to the occasion by revealing all the nobility, disinterestedness, and concern for the welfare of his fellow men which alone could justify the removal of the restraints of government? Or would the great experiment fail because of his selfishness, his inclination to seek his own advancement at the expense of the community, and his inability to fulfill the duties of citizenship? These were the questions raised by the Declaration of Independence.

Despite the contention of the democrats that if all were expected to fight for liberty, all ought to possess the right to vote, only two states

[2] In their first constitutions, only three states followed John Adams's doctrine of the separation of powers; the other ten invested a popularly elected assembly with authority and dispensed almost altogether with checks and balances. As the war progressed, however, the state governments increasingly reflected Adams's views.

applied the principle of no taxation without representation — the rallying cry of American patriots against the mother country — to conditions
at home. As a free and independent people, Americans continued to be
taxed without benefit of representation simply because they did not
have enough property to qualify as voters. These property requirements
were inherited from colonial days and were perpetuated in the United
States largely because conservatives believed that those who owned the
country ought to rule it.[3] Officeholders were required in most states to
be well-to-do: to qualify as governor, a considerable estate was needed.
In its higher branches, politics was a career open to money, not merely
to talent.

Property qualifications, however, were not in themselves sufficient to
hold back the democratic tide. Town workers might be debarred by
this means from exercising the franchise,[4] but probably a majority of
farmers held enough property to qualify as voters. And, as was pointed
out, during this period of American history "every workman who can
use his hands, may be looked upon as likely soon to become a man of
property." Therefore, it was still possible for the people to dominate
by sheer force of numbers if they were sufficiently aroused by public
issues to march to the polls; the ascendancy of conservatives was precarious and the dread of majority rule was always present in the custodians of property rights.

Most of the constitutions provided that the governor and members
of the senate or upper house were to be elected by the assemblies or by
an electorate of large property owners. This provision reflected the prevailing belief of conservatives that the people lacked sufficient judgment to be entrusted with the choice of higher officials and that, in the
interests of property rights, some branches of the government ought to
be removed from the direct control of the populace.

In adopting these constitutions, the most democratic procedure was for
the people to elect the members of a constitutional convention and to
pass upon the proposed constitution by means of a plebiscite. Nevertheless, only one of the revolutionary constitutions — that of Massachusetts
— was submitted to the people for approval; the rest were drawn up by
legislatures or conventions and put in force without recourse to a popular referendum.

Although in Pennsylvania under the constitution of 1776 the west
achieved equality of representation with the east, in many of the South-

---

[3] In one respect, however, an important gain was made. During the colonial period,
suffrage was based chiefly on land ownership; after the Revolution, most states tended
to put renters of land or houses on a level with freeholders. In states where taxpayers
were given the right to vote, no distinction was made between real and personal property. Four states retained the old system of requiring a freehold.

[4] As late as 1790, only about one in ten male residents of New York City owned
sufficient property to vote for governor.

ern states the constitutions perpetuated the domination of the east by denying westerners proportional representation. In South Carolina, for example, about one fifth of the population, residing in the eastern part of the state, governed the remaining four fifths of the people. Conservatives were taking no chances with the "wild men" of the west; the western brand of democracy found little favor among the conservative leaders of the rebellion.

Especially in three states — New York, Maryland, and Massachusetts — did conservatives succeed in writing much of their creed into the constitutions. High property qualifications for voting and office-holding, strong governors and upper houses to check the assemblies — these provisions represented a clear-cut triumph over the radicals.

But even where conservatives wrote the constitutions, they did not always succeed in ruling the state. In New York, for instance, where John Jay and other conservatives drew up the constitution, power passed into the hands of Governor George Clinton, a radical country lawyer, without pretensions to ancestry, who employed the authority vested in him as governor (he was the strongest executive in the United States) in the interests of the common people. Clinton left no doubt that a strong government could be directed against conservatism and that the masses had at least as much to hope as to fear from government.

Thus, in general, the revolutionary settlement left the "opulent minority" exposed to the bitter winds of democracy. Despite their efforts to impose curbs and restraints upon popular sovereignty, power still resided with the people and it only remained for them to recognize their strength and rise up in their majesty. Some Americans seemed bent upon sharing the wealth. "Would not a law for dividing the wealth of the state equally among the inhabitants, be . . . popular?" asked an agitated citizen. "Only set the thought on foot, and take a little pains to blow it about, and you will soon have legions of advocates for it. An estate of one hundred thousand pounds, would make a hundred beggars smack their lips." As conservatives perceived, the popular assemblies were potential instruments of majority rule.

The full force of this peril was not revealed until after the war was over. It remained for the postwar depression and the radicalism it generated to demonstrate conclusively to conservatives that too much power had been given to the people by the revolutionary settlement and that checks and balances against popular majorities must be raised if property was to be protected from the inroads of poverty-stricken farmers and town workers. "In our opposition to tyranny," said a revolutionary leader in 1787, "we forgot that the temple of tyranny has two doors. We bolted one of them by proper restraints; but we left the other open, by neglecting to guard against the effects of our ignorance and licentiousness."

During the Revolutionary War, Pennsylvania became a proving ground for democratic ideals — an experimental laboratory in government. Here, it was said, could be seen the workings of "unlimited democracy (the most horrid of all governments)." Here was being fought out one of the fundamental issues of the American Revolution: Could order and stability be reconciled with the rule of the people?

Pennsylvania, in drawing up its constitution, wholeheartedly adopted the views of Thomas Paine. Whereas most of the states carefully diluted their draught of democracy, Pennsylvania took hers straight. The constitution of 1776 established virtual manhood suffrage, dispensed with checks and balances, and established a unicameral legislature as the supreme power in the state. Benjamin Franklin, among others, urged the creation of this all-powerful legislature; two chambers, he said, would resemble a wagon with two teams of horses pulling in opposite directions.[5]

The Pennsylvania Constitution of 1776 vested virtually all power in the popularly elected assembly. As its critics complained, although there were scores of barriers raised against the tyranny of the executive, there was no protection against the tyranny of the assembly. In other words, minorities — and particularly wealthy minorities — were afforded little defense against oppression.

In the upheaval of revolution, the first families, to whom ruling the country had become one of the prerogatives of gentility, found themselves cast down from the seats of the mighty. Scotch, Irish, Germans, and Englishmen, recently arrived in the state and bearing none of the hallmarks — including family trees — of breeding, were now favored over those "whose ancestors had perhaps assisted in laying the first stone of Philadelphia" — to which the democrats answered that laying the first stones of Philadelphia gave no title to all subsequent erections. Conservatives called for "a union of the native and ancient citizens" against these lowborn interlopers upon the preserves of the best families. Had Pennsylvanians rebelled from Great Britain, they asked, to suffer the tyranny of the workmen of Philadelphia and the radical farmers of the western counties? They cried into their Madeira to see such a "Set of Scrubs" triumphant; in their eyes, it was the same kind of barbarian invasion that had overthrown Rome. It meant the end of all upper-class society, all distinction between rich and poor, all subordination — everything, in short, that made life pleasant and fruitful to the wealthy and well-born.

Conservatives lamented Pennsylvania's fall from "the first spot, not only in America, but upon the Surface of the earth" to the nether regions of democracy and levelism. The Declaration of Independence had

---

[5] This constitution was actually drawn up not by Paine and Franklin, as is often claimed, but by Timothy Matlack, Dr. Thomas Young, and other local leaders.

declared all men to be equal; and the Pennsylvania democrats seemed bent upon redressing any inequalities occasioned by superior talents in the art of accumulating worldly goods. "You would execrate this State if you were in it," Thomas Jefferson was assured by a friend, "the Supporters of their Government are a set of Workmen without any Weight of Character." A capitalist seemed no more likely to enjoy happiness in Pennsylvania than in present-day Moscow — meeting on every side the rude buffetings of outrageous democrats, there was no security or peace of mind for the opulent and wellborn.

The first democratic constitution in the United States was in some respects closer to the present Soviet conception of democracy than to the ideals upheld by this country today. It established a party line to which all voters and officeholders must conform. The so-called Test Act required an oath of allegiance to the constitution of 1776, and exacted a promise "not to do or say any thing, directly or indirectly, that shall be prejudicial or injurious to the Constitution." Those who refused to accept its principles were cast outside the pale and denied a voice in affairs. Not even the privilege of casting a dissenting vote was vouchsafed them. In short, every citizen admitted to participation in the government was required to hold certain beliefs upon pain of disfranchisement.

Defenders of the Pennsylvania Constitution maintained that this system was "*a good one for a poor man*" and that it was solely for this reason that the rich and wellborn hated it. They congratulated themselves upon having thrown off the rule of "*a few overgrown rich men*," and in making war upon "the Spirit of Aristocracy & Pride of Wealth." To justify their inroads upon liberty, they contended that democracy was fighting for its life and that, in order to survive, it must fight tyranny with tyranny's own weapons. Yet it is true that a large minority of Pennsylvanians — among whom were the Quakers, whose religious principles forbade oaths — refused to take this oath of allegiance to the constitution of 1776 and were in consequence debarred from voting. British "tyranny," it is fair to say, had not gone to this length.

The Test Act gave Pennsylvania a bad name among many liberals who, while sympathizing with the objectives of the Pennsylvania democrats, were unable to justify the means by the end. Richard Price, the English radical, for instance, roundly rebuked his Pennsylvania friends for aping the ways of tyranny in order to safeguard the rights of man. The purpose of all liberals, said Price, ought to be to enlarge the area of freedom; to suppress and disfranchise opposition was to take the road back to arbitrary government from which mankind had been struggling for centuries. Surveying the work of the Pennsylvania democrats, Price remarked: "I have, since the publication of my Observations on the American Revolution, heard so much that I do not like, that I have been sometimes afraid of having made myself ridiculous by what I have said of the importance of this Revolution." On their part, Pennsylvania conservatives sought to overthrow the constitution of 1776 and to establish in its stead a strong governor and senate capable of checking the overweening power of the assembly. In other words, they proposed to do for Pennsylvania what the Federal Constitution of 1787 did for the country as a whole: establish a government of checks and balances by which the "opulent minority" was protected from being despoiled by the majority.

This struggle between democrats and conservatives distracted the energies of Pennsylvanians from the war effort to a contest over who was to rule at home. Thomas Paine was apprehensive lest internecine strife destroy all patriotism in the country. "A man," he said, "may as well talk of loving a wife and a mistress, at one time, with equal felicity, as of jangling with his neighbours and yet joining with them in public defence." While Pennsylvanians quarreled over their constitutions, he warned, the British might conquer the state and leave them no constitution whatever to argue about. Nevertheless, even the danger that Philadelphia would become "the seat of *vermin* and *British beasts of prey*" failed to abate the rancor of conservatives and radicals; in the darkest days of the war, Anthony Wayne complained that the "sickly Constitution" of Pennsylvania was not worth defending.

It was not only in Pennsylvania that conservatives found cause for alarm: in many quarters they saw signs that "Down with the rich!" might become a slogan of the American Revolution. In North Carolina, where the people were smitten with a desire to embrace democracy in the manner of Pennsylvania, it was said that "every one who has the least pretensions to be a gentleman is suspected and borne down *per ignobile vulgus* — a set of men without reading, experience, or principle to govern them." In Virginia, the people were heard to say that after independence had been won, they would establish a government which, "by being independent of the rich men, every man would then be able to do as he pleased." A Virginia gentleman, outraged by such demagoguery, accosted a democrat and upbraided him for preaching against the rich. "I shamed the fool so much for it he slunk away," he declared; " — but he got elected by it."

Conservatives might well fear that in their zeal to break the ties with Britain they had opened the bag of the winds and that they themselves would be swept aside by the whirlwind of democracy. A new attitude toward the genteel and wellborn was making itself manifest in ways highly disturbing to upholders of the old order. For example, take the harrowing experience of Colonel Randolph of Virginia: seated with a few other gentlemen before a tavern fire one evening, he was startled by the entrance of some "peasants" who, crowding about the fire "began spitting, pulling off their country boots all over mud" without any re-gard whatever for the sensibilities of the gentlemen present. This inci-dent prompted Colonel Randolph to soliloquize upon the depravity of the times. "The spirit of independence was converted into equality," he declared, "and every one who bore arms, esteems himself upon a footing with his neighbors. . . . No doubt," the agitated colonel con-cluded, "each of these men conceives himself, in every respect, my equal."

This growing lack of deference toward the first families led a Euro-pean traveler to predict that "the advantage of distinction will never again exist in this country, in the same manner it did before the com-mencement of hostilities." There was a new spirit abroad in the land; and although the upper class retained its land and a large share of its political power, the American people, it was clear, did not suffer aris-tocrats gladly.

The ancient bulwarks of feudalism and privilege imported from Great Britain began to fall one by one before the advance of democracy. Quit-rents, the great estates of absentee proprietors, feudal tenure — all went down during or shortly after the Revolutionary War. Primogeniture and entail, the devices by which great estates were perpetuated, were like-wise abolished. Maryland took over the lands of the Baltimores; Penn-sylvania confiscated the property of the Penns; New York abolished the manorial powers of the patroons; and hundreds of thousands of acres were confiscated from banished Tories. A considerable share of this land passed into the hands of small owners, thereby strengthening the economic foundations of democracy in the United States.

Southern aristocrats seemed likely to be a serious stumbling block to the progress of democracy in the United States. John Adams feared the "Barons of the South" whose influence, he supposed, would be cast into the scales against the rights of man — for how could liberalism exist among drivers of Negro slaves? Between the "Monarchick and aristo-cratic spirit of the South" and the spirit of Great Britain, the New Eng-lander saw little to choose. In the South, he pointed out, "the gentry are very rich, and the common people very poor. This inequality of property gives an aristocratical turn to all their proceedings." John Adams, although he did not love unfettered democracy, was equally hostile to the arbitrary rule of an aristocracy.

Nevertheless, it was Southerners who took the lead in proclaiming the principles of equalitarianism and the inviolability of the liberty of the individual. A Virginian, Thomas Jefferson, was chiefly responsible for the Declaration of Independence; and the Virginia Bill of Rights, drawn up by George Mason in 1776, served as a model for the preamble to many state constitutions. In the light of these events, John Adams began to revise his opinion of the Southern "Barons": instead of distrusting them as reactionaries, he began to fear them as radicals. They seemed determined to make the United States unsafe for gentlemen; seldom had John Adams seen aristocrats more inclined to liquidate their own class.

Although the Old Dominion never carried its democracy to the extreme practised in Pennsylvania, the work of Thomas Jefferson made the state a beacon to liberals everywhere in the United States. Here the ideas of the Enlightenment were to be seen in their purest form; democracy and humanitarianism were indissolubly joined.

One of the most important achievements of the Enlightenment in Virginia was the establishment of religious liberty. Before the Revolution, the Congregational Church and the Church of England were in many colonies the recognized state religions. Toward the support of these churches, citizens, regardless of their religious beliefs, were obliged to pay taxes. These taxes were collected by the state and handed over to the church by a sort of check-off system: magistrates and clergy were allies in upholding the approved religion and in making life as burdensome as possible for those stubborn folk who remained outside the pale of godliness as defined by the authorities.

To dissenters, these established churches were fully as oppressive as any wrongdoing by the British Parliament. Downtrodden sects, such as the Baptists, persecuted by both New England Congregationalists and Southern Episcopalians, raised the cry at the beginning of the Revolution against "Spiritual tyranny, the worst sort of tyranny" and demanded that, as a price for their participation in the rebellion, complete religious freedom be established in the United States.

Fortunately for the cause of religious freedom, the position of the established churches, particularly that of the Church of England, was weakened by the Revolution. In the Southern states, many Anglican clergymen supported the mother country against the colonies, thus producing a schism between clergy and laity. Branded as a "disloyal" church, the Church of England was no longer able to withstand the attacks of the dissenters by whom the western part of the Southern states was largely peopled.

The demand for religious freedom in Virginia was carried forward by a small group of enlightened aristocrats aided by discontented westerners. Western farmers had long been restive under planter rule and they eagerly embraced an opportunity to overthrow the political, economic, and religious predominance of the low country. That a new spirit was stirring in the Old Dominion was evident in the altered appearance of the Virginia House of Burgesses, formerly the stronghold of the aristocracy. In 1776, observed a member, the legislature was "not quite so well dressed, nor so politely educated, nor so highly born as some Assemblies I have formerly seen." Patrick Henry, the leader of the western forces of revolt, was regarded by some Virginia gentle-men as "a coarse and common man, and utterly destitute of dignity." Nevertheless, Henry was elected governor of Virginia in 1776, defeat-ing Thomas Nelson, the candidate of the aristocracy.

These charges of low birth and want of refinement could not be brought against Thomas Jefferson, who, more than any other man, gave the Revolution in Virginia form and direction. Jefferson was emi-nently a gentleman; but this circumstance merely made his offense more heinous in the opinion of his peers. Henry, after all, was faithful to his class, whereas Jefferson seemed to be betraying those who had every right to look to him for support.

After his return to Virginia from serving in the Continental Congress, Jefferson presented his countrymen with a complete program to im-plement the democratic ideals he had incorporated in the Declaration of Independence. Broadly speaking, he proposed to establish religious freedom, equality of privilege, educational opportunities open to all, and reform of the criminal code — measures designed to confer the fruits of independence upon the common man.[6]

In his bill for establishing religious freedom, Jefferson took the posi-tion that only by a complete divorce between church and state could liberty of conscience be attained. Magistrates had no concern with re-ligious opinion, for the state had no power over conscience. "Truth," said Jefferson, "is the proper and sufficient antagonist to error, and has nothing to fear from the conflict . . . errors ceasing to be dangerous when it is permitted freely to contradict them."

This reform was doggedly, albeit vainly, resisted by the old guard of the Virginia gentry — "a half dozen aristocratical gentlemen, agoniz-ing under the loss of pre-eminence." The Virginia Declaration of Re-ligious Freedom quickly took its place as one of the great charters of human liberty. Few documents did more to raise the prestige of Ameri-cans in the eyes of European liberals or to give stronger hopes that a new day had dawned for mankind. Jefferson's handiwork, said Thomas Hollis, an English Whig, "surpasses for spirit and good sense anything of its kind in Europe and gives us example of what we may expect from men emancipated from subjection, perfectly free with the powers of the human mind, at full liberty to range through the civil and intellectual world, and pursue truth and knowledge and follow their dictates."

No doubt, the most important achievement of the Revolution in the field of religion was the separation of church and state. Except in Massa-chusetts and Connecticut, the severance was complete: public worship was sustained by the voluntary contributions of communicants rather than by taxes imposed by the state indiscriminately upon believers and

[6] A detailed study of Jefferson's reforms will be made in the next volume of this history, which deals with the period of the Confederation.

nonbelievers. Religion became a matter between man and his Maker over which the secular power had no power, and all sects were declared equal before the law.

Most of the states, however, imposed a religious test upon officeholders, usually a declaration of belief in the Christian religion as exemplified in the Protestant faith. Even Pennsylvania required an officeholder to swear his belief in God and the divine inspiration of the Bible. These tests discriminated against Quakers, Roman Catholics, Jews, and infidels. Catholics could hold office in eight states and Jews only in four states. For Catholics, these changes represented a vast improvement over their earlier status. As colonists, Americans had been distinguished by their uncompromising hatred of Roman Catholicism. Although it would be too much to say that Americans wholly relinquished their prejudices against Roman Catholics, during the American Revolution, it is significant that on July 4, 1779, the Declaration of Independence was celebrated in Philadelphia by a Te Deum in the Catholic chapel, in which members of Congress, civil officials of the government, military officers, and many citizens participated. Even Sam Adams, as vigorous a foe of "Popery" as any in the United States, was among those present. Old laws excluding Roman Catholics from the privileges of citizens were repealed; several Roman Catholics were elected to Congress; and in 1789, John Carroll of Maryland became the first Roman Catholic bishop in the United States.

WITH the consummation of the Franco-American alliance and the slowing down of the tempo of the war in North America, domestic politics came to the fore in the United States. Although the discord seemingly took its rise in Paris and revolved around international issues, actually it was part and parcel of the conflict that raged between conservatives and radicals over the kind of social and economic system that was to emerge from the American Revolution.

Not all Americans in Paris shared Franklin's fondness for the French capital and its people. The Paris of the philosophers, salons, and beautiful women had its seamy side which did not escape the attention of tourists: there were no sidewalks; the streets were ill lighted, "narrow, nasty, and inconvenient," "stinking extremely bad"; pedestrians sank up to the calves in mud or worse filth; the descending contents of chamber pots was an inevitable hazard in walking; and as one Bostonian remarked, "the whores are as thick as flies with us in summer, painted as much as possible." The only way to get about Paris with convenience, celerity, and a reasonable degree of sanitariness was by carriage. As the American commissioners soon found, it was necessary to keep one's own carriage, public vehicles being out of the question — they were so narrow that "two Englishmen cannot with any sort of ease sit on a side; but the natives having less beef and pudding about them, will cram six or seven together."

None could deny, however, that Paris was the arbiter of fashion. At a time when men dressed in silks and satins, laces and ruffles, wigs and high-heeled shoes, Paris was quite as much a mecca to the male sex as it was to the ladies. "The first thing to be done in Paris," John Adams observed, "is always to send for a tailor, peruke-maker, and shoemaker, for this nation has established such a domination over the fashion, that neither clothes, wigs, nor shoes made in any other place, will do in Paris." "You would have laught," wrote Captain Joseph Hyson, "to have seen me under the Barbers Hands when I first came here; to see the Fellow turn my Hair up before, fill my Head full of Powder, that I was obliged to submit to, but the next thing was to put a large Bag in behind but that I could not bear." In the name of Fashion, it would seem, men suffered quite as much as did women.

John Adams, who came to France early in 1778 as an American commissioner, surveyed Paris with the disapproving eyes of a Boston Puritan in Babylon: the frivolous, pleasure-seeking capital was not for him — and, he believed, it ought not to be for Frenchmen. He would have had the Kings of France lead lives as immaculate as those of Boston selectmen; he was so concerned over the morals of Louis XV that he urged that the pavilion of Madame du Barry at Marly be razed to the ground as "a monument of his Infamy." The people's preoccupation with amusement, he declared, kept them from the serious things of life; plays, balls, and fashions were their only interest. As might be expected, he did not score a social success in France; indeed, he made an uncommonly rusty courtier: reserved, proud, and inflexible, he condescended to no man and conformed to no fashion, however much to his advantage a little unbending might be. The result of his travels, he admitted, was to instill in him "a stronger Attachment to the Religion and Government of my native Country than ever." Benedict Arnold would never have become a traitor to his country had he first taken the Grand Tour, Adams once remarked; had he done so, his yearning to get back to the United States as quickly as possible would have driven all thoughts of treason from his mind. "I grow every day more and more wearied and disgusted with Europe," he wrote in 1780.

If French manners and morals excited Adams's disapproval, his sensibilities were even more affronted by the spectacle of an American joyously entering into the life of Paris. And if that American happened to be long past the age for such frivolities and holding a position of great dignity as the representative of his country abroad, and Adams's chief rival for the honor of being the United States' Number One Diplomat, it can be perceived what pangs the New Englander suffered. The cause of his perturbation was, of course, no other than Benjamin Franklin, now, with France and the United States formally allied, at the height of his popularity in France.

John Adams could not forgive Franklin for stealing the limelight from all other Americans in Europe. He winced to see Franklin and Voltaire in each other's arms, and he could not bear to hear it said — as it often was said in France — that Franklin's "electric wand had accomplished all this revolution." He found it commonly believed that Franklin "made all the American constitutions and their confederation; but" said Adams, "he made neither. He did not even make the constitution of Pennsylvania, bad as it is." Adams always resented that in writing the Declaration of Independence, Jefferson had run away with the glory; now, he complained, Franklin was making off with all the diplomatic honors. Apparently, the best that John Adams could hope for from history was a casual mention that John Adams was also present. While Franklin was acclaimed on every hand, the New Englander found that he was "a man of whom nobody had ever heard before; — a perfect cipher; a man who did not understand a word of French; awkward in his figure, awkward in his dress; no ability; a perfect bigot and fanatic." It is clear that Adams credited Franklin with one of his own weaknesses: when Adams was hailed by some enthusiastic Frenchmen as "the Washington of diplomacy," the New Englander's first thought was that "a few of these compliments would kill Franklin if they should come to his ears." That is by no means certain, but it is undeniable that the compliments paid Franklin almost killed Adams.

Of all Franklin's foibles, none gave Adams keener distress than the old philosopher's weakness for the fair sex. It jarred him to hear Franklin call Mademoiselle de Passy "his favorite, and his flame, and his love"; and as for those walks in the Bois de Boulogne, Franklin ought to be tending to business which, in Adams's opinion, he sadly neglected. Some New Englanders have taken pride that Franklin was born in Boston, but John Adams found no satisfaction in what he could only regard as an unfortunate aberration of nature.

It had occurred to John Adams — perhaps it was only one of those vagrant thoughts that sometimes fleet through the minds of the most moral — that an American minister to France "might possibly, if well skill'd in intrigue, his Pocketts well filled with Money and his Person Robust and elegant enough, get introduced to some of the Misses and Courtezans in Keeping of the statesmen in France" and do some good for his country. Not that John Adams himself ever intended to act upon this idea — Heaven forbid! But it outraged all his canons that Benjamin Franklin should aspire to play such a part in international affairs. However willingly the old philosopher might sacrifice himself in the cause, Adams begrudged him the honor.

"The moment an American minister gives a loose to his passion for women, that moment he is undone," said John Adams, and he was by no means alone in fearing that Poor Richard was a wolf in philosopher's clothing. Although perhaps less inclined to condemn Franklin's lapses, Thomas Jefferson was far from approving the doctor's roving eye; but his concern was lest Poor Richard should undo the state by his weakness. In the presence of a pretty woman, Franklin was notoriously voluble. Jefferson complained that Franklin had "too little guard over his lips. I have marked him particularly in the company of women where he loses all power over himself. His temperature would not be proof against their allurements, were such to be employed as engines against him. This is in some measure the vice of his age, but it seems to have increased also by his peculiar constitution." Such susceptibility seemed likely to lead the incautious old gentleman to whisper state secrets, together with sweet nothings, into the ears of glamorous female spies.

Inevitably, there were minor irritations in Paris which grated upon Adams and sunk Franklin ever lower in his esteem. When Adams first came to Paris he lived with Franklin at Passy to save rent; but Poor Richard was always taking the only carriage to go out to parties, leaving Adams at home to labor over accounts. "There was nobody," lamented Adams, "to do any business but me." He bought ledgers, applied himself strictly to business, and sought to master the French language. He urged his fellow diplomats to reduce their household expenses by dismissing their servants and getting along with one house and one carriage, particularly addressing his remarks to Franklin, who, he believed, needed frequently to be reminded of the wholesome maxims of Poor Richard. He even went so far as to suggest that Arthur Lee and Franklin live together to save expenses, but Franklin balked at such drastic measures, leaving John Adams to conclude that Franklin did not practice what he preached, at least when it was other people's money that he was spending.[1]

Although naturally a great talker, Franklin had the knack of shutting up like a clam whenever it suited his purpose. He was known to sit whole evenings without saying a word, "as silent as midnight." Much to John Adams's exasperation, Franklin frequently resorted to this provoking reticence in his relations with his colleagues in Paris; Adams complained that he could pin the shifty old philosopher down to nothing. "It is constant Policy," remarked Adams, "never to say Yes or No decidedly but when he cannot avoid it; his love of ease and dissipation will prevent any thorough reformation of any thing, and his silence and reserve render it very difficult to do any thing with him." Craft and guile seemed to be Franklin's distinguishing characteristics.

Acting as Franklin's secretary in Paris was his grandson, Temple Franklin, the son of the old philosopher's illegitimate offspring, William Franklin, late royal governor of New Jersey. The presence of this young man in Paris was an affront to John Adams's high Bostonian sense of propriety: Franklin ought to have hidden his shame instead of parading it by making his grandson his secretary. Adams stormed that "the Effrontery with which he has forced these Offspring [his son and grandson]

[1] Franklin spoke French fluently but, as he acknowledged, paid little attention to the niceties of grammar. John Adams, who admitted that the best he could do was to gibber something that he hoped sounded like French, was not willing to concede that Franklin spoke the language much better. The doctor's pronunciation, said Adams, "upon which the French gentlemen and ladies compliment him, and which he seems to think is pretty well, I am sure is very far from being correct."

up in the World . . . are Outrages to Morality and Decorum, which would never have been forgiven in any other American." Morality aside, said Arthur Lee, Temple Franklin was at best but "a young insignificant Boy as any in existence" and, having had a Tory father, might well prove to be a Tory himself. Stung by these reflections upon the probity of his grandson (Poor Richard was beyond feeling qualms over his own indiscretions) Franklin claimed to have saved Temple from Toryism and to have inculcated in him the faith of a firm republican. "It is enough that I have lost my *son*," he lamented; "would they add my *grandson?*"

For the most part, Franklin suffered Adams with good humor, although he confessed that no one, except Arthur Lee, gave him greater provocation. Admitting that Adams was a sincere patriot, utterly incorruptible and often wise, "sometimes, and in some things," he said, Adams was "absolutely out of his senses." Franklin ascribed Adams's resentment to envy and wounded pride; as in the case of other American diplomats, John Adams's malice seemed to Franklin to take its rise from the fact that the people of France "happen'd to respect me too much and him too little, which I could bear, and he could not." His enemies, Poor Richard remarked, resembled "those little dirty, stinking insects, that attack us only in the dark, disturb our Repose, molesting and wounding us, while our Sweat and Blood are contributing to their Subsistence."

Even before John Adams's arrival in Paris, the American commissioners were far from being one big happy family. A feud had already sprung up between Arthur Lee on one side and Silas Deane and Benjamin Franklin on the other. John Adams walked into this domestic fracas, but instead of restoring peace among the distracted diplomats, Adams joined in the quarrel on the side of the outnumbered Arthur Lee.

Arthur Lee was by all odds the least popular at Versailles of the American commissioners; indeed, he was perhaps the most undiplomatic diplomat ever to serve his country abroad. Arthur Lee was one of those patriots who confused Whiggishness with waspishness, and patriotism with peevishness. It is true that he did not condemn all mankind, yet he condemned most of the small part of it with which he came in contact; he seemed to act upon the principle that no man was to be trusted until thoroughly acquitted of the charge of being a villain. As Franklin said, Lee behaved as though he had never known an honest man in his life — except himself. Even those who admired his honesty and candor deplored his proneness to find fault with his fellow men; with his acid tongue and quick temper Lee, said John Adams, would "raise quarrels in Heaven." Thomas Jefferson reported that Lee, finding it impossible to stir up trouble among the men in Annapolis, entered into the quarrels of the ladies. "A ball being appointed by the one party on a certain night," Jefferson remarked, "he [Lee] undertook to give one, and fixed it precisely on the same night. This of course has placed him in the midst of the mud" — which was, Franklin suspected, his true element.

Although a Virginia blue-blood, Arthur Lee was a democrat, suspicious, like so many of his breed, of the motives of businessmen. In his eyes, Sam Adams — certainly not overburdened with gentility — was the greatest patriot of the times and Adams in turn regarded Lee as a watchdog of liberty, particularly valuable in tracking down profiteers. Lee found his best friends among New Englanders and generally acted upon the principle that "New England men are fittest to be trusted in any dangerous or important enterprises." Coming from a Virginian, that sentiment carried weight.

Deane and Franklin soon found that they could do very nicely without Lee — he was in fact the third member of a cozy twosome. Nor was he more welcome at Versailles. Vergennes even suspected that Lee was a British spy: "English to the marrow of his bones," and with numerous friends in England, he seemed to be the likeliest source of the leak through which the British government knew virtually everything that transpired between the American commissioners and the French government. Here, of course, Vergennes did Lee an injustice; his patriotism was never open to doubt.

To get Lee out of Paris he was sent by Franklin and Deane on long and futile missions to Madrid and Berlin. Dr. Franklin excused himself from undertaking these expeditions with the plea of old age and bad roads; Deane declared that he had pressing business in Paris; so the unwanted tasks were thrust upon Lee. It was, however, only Lee's stern sense of duty that induced him to leave Paris: in his own opinion, he ought to have remained in the French capital — "the centre of political activity" and the only proper theater for his talents — while Deane went to Holland, a more obscure post, and Dr. Franklin settled in Vienna, "the most respectable and quiet" capital on the continent and eminently suited to the old philosopher's declining years. Lee was the more reluctant to leave Paris because he suspected that his colleagues wished to pocket public money; he even believed that Deane, to accomplish this purpose better, was urging Vergennes to have him put out of the way.

Held up at the Spanish frontier by the refusal of the government to permit him to enter the country, Lee went to Berlin, where he became the center of some highly irregular diplomatic goings-on. If modesty was not among Lee's virtues, boldness and perseverance certainly were. He carried the banner of republicanism into the very citadels of European monarchy, and he refused to take "No!" for an answer even when it was thundered by outraged royalty.

Frederick the Great had never forgiven the British for having left him in the lurch in 1762, thereby compelling him to fight Russia, Austria, and France singlehanded. At one point in the war, Berlin was lost to the Russians and Frederick was hemmed in on all sides by enemies, when providentially the death of the Empress Elizabeth brought to the throne a weak-minded Tsar who admired the Prussian monarch so extravagantly that he called off the war. Prussia was saved, but no thanks were owing to England. After this experience, Frederick remarked that it was as probable that a good Christian would lie down with the Devil as that he would consent again to act as England's ally. Indeed, so deeply hurt was Frederick by this treachery (although he had been guilty of treachery to others many times over) that it was said that nothing but the division of Poland took the King of Prussia's "attention off from the injustice done him by Great Britain." [2]

Frederick's strong bias against England encouraged Americans to hope that he could be brought into their camp. The Prussian King might require a little working over, but his eventual adherence to the American cause seemed more certain than that of any European sovereign excepting, of course, His Most Christian Majesty.

To negotiate a treaty of commerce and procure the recognition of American independence from Frederick the Great, Arthur and his brother William Lee journeyed to Berlin. Two more crotchety, hot-tempered, and zealous diplomats could hardly have been found than this pair of Virginia Lees. Although they perhaps did not know it, there was no tougher diplomatic assignment in Europe. For Frederick, instead of proving to be an easy conquest for American diplomats, revealed himself to be a bitter and disillusioned old man who, however much he might hate England, had no sympathy for the ideals of the American republic. He was far more interested in seizing Bavaria or Poland than in aiding the American rebellion, and he had no intention of being drawn into war with Great Britain unless it redounded to the territorial aggrandizement of Prussia.

In Berlin, the Lees were subjected to rebuffs that would have discouraged less importunate diplomats. Frederick refused to see them; they were denied the standing of representatives of a friendly power; and they met with only evasion and delay from the Prussian foreign office. As Frederick told his friends, he intended "to procrastinate in these negotiations, and to go over to the side on which fortune shall declare herself." If Frederick hoped to weary Arthur Lee by such tactics, he mistook his man: Lee took the unkindest cuts in his stride; he dogged the steps of the Prussian foreign minister, begging for interviews with Frederick so persistently that the harried Prussian became apoplectic at the sight of the American representative. To add to the uproar that raged round the Lees, the British ambassador had one of his servants steal Ar-

---

[2] This was the first division of Poland (1772) among Prussia, Austria, and Russia. Ultimately, in the course of three different partitions, these powers devoured Poland altogether.

thur Lee's diplomatic pouch — which, after being thoroughly rifled, was returned to Lee's quarters.

The only concession granted the Lees by Frederick the Great was permission to buy clothing and arms in Prussia — not, however, from Prussian state armories, but from private merchants. Where he saw an opportunity to make a profit for Prussia by doing business with the Americans, Frederick was on his best manners, but it was strictly cash and carry — credits and loans were ruled out. Lee acted upon this permission but he was miserably swindled in his purchases: the cloth proved to be stock rejected by the Prussian government; the guns were so poor, Lee lamented, that even the American militia would spurn them — and he paid more for them than the best guns cost in France.

Nevertheless, Frederick rendered real service to the American cause, although in this instance he did good by inadvertence. To keep German manpower at home the better to fight Austria and other enemies, the Prussian King deliberately obstructed British efforts to recruit troops in the German principalities. He inveighed against the "dirty selfishness" of those German rulers who sold their subjects to the British "as one sells cattle to be dragged to the shambles." He refused passage through Prussian territory to any German soldiers in British service, and since Prussian territory extended along the Rhine and other important rivers, this directive caused the British serious embarrassment. True, he accompanied his order with assurances of good will for Great Britain, but, as a British diplomat remarked, "it is like kicking us, and at the same time telling us we are not to take it as any breach of his Regard or friendship." And equally unfriendly, from the British point of view, was Frederick's conduct in August 1777, when he told France that he would not begrudge His Most Christian Majesty any advantages he might gain if he chose to intervene in the war between Great Britain and the United States.

Finding himself left out of important negotiations, given the cold shoulder at Versailles, and sent off on forlorn missions, Lee became more sour and his view of his colleagues increasingly jaundiced. Arthur Lee was not a man to be snubbed with impunity; Deane and Franklin had seriously underestimated his power of injuring those who had incurred his enmity. He complained to Congress of the conduct of his colleagues towards him; he refused to sign the Franco-American alliance, on the ground that it contained clauses detrimental to the United States; and he publicly accused Franklin and Deane of having defrauded their country of millions of dollars. It was particularly against Silas Deane that he directed his undoubted talents as an exposer of wrongdoers.

Silas Deane found Paris vastly superior to Connecticut — here was one Connecticut Yankee who did not draw invidious comparisons between the manners, morals, and sanitary conditions of New Haven and those of Paris. On the contrary, he took to Parisian life with enthusiasm, not to say abandon. He lived expensively, indulged his taste for finery, and rented a luxurious apartment in the house of a woman "famous for her Galantries," who had been at one time mistress of Louis XV. Deane was quite at home in these somewhat anomalous surroundings until Vergennes warned him to move — his charming landlady was under suspicion of being a British spy. Believing that Marie Antoinette was friendly towards Americans and eager for war with Great Britain, Deane at one time contemplated the fascinating possibilities of a court intrigue. A timely gift, he believed, might win her over completely. "She loves riding on horseback," he wrote to Congress. "Could you send me a narrowhegansett horse or two, the present might be exceedingly well laid out." Much to Deane's disappointment, Congress did not see fit to try this experiment.

Most of Beaumarchais's dealings were with Deane, the only member of the American commission in Paris whom he wholly trusted. In Beaumarchais's eyes, Deane was a bulwark against a separate peace between the United States and Great Britain; the "masculine firmness of that republican," the French dramatist remarked, prevented "the insidious politician Lee, and the taciturn Doctor Franklin" from straying into the British camp.

Vergennes shared Beaumarchais's high regard for Silas Deane, preferring him even above Franklin. Poor Richard was too reserved and too fond of labyrinthine ways to suit the taste of the French minister; Deane, on the other hand, was an honest, straightforward individual who usually laid his cards face up upon the table. Deane kept Vergennes informed of all measures taken by Congress and of the intrigues — so far as he knew them — of British secret agents; and he made a point of frequently asking Vergennes for advice.

In 1776, it will be remembered, Deane and Beaumarchais entered into an agreement whereby Hortalez et Cie. was to supply the United States with munitions and implements of war to be paid for by the United States in tobacco, indigo, and other colonial products. The terms were easy: nothing down and eight months before the first payment would fall due. In exchange, Beaumarchais indicated that he wanted a monopoly of all commerce between France and the United States, but this Deane was neither able nor disposed to grant. That Beaumarchais expected to make a profit from these transactions is fully evidenced by the prices he charged Americans and by the transportation costs which he added to his bills. The French government might go in for philanthropy, but to Beaumarchais it was strictly business.

As far as the American commissioners knew officially, Hortalez et Cie. was a purely commercial house without connection with the French government. The Ministry deliberately attempted to keep the commissioners in the dark as to the source of the war materials with which they were being supplied. "We are scarce allowed to know," wrote the commissioners, "that they [the French government] give us any aids at all, but are left to imagine, if we please that the cannon, arms, etc. which we have received and sent are the effects of private benevolence and generosity." The commissioners, of course, knew better; yet they never received an explicit statement from Vergennes to the effect that the supplies furnished by Hortalez et Cie. were the gift of the French government. Congress had offered to pay for French aid; Deane and Beaumarchais had entered into a contract providing for payment; and here matters rested until October 1777.

In that month, perhaps to temper the blow of cracking down on American privateers in French ports, Vergennes told the American commissioners that no payment would be required of the United States for what had already been given by the French government in money and war materials. This was good news to the struggling states; but among the American commissioners in Paris it raised unexpected contention. Did this forgiveness of debt include the supplies shipped by Beaumarchais under the auspices of Hortalez et Cie., in which the French government had consistently denied it had any part? Arthur Lee insisted that Beaumarchais's supplies were a gift of the French government; Silas Deane declared that they must be paid for. Franklin at first sided with Lee, but later inclined to Deane's view that the war materials furnished by Hortalez et Cie. were, although drawn from French arsenals, not included within the free gift made by the French government to the United States.

To lend verisimilitude to the operations of Hortalez et Cie., Vergennes ostensibly charged the company for the munitions and implements of war drawn from the French arsenals. This, apparently, was for the record and was designed to cover up the part played by the French government in the business of supplying the rebels with contraband. It is quite possible, however, that the French government intended from the outset that the United States should pay for the aid it received through Hortalez et Cie.[3] Certainly, at no time — if the evidence of Arthur Lee be excepted — were the Americans told that this assistance was gratuitous; Beaumarchais, Deane, and Vergennes — the three men who drew up the terms of secret aid — agreed that the war materials sent by Hortalez et Cie. were to be paid for. Beaumarchais himself never left the Americans in doubt that he expected to be paid in full for his wares: in December

[3] From the point of view of the French government, it would have been wise to have insisted upon that stipulation: by obliging Americans to ship cargoes of tobacco and other colonial products to France in exchange for this aid, trade between the two countries would be stimulated and Americans would be bound more closely to France. As has been seen, the destruction of Britain's commercial monopoly over North America was one of the main objectives of French policy.

1776, for example, he warned the Committee of Secret Correspondence that he could not continue to send supplies to the United States unless remittances in the form of American raw products were immediately forthcoming. Deane chimed in by informing Congress that Beaumarchais was heavily in debt for the stores he was sending and could not long endure the financial strain.

There can be no question, however, that the money advanced by France and Spain to the Americans prior to the Franco-American alliance was intended as a gift rather than as a loan. The Bourbon monarchies deemed it beneath their dignity to set up as moneylenders to the American rebels; a gift could be more easily concealed than a loan and was therefore less likely to provoke war with Great Britain; and, as Vergennes pointed out, a gift was more likely than a loan to keep the Americans fighting. It is significant that these gifts of money (except, perhaps, for the initial grant of two million livres made in 1776) did not pass through Beaumarchais's hands: in the main, Hortalez et Cie. concentrated upon the secret aid dispatched by the French government.

Beaumarchais was not long content to act merely as the go-between for the Ministry in its dealings with the Americans; he began to take himself seriously as a merchant and to see in the American Revolution an opportunity not only to cover himself with glory but to put himself on easy street for the rest of his days. By taking advantage of his close connection with the government, he induced several French merchants and nobles to finance the shipment of supplies on private account to the Americans. In other words, Beaumarchais put two fingers in the pie — and with one, at least, he intended to extract some of the very juicy plums he saw therein. There was no lack of partners in this enterprise: even English manufacturers urged their goods upon Beaumarchais, although they knew full well the ultimate destination of his wares. Some of Beaumarchais's cargoes to the rebels were insured by London brokers. A man as closely connected with the government as was Beaumarchais had no difficulty in procuring credit from merchants and manufacturers; and Hortalez et Cie. was soon offering to supply American businessmen with "all those goods which promised to have the greatest sale on the other continent."

Thus Beaumarchais came to be both a government agent and a free-lance merchant trading with the Americans; some of his supplies were given him free of charge, others were purchased with his own capital. Where the bounty of the French government ended and the private speculations of Beaumarchais and his associates began could never be determined from the books of Hortalez et Cie. Beaumarchais lumped together all the goods he forwarded to the Americans, and insisted upon payment without exception.

In his zeal to do business with the Americans, Beaumarchais overtaxed his resources. By the end of 1777, Hortalez et Cie. had sent almost nine million livres' worth of supplies to the United States, little of which had been paid for by the rebels. Beaumarchais also alleged that almost two thirds of his ships carrying munitions and implements of war to the Americans had been captured or lost at sea, and that the meddling of the British ambassador had cost him dearly by obliging him to hold up cargoes in port, unload ships that were ready to sail, and pay inactive crews. As a result, in January 1778, the distraught dramatist informed Vergennes that he was "at the point of ruin as a merchant" unless he received four hundred thousand livres immediately from the government.

It was at this time that Lee trumpeted the good news to Congress that all aid from the French government, including that handled by Hortalez et Cie., was "given without expectation of any return." Arthur Lee claimed to have private information which, in his opinion at least, left no doubt that the French Ministry had intended from the beginning to give the Americans the munitions and implements of war forwarded by Beaumarchais. Early in 1776, Lee's story ran, he had been approached in London by Beaumarchais, who told him flatly that the French government had decided to send supplies to the rebels in America as a free gift. As Beaumarchais explained the deal to Lee, the French Ministry believed that it was getting ample return for its money merely by strengthening the hands of the rebels; its reward came from embarrassing and distressing Great Britain. Having thus plainly indicated the policy of his government, Beaumarchais had dropped his negotiations with Arthur Lee and gone back to Paris, where he and Silas Deane worked out the details of secret aid. Lee had been henceforth ignored — a slight which Lee never forgot.

As might be expected, this turn of events dismayed Beaumarchais. Trusting to his contract with Deane to ensure repayment, he had invested his own and his friends' money in supplies which he now found Arthur Lee picturing as a free gift. True, Beaumarchais did not stand to lose anything except perhaps freight on the supplies that had been given him from the French arsenals for shipment to the Americans; but if Arthur Lee succeeded in convincing Congress that everything bearing the name of Hortalez et Cie. was a present from the French government, Beaumarchais and his associates were out of pocket a considerable sum of money. All his rosy dreams of making a fortune from the American Revolution went glimmering when Arthur Lee exploded his bombshell.

Beaumarchais was quite equal to the occasion: an agent of Hortalez et Cie. was sent to Philadelphia to head off Arthur Lee's testimony by procuring a written promise from Congress to pay for goods already received and those to be sent by Hortalez et Cie. In April 1778, Congress agreed to these terms, and Beaumarchais could breathe easier.

Silas Deane was drawn into the affair by reason of his close connection with Beaumarchais and his partnership with Robert Morris, the
most powerful American businessman of the day. Silas Deane had come
to France in the dual role of an agent of the United States government
and a business partner of Robert Morris and other merchants. He was
expected to raise supplies and loans for the Continental Congress at the
same time that he handled the commercial interests of Willing, Morris
and Company — a service for which he was promised a commission of
5 per cent. Deane himself had been a merchant and he was not averse
to serving his own interests as well as his country's; and he was encouraged by Robert Morris to overlook no chances of lining his pockets in
France. "There is plenty of room," said Morris, "to make as much money
as you please." [4] Although Deane did not keep separate accounts (he
mixed private and public funds, records, and vouchers) most of his work
was done for the government rather than for his commercial associates.
About ten million livres of government money was spent by Deane for
supplies and ships; his private speculations, on the other hand, were comparatively small in scale and yielded him little in the form of commissions. And directly or indirectly, whether serving Congress or Willing,
Morris and Company, Deane was working toward the end of supplying
the United States with vitally needed war materials.

It was impossible for Arthur Lee to believe that those who differed
with him were anything but scoundrels and cheats. Having already
conceived a grudge against Silas Deane, it was easy for him to rank
Deane among those baleful enemies of the republic whom he saw on
every hand. Specifically, Lee charged that Deane was a partner in fraud
with Beaumarchais and Robert Morris. Lee even had at his finger tips
the exact profit made by Deane in his swindling operations: two hundred and fifty thousand dollars was Deane's share of the loot.

There is no doubt that Deane engaged in private trade on the side;
but that he used government money for that purpose is another matter.
Certainly, he did not as commissioner lay away a nest egg as Arthur Lee
supposed — he died a few years later in extreme poverty. Except for
living beyond his means and keeping disorderly accounts, John Adams
found no evidence of irregularity in Deane. Lee's suspicions remained
only suspicions; and in view of the long — and honorable — roster of
men who at one time or another were on Lee's blacklist (John Jay, John
Dickinson, Benjamin Franklin, to name only a few), it is unfair to con-
vict Deane upon such slender evidence.

Although he began by believing that Deane was "the author of all

---

[4] In the same manner, Morris established a connection between his firm and
William Bingham, the United States commercial agent at Martinique. This was a
highly lucrative arrangement for all concerned except, perhaps, the United States
government. Bingham retired with a fortune.

the mischief," Arthur Lee by no means absolved Franklin. In the eyes of this censorious Virginian, Franklin was "more devoted to pleasure than would become even a young man in his state": he neglected public business while he played the roué in Paris salons. Lee was not often invited to the salons, but his imagination readily supplied a picture of scandalous goings-on in which Franklin played the part of master of the revels. Carrying his suspicions a step further, he concluded that Franklin was hand in glove with Deane in speculating with government funds — a suspicion shared by John Adams and frequently repeated by British spies in Paris. Although there is no evidence that Franklin was in any way involved in shady deals, his grandson, Temple Franklin, was associated in commercial enterprises. It has yet to be proved, however, that he used government money.

This indictment stung Franklin to the quick. To these charges that he was living high, wide, and handsome in Paris on the taxpayers' money, he retorted that his only luxury was the Encyclopedia. But the more Lee's victims protested their innocence, the stronger grew his suspicions: he was soon accusing Franklin of being the master mind of the gang and of having made off with the lion's share of the loot. When Franklin consented to take care of a sealed trunk for Lee, the distrustful Virginian insisted that Poor Richard give him a receipt; and to make it binding he called in four witnesses to the transaction! It is perhaps understandable why Franklin should have felt that the severest trials in the career of an American diplomat were American diplomats.

To Franklin, Arthur Lee was almost too heavy a cross to be borne; seldom had his philosophy of live and let live been more cruelly taxed. "I consider him," said Franklin, "as the most malicious enemy I ever had (though without the smallest cause)." He could only conclude that Lee was headed for the madhouse: such unwarranted suspicions and wild fancies betokened a sick mind. Dr. Franklin prescribed for Lee a quiet, restful life without excitement or the responsibilities of office; but Deane protested that Franklin was being too charitable in ascribing to insanity what clearly emanated from venom and the "malignancy of his heart." Lee, said Deane, was a born calumniator of good men and a lover of mischief for its own sake.

By the time John Adams arrived in Paris, the quarrels of the commissioners were public knowledge. Every commissioner had his own house and retinue of servants, his own circle of friends and courtiers; the first time Franklin got Adams alone, he began to complain of the bad blood between the commissioners and to vent his resentment against Lee. "In my youth," said Adams, "I had often heard of the address and intrigues of the French Court, but I could sincerely say, I had found more intrigue and *finesse* among my own countrymen at Paris, than among the French." He thought seriously of going home, preferring to risk capture by British men-of-war rather than remain among his backbiting countrymen in Europe.

News of the wrangling of the commissioners astounded Congress. Was it possible that in Paris Americans could not find better things to do than to bicker among themselves? It began to appear that even "a residence at Paris will not exempt men from infirmities of the mind," and that "Schoolboy Jarrings" were the pastime of Americans abroad as well as at home. Since it was clear that Congress must take action before the situation got wholly out of control, Silas Deane was recalled to report to his government.

Upon Silas Deane congressmen pinned the blame for the inundation of foreign officers. They cursed Deane's fondness for handing out commissions and grumbled that he "could not say nay to any frenchman who called himself count or chevalier." Some of these officers were obviously "rank Cheats," yet they bore contracts signed by Deane — contracts which might often prove to be "inconsistent with each other, and all of them . . . inconsistent with the honor of our American Officers." Congressmen conveniently forgot that they had given commissions to many French officers, particularly the adventurers who had swarmed to Philadelphia from the West Indies like flies to honey. A scapegoat had to be found, and Deane was chosen for the unhappy distinction. Silas Deane, said Franklin, was "an able, faithful, active, and extremely useful Servant of the publick," exposed to almost irresistible pressure to provide for officers recommended by the French court; but Congress was not interested in justifications of Deane's conduct. Politics must be served.

The French Ministry took every precaution in its power to ensure that Deane came to no harm at the hands of Congress. He traveled in the company of Gérard, the minister to the United States, in a royal ship of the line and he carried the portrait of the King of France as a testimonial of that monarch's affection. In this manner, it was made plain to Congress that to disgrace Deane was to offend France.

The arrival of Gérard, the French minister to the United States, temporarily diverted attention from Silas Deane. Congress was ill prepared to receive visitors. The State House, converted by the British into a hospital during the occupation of Philadelphia, had to be cleaned up and, equally important, a code of ceremony had to be devised for the reception of the French minister. In this connection, one of the questions which agitated Congress was how far above the chair of the representative of Louis XVI that of the President of Congress ought to be raised; after long discussion, Congress settled upon two feet above the common level for the President and eighteen inches for the French minister.[5]

[5] Upon this occasion, Sam Adams wrote to a friend: "Would you think that one so little of the Man of the World as I am should be joyned in a Committee to settle

Transplanted to the United States, the controversy between Deane and Lee ceased to have much to do with French loans or the veracity of the two principals: it became part of the struggle for power between the businessmen and the representatives of Southern planters, Northern town workers, and the yeomanry of both sections.[6] Robert Morris and his associates, representing the big business of the times, were arrayed against Sam Adams, Richard Henry Lee, and other paladins of the common man. Deane's partisans, said the opposition, were "Tories, all those who have rob'd the public, are now doing it, and those who wish to do it"; the supporters of Arthur Lee, on the other hand, were denounced as demagogues and rabble-rousers.

This quarrel created in Congress parties the members of which were "as regularly marshall'd as hostile Troops." From the beginning, Congress had been the scene of conflict between radicals and conservatives: as early as 1774, Sam Adams began organizing the "left wing" of radical patriots. In Richard Henry Lee of Virginia, who, like Adams, was no friend of aristocracy, the New Englander found an able and congenial associate. Lee is the only Virginian on record who ever apologized to a New Englander for having been born in the Old Dominion; and he always regarded himself as more a New Englander than a Virginian. Never did he cease to regret that his lot was cast south of Mason and Dixon's line. "The hasty, unpersevering, aristocratic genius of the South suits not my disposition," he remarked, "and is inconsistent with my ideas of what must constitute social happiness and security"; only in Boston, he lamented, could these conditions be found.

The party led by Sam Adams and Richard Henry Lee, an alliance of New England and Virginia, was at first the dominant group in Congress, where, it was said, these men ruled as absolutely as did the "Grand Turk." Their control was challenged by a conservative bloc from the Middle states and Lee proved unable to keep his state true to the political alignment with New England. The aristocratic landowners and lawyers of New York were infinitely more attractive to Southern gentlemen than were Sam Adams and his town followers, and upon this foundation was established an alliance between New York and the Southern states which ultimately undermined the power of the New Englanders.

Never before the Deane-Lee controversy had the opposing groups

Ceremonials? It is however of some Importance that we agree upon Forms that are adapted to the true *republican* Principles; for this Instance may be recurred to as a Precedent in Futurity." It was widely feared that upon this occasion members of Congress would be tempted to exhibit "all the magnificence of Monarchy."

[6] This is often pictured as a conflict between the "landed" and the "monied" interests. It was that — and more. Men like Sam Adams and Tom Paine can hardly be regarded as spokesmen of the agrarian interests of the country; rather, they expressed the views of the town workers who, in this struggle against the businessmen, found themselves allied with the farmers.

lined up with such order and regularity or submitted themselves so implicitly to the direction of their leaders. For the first time, embryo parties appeared clearly in the Continental Congress; and the issue from which they sprang was largely the question whether businessmen or the people were to dominate the republic. Party strife raged so hotly in Congress that John Jay declared that there was "as much intrigue in this State House as in the Vatican, but as little secrecy as in a boarding-school." Lafayette deplored these "cabals and their everlasting barking" but he concluded that congressmen were "like husband and wife, incessantly quarreling, but re-uniting when the interests of the family are concerned."

Deane's books were almost as confused as those of Beaumarchais: indeed, between them, these two worthies succeeded in producing some of the most unbusinesslike bookkeeping on record. Moreover, Deane failed to bring with him to Philadelphia a copy of his agreement with Beaumarchais or the vouchers, invoices, and other data he had preserved. These had been left behind in Paris, he lamely explained, because of lack of space in his trunks; but Thomas Paine unkindly suggested that it was because he had come to the United States "burthened with forty changes of silk, velvet, and other dresses" in order to strut about the streets of Philadelphia and dazzle the citizenry with his Parisian finery.

Whenever there was a good fight going on, Thomas Paine could never resist the temptation to get in the thick of it. The Deane-Lee quarrel was cut to Paine's taste; he yearned to deliver a stout blow against the Deane faction — in his eyes, a pack of profiteers and monopolizers. Unfortunately for Paine, his position as secretary to the Committee of Foreign Affairs debarred him from taking part in the imbroglio, but Paine was never one to consult expediency or to permit official responsibilities to stand in the way of what he regarded as the cause of justice. Accordingly, he launched an attack upon Deane and quoted even from secret documents in the files of the Committee of Foreign Affairs to prove his point that Deane and his associates were trying to swindle the United States out of an immense amount of money.

Paine was gunning for bigger game than Silas Deane. "It has ever been my custom," said Paine, "to take the bull by the horns, and bring out the great offenders." In this case, the bull seemed to be Robert Morris, the wealthy Philadelphia merchant and profiteer; compared with him, Deane appeared hardly worth the shot necessary to bring him down. Robert Morris, said Paine, was the guiding spirit of the organization that had been set up to rob the public and to turn the American Revolution into a huge stock-jobbing operation.

The root of the evil, as Paine saw it, lay in permitting members of Congress to engage in private trade and to enter into commercial partnerships with American diplomats abroad. By this means, monopoly was fostered; a rich merchant like Robert Morris, enjoying access to state secrets as a member of Congress, could destroy freedom of trade if he were permitted to capitalize upon those secrets for his own profit. "To what a degree of corruption must we sink," Paine asked, "if our Delegates and Ambassadors are to be admitted to carry on a private partnership in Trade? Why not as well go halves with every Quarter-Master and Commissary in the army?" Every congressman with outside business interests ought to be brought under investigation, Paine declared, in order to ferret out all such unholy alliances as that between Deane and Robert Morris.

In his zeal to expose the corrupt practices of Deane and Morris, Paine brought to light secrets which the French government had taken considerable pains to conceal. Paine was shouting about Hortalez et Cie. from the housetops — or rather, what was infinitely worse, exposing it in the pages of American newspapers. Rather than endure this unfavorable publicity, the French minister demanded that Congress disavow Paine's statements. Congress consented, and although every member knew the contrary, it was solemnly asserted that the United States had received no aid whatever from the French government before the signing of the Franco-American alliance. This was done with a straight face; and even the French minister preserved, outwardly at least, his dignity in the affair, although at almost the same time that he was putting pressure on Congress to declare that it had received no aid from France, he was insisting that Congress pay Beaumarchais and the French government for that very aid. France was saying to Congress, in practically the same breath, "Pay up!" and "Deny that you ever received anything!" Unable to swallow such anomalies, and in hot water with Congress, Thomas Paine resigned as secretary to the Committee of Foreign Affairs.

Although the incident had ended happily from the point of view of the French minister, Gérard was not wholly satisfied with the outcome: he feared that he had made Paine a confirmed enemy of France. Manifestly, it would not do to have the ablest pamphleteer in the United States writing against the alliance; so Gérard sought to atone for having cost Paine his job by offering him a position at a higher salary in the service of France. He made Paine "a very genteel and profitable offer" of one thousand dollars a year. The only strings attached were that Paine was to publish nothing on political affairs without first submitting it to Gérard; no more attacks were to be made upon Deane, and state secrets were to be kept out of the newspapers. Paine gladly accepted the offer to serve as a paid propagandist for the French government. He had never been an enemy of France, he told Gérard — his only purpose was to show that it was the magnanimity of France rather than the intrigues of Deane that had produced the bountiful aid that had been given this country. Henceforth, Paine was careful to say that "there was a disposition in the gentlemen of France to have made America a very handsome present" — not that they had actually made it. During the war, the French minister to the United States had occasion to hire several prominent Americans to write as propagandists, but he never got more for his money than he did from Thomas Paine.

Weary of waiting for Congress to hear his case and fearful that he would not secure justice at its hands, Deane appealed to the people over the head of Congress. By this action, Deane won no popularity in Congress; many members resented his attempt to call a higher authority into the dispute. John Adams stormed that Deane's action was "like a dissolution of the Constitution" and that Deane was "a wild boar, that ought to be hunted down for the benefit of mankind." If every man who had a grudge against Congress were permitted to insult and decry its authority in the newspapers, where would Congress be? Nevertheless, a majority of Congress upheld the principle of free speech even against themselves; they declared that "there should not be the least restraint of the Liberty of the Press." Congress refused to punish Deane for his temerity, although Henry Laurens, President of Congress, resigned his office in protest.

After spending a year in Philadelphia waiting futilely for vindication from Congress and a settlement of his accounts, Deane returned to France, again as a partner of Robert Morris. Still his affairs did not prosper; Congress refused to pay his back salary, and John Hancock, to whom he had loaned three hundred pounds sterling, would not even answer Deane's letters requesting payment. He tried to borrow money from Beaumarchais but that chastened speculator swore that he was destitute, having ruined himself in the service of the "contemptible new born republic" which destroyed "all deserving men who have forwarded its interests." Broke, dispirited, and smarting under the charge of having "grown rich out of the public moneys," Deane lost faith in the American Revolution and went over to the British side. He volunteered his services as a propagandist, and although never apparently paid for his work, he was classed by his countrymen with Benedict Arnold as "a damned artful rascal." Robert Morris washed his hands of any connection with Deane, and Gouverneur Morris "hopped around upon one leg [he had lost the other in an accident], swore they had all been duped, himself among the rest."

Deane did a great deal of good for his country, and if he mixed profit with patriotism he was hardly unique among his countrymen. Left almost entirely to his own discretion, "without intelligence, without orders, and without remittances, yet boldly plunging into contracts, engagements, and negociations, hourly hoping that something will arrive from America," he had acquitted himself well. He joined forces with Beaumarchais to break the official red tape that threatened to halt the shipment of French war materials across the Atlantic; he encouraged French merchants to send supplies on their own account to the United States; and he acted as an intermediary between French and American businessmen. This work needed to be done and Deane did it capably. In furthering Franco-American commerce, he was far more successful than was Arthur Lee, whose stiff, dour nature made him unpopular among the French.

Arthur Lee's career as a diplomat was ended by his quarrel with Deane. Pronounced persona non grata by France and Spain — Gérard bluntly informed Congress that Lee did not enjoy the confidence of Louis XVI — he was recalled to the United States. It was a diplomatic triumph for Gérard to rid his country of Arthur Lee; yet it was not accomplished without cost. By making himself a party to the dispute, the French minister won the esteem of Morris and his friends, but in the eyes of Lee's supporters he had allied himself "with dirty Schemes of money making." Moreover, by intervening in the domestic concerns of its ally, France was laying itself open to the charge of treating the republic more as a client state than as an equal.

Arthur Lee's distrust of France developed into an acute case of Francophobia. Sent to Congress by Virginia, he warned his countrymen from this vantage point to be on guard against the machinations of their ally. The French, he declared, did not really wish to see the United States strong and independent — "we are made the dupes of their policy and the instruments of their ambition."

As for Beaumarchais, he continued to try to collect in full from the United States government. Precious little information was to be gleaned from his books, however; apparently he carried his accounts in his head. Of course, Beaumarchais had a sufficient excuse for his unmethodical bookkeeping: he was a man of letters and only by accident a businessman. In any event, all that Franklin could get from Beaumarchais was the vague statement that the United States owed him "a great deal of money." He wept profusely in Franklin's presence while he recounted his financial distress; but Franklin could pin down the lachrymose dramatist to few facts or figures. Beaumarchais could not, or perhaps would not, account for one million livres advanced him by the French government which, apparently, had not been laid out in supplies for the United States. Finally, he produced the figure of three million, three hundred thousand livres, which, he claimed, was owing him by the United States; but this figure was contested by Congress. Congress paid him three million livres outright, and after many years of haggling and litigation, the remainder of the bill was settled in 1835 with Beaumarchais's heirs for about ten cents on the dollar.

Benjamin Franklin, almost alone of those involved in the Deane-Lee controversy, landed neatly on his feet. After the recall of Silas Deane, Franklin was unquestionably the favorite of the French Ministry. Vergennes urged upon the Continental Congress the appointment of Franklin as sole minister to France and endeavored to make him the American plenipotentiary to the peace conference. Loans to the United States were pointedly made by the French government through Franklin; and Vergennes instructed the French minister in the United States to defend before Congress at all times the patriotism, zeal, and wisdom of the old philosopher.

Only by grace of a slender majority in Congress, however, did Franklin maintain his post as minister to France. In the opinion of many delegates, Franklin was too "Frenchified" to represent the United States at the French court; he seemed to be the dupe of the Bourbons — whether from his extreme age, his love of ease, or his fondness for the ladies, no man could say. Richard Henry Lee called Franklin "that wicked old man" who had made his headquarters in France a "corrupt hotbed of vice. . . . How long," exclaimed the agitated gentleman from Virginia, ". . . must the dignity, honor, and interest of these United States be sacrificed to the bad passions of that old man under the idea of his being a philosopher." Franklin's mind had long since given way, declared his enemies, and only his vices lived on. "There never I think existed a man more meanly envious and selfish than Dr. Franklin," said Arthur Lee. The indefatigable Virginian had the last word; Dr. Franklin had long since recognized the futility of attempting to reason with his enemy.

CHAPTER XIX

Spanish Mediation

AMERICANS had emerged triumphantly from "the times that try men's souls," but they did not endure prosperity as successfully. The alliance with France was followed by a letdown in the war effort that almost cost the United States the war. Under the conviction that peace and prosperity were just around the corner, Americans put the war behind them and settled down to enjoy the fruits of victory. As a result, in the midst of the struggle for freedom, we find the American people taking a long week-end and calling peace when there was no peace.

From the beginning of the war, Washington had bewailed the difficulty of persuading Americans "that there is, or can be, danger till the Bayonet is pushed at their Breasts. . . . When we receive a check, and are not quite undone we are apt to fancy we have gained a victory; and when we do gain any little advantage, we imagine it decisive and expect the war immediately to end." Alexander Hamilton observed that the people and the governments, if they should "get it into their heads that the enemy would remain idle for six weeks, would think they had a right to doze away forty days at least." Much of Washington's caution sprang from his fear that defeat would produce in the people "a total relaxation and debility . . . from which perhaps we should not be able to recover." After 1778, it began to appear that victory had the same untoward effects.

Americans were prone to view the French alliance as the beginning of a landslide that would eventually sweep all Europe into their camp. Other nations would hasten to align themselves with the republic against Great Britain; and opposed by a host of enemies, it could hardly be doubted that Britain would go down to crushing defeat. Thus the sixth of February, 1778 — the day on which the Franco-American alliance was signed —

would prove "a day memorable throughout the universe" as signalizing the end of the British Empire. "The East-India seapoy, the West-India carib, and the African negro, who had been deprived of life by the lust of wealth and dominion of Great Britain, rejoiced to see an end put to her depredations upon human nature by the union of France with America." In this frame of mind, Thomas Paine declared in May 1778 that the fighting was nearly over — "for Britain, made wicked and foolish has done her utmost. The only part for her now to act, is frugality." Sam Adams thought that the time had come to reduce the size of the American army; and many French officers packed up to go home, believing that the principal theater of war would henceforth be in Europe.

Accordingly, Americans began to devote themselves to pursuits that ought to have been strictly reserved for the postwar period. "We proceed as if we had totally vanquished the enemy," lamented a South Carolinian. "We have in a manner laid up our arms." "People here [Pennsylvania] are fast A Sleep," exclaimed a Continental officer; "its as perfect a peace as it was in '73 & there is nothing will Rouze them but Brittish Guns & Drums." Indeed, some Americans slept so soundly that it was to be feared that "their very Souls will be petrified so that the D——l himself cant wake them." Yet neither the British nor the Devil stirred, and Americans took their ease, "contenting ourselves," said Washington, "with laughing at the impotence of G. Britain which we supposed to be on her knees, begging mercy of us, and forgiveness for past offences." "Like a great beauty who has obtained a husband," lamented another patriot, "we have grown careless in our dress, and sluttish in our manner."

With victory seemingly assured, Americans fell to debating whether it was to the interest of the United States to destroy Great Britain utterly. Some patriots rejoiced in the prospect of the allies dictating peace in London, stripping that "proud wicked & tyrannical Nation" of its empire and leaving Englishmen to molder on their foggy island. "Britons," exclaimed Benjamin Rush of Philadelphia, "I hope will soon enjoy the heroic pleasure of dying in the last ditch" — and, he added, Americans ought not to deny them that pleasure. It was held to be Americans' duty to work for the complete destruction of Great Britain as they would labor to bring to justice a criminal who had terrorized society. After taking part in a skirmish against British troops, Thomas McKean of Pennsylvania wrote his wife: "These were the first guns I ever ordered to be fired agt human Beings, if I may be allowed to call the Enemies of Mankind such." Thomas Paine believed that the peace and security of the world demanded the liquidation of the British Empire: by their deeds in India — "not so properly a conquest as an extermination of mankind" — the British had proved that they were not fit to be trusted with the responsibilities of empire. "Extent of dominion," said Paine, "has been her [Great Britain's] ruin, and instead of civilizing others has brutalized herself." In losing their empire, Englishmen might find themselves; a dash of humility would sweeten the English character wonderfully.

However much they might believe Great Britain deserved it, many Americans could not bring themselves to wish for its complete ruin. Franklin, while admitting that the patriots had ample provocation, always counseled his countrymen not to seek Britain's destruction; and although John Adams observed that it "seemed to be the will of Heaven that the English should have success enough to lead them on to final destruction," he was ready to shed a tear for the former mother country. "The destruction of Old England would hurt me," said John Jay; "I wish it well; it afforded my ancestors an asylum from persecution." Nor was sentiment alone responsible for this reluctance to push Britain to the wall: it was held contrary to the interests of the United States to make France dominant in Europe. Was not the maintenance of a balance of power in Europe as essential to the United States as to Great Britain? If England went down in ruin, warned a member of Congress, "we might fall a prey to the Conqueror in our turn." "France able to dictate the law to Great Britain," it was said, "can do the same to us, and in a more imperious manner."

Many Americans rejoiced in the connection with France as presaging a new era in American civilization. It is significant that, shortly after the war, there appeared an ardently nationalistic school of American writers — the Hartford Wits. The idea that the United States was to be the new Athens of the arts and sciences had been frequently expressed during the Revolution. As long as they remained colonists, it was said, Americans had reflected all the prejudices and insularity of Britons; now, however, as free men they stood prepared to embrace the world, drawing inspiration from all cultures and all men. Indeed, in the eyes of some patriots the Revolution had come just in time; another generation of British rule, declared an American, and the colonists would have "learned to eat and drink, and swear and quarrel like Englishmen." Observing the world through the murky spectacles of John Bull, they might have gone on forever believing that "a French officer spends the morning at his toilette, puts on paint, and is scarcely in a condition to carry his fusee; that a British grenadier can put to flight a company of French soldiery by blowing on them; that the tallest among them reaches only to the shoulder of a Briton; that the kingdom of France has but imperfect manufactures; that her wines are weak and unwholesome; the nation enslaved, the Prince despotic." Happily, their eyes had been opened in time and they could now perceive that France was "the most enlightened nation in the world" and its people the most civilized and polite. France had polished and refined Europe; the next step was for this gifted nation to remove the last vestiges of rusticity from the United States.

The patriots' joy in the supposed imminence of peace, prosperity, and the renaissance of arts and letters was somewhat damped, however, by the stubborn and, as they thought, shortsighted refusal of the British to admit defeat. Americans were ready to make peace with this supposedly beaten enemy, but the British grimly hung on, seemingly bent upon bringing irreparable destruction upon themselves. Grudgingly, the patriots began to admit respect for the "Bull dog nature" of their enemy and to acknowledge that they had underestimated the resources as well as the tenacity of Great Britain, "whose government," said Alexander Hamilton, "has always been distinguished for energy, and its people for enthusiasm."

Thus, if Americans but had eyes to see, the war was far from being over and much hard fighting lay ahead. "There is blood, much blood in prospect," said the President of Congress. ". . . Britain will not be hummed by a stroke of policy: she will be very angry, and if she is to fall, her fall will be glorious. We, who know her, ought to be prepared."

⌒   ⌒   ⌒

The French alliance became the touchstone of American patriotism: to speak against France was to invite an accusation of Toryism and a visit from the mob. American politicians were quite equal to executing an abrupt about-face and leaping aboard the French bandwagon. For example, John Hancock, who had once remarked that "a Connection with France would ruin America," now distinguished himself by his zealous devotion to all things French. John Adams renounced his earlier opposition to an alliance with France, declaring that it was "a Rock upon which we may safely build." It was widely held to be a perpetual alliance of the two peoples; to the French, said Patrick Henry, he would be "everlastingly bound by the most heartfelt gratitude. . . . We are undone, if the French alliance is not religiously observed."

It was not foreseen, however, that France, as an ally, would interfere in the domestic and foreign policies of the United States. The Franco-American alliance was an alliance of equals: in no respect was the United States a client of the Bourbon monarchy. Nevertheless, the alliance was not a year old before France had begun to exert a powerful influence in the councils of the republic. It was soon demonstrated that the course of this alliance was not to run smoothly.

Canada was the first love of American expansionists; having almost effected its conquest in 1776, they could ill bear to surrender it to John Bull. Moreover, there was sound military reason for seeking to bring this colony within the American fold: the British were employing it as a base of operations against the United States, and from its confines issued a horde of Indians and Loyalists to ravage the American frontier. Only by possessing Canada, it was said, could the United States be secure "from the ravages of the savage Indians, and from the depredations of the more savage Britons."

After the conclusion of the French alliance, Congress conceived the idea of inviting France to help conquer Canada and Nova Scotia for the United States. With the aid of the French fleet, Congress anticipated the speedy overthrow of British power and the annexation of these provinces to the American union. France, it seemed, was to have the honor of helping to add two or three states to the confederation and thereby strengthening the republic against its foes. As an ally of the United States, it was presumed that His Most Christian Majesty would leap at the opportunity to do the United States such signal service.

Lafayette enthusiastically endorsed this plan: his romantic nature was captivated by the prospect of aiding his "oppressed brethren" in Canada to win their freedom, and his love of military glory made the adventure almost irresistible.[1] But the French government did not base its policy upon romantic knight-errantry: the statesmen at Versailles were governed by one paramount consideration — the advantage of France. To their minds, it did not serve French interests to help the United States conquer Canada. They hoped to make the United States the permanent ally of the Bourbon monarchy; calling a new world into being merely to raise up republicanism in the Western Hemisphere was foreign to their plans. Manifestly, if the alliance with the United States was to be preserved, the republic must not be permitted to become too strong lest Americans lapse into isolationism and, feeling themselves secure from their enemies, throw off the alliance with France as an encumbrance. Moreover, if all causes of friction between Great Britain and the United States were removed, Americans might revert to their former attitude toward the mother country and thereby undo, from the point of view of France, the main benefits of the American Revolution. Canada in British hands seemed a guarantee that Americans and Englishmen would never lie down together in peace, and that Americans would continue to look to France for protection against their troublesome neighbor in the North. There was no surer cement for an alliance than common danger; and this the French believed that the British admirably provided. Therefore, French policy was to ring the United States round with bad neighbors whose belligerence would forcibly remind Americans of their dependence upon France.

Although France did not wish the United States to acquire Canada, neither did it aspire to regain for itself this lost colony of the French

---

[1] Lafayette also believed that it would be good policy for the United States to acquire people who, presumably, would always be attached to France and might enable France to dominate the United States in case civil wars broke up the union. It is clear that Lafayette had much to learn about the French-Canadians, among whom loyalty to France is most imperfectly developed.

Empire. Early in the war, Vergennes informed the Americans that France had no designs upon Canada, and from this position he never departed. He recognized that if France took Canada, or allowed the least suspicion of such an intention to enter the minds of the Americans, the Bourbons would be in the same unhappy position in which they hoped to put Great Britain: they would become an object of jealousy and fear to Americans.

Perceiving the importance Americans attached to the acquisition of Canada, Vergennes walked carefully in thwarting their ambition to expand their frontiers northward. To let the Americans know that France was opposed to annexation of Canada would, said Vergennes, "be an offense they would never forgive us." Therefore, instead of speaking bluntly to the statesmen in Philadelphia, the French foreign minister moved deviously behind the scenes. Whenever Congress was seized with the Canada fever, Gérard and La Luzerne, the French ministers in Philadelphia, gently reminded congressmen that the British still had a powerful army in the heart of the United States, and that it would be well to clear the soil of their own country of the invader before embarking upon adventures in the North. Moreover, they encouraged the opposition of Southern congressmen to a conquest which seemed certain to strengthen the North against the South. Finally, the French took much comfort from the improbability that the republic could carry off a successful invasion without the aid of the French fleet.

In General Washington, the French found an ally in dashing cold water upon congressional schemes of conquering Canada. Though he acknowledged the importance of expelling the British from the North, Washington could not overlook the almost insuperable difficulties that militated against such a move. He warned Congress of the risk in detaching a large body of troops from the main army; of the unfriendliness of the Canadians; of the strong natural defenses of the country; and of the necessity of first eliminating the enemy's naval strength on Lake Ontario. Nor did he allow Congress to forget that Canada had once before swallowed up an American army and that starvation, smallpox, and humiliating defeat were still hazards of the Northern wilderness. These sentiments so pleased the French minister that he assumed that Washington had divined the purpose of France in keeping Canada in British hands; but it is more probable that the American commander was thinking solely in terms of the military obstacles that put Canada out of the reach of American republicans.

⌢ ⌢ ⌢

In reconciling the jarring interests of Spain and the United States, the French were notably less successful than in denying Americans the forbidden fruit of Canada. As regards Spain and the American republic, Vergennes was in the unhappy position of a man with two jealous mistresses, each of whom suspects that she is losing his affection to the other.

Spain, it has been seen, was outraged by the unilateral action taken by France in allying itself with the Americans; it was not often that France crossed Spain in matters of foreign policy, and Spanish pride rankled under the pact consummated with the republicans. "I observe with pain that this government [Spain] singularly fears the prosperity and progress of the Americans," reported the French ambassador in Madrid; "and this fear, which was in part the cause of its excessive ill humor at our engagements with them, may often turn the scale to the side of the English." Anti-French sentiment, always strong in Spain, now attained a point menacing to the Family Compact. Florida Blanca thundered that France had treated His Catholic Majesty "as a viceroy or provincial governor, to whom you put a question as if for his opinion, and to whom you then send orders!" Yet, on the other hand, he protested, "the American deputies are treated like the Roman consuls, to whom the kings of the East came to beg support."

Obviously, Spain was in no mood to be approached on the subject of making a third party to the Franco-American alliance. A cooling-off period was required before Vergennes could broach this topic; in the meantime, he was forced to be content with the neutrality of Spain, qualified by the secret aid which the Spanish government continued to send the rebels through Gardoqui and Sons.

France placed a high value upon Spain's participation in the war — a value which was hardly borne out by Spain's record in recent wars against the British and the Algerian pirates. It was true that Spain had forty ships of the line but, asked the French ambassador to Madrid, "how are they armed, and by whom are they commanded?" Spain, he pointed out, with its top-heavy empire and military weakness, might prove more a liability than an asset as an ally. Nevertheless, Vergennes bent every effort toward making Spain a belligerent on the side of France and the United States.

And well he might: Spain was deep in negotiations with Great Britain. In its anger against France, the Madrid government no longer consulted the interests of its partner in the Family Compact. His Catholic Majesty did not wear the livery of France; and if, against his advice, France chose to climb out on a limb with the Americans, he was prepared to saw off that limb. In brief, Spain decided to play a lone hand and to seek to further its own purposes at the expense, if necessary, of the French and Americans.

To Spain, the recovery of Gibraltar was a paramount national objective. Although this fortress had been British since 1713, Spaniards had never

reconciled themselves to its loss. In their eyes, it remained España Irri-
denta; therefore, when the Spanish government came to fish in troubled
waters, it was inevitable that it should cast its net for Gibraltar. Rather
than join France in war to win back the Rock, His Catholic Majesty
chose first to try the arts of diplomacy. In exchange for the cession of
Gibraltar, he offered to act as mediator between Great Britain and the
Franco-American allies.

At the price of surrendering Gibraltar to Spain, Great Britain might
have got out of the war with its honor, and perhaps its territories, intact.
As mediator, Spain proposed that while the United States was to be regarded as independent during the negotiations, the question of its permanent status should be left for future deliberations. Moreover, pending a
final settlement, the principle of *uti possidetis* should prevail, thereby leaving Great Britain in actual possession of strategic footholds in the United
States; and possession, in the peace negotiations, might prove to be nine
points of the law. It was a proposal in which neither the United States
nor France could take satisfaction, for it might well prove to be a sell-out
of American independence.

Spain's efforts to make Gibraltar a counter in international diplomacy
occupied its energies for over a year. As a result, the British, who were
ill prepared to sustain a vigorous attack from France and Spain in the
spring of 1778, were given an opportunity to prepare their defenses
against the combined strength of the Bourbon monarchies. This delay
caused Vergennes acute distress, but nothing could induce the Spaniards
to move faster than they chose to go. "God knows what can be attained,"
Vergennes exclaimed in despair in November 1778; only by the most
vigorous exertions in the war, he declared, could Spain ever atone for
the damage it had done by withholding its military aid in 1778.

Vergennes reluctantly gave his approval to Spain's mediatorial scheme.[2]
The Continental Congress likewise accepted its good offices; and although
Great Britain had not given the slightest indication of willingness to make
peace, Congress in effect took six months off from the war to draw up
peace terms. Ignoring Vergennes's warnings that the war ought to be
prosecuted more vigorously than before, the statesmen in Philadelphia
turned their attention almost wholly to peacemaking.

Congress talked peace but there was no peace in Congress: the Spanish
proposals precipitated an embittered sectional quarrel which, for the time
being, thrust the war into the background. The prospect of an early
peace caused each section of the union to demand that its interests be
accorded preferential treatment in the settlement. It was almost as difficult
for Congress to make peace as it was for that body to make war; and

---

[2] Vergennes did not, however, agree to the Spanish proposals of *uti possidetis*
coupled with a long-term truce between the belligerents. These were couched in the
form of an ultimatum served by Spain upon Great Britain in April 1779.

the effort to draw up acceptable peace terms revealed the tenuous nature of the fabric out of which the American union had been constructed.

To New Englanders, the right of participating in the Newfoundland and Nova Scotia fisheries was an indispensable part of any peace to be made with Great Britain. In their eyes, it was downright sacrilegious not to demand "what the Deity intended for us"; never willing to countenance impiety, they declared themselves ready to withdraw from the confederation unless Congress obeyed this divine mandate.

As British colonists, Americans had enjoyed fishing privileges in those waters and had landed freely upon the shores to dry their fish. With these advantages, New Englanders had built up an extensive commerce by supplying the markets of southern Europe and the West Indies with fish. The prosperity of pre-industrialized New England depended upon cod and haddock; and in an age when manpower for the fleet was drawn from the merchant marine, the naval power of the United States could not be separated from the question of fisheries. It was said that the fisheries were "more valuable to us than mines of Gold or Silver, without them we will have no navy, & consequently will make but a trifling figure in the history of the world." Indeed, in losing fisheries, the United States might forfeit the means of defending its independence.

To the West, the free navigation of the Mississippi along its entire length to the Gulf of Mexico was no less essential than were the fisheries to New England. Denied an outlet to the sea, the West might well remain an undeveloped wilderness; or, forming a separate confederacy, Westerners might ally themselves with the power that controlled "the Father of the Waters." Since 1763, British subjects had enjoyed the privilege of navigating the Mississippi River, and it was contended that the American people, as heirs of the British Crown, succeeded to this right. But a higher source than defunct British titles was found to sanction these claims: God and Nature, Americans argued, had ordained that the citizens of the republic should be permitted to use freely the great river that drained the interior of the continent. And so, to the western and southern sections of the United States — for the American West of this period was largely an offshoot of the South — the navigation of the Mississippi was a *sine qua non* of peace.

The power in possession of both banks of the Mississippi along part of its reaches — and therefore in a position to control its commerce — was not impressed by Americans' arguments. The intentions of God and Nature were very differently interpreted in Madrid and Philadelphia. In the opinion of His Catholic Majesty, the Mississippi had been specially designated as a barrier protecting the Spanish Empire from the land-hungry republicans of the United States; to open this waterway to their shipping was to invite an inundation of Yankees upon Spanish Louisiana, Mexico, and perhaps Peru. Therefore, the Spanish government was resolved to block American aspirations to navigate the Mississippi, and to this end, it sought to enlist the support of France.

Vergennes had always endeavored to soothe the fretful Spaniards with assurances that France had no intention of making the United States "the exclusive mistress of all that immense continent" and that the American republic and the Spanish Empire could forever remain at peace. It was fortunate for Europe, Vergennes believed, that Americans had deliberately chosen to live under a weak central government and to treasure their local liberties almost to the extinction of nationalism. Under a different form of government, the United States might become a menace to the established order; but as long as the Articles of Confederation endured, Americans seemed incapable of defending themselves, much less conquering the continent. And so Vergennes felt safe in predicting that the states would "always be a feeble body and capable of little activity."

Spain, however, did not rest content with Vergennes's prophecies of the future impotence of the United States; instead, it demanded that drastic measures be taken to make certain that the republic would remain for all time stunted and feeble. Republicanism, to His Catholic Majesty, was a menace not to be taken lightly.

Therefore, as a price for interposing its good offices to restore peace between Great Britain and the United States, Spain insisted that the Americans surrender their claims to the Floridas and to the navigation of the Mississippi where it passed through Spanish territory. It is clear that the cost of peace, if it were to be bought through Spain's mediation, would come high.

There was good reason why France should side with Spain rather than with the United States when the interests of these two powers came in conflict. Vergennes had little sympathy with the expansionist aims of the United States and he hoped to bring the two countries together in an alliance. France was eager to close the circle of alliances against Great Britain: with Spain and the United States formally joined, Vergennes anticipated that Spain would assume a larger share of the burden of keeping the United States in the war. Moreover, the alliance with Spain was prized more highly at Versailles than that with the transatlantic republic: Spain was a first-rate military and naval power, whereas the United States could hardly be accounted a second-rate power. Finally, Spain was a close neighbor and traditional ally. Less than twenty years before, His Catholic Majesty, at the instigation of France, had engaged in a disastrous war against Great Britain — with the result that his subjects were soured toward the Family Compact. If Spain was to be preserved as an ally, France must demonstrate that war against Great Britain could be made to yield dividends at the peace table. Another peace such as that of 1763 and Spain might be irrevocably lost to France as an ally.

For these reasons, the French minister in Philadelphia was instructed by his government to support Spain's claims against the United States. It was not pleasant for Vergennes to be compelled to choose between his allies, but there was never any doubt to which side he would incline if the choice had to be made.

Spain opposed the territorial aspirations of Americans: it remained for France to cast the weight of its influence against their claims to fishing rights in Newfoundland and Nova Scotia. France itself had vital interests in the North American fisheries: Breton seamen had been among the first to fish the Newfoundland Banks, and although France had lost its empire in continental North America, the fishery continued to be carried on. Of the wreckage of its colonial empire, France retained in these northern waters only the two small islands of Miquelon and St. Pierre. By treaty with Great Britain, France was permitted to fish in these waters and to dry fish upon specified parts of the Newfoundland coast; yet it was by no means certain that it would retain these privileges if Americans were allowed to participate in the fisheries.

The French minister labored in the congressional vineyard in behalf of Spain and his own government, marshaling his followers against the New Englanders, who would make no peace without the fisheries, and against the Southerners, who insisted upon navigation of the Mississippi. He lectured congressmen in private, urging them not to force His Most Christian Majesty to choose between Spain and the United States, because, in that event, Spain would certainly triumph, and warning that France would leave the United States to fight alone rather than protract the war in order to round out the American Empire. The only course open to Americans, Gérard declared, was to yield every point to His Catholic Majesty and thereby "to reconcile him perfectly with the American interest."

Gérard succeeded in drumming up some votes in Congress favorable to the Spanish claims of an exclusive right to the navigation of the Mississippi. Most of these votes came from Northern members of Congress, in whose eyes the navigation of the Mississippi was a purely Southern and Western concern which, if achieved, would make those sections paramount in the union. John Jay of New York, for example, took the position that "our empire is already too great to be well governed" and that the West ought not to be built up at the expense of the East. Moreover, the claims of powerful land companies, covering as they did a great part of the region north of the Ohio, damped the ardor of some Americans for pressing the case for free navigation of the Mississippi. It was difficult to persuade Americans to fight to make the West safe for American and British capitalists.

At the same time, Southerners were generally averse to alienating France and losing an opportunity to make an otherwise advantageous peace, merely because New Englanders insisted upon the fisheries. Such intransigence, they pointed out, might mean "the willfull Murder of thousands" — and it would be American, not French blood that would be spilled, the French having made clear that they would not fight for this objective. Because they supported New England's claims to the fisheries, Richard Henry Lee of Virginia and Henry Laurens of South Carolina were "squinted at as two monsters on the other side of the Susquehanna." It is significant that even at this early date some Southerners dreaded to build up the maritime strength of the North lest it be turned against them in some future conflict between the two sections.

France was at least impartial in its opposition to American aspirations: it opposed with equal inexorability the claims of all sections of the union. The obvious danger in this policy was that all sections might be united against France. Yet the immediate effect was that section was set against section and that Americans were divided at a time when unity was essential to victory.

However costly to American union, the diplomacy of the Bourbons achieved its objective. As a result of the lobbying of the French minister, neither the navigation of the Mississippi nor the fisheries were made absolute conditions of peace; instead, they were reserved for separate negotiations with Great Britain and Spain. Thus these disputed points no longer stood in the way of Spain's mediatorial efforts.

Nothing of the debate in Congress precipitated by Spain's proposal was known to the American people. Having been sworn to secrecy by Vergennes, Congress worked behind locked doors, and for six months the people were obliged to content themselves with rumors. It is true that some congressmen dropped hints that they had "some foreign Intelligence of great importance in our favour which was not proper *yet* to be divulged"; but so closely was the secret guarded that even Washington was not informed until the French minister, late in April 1779, laid the facts before him.

It was natural that the people, excluded from the confidence of Congress, yet at the same time assured that decisive matters were under discussion, should have been encouraged to believe that the war was as good as over. With the people eager for peace, the army suffering from shortages that sapped its fighting strength, and the paper money issued by Congress seemingly headed for utter worthlessness, many felt that peace on almost any terms was preferable to a continuance of the war, and even Thomas Jefferson was of the opinion that it would be better "to carry on a ten years' war some time hence than to continue the present an unnecessary moment."

By the time Congress had succeeded in agreeing upon its peace terms, Spain had dropped its role of mediator and had entered the war against Great Britain (June 1779). But not as an ally of the United States — Spain firmly declined to avail itself of the secret article in the Franco-

American alliance providing for the adherence of His Catholic Majesty. A separate alliance between His Catholic Majesty and His Most Christian Majesty was consummated, in which the United States was barely mentioned.

Spain's entry into the war against Great Britain had to be bought, and it could not be denied that the Spaniards drove a hard bargain. As Vergennes learned, "from Spain nothing is to be got for nothing. . . . The pretensions and expectations of Spain are gigantic." At Aranjuez, in April 1779, France agreed among other things, in exchange for Spain's promise to enter the war, to aid in the recovery of Minorca, Pensacola, Mobile, the bay of Honduras, and the coast of Campeche; and that no peace would be concluded without Gibraltar. In consequence, the United States, already bound not to make peace without the approval of France, now found itself obliged, without having given its consent or been consulted in any way, to remain at war until Gibraltar had been won.

Vergennes was willing to meet Spain's price for actively joining in the war because he feared that Great Britain, rather than face the combined sea and land power of the Bourbon monarchies, would attempt to purchase Spain's neutrality. He need have given himself little concern on that score, however. So contemptuous of Spain was the British government that it offered nothing to Madrid for its good offices as mediator, nor did it seek to tempt it with territorial concessions to remain neutral. To receive peace from the hands of Spain was insufferable to Englishmen; no foreign power, it was said, could rightfully interfere in "settling the terms to be granted by a sovereign to his rebellious subjects."

The participation of His Catholic Majesty in the war came as an anticlimax to the earth-shaking events predicted by Congress early in 1779. Congress put a good face upon the matter by hailing this new enemy of Great Britain as a power "well prepared for war, with fleets and armies ready for combat, and a treasury overflowing with wealth." And, as usual, many Americans gave free rein to the hopes which seemed to spring eternal in their breasts that the war was virtually over and that Great Britain could be written off as a great power. "The declaration of Spain effectually secures the downfall of G. Britain," said Richard Henry Lee. "A dreadful example to wicked princes and people abandoned to luxury. A mighty empire quickly crumbled to dust — An empire that five years ago terrified the world." Lee even began to look forward to "some wholesome Axe work in England": revolution would sweep the country and heads would roll in the sand. Also Washington permitted himself an optimistic look into the future. "If the Spaniards would but join their fleets to those of France, and commence hostilities," he said, "my doubts would all subside."

The abortive peace negotiations of 1779, however, marked the end of the honeymoon period in the relations of France and the United

States. The unmistakable favoritism shown by France toward the territorial demands of His Catholic Majesty and its own claims to the fisheries revealed that all was not bliss in the Franco-American household.
To many Americans, the unkind cuts of France were as unexpected as
they were galling: the good will of France toward its ally seemed to
have vanished with the signing of the treaties of alliance and commerce.
Not since the outbreak of the Revolution had France appeared so much
like one of those "corrupt, rotten despotisms of Europe." "Why," exclaimed Sam Adams, "should we tie our interests so closely to those of
France? Here, is where our independence should be consolidated."

It could not be denied that French influence had become a force to
reckon with in the internal affairs of the United States. Gérard and his
successor, La Luzerne, were much more than ministers of an ally: they
were the power behind the chair of the President of Congress. Gérard's
house was only a few steps from the State House where Congress met;
and he delighted to act the part of a good neighbor. Open house was
maintained for congressmen; a goodly store of French wines was kept
on hand; and in his private chambers the French minister met with his
followers in Congress, exhorting and reproving them in the manner of
a party whip. Congress might have its secrets from the American people,
but all its proceedings were known to the French ministers. A hard-up
congressman, John Sullivan of New Hampshire, was paid regularly for
information concerning its doings: and La Luzerne hired newspaper
writers to turn out propaganda favorable to France and French policies.
In 1780 he toured the New England states to urge a larger army upon
the legislatures; and in 1781 he was instrumental in defeating Arthur
Lee's candidacy for the newly created post of secretary of foreign affairs.
Occasionally, La Luzerne went too far even for the friends of the French
alliance: when he wrote a circular letter to the states exhorting them
to respond promptly to Congress's requests, Congress asked him to withdraw the letter as an encroachment upon its authority.

CHAPTER XX

The Campaigns of 1779

IF Sir William Howe had cause to complain of neglect by the home government, with much more reason Sir Henry Clinton could find fault. Clinton's letters are an unvarying dirge upon the difficulties and mortifications of a general always denied the reinforcements and supplies he deemed essential to victory. In 1778, when he assumed command of the army, he expected a reinforcement of twelve thousand men to be sent to New York; instead, the army under his command was reduced by fourteen thousand troops. The navy was even harder hit: only one third of the fleet that had sailed under Lord Howe now held the seas around New York. When to this is added the fact that the Howes had to fight only Americans, whereas Clinton was obliged to grapple with French, Spaniards, and Americans, the cause of his bafflement can be easily understood.

Whatever his merits, it is clear that Sir Henry Clinton did not share his predecessor's popularity in the army; he was not a magnetic leader, he did not possess lofty rank in the British aristocracy, and he was not a man of pleasure who knew how to put his officers and men in good humor by bluff heartiness and dogged courage. Sir Henry, unlike Howe, was devoted to business: austere, serious-minded, brooding, and painfully thin-skinned to criticism, he gave himself up to anxiety over the war and showed his disquiet in his bearing toward his staff. He was constantly on the lookout for slights and affronts — which, as might be expected, he found on every hand. Struggling against growing doubt that victory was possible, that the war was not already lost, and that he would go down in history as a miserable failure, he was at times almost a defeatist. Clinton, in short, got on everyone's nerves, including his own. Worry made him fussy, and Heaven protect an army from a fussy general!

Hedged round by apparently insurmountable difficulties, Clinton grew more and more despondent. He swore that he was weary to death of "this horrid war" which dragged on interminably — a boredom unbroken by either victory or defeat. Like Lord North, he yearned to be released from the torture of office, yet he was reluctant to step down from his post until he could quit it with honor. In the meantime, however, he labored under an oppression of spirit; he was exasperated by the wrong-headedness of the admirals Lord Sandwich sent to the American station; and he was driven to despair by his want of resources and the cavalier manner in which his requests for reinforcements were treated. Moreover, he found himself the object of the resentment of Sir William Howe's friends, in whose eyes he was practically a usurper of the post once held by Sir William. These officers taxed Clinton with being feeble, vacillating, and temperamental; and responsibility for every misfortune was laid by them at his door. "I know I am hated, nay, detested in the Army," Clinton said, "but I am indifferent about it, because I know it is without a cause."

As an additional irritant, Clinton's relations with Germain became progressively more strained. In the minister's opinion, the general was querulous, incompetent, and more prone than even Sir William Howe to magnify his difficulties. In 1779, without saying a word about reinforcements, Germain coolly instructed Clinton to annihilate Washington's army. Goaded beyond endurance, the unhappy general retorted: "For God's sake, my lord, if you wish me to do anything, leave me to myself, and let me adapt my efforts to the hourly changes of circumstances." To one of his subordinates, Charles Stuart, he unburdened himself without reserve; "with tears in his eyes," he exclaimed "that he was quite an altered man — that business oppressed him, that he felt himself incapable of his situation; . . . believe me, my dear Col. Stuart," he cried, "I envy that Grenadier who is passing the door, and would exchange with joy situations — no! let me advise you never to take command of an army. . . . I am determined to return home. The Minister has used me so ill that I cannot longer bear with this life."

Inactivity taxed the morale of the British troops; long periods of idleness, with nothing but drink, gambling, and women to take their minds off their homesickness, left the soldiers restless and ready for mischief. Many spent their time "dancing, card-playing, acting farces on mock stages, and decorating their pretty persons for the astonishment and delight of their female admirers," but others turned to less innocent diversions.

In the North, the war became an uninspiring catalogue of skirmishes, feints, and hit-and-run raids. Late in 1778, for example, a British fleet sailed majestically up the Hudson, landed troops at King's Ferry, where they "burn'd two or three small logged Houses with 9 Barrels of spoilt

Herrings," and then sailed majestically back to New York. Marches and countermarches, attacks upon storehouses, saltworks, farmhouses, and fishing smacks — these were the chief incidents of war in the eastern part of the United States. The American war had become that most deadly of all wars — a boring war. Recruits now joined the American army at the end of the campaign instead of at the beginning. Massachusetts sent about four hundred troops to Washington's army in 1779, among whom were a considerable number of children hired at fifteen hundred dollars each for nine months' service. It is apparent that Americans were willing to trust their security to the inactivity of the enemy rather than to their own efforts.

This otherwise tame and aimless war was enlivened by British terror-raids upon New England towns. Fairfield, Norwalk, and New Haven were partially destroyed by British troops under the command of Governor Tryon, who, said Washington, "in defiance of all the opposition that could be given by the Women and Children Inhabitants of these Towns performed this notable exploit with 2000 brave and generous Britons adding thereby fresh lustre to their Arms and dignity to their King." Angered by these depredations, Washington urged the burning of English towns in retaliation: but far from being able to accomplish this objective, he was unable to give adequate protection to the New England countryside. General Clinton, it is fair to say, took no pride in these achievements. "I have been a *buccaneer* too long," he declared. "I detest this sort of War."

During his long tenure of the chief command, Clinton, unlike Howe, made little effort to bring Washington to battle: although he waged war vigorously in the South, for the most part he remained strictly on the defensive in the North, content to wait for the enemy to make the first move. The American army also remained on the defensive at West Point, fearful of a British move up the Hudson. In May 1779, Clinton threatened West Point, but after capturing Stony Point, a small outpost on the Hudson, he brought his main army back to New York. "Mad Anthony" Wayne recaptured Stony Point in a surprise attack in which the Americans relied entirely upon their bayonets (as did the British in the Paoli Massacre two years before, in which Wayne's command had been almost wiped out), but lack of troops obliged the Americans to evacuate the post. Here the campaign in the North ended. Washington strengthened the defenses of West Point and Clinton dug in deeper at New York; but the two armies made no appreciable progress toward coming to grips with each other.

⌢   ⌢   ⌢

Along the frontier, however, all was not quiet. Here the war suddenly flared into violence as thousands of Indians took up the hatchet against the Americans and, led by Tories and British, began to devastate the settlements. Frontiersmen, unlike their more sheltered countrymen, entertained no illusions that the war was over; for them, its horrors had just begun.

Almost from the outbreak of the War of American Independence, Indians were in the thick of battle. During the siege of Boston, a contingent of redskins joined the Americans, but these were members of the domesticated tribes of Massachusetts and, Americans took pains to point out, more civilized than the "savage Britons." In 1776, however, Massachusetts enlisted several hundred Nova Scotia Indians; and at the same time Virginia began to take Indians into its armed forces. In May 1776, Congress authorized Washington to employ Indians as auxiliaries in the army; and the commander-in-chief, in pursuance of this authority, sent emissaries to the Cherokees and other tribes to secure five hundred warriors. Later in the war, however, Washington recommended that efforts to enlist Indians be dropped; the tribesmen ought to be informed, he said, "that all we require of them is their friendship and good wishes."

The British were not far behind the patriots in making use of Indians. General Thomas Gage, commanding the British forces at Boston, urged in 1775 that Indians be employed on a large scale against the rebels; "no time should be lost," he declared, "to distress a set of people so wantonly rebellious." Lord George Germain yearned to unleash the savages upon the rebels; nor did he draw the line at barbarities. "The Dread of the People of New England &c. have of War with the Savages," he said, "proves the Expediency of Our holding that Scourge over them." It became part of British strategy to crush the rebellion between redcoats on the seaboard and redskins on the frontier.

Accompanying the Indians were many whites, their bodies greased and painted, a collection of scalps dangling from their belts, and a brood of half-breed children in their tepees. By no means were all these gentry renegades — some of the "best people" were known to go native. For example, of Captain Christopher Carleton, nephew of Governor Carleton of Canada, it was said: "He paints his face, wears a ring in his nose and dresses like a savage." His wife was "My Lady" but he also had an Indian wife and, of the two, he much preferred his dusky spouse. Captain Carleton, undistinguishable from his companions, commanded the advance guard of Indians during Burgoyne's invasion of the United States.

The Continental Congress sent agents among the Indians, appointed commissioners to superintend Indian affairs, and dispatched committees to draw up treaties of alliance with the tribes. No efforts were spared to bring the tribesmen into the American camp. At Washington's headquarters, delegations of Indian chiefs were fairly overwhelmed with hospitality; the commander-in-chief personally escorted the warriors through the camp, entertained them at his own table, and smoked with them the pipe of peace. On one occasion, "a motley crew [of Indians] mounted on horseback, with his Excellency George Washington at their head," reviewed the American army. At another time, a group of Indian chiefs was saluted with thirteen cannon "which they received with a hideous Yell, but was much pleased with it." No doubt, the trigger fingers of some frontiersmen in the army itched at the sight of these visitors. Congress set aside a room for the reception of delegations of visiting tribesmen; and in 1775, when Captain White Eyes, a chief of the Delaware tribe, addressed Congress through an interpreter, after his speech congressmen crowded round the orator to shake his hand. Not to be outdone by rebels, George III permitted an Indian chief, complete with war paint and hatchet, to stand beside him reviewing troops on Wimbledon Common.

To win the support of the Indians, it was first necessary to control the frontiersmen, who in their zeal to acquire Indian tribal lands were little disposed to respect either the property rights or the lives of the aborigines. No "dam'd Injuns," they swore, would stand in their way — and so, regardless of consequences, they encroached upon Indian lands, ambushed Indian hunting parties, and wiped out Indian villages, indiscriminately killing women, children, and the aged. Indeed, they were, said a Continental officer, "a wild, ungovernable race, little less savage than their tawny neighbours." In 1779, Washington learned of a plot laid by frontiersmen to ambush a delegation of Delaware Indians, allies of the United States, on their way to a meeting with Congress. When the state of Pennsylvania offered in 1780 a reward for scalps, to induce citizens to turn out against the Indians, it was the friendly Delawares who stood in the gravest danger of having their scalps lifted. In Pennsylvania, the frontiersmen massacred the helpless Moravian Indians, even falling upon them while they were in the churches singing hymns. Washington concisely expressed Americans' attitude toward the Indians when he said: "The gradual extension of our Settlements will as certainly cause the Savage as the Wolf to retire; both being beasts of prey tho' they differ in shape."

In this struggle for the friendship of the Indians, the British enjoyed very considerable advantages over the Americans. In the wars waged by European powers for the mastery of North America, Indians had often held the balance of power and their alliance had been assiduously sought by the combatants. For over a century, the Iroquois, one of the most warlike tribes on the continent, had remained loyal to the British and had aided them in conquering French Canada. Since 1763, the British had acted the part of protectors of the tribes against the encroachments of white settlers and trappers. Moreover, the British were in a far better position to supply the Indians with such necessities as guns, powder, and liquor. Early in the war, the colonists made a rich haul of guns and ammunition consigned by the British government to southern Indians, but the Americans were never able to spare much of this equipment for their red allies. It was observed that the Indian captains in the British service were clad in resplendent uniforms and were loaded with presents, whereas the Indians who joined the Americans were naked and received "nothing but a little Whiskey" by way of recompense. Lacking worldly goods, the patriots sought to win the allegiance of the braves by appealing to their idealism, urging them to "join us who are their Brethren born, in the same Country against our common Enemies." This eloquence was wasted on the redskins, who displayed "very little taste for those heroic and elegant compositions which have been so much the wonder and admiration of the rest of the world." On the other hand, some Americans won considerable personal popularity among the Indians; for example, Anthony Wayne found himself "in a fair way of being adopted by one of the Kings" of the southern tribes — and, he added, "if I inclined might form an Alliance with the *Charming* Princess of the lower Creek Nation, which honor I shall decline."

The use of Indians against the rebels produced a bitter debate in Great Britain over the morality of employing such a terrible instrument of warfare. The English Whigs were horrified at the thought of waging a war of extermination against fellow Englishmen. They groaned to find scalping knives listed as one of the items of expense in the British army. If the object of the struggle was to reunite the empire, they asked, what part could tomahawks and scalping knives play in the contest? On this theme, Edmund Burke delivered a speech so fiery that it was said that it was fortunate the galleries of the House had been cleared, as otherwise the ministers might have been "torn in pieces by the people in the way to their houses." Chatham hobbled into the House of Lords to thunder against the government for "letting loose the blood-hounds and hell-hounds, the savages of America." Let England win her own wars, the old statesmen exclaimed; it was not by the tomahawk and scalping knife that Britain had become great; these base weapons had cast a stigma upon Great Britain — "a stigma which all the water of the rivers Delaware and Hudson would never wash away." No punishment was too severe, he declared, for the ministers who had "scoured all Germany and America, to seek the assistance of cannibals and butchers." [1]

To these outbursts, the Ministry replied that had not the British made use of Indians, the rebels would certainly have done so — with disastrous

[1] The ministers pointed out that it came with ill grace from Chatham to raise his hands in horror over the use of Indians by the British army. As Prime Minister, he had sanctioned the employment of Indians against the French during the Seven Years' War. To which Chatham replied that "savages might have been employed; but he denied he knew any thing of the matter."

results to the British cause. Lord North, who had no stomach for Indian massacres, declared that it was a "bad, but unavoidable" business; and Lord George Germain said that "we at worst but copied the righteous and infallible Congress, but with more success." On the other hand, one cabinet member, Lord Suffolk, openly justified the use of Indians, on the ground that the government would have been "highly censurable, if, entrusted as they were, with the suppression of so unnatural a rebellion, they had not used all the means which God and nature had put into their hands." "I see no distinction in point of honour," said another Tory, "whether he kills his adversary with a sword, or the more un-fashionable implement, a tomahawk." Yet it could not be denied that by summoning the Indians to take part in the civil war in the British Empire, the hope of a peaceful settlement suffered a grievous setback.

It is true that both sides attempted to mitigate the savagery of Indian warfare by paying a higher bounty for live prisoners of war than for scalps. The Continental Congress, for example, offered Indians one hundred dollars for every officer and thirty dollars for every private brought in as a prisoner; and the British sought by a similar system of rewards to keep the redskins from running amuck. This prompted Burke's famous sarcastic sally in the House of Commons when his parody of Burgoyne's talk with the Indians sent gales of laughter through the House and "almost suffocated Lord North himself with laughter." "Suppose there was a riot in Tower Hill, what would the keeper of his Majesty's lions do," asked Burke; "would he not fling open the dens of the wild beasts, and then address them thus? — 'My gentle lions, my humane bears, my sentimental wolves, my tender-hearted hyenas, go forth; but I exhort ye, as ye are Christians and members of a civilized society, to take care not to hurt man, woman, or child.' "

No name was more terrible along the frontier than that of Colonel Walter Butler, the "hell-hound" whose exploits, however tame and amateurish they may seem to a generation inured to mass killings, shocked his contemporaries. All told, Butler was responsible for the deaths of less than five hundred people — a record which, viewed in the perspective of history, sadly diminishes his reputation as a man of blood.

Whatever else he may have been, Butler was no outcast or renegade: he came from a good family of upper New York which had the misfortune to choose the losing side in the dispute between Great Britain and its colonies. The Butlers, father and sons, went to Niagara, where they joined the Rangers, a band of Tories that specialized in terrorizing the frontier settlements. Walter Butler saw service in 1777 with St. Leger in the Mohawk Valley; then, in 1778, he emerged as one of the boldest and most savage of the leaders of the partisan bands that harried the frontiers of Pennsylvania and New York.

Early in that year, Butler was placed in command of a band of Rangers whose purpose was to divert the attention of the Americans from Howe's army in Pennsylvania. Butler had a definite military assignment and his actions ought to be judged in that light; the thorough manner in which he carried out his instructions won him the plaudits of the British government. With about eighteen hundred men, Indians and Loyalists, he fell upon the Wyoming Valley in Pennsylvania, settled largely by Connecticut farmers. While his men killed the defenseless inhabitants, Butler surrounded the American troops in a small fort. Accompanying his demand for unconditional surrender of the garrison, Butler sent the outnumbered Americans "the bloody scalps of 200 of their late relations, friends and comrades." The American commander, recognizing the hopelessness of his situation, asked Butler for terms — to which Butler answered that the only terms he would grant were "the Hatchet." When the garrison finally surrendered, Butler proved as good as his word; he locked the prisoners in their barracks, which were then set on fire, and he and his men "enjoyed the savage pleasure of beholding the whole consumed in one general blaze." At another fort, the garrison was slaughtered while men, women, and children were burned to death in their houses.

Butler next struck at the New York frontier: at Cherry Valley he wiped out a small body of Continental troops that had been stationed to protect the settlers. Although he later claimed that he had attempted to restrain the Indians, over thirty people were killed in cold blood. In the telling, however, the "Cherry Valley Massacre" became another St. Bartholomew's and the terrified settlers fled their homes in such numbers that the frontier was depopulated beyond Schenectady. These, "the most Cruel Butcheries Ever Known," were widely publicized, and made Butler in the eyes of Americans one of the most bloodthirsty war criminals of the times.

From the point of view of Lord George Germain, however, Butler's tactics had succeeded admirably: the frontier was pushed back, hundreds of farms and settlements were burned, and the rebels were forced to fight on two fronts. Germain, indeed, regarded Butler's achievements as a vindication of his own farsightedness in having long advocated this kind of warfare to bring the rebels to "a sense of their duty." Many American Loyalists likewise were charmed by the deeds of Colonel Butler and his Rangers — in one campaign, it was said, he had struck more terror and wrought more devastation than had the British army during the entire war. If only Butler had a few thousand more men, his admirers predicted, he would make the rebels bleed from every pore. But in Butler's profession, one could hardly expect to live forever; before he was thirty years old, he had succumbed to an occupational ailment. His scalp dangled for several days from a pole at American headquarters before the trophy was finally taken down.

The key to the West, and with it the control of the Indians, was Niagara, which throughout the war remained in possession of the British. No post in the American West commanded the communications of so large an area; with a few hundred men and the aid of three small sloops, the British dominated Lake Ontario and the interior waterways of the continent. As long as the enemy held Niagara and were able to supply the Indians with arms and ammunition, the American frontier enjoyed no peace: to hold the line from Virginia northward against Indian incursions would have required the entire strength of the Continental army.

Westerners clamored for the capture of Niagara; but it was separated from the nearest American base by hundreds of miles of wilderness and numerous tribes of hostile Indians. Nevertheless, in 1779, a large expedition under the command of General Sullivan set out from the frontier of Pennsylvania to devastate the country of the Seneca Indians and drive the British from Niagara. Although Sullivan — notorious for his ill luck — was more fortunate in this enterprise than in others he had commanded, he failed to penetrate to Niagara. This failure seemed to put an end to all hope that the Continental army would be able to break the British grip upon the West. Washington flatly informed Governor Jefferson of Virginia that he could give no further aid to expeditions against Niagara or Detroit. "If the States would fill their continental Battalions we should be able to oppose a regular and permanent force to the enemy in every quarter," he declared. "If they will not, they must certainly take measures to defend themselves by their Militia however expensive and ruinous the System." [2]

⌒　⌒　⌒

Spain's entry into the war enormously complicated the task of the already overtaxed British fleet. It was necessary to reinforce immediately Gibraltar and Minorca, the great British-held fortresses in the Mediterranean; and, at the same time, the West Indies were endangered by the Spanish fleet at Havana and the French fleet and army at Santo Domingo.

The most immediate danger lay in the West Indies, where the French directed their attack against the British sugar islands. To reinforce the garrisons of these islands and the Floridas, Clinton was obliged to send eight thousand men from New York, thereby weakening the army

[2] With their power unbroken and with war supplies still furnished them by the British at Niagara, the Indians retaliated for the destruction wreaked by Sullivan and his army by resuming their attacks upon the frontier. In 1780, under the leadership of Sir John Johnson, the Indians ravaged the Schoharie Valley in New York, destroying wheat sorely needed by the American army. As late as 1782, the Indians were still burning up the Pennsylvania frontier and the state was calling upon Washington and the Continental army for aid.

under his command so gravely that he thought seriously of evacuating New York altogether. Asserting that a fatal blow had been delivered "to the hopes of any future Vigour in this Army," Clinton feared that he was condemned "to remain a mournful Witness to the debility of an Army." Although New York was held, it was found necessary to evacuate Newport. This station had been held against the combined sea and land forces of the allies in 1778, yet in the following year it was given up without firing a shot.

Britain's weakness in the West Indies enabled the French fleet commanded by D'Estaing to conquer island after island and to threaten even Jamaica, the headquarters of the British fleet and army in the Caribbean and, in the eyes of George III, one of the rarest pearls of his empire. By September 1779, Sandwich admitted that the Spanish and French forces in the West Indies were "more than sufficient to take Jamaica, almost without striking a blow." Grenada — the richest sugar island after Jamaica — fell in 1779 to D'Estaing, and "Foul Weather Jack" Byron was unable to bring the French fleet to decisive action. Instead of fighting Byron, D'Estaing sailed for the coast of the United States to have another try at aiding the Americans in dislodging the British army from their shores.

When Washington was informed that a French fleet was on its way to the United States, he immediately began to make plans for an attack upon New York, the loss of which, he remarked, "would be one of the severest Blows the English Nation could experience." With superiority at sea, he had high hopes of trapping the enemy forces on Long and Manhattan Islands; although admitting that the city could not be carried with less than thirty thousand men and he had only fifteen thousand in camp, he expected to make up the difference with the aid of French troops and American militia. Throughout October 1779, he was in almost hourly expectation of seeing D'Estaing off Sandy Hook. But no word whatever came from D'Estaing; though last reported off the coast of Georgia, it seemed to Washington that "some great convulsion in the earth has caused a chasm between this [New York] and that state that cannot be passed." Clinton was likewise at a loss for news of the whereabouts of the French fleet: from July to November, he heard nothing from Georgia. Finally the long silence was broken: D'Estaing was besieging the British garrison in Savannah and would be unable to aid Washington against the British in New York.[3]

[3] There were few regular channels for military intelligence. Often Washington learned of important battles or enemy troop movements from the newspapers. It was, for example, from a Charleston newspaper that he gained his first knowledge that D'Estaing was off the Georgia coast. It was not unusual for the public to know the news before the commander-in-chief was let in on the secret. The couriers bearing information to headquarters often drank and talked politics in the taverns along their route — keeping one's ears open in taverns was one of the best ways of procuring

Having cracked their heads against some of the strongest states in the union, the British, made cautious by misfortune, had singled out for attack the weakest state. Georgia was the most recently settled and the most isolated of the thirteen colonies; it contained only seventeen thousand whites, among whom lived thousands of Negro slaves who might be induced to revolt against their masters, and along its frontier were powerful tribes of Indians loyal to Great Britain and ready to take the warpath against the rebels. In the days of their prosperity they had not considered that such a weakling was worthy of their attention; now, having fallen upon evil days, they were happy to pick up any outlying provinces.

Charles James Fox compared the Ministry to gamblers who moved from table to table desperately trying their fortunes — and always losing. But in Georgia, they seemed at last to have struck a run of luck. In December 1778, Savannah fell to a British army under the command of General Prevost, and all Georgia seemed likely to follow the capital into the British bag. "The Inhabitants from all parts of the Province flock with their Arms to the Standard," reported a British officer, "and Cordially embrace the Terms which have been offered" — one hundred acres of land to every provincial who took up arms for the King. Encouraged by the quick collapse of resistance, the British began to think seriously of declaring Georgia in the King's peace and re-establishing civil government in the colony. "I think I may venture to pledge myself," said a British officer, "that I have taken a Stripe and Star from the Rebel flag of America." Shortly after this conquest, General Prevost marched his army almost to Charleston before being forced to turn back by the patriots.

The same weaknesses that were crippling the warmaking powers of the North were at work in the South. "A spirit of money-making has eaten up our patriotism," lamented a Southern Whig. "Our morals are more depreciated than our currency." Few soldiers could be tempted to enlist for depreciated paper money, and the militia would not submit to a draft. South Carolinians had stood by while Georgia was being overrun by the enemy, heedless of warnings that the calamities which the Georgians endured would soon be visited upon themselves. Even after the British had penetrated deep into South Carolina and threatened the capital itself, the people could not be awakened to their danger. "Our People begin to be as mad as before with the love of money & Speculation," said David Ramsay of Charleston. "We are again going to Sleep, though we have

---

firsthand military information. As a result, the transmission of military intelligence was apt to be painfully slow and uncertain — General Steuben, during the campaign in Virginia in 1780, exclaimed that he might as well be in Kamchatka as far as keeping in touch with Washington was concerned.

As for the British, Clinton had no ships in 1779 to carry dispatches to Georgia; after waiting six weeks, he finally found a privateer willing to open contact with the forces there. Unhappily for the British, this state of affairs was not uncommon.

every reason to believe that the enemy are preparing to visit us next fall." [4]

Franklin took consolation in the hope that "General *Fever*" would drive the British from Georgia, but the patriots could hardly wait for disease to dislodge the enemy. General Lincoln with some Continental troops and a strong body of militia was sent against the British in Georgia, and in September 1779, D'Estaing arrived off Savannah to coöperate with the American army. Against the French fleet the British defenders of Savannah had only four armed brigs. The American army outnumbered Prevost's force; and besides, several thousand seamen and marines were landed from D'Estaing's fleet to take part in the land fighting.

British commanders were seldom disposed to surrender merely because the odds were against them; moreover, it was not forgotten that this was the same D'Estaing who in 1778 had deserted his allies at Newport, Rhode Island. Prevost forced Negro slaves and citizens alike to work upon the fortifications of Savannah while he played for time by entering into surrender negotiations with the allied commanders. As the British hoped, the French and American commanders soon fell out: D'Estaing summoned the garrison to surrender in the name of the King of France, whereas General Lincoln insisted that the capitulation be made to the Continental Congress. But what saved Prevost and his army was the discovery, through a deserter, of the Franco-American plan of attack. This information enabled the British to mow down the allied troops as they charged the defenses of Savannah. Hundreds of French and Americans were killed, among them Count Pulaski, the Polish volunteer; D'Estaing himself was wounded. After this repulse, the allied forces made no further attack upon Savannah: the French fleet returned to France and the American army limped back to South Carolina, leaving the British to consolidate their conquest in Georgia. Thus another attempt to combine the operations of the French fleet and American army ended in defeat and recrimination.

---

[4] The conduct of South Carolina was no worse than that of Virginia. Although Congress urged Virginia to send troops to the South, the burgesses ignored its pleas on the ground that the danger was "altogether visionary."

CHAPTER XXI

❈

Crisis in England

FOR England, the worst crisis of the critical year of 1779 lay at home. Again Englishmen were confronted with the danger of invasion — this time by the combined fleets of France and Spain. It was now Englishmen's turn to endure "the times that try men's souls."

Spain declared war upon England in June 1779, but preparations had been made long before for a combined attack by the French and Spanish fleets. In accordance with this plan of operations the two fleets, in the summer of 1779, met at Corunna and a great armada, many times more powerful than that which had threatened England in the days of Queen Elizabeth, set its sails for the English Channel.

The combined Spanish and French fleets numbered sixty-nine ships of the line — "a force," observed a contemporary, "unheard of 'till now in history." In the French Channel ports, an army of forty thousand men was poised to cross the Channel when the British fleet should be eliminated. Against this armament, the British could muster only thirty-nine ships of the line under Sir Charles Hardy and a few thousand regulars who remained to defend the home islands. Thinly spread over the Atlantic, Mediterranean, and Indian Ocean, the British navy was inferior in numbers in almost every theater of the war. But the threat to the home islands themselves was by far the most serious danger; if England fell, the knell of the empire would be sounded.

In this crisis, George III sought to rally his subjects to a last-ditch fight, if necessary, upon English soil. He fully realized the danger but, as he said, "dejection is not the means of lessening it"; only boldness and vigor could save the country. Outnumbered as they were, Englishmen ought to remember that the odds had been against them many times in the past, and yet they had come through with colors flying. "It was," George remarked, "the vigour of mind shown by Queen Elizabeth and her subjects, added to the assistance of Divine Providence, that saved this island when attacked by the Spaniards." The King was prepared to emulate the great Tudor Queen if his subjects would but measure up to the heroic stature of Elizabethan Englishmen; placing his trust in "Divine Providence, the Justice of Our cause, the Bravery and Activity of my Navy," George declared that even if the French succeeded in effecting a landing upon the British Isles, they would have "thorough reason to repent of their temerity." But he had little doubt that the British fleet, outnumbered as it was, would have the victory; Sir Charles Hardy was ordered to put to sea without waiting for reinforcements and to seek out the enemy. The King declared that he had not "the smallest uneasiness" about the outcome if the fleet was able to make contact with the enemy. "I sigh for action," he said.

Lord North did not share the King's confidence that Providence could be counted upon to save England at the eleventh hour: Providence, he suspected, instead of reserving its smiles exclusively for Englishmen, sometimes showed distinct favor to Americans, Spaniards, and Frenchmen. Perhaps with this in mind, he remarked publicly, in August 1779, that he expected the invaders in a week. Plymouth, one of the largest naval bases in England, was almost defenseless, and it was here that Lord North looked for the French and Spaniards to make their landing.

In the case of the combined fleets of France and Spain, however, strength did not lie in numbers. This mighty armada proved to be merely a "huge mob of ships." The French fleet lacked four thousand men; the Spaniards were late in reaching the rendezvous where the two fleets were to join forces; no system of signals was worked out; the fleets were short of provisions; and an epidemic broke out before the ships had reached the English Channel. On August 16 the combined fleets were in sight of Plymouth, but half the crews were down sick; and although the ships of France and Spain rode the English Channel, they were in no position to do more than parade. Before Sir Charles Hardy could come to grips with the enemy, a gale drove them out of the Channel. Thus the Bourbons "talked big, threatened a great deal, did nothing, and retired"; as Marie Antoinette said, the expedition "cost a great deal of money to do nothing." The French admiral, D'Orvilliers, retired to a monastery, although it might be thought that the British ought to have been foremost in such signal acts of devotion.[1]

Thus, for the second time in two years, England was saved by the narrowest margin from an invasion which might well have meant ruin.

To stand on the defensive in the British Isles awaiting invasion was, in

---

[1] Disease had also weakened the English fleet. The source of the plague, Lord Sandwich explained, was the "pressed men & people from Jails that brought infection with them."

George III's opinion, to court disaster. He was well aware that time was not on England's side and that, in a war of attrition, the island kingdom was at a serious disadvantage, particularly when its command of the sea was insecure. Only audacity, he said, could preserve a great empire hard pressed on every side by its enemies. "We must risk something, otherwise we shall only vegetate in this war. I own I wish either to get through it with spirit, or with a crash to be ruined."

England had never played for higher stakes. "The dye is now cast," George said, "whether this shall be a Great Empire or the least dignified of the European States." While trusting in Providence, the King recognized that Heaven strictly limited its favors to those who helped themselves; and therefore his conviction that God had particular affection for the British Empire did not rob him of initiative. "Many men choose rather to despond on difficulties than see how to get out of them," he complained, but certainly the King was not one of them: fertile in expedients, he was constantly projecting plans to destroy his enemies. No Englishman, he said, except those "willing to sacrifice every object to a *momentary and inglorious Peace*," would ever grant America its independence — for, once the United States had proved that rebellion succeeded, other provinces would follow its example and Great Britain would be shorn of those overseas possessions from which she drew strength and greatness. Then would England dwindle into insignificance — most of her people would emigrate to the western world, and France and Spain would easily overrun the fortress island that for centuries had defied them.

All that George III asked was that Englishmen have faith in themselves and, however dark the hour, reveal the spirit that had saved England during every crisis of its fortunes. Perhaps George III was never greater than in losing his empire; in a better cause than waging war against the Americans he might have gone down in history as George the Lionhearted. He, for one, did not despair of the state. "However I am treated," he exclaimed, "I must love this Country," and his love was unquenchable.

The King found precious little of this spirit in his Prime Minister: had all Englishmen been cast in Lord North's mold, George might well have despaired of the state.

The outbreak of war with France disheartened Lord North: to bid Englishmen, already weighed down by defeat, to grapple with another foe was a task to which the Prime Minister did not believe himself equal. Both North and Germain prepared to leave office after the forging of the Franco-American alliance; and both had their eyes upon the same sinecure in which they proposed to spend their retirement — the wardenship of the Cinque Ports. Germain complained that his health was failing rapidly; the last session of Parliament, he remarked, had been extremely fatiguing and he yearned for peace and quiet. Lord North abjectly confessed that he was chiefly to blame for his country's extremity; he aspired to cut no great figure in history, he said, yet he feared that he had written his name in England's ruin. William Pitt had said of himself that he was the only man who could save England; Lord North seemed to believe himself the only man who could utterly destroy it. "Let me die disgraced for that I can not now avoid," he besought the King; "but let me not go to the grave with the guilt of having been the ruin of my King and Country. . . . I have been miserable for ten years in obedience to your Majesty's commands," he declared; and ten years in the purgatory of the prime ministership was as much as could be asked of any man.

As his difficulties increased, Lord North fell into a state of almost utter funk. To the King, he querulously complained that his faculties, never of the first order, were rapidly giving way under the strain of office. "My mind always weak," he said, "is now ten times weaker than it was, and I have difficulties ten times greater to encounter than ever I had." His "ancient indolence" was becoming a settled habit, making work of any kind impossible; his memory had failed to such a degree that it was no longer safe to entrust state papers to his care. "A letter of the first political importance," he said, "addressed to him by the King, which he had lost, after a long search, was found lying wide open in the water closet." The unhappy Prime Minister, thus verging fast upon his dotage, implored the King to rid himself of such an encumbrance; let not friendship stand in the way, he urged George, when the fate of the empire depended upon putting a stronger man at the helm. Although deeply affected by the monarch's confidence and friendship, North could hardly admire the royal perception in leaning upon such a weak reed as himself.

The fact is that Lord North had begun to lose confidence in British victory. Great Britain he believed to be in the right, but he doubted whether the right always triumphed. Sadly lacking in the spiritual fortitude of the King, he was a prey to misgivings that left him unnerved and irresolute. He made no effort to conceal from the King his opinion that "the advantages to be gained by this contest could never repay the expense," and he dragged out his tenure of power in fear and trembling lest some irreparable disaster should overtake British arms.

But the more Lord North urged his demerits upon the King, the greater waxed the royal affection for the Prime Minister. Decrepit as North claimed to be, the King infinitely preferred him to any other man in the kingdom; and he resolved to keep this shrinking violet at the head of affairs. He knew that he could never find a more loyal and obedient servant; on the other hand, to open the door to the Whigs would, he greatly feared, put an end to his own authority in the kingdom. Bound and gagged, he would be carried off in triumph by the Whigs and suffered to exist only as a *roi fainéant*. Confronted by this dire prospect, George clung to North with such tenacity that the disconsolate Prime Minister might well have felt that death alone could relieve him from the cares of office; as long as there was breath in his body, he could not escape from the prime ministership. Seldom has a man been stuck so solidly in that exalted office.

The King watched over North's health with a concern which hardly could have been exceeded by the Prime Minister's own physician. When North fell ill or — as was more frequent — complained of his multitudinous maladies, the King prescribed for him his own favorite remedies and insisted upon being kept in touch by special courier with the sickroom. In 1781, for example, George was worried lest "the turtle feast in this Warm Weather may have added some fuel" to North's feverish cold. Few ministers of the Crown have received more touching attention from their sovereign, but it may be doubted whether the King's prescriptions brought much comfort to the ailing minister, for George was a firm believer in the efficacy of *"Abstinence and Water."*

Into the faltering Prime Minister, the King sought to instill some of his own fortitude and dogged resolution. "Go on with Spirit," he urged North, while offering to stand by him to the bitter end, even against a hostile House of Commons. "If He would but hide his feelings and speak with firmness," George told the Prime Minister, everything would come right; and in every parliamentary crisis, the King lent his support to the North Ministry. George closely followed the voting in Parliament, doling out the loaves and fishes to the faithful and rebuking those who strayed from the fold. Thanks to these methods, Lord North was assured of a comfortable majority in Parliament. Yet even this did not stiffen the backbone of the Prime Minister.

In his eagerness to be relieved of his office, North actually went to the trouble of selecting from the opposition his successor as Prime Minister. Lord Chatham was the man to save England, North told the King; and the Prime Minister indicated that he would feel much easier about England's future if the change were made immediately. Indeed, Lord Chatham had no warmer supporter for the office of Prime Minister than the Prime Minister himself.

Chatham had once before saved his country: during the Seven Years' War, as William Pitt, the "Great Commoner," he had turned the tide of defeat and led England to triumph over the combined might of France, Spain, and Austria. Now, old and gout-ridden, he had long been in eclipse, emerging from retirement at infrequent intervals to denounce the men and policies that were leading the country to ruin.

Like George III, Chatham and his loyal follower, Lord Shelburne, saw the doom of England in American independence — "its splendor and glories would be no more, and she would be but a power of the second order in Europe." Therefore, the union with America must be preserved at all costs, but it must be based upon consent and mutual good will. That it was possible to persuade Americans to return to the empire if offered "a fair, honest, wise and honorable connection," Chatham did not doubt. Accordingly, his program was to withdraw all British troops from America and let time and British diplomacy do the rest.

To this, of course, the King would never consent. Nor could George accept Chatham as Prime Minister — the old statesman was too self-willed for the King's taste. At the head of the government George wanted a tractable man who would carry out the royal wishes; and certainly Chatham was not such a man. On the other hand, the monarch would have welcomed a ministry composed of "the Wise, the Virtuous and Respectable of all Parties," but he found fewer and fewer Whigs who met these specifications.

Despite the King's support, Lord North's knees continued to buckle under the blows of adversity. He slumped alarmingly in 1779, and the King almost reconciled himself to parting with his beloved servant: a series of resignations shook the cabinet, and although North survived the crisis, it was largely owing to the vigor and resolution of the King that North kept his place. George III, rather than the Prime Minister, guided the destinies of Great Britain; and the difficulties into which the country had fallen revealed the strength and courage of the King and the weakness and timidity of the Prime Minister. One of North's colleagues complained that "there is no energy, damn him, nothing can goad him forward." A crew has little confidence in a captain who is known to be planning to jump ship at the next port.

Yet North was reluctant to desert the King in a crisis; and it so happened that whenever North wished to resign, the King invariably discovered that there was a crisis. The Prime Minister was faced with the dilemma — posed by the King himself — whether he was prepared to abandon his post and thereby plunge the King and country into disaster, or to remain in harness and help pull the country to victory. In North's opinion, it was a question whether he or the country would succumb first. "These Crosses, & these alarms," he wrote the King, "are distressing, & absolutely drive Lord North to madness."

The unhappy Prime Minister might well have concluded that it would be safer to remain in office and to put up with all the torments it entailed than to resign and thereby risk punishment at the hands of the Whigs. Charles James Fox repeatedly declared that Lord North ought to be brought to the scaffold — proper punishment, said Fox, for a man who had almost singlehandedly ruined his country. In hours of parliamentary reverses, Fox found solace in the hope that North would not escape justice: if the law failed to punish, the people would take matters into their own hands and exact the full penalty from the First Lord of the Treasury and his fellow miscreants, no matter how highly placed. Lord North might repine at the cares and anguish of office, but it would seem that his life depended on sticking to his post. From which it can be seen that it was not only the American statesmen who signed the Declaration of Independence who had reason to fear that if they did not hang together they would hang separately.[2]

And so the tragi-comedy spun itself out: for eleven years, six of which were spent at war, Lord North served the King, if not the best interests of his country. Only after Yorktown did he relinquish the office that for many years he had regarded as a bed of thorns.

∩   ∩   ∩

Not the least of Lord North's difficulties was occasioned by the singular behavior of British generals upon their return to England after serving in America. Their exploits in the field rarely brought much pleasure to the Prime Minister, but he might have forgiven them their failures had they not made themselves so uncommonly troublesome at home.

There was no Mischianza awaiting Sir William Howe when he reached Great Britain in 1778. Much of his prestige had been buried in America; without having lost a battle, he was ranked among the most unfortunate of British commanders. In many quarters, he found himself scorned as the evil genius of the war — a lily-livered Whig to whom the lives of rebels were more precious than the integrity of the British Empire.

It was difficult for Englishmen to forgive Howe for waging a "soft" war against the rebels — for what had caution and forbearance to do with such a contemptible foe? "Your fits of caution were always strongest when the Americans were weakest," declared a critic; "and then strongest of all, when they were flying without any means of escape." Long Island, New Jersey, Brandywine, Whitemarsh, Valley Forge — a lamentable catalogue of missed opportunities! Howe seemed to have acted as if every hill in America were an inaccessible mountain and every thicket an impenetrable fortress. If America were lost, it was said, it would be chiefly owing to his "ignorance, dissipation, rapaciousness and treachery."

It was easier for many Englishmen to blame Howe than to acclaim Washington: it was incredible that "a Negro driver should, with a ragged Banditti of undisciplined people, the scum and refuse of all nations on earth, so long keep a British general at bay" unless that general was clearly incompetent. That Howe, a professional soldier, should be "puzzled and plagued for two years together with a Virginia tobacco planter" seemed incontrovertible proof that Sir William was a driveler. Indeed, Howe's failure seemed so unpardonable that in some quarters he was suspected of being a traitor: instead of trying to win the war, he had put politics above patriotism and had tried to embarrass the government by deliberately sparing the Americans.

[2] At the time of the signing of the Declaration of Independence, Benjamin Franklin is reported to have said: "We must all hang together, or assuredly we shall all hang separately."

From what he read in the newspapers, Sir William concluded that the Ministry was seeking to foist upon him the blame for the disasters of the campaign in 1777. He had expected no less, and his defense was already prepared. To the consternation of the Ministry, he demanded a parliamentary inquiry into the conduct of the American war in order to determine whether he or the government was responsible for the miscarriages in the field. As Lord North feared, the Whigs took this opportunity to marshal an impressive array of evidence demonstrating the incompetence of the government, the blunders of Lord George Germain, and the futility of persisting in efforts to conquer the Americans. British generals gave testimony to the effect that Americans were "almost unanimous in their aversion to the government of Great Britain"; General Gray declared that "the Americans were disloyal almost to a man," and Lord Howe testified that "almost all the People of Parts & Spirit were in the Rebellion."

For all the disasters of the war, the English Whigs pointed an accusing finger at Lord George Germain, the man who, they declared, had sent Howe to Pennsylvania, leaving him in ignorance of Burgoyne's march to Albany; who had concocted a plan of operations which an English schoolboy would have been ashamed to acknowledge; and who had attempted to run, from his office in Whitehall, down to the smallest detail, a war "carried on in the interior desarts of America, and at a distance of three thousand miles."

About this time, Burgoyne arrived in England as a prisoner of war on parole and, like Sir William Howe, found himself blamed for the miscarriages of the war. The newspapers charged him with rashness and folly, and he was denied admittance to the royal presence. From this, Burgoyne, too, deduced that the ministers intended to save themselves by throwing him to the wolves.

From the Whigs, Burgoyne received a very different reception: the opposition members of Parliament were always prepared to take unfortunate British generals to their bosoms and to acclaim them as brave and able officers sent to their doom by bungling ministers — a version of the Saratoga campaign with which Burgoyne heartily agreed. As a star witness against the Ministry, Burgoyne was a valuable acquisition to the Whigs. Charles James Fox hurried down to Plymouth to meet Burgoyne when he landed, and Edmund Burke praised the luckless general as a commander who delighted in "splendid acts of generosity and humanity."

Lest Burgoyne talk too much, the Ministry tried to get him out of the way as quickly as possible. The King's law officers questioned Burgoyne's right to sit in Parliament: as a prisoner of war, they ruled, he ought to be returned to the custody of the Continental Congress. Seldom in British history has the government been more eager to surrender a British general to the enemy. For Burgoyne, this was the final straw; he swore that he was being made the victim of a plot to frustrate a parliamentary inquiry into his expedition, and he asserted that the ministers of the Crown, to be rid of him, were even prepared to send him to his death. "To expose my constitution to the next American winter," he protested, "is in probability to doom me to the grave." Much to his relief, his good friends the Whigs came to his rescue, Fox in particular warmly championing the right of his "honorable friend" to remain in England. In the end, Burgoyne was not obliged to return to the United States — to the obvious disappointment of the cabinet.

All this while the Americans were doing their utmost to raise trouble in the home islands themselves — and succeeding much too well for Lord North's peace of mind. Of all the dominions of His Britannic Majesty to which Americans appealed to join them in rebellion, none seemed riper for revolt than Ireland. The Irish had religious, political, and economic grievances against Great Britain beside which the wrongs of the Americans seemed almost trivial. Irish industry was ruined by English laws; Irish farmers were exploited by landlords, many of them absentee Englishmen; the Irish Parliament was ruled in England's interest by means of corruption; and religious oppression was visited upon Irishmen, Catholics and Calvinists alike. To Irishmen, the ills of Ireland seemed to begin and end with England.[3]

England had few friends in Ireland, and little remained beyond the terror of its name and memories of the bloody suppression of previous revolts to preserve the loyalty of Irishmen. That this was insufficient was soon made evident. "A country enlightened as Ireland — armed as Ireland, and injured as Ireland," said Henry Grattan, "will be satisfied with nothing less than liberty."

By 1778, the Irish tinderbox had begun to crackle ominously. Demanding redress of grievances, the Irish accompanied their arguments with armed demonstrations and a boycott of British goods. Irishmen copied the example of the American republicans even down to tarring and feathering: to alarmed Englishmen, it seemed that the Irish were planning to "play off the American hand of cards, up from deuces to aces"; an Irish Congress would come next and then an Irish Washington to lead his countrymen against the enemy across St. George's Channel. John Adams found the prospect so encouraging that in 1780 he predicted that Ireland would achieve its independence before the United States. Franklin sent goodly quantities of propaganda promising support from the Americans

---

[3] It is true, however, that the American War of Independence crippled Ireland's last remaining industry — linen manufacture. After 1776, an embargo was clamped down upon the shipment of linen from Ireland to prevent supplies being sent to France or the French West Indies. Largely as a result of this drastic action, there were twenty thousand unemployed people in Dublin alone living on charity. It ought also to be pointed out that the Irish were old hands in staging rebellions against Great Britain. The Irish could rightly say that the American colonists were following in their footsteps in rising against British oppression.

if Irishmen rose against the tyrant. "It will be the true glory of America," it was said, "to preserve the liberty of Ireland."

The timing of these Irish demonstrations was happier than in previous revolts. To Englishmen, the empire seemed to be crashing about their heads; threatened with enemies on every side, they beheld Ireland seething with discontent and spawning armed men by the thousand. Lord North admitted that the Irish Presbyterians were "almost to a man favourers of the American Cause," and many of the Irish Catholics, although lacking the strong feeling of kinship with the American rebels felt by the Scotch-Irish, were ready to welcome any deliverer — French or American — from the oppression of England. But Vergennes had no intention of helping Ireland attain its independence and thereby relieving Great Britain of an incubus: he preferred to leave the Irish problem where it was — squarely in England's lap.

It was true that everything might have been brought right if England applied to Ireland the lessons that had been learned in America; but the trouble was that many Englishmen had learned the wrong lessons from the dispute with the colonies. "America hath been lost, and England almost ruined, by concessions" was the philosophy of the Tories; and whatever else happened, they were resolved not to fall into the same error in dealing with the Irish discontents. George III was averse to giving Ireland important commercial privileges — these ought, he said, to be granted "with a sparing hand, for experience has taught me that every favour granted there is only a reason to ask a greater."

Yet even Tories could perceive that a new approach to the Irish problem was imperative. With England's enemies closing in for the kill, the old blunt and forceful manner of disposing of Irish questions seemed outmoded; prodded by the English Whigs, the government began reluctantly to right Ireland's wrongs. It was difficult, as Edmund Burke found, to convince Englishmen that Ireland could not be prosperous except at their expense; nevertheless, some of the restraints on Irish industry were removed and a beginning was made toward granting religious liberty to Roman Catholics.

The easing of the burdens of Irish Roman Catholics was in part dictated by the necessity of drawing the manpower of Ireland into the British army.[4] Under existing laws, members of that faith had very little to fight for: they had been placed beyond the pale of national life and it was difficult for Catholics to regard the state as other than an inveterate enemy. They could not vote or hold office, their priests were liable to imprisonment, and they could not purchase or inherit land if any Protestant heir should lay claim to it. Manifestly, if they were to fight the battles of Great Britain they must be given some stake in victory; therefore, in 1778, the

---

[4] Roman Catholics could not hold commissions in the British army, but the government was no longer averse to recruiting Catholics for the ranks.

British government had begun to liberalize the laws regarding education and land ownership and even proposed to extend these measures to England and Scotland.

But to thousands of Englishmen the Roman Catholic Church was still the "whore of Babylon," and Popery was the abomination of abominations. There was, said Edward Gibbon, latent in England, particularly among the evangelical sects, a dark and diabolical fanaticism which he had supposed long extinct. The government's attempt to ameliorate the lot of the Roman Catholics brought to the surface the darkest depths of this fanaticism.[5]

The leader of the forces of bigotry was Lord George Gordon, a crazed Scotsman whose insanity took the form of a wild-eyed evangelical Protestantism and a fanatical hatred of Roman Catholicism. Wearing his hair lank and affecting the garb and piety of a Puritan of Cromwell's day, this "mad Lord" was at first laughed at; but when "No Popery" began to be chalked up all over England and when Gordon harangued his followers, "forty thousand Puritans, such as they might be in the time of Cromwell," it began to be seen that he was hardly more mad than thousands of honest, God-fearing Englishmen who followed him as if he were a Messiah. Gordon formed an organization known as the Protestant Association and threatened to march upon Parliament with one hundred and twenty thousand men at his back to demand the repeal of laws favorable to Roman Catholics.

When Parliament refused to be intimidated by these threats, Gordon called out his followers to overawe the Lords and Commons by a mass demonstration. Surrounded by a mob howling for repeal of the Roman Catholic laws, Parliament was besieged for several hours. The members barricaded themselves in their chambers and prepared to sell their lives dearly. Lord North, warned by Gordon that he would be torn to pieces by the mob outside, showed his mettle by walking through the crowd to his carriage. Other members of the cabinet and leaders of Parliament, however, did not escape so easily: Lord Sandwich was torn out of his carriage and was rescued by the Horse Guards just as the mob was preparing to wreak its vengeance upon him; Edmund Burke and the Duke of Richmond were chased through the streets; and the Bishop of London got out of harm's way only by scrambling over the rooftops.

This marked the beginning of a riot that terrorized London for almost a week. The original cause of the uprising was soon forgotten as the rioters turned their attention to procuring loot and drink instead of wasting their energies upon such unprofitable game as Roman Catholics. The

---

[5] John Wesley, the founder of Methodism, added fuel to the highly inflammatory state of mind of his followers by declaring that "no government, not Roman Catholic, ought to tolerate men of the Roman Catholic persuasion." He warned Englishmen that Roman Catholicism was making dangerous strides in the country.

Lord George Gordon riots, as they were known, became a great outpouring of the London slums; Newgate and King's Bench prison were carried by storm and the prisoners liberated to add their numbers to the lawless population of the metropolis. Fires burned all over the city; the Royal Exchange was attacked and the Horse Guards were forced to fight their way through Fleet Street. The Bank of England and the Inns of Court were in danger; Horace Walpole suspected that the rioters intended also to let loose the lions in the Tower of London and all the lunatics in Bedlam — the latter, he observed, would make excellent followers of Lord George Gordon.

The forces of law and order were at first utterly unable to cope with this eruption of the slums, but liquor began to exact its toll among the rioters. Hundreds lay dead drunk in the gutters and many killed themselves by overindulgence when they broke into the cellar of a Catholic distiller. Finally, after the city had endured almost a week of burning, looting, and drinking, British troops from all parts of the country began to converge upon London and "the pious ragamuffins soon fled . . . all their religion consisted in outrage and plunder." The metropolis, thus happily delivered, looked as though it had been sacked by an invading army: the French or Americans, said Walpole, hardly could have done more damage. The property damage totaled over one million pounds; the casualty list stood at four hundred and fifty dead and many more hundreds wounded.

Few of the rioters were tried and convicted, Lord George Gordon himself being acquitted of a charge of high treason. Gordon thereupon turned Jew, taking the name Israel Abraham Gordon, and lived as happily among the Jews of London as ever he had among the Calvinists of Scotland. It is a commentary upon English justice that although Gordon was not punished for instigating the riots that bear his name, in 1786 he was found guilty of libel upon the moral and political conduct of Marie Antoinette of France and was sentenced to five years in prison, where he died.

While freely admitting that London boasted as complete rascals "as were upon the face of the globe (*North America* excepted)," many Englishmen discerned in this riot the fine American hand of Dr. Benjamin Franklin. The doctor was believed to have agents stationed all over the British Isles ready to put the country to the torch at his bidding; and it was well known that the Continental Congress had called for the burning of English cities in retaliation for the destruction of American towns. Lord George Gordon was notoriously partial to the Americans and drank frequently to a rebel victory. All this seemed to indicate that Americans, as Walpole said, had been taught by the British how to burn towns and that Dr. Franklin had applied these lessons to London.

Franklin denied any part in the Lord George Gordon riots; they were, he said, the work of "a mob of fanatics joined by a mob of rogues!" Had the mob been instigated by love of liberty, he pointed out, it would have filled the empty prisons with members of Parliament — for where were there greater plunderers and oppressors of the people than in the Lords and Commons? It is true that Americans had hoped to see mobs of honest Englishmen crippling the power of the government by their riots in favor of liberty; but, as Franklin said, the Lord George Gordon riots were directed *against* liberty.

⌢ ⌢ ⌢

English conservatives dreaded the ideas promulgated by the rebellious colonists more, perhaps, than they dreaded the rebels themselves. The spectacle of republicanism starting up in the British Empire was as shocking as though today the Dominions should transfer their allegiance from London to Moscow. Lord North declared that the independence of the United States would mark the beginning of "a revolution in the political system of the world" which might sweep away the institutions of monarchical Europe; but if Britain triumphed, the Tories flattered themselves that the "thirteen-headed hydra" would be prevented "from doing any more mischief in this century at least." Clear-sighted conservatives perceived that their most formidable enemy was the philosophy of the Declaration of Independence.

It could not be overlooked that the English people, as well as the American colonists, suffered under injustice. In neither country was the principle of no taxation without representation applied. Twenty-nine out of thirty Englishmen had no vote; about six thousand voters scattered throughout Great Britain returned a clear majority of the House of Commons. Rotten boroughs, although they contained few or no voters, sent members to Parliament — of Old Sarum, the most notorious of these boroughs, it was said that the streets could be traced only by "the colour of the corn; and its sole manufacture is in members of Parliament." In the borough of Midhurst there were stones marked 1, 2, 3, 4, and so on, in the party wall of Lord Montague, the local magnate, who cynically remarked that they were voters and returned members of Parliament. The town of Banbury, with seventeen voters, sent Lord North to Parliament; Lord George Germain had a constituency of thirty electors. Moreover, because no important changes had been made in the system of representation since the days of Charles II, London and Bristol were underrepresented and several large manufacturing towns such as Manchester and Birmingham elected no representatives. The county of Cornwall returned almost as many members as did the whole kingdom of Scotland.

To these political grievances were added the evil of social and economic injustice. It is therefore understandable why, from the first sign of trouble in the colonies, English conservatives kept a watchful eye upon the lower classes in Great Britain lest revolutionary ideas, imported from America, should produce an upheaval in the heart of the empire. That the English people could be entirely immune from this contagion was hardly to be expected: a few years before, they had been wildly cheering "Wilkes and Liberty," and although "that devil Wilkes," as the King called him, had proved to be comparatively harmless, there was no security as long as it was "enough for any factious or desperate men to mouth and rant about liberty, to become the idols of the populace." In 1776, an Englishman complained that "the rabble, high and low, all over the nation, are absolutely drunk, or rather mad, with wild extravagant notions of liberty, inconsistent with all order and subversive of all government."

Although few Whig leaders were reformers by conviction, they saw no prospect of saving England as long as the Crown retained its power of corrupting members of the House of Commons. Parliament, it was charged, had been converted into a mere "registry of edicts" which enacted without question "every measure indiscriminately which came recommended by the servants of the crown." The House of Lords, although less inimical to American rights than the Commons, gave the government a handsome majority. (The presence of Scotch peers and pensioned English noblemen won for it the name of a "Hospital for Incurables.")

To break the King's grip upon Parliament, the Whigs were compelled to hoist the banner of parliamentary reform. Yet, because they believed that their own power depended upon preserving the system of partial representation, limited suffrage, and corruption, they did not seek to lay a heavy hand upon these abuses of English political life — rather, it was to be a job of feather dusting in which attention was confined almost entirely to the powers of the King. To make it more difficult for George to corrupt Parliament, it was proposed to clip the civil list; and Parliament was to be purged of contractors — Fox declared that North was in the habit of saying to contractors, "I give you a good contract on condition that you give me a good vote" — placemen, and pensioners. The King's household — likewise a fertile source of jobs and gifts — was to be reduced. Burke intended to leave at the disposal of the King sufficient money and offices for him to grant favors, but not enough for him to practice corruption. Englishmen, he said, ought to honor the King but not belong to him. As for the ease and comfort of the monarch, he was to enjoy as much magnificence as comported with the reduced and tax-burdened state of the country.

No radical changes were contemplated in this program of reform: Burke "swore Parliament was and always had been precisely what it ought to be, and that all people who thought of reforming it wanted to overturn the constitution." He admitted that he was "cautious of experiment even to timidity"; the rule of moderation in all things applied with special force to reform because, he insisted, "a temperate reform is permanent; and because it has a principle of growth." [6]

These measures tended to make Parliament independent of the King, but they did little to make that body truly representative of the people. It was the Whig aristocracy, rather than the people, that seemed destined to reap the real benefit of the proposed changes. Reform in the interest of the ruling class rather than in that of the masses was the Whigs' policy; in preventing England from becoming an absolutism, they did not wish to make it a democracy. So, in seeking to purge Parliament of King's men, they had nothing to say of duke's men, earl's men, and nabob's men, because these were for the most part Whigs. The Whig lords sent their own men to the House of Commons and thought it the best of all possible representative systems. Rotten boroughs were, as the Duke of Richmond said, "the very sink of corruption"; but since they were owned largely by Whigs, they escaped censure. "Very few men of great families and extensive connections," Burke said, "but will feel the smart of a cutting reform, in some close relation, some bosom friend, some pleasant acquaintance, some dear political dependant" — and Burke was resolved to spare the Whig magnates that bereavement. He would not lay violent hands upon private property, even when that property was a rotten borough.

Burke's program was intended to achieve economy as much as reform. During the war France set Great Britain an example of frugality and economy in finance. The "patriot king," Louis XVI, had consented to reduce the expenses of his court, and Necker sought to carry on the war without new taxes. Economy was the watchword in France. "For God's sake," exclaimed Burke, "let not this be the only fashion of France which we refuse to copy." In Great Britain, change was long overdue; inefficiency, waste, and graft ate up millions of pounds and the national debt increased apace. "Death," Burke asserted, "indeed, domineers over every thing, but the forms of the Exchequer. Over these he has no power. They are impassive and immortal."

Lord North stoutly opposed any substantial reform: he stood pat on the British Constitution, declaring that "every attempt to improve it, put in mind of the epitaph on the tombstone of the famous Italian valetudinarian: 'I was well, I would be better, I took physick — and died.' " As long as he remained Prime Minister, the country surely was in no danger of dying of an overdose of liberalism.

Besides the Whigs, there was a small group of radicals in Great Britain

[6] In Burke's opinion, there were no more dangerous reformers than the starry-eyed visionaries who sought to make the world over in twenty-four hours; by attempting to accomplish too much, they succeeded in nothing. He approved of the American revolutionaries because he thought the mother country was in the wrong and because he regarded them as conservative reformers. Reform in order to conserve was the principle upon which he acted.

who upheld the American cause. John Horne Tooke, Dr. Richard Price, and Joseph Priestley — all of whom had been clergymen at one time in their careers — went far beyond the Whigs in their zeal to give the Americans the blessings of liberty. Price ardently supported the American revolutionists as advance agents of the rights of man throughout the world. "I think it one of the most important revolutions that has ever taken place in the world," he declared. "It makes a new opening in human affairs which may prove an introduction to times of more light and liberty and virtue than have been yet known." He was even prepared to liquidate the British Empire upon the principle that "all dominion of one country over another is usurpation and tyranny." In England's misfortunes in the American war he and his fellow radicals saw a wholesome chastisement that might lead England to the pursuit of liberty instead of empire. Accordingly, they kept the rebels informed of British troop movements and the plans of the Ministry; and so well did they do this work that Sir William Howe complained that he could keep no secrets from the rebels if he sent information home. No doubt this was the reason why Howe imposed a blackout of news upon his movements, even to the extent of keeping the British Ministry in the dark.

For abetting the rebellion, Tooke landed in prison. A renegade clergyman of the Church of England, onetime friend of John Wilkes and founder of several radical organizations in Great Britain, he undertook in 1775 to raise one thousand pounds for the relief of the widows, orphans, and parents of the Americans who had fallen at Lexington and Concord, "inhumanly MURDERED by the King's Troops." Tooke was charged with libel against the King and the British army; but far from recanting when brought to trial, he declared that Lexington belonged in the criminal rather than the military annals of Great Britain — it was, he said, nothing less than "a premeditated massacre" in which English soldiers "plunged their swords into the bosoms of unarmed peasants." He tried to call witnesses to prove his contention that actual murder was done at Lexington, summoning Lord Germain, General Gage, and other high-ranking officials and military men. The witnesses refused to appear and Tooke was found guilty and given a year in jail to reconsider the right and wrong of the American Revolution.

Lest they be known by the company they kept, the Whigs dissociated themselves from all activities of the radicals. Burke branded them as "*visionary* politicians" who aspired to overthrow the English Constitution; for the Americans, Burke had good will, but toward the English radicals he bore the fear and antipathy which he was later to reveal toward the French revolutionists.

The meager measure of reform proposed by Burke did not satisfy the radicals or even many of the rank and file of the Whig Party. Finding that the Whig leaders had failed them, these liberals began to organize a reform movement of their own. They borrowed heavily from the American revolutionists, calling county conventions, appointing committees of correspondence, and summoning a general meeting of the committees in London which bore a disquieting resemblance to the Continental Congress. And their demands — annual Parliaments, extension of the franchise, and sweeping changes in the system of representation — seemed to herald a revolution in Great Britain hardly less democratic than that which had taken place in the United States. The authority of Parliament was threatened: the committees declared that no trust could be placed in that venal body ready to sell itself to the highest bidder, whether the King or the Whig lords.

Hoping that this might prove to be the long-delayed English revolution, Benjamin Franklin began to prepare to ship arms from France to the English committees. But Burke and most of the Whigs, alarmed by the specter of revolution they saw rising in England, disavowed the committees and the London Congress; as Burke said, they wanted to change the constitution whereas he wished only "a correction of it in the form in which it now stands." Charles James Fox, on the other hand, enthusiastically threw himself into the movement for reform, hailing the committees as proof that the spirit of Englishmen was not yet extinct. Fox addressed the Westminster committee — playing for the support of the rabble, said the Tories, in the hope of bringing back the days of Cromwell.

Meanwhile the Whigs pursued their time-honored policy of diverting popular discontent against the overweening power of the Crown. In April 1780, Dunning, a Whig member of Parliament, introduced a motion to the effect that "the influence of the Crown had increased, was increasing and ought to be diminished" — and the motion passed "the most corrupt and Tory Parliament that ever was" by a majority of eighteen votes. Stung by this defeat, the King's forces quickly rallied, the Whigs' program of reform was voted down, and Dunning's resolution remained unimplemented. "Had there ever been a circumstance so paradoxical," asked Fox, "as a parliament resolving that the influence of the crown ought to be diminished, without being able to effect a diminution?" Fox threatened to leave Parliament and to appeal directly to the people, but before he could carry out this plan, the reform movement had suffered a major reverse at the hands of Lord George Gordon and his gin-crazed "Protestants."

The Lord George Gordon riots temporarily put an end to the reform movement in Great Britain and strengthened the hands of the government. Dread of the rule of the mob became stronger than the fear of the King's influence over Parliament; Englishmen preferred to put up with the shortcomings of their political system rather than risk an uprising of "the dregs of mankind." The men of property who heretofore had been on the side of popular liberty were appalled by the violence and brutality that had welled up from the bottom of society; they now feared that liberalism might lead to the destruction of the monarchy and the establishment of "some wild scheme of Democratical government." Against popular lawlessness, the monarchy began to appear as a barrier. In short, reform was smeared with the Lord George Gordon riots, and in this unlovely guise it was forced to make its way among the English people.

As a result, conservatives and liberals began to close ranks against the "mobility": even John Wilkes and the King became chummy. At the royal levee, the King thanked Wilkes for his part in putting down the riots and inquired solicitously about his health. "To have heard the king," Wilkes later remarked, "one would have thought I was consulting a quack on the score of my health." Parliament was prorogued without acting upon Dunning's resolution, and the people who had signed petitions requesting that the King's power be abridged seemed thoroughly satisfied that Parliament had let the matter drop.[7]

Reflecting this changed temper of the English people, the general election of 1780 strengthened the position of the Ministry in Parliament: it was the Whigs who suffered a purge, not the Tories. It is true, however, that the Crown spent over one hundred thousand pounds in paying the expenses of government candidates, in buying boroughs from the borough-mongers, and in the other incidentals of purchasing a loyal Parliament. The King was staggered by the expense (it was twice as much as he had spent in any other general election) but Lord North blamed the Whig magnates who, he claimed, had hotly contested many boroughs with the Crown. Yet the King could hardly say that he had not got his money's worth: the administration was assured of a majority of well over one hundred members. Unless the war went badly, Lord North need not worry about Parliament; it was secure in the royal pocket.

Meanwhile, all that the English people seemed to be getting out of the war was taxes and yet more taxes: taxes on land, beer, wine, carriages, servants; stamp duties — everything, in short, that could be conveniently converted into a source of revenue. The war was not wholly financed, however, upon a pay-as-you-go basis: almost one hundred million pounds was added to the national debt by borrowing, leading Franklin to remark

[7] It was not until 1782, when the Whigs finally attained power, that Burke's program of reform was enacted. It is significant that many retrenchments which Burke and the Whigs had thought indispensable when they were in opposition were abandoned when they gained office. Even so, the power of the Crown to grant pensions, places, and jobs to political supporters was seriously impaired; among the casualties was Edward Gibbon, who lost his seat at the Board of Trade and was thereby given more leisure to devote to his history. But the influence of the King was far from destroyed; and the younger William Pitt, as Prime Minister, looked to the Crown for support much as had Lord North.

in 1780 that the national debt hung like "a Millstone upon the Neck of their Credit, and must ere long sink it beyond Redemption." Nevertheless, the credit of the British government remained the envy of Americans; and far from collapsing, it saw Britain handsomely through the war. Great Britain, prophets of doom to the contrary, had the longest purse in the world.

Having scraped through two invasion scares, Englishmen began to feel that they could take anything the Bourbon allies, together with the Americans, could offer. The coalition arrayed against England suffered, it was now clear, from all the weaknesses inherent in such marriages of convenience — and from this Englishmen might take comfort. And lastly, the cautious, apathetic war waged by the allies encouraged Englishmen to despise their enemies. "We seem to be able to cope with France," remarked Horace Walpole, "who makes war in our own piddling style. . . . It is a pickpocket war, and not a martial one and I never attend to petty larceny. . . . Numerous as our foes are, they certainly are very awkward. . . . We have done nothing that signifies a straw; but they have done less."

For some Englishmen, the war proved a bonanza; contractors, ship-owners, and merchants grew rich purveying to the armed forces. Taking advantage of the necessities of the state was not thought beneath the dignity even of members of Parliament; so many contractors sat in Parliament that it was said by a wit that giving a contract to any person except a member was a breach of privilege. Supplying drugs and medicine to the army was a monopoly held by the Apothecary General, his heirs or his assigns. The Paymaster of the British Forces, who held the most lucrative position in the government, was permitted to appropriate the interest on all moneys that passed through his hands. This netted him twenty thousand pounds a year; but Rigby, the fortunate incumbent during the War of the American Revolution, could not resist the opportunity to turn a dishonest penny on the side, with the result that when he left office at the close of the war there was a shortage of several hundred thousand pounds in his accounts. In the army itself, a few quartermasters, barrack masters, and commissaries made fortunes by fraud: they bought supplies at low prices and sold them to the government at exorbitant prices, using their positions to write the terms of their own contracts. With justice, British soldiers complained that they were being exploited by "the great men, who only want to fill their purses . . . to make hay while the Sun shineth."

Moreover, during the war, England experienced a crime wave notable even in the eighteenth century. Highway robbery, house-breaking, counterfeiting, and murder had rarely been more frequent; George Selwyn, one of the wits of the period, declared that he was "more struck with the terror of these insurgents than with any at a greater distance."

Although more than three hundred different crimes were declared punishable by death, fear of the gallows did little to dissuade Englishmen from a life of crime; on the contrary, it was said that "the procession and execution of criminals at Tyburn is considered as a kind of fair, and the frequent repetition of them so much hardens the unthinking multitude to them, that when it comes to their turn, it is only like playing a part that they have seen often rehearsed." When Lee, a notorious highwayman, was brought to the place of execution, he was dressed in a crimson suit with a gold-laced hat "which he pulled off to a young woman in a hackney-coach, genteely dressed in white, in Holborn, who immediately burst into tears." So brazen were these criminals that on a hanging day pickpockets practised their calling, punishable by death, in the shadow of the gallows. The Duke of Richmond declared that there was less danger "in passing the outpost of a besieged town than in making a visit a mile off" in England.

It was frequently pointed out that Englishmen did not allow the threat of a Bourbon invasion to upset unduly their round of pleasures. They took the danger so coolly, indeed, that some Englishmen suspected that their countrymen were too immersed in the delights of balls, theaters, and entertainments to pay proper heed to the perils that surrounded them. "Were you here," wrote Horace Walpole from London, "you would not be alarmed. You would see no panic; you would hear of nothing but diversions." All the disasters of the war, it was remarked, had not made "an alteration in the receipt at the door of a single theatre in London." An Englishman who toured the watering places while the French and Spanish fleets were riding the Channel declared that "from the extravagance, profusion, and luxury that prevailed there amongst all ranks of people, I should have been inclined to have believed that we were in the most certain security from any foe. . . . Whenever I spoke to a fine gentleman in the rooms of the present distressed state of affairs, he would say, 'I am no politician. I am just going to cut in, will you make one?' " When all other arguments failed, Englishmen fell back upon the comforting faith that "Providence has always saved us" and would do it again — "which argument, I suppose," said Horace Walpole, "is built on this simple hypothesis, that God made Great Britain, and the devil all the rest of the world."

The life of pleasure to which many Englishmen, particularly the upper class of the metropolis, had surrendered themselves led some observers to fear that England would be undone as much by its vices as by its enemies. While admitting that he was a true Englishman and therefore much more easily dissatisfied than pleased, Horace Walpole pronounced Great Britain to be "the sink of Europe," and lost almost beyond hope of redemption — "we shall moulder away piecemeal into our insignificant islandhood." Richard Price compared the manners and morals of Great

Britain with those of the United States and drew the moral that such debased creatures as Englishmen could never conquer the virtuous republicans in the colonies. "From one end of *North America* to the other," he pointed out, "they are FASTING and PRAYING. But what are we doing? — We are ridiculing them as *Fanatics,* and scoffing at religion — we are running wild after pleasure, and forgetting every thing serious and decent at Masquerades — We are trafficking for Boroughs; perjuring ourselves at Elections; and selling ourselves for places — which side then is Providence likely to favour?" It is possible that Price, had he been able to visit the United States in the grip of inflation and pleasure-seeking, would not have been quite so certain as to the designs of Providence.

Although the government could boast of few victories since 1777 over the rebels, it was far from discouraged by the posture of affairs in North America. For Americans, having fought the British army to a standstill, seemed on the verge of internal collapse. In its efforts to subjugate the republic, Great Britain found potent allies in the decline of nationalism and in the paralysis wrought by inflation in the United States.

AMERICANS distrusted all government but, above all, they feared centralized government. They established weak and inefficient state governments, yet they could with difficulty bring themselves to tolerate any national government whatever. It was from necessity rather than from choice that they consented to a central government; for the most part, their affections remained with their states.

The union under which Americans fought the Revolutionary War was created largely by British "tyranny." Before the British government undertook, with fatal results, to remodel the empire, the colonies were, in Thomas Paine's words, "a mere chaos of uncemented colonies." As recently as 1754 they had rejected a plan of union drawn up by Benjamin Franklin, designed to pool their strength and resources against the French and Indians. There was little thought, in the colonies, of forming an enduring union until they were brought together in 1765 under the slogan "No taxation without representation."

Americans' experience as British colonists had instilled in them a deep prejudice toward centralized government, and their attainment of independence did not weaken this antipathy. They exalted local liberty: the necessity of an efficient central government had to be learned through experience. The memory of their struggle with the British King and Parliament remained fresh in their minds. "Confidence should not wantonly be placed any where," it was said. ". . . It is but the other day, that we thought our liberties secure in the care of *Britain*." And so they snuffed the breeze from Philadelphia as suspiciously as they had tested the wind from Great Britain, resolved to swing into action at the first whiff of tyranny.

The problem of reconciling local liberty with centralized government

— the rock upon which the British Empire had split — now rose to vex Americans in their efforts to establish a government of their own. English statesmen had feared that the American doctrine of local rights would split the British Empire into infinitesimal fragments, each nursing pretensions to sovereignty and striving to undermine the authority of the government at Westminster. For the first thirteen years of existence, the United States seemed to bear out these apprehensions. Left to their own devices, Americans put their faith in liberty rather than in authority, and in local rights rather than in strong centralized government. They loved liberty more than they did empire; and to attain liberty they were willing to sacrifice even national greatness.

Among the warmest advocates of American independence were often found the foremost champions of states' rights. The first to urge war and separation from Great Britain, they were often the last to acknowledge the necessity of a strong central government, by which alone the war could be waged effectively. They were radicals as regards American rights against the mother country, but conservatives in their determination to suffer no diminution of the sovereign rights of the American states. Although acknowledging the necessity of union, at least for the duration of the war, they sought to keep that union as nebulous as possible. They sometimes seemed to regard the purpose of the Revolution as not only to win independence of Great Britain but to achieve the independence of the states from each other. Sam Adams, for example, declared in 1775 that each state "is and ought to be the sovereign and uncontrollable power within its own limits or territory." To Adams, the Revolution was above all a struggle for liberty, and this primary objective, he felt, ought never to be subordinated to the goal of creating a nation. "Patriotism in America," said a patriot of this school, "must always be partial to the particular States. Patriotism to the whole will never be cherished or regarded, but as it may be conducive or necessary to the other. . . . The virtue most cultivated will be that which will most distinguish a man in the State in which he resides. The grandeur and preeminence of that State will be the favorite passion of every man in it." "My affections still flow in what you will deem their natural order," said a New England patriot; " — towards Salem, — Massachusetts, — New England, — the Union at large." Patriotism, it can be seen, began at home and never strayed far from one's immediate surroundings.

Independence was declared before Congress seriously turned its attention to the problem of confederation. In the race between independence, foreign alliances, and confederation, confederation came out a bad third despite the opinion of many patriots that it ought to take precedence over all others. "Unless we confederate, we perish"; "We must apply for pardons if we don't confederate," were phrases frequently heard in 1775 and 1776. Everyone agreed that confederation was necessary, but when it came to determining the character and scope of the proposed union, agreement abruptly ended.

There was no dearth of plans of union. Franklin, who had drawn up such a plan for the British colonies in 1754, was the first to submit his ideas to Congress, but confederation in 1775 was judged premature and Franklin's views were too nationalistic to please many delegates. Franklin felt little of the pride of state that distinguished most Americans of his generation. A man of the Enlightenment, he took the world, rather than Pennsylvania or Massachusetts, as his province. He had little sympathy with the predilection of his fellow Americans for lavishing their affection and loyalty upon their states: in his eyes, they were Americans first, last, and always, and their only hope of salvation lay in the recognition of this truth.

A plan of union drawn up by John Dickinson in 1776 was rejected for the same reason: it was too national to win the favor of the powerful states' rights element in Congress.[1] The rejection of Franklin's and Dickinson's drafts made clear that the road to confederation was to be rough and thorny, and that the goal was far distant. The debate served to reveal differences of opinion between large states and small states, and between the sectional interests of the North and South, disheartening to the advocates of union. "We have done nothing with the Confederation for some Days," wrote a dismayed congressman in August 1776, "and it is of little Consequence if we never see it again, for we have made such a Devil of it already that the Colonies can never agree to it." Congress, it began to be feared, had been guilty of presumption in declaring the United States independent before a formal union had been achieved.

One of the most formidable obstacles to union was the fact that the states were of varying sizes, with more than half the population concentrated in the four largest states. State loyalty and pride burned as fiercely in the small states as in the great, and their citizens felt keenly the dangers of entering into a close union with the larger states. Lest they be swallowed up by their more powerful neighbors, the small states required guarantees that their sovereign rights would be respected. In particular, the smaller states demanded equality with the larger states in representation in Congress. Every state, they declared, ought to have the same number of votes, regardless of its population or wealth, in order to prevent the weaker members of the confederacy from falling victim to the aggrandizement of the strong. "Like another *Sparta*, may this little State be wise, and brave, and great," exclaimed a citizen of Delaware, ". . . holding its rank with unimpaired dignity in the scale of AMER-

---

[1] Dickinson's plan was more friendly to the sovereignty of the states than was Franklin's proposed union. For example, according to Franklin's draft, taxation and representation of the states in Congress were to be based upon population; Dickinson conceded that each state was to have an equal vote.

ICAN EMPIRE." Much of the debate over the Articles of Confederation represents an effort by the smaller members of the union to achieve
security against their larger, presumably aggressive partners.

On the other hand, the large states refused to enter into any scheme
which did not give due weight to their numbers. The effect of any other
arrangement would, they pointed out, whittle them down to "pygmy
size" and make it possible for a few small states, containing not more than
two hundred thousand people, to frustrate the will of three millions.
Representation on the basis of population meant majority rule, which to
the large states was the essence of republicanism. But to the small members of the confederation, majority rule was merely another name for
tyranny: they shrank from application of this principle as they had shrunk
from British oppression, and they insisted that the paramount concern
of any central government in the United States ought to be the protection of the rights of minorities.

Nationalists like Benjamin Franklin wished to see population made the
criterion of the number of representatives sent by each state to the
Continental Congress. "We are now a new nation . . . we represent the
people," said Benjamin Rush. "We have been too free with the word independence: we are dependent on each other, not totally independent
States." In his opinion, to give the states equal representation in Congress
would make the confederation a union of states rather than of individuals
and thereby defeat every hope that Americans would present a united
front to the world. Franklin suggested that if the smaller states wanted
equality in voting, they ought to contribute men and money to the
central government equally with the large states. "If they have an equal
vote without bearing equal burthens," he warned, "a confederation upon
such iniquitous principles will never last long."

To break the deadlock between the large and small states, Jefferson in
1777 proposed a compromise — looking forward to the solution finally attained in the Federal Constitution of 1787 — which would have created a
Senate in which the states enjoyed equality and a House of Representatives in which representation was determined by population. But Congress rejected all compromises which necessitated the creation of two
houses in the legislature. Instead, at the instigation of the small states, a
plan was adopted whereby each state, regardless of size or population, was
given an equal vote in Congress. The small states had triumphed: in the
Continental Congress, Rhode Island carried as much weight as Virginia.

Actually, however, the real danger to the stability of the union lay not
in the struggle between large and small states, but in the friction between
the sections that composed the United States. It had long been apparent
that the states, large and small, tended to group themselves into sectional
bodies, particularly the Northern and Southern interests. The American
union was an alliance of sections as well as a league of states. As early as

1778, Southerners were speaking of "the honor, interest and sovereignty of the south" as menaced by the North.

In 1776, Congress was riding the crest of its power; at no time during the war did it enjoy greater prestige and authority than at the beginning of the struggle. Its laws were enforced by hundreds of committees, the people looked to it for leadership, and its money financed the war effort. It was hailed as "that great luminary that gave light, beauty, warmth, and usefulness to all the colonies." The states were momentarily in eclipse. "What need for all this costly parade of governors, councils, and privy councils," it was asked; was it not wiser to concentrate power in a national government? When Rhode Island was threatened with attack, the governor of that state proclaimed that "every idea of partial and colonial defence ought to be given up. There was to be a supreme, superintending power, to exert and direct the force of the whole, for the safety and defence of all." Yet it was Rhode Island that five years later refused to give Congress the revenue that alone could make it function as a "supreme, superintending power."

The power and prestige of the Continental Congress soon reached a point alarming to the champions of states' rights. By failing to take advantage of the flood tide of nationalism, the friends of a strong central government in effect lost the battle: by 1777, when the Articles of Confederation were adopted by Congress, the tide had turned and states' rights were again in ascendancy.

It is significant that Congress drew up the Articles of Confederation without benefit of public discussion. Although it was suggested that a constitutional convention be called to frame a form of government, the Continental Congress refused to step aside; together with conducting the war, directing foreign policy, and settling the finances of the country, this overworked body drafted a plan of government for the United States.

The defect of the Articles of Confederation which prevented them from ever becoming an effective bond of union for the country was that the states were left sovereign in most essentials. The kernel of the Articles is contained in the second article, which provides that "each State retains its sovereignty, freedom and independence, and every power, jurisdiction, and right which is not by this confederation expressly delegated to the United States in Congress assembled." From this it can be seen that the United States began as a league of nations; the halting efforts that the world is making in the twentieth century to achieve a workable and enduring union were forecast by the experiences of the United States in the eighteenth and nineteenth centuries.[2]

---

[2] Often Americans did not think of themselves as one people, but as allies waging war against a common enemy. For example, a South Carolina patriot remarked in 1782 that there were at that time twenty states allied against Great Britain — the thirteen states of America and the seven nations of Europe at war with or contesting

Congress was given authority to make war and peace; but without the aid of the states, it was unable to wage war effectively. Congress could borrow money but it had no assured sources of income with which to repay its loans. State authority was evidenced everywhere: courts, magistrates, and civil officials taught the people to look to the states for justice, law, and protection, but Congress had virtually no officials to give visible embodiment to its authority.[3]

One of the cardinal shortcomings of the Articles of Confederation was that Congress was given no authority to tax. The power of levying taxes was reserved exclusively to the states; and although Congress could make requisitions upon the states for money, it had no means of coercing recalcitrant states into doing their duty. It has been said that the Articles of Confederation conferred on Congress the privilege of asking everything, and secured to each state the prerogative of granting nothing.

The same forces that had weakened the power of Parliament and the Crown in the British Empire now militated against the authority of the Continental Congress. Reasons which Americans had found conclusive against paying requisitions to the British Crown were now found equally conclusive against paying requisitions to the Continental Congress. Under both the empire and the republic, similar conditions prevailed: a central government menaced local self-determination. Against the British Parliament, in which they were not represented, Americans raised the cry of "No taxation without representation"; but this objection did not apply to the Continental Congress. Fundamentally, Americans were jealous of any superintending authority and averse to paying any taxes to any government other than their own state — and sometimes to that.

To discouraged Congressmen, it seemed at times as though the states deliberately flouted the requisitions of the Continental Congress in order to demonstrate their independent and sovereign status. Upon receiving a requisition from Congress, the state government debated whether or not it would comply; in what manner its compliance, if agreed upon, should be carried out; and when it should take effect — "by which means," exclaimed Washington, "scarcely any one measure is, or can be executed. . . . The contest among the different States *now*, is not which shall do the most for the common cause, but which shall do the least." No revenue could be depended upon with certainty: the states acted as they pleased and, as Robert Morris said, what money they might grant, and when they

---

the maritime claims of Great Britain. By this reckoning, the alliance of Massachusetts and South Carolina was on a par with the alliance of France and Spain.

[3] Congress was also given the power to regulate trade with Indians who were not members of any of the states; to regulate the value of its coinage and that of the states (but it had no control over the emission of paper money by the states) to act as a board of arbitration between one state and another, and between individuals claiming lands under conflicting grants; and to regulate the post office and weights and measures.

might grant it, were "known only to Him who knoweth all things." Sometimes, they even appropriated to their own use funds they had raised under the requisitions of Congress.

There was a strong tendency on the part of the states to conduct private wars with Great Britain rather than to unite their resources in the Continental army and navy. They maintained their own armies, navies, and boards of war; they competed with each other and with the Continental Congress for the available supply of war matériel; they attempted to buy arms and supplies from each other; and, increasingly, they put their own needs first and the necessities of the armed forces of the nation last. Americans had imperfectly learned the lesson that their strength and safety lay in union. To rely for protection exclusively upon the Continental forces was difficult for a people steeped in the traditions of provincialism. A strong army and navy at home, on the other hand, gave assurance to a state that, come what might, it would be saved. In pronouncing the name "The United States," the accent was on "States."

States raided each other's manpower resources to build up their own defenses. In 1776, for example, when South Carolina was unable "to find Men in their province," it recruited troops for home defense in North Carolina and Virginia by offering higher bounties than these states were prepared to pay. In 1778, in the middle of a drive to fill the ranks of the Continental army, it was found that agents from Massachusetts had induced a large number of New Hampshire men to enlist in the service of the Bay State by presenting them with a bounty of five hundred dollars for eight months' service. "We could not get a man after that to enlist," remarked a disgruntled New Hampshire recruiting officer.

Every state except one boasted its own navy. Even more than in the case of the army, the navy fell victim to that dispersal of effort which characterized the conduct of the war by the United States. Thirteen different navies (including that of the United States) plowed the seas or, more exactly, the creeks and sheltered inlets. These navies were composed of a highly miscellaneous collection of barges, galleys, luggers, and sloops, and it was a hardy mariner indeed who trusted himself to these craft beyond comfortable swimming distance from land. Nevertheless, citizens could point with pride to "our navy" and find in it visible embodiment of the sovereignty of their state. Then, too, each state had its own admiralty board which acted in the full panoply of sovereign independence. And each state issued letters of marque and reprisal to privateers — a privilege usually accorded only to independent sovereign nations.

For the most part, the Continental army was composed of separate armies or lines furnished by the respective states. There were thirteen different lines, but all were under the command of general officers appointed by the Continental Congress. Like the Articles of Confederation, the Continental army represented a compromise between the necessity for union and the strong predilection of Americans toward exalting their states.

Even in the Continental army, nationalism was threatened by the rising tide of states' rights feeling. At the beginning of the war, it had been proposed that Congress be given the right of appointing all officers in the Continental army — a measure intended to break down provincial distinctions and make the army truly national. But the champions of states' rights defeated this proposal: instead of Congress, it was the states which appointed for their respective lines all officers below the rank of general. Washington never ceased to regret this "fatal vote of Congress" by which appointments were thrown into the hands of the state legislatures, notoriously partial to the military pretensions of politicians and their nominees.

In the later stages of the war, there was grave danger that the Continental army would become an assemblage of thirteen different armies, each under the control of its respective state. In 1778, the Continental Congress itself took a long stride in this direction by directing every state to provide arms, ammunition, and clothing to its own line in the Continental army. Thus Congress yielded to the states the powers which made the Continental army truly national.

Frequently the states shared their supplies with the Continental army on a lend-lease basis. But they insisted upon being repaid for such loans; and if the Continental Congress was unable to satisfy them they unceremoniously seized what they wanted. In the summer of 1779, for example, a ship arrived in Virginia carrying arms consigned to the Continental Congress. Because the Continental Congress had never returned to Virginia arms loaned the army by the state, the government of the Old Dominion retained what it conceived to be its just due — an action that was condoned by Governor Thomas Jefferson.

In keeping with their position as independent sovereignties, the states tried to borrow money on their own account in Europe. South Carolina, for instance, instructed its agent in France to procure ships of war, to use the state's credit for the purchase of war supplies, and to raise a foreign legion to serve as a home guard. Here they came into competition with the agents of the Continental Congress. Franklin protested that "the Agents from our different States running all over Europe begging to borrow Money at high Interest, has given such an Idea of our Poverty and Distress as has exceedingly hurt the general Credit" and placed new obstacles in the way of securing loans. At least three states applied to the French government for arms, ammunition, and clothing; and when they were turned down, they asked Franklin to intervene on their behalf. But Vergennes declined to deal with separate states; he sought to strengthen the central government of the United States, not to encourage the already too powerful centrifugal forces at work in the republic.

As a result, these agents procured little for the states in the way of supplies or loans of money. The states were usually ill served by their representatives — hardly surprising in view of the fact that, as Franklin said, the states made a practice of putting their faith "in every Adventurer, who pretended to have Influence here, and then when he arrived, had none but what our Appointment gave him." The agent appointed by Virginia to borrow money at the court of France ended by going broke and absconding from his creditors, leaving Franklin to pay the bills. Pennsylvania sent a local politician abroad whose conduct in Paris aroused grave doubts as to his sanity.

⌢ ⌢ ⌢

Congressmen were swamped with work: in many ways, an election to that body was equivalent to a sentence at hard labor. Compared with Congress, exclaimed a distraught member, the army was "a Bed of Ease, a Pillow of Down"; no matter how hard they worked or how long hours they put in, congressmen were always behind in their work. For the most part, they were bogged down in drudgery and "worn out by business that could be much better done by clerks." Committee meetings began at six in the morning and ran far into the night. Some members broke down under the strain of hard work and late hours. Gouverneur Morris declared that he got no exercise from one week to another except walking from his house to the State House and back again, a distance of about fifty yards. "My constitution sinks under this and the heat of this pestiferous Climate," he cried out, but because Congress met throughout the year, there was no relief from this burden but to plead ill health and go off on a vacation. Many members adopted this course, spending the winter at home and returning to Philadelphia in the spring with the swallows.

No member of Congress was more overworked than James Lovell, who for many months was the only member of the Committee of Foreign Affairs, his colleagues having resigned or gone home for long vacations. Lovell's industry was a marvel to his colleagues. "He writes Morning, Noon and Night," reported Elbridge Gerry, "sickens once a Fortnight, and devotes a Day to Sleep, after which, like the Sun from behind a Cloud, he makes his Appearance with his usual Splendor." As long as his strength held out, Lovell conducted the foreign affairs of the United States as well as could be expected of one man, although he complained particularly of the perpetual stream of visitors who knocked at his door, "except indeed Foreigners," he said, "who give nobody the Trouble of asking 'who is there,' but bolt into your Bed Room." Midnight, he found, "only is Secure for drawing up Reports" — which was hard on a man who had to be up betimes to attend his multitudinous duties in Congress.

It should be supposed that these overburdened and harassed statesmen were so borne down by the cares of office as to leave no time for relaxation. John Hancock, the President of Congress, lived a gay life in Philadelphia, dining out with the best people, drinking the best wine, and dazzling his contemporaries with the splendor of his table and the prodigality of his parties.[4] His career in Philadelphia compelled many people to revise their ideas of New Englanders. Benjamin Harrison of Virginia found the girls of Philadelphia not unkind; he had, he wrote Washington, made a date with "little Kate the Washerwoman's Daughter over the way, clean, trim & rosy as the morning," and added that he would "relish a Week's longer stay," if she should keep the tryst.

The mills of the Continental Congress ground slowly, and although wordy congressmen furnished plenty of grist, the yield in actual legislation was small. Members eager to get on with business were often mortified by the dilatoriness of their colleagues. Charles Carroll of Maryland pronounced Congress "a weak assembly, fond of talking, and not much addicted to thinking"; and Gouverneur Morris complained that congressional proceedings were distinguished by "such exquisite tediousness of Debate, that the most precious Moments pass unheeded away like vulgar Things." The only occasion when Congress acted swiftly, it was observed, was when it was ignorant of the subject: a smattering of knowledge was almost always fatal to celerity. "If you could submit to spend a whole life in dissecting a fly," exclaimed an impatient patriot, "you would be in their opinion one of the greatest men in the world." Congress sometimes spent as much as three months in framing a recommendation to the states; and the states might take six months more in approving or rejecting the proposal.

Throughout the war, Congress worked behind a veil of secrecy: the doors of the State House were barred to visitors, and every congressman took an oath not to reveal debates or proceedings which a majority decided ought to be kept secret. So strictly was this rule enforced that congressmen could not even consult with their states upon pending legislation. While under discussion by Congress, the Articles of Confederation were not laid before the people: only a sufficient number of copies of the proposed form of government were printed for the members of Congress. Little information of what was going on in Congress was to be gleaned by the public from the Journals printed by Congress. At first the yeas and nays were printed in the Journals, but this practice was soon abandoned on the ground that "the enemy learned from them that Congress were not so unanimous as it was politic in us to make them believe." And for two years — from 1777 to 1779 — the publication of the Journals was sus-

---

[4] Hancock was president of Congress from May 1775 to October 1777.

pended, with the result that the workings of Congress were "as unknown to their constituents as the edicts of the Great Mogul." Little effort was made by Congress to give publicity to its resolves; the art of press-agentry was sadly neglected by the revolutionary statesmen.

The secrecy with which Congress invested itself struck many Americans as a denial of the liberties for which they were fighting. "What is the use of a *freedom in speech*," it was asked, "without a *freedom of hearing?*" Even in Great Britain — "that land of the most newfangled oppression and slavery" — such inroads upon the rights of the people were not tolerated. Jefferson asserted that Congress, by denying the people information, was undermining its own authority. "Our people, merely for want of intelligence which they may rely on, are become lethargic and insensible of the state they are in." Nevertheless, every effort to admit the public to the debates of Congress failed of success.[5]

As the struggle went on, a serious falling-off in the quality of members of the Continental Congress began to be noted. "The great men who composed our first council," declared Alexander Hamilton, "are they dead, have they deserted the cause, or what has become of them?" The answer in most cases was that they had returned to their states to make their political fortunes at home.

In the eyes of ambitious state leaders, the Continental Congress had become little better than the graveyard of reputations; prominent men frequently declined to accept seats in Congress, preferring to display their talents upon the local stage. Service in Congress was regarded as "thankless bondage" and few were willing to do time in the State House in Philadelphia when they might be feathering their political nests at home. As Secretary of Foreign Affairs, Livingston found his salary woefully insufficient, his estate dwindling as he dipped even deeper into his capital, and his only hope of repairing his fortune, political and otherwise, in his own state "where," he said, "I have something to hope from my connexions and the favor of my countrymen." Even the office of President of Congress went begging in 1781, only one member being found willing to accept the honor.

Congress was reluctant to summon public opinion to its support against the states; it stood in awe of those sovereignties from which, by the usually accepted theory of the times, it derived its being. Congress itself helped to cast a blight upon the nascent nationalism in the United States. In every

---

[5] During the war, news consisted in large part of rumors and fabrications, sometimes deliberately manufactured by speculators to serve their purposes. To protect the people, Washington wished to purchase a small portable press to be used in issuing communiqués from headquarters. This, he pointed out, would give Americans trustworthy as well as "speedy and exact information of any Military transactions that take place with proper comments upon them." But this suggestion was never carried out; perhaps Congress, in its jealousy of the army, did not choose to put Washington too directly in the limelight.

crisis, it hesitated between addressing the states with "decisive plainness" or with the humility due sovereigns; and usually it chose the side of humility. Instead of combating vigorously the encroachments of the states, it surrendered its authority tamely. In April 1777, Congress resolved that all sovereign power was in the states separately, enumerated powers alone belonging to Congress, and that "in all things else each State would exercise all the rights and power of sovereignty, uncontrolled." Congress acted within the boundaries marked out by the Articles of Confederation, but the states in return steadily encroached upon its authority, leaving it in the end a thing of shreds and tatters.

෴ ෴ ෴

In the decline of American nationalism, Englishmen found much comfort; but they rejoiced in an even more powerful ally in their war against the United States — financial chaos. Where British armies had failed, inflation might succeed; in 1779, a Hessian officer declared that the collapse of American currency was worth forty thousand men to the British. Lord North's flagging courage was bolstered by the rebels' distress. "Thinking men in this situation," he remarked, "will be inclined to peace on just and reasonable terms." Lord George Germain, to whom was given an invincible optimism, composed himself for the expected news that the rebellion had ended in financial wreck. Loyalist propagandists delighted to remind Americans that they were as good as bankrupt. "Your grain, your tobacco, your produce of every kind, your cattle and lumber," they told the patriots, "must go for vile paper dollars, which are no better than so many old rags!" The phrase "not worth a Continental" promised to become the epitaph of the short-lived American republic.

"America is safe, but from the damned Situation of our Money," exclaimed the patriots. "Every Person seems afraid of it." The failure of the people to support their own money constituted, to Washington's mind, the greatest danger to the American cause and occasioned him more despondency than did British victories. "We now stand upon the brink of a precipice from whence the smallest help plunges us headlong," he asserted in May 1779. "At this moment, *our Money does but pass*."

No less alarming was the change which had come over the American people: the spirit of '76 seemed to have almost wholly vanished from the land. "In every town on the continent," said Henry Laurens in 1778, "luxury flourishes as it would among a people who had conquered the world, and were about to pay for their victories, by their decline." "Virtue and patriotism are almost kicked out," lamented Washington. "Stock jobbing, speculating, engrossing, &c. &c. seems to be the great business of the day, and of the multitude, whilst a virtuous few struggle, lament, and suffer in silence, tho' I hope not in vain." To the dismay of these patriots, it began to appear that the American people confused the pursuit of happiness with the pursuit of dollars.

How the United States reached this lamentable state of affairs requires some explanation.

In order to finance their war for freedom, Americans had early resorted to paper money. As British colonists, they had become familiar with this medium of exchange, having frequently used paper money for war purposes in the struggle between France and England for mastery of the North American continent. But Americans printed money in peace as well as war — and in so doing ran foul of powerful interests in the mother country. Because they insisted upon paying their debts to British merchants with depreciated colonial paper money, the British government in 1764 prohibited the provincial governments from emitting paper money to be used as legal tender. There was an immediate outcry of "tyranny" in the colonies, but the law stood and Americans were obliged to get along with the meager stock of hard money they were able to scrape together in the course of trade.

To raise and equip armies against the mother country, the Continental Congress began in 1775 to print paper money. This was fiat money; outside its treasury, Congress might have hung this sign: "Gold and silver have we none, but our supply of paper is unlimited." For, although Congress issued millions of dollars in paper money, its coffers were bare of specie; and its paper money had no backing other than its promise to exchange paper for gold and silver at some future time. To give currency to this paper, Americans were expected to invoke their patriotism and their confidence in the future financial stability of the republic. Certainly, the only security offered by Congress was its good name and the purity of its intentions: that the British might win the war and thereby turn all its money into waste paper was a chance taken by every person who handled it.

Paper money was an easy way of financing the war — too easy, in fact, for Americans' own good. Literally, it was a case of from rags to riches; for, as long as the supply of rags held out, the presses could produce the money. Americans were struck by "the Charm of converting a piece of paper not worth a farthing into a 30 dollar bill" — here was another of those wonder-working providences which proved that Heaven was on the patriots' side.

Paper money was the course of least resistance; printing presses became the "Peru and Mexico" of the United States, and the success of this makeshift system led Congress to postpone until too late the establishment of a sound financial structure. It built a house of paper — and inflation blew it down.[6]

---

[6] Some of the earlier issues assigned a definite date for the exchange of paper for silver or gold, but even this slender comfort was omitted by Congress after 1776.

With perhaps one third of the population hostile or indifferent to the cause of American independence, it was inevitable that paper money should be distrusted in many quarters. Yet few individuals dared refuse it: the patriot committees had a way of dealing with recalcitrants that quickly brought them to think better of turning down a paper dollar. Congress declared that those who refused to give currency to its money were to be treated as public enemies, and Washington was of opinion that they ought to be hung. And so paper money circulated — but only so long as the patriots kept their tar and feathers handy.

In the beginning, paper money invigorated and extended the revolutionary movement; in fact, the Revolution made its way partly on the strength of the prosperity this money created. Hard times did not strike the country until the inflation had run its course: while the price spiral was going up, employment, high prices, and prosperity, however fictitious, aided in spreading the revolutionary gospel. It was not until the deflation began, in 1780, that the people as a whole tasted adversity.

With twenty million dollars of Continental notes in circulation, the country was prosperous, and the demands of the army kept production at a high level. Paper money seemed to be the "poor man's friend"; to it were ascribed the full employment and the high price of farm products that prevailed during the first years of the war. By 1778, for example, the farmers of New Jersey were generally well off and rapidly getting out of debt, and farms were selling for twice the price they had brought during the period 1765–1775. Trade and commerce were likewise stimulated; despite the curtailment of foreign trade, businessmen had never been so prosperous. Above all, paper money made it possible to draw forth the resources of the country in support of the war effort; without its aid, it is doubtful whether the war could have been carried on.

In establishing a central government, the states by no means surrendered their financial autonomy to the Continental Congress: as separate sovereignties they insisted upon discretion in money matters. Each state therefore issued its own paper money, thus making fourteen different currencies in the United States; and although Congress asked the states in 1777 to stop printing money and to rely wholly upon Continental money, the request went unheeded. Between these state currencies there was little uniformity: the dollar had different values in relation to gold and silver and was figured in such exotic coins as doubloons, ducats, and pistoles — more suited, one might suppose, for Captain Kidd and the Spanish Main than for prosaic American businessmen and farmers. At first, this money

---

Of this paper money, quotas were assigned to the various states (the amount being determined by their population) with the request that each state "provide ways and means to sink its proportion" — an event which, in the case of the earlier issues, was to be accomplished by 1782.

circulated generally among the states, but before the war was over, every state had moved to protect itself against the depreciated paper of its neighbors. "Rhode Island in particular," observed a New Englander in 1777, "must be watched most narrowly, or she will drown New England with paper." Soon Rhode Island's paper money was not honored outside the state's own borders.

It was owing to paper money that Congress became the financial center of the United States and thereby acquired an importance and influence which had no sanction in the Articles of Confederation. The states looked to Congress as a cornucopia of plenty from which they might draw money to finance the war. The federal government was a rich uncle to thirteen nephews — this happy family group took form from the very beginning of the War of Independence. Every state wished the central government to assume the costs of the war within its borders, on the ground that a national war ought to be paid for by the United States. And Continental paper money alone circulated throughout the country as a whole.

From the beginning of the Revolution, powerful inflationary forces were at work. Inevitably, shortages were produced by the virtual cessation of trade with Great Britain and Europe, and upon these profiteers battened. To compensate for the risks and increased costs of doing business, importers of foreign merchandise began to raise their prices, and every retailer promptly followed suit. "It is incredible," exclaimed a Boston patriot, "what a profit the merchants take on their wares — double is the very least. So if I buy something fourth hand, I can count upon paying almost sixteen times as much as it cost first hand." During 1775, to beat the deadline set by the Continental Congress upon the importation of British manufactures, the merchants bought huge stocks of merchandise which they held until the scarcity had become acute and the people were desperate for goods. Profits as high as 700 per cent over cost were made in this way during the first year of the war. With these profits, the merchants were able "to roll the snowball of monopoly and forestalling"; riches bred riches and prices went ever upward.

Goods were often so scarce that it was comparatively easy to corner the available stock of such articles as clothing, rum, shoes, and the like. In 1777, for example, some Maryland merchants bought up the entire supply of shoes in North Carolina and thereby obliged the government and people to pay exorbitant prices. The demand for merchandise had never been greater; millions of dollars of paper money were in the hands of the people, and the armed forces were buying heavily in the open market. Under these conditions, supply could not match demand.

Never before had American businessmen enjoyed such opportunities of getting rich quick — not through a lifetime of saving and hard work, but as a result of lucky speculations, holding for a rise in the market, cornering the available supplies of commodities, and taking advantage of the public necessities.

Profiteering was not, however, without its hazards: the merchants made immense profits but their victims sometimes reacted violently. For example, Thomas Boylston of Boston, who was reported to be hoarding a hogshead of coffee for a rise in price, found his place of business surrounded by a crowd of men and women who demanded the keys to his warehouse. Boylston stoutly refused to give up his keys; whereupon one of the women "seized him by his neck and tossed him into the cart. Upon his finding no quarter, he declared the keys, when they tipped up the cart and discharged him; then opened the warehouse, hoisted out the coffee themselves, put it into the truck, and drove off." "Poor Boylston was never so swetted since he was born," said a bystander; "he was very roughly handled."

Everything was going up. It required no special business acumen to wax rich in such a market; all that was required was a readiness to gamble in commodities, staking one's fortune on the chance — virtually a certainty — that prices would continue to rise. That this was betting against the welfare of the country seems hardly to have entered the minds of speculators. Because their profits depended upon driving down the value of paper money, they worked ceaselessly to undermine the currency. Yet, as every citizen knew, the fate of American independence was inextricably bound up with paper money. It was the only medium by which the army could be supplied and the soldiers paid. Without paper money, said Washington, there would be "a general crash of all things."

Price fixing had been attempted at the outset of the war by the revolutionary committees which ruled the country during the interregnum between the dissolution of the colonial governments and the creation of the states. In some respects, these revolutionary societies were more powerful than the state governments by which they were succeeded: they became the terror of would-be monopolists who, haled before revolutionary tribunals, were forced to disgorge their hoarded goods and to observe ceiling prices. Price fixing was rigidly enforced by the Committees of Inspection and Observation; and to back up their decrees, there was always the threat of mob action.

This auspicious beginning in price fixing came to an untimely end, however, when the Philadelphia merchants complained to Congress that the inquisitorial practices of the committees were driving trade from the city. Congress came to the aid of the merchants by ordering the committees to halt all price-fixing activities with the exception of those relating to salt. Whereupon the merchants, freed from all restraint, raised prices faster than before. Like the breaking of a dam, the ending of price control in Philadelphia let in "an inundation of rapine and extortion." When

Congress again came to wrestle with the problem of inflation, it had grown to gigantic stature.[7]

The New England states — far more of a nation in themselves than was the United States as a whole — formed a united front against inflation late in 1776. Under the pressure of skyrocketing prices, a convention of delegates from all the states east of the Hudson was held at Providence, Rhode Island. This meeting, needless to say, gave promise of far more effective measures of price control than had hitherto been made by the local committees which up to this time had directed the fight against inflation. From the Providence meeting issued a complete program of price control: a schedule of price ceilings for every commodity and of wage ceilings for almost every occupation was drawn up. Violators were to be regarded as enemies of the country and prosecuted as such in the courts; and one half of the fine imposed upon profiteers was to go to the informer. Thus the first serious trial of price fixing was launched and the entire country waited the outcome of this experiment.

Congress did not at first view kindly this action by the New England states — it smacked too strongly of a usurpation of powers belonging to Congress. But ultimately Congress voted approval of the New England Convention and recommended similar regional meetings to the rest of the country. As a result, a conference of delegates from the Middle states met at York, Pennsylvania, early in 1777 but, as a patriot said, "a *mistaken* principle of leaving trade to regulate itself broke them up without doing anything." Pennsylvania and other states adopted price fixing, but there was no concerted action by the states as a whole to uproot the evil of inflation.

Commodities were generally fixed at prices allowing a generous margin of profit to farmers and merchants: the legislatures acted upon the principle that "where Prices are limited they ought to be generous and to fall in with the avarice of the Times in some Degree in order to check its Progress rather than to attempt the tearing it up by the Roots." For example, an increase of 25 per cent over cost was allowed in Pennsylvania. But even this profit was not sufficient for men who could make up to a 1000 per cent simply by breaking a law — no more a crime in their eyes than was the violation of the Volstead Act to Americans in the 1920's.

It was soon evident that the state governments of the revolutionary period, purposely rendered weak and ineffective by their creators, were utterly incapable of meeting the demands now made upon them. The enforcement of price and wage laws was far beyond their powers; and,

[7] Price fixing was also practised by the British during the war. "No sooner do they get possession of a small island," it was remarked in 1779, "but an ordinance is immediately published, limiting the price of all kinds of produce, manufactory and merchandise."

as a result, attempts at price fixing merely served to teach Americans "the dangerous lesson, that laws may be broken with impunity."

To defeat price fixing, the profiteers were not content to rely upon theoretical arguments drawn from the rights of man or the laws of economics: they adopted the more effective expedient of organizing a black market. In many instances, the merchants and farmers refused to sell at fixed prices, declaring that "none of these articles are to be had: we have all sold out, &c." On the other hand, there was little that could not be bought by slipping a few extra dollars under the counter or by bartering commodities. Trade in the usual sense of the word came to an almost complete halt: few were willing to sell their goods because, expecting price fixing to fail, they intended to unload at inflated prices after controls had been removed.

In Pennsylvania, as a result of efforts to regulate the price of salt, that commodity was driven from the open market and the price rose from one dollar to thirty-six dollars a bushel. "We regulated the price of flour till there was none in the market," lamented a patriot, "and the people were glad to procure it at any price."

But merchants were by no means the only offenders: farmers steadily raised the prices of their products as their confidence in paper money ebbed. In fact, merchants and farmers tried to overreach each other by raising prices — striving to gain the advantage in a price war that raged between town and country.

And so, exclaimed a patriot, Americans came to resemble "the infernals whose character is to devour one another; . . . unless heaven interpose, we shall all turn Sharpers . . . Slaves to the worst of passions, Covetousness." At the beginning of the Revolution, it was pointed out, "no one then even dreamt, that our struggles against the common oppressor would involve us in mutual oppressions of each other."

In Boston, the price war between town and country culminated in an attempt by the farmers to starve the townspeople into lowering prices. Almost as much suffering resulted from this struggle as from the efforts of the British government to reduce the Puritan metropolis by famine through the operation of the Port Act of 1774. The war with Great Britain was almost totally forgotten by Bostonians in their preoccupation with the more vital question of where their next meal was coming from. Benedict Arnold found Boston almost defenseless — "one fifty gun Ship," he said, "might take, Plunder & burn the Town, — which is in the most perfect Security, the only Contest they seem to have is with the Farmers, (abt eggs, butter &c.) who have nearly Starved them."

Soon the markets were so bare that it was said there was more quarreling over a pound of beef "than ever took place at a gambling table." "I doubt whether Egypt, during the seven years of famine," exclaimed a hungry Bostonian, "was in greater distress than this unhappy town." "Our

Farmers are as cruel as Death," groaned a citizen. ". . . They don't consider the suffering sea ports. I believe in General they have no feeling for us, but want all our money, goods, houses & then our selves to be their Servants." "Almost pinched to death by the unreasonable Farmers," many Bostonians were obliged to "set cooled and go with Hungry Bellies." Bostonians exclaimed that they had been brought to this plight "by the rascality of a people, in word only patriotic"; but at the worst, the townspeople were better off than was the Continental army, which, too, was being consigned to starvation by ungrateful and unpatriotic people.

It was a peculiarity of price fixing that one regulation led to another; and instead of solving the problem once and for all, price regulation created a host of new problems which cried out for cure. The states in which regulatory schemes were in force were always outnumbered by those which tolerated unrestricted inflation. States which tried price fixing found that their citizens soon hit upon the expedient of selling goods in neighboring states where price laws did not prevail. Inflation was a national problem and could be attacked successfully only on a national, or regional, scale — certainly not by a single state. By acting alone, a state was almost certain to injure itself and to profit neighboring states where price ceilings did not prevail.

Upon every state where price-fixing laws were in force, a host of speculators descended, "as thick and as industrious as Bees, and as active and wicked as the Devil himself." By buying up commodities for export to states where prices were unregulated, they drained the state of its supplies, deprived the army of necessities, and made fortunes for themselves. In New York, for example, the price of wheat was set at twenty dollars a bushel, whereas in Pennsylvania, where no ceiling was imposed, it reached seventy-five dollars a bushel. The troops in New York might be desperately in need of flour, but there was none for sale at the fixed price which the quartermaster's department was instructed to pay — it had all gone to Pennsylvania. Connecticut, which persisted in price fixing long after it had been abandoned by the other New England states, almost brought ruin upon itself and the Continental army. Although the army largely depended upon Connecticut for beef, and although beef was plentiful in the state, none could be procured at the price established by law: it was either withheld from the market or it went to other states, where it brought high prices in the open market.

Therefore, in order to enforce price ceilings without at the same time driving away business, the states found it necessary to impose embargoes upon the exportation of merchandise beyond their borders. As an invasion of the liberty of the individual, embargoes were highly unpopular among businessmen; moreover, they served only to clog the channels of regular trade and to divert an even larger share of business into the black market. Against the opposition of merchants, embargoes proved unenforceable;

long experienced in running cargoes round the King's customhouse, the merchants now turned their talents to smuggling goods out of the state in defiance of the embargo. For instance, one ship was disclosed to have sailed from Philadelphia contrary to the embargo, carrying three hundred barrels of flour covered over with dirt. And, as a result of these state embargoes, the country was broken up into antagonistic segments which, instead of uniting against Great Britain, waged economic warfare with each other.

In the hope that more laws and stricter enforcement of ceiling prices by the states would cure the evil, Congress recommended to the states that laws be passed for the seizure of all large stores of grain and flour. It was held that possession of such stores could be deemed evidence of an intention to monopolize. In 1779, Congress advised the states themselves to undertake the purchase and export of grain and flour, thus taking this branch of trade entirely out of the hands of private merchants.

To bolster the value of paper money — and thus bring down prices — the states resorted to punitive laws. Before the end of the Revolutionary War, the statute books fairly bristled with pains and penalties to be inflicted upon those guilty of undermining confidence in paper money. In some states, to speak disrespectfully of paper money was to risk punishment as a public enemy. In order to force this money upon recalcitrant creditors, tender laws were enacted by which the mere tender of paper money, no matter how depreciated, sufficed to extinguish the debt. It availed nothing for a creditor to refuse this money: the debtor was free if he succeeded in catching his creditor in an unguarded moment and thrusting the notes upon him. Thus was worked the miracle by which debtors pursued their creditors.

Meanwhile, New Englanders' efforts to combat inflation were proving ineffective because of the refusal by merchants and many farmers to submit to control. Only the town workers enthusiastically supported price control. "The merchant scolds, the farmer growls, and every one seems wroth that he cannot grind his neighbor," said Mrs. John Adams. Eight months after the meeting at Providence, a second conference of delegates from the New England states recommended that the scheme be abandoned and a free economy be restored. The market place had triumphed, and the money-changers drove the politicians from the temple.

By 1778, price fixing, at least in the partial and halfhearted manner in which it had been carried out in the United States, seemed such an unequivocal failure that Congress recommended that the states abandon the scheme. Congress itself moved to exorcise the demon of inflation; two days of every week were devoted to study and debate of the financial crisis. But the evil had long since passed beyond the stage of debate; only vigorous and immediate action could avert disaster.

Labor was not one of the beneficiaries of inflation; on the contrary, the workingman was one of the chief victims of the scourge. Although wages had doubled by 1777, labor was the loser because the cost of living had increased during this same period three and four fold. Caught between the upper and nether millstones — the farmers and the merchants — the town workers experienced in some measure the hardships visited upon American soldiers during the War of Independence.

It is hardly surprising, therefore, that American workmen were restless and prone to strike for higher pay. In eighteenth-century America, skilled labor was scarce and commanded higher wages than anywhere else in the world. Yet, confronted with a steadily rising cost of living, these work-men saw their high wages being undermined by inflation; accordingly, they demanded higher pay, and when it was refused, went out on strike. The gunsmiths of Lancaster County, Pennsylvania, struck in 1776; they won their demands and Americans were soon lamenting the "shocking prices" asked for guns. Laborers working for the government on defense projects walked out when their demands were refused. Carpenters engaged in constructing naval vessels laid down their tools in 1776, declaring that it was better that wealth be "shifted out of the hands of Numbers (who now Possess large Quantities of it) even to ship carpenters, than that they should much longer enjoy it." In 1779, the carpenters at West Point, learning that wages were higher in Philadelphia, struck in protest. Team-sters sometimes refused to transport supplies to the army unless paid in advance — a demand that became increasingly common as the war pro-gressed. Paper money depreciated so rapidly that if payment was long postponed, the money retained only a fraction of the purchasing value it possessed when earned. Labor difficulties ultimately forced the Con-tinental Congress to use enlisted men in the war factories — the civilian workmen, it was said, were "transient, clamorous, ungovernable, and extor-tionate." Yet the soldier workmen soon complained that they were obliged to work for one tenth of the pay given civilians doing the same job.[8]

From the employers' point of view, the workers' demands for higher wages were extortionate. "Wages is so very high, that it raly scares mee every day," exclaimed a merchant in 1776. John Holt, a New York pub-lisher, was so disgusted that he thought seriously of going out of business. "The increasing Wages demanded by my people, without end or Limita-

---

[8] Business enterprise had, from the settlement of the colonies, been sharply curtailed by the high price of labor. As long as land was abundant and cheap, it was almost impossible to keep wages down to a competitive level with those of Great Britain and the European continent. The problem during the colonial period was not how to keep Americans down on the farm, but how to get them to leave their farms for workshops and factories. The early history of American manufacturing is largely the record of a struggle between capitalists and high-priced labor — with the capitalists generally on the losing end. Three attempts were made from 1740 to 1775 to estab-lish a nail factory in New England, but each time the enterprise failed because nails could be imported from Great Britain cheaper than they could be manufactured in the colonies.

tion," he said, "the enormous & continued advance upon every article either for Living or Business, & the great Difficulty in procuring paper & the Distance of bringing it are extremely perplexing." John Adams declared that his salary for four years' service in Congress was insufficient to pay the hire of a farm hand in Massachusetts.

The servant problem — always acute in wartime — for many Americans took the joy out of the frenzied prosperity of the Revolution. Servants went into more profitable lines of work or reflected the spirit of the times by becoming insubordinate and saucy. "There is no person, white or black, old or young, to be had at any price," lamented Christopher Marshall of Philadelphia. A short time later, he shaved himself for the first time in thirty years because his barber "was got so impertinent and extortionate it was time to try." Thomas McKean, Chief Justice of New Jersey, broke the bad news to his wife in this manner: "I have tried to get you a maid, but in vain. I offered 20s. a week but the Jades won't leave Town." The army was stationed near-by and "the Jades" were otherwise engaged.

In Philadelphia, the industrial heart of eighteenth-century America, the workers took the fight against inflation into their own hands. Profiteers had little to fear from governmental control — price ceilings and embargoes could be broken with impunity — but there was still the mob to be reckoned with. It was the Philadelphia mob, composed of artisans, seamen, dock workers, and other victims of the inflation, which in 1779 tried to force down the cost of living by terrorizing businessmen.

Businessmen were not the only object of the townspeople's wrath: their temper was soured by the leniency shown the Tories who had remained in Philadelphia after the British evacuation. Instead of being punished by means of fines, confiscations of property, and prison sentences, many Tories were coddled by the Whigs and permitted to make fortunes by profiteering. Attempts to bring the Tories to book by legal means failed: treason trials ended in acquittals and the worst that the Tories suffered was to be seized by the mob and forced to parade through the streets to the "Rogue's March." The workingmen and small shopkeepers of Philadelphia were not satisfied with such a meager measure of retribution against these internal enemies who stood chargeable with a large part of responsibility for the depreciation of paper money and for the coming of the British army to Philadelphia. There was, therefore, a heavy score to settle with the Tories, and the people saw no way of effecting it except by taking direct action.

Robert Morris, the leading businessman of Philadelphia, combined private profit with patriotism: at the same time that he served his country he served himself, and while he gave unstintingly to the cause, he obliged the country to pay handsomely for his time and effort. As a delegate to Congress he insisted that he still retained his right as a businessman to pursue profit, and he used the inside information gained by serving upon key committees to further his own enterprises. As a result, Morris helped materially to save the Revolution and became, in the process, the richest man in the United States. Apparently he never doubted that patriotism and profiteering were perfectly compatible; certainly he never admitted the conflict or ceased to profiteer because the good of the country required it. To withhold needed supplies in the hope of a rise in price was in Morris's opinion nothing more reprehensible than shrewdness; to sell to the French army and navy for cash while the Continental army, with only paper money to offer, went hungry was to him not discreditable; to gouge the consumer by monopolizing necessities was sanctified in his eyes as "business." The greatest businessman of his times was no moral crusader; without the hope of profit, mankind, in his eyes, was as nothing. Certainly he required copious doses of that particular stimulant.

Morris's enterprises were almost as varied and far-flung as the industrial empires of later American family dynasties. His firm, Willing, Morris and Company traded in Europe, America, and Africa, selling American raw products for European manufactures and war supplies. It was Morris who introduced into the United States such luxuries as the ice house. He was deeply interested in Western lands, mines, and the nascent industries of the United States. His privateers ranged the seas, capturing ships and cargoes and adding to his already swollen wealth. It was said in Philadelphia that if Morris was unduly serious on a Sunday at church it meant that one of his privateers was overdue and not heard from. Like the merchant prince he was, he lived in one of the finest houses in Philadelphia, later occupied by President George Washington when the national capital was located in the Quaker City.

Morris has gone down in history as "the financier of the Revolution," but his contemporaries knew him by a less flattering title. As one of the greatest profiteers in the country, he was anything but a household god to many thousand of American families. As he said during the Revolution, "There never has been so fair an opportunity of making a large fortune since I have been conversant in the World," and he advised his fellow businessmen to make the most of it.

To the unhappy Philadelphians, there seemed no limit on prices short of the sky. The more goods that reached the city, the higher prices soared; when one of Robert Morris's ships arrived in port with a rich cargo, prices rose sharply. "It takes all the country peoples' money to go to the shops with, and all the town peoples' money to go to the markets with," exclaimed a Philadelphian; ". . . I have more money than I ever had, but I am poorer than I ever was."

It had long been predicted that the exactions of the profiteers would "go near to driving the poorer sort to desperation." The plain people of Philadelphia were in no mood to suffer themselves tamely to be "eaten up by monopolizers and forestallers" while they waited for the state to curb the merchants' money-making activities. Taking matters into their own hands, they appointed a Committee of Prices to fix prices in Philadelphia; and in many townships and counties similar committees went into action. Handbills appeared in Philadelphia threatening vengeance upon profiteers. "In the midst of money we are in poverty," they declared, "and exposed to want in a land of plenty. You that have money, and you that have none, down with your prices, or down with yourselves. For by the living and eternal God, we will bring every article down to what it was last Christmas, or we will down those who oppose it."

Ordinarily a well-behaved town, Philadelphia rose in a riot that would have done credit to Boston in its most unruly days. The mob, hundreds strong, after listening to inflammatory speeches against Morris and the Tories, paraded through the streets, terrorizing the burghers, most of whom hastened to get indoors. Screaming that they would "hang and bury the Tories" and have the blood of profiteering merchants, the rioters attacked the house of James Wilson, a prominent lawyer and patriot who had distinguished himself by defending the Tories in courts. Wilson's friends, about thirty in number, fearing that their turn would come next, barricaded themselves in Wilson's house. A hot battle was soon raging, the defenders shooting through windows at the crowd below and doing considerable execution among the rioters. But Wilson and his friends had only a limited store of ammunition, and it was soon apparent that they could not hold out long against their enemies. Just as the mob was on the point of breaking into the house and putting its defenders to death, Joseph Reed at the head of the Philadelphia Light Horse — the silk-stocking cavalry of the city — arrived upon the scene and struck the rioters with the flats of their swords; whereupon the mob "scampered off instantly."

Philadelphia continued to simmer for a week after this riot. Many of the rioters were thrown into jail, but as the Germantown militia threatened to march to Philadelphia to batter down the prison walls and release their comrades, it was deemed prudent to release them on bail. Conservatives could take little satisfaction in the outcome of this uprising; true, the rioters had got the worst of the first encounter, but there was good reason to fear that they would soon be back for another trial of strength. Momentarily, at least, Philadelphia had become the hottest spot in the country for profiteers and conservatives of every cast; even in Boston, the citizens were urged to "rouse and catch the Philadelphia spirit; Rid the community of those Monopolizers and Extortioners, who like cankerworms, are gnawing upon your vitals."

In effect, this outbreak served notice that the mob, long the terror of the Tories, was now becoming the scourge of all conservatives, and that American businessmen seemed likely to be the chief sufferers at its hands. It was evident that "the lusty Mobility, grand *Exciter* & *Finishers* of every

Revolution," was bent upon carrying the Revolution a great deal farther than conservatives intended and that it had constituted itself an instrument of social justice, directing its wrath against those who offended against the well-being of the community.

The Philadelphia rioters had been balked of their prey; because of the unexpectedly stiff resistance at James Wilson's, the mob had been compelled to call off the visit it had intended to pay Robert Morris. Fortunately for that merchant prince, it was decided to punish his transgressions by orderly, legal means. Believing that they had "the goods" on Morris, the patriots decided to bring down this high-flying profiteer by exposing him as a common lawbreaker.

A committee was appointed to investigate the charges against Morris, and Thomas Paine, much to his satisfaction, was appointed a member.

The revelations brought to light by the Deane-Lee affair had convinced Paine that Morris was one of the chief practitioners of those *"low dirty Tricks"* of trade by which a few merchants and speculators were amassing fortunes. Paine's presence on the committee, therefore, spelled bad news to Morris. "Paine," said Morris's friends, "like the enthusiastic Madmen of the East, was determined to run the Muck."

Thomas Paine had refused to dive with his compatriots into the fleshpots. An uncompromising idealist, he fought in the army, pursued the Muse of propaganda, and served as secretary to the Committee of Foreign Affairs — yet in everything he did, he was completely indifferent to money-making. He walked the streets of Philadelphia a poor man — spiritually still living in 1776, a strangely anachronistic figure. He boasted that his salary as a public officer was not equal to the pay of a common soldier and that, as a result, he was finally brought to the verge of starvation. A man of letters did not fare well in wartime America, particularly if he was a high-souled patriot who failed to look out for his interests in the inflation. But at least Paine could look the profiteers of Philadelphia in the eye, which was perhaps more than they could do in return.

Paine was a gadfly, buzzing in Americans' ears that they were in the midst of a war and a "glorious revolution" and that to relax was to court disaster. The cause of America, he exclaimed, "originally rested on honour and principle," not upon loaves and fishes; and with the fate of mankind in the balance, it was no time to think about making money at the expense of the government or of one's fellow citizens. Still, he could not ignore the fact that Americans had suffered a serious backsliding from the heights they attained in 1775 and 1776 and that they were "extinguishing by stages the ardor we began with, and surrendering by piece-meal the virtue that defended us." Declaring that "our first days were our days of honor," Paine tried to revive "something of that virtuous ambition which first called America into the field." To this end, he rehearsed the record of British atrocities in America and ransacked British history for "the most

shocking instances of cruelty ever practiced." But more and more, Paine
began to resemble Savonarola, flaying Americans for their vices and warning them of the wrath to come. He never lost faith in the rightness of the
Revolution or in ultimate victory, but, on the other hand, he never ceased
to deplore the iniquities of the times. His voice was one of the most
powerful in the United States. "I think," said General Steuben, "that a
pamphlet written by Common Sense . . . would produce a better effect
than all the recommendations of Congress in prose and verse" — yet even
he could not resurrect the spirit of 1776, buried as it was under an ava-
lanche of paper money.

To conserve flour for the use of the Continental army, Pennsylvania
had in 1779 imposed an embargo upon the shipment of flour outside the
state. Nevertheless, there was such a shortage of grain that the citizens
complained that they were obliged to eat "musty English Flour" which
before the war they would not have fed to cattle. Obviously, somewhere
there was a leak in the embargo, and it was suspected that Robert Morris
was at the bottom of it. Morris ostensibly was engaged in buying flour
for the French fleet; actually, some believed, he had cornered the supply
of flour in order to force the famished citizens to pay his own price. For
Morris, the prospect was black: when one of his supporters tried to
address a meeting of the citizens of Philadelphia in the State House yard
he was hooted down by a hundred men armed with clubs "who had
marched in array, under their officers, with fife and drum, and placed
themselves near the stage."

Morris was summoned by the committee to give testimony, but he
declined to appear before the tribunal. Thereupon the committee seized
Morris's stock of flour, and they were preparing to seize Morris himself
when the whole case blew up in the faces of Paine and his fellow committeemen. It appeared that Morris had actually been buying flour for
the French fleet, and the precipitate action of the patriots threatened to
disrupt the military and naval strategy of the allies. The French minister
personally complained to Congress of the meddling of the Philadelphia
patriots. As a result, the tables were turned, and Morris emerged from the
affair as the innocent victim of abuse and misrepresentation. It was now
Tom Paine's turn to suffer obloquy: his enemies charged him with being
a British spy hired to foment discord in the United States in order to
smooth the way for conquest.

Strengthened by this victory, Morris and his fellow merchants procured
the removal of the Pennsylvania embargo in the spring of 1780; and freed
of all restrictions, a brisk trade in flour sprang up between Philadelphia
and the West Indies. For the first time in years, European merchandise
began to appear in plentiful supply in the shops of Philadelphia; and the
production of flour was stimulated to such a degree that by the summer
of 1781, Morris declared that he could buy ten thousand barrels at any

time — and at a price cheaper than in the days of artificial restraints on trade. From these results, he drew the conclusion that "commerce should be perfectly free, and property sacredly secure to the owner" in order to achieve the "Universal plenty" at which the United States aimed. "Whenever these maxims have their proper force in our governments," he declared, "these United States will abound with the greatest plenty of their own produce of perhaps any Nation in the World."

⌢ ⌢ ⌢

It was not always the old-established business houses that prospered in this new era of easy money: a new class of businessmen was rising to the surface, churned up by war, revolution, and inflation. Peddlers became merchant princes: from pushcart to State Street was the success story of the Revolution. For example, a carpenter sold his tools and bought a hogshead of rum which he sold to the soldiers at Kingsbridge. Within twelve months, so spectacularly had his business prospered, he was making over twenty thousand dollars a year. Farm hands quit their jobs to turn traders. A hawker, beginning with a few barrels of rum and an inexhaustible store of low cunning, soon "amassed a fortune, leaped, as it were, at once from the barrow to a chariot." One farmer, after meeting his former hired man, said that the man no longer valued the wages offered laborers: "he had money enough to buy my farm, and asked the price; he had been trading in partnership with a baker, who had turned merchant, and could not read, and gave him half the profits for keeping the account." No business ethics stood in the way of these "rascally upstarts in trade"; their motto was "Charge everything the traffic will bear."

Of all the ways of getting rich quick during the War of American Independence, few were more popular than privateering. Their imaginations fevered by the great piles of booty lining the wharves of American seaports, many patriots began to go down to the sea in privateers. A stout ship and a daredevil crew — here was the way to make one's fortune. Some laid plans to intercept the Hull ships carrying woolens to Amsterdam and Rotterdam; others fancied the Irish linen ships; Indiamen, whether inward or outward bound, were certain to be richly laden; Hudson's Bay ships and West India sugar ships — treasure everywhere, and theirs for the seizing! In Philadelphia, almost every vessel capable of being converted into a privateer was fitted out with guns and sent to sea; South Carolinians sent agents to New England to recruit five hundred sailors for the privateers being fitted out in Charleston.

The result was an acute labor shortage at home. "You can place no dependence on your workmen," lamented a businessman in 1779; "to-day they are with you and to-morrow on board of a privateer, with hopes of making their fortunes." Robert Morris complained that as a result of the mania for privateering, he could get few ships, and that "the scarcity & insolence of Seamen, are beyond bearing."

Soldiering could not compete with privateering; the way to wealth in the United States lay not in shouldering a musket but in sharing in the fortunes of a stout-keeled privateer. In the seaports and even in the country, where reports of these fabulous riches had penetrated, it was almost impossible to enlist men for the army — every able-bodied man had signed on board a privateer; in 1779, Washington complained that "no Man can be obtained for any other purposes" than trade and privateering. Even during the retreat across New Jersey in the black days of 1776, General Greene reported that "the success of privateering has set all the troops distracted. . . . Were I at liberty," he added, "I think that I could make a fortune for my family. But it is necessary for some to be in the field to secure the property of others in their stores." Only by imposing embargoes upon the sailing of privateers and by impressing seamen could men be recruited in the seaports for the Continental army and navy. Had Americans enlisted in the army with the alacrity with which they took to privateering, the war might have been won in the span of a few years. In 1776, Rhode Island had twelve hundred men at sea in privateers — a considerable part of the available manpower of the state. All told, about twenty thousand men were on board the privateers — a larger force than Washington usually commanded.

To share in the booty captured by a privateer it was not necessary to ship before the mast: without stirring from home, one might benefit from the good fortune of the voyage. Shares in privateers were hawked about the country; even in the army, officers and men, when they could scrape enough cash together, often bought an interest in a privateer. Shrewd investors distributed their capital over many different privateers to hedge against excessive loss: the most successful privateers were sometimes men who had never set foot aboard ship.

Despite its undoubted services in hampering British commerce, privateering took men's minds off the real business of the Revolution — winning the war against Great Britain. Like the inflation, it disorganized the war effort and nourished Americans' ambition of making their fortunes by some lucky stroke. Privateering became less a means of distressing the enemy than of making money; it was a brutalizing and unsavory pursuit of wealth. "No kind of Business can so effectually introduce Luxury, Extravagance and every kind of Dissipation," it was pointed out. "Those who are actually engaged in it soon lose every idea of right and wrong." It led Americans to neglect regular commerce for the greater profits to be found in privateering; partly for this reason, little tobacco, indigo, flour, and other American products reached Europe in payment for importations of war supplies. In Rhode Island, no cannon could be cast in 1776 because the workmen went off privateering. "They have sacrificed every other Object public & Private to it," declared Robert Morris. It is significant that Benjamin Franklin advocated the abolition by international law of privateering in future wars.

As a result of privateering, the American aristocracy, particularly in New England, received a strong infusion of men who had made their fortunes on the quarter-deck, barking orders at a crew that would have warmed the heart of Captain Kidd, or who had been fortunate enough to invest their money in successful privateers. It grieved the old families — those who had not been exiled as Tories — to be obliged to rub shoulders with these rough-and-ready characters lately risen from the sea; but the prerogatives of wealth could not be denied; and, indeed, the fortunes of some of the first families could be traced back to some hardy smuggler who knew his way round the British customhouse.

Like the stock market in 1929, privateering crashed and wiped out in its fall hundreds of speculators who had believed themselves securely on easy street. The black days of American merchantmen and privateers came after Yorktown, when, because of the withdrawal of the French fleet to the West Indies, American ships were left at the mercy of British cruisers. Taking full advantage of this opportunity, the British navy and Loyalist privateers proceeded to reap a rich harvest of American shipping before peace should put an end to their opportunity for prize money. The privateering strongholds along the New Jersey coast were wiped out and privateers were ruthlessly tracked down at sea. Within six months, Philadelphia alone had lost almost one million pounds sterling in ships and cargoes to the British and Loyalists. Privateering strongholds like Marblehead and Beverly ended the war with only two or three vessels afloat. A Frenchman visiting Philadelphia at the end of the war observed that "there was scarcely a captain, or even a common sailor, who had not been taken six or seven times during the war, nor a merchant who had not been more than once rich and ruined." It was not uncommon, said De Chastellux, another French traveler, to find a man worth forty or fifty thousand pounds reduced in one day to bankruptcy. American merchants had been able to show a profit if one ship out of three arrived safely in port; but now, owing to the vigilance of the British cruisers, scarcely one in seven penetrated the blockade.

⌒ ⌒ ⌒

There were many businessmen who deplored the practices of the profiteers, but the business community tended to sink to the level of its most unscrupulous members. Merchants who wished to deal fairly by the consumer and government learned that "if they trade at all, they must swim with the stream." Patriotism, if carried to the length of supporting the value of Continental paper money, was ruinously expensive: the penalty of public spirit and self-sacrifice might well be the ruin of one's business.

Speculators had little scruple in holding up the government for high prices, although they knew that they thereby were adding to the hardships of the soldiers. Government agents were often obliged to bid against private speculators for scarce commodities — with the result that the government usually came away with empty hands. Iron, for example, was at one time almost entirely in the possession of the speculators; none could be procured by the government for the use of the army. When a ship arrived in port, the get-rich-quick gentry swarmed down to the wharf and made off with the cargo. Moreover, after buying up everything in sight, they were in no hurry to sell to the government; and if they did consent to part with the merchandise, it was only at exorbitant prices.

In November 1776, the Continental Congress, learning that all the supply of shoes, stockings, and many other necessities had been cornered by profiteers "whilst the soldiers of the Continent, fighting for the liberties of their country, are exposed to the injuries of the weather," was obliged to appeal to the people of Philadelphia to contribute blankets and woolen stockings for Washington's troops. In 1779, Congress declared that some merchants were asking one hundred dollars for goods that had cost them less than five dollars. "There is such a thirst for gain," exclaimed Washington in 1778, "and such infamous advantages taken to forestall, and engross those Articles which the Army cannot do without, thereby enhancing the cost of them to the public fifty or a hundred percent, that it is enough to make one curse their own Species, for possessing so little virtue and patriotism."

Washington, laboring to hold his army together, saw his efforts thwarted by this "tribe of black hearted gentry," whom he regarded as "a hundred times more dangerous to our liberties and the great cause we are engaged in" than the whole military might of Britain. "These murderers of our cause," he exclaimed, "ought to be hunted down as the pests of society, and the greatest Enemys we have to the happiness of America. I would to God that one of the most atrocious of each State was hung in Gibbets upon a gallows five times as high as the one prepared by Haman." Indeed, no punishment was too severe, in Washington's eyes, for the monopolizers and profiteers who, he declared, were "preying upon our very vitals, and, for the sake of a little dirty pelf, are putting the rights and liberties of the country into the most imminent danger."

The American people had not taken up arms to make the United States safe for profiteers and monopolists. To establish an equalitarian society as a result of the separation from Great Britain was the goal of many revolutionists. Yet, in attaining their freedom, Americans seemed to be losing the equality without which, it was agreed, liberty would prove an empty name. By creating a class of rich men, the Revolution was in fact undermining democracy, for, as a patriot pointed out, "*riches* and *wealth* ever lay human nature under the strongest temptations to grasp at the reins of government; and, when obtained, to lord it over the honest commonalty in society." And their rule promised to be far more oppressive than any tyranny Americans had experienced at the hands of Great Britain. "Cunning subtle long-headed gentry" seemed destined to become the material heirs of the Revolution: while others fought, the profiteers, smugglers, black-market operators, speculators, and monopolists appropriated the riches of the commonwealth.

The "speculating miscreants — sucking the blood of their country" committed their crimes in the name of liberty. Surely, it was said, businessmen ought to enjoy the same freedom from state control as did other members of the community. They reminded the patriots that one of the aims of the Revolution was freedom of trade. "On this foundation," they observed, "we were to build the future wealth, grandeur, and power of the United States." Robert Morris demanded an end to "the whole detestable tribe" of regulations. "Let the people," he exclaimed, "be put in possession of that freedom for which they are contending. . . . Perfect freedom makes the people easy, happy, rich, and able to pay taxes." To his way of thinking, trade always regulated itself and Americans would find their greatest felicity in adhering to that maxim. "Trade must regulate itself, can never be clog'd but to its ruin, and always flourishes when left alone," said the merchants; "it is justly compared to a coy mistress, she must be courted with delicacy and is ruined by force." Ruin awaited the people that allowed prices to be determined "according to the *Opinion* of a Set of pettifogging Lawyers, instead of the *Quantity* at Market." The temples of the merchants were, for the state, forbidden ground: the "No trespassing" signs were up and let the state take notice!

Thus the patriots found that liberty meant laissez faire and laissez faire meant in practice monopoly and ruinous inflation. This was unforeseen: the patriots had never intended that liberty should provide a shelter for profiteers and other public enemies. Clearly, the presence of these malefactors in the body politic made imperative a revision of the philosophy of 1776. To some Americans, the lesson was clear: the people were not all virtuous and in every society there was an unscrupulous minority which put private gain over public good. Unless these self-seekers were strictly controlled by government, they would bring down the entire fabric in ruin. Therefore, mankind — and particularly businessmen — could not be trusted with complete freedom of action: the state must keep businessmen under close scrutiny lest they revert to those harmful practices to which they seemed peculiarly prone. The state must exert its authority unless "this young Empire become . . . a den of thieves, which requires a divine Arm to overset the tales of these avaricious money changers." Some radicals went so far as to favor banning all private trade for the duration, leaving only public agencies to carry on buying and selling. Whatever methods were devised to combat the evil, Americans must choose between liberty and economic equality — never the twain would meet.

And so Americans were confronted with the alternative of jettisoning their prejudices against strong government or suffering a runaway inflation and all the ills that followed in its train. Strong government, once condemned as the instrument of tyrants, was now called upon by democrats to aid the cause of liberty; some of the very men who had been so intent upon protecting the liberty of the individual that they had denied adequate powers to the state were among the first to admit the necessity of strengthening government in the interests of the common man. "I am fighting," exclaimed a patriot, "against men having *liberty* to do *wrong*, and every kind of oppression under the sun." A new emphasis was placed upon the state as the guardian of the many against the few, and law was invoked to restrain "the Narrow Monopolizing Views of short sighted Merchants" and to effect "a general reformation in the people, to suppress every licentious oppressive spirit." Increasingly, the doctrine that civil government was instituted largely to prevent practices detrimental to the common good gained ground; as the Continental Congress said, laws were necessary "to supply the defect of public virtue, and to correct the vices of some."

⌒　⌒　⌒

Price fixing and embargoes had been tried and found wanting; there remained taxation as a stopgap to inflation and as a means of financing the war. From the beginning of the struggle, a few Americans had advocated taxation as a means of supporting the paper money issued by Congress and the states. In the Virginia Convention of 1775, George Mason had urged the imposition of as heavy taxes as the people could bear; and John Jay of New York advised his friends to demand taxation as a boon. "Will no one ever think of Taxes?" he asked his friends early in 1776. "The ice must be broken, the sooner it is begn & more insensibly performed the better. I tremble for the Delay." Yet there was good reason why, in this struggle for freedom, Americans should not think of taxes.

It was said that, during the War of Independence, Americans showed every kind of courage "except the courage to Tax themselves." The Continental Congress could not, and the states generally would not, impose taxes. Americans had risen in rebellion against taxation, and the new-fledged state governments dared not risk alienating citizens by taking money out of their pockets. Taxation was a horrid word to Americans, and as the Continental Congress said, "the contest being upon the very question of taxation, the laying of imposts, unless from the last necessity, would have been madness." Taxation had connotations of oppression, arbitrary government, and all the other evils Americans associated with British imperialism. Yet, as British subjects, it must be confessed that they had merely a nodding acquaintance with that dread visitant, the tax collector.

Americans were lightly taxed; they rose in rebellion against evils which they apprehended rather than experienced. The very lightness of the burden they had borne as British subjects ill conditioned them for the obligations they necessarily incurred in the War of Independence. Even while fighting for liberty, they did not fail to protest against taxation: it seemed as though they intended to abbreviate their slogan of "No taxation without representation" into "No taxation." Because Americans erected governments based upon the principle of consent, the people themselves were left to determine when taxes should be resorted to. "In what country of the world shall we find a nation willing to tax themselves?" asked Robert Morris. "Certainly not in America," he hastened to answer.

During the early period of the war when inflation was fastening itself upon the country, taxation was objected to on the ground that the people could not stand it. "This," exclaimed Thomas Paine, "has been the most expensive doctrine that ever was held out, and cost America millions of money for nothing," because under the influence of this delusion, the United States "could not bear to pay a penny to save a pound." In consequence, the government "paid a pound for a penny," the army was starved, and Americans were "hunted like partridges on the mountaines" by British and Tories. Of those who said that the country could not afford to bear taxes, Paine asked if it could bear to be "over-run, ravaged, and ruined by an enemy."

Many patriots, foreseeing the inevitable smashup at the end of the inflationary joy ride, prayed for taxes and yet more taxes. For the first time in their lives, they regarded taxes as a blessing. "O!" exclaimed a patriot, "that our legislature would tax us 'till we fought after the money." John Adams instructed Mrs. Adams to "pay every tax that is brought, if you sell my books or clothes or oxen, or your cows, to pay it." The people must be convinced, said John Adams, of "this sacred Truth, that it is their Interest to pay high Taxes!" — just as truly as a few years before, when as subjects of George III it had been their interest to refuse to pay high taxes. Thomas Paine thought it a pity that no "other word beside taxation had been devised for so noble and extraordinary occasion. . . . The man who paid his taxes," said Paine, "does more for his country's good than the loudest talker in America." Taxes ought to be regarded as "an offering in the holy temple of liberty."

Until 1779, few Americans would have known from their tax receipts that they were engaged in war with one of the most powerful nations on earth. Their joy in making money was unalloyed by the realization that much of it would have to be handed over to the government in March.

In November 1777, the Continental Congress, driven from Philadelphia by the British army, urged the states to levy taxes in aid of the war effort. Congress, however, could not command: the sovereign states could be addressed only in the tone of entreaty or reproach. Left to their own discretion, some states complied with this recommendation, others ignored it. Virginia did not seriously undertake the collection of taxes until 1782; Connecticut and Massachusetts, on the other hand, began in 1777 and 1778 and continued to levy progressively higher taxes as the war went on.[9]

When finally imposed, taxes yielded disappointingly small revenue: frequently a tax scarcely paid the cost of collection, and always the rapid depreciation of money left the needs of the state unsatisfied. Particularly in the Middle states — "the enemy's country" — many citizens declined to regard taxpaying as a patriotic duty. In Pennsylvania, for example, from 1778 to 1781, less than half the taxes assessed were collected: it was not uncommon for citizens to slam the door in the tax collector's face — and get away with it. Lacking adequate machinery to enforce its laws, the state was often unable to punish defaulters. Lancaster County, one of the richest counties in Pennsylvania, paid little to the state treasury although many of its citizens were known to be hoarding gold and silver — "too sacred to be touched for taxes." Until 1780, Americans were not asked to pay in gold and silver — paper money, depreciated almost to the point of worthlessness, was gladly accepted by the states; but many citizens refused even to part with this despised currency to aid their governments. New England, on the other hand, encountered little opposition in collecting taxes — until they were made payable in hard money.

Little of the tax money collected by the states ever reached the Continental Congress or the Continental army. The states made it a rule to provide for their own needs first, and if anything was left over, to turn it over to Congress; but rarely was there something to spare for Congress. That did not mean that the state governments were basking in affluency while the central government was reduced to beggary: the government of Pennsylvania, for example, was in 1780 compelled to live from hand to mouth on money borrowed at high rates of interest from businessmen. The people might be prosperous, but their governments did not share in the blessing. Moreover, recalcitrant patriots rose in arms against taxation when the days of cheap money were over. In 1780, the president of Pennsylvania declared that "the people of this State would, if too heavily pressed, more readily renew their connexion with Great Britain, than any State now in the Union." And in Massachusetts a taxpayers' strike, led by Richard Ely, developed into an armed revolt against the state — an

---

[9] In Massachusetts a tax of one million pounds (Massachusetts money) was laid in 1778; and two million, eight hundred thousand pounds was collected in 1779. "We deal in our Millions as well as Britain, and raise them as easily," boasted a Bostonian.

unmistakable warning to the states of the peril of attempting to tax their citizens.

Nor could Americans be persuaded to loan the government any large sums of money. For the convenience of patriots who wished to lend money to the government, so-called loan offices were established throughout the country. Here Americans could buy certificates (today they would be called war bonds) paying 4 per cent interest. In this way, Congress hoped to finance the war by borrowing from American citizens, and to head off inflation by drawing off the excess purchasing power of the country. But this plan ran into an unexpected obstacle: the states began to compete with the Continental Congress for the favor of investors by issuing certificates yielding higher interest than those of Congress. Reluctantly, Congress raised its rate to 6 per cent but met with little success until France, in 1778, undertook to pay, partly in specie, the interest on Continental certificates. This, together with the depreciation of paper money — for the government accepted at face value almost worthless currency in exchange for certificates — made them attractive to investors, speculators and patriots alike. Nevertheless, certificates depreciated as did paper money and, circulating from hand to hand, served the purpose of additional money rather than of war savings bonds. In 1780, Congress closed the loan office and in 1782 suspended interest payments; and not until the funding and assumption measures of Alexander Hamilton did the certificates, both state and federal, recover their value.

⌢　⌢　⌢

People living on fixed salaries or income suffered cruelly during the inflation. "In faith when the war is over," exclaimed a patriot, "I for a maintenance must take to the Highway, & Politely, with a Pistol, ask Charity of Passengers." Many clergymen fell into more than apostolic poverty, and they learned during the inflation, if they did not know it before, that their flocks were "generally more careful of their bodies than their souls" and that, whereas a doctor of medicine could cope with the high cost of living by raising his fees, a doctor of divinity "would soon lose his employers and be turned adrift" if he asked for more. They were happy if paid their salaries in food: in their extremity, nothing so rejoiced the hearts of these men of God as to see a parishioner settling his tithe with a fat sow.

Government job holders were in much the same plight. Timothy Pickering complained in 1779 that his expenses were at least fourteen thousand dollars a year more than his salary as a member of the Board of War, and that he had bought no new clothing for years; but, he added, "I must buy *some* clothing, for my old clothes I have already worn on both sides." Some public officials, it is true, amassed fortunes during the war; but most of them risked beggary by remaining at their posts. Even when Congress and the states raised salaries to compensate for the depreciation of the currency, the increase fell far short of the rise in the cost of living. An assistant quartermaster claimed in 1780 that his salary of one hundred and sixty dollars a month had the purchasing power of three dollars and a half in specie.

Furthermore, it could hardly escape attention that the inflation was adding an immense burden of debt to the country and wrecking its economy. If the currency continued to depreciate, it was doubtful whether the United States could keep an army in the field; as early as 1777 it was being said that "the mines of Peru would not support a war at the present high price of the necessaries of life." By 1779, the public debt exceeded two hundred million dollars. One of the reasons advanced for leaving the British Empire was the huge national debt of Great Britain, at least part of which, it was feared, the government was planning to foist upon the colonists. Now Americans seemed destined to carry the burden of an equally oppressive debt; the price of independence, measured in dollars and cents, was costly beyond all expectations. And Americans were soon brought to see that inflation, instead of bringing prosperity to all, enriched a few and impoverished the many. In this lottery, the great majority drew blanks; the prizes went only to a handful of unscrupulous individuals.

An agricultural country such as the United States of 1780 could better withstand the ravages of inflation than could a highly industrialized society dependent upon money as a medium of exchange. Partly for this reason, some Americans took comfort in the assumption that inflation acted as a tax upon the people and therefore was not wholly evil. Franklin, for example, said that "every man has paid his share of the tax according to the time he retained any of the money, and to the depreciation within that time." And it was an equitable tax because "those people paid most, who, being richest, had most money passing through their hands."

If inflation really was a tax upon Americans, it thrust the burden upon the shoulders of those least able to bear it. The unpatriotic, business-as-usual men, far from sharing the load with their weaker neighbors, profited from the inflation and feathered their nests at the expense of the community. It was primarily taxation of the poor and the patriotic. "Whilst some have contributed more than twenty times their just proportion," it was observed, "others have been great gainers, or, at least, have contributed nothing." The War of American Independence was carried on by taxation of the most inequitable and oppressive kind — and largely because many people preferred to take their chances in an inflation rather than submit to taxation and price control.

In the beginning, the upward trend of prices was largely owing to scarcities produced by the stoppage of normal channels of trade; but after 1776, the inflation assumed a more sinister aspect. It began to take the form of a flight from the dollar — a flight that ultimately reached the stratosphere. This phase of the inflation was the result not of shortages in the supply of goods but of lack of confidence in the ability of the government to redeem with silver and gold the paper money that had so prodigally issued from its presses. It ended in the utter collapse of the paper dollar as a medium of exchange.

That the government could not continue indefinitely to print paper money backed only by its promise to pay gold for paper, when everyone knew it had no gold, was obvious to many Americans. As early as 1775, for example, Benjamin Franklin pointed out the pitfalls of depending upon fiat money, but Congress failed to heed the admonitions of Poor Richard. The war, it was generally supposed, would be short. And "it was imagined," said an American, "that the Justice of our cause, and the united ardor and patriotism of the people would preserve the value of these bills during the contest." In short, paper money was backed chiefly by hope — hope that the war would be short and that the American people would be patriotic.[10]

The value of American paper money was not determined by the fortunes of war: it was the quantity of paper money in circulation, rather than military victories or defeats, that was responsible for its depreciation. By flinging millions of dollars upon the backs of other millions without providing for taxation or a specie reserve — sending its money into the world naked, as it were, except for a promise to redeem it at some future day with silver and gold — Congress was imposing a heavy strain upon the patriotism of the people. It was not until the amount of Continental paper in circulation exceeded thirty million dollars that the rise in prices really got out of hand. The true inflation of the Revolutionary War did not come until the people began to lose confidence in the currency; and they lost confidence primarily because of the excessive amount of paper money put in circulation by the states and by the Continental Congress.

In 1779, paper money suffered an unprecedentedly swift collapse. Prices rose to unheard of levels: tea was forty dollars a pound; meat two dollars a pound. The price of imported merchandise rose almost 2000 per cent over the price level of 1775. Of course, these prices were low in comparison with what was to come, but already Americans began to have the uneasy feeling that there was no bottom to the rapidly falling Continental paper money. Moreover, nothing escaped the blight of inflation. Largely

[10] In September 1775, it was proposed, but not seconded, in Congress that all the conventions and assemblies be instructed to print no more paper money without permission from Congress; and in December 1775, a committee of Congress recommended that Congress stop its presses.

shut off from West Indian rum by the war, Americans, hitherto a nation of rum drinkers, turned to whiskey as a substitute. But now the high price of grain put even whiskey beyond the reach of many. And prices were still going up. "Our dollars pass for less this afternoon than they did in the morning," lamented the patriots; in May 1779, prices in Philadelphia increased 100 per cent in three weeks. In August 1778, a Continental paper dollar was valued (in terms of gold and silver) at about twenty-five cents; by the end of 1779, it was hardly worth a penny. The money consigned to the army, said General Greene, was "no more equal to our wants than a sprat in a whales belly."

There was nothing in the war news to warrant this swift decline: indeed, the news had never been better. France had allied itself with the United States, and Spain seemed likely to enter the war at any moment; the British had withdrawn to New York apparently intending to abandon the American war as a bad job. It was portentous that paper money failed to respond to this favorable turn of events on the military and diplomatic fronts; the patient was obviously beyond cure by cheerful news. As a congressman remarked in 1780: "For some time past we have resembled a patient far gone in disease, given up of his physicians and left to the mere efforts of nature." Now it began to appear that nothing could check the disease.[11]

Under these circumstances, the shrewd and farseeing began to invest their paper money in goods and lands, thereby helping to aggravate the evil of inflation. For if Americans had no more faith in their own money than to convert it into tangible property in the shortest possible order, how could they expect it to retain its value? Nevertheless, daily experience proved that he who held paper money was lost; therefore, to get rid of the depreciating paper as fast as possible and to invest it in property became one of the absorbing passions of the day. Undoubtedly, land was the safest investment; Washington observed that "there is scarce a possibility of their [lands] falling in price, but almost a Moral certainty of their rising exceedingly in value." He therefore advised his friends not to part with their land for paper money.

Paper money was the cornerstone of the authority of the Continental Congress. Congress, while its paper money held out, was at least a sovereign among sovereigns: its bank roll permitted it to move in the company of the states, even though they were not wholly prepared to accept it as an equal. To lose paper money, in short, was for Congress to cut off its right hand; yet the amputation of a limb, it was pointed out,

---

[11] Even Alexander Hamilton was taken unawares by this unexpectedly swift fall in the value of paper money. In November 1778, Hamilton cautioned his friends against taking too gloomy a view of paper money. "I think, bad as it is," he said, "it will continue to draw out the resources of the country a good while longer." Like many other Americans, Hamilton supposed that the end of war was in sight.

was preferable to the untimely end that seemed to lie in store unless paper money were quickly cast off.

Bankruptcy so closely crowded upon the heels of Congress that there was no time to pause to establish a stable system of finance. As a result, Congress could do little more than improvise defenses against inflation, hoping that by thus palliating the evil, the country would somehow scrape through.

To this end, Congress on September 1, 1779, resolved to put a ceiling upon the amount of paper money in circulation. Not more than two hundred million dollars, Congress decided, should be printed; and since it had already issued more than one hundred and sixty million dollars, only about forty million additional could be emitted — a mere pittance at the current value of the dollar.

Upon this mountain of paper, Congress resolved to make its final stand — it would issue no more money, yet it would defend to the last what it had already printed. But Congress had been too deeply involved in wild-cat schemes to make convincing its promise to turn over a new leaf. Its efforts to maintain the value of the dollar failed ignominiously: the defiant proclamation of September 1779 proved the signal for another sharp selling wave in Continental money. By January 1780, the army was paying for supplies twice what it had paid in September 1779; and by March 1780, prices had risen four times above the level of September 1779.

Congress had no better luck in its efforts to raise a loan. Even when it offered 50 per cent interest on short-term loans there were no takers. Few individuals in the United States had a poorer credit rating than had the government of the United States.

Congress tried economizing: by trimming sails in the financial storms, the statesmen in Philadelphia hoped to get safely over the shoals. The expenses of the President of Congress were closely scrutinized by Congress: Richard Henry Lee demanded to know how much the President was spending on his table, reputedly one of the best in Philadelphia. Congress busied itself in investigating the quartermaster's and commissary's departments, into which vast sums had been poured with little to show in the way of supplies for the army. But this hue and cry after officials in departments of supply merely led Congress down a blind alley — the causes of inflation and its cure were not to be discovered there.[12] The army spent millions of dollars because prices were high; there was nothing to be gained from saying, as many congressmen did, that prices were high because the army spent so much money. Nor did it profit

---

[12] True, the commissary's and quartermaster's departments seemed a bottomless gulf into which the wealth of the country was being poured. In 1776 the expenses of both departments were a little over five million dollars; in 1779 they were consuming one hundred and twenty millions a year and crying for more.

Congress to hold the Tories accountable for the depreciation of the currency and to summon the people to hunt down the malefactors. The source of the evil lay at home: Congress was struggling against "the malice of our enemies and the avarice of our citizens" but, of the two evils, avariciousness was the greater.[13]

With its money expiring upon its hands, Congress, in November 1779, advised the states to go back to price fixing. Regional conferences were called and price-fixing laws were again enacted. These experiments proved, however, that the evil had gone too far to admit of cure by such devices: prices, climbing steadily as paper money depreciated, broke through every ceiling that could be erected.

Taxation, even if it could have been adopted over the prejudices of Americans, was now of little avail: during the interval between laying and collecting taxes, the money depreciated so rapidly that what originally had been a heavy tax became almost inconsequential in its effects. There were simply no brakes left; the best that could be hoped was that the smashup, when it came, would not shatter the government utterly.

Waging war was a simple matter, Congress found, compared with struggling with the intricacies of finance. "Never was a poor fly more completely entangled in a cobweb than Congress in their paper currency," mourned a member. The spectacle was not reassuring to people who looked to Congress for salvation. "I wish I could say that there was one member of Congress adequate to the important business of Finance," said General Schuyler.

Apparently, all that remained for Congress was to hoist the distress signal — "Sinking with all hands" — and wait rescue by the states. This, admittedly, was the counsel of despair; it was evident that most of the states cheerfully entrusted the care of the central government to Providence while they sought to save themselves. As a result, the best — indeed, the sole — hope of succor lay in foreign aid. Its necessities compelled Congress to look abroad, thereby creating what might be called an international outlook, although it must be confessed that the gaze of the impecunious statesmen in Philadelphia was fixed principally upon the pocketbooks of their European friends and allies.

The needs of Congress were so pressing that it could not wait upon loans from friendly European powers; it must anticipate loans, relying upon "the favourable disposition of most of the States in Europe towards

---

[13] This is not to say that the Tories had no hand in the undermining of confidence in patriot paper money. Counterfeiters worked overtime at New York, and anyone who was willing to risk spreading the money in patriot-held territory could have it for the asking. Two emissions of Continental money were found to be so extensively counterfeited that Congress was obliged, in 1779, to order the money taken out of circulation. In the same year, the entire Virginia currency had to be called in and new plates and paper procured. To stop this practice, the death penalty was sometimes meted out to counterfeiters.

these States." Certainly Congress put the favorable disposition of its friends to a severe test. In June 1777, it began to draw drafts upon its ministers abroad, in the hope that by the time the drafts reached them, they would have secured a loan from those governments sufficient to cover the amount already expended by Congress. In this way, Congress began to mortgage the future and to live upon its expectations. Actually, this meant living upon the treasury of France.

Congress drew these bills in the knowledge that if they ever bounced back across the Atlantic, its credit would be at an end and, for all practical purposes, the United States would be insolvent. Perhaps it was for this reason that Congress made so bold with its drafts — surely France would pay the bills rather than see its ally crash into bankruptcy in the middle of the war. It was, at least, a fair calculation that the United States would not be repudiated by its ally; and therefore Congress vigorously exploited this vein of ore. Some congressmen felt that France was not doing enough in the way of loans to the United States; drawing drafts was an effective method of gaining entry to the Bourbon treasury, which, Americans supposed, contained inexhaustible riches.

But it would be a mistake to suppose that Congress as a whole intended any chicanery or sought to take advantage of France; there were simply no other means of raising the money necessary to carry on the war. To keep its head above water, Congress clutched at straws — or, more precisely, at the pocketbook of its ally. On the other hand, had it been supported by the states, Congress would cheerfully have relied upon the internal resources of the country as far as possible; there was little satisfaction in running up "an enormous national debt to foreigners, who may hereafter claim the honor and merit of our whole salvation as due to them and surprise us with unexpected demands."

Franklin was so vexed by these bills that he was frequently unable to sleep nights from worrying how he was to meet the next day's crisis. There was, of course, only one course open to him: to go to Versailles and beg aid of Vergennes. He was never consulted about these bills or informed of the total amount drawn upon him; always under pressure to meet a deadline, he never knew what might be demanded of him. "Ever since I entered into office," Franklin protested, "they [the bills] have not only plagued and perplexed me, but they have invariably consumed the resources on which I have formed a reliance." His own pay as minister early went into the pot.

Congress seemed bent upon making Franklin a mendicant at the court of Louis XVI; but nothing in Poor Richard's philosophy sanctioned raising oneself in the world by touching one's friends. Franklin came to hate these little journeys to Versailles: the only thing he lacked to make his role complete was a tin cup. He rebelled at the idea of his country living off the bounty of France. One of his favorite maxims was "God helps them that help themselves." That his countrymen were exerting themselves vigorously in the cause for which they had taken up arms, Franklin emphatically did not believe: he knew too well how much money was being expended by Americans upon European luxuries to credit their stories of destitution and insolvency. "It is absurd, the pretending to be lovers of liberty while they grudge paying for the defense of it," he exclaimed. "Increase of industry in every American, male and female, with a small diminution of luxury," he predicted, "would produce a sum far superior to all we can hope to beg or borrow from all our friends in Europe." Moreover, he saw danger in relying upon France too exclusively: Americans might ride a free horse to death.

The unsoundness of the French financial structure led him to fear that his countrymen, by their improvidence, might bring it down in ruins. France, he observed, was itself borrowing money to finance the war: contrary to Americans' belief, the treasury of France was not an overflowing cornucopia. Knowing this, he became thoroughly ashamed of showing his face at Versailles; despite all that France had done for the United States, he complained, "I am obliged to worry them with my solicitations for more, which makes us appear insatiable."

As might be expected, Franklin did not meet with a warm welcome at Versailles when he came with his pockets full of bills. Vergennes was not willing to give his allies a blank check upon the French treasury, for he suspected that the Americans intended to saddle France with most of the cost of the war; if by a stroke of pen they could procure unlimited supplies of gold and silver, he had little doubt that they would take their ease, leaving France to pay for as well as fight the war. Nevertheless, he paid these bills, always protesting that Congress was taking unfair advantage of France, and always threatening to stop further payments.

To pacify Dr. Franklin, Congress frequently promised that this would positively be the last time that he would be sent begging to Versailles — and then, a few weeks later, it found itself obliged to impose on him again. As John Jay said, nothing would ever stop Congress from working the pump except "Proof that its Well has a Bottom." Vergennes himself tried to make Congress understand that the bottom had been reached. Early in 1781, the French minister declared that France would no longer honor drafts drawn upon American ministers abroad; and in August 1781, Franklin promised Vergennes not to accept any bills drawn on him after April 1782, under pain of default. But still the bills poured across the Atlantic and the French government continued to make them good.

Congress was not alone in pestering Franklin with bills; John Paul Jones, among others, drew upon him to keep the American navy afloat in European waters, until Franklin cried out: "For God's sake be sparing, unless you mean to make me bankrupt, or have your drafts dishonoured for want of money in my hands to pay them." Every American commercial agent in Europe took the liberty of presenting Franklin with drafts which they had already cashed *in his name*. Nor did the states long overlook this source of ready money: when Pennsylvania sent an agent abroad in 1780, the state drew one thousand pounds sterling on Dr. Franklin to cover the traveling expenses and incidentals of its emissary. Franklin's countrymen did not doubt that he would be able to scrape up the money; certainly, there was much to be said for dumping the financial problems of the United States into the lap of Poor Richard. The author of "The Way to Wealth" ought to be able, if anyone could, to lead his countrymen out of the financial wilderness. Thus, said Franklin, it was made his duty to draw water "for the whole congregation of Israel" — and a thirsty lot they were. Sweating at the pump, he found, was his principal labor as minister.

Congress likewise drew drafts upon John Adams and other American representatives abroad, although they had not been received as ministers by the countries to which they were accredited. They were empowered to raise loans and this was held sufficient to warrant making drafts upon them in anticipation of future blessings. When he arrived in Madrid in 1780, John Jay found a flock of bills waiting for him which he was utterly without means to pay. John Adams attempted to meet the drafts drawn upon him by floating a loan in Holland, but his success was so slight that, instead of sending the money home, he used it to make up part of a down payment on a house he purchased in The Hague. Although he was so destitute that he was obliged to look to the French government for his salary, Adams found that Congress continued to send him hundreds of thousands of dollars in bills for payment. Congress even drew a bill of exchange upon Henry Laurens while he was on his way to Holland, in the expectation that the minister would not find the Dutch hardhearted. Laurens, however, was captured en route by the British and was thrown into the Tower of London, where his chances of floating a loan were hardly bright. Ultimately, the bills were redeemed by France, but not before Congress had succeeded in advertising its poverty to the world.

Drawing bills became the bane of American finance. Anyone in official position who had expectations, however slender, of coming into money was likely to find himself swamped with these notes. General Lincoln, in command of the Southern army, drew bills upon the President of Congress. The states drew bills upon Congress, and Congress drew bills upon the states. But, except for those paid by France, this method yielded little. The state treasurers honored only a small part of the bills drawn upon them, leaving Congress holding the bag. And when Franklin had the temerity to draw a bill upon Congress, it promptly went by default.

The bills drawn upon the ministers abroad were used by Congress to buy supplies for the army. Well aware that Congress had no assurance that the bills would not be protested, the merchants discounted them sharply

and, passing into the hands of speculators, they depreciated sometimes
as much as half of their face value. Everything that Congress touched
seemed to turn to dross.

⌒   ⌒   ⌒

By 1780, the day of reckoning could no longer be postponed. It was
observed at this time that congressmen were seldom seen to smile — you
could pick them out in any company by the glumness of their expres-
sions. And glum they might well be, for they were looking at the specter
of repudiation and all the evils that walked in its train.

Hitherto Congress had indignantly rejected any suggestions that it
default on its promise to exchange paper money for gold. "A bankrupt
faithless republic," it declared, "would be a novelty in the political world,
and appear among reputable nations like a common prostitute among
chaste and respectable nations." Repudiation was regarded as the "unpardonable sin" that would brand American democracy for all time. "Let
it never be said," exclaimed Congress, "that America had no sooner become independent than she became insolvent." How could loans be raised
in Europe if the republic appeared in foreign courts as an absconding
debtor, fleeing the wrath of its own defrauded citizens? Such a course
would be "madness, atheism and suicide"; only Tories could be base
enough to suggest that Congress intended to repudiate its paper money.

Yet to redeem paper money at its face value might well bankrupt the
country: the interest alone on the national debt promised to be a
"*devouring monster*" eating Americans out of house and home. And to
benefit whom? Whom, indeed, but speculators, "some of the greatest
Rascals that ever disgraced humanity," who had bought up paper money
at one cent on the dollar in the expectation that Congress would pay them
full value in gold. To aggrandize this "black tribe of speculators," thousands of American farmers and workers would be "reduced to beggary
by taxes." With their ill-gotten millions, these men would make themselves lords and masters of the country, and Congress would be cursed by
thousands of Americans for having fastened upon the country a more
oppressive oligarchy than that of the Tories.

With such arguments, Congress salved its conscience in taking a step
which, a few months before, it had decried as treachery to the people of
the United States. On March 15, 1780, Congress declared that forty paper
dollars were equivalent to one dollar in gold.

With a stroke of the pen, it thus reduced the national debt from about
two hundred million dollars to five million, exclusive of foreign debts and
obligations incurred by the states. Congress congratulated itself upon having thrown off "an unjust and cumbrous load of debt which threatened
for ages to clog the industry of our people" — and, truly, it seemed to be a

piece of legerdemain almost as spectacular as the creation of money from rags. As a result of this action, by the end of the war it was estimated that sixty million dollars represented the price of freedom to the American people — forty million dollars owing by Congress and twenty million dollars by the states.

By this devaluation, Congress expected to stabilize the value of its paper money at forty dollars in paper to one dollar in gold or silver. Upon this line the inflation would be halted and a new emission of paper money, safeguarded by taxation, would be issued to replace the discredited Continental notes. But there was no opportunity to try the effect of soundly backed paper money: the inflation was not to be halted even at the ratio of forty to one.

Continental paper fell through every flooring Congress sought to interpose: it was soon quoted at sixty to one, then seventy-five to one, then one hundred to one. "Though many have died of disease," it was observed, "yet not a few have died of the Doctor."

Congressmen were not the least to suffer from the drying up of the financial wells: living upon inadequate salaries in the most expensive city in the United States, they were among the chief victims of the inflation. As early as 1777, John Adams, dismayed by the size of his expense accounts as a member of Congress, expressed alarm lest his constituents suspect that he was conducting himself in Philadelphia in a manner that would not bear scrutiny in Boston. In order to nip any possible scandal in the bud, Adams protested that he was keeping nothing more compromising than a horse, and as for the rest, it was all chargeable to the high cost of living. To Adams's mind, keeping horses was a justifiable expense for an American statesman: the enemy might be at the gates of Philadelphia any day, and in that event, horses would be at such a premium that, as he pointed out, a person would not be able to "obtain one to ride fifty Miles for Love nor Money."

For that reason, he deemed it his duty to instruct his cousin Sam Adams, likewise a delegate to Congress, in the art of horsemanship when the two men found themselves traveling companions on the road to Philadelphia in 1775. Sam had scarcely ever been on a horse before, but under John's coaxing he was persuaded to mount "a very genteel and easy little Creature," and John painstakingly taught him to mount and dismount without the aid of the two servants he usually required. During the first few days of travel, Sam Adams suffered from the soreness inevitable to an inexperienced rider, but his cousin induced him to continue. At John's suggestion, Sam bought some linen cloth which their landlady made into "a Pair of Drawers" which eased the friction and "entirely healed the little Breach which had begun." Before the travelers had been many days on the road, their servants, who rode behind in a carriage, were remarking upon Sam's superior horsemanship; and by the time they reached

Philadelphia, John had the mortification of hearing it said that Sam rode 50 per cent better than he.

During the course of the war, John and Sam Adams turned their equestrian skill to account by making several quick getaways from Philadelphia in which they handsomely outrode the British. But no congressman could outride the inflation — go where he would, there was no escape from the plague of high prices.

With the stoppage of the printing presses, congressmen found themselves squeezed unmercifully by the inflation. As long as the government continued to print paper money, they had drawn their salaries directly from the Continental treasury; now, like the army, they depended wholly upon the states or private means, if such they had, for survival. Yet the states showed little concern over their fate; abandoned without funds to the mercies of Philadelphia landlords, tavern keepers, and other creditors, congressmen began to feel like orphans in the storm.

After March 1780, few congressmen boasted a sufficiently large private income to enable them to live like gentlemen in Philadelphia. In 1775 and 1776, board and lodging had stood at "four dollars per week exclusive of liquors"; by 1779 it had risen to "100 dollars per week, liquors 60 dollars"; and in 1780 it reached "£270 Continental money a week for a gentleman and Servant exclusive even of Table beer" — from which it can be seen that at least the country was still liquid.

A New York delegate estimated that his ten months' service in Congress had cost him fifty-seven thousand dollars and that to pay his bills he had incurred a personal debt of twenty-five thousand dollars. Some congressmen borrowed heavily upon their own property to see them through their term of service; James Madison of Virginia described himself as "a pensioner on the favor of Haym Salomon, a Jew broker." During these trying days in Philadelphia, a particularly lean and hungry individual might reasonably be supposed to be a congressman. No doubt, the best way to do your congressman a good turn was to take him out to dinner.

Congress seriously considered leaving Philadelphia for less expensive parts — a fugitive from the high cost of living. Individual congressmen stranded in the city frequently threatened to come home with or without the consent of their constituents; but had they taken to the road it would probably have been as hitchhikers. Without money, and narrowly watched by their landladies and other creditors, it was no easy matter for them to wipe the dust of Philadelphia from their feet. One delegate, surveying his debts to his landlady, tailor, and shoemaker, lamented: "I have no horse, or I might ride away from these great debts, and ask charity on the road." Another congressman found that "several thousand Pounds continental money . . . perished in his hand in one Week and would not enable Him to travel 50 miles." A third lamented: "I owe about 4000 for

Board & have not a farthing to pay it with"; a fourth that he faced the prospect of being "an Embassador and a Beggar at the same time." It was vain to look to the states for rescue: some states had not a dollar in their treasuries with which to ransom the congressmen from their creditors.

Congress might well regret the first drink it had taken of the heady wine of inflation. To this pass had it been brought: from riches to rags in five years — an inversion of the American Success Story.

⌒   ⌒   ⌒

The effect of the inflation was to sink American patriotism as low as American money. "Our morals are as much depreciated as our currency," was one of the most common laments of the times. Thomas Paine pointed out that in an inflation "every principle of justice is put to the rack, and the bond of society dissolved" — it is every man for himself and the devil take the hindmost. Money-madness tended to crowd out all thought of public welfare; in that "sordid and avaricious Spirit which infected all ranks and conditions of men," there was no room for patriotism, loyalty, and self-sacrifice. Refugees fleeing from Indian massacres on the frontier complained that they were so unmercifully overcharged by profiteers that the Indians themselves could hardly be more cruel. The deluge of paper money swept away the old morality and love of country; like a cancer, inflation ate its way into the heart of American patriotism, leaving only the husks of money-making and pleasure-seeking behind.

The patriots found that, far from ushering in a reign of virtue, the American Revolution had made the people less moral, less frugal, and less chaste. It was a net loss in all the qualities that were held necessary to the greatness of a nation. "On the whole," said David Ramsay, a contemporary historian of the American Revolution, "the literary, political and military talents of the citizens of the United States have been improved by the revolution, but their moral character is inferior to what it formerly was."

Benjamin Franklin was under the happy impression that his countrymen would gird themselves for battle with the maxims of Poor Richard. In declaring their independence, he believed that Americans were erecting a barrier against the vices of Europe and were ushering in a golden age of the homely virtues. He supposed that they would devote themselves wholeheartedly to serving their country; public spirit would really exist in the United States, in contrast to Great Britain, where, he remarked, "it is universally deemed a Non Entity, and whoever pretends to it is laugh'd at as a fool, or suspected as a Knave."

During the first year of the war, the American people did not disappoint these high expectations; they fitted neatly into the heroic mold in which they had been cast by the patriot leaders. Public fasts were proclaimed by

Congress and the states, and even New Yorkers, who were accustomed to sneer at New Englanders' fasts, now went supperless and betook themselves to their prayers. Instead of drinking coffee, tea, and sugar, many Americans followed John Adams's prescription of a glass of milk for breakfast. Bans upon horse racing, gambling, and public balls and theaters were enacted; the people renounced tea drinking and expensive clothing and became almost as puritanical as even Sam Adams could have wished. When, in November 1775, Mrs. Washington passed through Philadelphia on her way to Cambridge to join the general, some admiring citizens tried to arrange a ball in her honor. But because the Continental Congress frowned upon such entertainments and some outraged citizens threatened to wreck the tavern where it was planned to hold the ball, the Philadelphia Committee of Safety declared against the ball or any other entertainments "while these troublesome times continued." A committee was therefore sent to Mrs. Washington to request her not to attend, and she graciously consented — much to the disappointment of several Southern congressmen who insisted that the ball was "legal, just and laudable."

Moreover, the people seemed prepared to make any sacrifices demanded of them in defense of liberty. Life and property were slightly regarded in comparison with liberty; on every side, patriots spoke of dying for freedom — "forty thousand lives would be cheaply thrown away," it was said, in exchange for liberty. Any man who was not willing to die to save his country was held unworthy to be an American; Congress declared that millions of Americans were ready to die as free men rather than to live as slaves; and a Virginian asserted that there was not a mother in the Old Dominion "who would not put the sword into the Hand of her only son to fight the Cause of God and our Country." In 1775, it was observed that in Philadelphia every person was "willing to sacrifice his private interest in this glorious contest"; and years later, Washington remembered his countrymen saying at this time: "We should be compleatly satisfied, if at the expense of one half we could defend the remainder of our possessions."

American patriots loved to draw comparisons between the luxurious, vice-ridden mother country and the vigorous, virtuous colonists, unspoiled by European corruptions. But as the war progressed and the inflation fell like a blight upon American morale, the dreadful truth dawned upon the patriot leaders: Americans were no better than Englishmen. In fact, Timothy Pickering went so far as to say that he sometimes doubted whether Europe exceeded America in crimes. "The *virtue* of Americans is often sounded in our ears," he said; "I wish there was more reason to boast of it." A Virginian declared that he had given up all hope of greatness from the revolutionary generation — "they are too much infected with the views of Britain"; and a South Carolina clergyman preached "a most excellent sermon upon the vices and immorality, want of honor, honesty, and everything that is virtuous, of South Carolina." One dis-heartened patriot suggested that Americans would soon be so corrupt "that even the tyrant of Britain will not accept of us as slaves, nor suffer his British subjects to be contaminated by a union with us." Washington, although not prepared to admit that his countrymen had yet sunk to this low level, confessed that "*we* that are not yet hackneyed in vice, but infants as it were in the arts of corruption . . . find it almost, if not quite impossible to preserve virtue enough to keep the body politic and corporate in tolerable tune."

Surprisingly enough, British morale seemed to be superior to that of Americans — these despised British were showing that they were made of sterner stuff than were Americans. "Is it not strange," remarked Charles Carroll of Maryland, "that the lust of domination should force the British nation to greater exertions, than the desire of liberty can produce among us?"

The war-rich made a dazzling display with their expensive clothes, gaudy chariots, and sumptuous feasts. In 1779, an awed dinner guest in Philadelphia reported that he had sat down to a repast consisting of one hundred and sixty-nine dishes. That the army was going hungry at the time affected not a whit any of the guests' appetites nor lessened the deference in which they held their host. As Washington said, these dinners and other entertainments "not only take Men off from acting in but even from thinking of this business." The United States seemed to be flowing with fun and whiskey; and if there was a war going on, it appeared to be arranged expressly for the benefit of profiteers and others of the get-rich-quick fraternity.

Americans began to copy the views of upper-class Europeans regard-ing affairs of honor as well as the cut of their satin breeches. Dueling, hitherto frowned upon in the colonies as a product of European depravity, grew popular in the United States. Americans suddenly became excessively touchy about their "honor"; upon the slightest affront, men were called out to settle the affair by the code of gentlemen. Philadelphia, for example, had nine duels in one week; the fields around the city fairly crackled to pistol fire as offended gentlemen, most of them army officers, tried to bring each other down. Even the French minister, Gérard, was startled by the frequency of these affairs of honor. Fortunately, the fatalities were few; either these duelists were uncommonly poor shots or their honor was satisfied by the burning of a little powder.

Americans enthusiastically took up French fashions. Some Philadel-phians aspired to make their city the American Paris by sedulously copying the fashions and manners of the French capital. They looked to the French Ministers, Gérard and La Luzerne, as arbiters of good taste sent to redeem Americans from rusticity and provincialism; and the French ministers obligingly undertook to teach these willing republicans how to be men of the world. Twice a week, Gérard's house was the scene of balls, entertainments, and parties where Americans might acquaint themselves with the latest modes from Paris; and soon these fashions were seen in all the drawing rooms in Philadelphia. Among the ladies, it was observed, "French hair dressers, milliners, and dancers are all the *tone*. The *Virginia-Jig* has given place to the *Cotillon*, and minuet-de-la-cour." And everywhere "every Lady & Gentleman were Endeavouring to outdo the other in Splendor and Show."

On the other hand, not all Americans were willing to carry intimacy with France to the point of sending their sons to Paris. Mrs. Mercy Warren of Boston, for example, warned her son to beware of France, "the seat of dissipation, where luxury is refined upon, and enormities are fashionable that would put a savage to the blush." Probably no advertising could have been more effective in stimulating young men to complete their educations in Paris.

While the ladies were piling switches and ornaments on their heads until getting safely through doorways almost became a serious problem in navigation, the men, in accordance with the precepts of republican simplicity, were giving up wigs and powder and exposing their own hair — or lack of it — to the public gaze. For those blessed with a fine head of hair, the sacrifice was not perhaps disadvantageous, but to the bald the fashion was hardly welcome. "Neither powder nor pomatum has touched my head this twelvemonth, not even to cover my baldness," declared Timothy Pickering, a martyr to the new mode.

It was remarked of Philadelphia in 1782 that this city, formerly renowned for its austerity, would now "vie with the first Courts in Europe for dissipation, luxury & extravagance"; at a celebration given by the French minister in honor of the birthday of the Dauphin, "few gentlemen appeared in less than Silk & Embroidery." The Prince de Broglie, visiting Boston in 1782, complimented the descendants of the Puritans upon their breeding. "They have capital wines and also napkins," he reported. "At table everybody drinks out of his own glass, and the plates are changed as often as can be desired. It is in fact downright magnificence." [14]

It is equally clear that French refinement had scarcely reached rural America. A French nobleman, stopping at a New England farmhouse, might expect to be asked to cut the children's hair — all Frenchmen being thought to be either barbers or dancing masters. In Virginia, the common people found amusement in cockfights and boxing matches — of which latter sport, De Chastellux remarked that "the ferocious practice of stage-

[14] The Prince de Broglie had a narrow escape in Philadelphia from which he learned the importance of informing himself of American customs. "I partook of most excellent tea," he wrote, "and I should be even now still drinking it, I believe, if the Ambassador [Luzerne] had not charitably notified me at the twelfth cup, that I must put my spoon across it when I wished to finish."

boxing in England, is urbanity, compared with the Virginian mode of fighting." The "innate ferocious disposition" of the lower classes in Virginia left De Chastellux doubtful whether civilization had penetrated very deep in the Old Dominion.

Many Congressmen enthusiastically threw themselves into the night life of Philadelphia, gaming, dancing, and feasting until the small hours and easing themselves the next morning into their seats in the State House somewhat the worse for wear. It was whispered that the reports of committees were sometimes delayed because the members had been carousing most of the night. No doubt, after a night spent in revelry, many were ready to agree that there was something to be said for a life of sobriety, and perhaps it was in this chastened frame of mind that they passed their resolutions calling upon the American people to practice the Spartan virtues. On the other hand, Congress celebrated the Fourth of July by "drinking Madeira Wine from 5 to 9 o'clock, then sallying out to gaze at fireworks, and afterwards, returning to Wine again," And the President of Congress lived with almost princely ostentation, a "sumptuous Equipage, & every Appurtenance," together with one of the finest houses in Philadelphia, being placed at his disposal. The Tory landlord of the President's house refused to accept his rent in paper money, with the result, a patriot reported, that "all Rents immediately were demanded in hard money, & many a poor Whig has been obliged to leave his House because he had only paper to pay his Rent." Yet, in 1778, in a sudden access of virtue, Congress resolved that since theatrical entertainments diverted the people from the war effort, anyone holding office under the United States should be dismissed if he acted in or attended the theater.

Ugly rumors began to be heard that some Congressmen were using the confidential information they derived from service on committees to further their speculations in trade. It was charged that many members had turned speculators and monopolists and that men in almost every important department of government were making their private fortunes in commerce and trade. In the case of one member, at least, the evidence is clear: upon learning that the French fleet was coming to the United States and would be in need of flour, Samuel Chase of Maryland bought so heavily that he raised the price more than 100 per cent.

John Hancock was a particularly flagrant offender against the moral code that was supposed to distinguish all good republicans. As a gay young man about Boston, his money and connections had been useful to the patriots, and Sam Adams had helped put him in the front rank of patriot leaders. Adams soon had reason to regret his action. Hancock, after his elevation to the presidency of Congress, began to affect "all the pageantry and state of an Oriental prince," dashing through the streets of Philadelphia in an elegant chariot, emblazoned with heraldic devices, and attended by servants in livery and fifty horsemen with drawn sabers.

After resigning the presidency of Congress, Hancock returned to Massachusetts and served as a general during the attack upon Newport and stayed "Just long enough to gain among the Multitude the popular Eclat." Fortified with a military title, he went into state politics, seeking to become the first governor of Massachusetts under the constitution of 1780. And, to the dismay of Sam Adams and other straight-laced patriots, the people preferred the flashy, fast-living Hancock to old-fashioned leaders of the vintage of '76.

Hancock was inaugurated with balls, assemblies, entertainments and feasts — "equal," groaned a patriot, "to anything you can tell of in Europe." Even the deacons and other good people of the one-time Puritan metropolis joined in the festivities, and, although seldom seen at their devotions, were often found "in the dancing or drawing room at a Game of Whist or leading down a Country Dance."

Those who summoned the people to return to the "spirit of '76" found themselves derided as "old-fashioned Whigs," professional kill-joys, narrow-minded Puritans. "I could never have thought," lamented Joseph Reed of Pennsylvania, "that in five short Years I should have heard publick Frugality, Spirit, and Patriotism laugh'd at, but so it is." Lafayette found that patriotism had become almost ridiculous in the eyes of some Americans: fighting in the cause of liberty was good enough for "suckers," they seemed to be saying, but smart people feathered their nests during a war. Instead of exerting themselves to save the Continental currency, the people acted "as tho' they had agreed to plunder the State between them, each exerting himself to get the greatest share of booty." "The Commonwealth lay like a Ship stranded," declared a patriot, "whose mariners instead of exerting themselves to save her were wholly employed in securing to themselves as much of the Cargo as possible, leaving her to the mercy of wind and waves."

The root of the evil was inflation, which, as Benjamin Rush of Philadelphia said, would "corrupt a community of Angels." The American people, being only mortal, quickly fell victim to its poison. Inflation became "the real plague of America," said the French minister — and from it stemmed most of the evils of the time: the distress of the army, the preoccupation of the people with money-making, and the decline of revolutionary idealism.

Nothing discouraged Washington as much as the indifference of his countrymen toward the war. The lack of patriotism of the American people, he declared, was "infinitely more to be dreaded than the whole force of G. Britain, assisted as they are by Hessians, Indians, and Negro Allies." Although he never doubted that the people were eager for independence, their reluctance to make sacrifices and their supineness (which he came to regard as a national characteristic) led him to doubt that they would ever attain that happy state.

If Americans continued in this course, lamented the patriots, they would not long enjoy their freedom. Without ideals, they warned, the United States could not endure; unless Americans dedicated themselves to the public good, the commonwealth would be short-lived. "Recluses and Enthusiasts may vainly flatter themselves with democratical Constitutions on paper," said Alexander McDougall, "but the present Manners and forms of Government, will not long exist together." In 1779, John Adams expressed the fear that his countrymen "after having astonished the Universe by their Wisdom and Virtue, will become a Spectacle of Contempt and Derision to the foolish and wicked . . . and all this in the Space of a few Years." Americans were not fighting merely for the material grandeur and power of the United States; the patriots of '76 had striven to make the republic a moral force in the world, dedicated to propositions which proclaimed the dignity of the common man and his inalienable rights as a citizen. Now, however, it seemed certain that "no Country ever Catched the vices of others and degenerated so fast"; it might prove to be the melancholy distinction of the American republic that it fell faster and farther, in its short career, than any other country in history. "Like the great Roman empire we may fall from the summit of greatness and be buried in ruins," exclaimed a patriot.

Observing the American people thus fallen from grace, many patriots began to question whether such a people ever could storm the heaven of democracy. "There is so much Rascality, so much Venality and Corruption, so much Avarice and Ambition, such a Rage for Profit and Commerce among all Ranks and Degrees of Men even in America," said John Adams, "that I sometimes doubt whether there is public Virtue enough to Support a Republic." The French minister to the United States in 1778 declared that "the spirit of mercantile cupidity forms perhaps one of the distinctive characteristics of Americans" — hardly a sound foundation upon which to build a democratic society.

Already, it was known, French officers were saying of Americans that "money is their God, money is the controlling idea in all their actions, they only think of how it may be gained; every one is for himself, no one for the general good. . . . There is not a coffee-house in Paris where there is not to be found a hundred times more enthusiasm for this revolution, than in all the United States together."

And yet not all patriotism had fled the United States: there were, as Washington said, "a virtuous few" who kept the flame of resistance alive and who upheld the ideals of the Revolution amid the "Vanity, Vice and Folly" of the many. "Remove the personal influence of the few," it was said, "and they are a lifeless, inanimate mass, without direction or spirit." These steadfast spirits — most of whom were in the army — held the Revolution on its course and brought it to safety and success.

CHAPTER XXIII

Continental Army

IT was the army which bore the brunt of the inflation and the exactions of the profiteers. Wherever the army went, said General Henry Knox, prices were raised in order to effect as speedy a transfer as possible of the soldiers' pay into the pockets of the civilians. This phenomenon was observed first in New England, then in New York and Pennsylvania, and finally in Virginia. Let the army but appear on the scene, and watch prices skyrocket! "How unmercifully We poor Strangers are flead alive by the people of this country," exclaimed General Steuben in Virginia. By the summer of 1776, prices had risen to such a degree that General Knox declared that the soldiers' pay would not afford them decent clothing and there was "nothing to remit to their families except they go as ragged as beggars."

Shoddy merchandise which could not be sold elsewhere was unloaded upon the army — no doubt upon the principle that the army was fortunate to get anything whatever. On Arnold's expedition to Quebec, for example, the boats were found to be so poorly made that they swamped and ruined most of the provisions. "Could we have then come within reach of the villains, who constructed these crazy things," exclaimed one of Arnold's men, "they would fully have experienced the effects of our vengeance. . . . Avarice, or a desire to destroy us, perhaps both, must have been their motives — they could have had none else. . . . These men could enjoy the sweets of domestic ease, talk about liberty and the rights of mankind, possibly without even a recollection of their parricidal guilt." In 1776, incensed by the profiteering of New Englanders, the soldiers in reprisal cut down the fine groves of Cambridge and threatened to pull down the houses. General Steuben would not have stopped at these lengths; "I believe that in order to reconcile Heaven to us we should begin by hanging some Merchants who have troubled our affairs," he said. Certainly it would not have been healthy for a profiteer to trust himself near an army camp.

The morale of the soldiers was severely tried as they saw rags and a lean, hungry look becoming the emblems of an American fighting man. The question that never ceased to agitate American soldiers was why they starved and went naked in the midst of plenty. "Can the Country expect Spartan Virtues in her Army," asked General McDougall, "while the people are wallowing in all the luxury of Rome in her declining State?" "I despise my Countrymen," declared a soldier; "I wish I could say I was not born in America. I once gloried in it but am now ashamed of it"; why should he risk his life, he asked, "for my Cowardly Countrymen who flinch at the very time when their Exertions are wanted, and hold their Purse Strings as tho' they would Damn the World, rather than part with a Dollar to their Army"? During the winter of 1779–1780 — for the Continental army the worst winter of the war — in Philadelphia and other towns life went on "as if everything was in the most comfortable time of profound peace and Security." While the army starved and froze in 1777–1778, more fortunes, it was estimated, were made in the United States than in any other year since the founding of the colonies.

Freedom threatened to turn sour before it could be savored by the soldiers: while they fought and bled, profiteers, "Like Canker Worms to our Country," were "skulking about to hoard up and depreciate our money, and to avoid their duty in the field. . . . Others were basking in the sunshine of monopoly, forestalling and extortion, and withal pampering their vile natures in ease, superfluities and luxury." In this way, it was said, "millions were become poor in order to enrich a few."

Confronting the soldiers was the bitter prospect of returning to civilian life after the war, to find that the shirkers and draft-dodgers, speculators and profiteers, had become a privileged aristocracy while they — the men of the Continental army who had suffered and bled for liberty — were cast naked upon this alien world. "What encouragement to the soldier to risque his life, by braving death in defence of his country," it was asked, "when, after the war is over he will be obliged to support a miserable existence on the crumbs that fall from the table of those who have created fortunes from the distresses of the army?" Soldiers alone seemed destined to suffer "from that glorious revolution which they are the principal instruments of effecting"; for, as a result of their self-sacrifice, they were "involving themselves in debt, and laying the foundation of dependence on those whose liberty and affluence they are struggling to establish." They beheld civilians "sauntering in idleness and luxury, who at the commencement of the war, would not have been honoured with the rank of a non-commissioned officer in any of our corps." And these civilians were the first, bitterly exclaimed a soldier, "to despise our poverty and laugh at our distress."

Soldiers returning to Philadelphia on furlough found it hardly recognizable from pre-war days; it had become the most "genteel and elegant spot on the continent." "My God," exclaimed a veteran, "what Swarms of fine Girls in this Town." "You will hardly dine at a table," said a returned officer, "but they present you with three Courses, and each of them in the most Elegant Manner." Indeed, this relentless round of pleasure undermined the constitutions of the most hardened campaigners: men toughened by the rigors of the field broke under the strain of feasting and gaiety. General Nathanael Greene, visiting Philadelphia in 1779, was soon worn out by the feverish pace of the city's social life. "It was hard Service to get through the duties of the day," he said. "I was obliged to rise early and go to bed late to complete them. In the morning a round of Visiting came on — Then you had to prepare for dinner after which the Evening Balls would engage your Time until one or two in the Morning." William Erskine, back from the wars with a game leg, after a few weeks in the swirl of Philadelphia society found that he would have to leave town if he ever expected to recuperate.[1]

Yet the glitter and gaiety of Philadelphia palled upon soldiers who remembered what they had suffered and what their comrades were still suffering in the field. When Washington visited Philadelphia in 1779 and was treated to a dizzy round of balls, feasts, and receptions, it was, said General Greene, his companion, "such a Scene of luxury and profusion it gave him infinitely more pain than pleasure."

Perhaps it was only because he had been long in the field, but one young colonel found the Philadelphia girls much altered as a result of the war: they had, he remarked, "lost that Native Innocence in their manner which formerly was their Characteristick," and had "really got the Art of throwing themselves into the most Wanton and Amorous Postures." The susceptible colonel went home profoundly disturbed by what he had seen. "By Heaven," he exclaimed, " 'tis Almost too much for a Healthy, Vigorous, Young Soldier to bear; to be plac'd on an Elegant Sofa along Side of one of them, when they are displaying both the Artillery of their Figures and Eyes." British artillery had never done half so much execution.

The winter of 1779–1780 saw the army in worse plight than at Valley Forge. The War of American Independence never ceased to try the souls of American soldiers: the time for "heroic patience" lasted as long as the war. Hunger stalked the American camp; the magazines were completely

---

[1] But Philadelphia was by no means unique in its preoccupation with pleasure. After a tour of duty in Virginia, in which scarcely an evening passed without a dance, Colonel Walter Stewart was prepared to admit that he was never "amongst a People who studied more to please, or who Paid more attention to pleasure than the Virginians." But, he added, "I must still call it [Philadelphia] the most Agreeable place I was ever in."

empty of supplies. The men were obliged to spend much of the winter in tents, and, as at Valley Forge, they built their quarters in the dead of winter. What made this winter more unendurable was the extreme cold that gripped the country for many months. It was one of the coldest winters on record, and veterans of Valley Forge might well have regarded that encampment as a lesser purgatory than West Point and Morristown. "Many a good Lad," it was said, stood in the knee-deep snow "with nothing to cover him from his hips to his toes save his Blanket." Washington said in the winter of 1779 that the prospects of the Continental army had never been blacker: "We have never experienced a like extremity at any period of the war." At one time, it seemed inevitable that West Point would have to be abandoned and the troops dispersed to prey upon the countryside for food. Several Maryland brigades kept themselves alive by fishing for herring with nets loaned them by the inhabitants. At one time, the soldiers ate even the horses' food, although they drew the line at hay.

Yet, at this very time, the flour mills in New York, suffering from a shortage of water power, refused to grind except "for the ordinary consumption of the Inhabitants." In Pennsylvania, the government had collected over five thousand cattle for the army which could not be killed and preserved because of the lack of salt "of which," said the president of the state, "we cannot get a Bushel as we have neither Specie nor Continental Money & our Merchants will not touch State Money." Others refused to sell supplies to the army except for hard money or in exchange for such scarce commodities as sugar and salt, of which the army purchasing agents had none. The merchants had large quantities of clothing on hand which, so far as it benefited the army, might have been in another hemisphere.

The American army drew its flour chiefly from the Middle states and its meat from New England. From this circumstance sprang much hardship to the troops. Because the British controlled the sea, Americans were compelled to depend almost entirely upon land transportation, lamentably inadequate to the strain thus imposed upon it. Before the war, Americans had been accustomed to move their goods by water; as a result, roads had remained comparatively undeveloped. Particularly was this true of the South, where, because of the primitive state of the roads, the entire region, so far as supplies for the army were concerned, was almost cut off from the rest of the union. South of Pennsylvania, the north-south highway petered out into little more than a rutty and sometimes impassable wagon trail. A French officer who made the trip overland with Lafayette from Charleston to Philadelphia declared that "no campaign in Europe would be harder than this journey. . . . Our miseries increased every day, and had no other relief than the hope of arriving at last at Philadelphia." While the army was in New Jersey, the cost of transporting wheat from the

states south of Mason and Dixon's line was prohibitive: the teams consumed more in forage and food than they brought to the troops. To bring
flour from Annapolis to Boston overland was so expensive that General
Greene declared that it would be cheaper to send it by water in small
vessels; even "if only one out of four of these vessels should arrive safely,
it would afford a saving in point of expense." Indeed, so insoluble appeared
the problem of maintaining the army during the winter that General
Gates advocated sending the troops of each state home to be quartered
on their families and friends; if this were done, he predicted, "they would
come out Hearty, & Fat, in the Spring."

The bottleneck in land transportation was rendered more acute by
shortages of teams and wagons. The army found itself unable to bid for
horses against private buyers: in 1779, a quartermaster reported that in
Philadelphia a good horse, "(so great is the Demand for them) is comparatively as great a prize as the taking of a fort, tho' not so much honor
acquired in this acquisition." Horses were usually employed in civilian
work, where the profits were larger than in government service; as a result,
it was sometimes necessary for the men to harness themselves to wagons
and draw them through the snow. Through some error, virtually all the
horses belonging to the government were sold at the end of the campaign
of 1779, leaving the army dependent upon hired teams. Its money and
credit almost at the vanishing point, the army could not compete with
businessmen.

For American soldiers, this was truly a war of survival — survival against
starvation, hunger, and disease which fell to their lot, as defenders of
liberty, in a greater degree than to any other part of the population.
At few times in history from the Battle of Marathon to the Battle of
Britain have so many owed so much to so few. "Amidst all this boasted
Patriotism," said an American general, "the burthen has & must hang on
a handful of worn out worried Continentals." Gérard, the French minister, declared that outside the army there were few evidences of patriotism
in the country. "I have always thought our best Men were in the Army
— without are dogs," said a patriot. It never ceased to be a source of
wonder to Washington that men could endure so much for the sake of a
cause. The Continental army, he believed, had "done more and suffered
more than any other Army ever did in the defense of the rights and
liberties of human nature." The men were often half starved "always in
Rags, without pay, and experiencing, at times, every species of distress
which human nature is capable of undergoing." Lafayette hoped that the
sufferings which the troops endured would be put to their credit in the
next world "as a sort of purgatory"; sinners who had done time in the
Continental army ought to get off with a lighter dose of hell-fire.

Regardless of the fate of the soldiers in the next world, the Continental
army was in danger of losing whatever semblance of a regular army it had

slowly and painfully attained. Starving, freezing, and homesick men do not make good soldiers; the shortest way to make the army turn into a mob of freebooters was to subject it to suffering such as it experienced at Valley Forge, Morristown, and West Point. That the countryside was not ravaged by bands of marauders was a tribute to the discipline and patriotism of the officers and men. Perched upon these desolate heights, the army shivered, fasted, and swore throughout the winter, obliged sometimes to take provisions at the bayonet point but usually maintaining a discipline and moderation which under the circumstances was astonishing.

Military coercion of supplies was not Washington's choice: he was driven to it by necessity. It was only after persuasion, entreaty, and requisition had failed that he was reconciled to the use of force. At best, impressment meant an uncertain supply; at worst, it gave rise to disputes with the civil authorities and bred bitterness among the people. "We begin to hate the country for its neglect of us," said Alexander Hamilton in 1780. "The country begin to hate us for our oppressions of them." In some parts of the country, the people determined to "oppose Force to Force," threatening to precipitate civil war at the very time Americans were in danger of suffering defeat at the hands of their enemies.

As Washington frequently reminded his countrymen, there was a point beyond which the patience and fortitude of the soldiers could not be pushed. Civilians who dreaded "military license" and dictatorial rule were, by their neglect of the well-being of the army, ensuring the evils which they deplored. "The long and great sufferings of the Army is unexampled in History," he observed; "but there is an end to all things."

Except for the areas devastated by war, the country was becoming steadily more prosperous. More cattle were to be found in Massachusetts in 1779 than ever before, despite the fact that large numbers had been slaughtered for the army. If Americans were ruined, they were, it was said, "ruin'd in the midst of the most desirable plenty." In reality, however, it was only the army that experienced the pangs of hunger. It is ironical that the United States, one of the richest and most productive agricultural regions of the world, which before the war had exported a huge surplus of food products, should not have been able to feed adequately an army of a few thousand men. No one contended that there was any actual shortage — it was simply that the food did not reach the army. The troops were fairly well supplied with weapons and ammunition — thanks to France — but they were wretchedly supplied with food — thanks to the inefficiency with which the war was conducted, the breakdown in transportation, and the inflation which deprived the government of its vigor and the people of their patriotism.

It is worthy of note that the French forces in the United States suffered no lack of supplies. The American army might be reduced to a harrowing degree of destitution, yet a short distance away French troops would be living on milk and honey, owing, of course, to the fact that the French offered the farmers and merchants gold and silver, whereas Washington could offer only paper money or certificates. That is not to say, however, that there was no profiteering at the expense of the French; the merchants did not dispense with the time-honored principle of charging all that the traffic would bear merely because the French were allies. It was the custom to raise prices sharply just before the arrival of the French fleet in America; and the merchants, among them Robert Morris, made a killing by this strategy. When the French army was in New England, it was estimated that it expended at least sixty million French crowns — with a profit of at least three million crowns to two enterprising Yankees who helped supply its necessities. In 1779, while the American army was in its usual state of living from hand to mouth, the French minister was embarrassed by the quantity of flour offered in Philadelphia for the use of the French fleet; he hesitated to accept lest there be nothing left for the army of the United States.

Because paper money was inadequate to meet the demands of the armed forces, the army resorted to certificates — I O U's which the government stood pledged to redeem. But when these certificates fell due, the quartermaster and commissary departments were unable to meet their obligations; consequently the certificates went the way of paper money, debased and scorned. By 1778, speculators were purchasing them for a mere fraction of their original value; by 1781, they had almost ceased to pass at all. Few methods of raising supplies could have been more costly in good will of citizens; again it was the patriotic who were penalized for supporting the war effort.

Certainly the shortages that plagued the Continental army were not owing to any lack of manpower in the quartermaster and commissary departments. In 1780, the French minister to the United States estimated that at least nine thousand men were employed in handling the provisions of the army, drawing salaries and helping to consume the provisions they gathered. These men, for the most part, lived the life of "Gentlemen of pleasure and Gallantry," and so many held high rank that a French officer remarked that "one risks nothing in calling colonel a stranger who accosts you with confidence (for the inferior officers are more modest). The army swarms with them." Congress was agitated by the spectacle of these "Legions of Continental Sinecures who appear in Swarms like Locusts . . . rioting upon the blood and treasures of the virtuous Citizens (if any Such there be) in these united states." But if this state of affairs was disturbing to Congress, it was doubly so to the troops. Stout fellows strolling about camp, flaunting their finery and their full rounded bellies while those who did their duty in the field went hungry and in tatters — this spectacle was not calculated to reconcile the soldiers to their lot.

No doubt, the most conspicuous failure of the Continental Congress during the war was in supplying and organizing the Continental army. Lack of executive skill, the constantly shifting personnel of Congress, and the ignorance of military matters on the part of many members contributed to the distress and confusion in the army. While American soldiers were going almost naked, ample clothing consigned to Congress was rotting in the West Indies. The ordnance, clothing, and hospital departments were chronically in a state of chaos. Inefficiency, waste, and graft took their toll — always with the common soldier as the prime victim.

It was easy to blame the Continental Congress for the ills of the army. Congress was declared to present "a shocking Spectacle of Corruption & Deceptions" — a nest of intriguers and villains given to saving money at the expense of the army. "Popularity," said General Greene, "is the bane of American Liberty, and if a different policy is not pursued hereafter, ten to one but it proves our ruin. Such wrong headed politicks will either sooner or later like repeated fits of the apoplexy destroy the political existence of these States."

As might be expected, officers and men often grumbled at the wrong-headed interference of Congress in military matters. Let the civil authority appoint able men to command the armies and then let them fight the war unhampered by politicians was the cry. General Greene protested against a system which, he said, made gentlemen of the sword "subject to the censure and reproach of every dirty little politician, ignorant of every circumstance necessary to form a right judgment."

In 1780, Washington declared that the army was "distracted and almost torn to pieces by irregular promotions and disputes about rank." "We now see boys of yesterday's growth," it was remarked, "raised to the command of veterans, who have distinguished themselves in war before these striplings were born" — and all because they had friends in Congress or in the state legislatures. One officer, upon learning that a "Dutch Tavern Keeper, & a fat Son of Epicurus" had been promoted over his head, set out for Philadelphia, vowing that he would make a "Devil of a *Splutter*" in Congress. At one time, the army could not even parade without provoking controversies over rank and precedence; and many officers refused to do duty rather than be commanded by men they regarded as their inferiors. Officers complained that "not a fellow will shoe a horse or skin a beef unless you flatter him with a *Captaincy* at least; and he who retails whiskey, and chops up provisions for the soldiers must be dubb'd a *Colonel*."

The Continental Congress at first had refused to furnish any clothing whatever to the soldiers; then, after having reluctantly assumed this obligation, it largely shifted upon the states the burden of finding clothing for the troops of the various lines. As a result, while the troops of one state might be well and warmly clothed, the troops of another state were shivering in rags. At Valley Forge, for example, the Connecticut troops actually had a surplus of clothing which the state authorities hoarded, while the soldiers of other states went half naked in the snow. By 1779, the Pennsylvania Line was one of the best clad in the army, but Pennsylvania refused to grant Washington's request that its stores of clothing be turned over to a common stock from which all the states could draw. "We think it reasonable and just," said Pennsylvanians, "that our troops have the benefit of our care and diligence" — let other states take care of their own.

And so, to the discontent produced among the soldiers by the spectacle of civilians taking their ease in the midst of war, were added the gall and wormwood of inequalities in the army itself. Had all been upon an equal footing, misery might have been more easily borne; but the troops of a state that had hardly a good blanket or a whole pair of breeches among them had only to look to another cantonment to see troops of another state clad in warm clothing and, in some cases, elegant uniforms. The officers of the Pennsylvania Line, finding the officers of some other states "supplied with almost every necessary suitable for a gentleman and officer at a moderate cost" while they were obliged to pay six times as much for the same articles, resolved in 1779 to resign in a body unless their grievances were redressed. This threat of collective action turned the trick: supplies were sent to the camp by the state, to be sold to the officers at cost. The officers of the Pennsylvania Line were now the envy of the officers of less generous states, and were on "a footing equal to the British Establishment, & Superior to any others on the Continent." With the arrival of French troops in the United States, however, all American officers enviously contrasted their own shabby uniforms and meager fare with the resplendent clothing and well-laden tables of their allies.

Although promised uniforms as a bounty for enlisting, comparatively few soldiers ever actually received them. Failing uniforms, many soldiers would have settled cheerfully for a suit of clothes, a pair of shoes, or a blanket. Some served for years without receiving so much as a blanket. Anthony Wayne expressed alarm lest the country leave the troops "uniformly bare headed — as well as bare footed — & if," he added, "they find that we can *bare* it tolerably well in the two extremes — perhaps they may try it in the *Center*." Washington often deplored the "nakedness" of his troops; and although this adjective was perhaps not meant to be taken literally, the appearance of the men certainly bordered upon nudity.

Without uniforms, it was difficult to teach Americans to regard themselves as soldiers rather than as armed civilians. Washington believed that without military pride nothing could be expected from the army, but his efforts to inculcate soldierly virtues were impeded by a shortage of uniforms "painful to humanity, dispiriting to [the men] themselves, and discouraging to every Officer." "No man will think himself bound to fight the battles of a State that leaves him to perish for want of covering," said General Nathanael Greene; "nor can you inspire a soldier with the sentiment of pride whilst his situation renders him more an object of pity than envy." "I would soon risque my Life, Reputation and the fate of America at the Head of five thousand Troops neatly Uniformed," said Anthony Wayne, "than with double that number equally armed & disciplined, covered with rags and Crawling with Vermin."

Americans sometimes wore British uniforms handed down from the French and Indian War or confiscated from British supply ships. The result was that red coats were found in both armies; friend and foe were indistinguishable, and whole bodies of men were sometimes cut off by men they took to be friends. This fondness for red coats often cost Americans dear: three officers were scalped by friendly Indians in 1778 because they were in the uniform of British officers; and in a skirmish late in 1777, the Connecticut Light Horse, wearing cloaks similar to those worn by British cavalrymen, were surrounded by the enemy. Finally, in 1781, Washington forbade the wearing of red coats in the American army.

Because of the shortage of uniforms, officers were able to give free scope to their fancy in devising hats and other apparel. "I must acknowledge that I have an Invincible Prejudice in favor of an Elegant Uniform & Soldiery Appearance," Anthony Wayne confessed; and of his passion for elegance there can be no doubt. He wore a hat (his own creation) with "a white plume and a comb of flowing hair" — the general was hardly visible for the feathers. He was so encouraged by the effect that he immediately began "the experiment of making three short coats out of three old battered ones," which, if not a triumph of sartorial art, at least kept him occupied on long winter evenings.

In general, the American army looked as though it had been outfitted by an old-clothes dealer whose stock consisted of torn and tattered hand-me-downs. Men without breeches, men without shoes and stockings, men without shirts — these were the soldiers of the Continental army. Below the rank of colonel, most of the men wore their ordinary work clothes, stained and threadbare from hard usage in the plowing field as well as the field of battle. A man in uniform was likely to be a high-ranking officer, although anyone with a whole pair of breeches might qualify. General Sullivan declared in 1778 that he did not have enough clothes for another campaign, and that his pay was insufficient to permit him to buy new clothing. Unlike a private soldier, the general could hardly stalk about in a blanket.

This host in coats of many colors moved through the countryside the terror of crows. Shirtless and breechesless, they swarmed to the attack, spitting lead like so many furies. For many years of war, this was the plight of the American soldier; it was not until 1781 — six years after the commencement of hostilities — that the American army appeared like something more than farmers called out of their fields to repel an enemy. In that year, Count Rochambeau complimented Washington upon having "a Prussian Army" — the greatest compliment the Count could pay. The tattered hats, the patched coats and breeches, the stained hunting shirts, and the broken shoes were sloughed off; in the final campaign of the war, the army was clothed decently in uniforms. The troops still looked as though they badly needed a square meal but they were no longer naked — they wore trousers and shirts like other Christians, and the American camp was at last open to the inspection of ladies.

The sufferings of the army were well known to civilians; in fact, it was no doubt partly for this reason that so few civilians were willing to join the army. The toll taken among the troops by pestilence, particularly during the first years of the war, was sufficient in itself to make civilians rejoice that they were snug at home. The men who straggled homeward from the American camp, broken in body by disease, chilled the martial ardor of even the patriotic. Of the two thousand men who went to Ticonderoga with Anthony Wayne in 1776, less than nine hundred returned "and the most of these Emaciated, worn out and unfit for further duty."

The state of colonial medicine was not greatly inferior to that of Europe; most medical discoveries promptly made their way across the Atlantic and were incorporated in the lore of colonial physicians. Purging, bleeding, emetics, blisters, and the like were the doctors' stock in trade; and in the case of some patients it may reasonably be assumed that if they survived, it was in spite of the doctors. Quacks and nostrums flourished here as well as in Europe, and the remedies were equally ineffective. There was a serious shortage of doctors in the United States; in 1776, there were only two medical colleges, one in Philadelphia and the other in New York, to supply the country with trained physicians. Some American practitioners boasted degrees from such medical schools as the University of Edinburgh, but these trained men were far too few to cope with the emergency created by the war.

There was no sight more welcome to recruiting officers than that of a stout, pock-faced recruit. The pockmarks meant that he was immunized to one of the worst scourges of the army — smallpox. In the American army, vaccination was frequently resorted to; but as it necessitated a period of convalescence lasting several weeks, Washington hesitated to vaccinate his men lest the enemy take advantage of their temporary indisposition. Sometimes the troops themselves arranged to be inoculated for smallpox immediately after reaching camp, thus putting themselves out of action for almost a month — when their term of enlistment expired.

The catalogue of diseases, any one of which might prove mortal, that afflicted the troops was truly appalling. Smallpox, dysentery, jaundice, whooping cough, measles, cholera morbus, venereal disease, and typhoid — to name only a few — exacted a higher toll than did actual combat.

"What a frail, dying creature is Man," mused an army surgeon. "We are certainly not made for this world — daily evidences demonstrate the contrary." Disease was particularly rampant during the campaign of 1776 when, in New York, over eight thousand troops — one third of Washington's army — were down sick. The necessity of frequently moving the sick and wounded added greatly to their misery. So high was the death rate that Washington began to fear that the army would be consumed before the end of the campaign; the United States did not have sufficient manpower, he declared, "to allow of such a Consumption of Lives and Constitutions as have been lost." "Disease," said John Adams, "has destroyed ten men for us where the sword of the enemy has killed one."

Few American soldiers in this war experienced the exultant feeling of "Now I'm out of it" when nicked by an enemy bullet. In view of what they had to undergo in the hospitals, the wounded had better reason to resign themselves to death than to look forward to an early return to civilian status and happy reunion with their families. "Hospitals are the sinks of human life in an army," declared Benjamin Rush. "They robbed the United States of more citizens than the sword."

In its anxiety to economize, Congress adopted what General Charles Lee called "a little narrow dirty economy in all things relating to the Hospital." The pay of army doctors was set so low that Washington protested that "no man, sustaining the Character of a Gentleman, and who has the least Medical Abilities or Skill in the profession can think of accepting it." At first, Congress declined to give army nurses any pay whatever; finally, in 1776, they were given one dollar a week. Moreover, the pay of doctors and nurses, small as it was, was usually long overdue — the government owed some doctors for as much as two years' services. In 1781, the director general of hospitals complained that the expense of postage incidental to his office swallowed up all his pay. Under these circumstances, it is not surprising that many doctors, as Washington remarked, proved to be "very great Rascals, countenancing the Men in sham Complaints to exempt them from duty, and often receiving Bribes to Certifie Indispositions, with a view to procure discharges or Furloughs."

The medical service was especially unfortunate in its directors. Dr. Benjamin Church, its first head, proved to be a traitor; but even before his treason was detected, it was charged that he was neglecting his duties. His successor, Dr. John Morgan, a professor of medicine in the medical school of the College of Philadelphia, was dismissed from the service in 1777 by Congress; but, as Congress later acknowledged, it acted precipitately in holding Morgan accountable for many of the shortcomings which its own interference had produced. The next director of hospitals, Dr. Shippen, incurred the suspicion of Dr. Benjamin Rush — a gadfly of all evildoers (and of many whose only fault was to disagree with him). Rush asked how Shippen, on a salary of six dollars a day, was able to "vie with the minister of France in the magnificence of his Equipages & feasts." To Rush, Shippen's extravagance and display were prima-facie evidence that the director was embezzling public money; he even accused Shippen of "bargaining with tavern keepers in Jersey and Pennsylvania for the sale of madeira wine from our hospital stores, bought for the use of the sick." On the other hand, Robert Morris defended Shippen against these charges, although he admitted that the doctor was "too great a devotee to Convivality for a Man of business (this probably," he added, "is giving myself a Slap in the Face too)." Shippen ultimately was acquitted by a court-martial, but the long and bitter controversy between Shippen and Rush disorganized the medical service; while the doctors wrangled, soldiers died.

"All hope abandon, ye who enter here," might properly have been inscribed over the portals of military hospitals. Lacking adequate medicines, doctors, and even food — for hospital patients were frequently on the same rations as the rest of the army — these institutions were lamentably unfit to provide for the needs of the sick and wounded. At the Continental hospital in Massachusetts, the patients were without medicine for over a year; amputation cases had nothing to eat except bread; and hundreds of wounded would have died of malnutrition had it not been for public donations of food. In 1776, over two hundred New York soldiers were pronounced unfit for duty because there was no sulphur "to cure them of the itch." Sometimes the sick, wounded, and dead were thrown together. At Ticonderoga in 1776, Anthony Wayne reported that "the Dead and dying laying mingled together in our Hospital or Rather House of Carnage is no uncommon Sight." "The first object that presented my eyes," reported an officer, "was one man lying dead at the door, the inside two more laying dead, two lying dying between them, the living with the dead, had so laid for four and twenty hours."

The wounded sometimes lay for many hours at the scene of action unattended by surgeons. And when medical assistance finally arrived, its ministrations were often excruciatingly painful; it took British surgeons forty minutes to amputate a man's leg — of course, without anesthesia, which was unknown. Even so, Dr. Benjamin Rush acknowledged that wounded American soldiers who fell into the enemy's hands received better medical care from British army doctors than from those of their own army.

These sufferings intensified the bitterness of the soldiers against merchants who had turned the war into a huge stock-jobbing operation. "The country abounds with everything we want," exclaimed the senior surgeon of the army, "and yet it is truly mortifying that those should be the only sufferers who are the most deserving." A visit to an army hospital left patriots boiling with anger at the sight of so much needless suffering: General Nathanael Greene declared that he had never experienced greater distress than that produced by the spectacle of wounded soldiers. In 1782, the wounded lived on a diet of beef and bread, and the bread was usually sour, while, said Timothy Pickering, "the citizens in general of the United States indulge a luxury to which, before the war, they were strangers!"

It was not all grim starvation or stark boredom at the American camp: it was observed of the Continental troops that although they sometimes went several days without a square meal "their Spirits are good under every Difficulty, and they will be a frollicking," particularly if handed out a stout ration of rum. Occasionally, a contingent of local belles who, it was remarked, were "very fond of the soldiers, but much more so of officers," were brought into camp, where they were taught games by the officers which always ended in the girls being taken prisoner and afterwards released — at a small price — on parole. Suppers with dancing which lasted far into the night were the favorite amusements of the officers; a ball given on New Year's Eve in 1778 lasted until three o'clock — "thus," it was said, "have the gallant Virginians commenced the new year." In 1780, some of the officers stationed at Haverstraw, New York, dressed in women's clothes "and had a genteel Country Dance." The chief social events of the season, however, were the balls presided over by Mrs. Washington, Mrs. Knox, and the wives of other generals, and usually opened by General Washington himself. There were also less decorous affairs such as the dinner given Washington and his staff in 1776 when the guests drank such bumping patriotic toasts that "our good general Putnam got sick and went to his quarters before dinner was over, and we missed him a marvel, as there is not a chap in the camp who can lead him in *Maggie Lauder* song."

The commander-in-chief was a great favorite with the ladies and he fully returned their admiration; although not as much of a ladies' man as Benjamin Franklin, he certainly cut a more impressive figure than did old Ben in a ballroom. It was at balls, indeed, that Washington shone: his tall, graceful form was never better displayed than when he was whisking some belle about the floor. It was his fear of making a poor showing before the ladies of France that he gave as a reason against going to France after the war; he spoke no French, he explained to Lafayette, and "to converse through the medium of an interpreter upon common occasions, especially with the *Ladies* must appr. so extremely aukward, insipid, and uncouth, that I can scarce bear it in idea." Too, he might have added that Franklin had already pretty well covered the field. "He admires pretty women," noted an approving French officer, "and even notices their gowns and how their hair is dressed. He does it quite openly and before his wife, who does not seem to mind at all." Perhaps it was Washington's inability to tell a lie that accounts for Mrs. Washington's broadmindedness.

During the inactive season, Mrs. Washington usually joined her husband in camp; when the time to open the campaign arrived, she marched back to Mount Vernon. Martha Washington became a good trooper; she often remarked "what pleasure she took in the sound of the fife and drums, preferring it to any music that was ever heard!" The general took good care to make her stay with the army comfortable: in 1779, for example, not knowing where his headquarters would be pitched for the winter, Washington told his wife to "hire lodgings in some genteel (but not common boarding) house in Phila."

New England democrats might cavil at Washington's aristocratic bearing, but most Europeans who met him were charmed by his lofty manners, his cold and polished demeanor, and his stately, military carriage. "His manners," said the Baron du Bourg, "are those of one perfectly accustomed to society, quite a rare thing certainly in America." He looked as though he expected deference as his due — and usually he received it. It was noticed that Washington at all times treated his officers with great politeness, but they seldom attempted any familiarity with him. Most people, he kept at arm's length, and there were few who braved his displeasure by seeking to intrude upon his austere and forbidding privacy.

Most observers were struck by Washington's grave and careworn air: not until after victory was won did he relax "the contracted, pensive phiz" that he wore during the siege of Boston. "A shade of sadness overshadows his countenance," said De Fersen, a Swede serving in the French army, "which is not unbecoming, and gives him an interesting air." To many, he seemed silent and heavy — a dull man who took refuge in silence to cover up his want of wit; and it is true that in a large company Washington was seldom lively or entertaining. He aged rapidly during the war, and in 1779 he spoke of himself as an old man; when Washington was only fifty-three, a visitor remarked upon his "noble and venerable appearance." But this grave and silent man let down his reserve when, after dinner at headquarters, he sat with his staff, cracking nuts and drinking toasts. Mellowed by wine, he was at times almost witty. Certainly, the toasts were numerous enough to put even the most phlegmatic in sparkling good humor: they drank to the King of France, the Queen, to the United States, to a host of assorted dignitaries, "to our triumphs in war and in love," and so on, until the war seemed very far away.[2]

As commander-in-chief, Washington risked his life almost as freely as when he had served as a colonel of Virginia troops under Braddock's command. A Continental soldier said that he always ducked whenever he heard a bullet go by — until he saw Washington "stand on the Parapet of Fort Putnam, & with a Glass view the Motions of the Enemy, and with

[2] "They drank twelve or fifteen healths with Madeira wine," said a French officer. Frenchmen, before they learned to sip rather than to empty their glasses at every toast, were in danger of passing out before the toasts were half through. All the evidence indicates that Washington was temperate in his drinking.

the utmost Composure, while our men & the Enemy were contending with each other within Gun-shot of the Fort. . . . I caught the Example," exclaimed this veteran, "my Fears fled, & I think they are forever gone!"

If Washington was fighting to be a free man, the war was, he complained, making of him "a perfect slave." He supervised the training of the troops, drew up the plans for the campaign, and at various times acted as commissary general, quartermaster general, and clothier general. Lacking adequate maps of the country, he was forced to rely upon sketches of the terrain drawn by himself and his staff. He even performed all the duties of the intelligence section, writing letters to spies with secret ink and directing their movements.

Washington, a Virginia gentleman who rode to the hounds and kept a large stable, was an excellent judge of horseflesh. Like Cromwell, he was a country gentleman born to the saddle. Virginia bred fine horses and fine women but there was some doubt where the affections of Virginians really lay: it was said that during the Revolutionary War "anybody would as soon have lent his wife as his horse." Among the oddities of behavior that struck travelers in the Old Dominion was the readiness of the people to walk two miles in order to ride a horse one mile. At the track at Williamsburg — the best in the United States — races lasting a week were held every spring and summer, at which, it was said, "very capital horses are started, that would make no contemptible figure at Newmarket." Virginia gentlemen lived in their saddles; Jefferson, in recommending the formation of a cavalry corps, pointed out that "this service opens us a new fund of young men, who have not yet stepped forth; I mean those whose indolence or education, has unfitted them for foot service." In this type of young man Virginia abounded.

Given this background, it might be supposed that Washington would lose no time in organizing a strong force of cavalry, particularly as decisive superiority in cavalry might have brought victory to the Revolution. Such superiority could have been employed in harassing enemy lines of communication, gaining intelligence of troop movements, reconnoitering, and in cutting to pieces a routed army. Yet, in fact, Washington made little use of cavalry; and except in the Southern theater of war, where he was not in immediate command, mounted men took a distinctly minor part in the fighting.

The neglect of cavalry in the North was owing primarily to the difficulty of providing fodder for a large number of horses over any considerable length of time. Want of forage obliged Washington to scatter his cavalry and draft cattle over the countryside; in the winter of 1778, for example, the cavalry had to be divided into four parts and distributed among the states from Connecticut to Virginia. Cavalry had not been used extensively in the wars fought upon North American soil between the French and British: the great stretches of wilderness through which the armies marched offered so little sustenance to horses that it was almost impossible to feed the teams that hauled the wagon trains of the armies. Moreover, in New England, oxen rather than horses were commonly used in farm work and in transportation. Such horses as New England possessed were not cavalry material: they were mostly plow horses and nags which, said a British officer, "of all the various breeds of that noble animal, certainly are the most peculiar and diabolical," being distinguished by "an unaccountable wriggling gait, that till you are accustomed to it, you are more fatigued in riding two miles, than a whole day's fox-chace." No gentleman, it was observed, could mount such scurvy steeds — although in the opinion of British officers they were eminently suitable for Yankees.

The British cavalry, like that of the Americans, was hampered by shortages of horses, fodder, accouterments and saddles. The difficulty of transporting horses across the Atlantic in the slow-sailing transports of the time was staggering: fifty days or more at sea were bound to take a heavy toll. Most of the horses that survived the passage or were purchased or seized in the United States were used as draft animals by the British army to transport supplies, cannons, and baggage; few could be spared for such a comparative luxury as cavalry. The army, after all, moved by the aid of horse-drawn wagons; without the commissariats and quarter-masters' departments, the troops could not have taken the field. It is not surprising, therefore, that not more than six hundred cavalrymen served with the British army in the North and that not all of them were equipped at the same time with horses. A dismounted dragoon was a common sight.

As a result, cavalry remained one of the weakest branches of both armies. Not even a regiment of horse was attached to Washington's army, and no uniform system of maneuver or discipline was ever adopted. During the early part of the war there was no single officer in command of all the cavalry; when Count Casimir Pulaski, late commander of the Polish patriot army, was made chief of the cavalry by Congress, native-born Americans so hotly resented his elevation that he threw up his command in 1778.

After retiring from command of the cavalry, Pulaski formed a "Legion" composed of mixed cavalry and infantry, recruited in part from British prisoners and deserters; and various other leaders followed his example. But these Legions soon won a bad name for themselves. Unlike the lines in the Continental army, they owed no allegiance to any particular state and they were wholly dependent upon the Continental Congress for support. When supplies failed, they began to conduct themselves like freebooters, foraging indiscriminately upon the inhabitants to such a degree that Pulaski was ordered, in 1779, to leave Pennsylvania with his men before civil war broke out between his Legion and the embattled farmers of Lancaster County. Pulaski was killed shortly after at Savannah, and his Legion was incorporated in that of Colonel Armand, a French soldier of fortune.

At first, few women followed the army, and in consequence the troops became ragged and dirty, and "thinking it rather a disparagement to them, chose rather to let their linen etc., rot upon their backs than to be at the trouble of cleaning 'em themselves." The army badly needed the feminine touch — and soon got it with a vengeance. When it became apparent that the war was not to be a summer's campaign, wives of the soldiers and ladies of easy virtue took up quarters with the soldiers until, by the campaign of 1777, Washington was complaining that "the multitude of women . . . especially those who are pregnant, or have children, are a clog upon every movement." When the Continental army marched through Philadelphia in 1777 to meet Howe on the Brandywine, Washington ordered that the female camp followers were to be kept out of sight — the good people of Philadelphia might not understand. In 1781, when Washington made his dash to the Chesapeake to attack Cornwallis, he ordered the troops to leave at West Point "such of the Women as are not able to undergo the fatigue of the frequent marches."

Although an encumbrance in time of active war, these women were indispensable during the long periods of siege warfare which marked the conflict after 1778. They washed the soldiers' clothes, darned their socks, and made camp life tolerable to men who were notoriously partial to the comforts of home. Washington recognized that he must either give army rations to the women and children who accompanied the army or lose by desertion, "perhaps to the Enemy, some of the oldest and best Soldiers in the Service." [3]

Liquor was a staff of life in the American army: it was the comforter of the weary, medicine for the sick, balm to the heartsore, and the great reinvigorator of morale. Rum, John Adams said, was an indispensable ingredient in the American Revolution; it was likewise an indispensable ingredient in the American Revolutionary army. "Rum is as necessary to the Health of The Soldier as good Food," said General Gates; without rum, the consequence would be "Full Hospitals & a Thin Army." Lack of liquor was a potent cause of mutiny and desertion. "Experience has taught me," said General Robert Howe, ". . . that when men have been stinted in the Rations they have a just claim to, the only quieting Draught was the serving out to them a small Portion of Rum." Conditions in the American camp bred hard drinkers. "He is just what I should like for a military parson," said Alexander Hamilton of an acquaintance, "except that he does not drink." Of course, many officers, as befitted gentlemen, preferred wine to grog, but wine was in such short supply that sometimes

---

[3] In 1779, Margaret Corbin, who was wounded in the defense of Fort Washington "whilst she heroically filled the post of her husband who was killed by her side serving a piece of artillery," was given a pension by Congress.

even Washington and the general officers were obliged to make do with grog. When wine was available, however, the officers partook freely — so freely, indeed, that they became "as sociable as any sons of Bacchus in any Quarter of the World." "I was not half thawed," said Anthony Wayne, "until I put one Bottle of wine under my Sword Belt at Dinner."

Although Washington disapproved of the troops' "vile practice of swallowing the whole ration of liquor at a single draught," he never thought of denying his men their rations of rum. "The benefits arising from the moderate use of strong Liquor," he said, "have been experienced in All Armies, and are not to be disputed." In 1777, he urged Congress to erect distilleries for the army so that it would be sure of a cheap and abundant supply.

But this much-desired state of affairs was never attained: for soldiers, liquor was scarce and dear, although they often saw the country swimming in cider and whiskey. In an evening, a convivial civilian might toss down as much liquor as a soldier received in a month's rations. To the troops, the high price of liquor was one of the most trying aspects of the inflation. A month's pay was called "three Drunks" by the soldiers. Rum sold for thirty dollars a gallon in 1779 and it was "so weak that half a pint of it makes but a Pint of what they stile Grogg." A soldier's pay was good for only a quart of whiskey a month; yet, often as not, the men received no pay whatever and were obliged to depend wholly upon the consolations of philosophy and cold water. His men were falling sick for want of alcoholic refreshment, lamented General Heath, "while our country abounds with a variety and plenty of liquors." This was the recipe for mutiny if there ever was one. The troops deserted, plundered civilians, and raided taverns because, said Anthony Wayne, they would take by force "an article as necessary in the eyes of a Soldier as provisions & Clothing."

As might be expected, profanity was freely indulged in by the soldiers. A Georgia private, for example, addressed his colonel in this wise: he declared, said the colonel, that "I was a dam'd Lyar that I might do my worst God Damn me he cared not a damn for me." The vocabulary of this Georgia private, it would seem, was painfully limited; more picturesque profanity than this was to be heard in the American camp. Washington, however, had no ear for these niceties of speech: he was greatly disturbed by the prevalence of profanity and frequently signified in general orders his disapproval of the practice. "We can have little hopes of the blessing of Heaven on our Arms," he declared, "if we insult it by our impiety and folly." Washington wanted God-fearing fighting men and he bent every effort to inculcate piety and improve the morals of his troops. Chaplains were attached to each regiment; the soldiers were required to attend divine worship regularly; gambling was strictly forbidden. Washington even went so far as to banish cards and dice from camp whether or not they were used for gambling; officers, he said, ought to drill their men or read military treatises instead of whiling away their time over dice and cards.

Closely following the army were private traders or sutlers who sold rum, clothing, and food at excessive prices to the soldiers. These sutlers, said General Schuyler, were "in the Army what tippling-houses are in the cities: the receptacle of the abandoned, where mutiny, disorder and every vice takes place." Here soldiers were remorselessly stripped of their wages while the sutlers grew rich and advanced to the dignity of merchants and men of consequence in the community. The soldiers were loud in their complaints that "by the exorbitant prices of the necessaries sold by the sutlers, they have been obliged to expend the whole of their wages to prevent them from starving," but manifestly, it was better to be cheated by sutlers than to starve to death without them. Owing to the failure of regular supplies, the sutlers sometimes saved the army from dissolution — at, of course, a price. Moreover, the sutlers aggravated the inflation by offering high prices for goods which they were sure of selling to the troops at an even higher figure; they were, it was observed, "indefatigable in purchasing every thing, they don't care at what price" — with the result that the government usually found necessities preempted by the private traders.

When the soldiers received their pay — usually only a small installment of the sum owing them, for despite the vast sums of paper money printed by Congress there was little to spare for the army — they often as not found the money virtually worthless. By 1779, four months' pay of a private was equivalent to the price of a bushel of wheat; soap was far beyond the reach of enlisted men, although Washington pointed out that uncleanliness was one of the prime causes of the spread of disease; and even a moderate indulgence in the pleasures of life was likely to leave nothing to send home for the support of their families.

It was a subject of much dispute in the Continental army whether the officers or privates were the worse off. Sometimes officers were so deficient in clothing that they could not appear upon parade, and when ladies visited the camp, they were forced to beat a hasty retreat to quarters, taking particular pains to back away. Unlike a private, an officer was expected to support and clothe himself largely from his pay or private means. As a result of the inflation, the officers' pay and allowance were woefully inadequate: until 1778, they were given only eight pence a day for maintenance. Moreover, the states made no provision for supplying the families of officers with necessities. "There is no set of Men in the United States," said Washington, "(considered as a body) that have made the same sacrifices of their Interest in support of the common cause as the Officers of the American Army." Under the existing system, he complained, officers could not live up to their position as gentlemen; they could not offer a French officer or a friend better hospitality than "stinking whiskey (and not always that) and a bit of Beef without Vegetables." In some cases, even to eke out this humble fare, they were obliged to borrow money from civilians "and run in debt to them for necessaries upon promises of payment in a short time." And officers' feelings might easily be imagined, observed a Continental general, "when they are dunned by the peasants for small sums, and at a loss what answer to give them."

On the other hand, officers were free to resign at any time they desired, whereas privates had to remain in the army for the full term of their enlistment or incur the risk and odium of desertion. Hundreds of officers took advantage of this privilege by throwing up their commissions and retiring to private life, sometimes in the midst of a campaign. Washington was seldom without fear that his officers would leave him, singly or in a body; indeed, it seemed largely to be a question whether the soldiers or the officers would abandon him first. Many left the service in order to save themselves and their families from the inflation that was devouring their substance. "It is high time," remarked an officer in 1780, "for me to turn my attention to some way of Business to prevent my being a Beggar." Even some generals found that without private fortune they could not afford to remain in the army.

In the British army, officers' commissions were freely bought and sold; in the American army, on the other hand, trading in commissions was strictly prohibited. This, it might be supposed, worked little hardship upon the officers — a ticket to the poor house and a commission in the army seemed equally unsalable. Nevertheless, in their destitution, many officers asked that their commissions be made salable: when retiring from the army they might raise by this means at least enough cash to speed them on their travels homeward. But Congress refused to consent to this arrangement; whereupon the officers demanded that after the war they be given half pay for life.

Pensions of this kind were awarded officers in the British army, and Americans insisted upon being placed, in this particular at least, upon the same footing as the enemy. And, as Washington pointed out, the officers had made such heavy sacrifices for the cause that half pay for life represented only a small part of the losses they had sustained: to ask them to continue to give up their ease and comfort without hope of reimbursement "when their companions and friends are amassing large fortunes, is viewing human nature, rather as it should be, than it really is. . . . Few men are capable of making a continual sacrifice of views of private interest, or advantage, to the common good." The salvation of the cause, Washington bluntly told Congress, depended upon granting half pay for life to the officers; if this were denied, he predicted that the upper ranks of the army would "moulder away to nothing, or be composed of low and illiterate men void of capacity for this, or any other business."

To many congressmen, however, pensions smacked of a standing army and a privileged officer caste — abominations which ought never be tolerated in the home of the free and the brave. They thundered that "this *was* in the beginning a *patriotic* war"; had the officers forgotten, they asked, "that we drew the Sword in defence of freedom"? Henry Laurens, the president of Congress, declared that half pay would "compel thousands of poor industrious Inhabitants by contributions to pamper the Luxury of their fellow Citizens"; it would raise up "a set of haughty imperious Scandalizers of industrious Citizens & Farmers" and would rivet the most hateful of all aristocracies upon the country.

Nevertheless, Congress was hardly in a position to humor its prejudices against standing armies: the country was at war and the officers were throwing up their commissions and retiring to civilian life. After a long and heated debate, Congress in 1778 voted to give the officers half pay for seven years after the war — a compromise which removed some of the sting of having been forced to accede to the demands of the military under the threat of mass resignations. With this, the officers were forced to be content, although many grumbled that Congress was playing its usual niggardly game with the army.[4]

In 1775 and 1776, the American army contained a far larger proportion of yeomen and substantial citizens than later in the war. The army that gathered to repel the British at Boston and New York was no "rabble in arms" but men of property and standing in the community, mixed, it is true, with rougher elements of the population drawn from the seaport towns. In these years, the American army found it easier to raise men than at any other time during the war.

Obviously, it was not merely pay or bounties which led these men to enlist. "Something must be attributed," said General Knox, "to a rational, manly desire to be instrumental in the defence of the liberties of this country." As the soldiers themselves said, "nothing but a kind of enthusiasm, in the sacred cause of freedom" sustained their courage. Nothing less could have enabled them to endure the hardships of the fighting front. "Seven Years of painful life in the Field" was the lot of those who stayed for the duration. "I say in the Field," added Washington, "because they have not during that period any thing to shelter them from the inclemency of the Seasons but Tents, and such Houses as they could build for themselves." These veterans, said Lafayette, "have a patience in their misery which is unknown to European armies." It was this steadfastness of his men which helped to sustain Washington's courage "amidst every perplexity and reverse of fortune" and the discouraging state of the home front.

---

[4] The grant of half pay for seven years proved so unsatisfactory that in 1780 Congress was obliged to extend half pay for life. In 1783, this was commuted into five years' full pay in a lump sum.

With the fading of the first flush of enthusiasm and with the prospect of a long and grueling war before them, there came a distinct falling off in the quality of the men who entered the armed forces. "Men without education, without experience and without influence," took the places of the patriots who at the beginning of the war had seized their muskets and rushed to do battle with the enemy. By 1777, Washington had come to the conclusion that the country was "pretty well drained of that class of Men, whose tempers, attachments and circumstances disposed them to enter permanently, or for a length of time, into the army." The men who remained — those who could be brought to enlist only by the offer of large bounties — were not generally the pure-souled patriots who are pictured standing in defense of liberty: one Continental officer declared that the army was in part composed of "the Greatest villains in the world" and that it could not properly be called an army until it was purged of "the Scum of human Nature." It became increasingly true that only those who preferred "the soldiers life to that of Labour, knowing they will be Cloathed & fed," joined the army. Congress, as early as 1776, was disturbed by the number of "apprentices, small Debtors and Infants" enlisting in the army; and even some civilians were heard to complain of the quality of men who volunteered — which, to the troops, might well seem the final insult heaped upon them by the paladins of the home front.

It is apparent that the rolls of the Continental army were far from being the social register of the times. General Charles Lee complained that "the arms of a Republic get into the hands of its worst members . . . the most idle, vicious, and dissolute part of every society." "Idle lurking fellows to be found about the Wharves of Philadelphia" composed part of the Pennsylvania Line. "I always found the Philad. Recruits the worst sent into the army," said a recruiting officer. "I look upon one sprightly young fellow from the Country worth ten to be found in Cities." Washington admitted that some entire regiments in the army consisted of "vagrant foreigners." These rough-and-ready gentry serve admirably today as ancestors; but during their lifetimes they were definitely not parlor company. The army attracted the zealous patriots, the adventurous, the devil-may-care young men; but it also drew upon the down-and-out, the drifters, and the outcasts of society.

There was a criminal element in the army not easily kept within bounds. The army offered a refuge to jailbirds — whose service to their country was entirely incidental to such private matters as dodging sheriffs and the like. Housebreaking, burglary, and robbery were too common in the army to make credible the assertion that it was wholly composed of patriots without fear and without reproach. Washington was "shocked at the frequent horrible Villainies of this nature committed by the troops." Whigs and Tories were plundered indiscriminately — in fact, a rich Whig was preferred to a poor Tory. "We complain," said Washington in 1777, "of the cruelty and barbarity of our enemies; but does it equal ours? They sometimes spare the property of their *friends*. But some amongst us, beyond expression barbarous, rob even *them!*" Even a private who bore the disarming name of Hate-evil Colston was found guilty of robbery.

To suppress these disorders, Washington acted with decision. Soldiers caught red-handed in plundering and robbing were summarily executed — which led some tenderhearted civilians to accuse Washington of unnecessary cruelty. In fact, however, Washington did not usually inflict the full measure of punishment — of three deserters, for example, he executed one and pardoned two. When there was ground for reasonable doubt, he withheld punishment, for he acted always upon the principle that if errors were committed in matters of this kind, they ought to be on the side of mercy. His intent was to make examples of offenders rather than to administer wholesale punishment. "Soldiers," he said, "are restrained more by fear, than by argument; by severe and well timed examples, than by cool and lenient measures."

By the military articles, the severest corporal punishment, other than the death penalty, was one hundred lashes, compared with one thousand lashes sometimes administered in the British army. One hundred lashes, to the tough, rawboned troopers in Washington's army, were lightly borne: they put a lead bullet between their teeth while under the lash and suffered the stripes without a groan. Therefore, Washington felt obliged to inflict the death penalty upon hardened offenders; in fact, he had no alternative between meting out a light punishment and death. Upon his recommendation, Congress changed the army regulations in such a way that more severe corporal punishment was permitted. After this reform, there were fewer executions.

Nevertheless, Washington failed to stamp out the criminal element in the army largely because of the laxity of the officers in carrying out his orders. It was of little avail to threaten severe punishment upon offenders if officers winked at irregularities or were themselves engaged in unsavory practices. Discipline was little regarded. "There seems to be a total ignorance of and attention to this system," said Washington, "so necessary to render an army formidable. . . . If I send an Officer to collect the Sick or Scattered of his Regiment," he went on, "it is ten to one but he neglects his duty, goes home on pleasure or Business and the next that I hear of him, is, that he has resigned."

As late as 1780, Congress dealt on paper in impressive numbers of soldiers; thirty-five or even fifty thousand men were demanded of the states, but Washington accounted himself fortunate if he had seven or eight thousand regulars in his army. Finally, in 1781, Congress was driven to admit that it was unavailing to call for a large army. In that year, the number of regiments in the Continental army was reduced from one hundred and sixteen to fifty in the hope that the states would fill this reduced number of regiments.

During most of the war, the Continental army was maintained wholly by volunteering. Recruiting officers were paid ten shillings for every man they sent up who passed muster. To guard against the temptation to enlist men who were "only Food for Worms — miserable sharp looking Caitiffs, hungry lean fac'd Villains &c. &c.," it was provided that the men must be healthy, able-bodied, not under sixteen years old, and at least five feet two inches in height. Before being admitted to the army, recruits were passed upon by boards composed of civilians. Often, however, to these boards, a man was a man for all his infirmities or age; in consequence, hundreds of "old Men, mere Children, disordered and decrepid persons" were sent to Washington as prime military material.

Recruiting was a pleasant interlude in the lives of many officers. They were freely permitted to leave camp in search of recruits, and sometimes they remained away for weeks. When they returned, no questions were asked: it was expected of them only to tend to the business of recruiting "as well as strong drink and women will permit them." There were some officers who spent most of their time recruiting — a labor which took them frequently into taverns and necessitated much drinking with prospective soldiers. "Every country village in the vicinity of camp," it was observed, "you will find crowded with pot-valiant heroes and fire-side soldiers." Rather than let a promising recruit slip through their fingers, they would sit and drink with him all night and they accounted it an evening well spent if, before he slipped under the table, the recruit signed the articles. Taverns did a roaring business. After the recruit had been paid his bounty, the tavern keepers plied him with liquor as long as the bounty money held out, and "when it is gone, they encourage him to enlist for the sake of the bounty, then to drinking again; that bounty gone, and more money still wanted, they must enlist again with some other officer, receive a fresh bounty and get more drink, &c."

Early in the war, Washington recognized that patriotism alone could not be depended upon to fill the army. "A great and lasting war can never be supported on this principle alone," he said in 1776. "It must be aided by a prospect of Interest or some reward." Mankind, he concluded, was governed by self-interest — "the few . . . who act upon Principles of disinterestedness, are, comparatively speaking, no more than a drop in the Ocean." From the premise that mankind in the mass was governed by base motives, he reasoned that bounties were essential to spur enlistments in the army; and Congress was reluctantly compelled to agree.

Accordingly, as has been seen, Americans were given a bounty upon enlisting in the army, but these bounties could not keep pace with the inflation and with the swift decline of martial ardor that marked the later stages of the war. Bounties had to be raised steadily, and land and clothing as well as money held out to prospective recruits. John Adams declared as early as 1777 that the venality and greed of the people was "the most dreadful and alarming enemy America has to oppose. . . . This predominant avarice will ruin America, if she is ever ruined. . . . I am ashamed of the age I live in." By 1779, Virginia was offering four hundred dollars and three hundred acres of land to every volunteer — with few takers. In 1782, to raise a corps of riflemen for two months, the state of North Carolina offered as bounty a cow and calf. Even these heroic measures failed to draw forth the manpower of the country; as Washington said, "all the allurements of the most exorbitant bounties and every other inducement, that could be thought of have been tried in vain, and seem to have had little other effect than to increase the rapacity and raise the demands of those to whom they were held out." At best, bounties were "given to little better purpose than to hire the populace to visit the army" and, after looking about, to go home satisfied that they had not engaged for a longer period. Well assured that bounties would be increased, prospective recruits held back until they were offered more money, land, and clothes.

High bounties hardly proved that American soldiers were mercenary; compared with the inflationary increase in prices, bounties remained low. As early as July 1776, the complaint was general in the army that prices were so high that the purchase of a few necessities took the soldiers' entire pay. The soldiers' pay remained the same, yet the cost of living had advanced at least 25 per cent since the previous year. "Do you desire us to go to war," asked the soldiers of civilians, "and receive from you but one half of what we had when we first engaged?" Supplied by the government with bare necessities, the troops could survive despite the inflation, but their families were not so fortunate. It was through their wives and children at home that inflation most acutely struck the men of the Continental army. "Not a Day Passes my head," said an officer, "but some Soldier with Tears in his Eyes hands me a letter to read from his Wife Painting forth the Distresses of his family in such strains as these, 'I am without bread, and Cannot get any, the Committee will not supply me, my Children will Starve, or if they do not, they must freeze, we have no wood, neither Can we get any. *Pray Come home.*'"

Without bounties, the army could not have been maintained. In themselves, the rigors of military life were quite enough to dissuade most civilians from enlisting; and as the war spun itself out, the sweets of civilian life became progressively sweeter. Under the spur of inflation, wages advanced to such a point that by 1780 a day laborer was receiving for one day's work as much as a soldier received in a month. As Washington perceived, high wages at home were one of the army's worst enemies: "the class of men who are willing to become soldiers" were alienated from the service. It was difficult to make the army attractive at a time when the worst-paid drudgery in civilian life was more rewarding than the pay and rations of soldiers, or when common laborers were receiving higher wages than were officers in the Continental army. Although the states were ultimately forced to aid soldiers' families and to adjust the pay of the troops to the inflationary price level, few men would choose the army as a career offering material rewards commensurate with the risks and sacrifices it entailed.

It was necessary to supplement the strength of the Continental army with recruits sent up by the states for a brief tour of duty. These men were short-term recruits, sometimes enlisted for as short a period of time as three months. In Washington's opinion, such soldiers were hardly superior to the state militia. Twelve months was deemed necessary to train a soldier for combat; yet most recruits remained only a few months before they left the army for the greener pastures of civilian life. By the time their term had expired they had not yet been broken to harness: they were still, said Washington, "uneasy, impatient of Command, ungovernable; and claiming to themselves a sort of superior merit, generally assume, not only the Priviledge of thinking, but to do as they please." To Washington's mind, the curse of the American army was short enlistments; if the war should be lost, he was prepared to ascribe defeat primarily to this cause. It vastly increased the cost of the war, rendered impossible the planning of offensive operations, and made it necessary to feed and supply two armies at the same time — the discharged men on their way home and the new troops coming in. In later years, he always regretted that Congress had not recruited a permanent army in 1775–1776 "when zeal and patriotism ran high, and men were eager to engage for a trifle, or for nothing. . . . Had we kept a permanent Army on foot," said Washington in 1780, "the enemy would have had nothing to hope for, and would in all probability, have listened to terms long since."

But this opportunity was missed. Only a comparative handful of men enlisted for three years or the duration; in 1780, for example, three fourths of the troops were men enlisted for nine months or less. One of the severest trials of these long-enlisted men was to see the nine-months men leave happily for home; and their discontent was aggravated by the knowledge that they might soon "see those very men returning to the Field after exacting a much larger bribe for a few Moments Service." In short, the way to wealth in the army was to enlist for as brief a period as possible, pocket one's bounty, and re-enlist — a procedure followed by many Americans during the war. Thus the instrument placed in Washington's hands to win the war was a temporary, short-term army precariously supplied and poorly paid; an army in which the commander-in-chief had no confidence would effect "this great revolution." As early as 1777 he declared that it was "impossible, that any Army so unprovided can long subsist," yet the situation of his army became progressively worse as the war dragged on.

Despite the large number of guns imported from France — thirty thousand were sent in 1777 alone — the American army chronically suffered a shortage of arms. In 1780 the Board of War reported that there were only five thousand reliable muskets in the military stores of the United States; and in this same year two hundred men were returned unfit for duty in Washington's army because they lacked guns. This deficiency was primarily owing to the rapid turnover in the American army: discharged soldiers and deserters often walked out of camp with their guns and, presumably, hung them up over the fireplace as souvenirs of a glorious military career. Militiamen and short-term troops were particularly grievous offenders in this regard; thousands of serviceable muskets were carried off by the recruits, many of whom hardly remained long enough in camp to learn how to shoot. As Washington said, "the loss of arms is among the innumerable and unavoidable ill consequences of limited enlistments."

Nevertheless, it cannot be denied that this system of short enlistments created a large number of men who had seen action of some sort, if only a skirmish, and had undergone the baptism of fire. By dint of attacking foraging parties, the Americans were gradually accustomed, the British admitted, "to look us in the face, and stand fire which they never have dared to attempt in the field." These men, superior to raw recruits, formed a large reservoir of trained men for the Continental army; in 1781, Lafayette observed that many of the recruits coming into the Continental army were veterans and had seen more action than three quarters of the European soldiers.

A large part of these half-trained soldiers were deserters. Even short enlistments proved too long for Americans who could not wait to return to civilian life or, perhaps, to re-enlist in the army for another bounty. American soldiers seemed possessed with "the Devil of Desertion," and the only way to exorcise this demon, officers learned, was to give way to the troops' demands that they be permitted to go home; otherwise they would go off without leave. To pursue deserters was futile because the local magistrates and the people refused to aid in tracking them down, and the West offered a secure refuge to deserters as well as to outlaws. As early as February 1777, Congress was alarmed by the prevalence of desertion, and to stamp out this evil — "the most pernicious Vice that can possibly prevail in an Army" — Washington applied lashes, tar and feathers, the gantlet, and finally the death penalty. In the Continental army, the mischief was brought under control, but in the state armies and militia it was rampant until the war itself was brought to an end.

Most deserters from the American army made tracks for home; comparatively few went over to the enemy. They were not turncoats; rather, they suffered from war-weariness and homesickness, and they did not recover their morale until they were snug at home. It was observed, how-ever, that in taking their departure from the army they managed to make off with a considerable part of the belongings of those who remained behind. In this way, the baggage of officers and the hospital stores were pillaged. "Even the Quarters of General Officers," said Washington, "are not exempt from Rapine." It was apparent, a Maryland colonel remarked, that many of these deserters enlisted only with a view to "flight and plunder, both of which they are extremely dexterous at."

Perceiving the failure of the bounty system to bring the manpower of the country into the army, Washington advocated drafting men into the service. A draft was certain to be unpopular in the United States, and many of the state governments, their authority weak and untried, hesitated to attempt the experiment. Thomas Jefferson said that Americans "had learnt to consider it [the draft] as the last of all oppressions" and had refused to submit to it while subjects of Great Britain. Washington himself admitted that a draft might produce "Convulsions in the People"; nevertheless, he saw no other method of preventing the prostration of the American army.

With the Continental army steadily dwindling in strength, the states could no longer postpone drafting men for the field. This draft, however, was halfhearted and partial: militia were drafted for short terms to fill incomplete regiments in the Continental army. It failed to solve the most insistent problem of the war — how Americans could be induced to take their places in the armed forces of their country.

To an ever-increasing extent, it was not native-born Americans but "foreigners" who were shouldering muskets in the Continental army and paying the full measure of devotion to the cause of freedom. Of all the foreigners in the American army, the Scotch-Irish were by far the most numerous. Having recently left Ireland rankling under British oppression, the Scotch-Irish were often more bitter enemies of Great Britain than were native-born Americans. Many had risen against their landlords in Ireland; now it seemed that the British government was seeking them out in their refuge across the Atlantic in order to drag them back to Ireland to stand trial. Certainly, the Scotch-Irish did not need to be told by Americans of British tyranny. Man for man, they were more eager to take up arms against the mother country than were American "Sons of Liberty" to whom British tyranny was remote and apprehended rather than experienced.

Aware that the Scotch-Irish were one of the chief pillars of American resistance, the British made a special effort to conciliate these formidable antagonists. The Scotch-Irish were tempted to desert from the rebel army by means of offers of bounties in lands and money; and Scotch-Irish brigades were formed with Lord Rawdon, himself an Irishman, and reputed to be "the ugliest man in England," at the head of the corps.

Washington put his faith in native-born Americans as defenders of the country; if substitution were allowed, he urged that the substitutes be Americans rather than "vagrant foreigners." But the commander-in-chief took what he could get and was thankful for it. Before the war was over, he was taking a great deal worse than foreigners into his army.

Comparatively early in the war, British deserters and even prisoners of war were enlisted in the American army. These men received the same bounty, clothing, and pay given volunteers. No one claimed that they fought well: for fear of falling into the hands of their former comrades they hung back from battle or they deserted to the British on the eve of battle "especially," remarked an American officer, "when a pardon was proclaimed for returning Deserters or we had it not in our power to give them Rum." Or they carried to the British information of American troop dispositions or plans of attack, hoping thereby to save their skins. Except for filling the depleted ranks of the American army on parade, they were of little use to the rebels. Therefore, both Washington and the Continental Congress strictly forbade the enlistment of prisoners of war.

Nevertheless, despite this prohibition, British prisoners continued to be enlisted in the American army. Recruiting officers often acted upon the principle that the fewer questions asked about a man's past the better. Moreover, the failure of patriots to turn out for military service obliged the recruiting officers to send to headquarters anyone capable of carrying a gun and knapsack. Many Massachusetts towns enlisted British soldiers for service as substitutes in the Continental army for Whigs who had pressing business at home. Some British prisoners were taken out of jails and sent to the army as recruits. A large number of prisoners from Burgoyne's army, the so-called "Convention Troops," were eventually brought into the American ranks — which, in effect, Washington caustically observed, was giving back the British the men they had lost. In 1778, the Pennsylvania Line was said to be composed in a large part of deserters who, Washington warned, "will embrace the first opportunity of escaping with our Arms." There were so many British prisoners in the crew of the American frigate *Alliance* that an American diplomat, on his way to Europe, feared to trust himself on board ship. Captured English seamen were often forced to serve in American privateers or condemned to the American galleys. In the Southern states, both sides employed prisoners and deserters so freely that the armies began to resemble warring groups of expatriates.

By 1782, the manpower shortage had become so acute that Washington was constrained to drop his objections to the enlistment of prisoners of war. He now declared that German prisoners in particular would make "exceedingly cheap and valuable Recruits" and, being veterans, would strengthen the American army. Congress accordingly authorized the enlistment into the United States army of German prisoners who, by taking the oath of allegiance, became citizens of the United States.

Meanwhile, Americans had turned to the large Negro population of the United States as a source of manpower. Almost one fifth of the population of the United States was black, and most blacks were slaves. Every state sanctioned slavery; although more strongly established in the South than in the North, it was by no means the "peculiar institution" of any one section. At the beginning of the Revolution, slavery was national — for the blacks, there was no dividing line between liberty and slavery.

In writing the Declaration of Independence, Thomas Jefferson was keenly aware of the discrepancy existing between the ideals he was setting forth and the actual conditions that prevailed in the United States. He therefore included in the Declaration an indictment of George III for negativing laws passed by the colonial legislatures prohibiting the importation of slaves. But he quickly learned that slavery, although weakened in Virginia by declining profitableness and revolutionary idealism, had vigorous champions in South Carolina and Georgia, where it was neither unprofitable nor regarded as wrong. At the insistence of Georgia and South Carolina and the Northern slave traders, the offending passage was stricken out. Although willing to blame George III for every other evil that had befallen the colonies, the Southern plantation owners and Northern slave traders could not bring themselves to enumerate slavery — in their eyes, a positive good — among the crimes of the British King.[5]

Believing that slavery was the most vulnerable weakness of the rebellion in the Southern states, the British early in the war offered emancipation to the slaves. All who volunteered to serve with the British army were promised their freedom. By this means, the British expected to procure the services of thousands of laborers — it was not intended to make the freed blacks combat troops — and to ruin the patriot slaveowners by depriving them of their labor force. But slaves were valuable property, and British officers were tempted to seize Negroes not in order to give them the blessing of liberty but to sell them into a far worse slavery in the West Indies than that from which they had been forced. Slave stealing became a lucrative side line of some British military men; a post in the Southern states sometimes meant a small fortune from the capture and sale of slaves. In 1781, Cornwallis raided Jefferson's plantation and

---

[5] Depressed tobacco prices and mounting costs owing to soil exhaustion had deeply cut into the profits of the Virginia planters for twenty years before the Revolutionary War. Many planters, in consequence, were complaining of the ruinous expense of maintaining their slaves and extolling the advantages of free labor. Virginians, said a traveler, "seem afflicted to have any slavery, and are constantly talking of abolishing it. . . . The philosophers and the young men . . . regard nothing but justice, and the rights of humanity." Many went along with the institution because they saw no practicable alternative. "I am master of Slaves of my own purchase," confessed Patrick Henry. "I am drawn along by the general Inconveniency of living Without them. I will, I cannot justify it."

carried off about thirty slaves. "Had this been to give them freedom," remarked Jefferson, "he would have done right." General Clinton said that the prospect of dividing masters from their slaves was a "principal support" of the British cause in the South; but Burke protested against inciting racial war. After the Negroes had risen "and made themselves masters of the houses, goods, wives, and daughters, of their murdered lords," he pointed out, the British would be obliged to suppress the Negroes in turn, thus beginning a vicious circle of massacres and counter-massacres.

In the North, from the early days of the war, Negroes fought beside whites in the patriot army. As the war went on and the ranks of the army grew thinner, an increasing number of Negroes took the places of the whites, until it began to appear that Ethiopia as well as America was in arms. In Washington's army there was an average of about fifty Negroes to each battalion; and at the battle of Monmouth Courthouse in 1778, at least seven hundred Negroes were on the American side. So many Negro troops were raised by Massachusetts that in 1778 it was urged that a wholly black regiment be incorporated, but although Connecticut enlisted a separate Negro regiment, Massachusetts continued to mix white and black troops in its armed forces.

Inevitably, the presence of hundreds of blacks in the American army, fighting for liberty alongside the whites, smote the conscience of many patriots. Negroes were giving their blood for the rights of man: how could they be denied participation in those rights? How could white Americans, shunning the duty of a citizen to bear arms, employ slaves to fight their battles for them? The least that could be done, it began to be said, was to give the slaves their freedom when they entered the army. "It is justifiable that negroes should have their freedom . . . as freedom and liberty is the grand controversy that we are contending for." Give them freedom with their muskets, exclaimed Alexander Hamilton; secure their fidelity and animate their courage by endowing them with the dignity of free men. This was done by some Northern states: upon entering the army, slaves were promised their freedom on condition of serving three years or more. At the same time, slaveowners were compensated for their financial losses.

Most of these slaves owed their presence in the army to the fact that their masters preferred to hold down the home front while they sent their slaves to battle. Thanks to the substitute system, a patriot allergic to the smell of gunpowder might send his slave to war either in the militia or in the regular army. There was no obloquy attached to such substitution; on the contrary, to sacrifice one's bondservant for the cause of liberty was regarded as highly meritorious. And no one could deny that it was better to send a stout black man to the wars than to "fill up our battalions with [British] runaways and deserters" whose services as substitutes were also available to gun-shy patriots. Indeed, it was no doubt true in many instances that a Negro slave, inured to fatigue and hardened and disciplined by slavery, made a better soldier than his master. No observer ever went on record that the blacks broke in panic any quicker than did the whites.

Some Southern congressmen wished to draw the color line in this fight for freedom: lest Negroes imbibe ideas of liberty and racial equality by serving in the army, they demanded that the blacks be kept "in their place" — by which was meant, of course, at the very bottom of society. In 1775, for example, a South Carolina delegate moved in Congress that Washington be ordered to discharge all Negroes, whether slave or free, in the Continental army.

During the early period of the war, Congress, in deference to the sensibilities of slaveowners in both North and South, declined to advise the states to enlist slaves in the army. It was of course admissible for patriots to send their slaves as substitutes, but no state adopted the policy of raising slaves en masse. In 1779, however, with the British making rapid strides in the South against little opposition from the white inhabitants, Congress recommended to South Carolina and Georgia that three thousand Negro slaves under white officers be taken into the army. Slaveowners were to be given one thousand dollars in compensation for every slave they donated to the cause. John Laurens, son of the President of Congress, was appointed Lieutenant Colonel of the Negro regiments and sent to the South to take command of his troops.[6]

But Congress had reckoned without the strong aversion of Southerners to arming Negroes. When Colonel Laurens reached South Carolina he found that the plan was "received with horror by the planters"; only fifteen votes could be mustered for its support in the South Carolina Legislature. Rather than utilize slaves as soldiers, it was proposed in the South Carolina and Virginia Legislatures that the enlistment of whites be stimulated by offering every volunteer a Negro slave as a bounty.

Because of the reluctance of whites to fight the battles of freedom, the question would not down: could Americans retain their racial prejudices and, at the same time, win their liberty? Colonel John Laurens declared that five thousand black soldiers would ensure victory to America. "Men, who have the habit of subordination almost indelibly impressed on them," he remarked, "would have one very essential qualification of soldiers." George Washington, on the other hand, questioned the wisdom of enlisting slaves, lest a race in arming slaves be begun with the British. In that event, he asked in 1779, "where are our arms?" And as a slaveholder, he feared that if large numbers of slaves were freed be-

[6] In 1776, Congress had approved the enlistment of free Negroes in the Continental army.

cause of military service, slavery would become intolerable to those who remained unemancipated.

Necessity, more than idealism, overcame prejudice. In 1781, Maryland raised seven hundred and fifty Negro soldiers to be incorporated with whites; and Virginia freed all Negroes who had served honorably in the war. Even in South Carolina, Negro troops were used extensively in transport services and as labor battalions. General Sir Henry Clinton, upon observing the large number of Negroes in the American army, expressed his fear that this policy would reconcile the slaves to their lot and give Negro soldiers an interest in defending American soil. "Thus, my Lord," he told Germain, "are we deprived of another principal support."

Not content to stop with the emancipation of Negro soldiers, some patriots sought to turn revolutionary idealism against the institution of slavery itself. There was sting in Dr. Samuel Johnson's sarcastic query: "How is that we hear the loudest yelps for liberty from the drivers of negroes?"

Against the rights of man, conservatives placed the rights of property. Slaves were property, they insisted, and Americans had taken up arms in defense of the rights of property. Moreover, their labor was essential to the war effort; emancipation would alienate the South and perhaps break up the confederation. Sectional conflict loomed ahead, and for that reason some Northern patriots hesitated to advance too rapidly along the path of reform.

Nevertheless, in the Northern states, where slavery was less fundamental to the economy than in the South, the institution went down to defeat. For many years, the Quakers had held slavery in abhorrence and had attempted to purify their sect from its contamination; now, with the outbreak of the Revolution, a full-fledged antislavery movement sprang up in the North. William Gordon of Massachusetts, one of the most liberal men of his generation and later a historian of the American Revolution, turned the Declaration of Independence and the Virginia Bill of Rights against the institution. He advocated not merely freeing the slaves but giving them the right to vote and every other right accorded white citizens. Was it not unjust, he asked, "to exclude *freemen* from voting for representatives and senators, though otherwise qualified, because their skins are black, tawny or reddish? Why not disqualified for being long-nosed, short-faced, or higher or lower than five feet nine? A black, tawny or reddish skin is not so unfavourable an hue to the genuine son of liberty, as a Tory complection." Henry Laurens of South Carolina declared that he was not "one of those who dare trust in Providence for defence and security of their own liberty while they enslaved and wish to continue in slavery thousands who are as well entitled to freedom as themselves." Until Americans lived up to their principles and emancipated their slaves, said John Jay of New York, their "prayers to Heaven for liberty will be impious."

By the end of the war, Vermont, Massachusetts, and New Hampshire were free soil, and Pennsylvania, Rhode Island, and Connecticut had adopted schemes of gradual emancipation. On the other hand, slavery resisted stubbornly in New York, one of the last of the Northern states to take action against slavery. It was not until 1799 that New York adopted a plan of gradual emancipation.

Slavery survived in the South the assaults of the humanitarians, but not so the slave trade. As British colonists, Americans had protested against the slave trade and had blamed the King and Parliament for its continuance; now, with independence achieved, George III and Parliament could no longer serve as scapegoats. Americans were free to destroy what they had long denounced as an abuse; and, in general, they acted in conformity with their principles. During the war, every state except South Carolina and Georgia prohibited the traffic in slaves; and in 1808, the slave trade was officially abolished throughout the United States.

CHAPTER XXIV

The Revolution Falters

AMERICANS' assumption that the war was as good as won was rudely shattered in 1779–1780 by the British conquest of Georgia and South Carolina and the destruction of two American armies, each as large as the force that Burgoyne had surrendered at Saratoga. By shifting their attack from the North to the South, the enemy, in short, not only revived the American war but scored successes that brought the patriot cause to the verge of disaster.

The allied failure at Savannah in 1779 and D'Estaing's subsequent return to France opened the way for a large-scale British attack upon the Southern states. In December 1779, with Georgia firmly in British grasp and with the French fleet no longer menacing their lines of communication, a great fleet and army left New York. Their destination was Charleston, South Carolina — hardly a place of happy memory to British soldiers and sailors.

To Englishmen, the South seemed to be the most vulnerable part of the United States — had Lord North possessed Winston Churchill's gift of felicity of phrase, he might have called the South "the soft underbelly of the rebellion." Weakened by the presence of thousands of black slaves in their midst and powerful tribes of Indians on their frontiers, and possessed of a disproportionately small share of the war material that made the North formidable, the South invited attack by the enemy. Relying largely upon militia, Southerners had neglected, even to a greater degree than had Northerners, to recruit troops for the Continental army. Because militia were notoriously unwilling to fight beyond the borders of their state, it seemed likely that each state in the South could be conquered singly. Moreover, the social system of the country — great planters opposed by the small farmers of the uplands — afforded hope to the British of driving a wedge between classes. An English official pointed out, for example, that "it might have been in the power of Two or Three of the most eminent of Virginia Families to have stopt at their Frontier, the course of these pestilential blasts from the North & so the whole Explosion might have evaporated in partial Remonstrances." Even at this late hour, perhaps it was not too late to divide and conquer the South.

Moreover, owing to their command of the sea, the British were assured of easy access to the most vital parts of the South. And once the region was conquered, Clinton pointed out, it was unlikely "to be rescued from the Commanders of the Sea." The numerous bays and rivers permitted men of war to penetrate into the heart of the country; cut off from the North by deep rivers and vast expanses of forest, the Southern states could be easily isolated from the rest of the union and subdued at the leisure of the British fleet and army.

Nevertheless the British force in New York had been so gravely weakened by the necessity of reinforcing the West Indies and the Floridas that Clinton hesitated long before opening a new theater of war in the South. He feared for the safety of New York; he feared that the defenses of Charleston would prove too strong for the British fleet and army; and he feared that even if Charleston should fall, the rest of the country would continue to resist. Sir Henry had not forgotten the rough handling he had received on his first visit to Charleston in 1776; another failure in that quarter might bring the war to an inglorious end. "If we cannot . . . destroy the spirit and resource of the province," he declared, ". . . we shall accomplish nothing substantial for Great Britain. The strength of North Carolina, and the neighboring provinces, will keep gathering round us, till we shall become contemptible in the eyes of Europe, or fall an easy prey to a combined operation."

But Germain and Cornwallis — the latter faced with the disquieting prospect of going to the West Indies unless South Carolina was invaded — egged on the reluctant commander-in-chief. Germain had long been eager to try the fortunes of war in the Southern states; in March 1778, he had drawn up plans for an attack upon the Carolinas and Georgia to compensate for the loss of Philadelphia. The British Colonial Secretary was confident that if the Carolinas and Georgia could be overrun, "all America to the south of the Susquehanna would return to their allegiance, and . . . the northern provinces might be left to their own feelings and distress to bring them back to their duty."

Germain did not doubt that the weak resistance encountered by Prevost in Georgia and on his raid into South Carolina was "indubitable proof of the indisposition of the inhabitants to support the rebel government." The minister saw thousands of Loyalists in the South languishing for an opportunity to throw themselves into the arms of a victorious British general. As was his wont, he could not see the patriots for the Loyalists.

Clinton, too, hoped to find in the South the Land of Tories he had vainly sought in the North. He envisaged the expedition as an experiment — probably the last of its kind in the American war — which would decide whether Great Britain retained the loyalty of any large number of Americans. In his opinion, the South promised the best hope of such loyalty: it was inhabited by "a People who can & will be controuled when conquered, a people not politically but from the Ambition of a few connected with the Northern Districts and not without Jealousy of the designs of France upon them."

A close study of Loyalism in the United States had satisfied Clinton that it was only where the people were assured of protection or chastisement by the British army that affection for Great Britain flourished. "There remains doubtless in the hearts of many a Something British which draws them to our Standard," he remarked, "But fear interest and family ties are the main Springs of Mens' Actions."

Above all, Clinton was resolved not to abandon the Loyalists who came forward in Britain's behalf. Too often he had seen Americans rewarded for their loyalty to the mother country with banishment, confiscation of property, and all the pains and penalties devised by revengeful patriots. This time there was to be no repetition of the fate of the Loyalists in New England, New Jersey, and Pennsylvania: what the British army conquered it must hold, and the Tories must be made to see that they need never fear to be left undefended after they had espoused the cause of King and country.

In concentrating their forces against the South, the British were abandoning their earlier strategy of forcing a decisive battle upon Washington in the North. That strategy had signally failed of its objective and now Clinton was too weak to challenge the rebel leader to battle. Clinton was not eager to seek an engagement among "the perfidious Thousands of the Jersey & of New England who singly take the field against us from every tree & house & who tho driven from our front close in with redoubled inveteracy in our Flank & Rear." In the North, Washington was near his supplies and reinforcements — armed men seemed in emergencies to spring from the soil; and even though Washington had been defeated in battle, there always remained a hard core of resistance against which the British could make little headway.

It is significant that a British invasion of the Southern states fulfilled Washington's worst fears. Hitherto, he had found little cause for complaint in British strategy: it was usually obvious and straightforward; above all, it had concentrated the fighting in the Northern states, where Americans were best able to resist. To shift the scene of action to the South meant that Washington and the bulk of the Continental army would be out of action, for Washington had always refused to march his troops south. Moreover, if Washington was to maintain an army in the North, he could spare little or no aid for the South: inadequate for his own needs, his force did not admit of further depletion.

For these reasons, Washington had little hope that the Southern states would be able to beat off a British attack: "their internal weakness, disaffection, the want of energy, the general languor that has seized the people at large" would, he feared, prove the downfall of the South. Only a French fleet and army seemed capable of warding off a British attack. For once, the British appeared to have hit upon the right strategy. "I see no better purpose to which they can apply their army in America," Washington unhappily admitted.[1]

Clinton's plan was to deliver a two-pronged attack upon the South. The main blow was to fall upon Charleston, with a diversionary attack upon Virginia designed to keep the forces of the Old Dominion occupied at home. This was the strategy pursued by Clinton until Lord Cornwallis's march to Virginia compelled him to revise his plan of operations.

In Charleston Harbor, the British faced the same formidable fortifications of cannon-ball-proof palmetto logs that had worked their undoing in 1776. Now, in 1780, however, the British ships took advantage of a heavy gale and thunderstorm to run past Fort Moultrie without sustaining serious damage from the American batteries. The same caution was observed by the British in their attack upon Charleston itself: throwing siege lines around the city, they inched forward, pounding the American positions with cannon balls, scrap iron, and glass, and firing red-hot shot into the city to set fire to houses.

As soon as considerable fires had been started, Clinton ordered his batteries silenced "in order to give this stubborn people time to think it over." He gave them plenty of time to consider their position: in April 1780, three months after laying siege to the city, Charleston was completely surrounded and the British lines were within easy artillery range of the city.

All told, the siege of Charleston lasted over four months – a sufficient period, it might be supposed, to enable the Americans to bring up reinforcements and drive the British back to their ships. But lack of transportation, the weakness of the state governments, the ruinous state of the currency, and the reluctance of Americans to take action until danger was at their very doors combined to prevent aid from reaching the besieged city. Only a small part of the manpower of South Carolina itself was engaged in the defense of Charleston: many Virginians and North Carolinians objected that they had no business fighting the battles of South Carolinians.

Although Congress and the Southern states voted to send nine thousand

[1] Some Americans saw a ray of good in this event; it was well, they believed, that the Southern as well as the Northern states should "taste the Chastisement of the War, & be forever weaned from Britain by a Taste of British Clemency & Cruelty."

men to Charleston, less than two thousand actually arrived in the city. Washington refused to weaken further his army at Morristown but he sent Du Portail, a French engineer, to supervise the construction of the city's defenses. By the time Du Portail arrived, however, Charleston was doomed and he was captured with the garrison.

General Lincoln, in command of the defense of South Carolina, threw his entire army into Charleston, thus involving the fate of the state with that of the capital. This may have been the course of valor, but it was hardly that of wisdom. On the ninth of May, 1780, the British opened a concentrated bombardment upon the American positions. In two days of almost continuous firing, over a thousand cannon balls were hurled against the Americans — and there were exactly five casualties in the American army. Nevertheless, the garrison had no heart for continuing the struggle; surrounded by the enemy and apparently abandoned by their country-men, many troops threw down their guns. The townspeople urged General Lincoln to surrender before the British stormed the city. Lincoln had no alternative but to seek the best terms possible; on May 12 he signed articles of capitulation by which the Continental troops in Charleston became prisoners of war and the militia were given freedom to return to their homes.

At Charleston, the British captured an army of over five thousand men (two thousand of whom were Continentals), including three generals — a force larger than the Americans had taken at Saratoga. Over three hundred cannon, two frigates with their guns intact, and military stores of all descriptions fell into the hands of the victors. It was by all odds the most serious reverse, until Bataan, ever suffered by the United States army. Yet this blow was necessary, Washington thought, "to rouse us from the more than thrice unaccountable state of security in which we were sunk."

Had it done so, it would have been cheaply bought.

Clinton's first step was to seek to win the rebels by leniency. Resolved not to permit looting and atrocities to doom at the outset this experiment in regaining the allegiance of Americans, he kept the army tightly under control, and pillagers were shot without mercy. At the same time, mercy was held out to the rebels: even some of the chief fomenters of rebellion were given certificates by the British commander warranting them to be true and loyal subjects of George III and entitled to the protection of the British army. The Tories protested that this generosity would not beget gratitude and affection among rebels, but Clinton paid no heed to their objections. Paroles were so freely granted to the inhabitants of South Carolina that the patriots began to fear that the British would conquer the entire South by this means. Rebels were disarmed and, after giving their parole to remain peaceably at home, were promised the protection of their conquerors. It began to appear that if paroles were strictly ob-served, there would soon be no one left to resist the invaders.

Down to the fall of Charleston, the British had taken possession of many state capitals without conquering the states themselves; but South Carolina promised to be a notable exception. After the capitulation of Charleston, the country between Charleston and Savannah hastened to make its peace. "The most violent Rebels are candid enough to allow the Game is up," observed a British officer. More than two thousand men voluntarily came to British headquarters to offer their services to the King, asking only that they be permitted to fight Frenchmen and Spaniards rather than their own countrymen. Two hundred citizens, declaring themselves to be "the principal and most respectable inhabitants" of Charleston, congratulated Clinton upon his conquest of the city. The British succeeded in raising a large body of Tory militia to hold down the country while the army moved on to new conquests; even many of the American prisoners taken at Charleston were induced to take the oath of allegiance and serve in the West Indies with the British army. "There are few freemen in South Carolina who are not either our prisoners or in arms with us," reported Clinton; and in his jubilation, he informed the government that it was "very possible, we may have conquered the two Carolinas in Charles Town." With Georgia and the Carolinas "restored to allegiance, and three stripes lost from the detestable thirteen," Clinton began to believe that the experiment in the South would prove an unprecedented success.

It was Clinton's intention to establish civil government in South Carolina after the military had brought the state under control — a project warmly seconded by Germain. The British minister was now eager to persuade Americans that the mother country intended no abridgment of their former liberties and that the principal objective of the war was "the Restoration of the Constitution." For this purpose, the one-time lieutenant governor of the royal province of South Carolina was sent to Charleston in 1780 to resume the reins of government; but when the war took an unfavorable turn, the plan was shelved. The patriots, however, maintained their government throughout the struggle for South Carolina; led by Governor Rutledge, the patriot government continued to raise troops and procure supplies for the army, standing to the last as a symbol of the unconquerable spirit of the Revolution.

Clinton was not permitted to conduct the British efforts to establish civil government in South Carolina; shortly after the surrender of Charleston he was obliged to return to New York to hold Washington in check. Upon his second-in-command, Lord Cornwallis, developed the leadership of the army and the responsibility of restoring British rule over the South.

Lord Cornwallis, destined to occupy the limelight in the American war until the final blackout at Yorktown, was the most promising of the younger generals in the British army. Although he had upheld the American cause in Parliament, he gave the rebels no comfort when he took the field against them — the English Whigs complained that he was as eager as any Tory to harry the patriots. In 1776, after his triumph in New Jersey, little doubting that the war was over, he had planned to return to England; but it was not until 1779 that he finally found an opportunity to go home. His earlier optimism had now completely vanished; he was convinced that the American war would prove the graveyard of reputations and that he was well to be out of it. He was drawn back to the struggle largely by the prospect of succeeding Sir Henry Clinton as commander-in-chief when that worthy should have had his fill of the disappointments and frustrations incidental to his office.

At first, Cornwallis met with success on every hand in South Carolina. Almost the entire state was brought under British control; fortified posts were established along the frontier, and what remained of patriot resistance was largely driven underground. The guerrilla leaders, Marion and Sumter, together with their bands, were forced to take refuge in the swamps. Unexpectedly, however, this prospect clouded over.

Although the British army could be held in leash, not so the Loyalists. Having suffered for years under the rule of the patriots, the Loyalists now began to take revenge upon their former oppressors; and strive as they would, the British could not prevent the state from being drenched in blood.

Patriots and Tories were so evenly divided in the Carolinas and Georgia that this civil war was not, as in New England, a mere matter of mobs hounding a few outnumbered Tories, but war without quarter in which both sides committed gruesome atrocities. "The people," it was said, "by copying the manners of the British, have become perfectly savage." Whigs and Tories were shot down in the streets of frontier towns, ambushed in the woods, burned alive in their houses, and plundered of all their worldly goods. The patriot militia of North Carolina refused to march against the Indians because they had heard that the plunder in the Tory Scotch settlements was so much better than in the Indian villages. "I have been so long here amongst the wretched, dam'd and disaffected," wrote a Continental officer in the South, "I have almost lost every feeling of humanity." Years after the Revolution, there was living in Carolina a venerable justice of the peace who declared that "he had during the war, shot, at different actions, and in cold blood, ninety-nine tories, and felt unhappy he had not accomplished the complete hundred."

Thus the forbearance and leniency of the British commanders was undone by the Loyalists, and the so-called "conquered provinces" turned into hotbeds of civil war. The dismayed British found "such a fund of Hatred and Animosity in the Hearts of the People, as Time only can extinguish." Although many men were cowed and dared not speak their minds, still, it was observed, "the Women make full Amends for their Silence, they amuse themselves by teaching their Children the principles of rebellion, and seem to take Care that the rising generation should be as troublesome as themselves." Detected in underground resistance, some citizens of Charleston who had given their paroles not to take any further part in the war were incontinently put aboard prison ships and sent to St. Augustine for safekeeping.

Undeterred by this severity, hundreds of those who had taken the oath to the King went over to the rebels upon every British reverse and turned against the redcoats the guns they had been given as Loyalist militiamen. Such treachery forced the British to retaliate: Cornwallis ordered that any provincials taken in arms after having sworn fealty to George III were to be summarily hanged; and Lord Rawdon issued a proclamation offering "ten guineas for the head of any deserter belonging to the volunteers of Ireland, and five guineas only if they bring him in alive."

In the South, the art of war as practised upon European battlefields stood British generals in poor stead. The vast distances, the rivers, swamps, and forests, and the sparse population which distinguished this region challenged the resourcefulness and skill of English commanders. It is clear that they were now far better equipped to cope with these conditions than they had been at the beginning of the conflict. Experience had taught them many salutary lessons. The troops were instructed in marksmanship; British officers ripped off their gold braid and epaulets; and dandies cut their hair short, observing that "however some of the men may prize effeminate length of hair, short hair is certainly better for actual service." Rogers's Rangers were organized to fight the rebels in the forests; [1a] and Major Ferguson, the inventor of a breech-loading rifle, was put in command of a special corps known as Ferguson's Riflemen. In short, the whole character of warfare began to undergo change: light troops and skirmishers were thrown out in front of the army, and riflemen were posted to thin out the enemy ranks. Maneuverability and speed were given greater emphasis, and the British army became more flexible in its tactics. By the end of the war, it had left behind the stiff, formal methods to which it had paid obeisance in 1775. In 1785, Lord Cornwallis, after reviewing the Prussian troops on maneuvers, remarked that any English general who employed such antiquated tactics would be derided as an old fogy.

In only one respect were the British at a serious disadvantage: they lacked a sufficiently powerful force of cavalry to hold down the country. War in the South was carried on largely by mounted men; to a Southerner a horse was almost as essential as a gun. Without cavalry, the armies could not forage supplies, bring up reinforcements, reconnoiter, or travel quickly over the great distances that usually separated them from their objectives.

The bands of Sumter and Marion were composed of mounted men

[1a] Rogers's Rangers were raised as early as 1776. In that same year, Rogers was deprived of his command and was succeeded by Captain John G. Simcoe.

who raided British outposts, scouting parties, and lines of communication. Against these guerrillas, the British had no certain defense. Cornwallis declared that he had little fear of the rebel army, but the activities of the guerrillas and the insurrections they inspired far behind the British lines kept the country in constant alarm and made necessary the presence of British regulars everywhere in the conquered regions.

Not all of these guerrillas were fervent patriots who fought from conviction; some sought revenge upon the Tories and British, but others aspired only to plunder their neighbors and British wagon trains and detachments. "The first," said General Greene, "are the best of citizens and the best of soldiers, the last are the dregs of the community and can be kept no longer than there is a prospect of gain." Loot did not come easily, however, and what they gained was usually purchased with blood. It was the hardest kind of warfare; much of the time, Marion and Sumter had no medicines, and the wounded often bled to death for want of care. There were so many desertions that both Sumter and Marion wished to throw up their commands in May 1781; and there was always danger that these bands would turn mere freebooters.

Although South Carolina was already beginning to seethe with discontent, Cornwallis began to look for new provinces to conquer. North Carolina, he believed, would prove an easy victim — its large Tory population presumably waited only the signal of a British invasion to rise up against the patriots. But it was now clear that the rebels were ready to fight to regain the South and that Cornwallis must defeat the American army before his gains would be secure.

To meet the menace raised by the British invasion of the South, General Gates was called out of the semiretirement to which he had been consigned after the Conway Cabal. Gates had been long stationed in Boston, where he was almost as much out of the war as though he had been retired from the active list. In the Puritan metropolis, the general became involved in the political wars that raged between Adams and Hancock; and Mrs. Gates added to his worries by trying to crash Boston society. Gossip said that she was always needling her husband: whenever he wished to relax contentedly upon his laurels, Mrs. Gates spurred him on to new exertions. "That Medusa his wife governs with a rod of Scorpions," said General Lee, who was in a position to know the domestic tribulations of his colleague. In any event, Gates accepted the command of the Southern theater — with disastrous results to the reputation he had won at Saratoga.

Most of the troops under Gates's command were militia: he had only about thirteen hundred Continental troops from the Maryland and Delaware Lines. For Gates, this was hardly a hardship: he had employed militia with spectacular results against Burgoyne and he had often expressed the opinion that militia, if properly led, were scarcely inferior to regular troops. But the militia that now followed his standard bore little resemblance to the men he had commanded at Saratoga. Though the back-country militia of the South was a formidable fighting force, the troops Gates commanded came chiefly from the lowlands and were ill fed, ill armed, and ill disciplined. Many had never seen action and were weakened by the rigors of the march before the battle began. New Englanders did not fail to point out, after Gates's defeat, that if John Stark and the Northern militia had been on hand, the outcome would have been very different.

But the greatest weakness of Gates's army was its lack of cavalry: virtually his only mounted men consisted of Colonel Armand's Legion. There is nothing to show, however, that Gates was greatly concerned about the absence of cavalry; he had won against Burgoyne without cavalry and apparently he expected to repeat his success against Corn-wallis. It is patent that, although warned early in the campaign that his cavalry could not take the field without suffering certain defeat, Gates did not allow this weakness to affect his strategy.

Yet Gates could hardly fail to appreciate the magnitude of the task before him. Lacking provisions, arms, and transport, and in command of an army without discipline and organization, he found himself expected to work the same miracle that he had achieved at Saratoga. There were no depots of food or arms; the troops lived from hand to mouth, even going without flour for weeks at a time. Green apples, peaches, and corn were the staples of the army. There were no tents; the troops lay exposed to rain day and night. "Instead of rum," lamented a soldier, "we had a gill of molasses per man served out to us, which instead of enlivening our spirits, served to purge us as well as if we had taken jallap." The country through which Gates passed had been stripped by British and American foraging parties; the little that remained to the people, they would not part with "for love nor for Money." Gates had no money with which to tempt them; the treasury of Virginia upon which he relied for finan-cial aid contained at this time not a single dollar. In a moment of despond-ency, Gates compared his army to "a dead Whale upon the Sea Shore," left to rot by the citizenry.

Fortune, however, unexpectedly smiled — or, rather, seemed to smile — on Gates. On August 13, 1780, the American commander was joined by almost three thousand militia from Virginia and North and South Carolina. This accession of strength raised his army to about five thousand men, double the size of Cornwallis's force. Washington once said that the chief object of a commander in the Southern states ought to be to have a good army rather than a large one, and to the commander-in-chief a good army was one composed of regulars. He had never supposed that with militia Gates could win a victory over Cornwallis; a large number of militia were more to be dreaded than wished for, he remarked, because Gates might be encouraged to attempt too much and thereby lose everything.

That these fears were not groundless was evidenced by Gates's conduct after the Southern militia had joined his army.

Made bold by numbers, Gates now determined to attack the British at the earliest possible moment. Despite the deficiencies of his army, Gates never ceased to seek out Cornwallis — indeed, he could hardly stop without danger of sacrificing his men to starvation.[2] But weak as he knew himself to be, he believed that Cornwallis was weaker; and with a confidence born of his victory over Burgoyne, he spoke confidently of driving the British back to Charleston.

Believing that the British had weakened their position at Camden, South Carolina, and that Lord Cornwallis had gone to Savannah, leaving Lord Rawdon in command in South Carolina, Gates advanced boldly upon the enemy. British advance parties fell back before him, and Gates was drawn ever deeper into the enemy's country.

There was some warrant for the American commander's confidence. The British were seriously alarmed by the approach of Gates's army; their entire position in the Carolinas was endangered because, as the American army advanced, the patriot underground went into action in regions supposedly safely conquered by British arms. Scarcely an open friend remained to the British in North Carolina; none dared to send information of the size or movements of Gates's force, and many of those who had taken the oath to King George now renounced their allegiance. Cornwallis declared that unless events quickly took a favorable turn, the country between Camden and Charleston would soon be swarming with rebels. Sumter and his men were menacing the British rear, threatening to cut off communications. Loyalists' plantations were being burned and their slaves driven off. In short, the patriots seemed to be getting the upper hand, and a defeat at the hands of Gates might lead to the annihilation of the entire British army in the South.

In one respect at least, the British were not so weak as Gates supposed: Lord Cornwallis, instead of going to Savannah, had rejoined his troops near Camden on August 14. Gates was going up against the champion himself: it was the conqueror of Burgoyne versus the "English Hannibal." Cornwallis, always eager to meet the rebels in pitched battle, could hardly have asked for more.

Nevertheless, the British commander hesitated. Despite his confidence in the prowess of British regulars, it was perhaps too much to ask them to overcome an army over twice their number. On the other hand, he knew that to turn back might cost the British all their gains in the South and leave the Loyalists at the mercy of the patriots. Moreover, he had

---

[2] Gates's strategy, it will be observed, was very different from that which he had followed against Burgoyne. The precarious state of his supplies, the necessity of striking a blow before his army disintegrated, and perhaps overconfidence account for this difference.

eight hundred sick together with valuable stores at Camden which he would be obliged to abandon in case of a retreat. And so, "seeing little to lose by a defeat and much to gain by a victory," Cornwallis resolved to stand his ground.[3]

Gates planned to force an engagement by taking a strong position protected by a swamp near Camden. So certain was he of victory that he made no provision for a retreat. Cornwallis, however, did not permit Gates to choose the time and place of the action: before the Americans were ready, at two o'clock in the morning, the British cavalry "made a most violent onset Huzzaing all the time." This charge was repulsed, but the enemy resumed the attack with light infantry, and against these troops the patriot militia could not stand. After firing one volley, the Virginia militia took to their heels, spreading panic as they fled. Many militiamen ran without firing a shot and threw away their guns to run the faster. Through the breach left by the fleeing militia, the British regulars poured in upon the rear of the Continental troops, who still were doggedly resisting. The Maryland Line was broken and pursued into the swamps, where most of the soldiers were killed, wounded, or captured. The British cavalry had a field day flushing the broken remnants of the army out of swamps and forests.

Gates meanwhile was attempting to rally the militia but the panic-stricken farmers brushed him aside in their flight. "They ran like a Torrent," he said, "and bore all before them." Finding that the militia would not stand, Gates likewise took wing, leaving his Continental troops behind to fight their way to safety if they could. Few were as fortunate as was Gates. Of the Continental troops engaged at Camden, almost half were casualties. As for the militia, most of them suffered nothing worse than palpitations of the heart brought on by fright or too much running.

With a guard of six men, Gates fled to Hillsborough, North Carolina, some two hundred and forty miles from the battlefield, and from Hillsborough he broke the news to Congress that he had suffered a "total Defeat." It would have been better for his reputation had he been killed or captured at Camden. In that case, he would have gone down in history as a brave commander ruined by "ye damned rascally behaviour of ye Militia"; instead, by displaying such ill-timed concern for his personal safety he disconcerted even his admirers. "Doubtless," said Mrs. Warren of Massachusetts, "this honest Republican rode off rather too fast for his own reputation." "Was there ever an instance," asked Alexander Hamilton, "of a general running away, as Gates has done, from his whole army?" His speed was astonishing — almost two hundred miles in three days. "It

---

[3] At Camden, the Americans had about thirteen hundred Continentals and slightly over three thousand militia; the British had fifteen hundred regulars and five hundred militia. It will be observed that, in regulars, the British outnumbered the Americans.

does admirable credit to the activity of a man at his time of life," was Hamilton's sarcastic comment.

Camden pricked the bubble of Gates's reputation: his victory over Burgoyne was forgotten in his humiliation at the hands of Cornwallis. "Misfortune," Gates learned, "is construed into Wickedness or Weakness." For the crime of being unsuccessful, the penalty was obloquy and disgrace; Congress removed him from his command, ordered a court of inquiry, and directed Washington to send another major general to take command of the Southern army.

What was left of the Southern army lay huddled at Hillsborough, North Carolina. The heavy loss of Continental troops and arms at Camden made further resistance to Cornwallis impossible; and the people living in the vicinity of Hillsborough, by refusing to sell their produce to the starving troops, almost sealed the doom of the army. For ten days the soldiers had no bread. The beaten survivors of Camden enjoyed little honor among their countrymen.

The defeat at Camden was not the full measure of American disaster. Shortly before the battle in which Gates suffered rout and ruin, General Sumter and his guerrillas had captured a British wagon train. Encumbered with spoil, they were making for safety when they were caught by surprise by Tarleton, the British cavalry leader. The Americans were overwhelmed and Tarleton recaptured the wagon train. Thus the British could congratulate themselves upon having eliminated two rebel armies almost at one blow.

The news of British successes in the South saved the ministry of Lord North from a parliamentary crisis. For many years, Englishmen complained, "we have dined on meals to come, and had little to pick but the bones of provinces we have lost"; and Lord North, Germain, and Sandwich were blamed by an increasing number of Britons for this hard fare. Now, however, the hard-pressed ministers could give the country a substantial and perhaps decisive victory. Lord Sandwich, as was his custom, unhesitatingly climbed out on a limb by predicting that this "fatal blow" would end the rebellion forthwith.

Camden was hailed as a victory "as glorious, compleat and critical as has been obtained by the Arms of Britain for Ages" — nobody, it was said, talked of anything else for a fortnight. This was the kind of battle the Ministry had long promised England: rebellious peasantry stampeding for safety and cut to pieces by the pursuing regulars. It was generally assumed that such poltroons would soon beg for peace. This was the aspect of Cornwallis's victory that the English Whigs most deplored: John Wilkes, for example, refused to support a vote of thanks in Parliament to Clinton and Cornwallis because, he explained, their victory would merely prolong a ruinous war. Immediate peace with America, cried Wilkes, could alone save England from rushing upon destruction. And, he observed, "not a single Frenchman or Spaniard in arms against us fell at this most glorious victory at Camden" — the only casualties were cousins. So vehement became the Whigs in their condemnation of this victory that it was necessary for Lord North to remind the Commons that "Lord Cornwallis was fighting, and fighting not against, but for his country."

⌒   ⌒   ⌒

What recalled Clinton to New York from this promising experiment in the Carolinas was the menacing situation which had arisen as a result of the activity of the rebels around New York and the dispatching of a French fleet and army to the United States.

Vergennes had come to the conclusion that little could be expected from the Americans unless France took an active part in the war in the United States. By the Continental Congress, Franklin, Lafayette, John Adams, Washington, and many others he had been informed of the necessity of naval superiority in North American waters, and he was now prepared to act upon their advice by sending a large fleet to the United States. In fact, he was willing to do more for the Americans than they had asked: together with the ships, he sent troops to reinforce the American army. Thus the war seemed destined to become, on land as well as on sea, a French show, with the Americans largely relegated to the position of spectators. Early in 1780, a French fleet under the command of De Ternay and five thousand French soldiers under Rochambeau sailed from France for the United States.

When the French fleet dropped anchor in July 1780 at Newport — abandoned, it will be remembered, the previous year by the British — Clinton planned to lead an amphibious attack upon them before they could establish themselves on the island. The British navy failed to give him proper support, however, and the French took undisturbed possession of the former British base. Yet, if the British could not keep the French from entering Newport, they could at least prevent them from leaving that base. The timely arrival of a fleet from England gave the British such decisive superiority at sea that they were able to blockade the French squadron in Newport — with the result that it was kept out of action for almost a year.

The French military and naval force in Newport was merely the first installment of the aid His Most Christian Majesty intended to send to the United States in 1780. It was planned to dispatch about ten thousand French troops to the assistance of the Americans; but, unfortunately for the allies, the remainder of the expedition was blockaded in Brest by a British fleet and was unable to reach the United States in time for the campaign of 1780. Thus two French fleets were bottled up; and instead of the ten thousand French troops and powerful fleet Americans had been led to expect, only five thousand troops and eleven men-of-war actually arrived.

Americans had asked for French money, implements of war, and ships — French soldiers fighting on American soil was more than they had bargained for. After boasting of the legions of freemen that would spring to arms against the invader, it was painful for American patriots to see upon American soil thousands of soldiers wearing the white uniforms of the House of Bourbon, outnumbering the Continental army itself.

It had been Americans' pride that they fought their own battles instead of scouring Europe, as did the British, for mercenaries. "It was my pride to get rid of the enemy without foreign aid," said General Nathanael Greene. "I am fond of an alliance; but I wish for the honor of America that liberty may effect her own deliverance. I should like supplies from our friends, but wish to fight all the battles ourselves." Yet it was the failure of Americans to fight their own battles effectively that impelled the French to send troops to the United States.

Washington began to fear that he would yet experience the final humiliation of "seeing the cause of America, in America, upheld by foreign Arms." That Americans could ever live down that disgrace, he did not believe; yet his own army was so weak that his principal reliance was the inability of the enemy to take advantage of its opportunities. In fact, Washington might have had no army at all had not some Philadelphia merchants, at the instigation of the French minister, pooled their resources to form a "bank" by which the army was supplied with necessities. Repayment, with interest, was promised by Congress, but the merchants, having had some experience with the promises of Congress, took care to discount its pledges, particularly those of a financial nature.[4]

Even supposing that great numbers of citizens had rallied to arms, Washington acknowledged that he would not have known how to feed them. From long and painful experience, the army expected to starve during the winter, but in 1780 it was on short rations most of the summer: at times, the troops went "five or Six days together without Meat; then as many without bread, and once or twice, two or three days together without either." Washington was obliged to dismiss most of the militia lest they starve on his hands. Although it grieved him to see the army "assume the odious character of the plunderers instead of the protectors of the people," he was compelled to order his men out on foraging ex-

---

[4] Thomas Paine gave this account of the so-called "bank" organized in Philadelphia in 1780: "The only thing that now remained, and was capable of reaching the case, was private credit, and the voluntary aid of individuals; and under this impression, on my return from the house [the legislature of Pennsylvania], I drew out the salary due to me as clerk, enclosed $500 to a gentleman in the city and urged him to propose a voluntary subscription among his friends. . . ." This subscription was intended as a donation, and was to be given in bounties to promote the recruiting service.

peditions. As a result, farmers living near the American camp were reduced to poverty; even milk cows were slaughtered for meat by the famished troopers. This means of sustaining the army soon came to an end. "Military coercion is no longer of any avail," Washington reported, "as nothing further can possibly be collected from the Country . . . without depriving the inhabitants of the last morsel." As at Valley Forge, lack of transportation was in part responsible for the misery of American soldiers. There were, for instance, over two thousand barrels of salted meat in Connecticut in 1780 which could not be moved to the American camp because the quartermaster department had no money to pay for teams and few farmers were willing to donate their services or equipment to the cause.

In fact, the shortage of horses and wagons was so acute that Washington, even with his handful of men, could hardly have got to the field of battle: the only way he could fight was for the British to seek him out.

Before the French troops were sent to the United States, Franklin agreed on behalf of his government to furnish them with provisions without charge. Franklin expected that his action would meet with the approval of Congress, but in this he was disappointed. However generously disposed, Congress's straitened means grievously curtailed its hospitality; so the French soldiers became strictly paying guests in the United States.

With the arrival of French naval and military aid, even Washington permitted himself to hope, contrary to all previous experience, that the states would act vigorously and provide him with the means of winning the war. "This is the time," he said, "for America by one great exertion to put an end to the war. . . . The sparring system has been too long tried, till it has brought us to a crisis little less than desperate." If the states acted, he planned to attack New York, the key to the arch of British military power in the United States. The commander-in-chief soon recognized how insubstantial was his hope — having repeatedly let down their army, the states let down their ally. Six weeks after the deadline set for the state levies to be in camp, less than thirty recruits had straggled into headquarters. By the middle of July, only about one thousand men had joined the colors — and it was time for the campaign to begin.

Outwardly, Washington took these blows with the imperturbable calm which distinguished him throughout the war. "The great man is confounded at his situation," reported his friend Nathanael Greene, "but appears to be reserved and silent." As long as hope remained to Washington, he fought the good fight; but in 1780 even this last resource began to fail him. "I have almost ceased to hope," he said. "The Country in general is in such a state of insensibility and indifference to its interests, that I dare not flatter myself with any change for the better." It is significant that it was the condition of the home front rather than the military situation that shook momentarily Washington's faith in ultimate victory and tormented him with the "Blue Devils" that plagued American patriots during the war.

Washington's complaints were matched by those of Sir Henry Clinton: the two commanders would, indeed, have derived much consolation from reading each other's mail — from which they might have drawn the moral that bad as things were, there was always someone a bit worse off. "For God's sake," exclaimed Clinton, "send us Money, Men, & Provisions, or expect nothing but Complaints. Send out another Admiral, or let me go home. . . . My Wish is to retire from a Situation the most irksome that ever Man was placed in." Except that Washington did not have an admiral to find fault with, the words might have been the American commander-in-chief's.

The French remained at Newport, eating their hearts out with enforced inactivity — "like an oyster in his shell" was the way one French soldier described their situation. They did not, however, lack for supplies: French money worked wonders in bringing provisions of all kinds to camp, although Washington's army, at this very time, was living from hand to mouth. The French soldiers, however, accustomed to living well, were not like the American troops in regarding three square meals as the very summit of happiness: time hung heavy on their hands and some could not find solace even in the Rhode Island girls. They missed their "mistresses and the pleasures of Paris; no theatres, no balls; they are in despair; only an order to march upon the enemy will console them," said a French officer.

The fact that a large body of French troops could be stationed in the United States and live in amity with the American people confounded Englishmen who had comforted themselves with predictions of the early end of the Franco-American alliance. It was an object lesson in international relations: the more the French and Americans saw of each other, the better they seemed to get on. After the war, a traveler found the young ladies of Newport pining for the departed warriors. "We had the flower of the French army," they reminisced, "some very elegant young men." One Newport belle declared that she wished there would be more war if it could be waged without bloodshed. "They had a little fighting, to be sure, in the summer, but when the winter came they forgot all the calamities of war and drowned their cares in assemblies, concerts, parties, etc." It was many years before Newport saw the likes of these accomplished Frenchmen.

It must be confessed that it required time and experience for French soldiers to adjust themselves to the manners of American women; their experiences in France were not a safe guide in the United States. For example, a French officer set down for the edification of his friends the wisdom he had acquired — perhaps with the aid of a slap or two — among the Pennsylvania belles. "Here a woman will kiss you all day," he said, "will do a thousand foolish things with you — crush your foot, make your arm black and blue by dint of pinching you while walking with you, and will give you in a single day the same provocations which one of our women could not do, without being thought too free, after a month's acquaintance. You are often no further advanced with them for all that. It all vanishes like a dream, and they are laughing at you." Ascribing this singular conduct to nothing more than curiosity "to see how the French go about it when making love," he resolved to steer clear of foreign entanglements.[5]

These amours, however unsuccessful, were a welcome relief from the drudgery and tedium of uneventful war. Despite the high hopes with which the campaign had opened, no battles were fought and the year ended with the positions of the adversaries unchanged in the North. The British were still firmly established in New York City and Long Island and they continued to enjoy a comfortable margin of naval superiority. The Americans had marched out bravely and feinted at the defenses of New York and then marched back to camp again. "All this," exclaimed Lafayette, "is as dull as an European war." Unhappily for the United States, this could not be said of the war in the Southern theater, where the British were engaged in a whirlwind conquest of the Carolinas.

The abortive campaign of 1780 was essentially a lesson in the vital role played by sea power in the War of American Independence. Without naval superiority, the land armies of France and the United States could do little more than fight a defensive war; and there was small prospect that defense would win the war. To an ever greater degree, Washington was learning to rely upon the French rather than upon his countrymen for aid: he had been disappointed too often by the states to have much confidence in their abilities or, indeed, in their good intentions. "Unless our allies can lend us largely we certainly can attempt nothing," he confessed.

⌢   ⌢   ⌢

Despite the hardships experienced by the army as a result of inflation and the indifference of civilians, remarkably few officers went over to the

---

[5] For what it is worth, I append the information that the young lady who led him on so tantalizingly only to jilt him in the end was a New England girl visiting friends in Philadelphia. A Philadelphian traveling in New England in 1775 reported experiences not wholly dissimilar to those recounted by the disillusioned French officer quoted above. "Such is the custom amongst even the genteel young ladies," remarked this observant traveler, "that they will look at you with a pleasing countenance, and if your admiration excites a smile, they will answer it, and if you should speak they will familiarly answer you. This behaviour of ladies, we knew were modest and virtuous, appeared to us extraordinary and for a short time very amusing." On the other hand, Rebecca Franks of Philadelphia, commenting on the change in women's manners during the war, remarked that "to all appearances, 'tis the ladies and not the gentlemen, that shew a preference nowadays! 'Tis here, I fancy, always leap year."

enemy. In all the vicissitudes of the struggle, it was pointed out in 1779, "no character of any considerable trust or consequence in the army has betrayed it." The patriots boasted that the United States had given the world an example of fidelity "unparalleled in civil wars. In other armies, discontent, mutiny, and sedition are the certain consequences of want of pay, cloathing . . . but not so in the armies of America." Such vaunting was premature: Americans were soon to see both treason and mutiny in their army.

Badly lamed in the fighting against Burgoyne, Benedict Arnold was obliged to give up his field duties and accept a less active command. For this reason he became American military commander of Philadelphia and here he took the first steps that led to his treason. Arnold found himself in the gayest city in the United States, where wine and easy money flowed profusely and people forgot the war in a giddy pursuit of pleasure. The atmosphere of Philadelphia was, to put it mildly, relaxing; and Arnold, like most soldiers returned from the wars, was eager for a respite from active duty.

Arnold quickly abandoned himself to the gaieties of Philadelphia. His pride wounded by the failure of the people to acclaim him as the military hero of the Revolution and sore from his collisions with Congress, he succumbed easily to the popular passion of the day — money-making. If he could not win the glory that he believed his right, he could at least line his pockets, as thousands of civilians were engaged in doing. His only purpose was to make as much money as possible without scruple as to the means. To that end, he speculated in privateering, dabbled in real estate, and used his official position to gain possession of merchandise left in Philadelphia by the departed Loyalists.

Like most of the get-rich-quick gentry of the Revolution, Arnold spent his money as freely as he made it; in fact, his expenses were considerably more than his income. He aspired to move in the best circles in Philadelphia, but his comparatively slender means, even though eked out by graft, could not maintain him in the splendid style of the profiteers. That is not to say, however, that Arnold did not make an impressive show. Establishing himself in the house formerly occupied by General Howe, he dashed about Philadelphia in a coach and four with liveried servants, quite in the style of John Hancock when that worthy was President of Congress. But Hancock had the wherewithal to be a playboy, whereas Arnold was soon reduced to borrowing money to maintain the figure which he aspired to cut as military governor of Philadelphia.

In seeking out the "best" people in Philadelphia, Arnold inevitably found himself in the company of the Tories and conservative Whigs who composed the upper crust of society in that metropolis. There were comparatively few ardent patriots among the socially elect of the city; and Arnold, having himself become something of a social butterfly, saw no reason to draw a political line in choosing his friends and acquaintances. It was difficult, at best, to determine the line between Tories and conservative Whigs, and Arnold, in his new role of society-crasher, was concerned only with the family connections and wealth of the people he hoped to mingle with as an equal. When he gave a ball, for example, he invited Tories as well as Whigs; and even the wives and daughters of men who had been proscribed by the government and had taken refuge with the British graced his entertainments.

Above all, Arnold swore that he would not make war upon women for their political opinions — a pretty woman, whether of Whiggish or Tory complexion, was always welcome at his house. Pleasure before politics seemed to be Arnold's motto.

Unfortunately for Arnold, the wealthy and conservative citizens with whom he had thrown his lot were no longer the rulers of Pennsylvania. Their power had been largely usurped by democratic leaders who, by means of the bloodless revolution consummated by the Pennsylvania Constitution of 1776, had established a government far more popular in character than that which Pennsylvania had enjoyed under the proprietorship of the Penn family.

Arnold had scarcely installed himself as military commander of Philadelphia before he found himself at odds with the ruling powers of Pennsylvania. This incident, unimportant in itself, might aptly be called "The Strange Case of Major Franks's Barber." It happened that Timothy Matlack, one of the leading politicians of the state, had a son serving in the Pennsylvania militia as a sergeant. Major Franks, one of Arnold's aides, ordered young Matlack to call a barber — whereupon the affronted sergeant went home and told father that he had been insulted by a Continental officer. Matlack sire hit the roof when he learned to what indignities his son had been subjected; as a democrat, he could not bear that his son should be sent running after barbers by Continental officers. To his mind, free men, even though they were in uniform, ought not to be required to do the bidding of their officers. "Even the *common soldier,*" declared Matlack, "retains *some right* to judge of the propriety of the order which he has obeyed, and to *demand satisfaction* in cases where improper, or unnecessary, orders have been given. And freemen *will judge* for themselves, and will speak their Sentiments with *decency and firmness.*" Above all, Continental officers must not order militiamen around like inferiors: to Matlack and his fellow democrats, the militia was a more respectable and honorable service than was the regular army.

Arnold was brought into the case by Timothy Matlack's insistence that he order Major Franks to apologize to the offended sergeant of militia. Matlack threatened to throw the whole case into the newspapers unless Arnold gave satisfaction, but a veteran of Quebec and Saratoga was not likely to be intimidated by such tactics. He denied the justice of Matlack's grievance, declaring that no soldier could expect to carry over into the army the rights and privileges of civilians. A soldier must obey orders or the army would cease to exist, Arnold pointed out; therefore the duty of Sergeant Matlack was to do as directed without questioning its propriety.

With this the affair rested, but Arnold's enemies did not forget Sergeant Matlack and Major Franks's barber: in the charges leveled against Arnold by the Pennsylvania Council in 1779 was the accusation that he had imposed "menial offices upon the sons of freemen of this State." It was a small matter, perhaps, but it served the purpose of helping to raise a hue and cry against him.

Although Arnold was seemingly unaware of it, his situation was fraught with danger: the Pennsylvania democrats could not brook any semblance of superiority in the military power, as many officers before Arnold had learned to their cost. Count Pulaski had been virtually driven from the state because his men violated the law prohibiting the impressing of wagons or provisions without the consent of the Pennsylvania Council; and General Wayne had been charged with disrespect to the civil government when he refused to admit to his lodgings in Philadelphia "a dirty looking fellow" who came in the middle of the night to clap a warrant upon him. These brushes with the military had made the Pennsylvania politicians as touchy as a gouty foot, "which," an officer remarked to General Greene, "*I* know, if *you* do not, will wince at the approach of even a feather."

Arnold was in no position to tangle with such vindictive and resourceful enemies; his career was not an open book free from reproach. Arnold may have been a knight-errant of liberty but already his armor was tarnished by charges of graft and corruption that had cropped up persistently during his career. At Montreal, he was alleged to have sold for his own profit goods captured by the American army; and after the British evacuation of Philadelphia he was accused of having seized a large part of the merchandise left behind by the British and Tory merchants. Arnold, by his undoubted services to his country's cause, might have lived these charges down, but instead they were swallowed up by the greater enormity of his treason. Perhaps Arnold was not guilty of dealing in stolen goods (his later career, however, hardly gives him the benefit of the doubt), but the fact that he was so accused strengthened his conviction that he was being made the victim of unmerited persecution. "I cannot but think it extremely cruel," he exclaimed, "when I have sacrificed my ease, health, and great part of my private property in the cause of my country, to be calumniated as a robber and thief, at a time too when I have it not in my power to be heard in my own defence."

In his contempt for his enemies, Arnold gave them the opening they sought. He used teams and wagons belonging to the government for his own purposes, and although he paid for their use and they were not needed for public purposes at the time, the Pennsylvania democrats availed themselves of this incident, among others, to demand that the Continental Congress punish Arnold for his transgressions.

Arnold swore that he was being made a scapegoat of vindictive politicians; nevertheless, the charges of the government of Pennsylvania could not be passed over lightly and he was ordered brought to trial. And to ensure that Arnold was punished, Joseph Reed, the president of the Pennsylvania Council, declared that in case of an acquittal Pennsylvania would furnish no wagons to the army "be the Emeregency what it may." The trial, although a court-martial, was actually, he said, "Arnold vs. the Freemen of Pennsylvania" and the accused must be humbled in the dust before the sovereign power of the people.

As a victim of the malice of Pennsylvania democrats, Arnold won the sympathy of conservatives and army officers who had experienced something of the difficulties of getting along with jealous civilians. In fact, he became in some quarters the public hero he had always wished to be. Arnold, the Hannibal of the American army, had fallen, said his admirers, "into the unmerciful fangs of the Executive Council of Pennsylvania"; and General Charles Lee exclaimed that Arnold was being attacked by "a Banditti of ignorant mercenary Clowns."

To Arnold, however, this persecution merely strengthened his conviction that he was surrounded by relentless enemies. Others might commit with impunity far greater crimes than those with which he stood charged; but let him make the slightest misstep and his enemies were upon his back.

It is not extraordinary that Arnold lost faith in his countrymen and, indeed, in human nature. "I daily discover so much baseness and Ingratitude among Mankind," he wrote Peggy Shippen, "that I allmost blush at being of the same Species."

Saturnine, restless, goaded by an ambition which fed upon disappointments, Arnold found even the Philadelphia ladies cold: he said that they needed to be taught how to kiss. Nevertheless, Arnold fell in love with a Philadelphia beauty and she did not prove frigid. Arnold's success in love was his final undoing. He wooed and won Peggy Shippen, daughter of a wealthy and conservative family. The Shippen family had remained in Philadelphia during the British occupation and although Peggy had not held herself aloof from the gay social life provided by the presence of hundreds of British officers, she had not attended the Mischianza because her father was scandalized at the idea of his daughters wearing Turkish trousers.

As a result, when the Americans came back to Philadelphia, the ladies who attended the Mischianza — "equally noted for their Tory principles and their late fondness for British debauches and macaronies" — were not immediately accepted within the pale of Whig society; but the Shippen girls, because they had not been present at that entertainment, were held in bounds for Continental officers. Arnold, when he married Peggy Shippen, was thirty-eight and she was only eighteen, but this hard-bitten campaigner was peculiarly attractive to women. As General Knox said, the marriage proved what he often had occasion to point out: that "the girls are the same everywhere — at least some of them; they love a red coat dearly."

Peggy Shippen brought no surcease to Arnold's financial worries; on the contrary, she was an expensive acquisition to a military man already living much beyond his means. Accustomed to every luxury, she did not expect to step down in the world by marrying Arnold; nor did Arnold intend that his wife should suffer any lack of the amenities she regarded as her due. He was now launched into Philadelphia society and he was resolved to make a splash that would put to shame the merchant princes and profiteers with whom he consorted. Accordingly, he bought for his bride an estate on the Schuylkill called Mount Pleasant, and there he settled down to a life that, had he possessed the money to maintain it, might have been idyllic.

Marrying a pretty girl and buying an expensive house are hardly the acts of a man who contemplates treason. Nevertheless, within two months of installing Peggy and himself in the suburbs of Philadelphia, Arnold, with the knowledge of his wife, had opened a correspondence with the British military authorities in New York and had offered to sell his services to the British Crown.

This astounding action on the part of a man who had many claims to be regarded as the outstanding military genius of the war sprang from the vexations Arnold had experienced at the hands of Congress and the government of Pennsylvania, and from the acute financial embarrassment in which his penchant for high life had involved him. He saw no prospect, by remaining an honest man, of ever attaining the wealth upon which he had set his heart. Already he had begun to touch his friends and had even approached the French minister, hinting that unless a loan was forthcoming he would be forced to leave the army. La Luzerne, although anxious that Arnold remain in uniform, could not oblige him with a loan—had he done so, a large part of the army might have camped at his front door.

So Arnold was driven to sell the last commodity on which he could raise money — his honor.

It is significant that Arnold did not wait for the decision of the court-martial before he opened negotiations with the British. In June 1779, his trial took place; and although Arnold was acquitted of any deliberate wrongdoing in using for his own purposes wagons belonging to the government, his conduct was held to be "imprudent and improper." He was therefore sentenced to receive a public reprimand from Washington. Characteristically, Arnold regarded this reprimand as an unwarranted insult: he declared that he had been punished not for doing wrong but because he might, had the circumstances been different, have done wrong — "or rather," he added, "because there was a possibility that evil might have followed the good I did." Arnold's sensitivity had reached the stage where a pinprick goaded him to fury; yet it is doubtful whether even complete exoneration by the court-martial would have affected his decision to sell himself to the highest bidder.

For over a year, beginning in May 1779, Arnold haggled with the British over the price of his treason. He was resolved to extract the last shilling from his villainy: Arnold was selling himself for the sake of money and he left the British in no doubt that an American major general could not be bought for thirty pieces of silver. Although he spoke of Great Britain as "his country" and declared that he was eager to do his duty by returning to its allegiance, it is clear that his love of country was overmatched by his love of money. His motives were mercenary and no amount of whitewashing could conceal that personal profit was at the bottom of his treason.

In his negotiations with the British, he referred frequently to such matters as indemnification, annuities, and pensions, and he set a value of ten thousand pounds sterling upon the property he stood to lose if the British failed to crush the rebellion with his aid.

Having resolved to go over to the British, Arnold took steps to make himself as valuable as possible to his prospective purchasers. To that end, he procured the appointment of commander at West Point. Now he was in a position to sell not only himself but a fortress of great strategic importance; twenty thousand pounds for West Point was, he assured General Clinton, "A cheap purchase."

To the British, West Point was worth everything — and more — that Arnold asked for it. Washington declared that West Point was the most important post in America and that its loss "must have given the American cause a deadly wound if not a fatal stab." The fortress had been begun after the campaign of 1777 when Clinton had succeeded in knocking out the American forts near Haverstraw and had penetrated almost to Albany; with West Point in their hands, the British might command the Hudson and thereby achieve the long-deferred objective of isolating New England and starving the already hard-pressed Continental army.

In changing his allegiance, Arnold of course believed that he was choosing the winning side. He had given up hope of American victory: later he likened the patriot cause to "the pangs of a dying man, violent but of short duration." In May 1780, Charleston, South Carolina, fell to the British; and in August of the same year, Gates went down to humiliating defeat at Camden. France, Arnold was satisfied, had proved itself incapable of winning the war for the patriots; and with the failure of its ally had vanished the last hopes of the United States.

Until the autumn of 1780, Clinton had no way of knowing whether he was actually corresponding with Benedict Arnold; many letters had been received at headquarters purporting to come from his hand, but no British officer had ever heard from Arnold's lips that he was ready to betray the cause. Clinton craved certainty: his plans must perforce remain unsettled until he knew that Arnold was ready to deliver West Point. For that purpose, he decided to send his aide-de-camp, Major André, to meet Arnold behind the American lines and to arrange for the surrender of the fort.

John André was Clinton's right-hand man. "By God," exclaimed a British officer, "Sir Harry Clinton's a mere old woman without him." Like many of his class, he was a polished gentleman, the delight of London drawing rooms and a brilliant wit. André was the author of a satirical poem entitled "The Cow Chace," in which the courage of American soldiers was derided in the manner fashionable among English officers. Among other American generals, he had held Arnold up to contempt: —

> "Canada immortaliz'd
> The Vender of the Pill."

He suggested humorously — although the joke was already wearing rather thin — that whatever valor Americans displayed was owing chiefly to the rum they imbibed plentifully before battle. Congress shared this predilection for the bottle, he said; but whether the members of that body were most fond of "Heresy, Sedition, or Strong Toddy" he could not say. In any event, these pot-valiant rebels were beneath the contempt of an English gentleman.

Meanwhile, the plot was moving smoothly: not a hitch occurred in Arnold's plans, nor did anyone get wind of his intentions. No special precautions were taken at West Point; the campaign was over and the army settled down to the inactivity that now characterized the war for nine months of the year. Many troops had gone home, leaving West Point dangerously weak. "I would stake my Salvation that I could have taken the place with 300 Men," declared an American general, "Just in as much time as it would take to March round the Redoubts." Even Washington was out of the way, conferring with Rochambeau at New London, Connecticut.

With fortune thus playing into his hands, André went up the Hudson in the British ship *Vulture* and, at the appointed spot, went ashore to interview Arnold. In the middle of their conversation, American batteries opened fire upon the *Vulture* and obliged it to raise anchor and slip down the river. This left André with no way of retreat to the British lines except by land; and although Clinton had enjoined him to wear his uniform at all times and not carry incriminating papers on his person, Arnold persuaded him to assume a disguise and to carry back to Clinton documentary evidence of the bargain that had been concluded. Before he reached safety, however, André was captured and his papers examined. Luckily for Arnold, he learned of his confederate's fate before the Americans were ready to apprehend him; without a moment's delay he got aboard the *Vulture*, which had remained near by, and made his way to New York, leaving André to get out of the scrape as best he could.

Indubitably, the circumstances under which André was captured made him a spy: he was disguised, he carried incriminating papers, and he was captured within the American lines. The penalty usually meted out to spies was death; and even though Washington recognized that André was more unfortunate than criminal in the affair, and Clinton threatened to execute American prisoners if André were put to death, he refused clemency. There were far too many British prisoners in American hands for Clinton to carry out his threat, as Washington well knew; but even if his decision were to lead to executions and reprisals, the American commander was resolved that André must die.

André was not permitted to die by musketry: as a spy, he met death by hanging. He departed this life with a quiet heroism that abashed his executioners: he was determined to show these rebels what stuff an English gentleman was made of and how proudly he could die. Dressed in full regimentals, he walked to the place of execution "with as much ease and chearfulness of countenance as if he had been going to an assembly room." He helped the hangman adjust the halter around his neck and tied the handkerchief around his eyes. "He died lamented by all the spectators," wrote an observer; "he seem'd to the last to value his Honour more than his Life, and met Death with the courage of a Hero, and the Calmness of a Philosopher . . . had he been tried by a Court of Ladies, he is so genteel, handsome, polite, a young gentleman, that I am confident they would have acquitted him."

Few Americans would not have preferred to string up Arnold rather than André; but Arnold was safe in New York, bickering with Clinton over the price of his treason. Although actually he was heavily in debt when he went over to the British, he coolly asked for ten thousand pounds as indemnification for sacrificing his estate and emoluments; nevertheless, Clinton refused to award him more than six thousand, three hundred and fifteen pounds as damages. Altogether, in indemnifications, annuities to his family, pensions, and so forth, the British government paid Arnold and his family a princely sum, yet Arnold still clamored for more. Apparently he would have been content with nothing less than a blank check upon the British Exchequer. In fact, however, Benjamin Franklin pointed out, Arnold had not driven a sharp bargain; "Judas," he observed, "sold only one Man, Arnold three Millions. Judas got for his one Man 30 Pieces of Silver, Arnold got not a halfpenny a Head. A miserable Bargainer!"

One of Arnold's first acts was to point out to the British all the American spies in New York of whom he had knowledge. As a result, Washington's intelligence from New York abruptly ceased; even those who escaped detection were too frightened to send information.[6] And within the American lines, every man scrutinized his neighbor more closely after Arnold's treason; in particular, Arnold's friends were brought under suspicion.

Arnold had left his wife behind as a hostage to fortune. He described her as being "as good, and as Innocent as an Angel," but whatever she might have been, she was not Arnold's good angel. Knowing all along of Arnold's intentions, she made no effort to dissuade him from his course. Nevertheless, she passed among her contemporaries as a sweet young thing who had had no part in her husband's villainy; and under this guise she was permitted to join Arnold in New York. Except for his wife, Arnold had no confederates: apparently there was no man in the American army whom he could trust to follow him into treason.

If Arnold could not be the most loved man in the country, he could be the most hated; although the popularity he sought so ardently had eluded him, few men have ever received a greater measure of obloquy. Together with the devil, he was burned in effigy all over the country: in one hand he was depicted holding a long purse and in the other hand a mask. Anthony Wayne protested against the practice of putting Arnold cheek by jowl with Satan — it was not fair to the devil, he said, to be associated with a fellow who had acted "in so dirty a manner that would make even the Devil blush."

Characteristically, after his treason Arnold proposed to the British that the American army be bribed to surrender en masse. Judging his countrymen by his own mercenary standards, Arnold believed that British guineas would prove a more potent weapon than British bullets. "Money," he said, "will go farther than arms in America." To eliminate the American army, he told his new comrades, it was necessary merely to offer to make good the arrears in pay of American troops, award two hundred acres of land to every private, ten thousand acres to every general, and twenty guineas in cash — and then watch the greasy rebels scramble for the

---

[6] Washington lacked funds to buy the services of many first-rate spies. Usually, the practitioners of this devious trade demanded hard cash with a down payment in advance — which, of course, put an end to all negotiations with the chronically hard-up American commander-in-chief. Until 1778, there was no organized secret service attached to the American army; as a result, little more than rumor and hearsay reached headquarters. Little reliance could be placed upon information gained from deserters, country people, and the like; notoriously given to exaggeration and falsification, these people deceived more than they informed the American army. This situation led in 1778 to the creation of a regular spy service which, particularly in New York City and Long Island, functioned smoothly in relaying military information to Washington.

largess. According to Arnold, every American had his price and, it would seem, could be purchased for considerably less than he himself had gone for.

⌒　　⌒　　⌒

In its consequences, Arnold's treason fell far short of his expectations: American morale was not shattered, and the patriot leaders did not trample each other in their haste to go over to the British side. Although mutiny broke out in the American army a few months after Arnold joined the enemy, this was the result not of Arnold's treason but of conditions in the American army that for many years had been generating such an outbreak. What is chiefly remarkable about the mutiny of 1781 is that it did not occur earlier.

The collapse of the currency brought Congress face to face with a question which admitted of no evasion: how were the soldiers to be paid and the army supplied without money? The campaign of 1780, it was estimated in 1779, would cost at least three hundred million dollars, assuming that the currency remained stable. As everyone knew, it was not stable — in fact, it was rapidly sinking from sight. It seemed likely that the army would follow paper money into oblivion; when Congress could no longer pay the soldiers, it was observed: "We must suppose them to be perfect Ideots if they do not disband themselves." John Adams would have had Americans "march out all at once, and crush the snakes in their Nest" — but the veterans had no intention of flinging themselves upon British bayonets in a death or victory charge.

With the Continental dollar valued at a penny or less, and the army on the verge of starvation for want of supplies, Congress decided, in February 1780, to break away from its well-nigh worthless paper by asking the states for supplies in actual commodities rather than in money. Millions of dollars were being expended for a pittance of supplies; at this rate, the country would soon be saddled with an unbearable debt. The road to ruin, it was now clear, was paved with paper dollars; this highway that in the beginning had stretched out so smoothly and invitingly had led straight to the slough of despond. An empty treasury, a ruined credit, an army that had already suffered almost beyond human endurance — with these Congress must save the country from the enemy at the gates. True, the states owed Congress more than fifty million dollars in quotas due and overdue; but Congress had learned not to put its trust in its accounts receivable.

In resorting to "specific supplies," Congress was sanctioning barter as a method of exchange. Throughout the country, barter had largely replaced the exchange of goods or services for money. Congress belatedly recognized what the people had long known — that paper money was ceasing to function as a currency. At the same time, Congress abdicated in favor of the states the function of supplying the army. There were now thirteen different legislatures to which the army must look for necessities — a notable victory for states' rights! Centralized government had broken down and the states picked up the reins of authority dropped by Congress.

Little good came from Congress's surrender of authority to the states: the system of specific supplies yielded less than did paper money. Requisitioning commodities rather than paper money from the states merely proved to be another, and more effective, way of starving the army and sinking the prestige of Congress in the process. Through a fatal oversight, Congress failed to provide adequate means of transportation for the supplies furnished by the states. The states were obliged merely to bring their contributions to some central depot; there their duties ended, and there, as often as not, the supplies remained. Certainly, only a thin trickle ever reached the Continental army; and, as Washington said, the government was charged with double the amount it actually received, and for what it received it was charged double. Underweight and runt cattle came as prime steers; moldy wheat was first grade; worn-out clothing was finely woven uniforms. Moreover, it was found that the cost of transporting this material to the army was frequently greater than the original cost. "It is a vain thing to suppose that wars can be carried on by quibbles and puns," said Robert Morris, "and yet laying taxes and payable in specific articles amounts to no more, for with a great sound they put little or nothing in the Treasury."

It was apparent that American soldiers, driven to desperation by the indifference of civilians, were "verging to that state which . . . will make a wise man mad." Fearing military despotism, the citizens adopted the surest means of making it a reality: an American soldier could be made an instrument of the tyranny of some Caesar or Cromwell only by the kind of mistreatment inflicted during the War of American Independence. It is not surprising, therefore, that the troops began to plunder without compunction these fat and frolicsome civilians. In 1780, the Pennsylvania Line fell upon the countryside with a violence which General Greene declared was equal to the worst atrocities of the Hessians; one body of soldiers pillaged a house in the presence of their officers, who dared not intervene lest they be cut down. Scores of offenders were punished, but manifestly the cure for this misconduct lay not in executions or whippings but in giving the soldiers enough to eat and in keeping them in clothes and liquor. In the summer of 1780, heralding events to come, a mutiny broke out among the troops which was suppressed only when the officers agreed to give up their rations of meat and live on flour, thereby helping the soldiers to resign themselves to their own lot.

This was at best merely a temporary expedient: it is poor consolation to starving men to see others starve.[7]

The Pennsylvania troops, besides the grievances common to all the soldiers, nursed a special sense of injury. In particular, the soldiers claimed that they had enlisted for three years, whereas the state authorities insisted that they had enlisted for the duration of the war. This difference of opinion, certain to make trouble when the three years were up, had not been settled by 1781, the year the troops regarded as terminating their service. "The Ides of January," Anthony Wayne warned his friends, would bring the showdown.[8]

The Pennsylvania Line contained a higher proportion of foreigners (chiefly Scotch-Irish and English) than did the line of any other state; and a number of British deserters had been enlisted in the Pennsylvania ranks. Later, this fact was to be used to prove the point that "human patience has its limits, but that citizen soldiers are much more patient than foreigners."

During the winter of 1780–1781, the greater part of the army was cantoned at West Point (Washington's quarters were at New Windsor) while the Pennsylvania troops were quartered at Morristown and the New Jersey contingent was stationed at Pompton, New Jersey. Here, on New Year's Day, 1781, the Pennsylvania troops ushered in the new year in a manner that shook the American cause to its foundations. A ration of rum was passed out to the men and they promptly got riotously drunk.[9] They refused to obey their officers; two captains and a lieutenant who attempted to compel obedience were killed and other officers were injured by blows

---

[7] Over a period of several years there had been brief flare-ups in the army. In 1779, with their pay six months in arrears, and on quarter allowances of meat, the Connecticut Line mutinied and prepared to march out of camp — a maneuver which was prevented by the bayonets of the Pennsylvania Line, which, fortunately for the Continental army, remained loyal. In January and May, 1780, there were other outbreaks when the troops declared that they would lay down their arms rather than endure the torture of starvation. These revolts were put down by the Continental officers; but to a delegation of Congressmen appointed to investigate conditions at camp, "with tears in their eyes, they stated their apprehensions that the dissolution of the army was at hand, unless constant supplies of *provisions* at least were kept up."

[8] In February 1780, Washington gave this explanation for the discontent of the Pennsylvania troops. They were, he said, "from the commencement . . . almost universally engaged for the war. When they saw the Eastern [New England] levies in the beginning of last campaign who had received enormous bounties (many a thousand pounds and upwards, for a few months) they began to compare situations to murmur and to dispute their engagements. To remove these discontents Congress, at my instance, were pleased to order a gratuity of 100 dollars to all men enlisted for the war previous to the 23d of Jany. 1779. The intention of this gratuity was clearly explained, the men received it and gave receipts expressive of that intention. They begin now to revive their former dissatisfaction and many desertions have taken place in consequence."

[9] Washington believed that the "Licentious conduct of that line [Pennsylvania's] was . . . more the effect of an over charge of spirits on the first of January than of premeditated design."

from muskets, bayonets, and stones. Fearing that the troops, almost fifteen hundred strong, would seek to join the British in New York, Wayne and a few officers took a position on the road leading to that city, "producing a conviction to the Soldiery," Wayne wrote the next day, "that they could not advance upon that route but over our dead bodies." The mutineers turned back toward Princeton, where they made camp. Under the command of their sergeants, they maintained strict order and discipline, but no outsiders were permitted to approach their encampment except under a flag of truce.

General Clinton, learning of the mutiny in the American army, immediately attempted to capitalize upon it. A large number of troops were put under arms and ordered to be in instant readiness to march; and emissaries were sent to the mutineers promising that "in this struggle for their just rights and liberties, they will be assisted by a body of British troops, that if they will lay down their arms they shall be pardoned all past Offences, be paid all the pay due them by Congress, and not be required to serve unless they chuse it." Clinton did not dare to go beyond this offer lest he "alarm their jealousy, mar all, and reunite them to their late tyrants."

The mutineers soon made clear that their quarrel was strictly a family affair and that the interference of outsiders was not wanted. The spies sent them by Clinton they turned over to the Pennsylvania authorities, who hanged them incontinently; and when Wayne begged the troops not to go over to the enemy "they declared it was not their intention, and that they would hang any man who would attempt it, and for that, if the enemy should come out in consequence of this revolt, they would turn back and fight them" — proving, said an American, that although Clinton could "bribe such a mean toad-eater as Arnold, it is not in his power to bribe an American soldier."

Congress and the Pennsylvania authorities were reluctant to use force against the mutineers; and indeed it was not clear where a force capable of overcoming fifteen hundred armed men was to be found. The militia certainly could not be depended upon: the militiamen either sympathized with the soldiers or had no stomach for tangling with these hard-bitten veterans. Yet, had the mutineers attempted to march to the British lines, there is little doubt that the militia would have gone into action. Fearful of driving the Pennsylvania troops into the hands of the enemy, Congress continued to supply them with provisions and sent a committee to camp to hear the demands of the soldiers. This, some officers grumbled, was standing on too much ceremony with "the Gentlemen Mutineers" — a whiff of grape ought to be the portion of men who struck down their officers and turned their arms against the authority they had sworn to uphold. Washington refused to march to the scene of trouble with the troops at West Point — "the civil authority having undertaken to settle

the dispute," he said, "there would have been an impropriety in my interfering in their conciliatory measures."

The upshot of these negotiations was that the mutinous troops virtually
wrote their own terms for laying down their arms. One half of the
Pennsylvania Line was discharged, and the rest were given furloughs; but
none were held to their engagements to serve for the duration of the
war. Many of the Pennsylvania troops went to Philadelphia, where they
swaggered about the streets, insolently provoking officers they encountered and boasting that they were now free men with money in their
pockets. Finally, what remained of the Pennsylvania Line was ordered,
in March 1781, to march to Virginia.

Perceiving the success of the Pennsylvania troops, the New Jersey Line
staged a mutiny despite the fact that the government was making every
effort to redress its grievances. As in the Pennsylvania Line, many of the
New Jersey soldiers were foreigners. Again the British in New York attempted to turn the mutiny to their advantage, although General Robertson of the British army expressed the fear that "the appearance of John
Bull might lead the quarreling dogs to a reconciliation." This time, however, Washington was resolved to use force to break the mutiny; to permit soldiers to dictate terms to the country was certain, he said, to
"subvert the whole army, if not quelled by a decisive effort of authority."
Washington therefore directed the troops at West Point to subdue the
uprising, with orders to execute the leaders as a warning to the rest of the
army.

The troops at West Point, mostly New Englanders, showed no inclination to join the mutiny, although several soldiers swore that they
would not fight against a brother soldier. But there was no outbreak or
demonstration — nothing, that is, said an officer at West Point, that
could not be quieted by a little rum. This, however, was not readily
supplied; a soldier said the garrison was "Dam'd scarce of Grog — touch &
go with provision. . . . Add the whole together & you'll find it pretty
tight living here."

The mutiny of the New Jersey Line was much less formidable than
that of the Pennsylvanians: only about two hundred men took part in this
latter uprising, the rest refusing to participate. Therefore, it was comparatively easy for the troops from West Point to suppress the mutiny.
As Washington had directed, two of the ringleaders were executed on the
spot.

Congress attempted to use the mutinies to drive home to the states the
moral that the army could not be held together unless requisitions were
promptly complied with. Responsibility for the outbreaks, said Congress,
lay not with the soldiers who revolted against intolerable conditions, but
with the states which had permitted them to fall into this plight. As
Washington said, "having punished guilt and supported authority, it now

becomes proper to do justice." The conditions that had produced the mutinies must be removed if the army was to take the field. "It is vain to think an army can be kept together much longer," he declared, "under such a variety of sufferings as ours has experienced." And, for the moment at least, the states were frightened into taking action for the relief of the troops. "I find," said General John Sullivan at the end of January, 1781, "that Congress & assemblies begin to Rouse from their Slumber & Individuals are now alarmed for the Publick Safety who have for years past been Employed in amassing wealth." As a result, the "strike" of the Pennsylvania troops brought benefits to soldiers in other state lines. Upon receiving news of the mutiny, for example, some of the New England state legislatures voted cash presents of twenty-four dollars to the soldiers.[10] And, shortly after the mutinies, a series of events contrived to give a more hopeful aspect to the American cause: Maryland acceded to the Articles of Confederation, a new loan was promised by France, Congress reorganized the departments of Foreign Affairs, Finance, and War, and Robert Morris was appointed superintendent of finance. The mutinies of 1781 were the low-water mark of the American Revolution.

[10] The reaction of the New Hampshire Legislature was typical. "The Horrible Revolt of the Pensilvania Line gives us much Anxiety," wrote a member, "The Genl Court have determined to Send forward some hard money by way of a present to our troops who it Seems have had no pay for near twelve Months."

AT this juncture of the war, Americans could ill afford to quarrel among themselves: Georgia and South Carolina had been overrun by the enemy and, to make the peril more acute, Cornwallis had turned northward, seeking to eliminate the last scattered elements of resistance in the Southern states.

With the American army routed and disorganized, Cornwallis summoned the North Carolina Loyalists to arms, urging them to fall upon the beaten rebels. The Loyalists, however, were wary; not until they saw a British army in their midst would they risk showing themselves in arms against their enemies. They had vivid memories of the defeat suffered at the patriots' hands in 1776 at Moore's Creek Bridge, and of the unhappy consequences of a premature rising made in June 1780 when, encouraged by the approach of Cornwallis's army, they had taken up arms only to be promptly vanquished by the patriots — a disaster which forced many Loyalists to take refuge with Cornwallis's army.

Despite these setbacks, they promised to join Cornwallis in the field as soon as his army had established itself in the state. As Cornwallis discerned, here was the acid test of the experiment which had brought the British to the Southern states: Could the Loyalists be depended upon for military aid? After the battle of Camden, everything encouraged Cornwallis to believe that the Loyalists would take an active part in the final struggle against the rebels, and it was with this expectation that he resumed his march northward.

Cornwallis had not proceeded far, however, before the military situation in the South was changed by two unexpected reverses sustained by British arms. After being twice victorious over the rebels, the British themselves were defeated at King's Mountain and Cowpens.

Cornwallis had detached Major Ferguson with eight hundred Tory militia and one hundred British regulars to eliminate the patriot bands that were playing havoc with British lines of communication. Finding the country swarming with armed men, Ferguson took a position on King's Mountain, a steep and wooded promontory in western South Carolina. Here he was attacked by fifteen hundred mounted riflemen who, heavily outnumbering the British, broke through Ferguson's defenses, killing the British commander in the charge. Even after the British and Tories had raised the white flag, the Americans continued to fire upon them in retaliation for the Tories' practice of denying quarter when they had the upper hand. Although American officers finally succeeded in stopping the killing, after the battle the patriots executed nine Loyalist militiamen and forced the remaining prisoners to march two days without food. For sheer savagery and brutality, the struggle in the Carolinas between patriots and Loyalists equaled anything in Indian warfare.

Crowding closely upon this blow came the defeat at Cowpens, where Tarleton, the British cavalry leader, made incautious by repeated success, attacked the Americans with the light troops of Cornwallis's army. Although outnumbering the rebels, Tarleton's regiment of cavalry, known as the British Legion, was composed partly of American prisoners taken at Camden who, finding themselves opposed by their former comrades, turned and fled, leaving the infantry to be surrounded and captured by the enemy.[1]

King's Mountain and Cowpens exposed to attack the British post at Ninety-six, the key to western South Carolina; deprived Cornwallis of the light infantry upon which he relied heavily in his invasion of North Carolina for scouting, flank attacks, and foraging; and revived the flagging spirits of the rebels throughout the South. To the British, the very earth seemed to sprout rebels: entire districts where all evidence of disaffection had been suppressed now went over to the patriots, and British outposts, hitherto believed secure, were menaced by guerrillas. Many of those who had sworn fealty to George III emerged in their true colors as unreconstructed rebels. In short, these reverses were, as Clinton said, "the first Link of a Chain of Events that followed each other in regular Succession until they at least ended in the total Loss of America."

Nevertheless, Cornwallis did not halt his march into North Carolina. King's Mountain and Cowpens merely strengthened the British commander's determination to subdue North Carolina, because from these defeats he learned that as long as the rebels held North Carolina and Virginia, the British position in South Carolina and Georgia would be

---

[1] On the other hand, there was frequent desertion from the Americans to the British. General Marion complained that the enemy force was composed in part of men who had recently fought with him.

insecure. The vast extent of frontier and the rebellious temper of the people, together with the small numbers of British troops available for garrison duty, persuaded Cornwallis that it was necessary to master the entire South if any part of it was to be held in peace.

Cornwallis could hardly hope to occupy North Carolina without a fight. The American army under General Nathanael Greene was moving into the state quite as though it had never heard of the battle of Camden. Greene had completely rebuilt the Southern army, procuring at immense effort the services of "some few of the many thousands who," he remarked, "are idle at home." Everywhere he found the people "engaged in matters of interest and in pursuit of pleasure, almost regardless of their danger . . . every man excusing himself from giving the least aid to Government, from an apprehension that they would get no return for any advances." Greene's chief concern was the inertia of the home front. "Three years ago our springs were rusty, on account of their not being used," remarked a patriot in 1780; "they now are worn out."

Unlike Gates, Greene prayed to be delivered from militia, among whom, he observed, "everybody is a general," but American generals took what they got in the way of soldiers and were thankful even for militia. Greene's army was of necessity composed largely of militia — there were not enough Continentals in the entire South to form a respectable fighting force; and to Greene's entreaties for reinforcements, Washington answered that if he parted with any troops he must accompany them himself or have none left to command, since his entire army was barely sufficient to garrison West Point.

The Southern states, instead of filling their Continental lines with long-term troops, persisted in maintaining vast bodies of militia which, said Greene, "like the locusts of Egypt, have eaten up everything, and the expense has been so enormous, that it has ruined the currency." He believed that North Carolina alone had enough militia to devour all the revenues of the United States since "every man draws and wastes as much as he pleases."

Suffering from the same shortages of food, arms, and trustworthy troops that had beset Gates, Greene shelved his predecessor's strategy of attack in favor of the Fabian policy that Washington had been compelled to adopt in the North.[2] He resolved never to risk a pitched battle with the enemy except on ground of his own choosing. Greene ascribed Americans' ill fortune in the South partly to the "commanding officers

---

[2] But Greene had one important advantage over Gates: he had a strong force of cavalry under the command of William Washington and in Lee's Legion he possessed a corps of hard-riding mounted troops. When necessary, he seized horses from the inhabitants and he urged the same course upon other American commanders. "Enlarge your cavalry, or you are ruined," he said. "Don't pay any regard to the murmurs of the people. They will bless you when they find they derive security from them."

risking battle in compliance with the wishes and impatience of the in-habitants" and to the officers' failure to recognize that "it is equally dangerous to go forward as to stand still for if you lose the confidence of the people you lose all support, and if you rush into danger you hazard everything." His purpose was to steer a middle course between these two evils, striving to keep the people's support without at the same time jeopardizing the cause by gambling everything on a quick victory.

Therefore, Greene fell back before Cornwallis as the British advanced into North Carolina; rather than stand and fight, he allowed himself to be chased out of the state. The campaign turned out to be little more than a foot race between Cornwallis and Greene; and although Greene won, the prize — North Carolina — went to Cornwallis. The British were now masters of every province south of Virginia; only the guerrilla bands of Morgan, Sumter, and Marion continued to keep patriot resistance alive. Therefore Cornwallis triumphantly raised the King's Standard at Hillsborough, North Carolina — the heart of the Loyalist country — and summoned the citizens to take the oath of allegiance and to engage themselves as volunteers in the King's cause.

But, to the chagrin of the British commander, the Loyalists held back; few joined the British troops at Hillsborough, although hundreds came to wish them success. The Loyalists were not yet persuaded that the British had won the war in the South and that it was safe for them openly to join the royalists: Greene's army was poised on the frontier, the guer-rilla bands were still active behind the British lines, and the British army — less than three thousand strong — seemed far too small to protect Tories from the rebels.

These cautious well-wishers of the British cause soon had reason to congratulate themselves upon their prudence: Greene returned to North Carolina and this time he made clear that he did not intend to yield the state without a fight. In March 1781, at Guilford Courthouse, North Carolina, the two armies finally met. Although Greene's army outnum-bered the British three to one, the American commander had only five hundred veterans, the remainder being militia. The Americans took a strong position, but it was Cornwallis, as usual, who made the attack. Behind rail fences and in shallow trenches, the Americans mowed down the enemy columns, but the British came on doggedly. The American cavalry under Colonel Washington sustained three assaults by British in-fantry, inflicting heavy casualties upon the enemy, but the militia by their cowardice nullified these advantages. Before the engagement, Greene had made a bargain with the North Carolina militia that if they fired twice they were at liberty to run away — "Two rounds, my boys," he said, "and then you may fall back" — and he had posted his militia in the front lines in order that they might execute this maneuver. The North Carolina militiamen did no more than they had agreed: two volleys and they were through for the day. Although the Continental troops and some of the Virginia militia continued to fight, falling back to the forests and fighting Indian fashion from behind trees, resistance was not long continued after the North Carolina militia struck for home.

The British carried the field, but their losses were staggering. Like Bunker Hill, this action, said a British officer, was "that sort of victory which ruins an army." And Greene remarked that he was ready to sell Cornwallis another field at the same price. About one third of the British forces engaged at Guilford Courthouse were killed or wounded. Exhausted by the battle and burdened with wounded, the British were unable to exploit their victory: while they re-formed their shattered ranks, the American army merely retreated a few miles and waited for Cornwallis to make the next move.

As Sir William Howe had often said, the British army could not afford to win battles in America at the cost of heavy casualties; and Cornwallis, cut off by hundreds of miles from reinforcements, could stand these losses less well than could Howe, who always remained in close contact with the British fleet. By winning battles, Cornwallis was in danger of losing the war.

After the battle, Cornwallis could not remain at Guilford Courthouse: his supplies were running low and the countryside did not afford enough food to keep his troops alive. Leaving the badly wounded behind, Cornwallis set off on a two-hundred-mile march to Wilmington, where supplies and British ships awaited him.

Greene closely pursued the retreating British, but now it was Cornwallis's turn to outrun the Americans. The American commander was somewhat handicapped by the eagerness of many of his troops "to return home to kiss their wives and sweethearts." Traveling by forced marches and sometimes leaving his dead unburied, Cornwallis left Greene far behind. Although Cornwallis had just won another victory over the Americans, and was passing through a supposedly Loyalist stronghold, the people showed no inclination to join the British cause. "Many of the inhabitants," Cornwallis reported, "rode into camp, shook me by the hand, said they were glad to see us, and to hear that we had beat Greene, and then rode home again, for I could not get 100 men in all the Regulators' Country,[3] to stay with us, even as Militia."

The Loyalists could hardly be blamed for consulting their own safety. Cornwallis and his men, on their retreat to Wilmington, hardly looked like the conquerors of the Carolinas. The British army resembled a mobile hospital; one third were sick or wounded, few had shoes, and all were ragged and dirty. In short, the British army had come to bear a striking resemblance to the American army. When the troops finally stumbled

[3] The Regulators — so called from their unsuccessful attempt to regulate the government of North and South Carolina in 1770 — were Loyalists.

into Wilmington, footsore and bedraggled, the wounded in litters, it might have been supposed that the invaders had just sustained a crushing defeat and that these were the survivors of the disaster. Of the three thousand men with whom Cornwallis had entered North Carolina, barely seven hundred remained; two thirds of his troops had been lost by battle, disease, and desertion.

True, Cornwallis could take pride in an impressive string of victories over the rebels. Commanding one of the best armies that Britain ever put in the field, he had waged war brilliantly under conditions of terrain and climate that would have taxed the ability of the greatest captains. Tactically, his battles were superb: catching the Americans off guard, always forcing the fighting no matter what the odds, and vigorously attacking at the weakest spot, he had driven the enemy from every battle-field, sometimes in complete rout. Under Cornwallis's leadership, the British regular soldier had repeatedly demonstrated his superiority over the Americans, whether Continentals or militia. Cornwallis was a natural leader of men; his troops swore that they would "carry the world before him." "His army," it was said, "is a family, he is the father of it. There are no parties, no competitions."

Cornwallis had written some brilliant chapters in English military history and had added immeasurably to his own reputation by his campaign in the Carolinas, but his conquests soon vanished into thin air. He had marched six hundred miles through two provinces, "a meteor of devastation" flashing across the countryside. All his activity, said Burke, had been "a continual series of marching and countermarching, of taking and evacuating." "Our March thro' this Country," remarked one of his own officers, "may be compared to the passage of a Ship thro' the Waves which give way on the least Impulse, but immediately close when the Body has passed."

General Greene had not defeated Cornwallis in battle — indeed, during the entire war, Greene did not win a general action — but he had fought skillfully and had forced the British to pay a heavy price for their triumphs. His army was still in the field, and could he have caught Cornwallis during the retreat to Wilmington, he might have tripped up the English Hannibal before he met his doom at Yorktown. But instead of pursuing Cornwallis all the way to Wilmington, Greene turned south, hoping by threatening South Carolina to force Cornwallis to return to Charleston. At all costs, the South must be reconquered: if he turned northward, Greene said, "the Southern States thus cut off will die like the tail of a snake."

At Wilmington, Cornwallis was confronted with the problem that had bedeviled him throughout the campaign in the South: where should he go from here? To return to Charleston was perhaps the counsel of prudence and certainly in accord with Clinton's wishes; but Cornwallis was little inclined to pay much heed either to prudence or to General Clinton.

To battle up and down the Carolinas no longer had charm for Cornwallis, and a mere defensive strategy he deemed "ruinous and disgraceful to Britain." He was, moreover, weary of this inhospitable region of swamps, forests, and rivers, and eager to seek a decision upon more congenial ground. It was the country, as much as anything, Cornwallis decided, that had robbed him of the fruits of victory. Sparsely settled, producing little that could sustain an army, plundered by both friends and foes, and plagued with snakes, heat, mosquitoes, endless pine woods and creeks which, the British commander remarked, would be called rivers in any other country — how could warfare be carried on in such a region, and victories, when gained, be turned to account against a foe that slipped away into the swamps and forests after every defeat only to emerge stronger than before?

All this led him to believe that his only hope was to track down the rebellion in the South to its final lair in Virginia. There he would destroy the seat of resistance that had kept the war alive in the Carolinas and Georgia and had made his splendid victories go for naught. By conquering Virginia, he reasoned, the provinces to the southward of the Old Dominion would be forced to cease resistance; but if Virginia was left unsubdued, the rebellion in the Carolinas and Georgia could never be extinguished. British attacks upon Virginia had hitherto been on a small scale and had proved to Cornwallis's satisfaction that "small expeditions do not frighten that powerful Province," but against a great army Cornwallis did not doubt that the Virginians would quickly wilt. The force under his command in North Carolina was too small to conquer the South; but if allied with the five thousand British troops already in Virginia and if reinforced from the British army in New York, he would have an army worthy of a conqueror. Virginia, indeed, had suddenly become so important to Cornwallis that he later urged Clinton to abandon New York if necessary, in order to force a final showdown with the rebels in the Old Dominion.

In turning to the greener pastures of Virginia, Cornwallis was doing what he had sworn he would never do: abandoning the Loyalists to the mercy of their enemies. He felt little reluctance, however, to leave such "dastardly and pusilanimous" friends as the Carolina Loyalists to their fate. He was completely disillusioned by their timidity: only about two hundred North Carolina Loyalists had been persuaded to follow his army as provincial troops and militia. The outcome of the great experiment in North Carolina was unqualified failure.

There was nothing novel in Cornwallis's plan of marching to Virginia: Clinton and Germain had both recommended this strategy. The concentration of large forces in the Chesapeake offered excellent prospects of reducing the colonies from Virginia southward to British control. But it had always been assumed by Cornwallis's superiors that when he turned his attention to Virginia the conquest of the Carolinas would have been completed; that he would march to the Chesapeake leaving the enemy strongly posted in his rear and threatening to wrest the Carolinas from British control was never anticipated. Yet when Cornwallis decided to go to Virginia, Greene was threatening the British base at Camden, opposed only by Lord Rawdon and a few thousand British troops. Admitting that a single defeat might cost the British their hold upon South Carolina, Cornwallis nevertheless deliberately weakened the army defending that province in order to carry the war to Virginia.

By advancing into South Carolina after the battle of Guilford Court-house, Greene had left the way open for Cornwallis to march northward from Wilmington into Virginia; thus the trap into which Cornwallis incautiously stepped was invitingly baited. An easy, unopposed passage to Virginia was the first lure cast before him. He swallowed it without hesitation: marching overland to Virginia, he made contact with the British forces in that state on May 20, 1781. It was the "good Genius of America," lamented Clinton, which drew Cornwallis, like Burgoyne before him, to his doom. The only difference between these unfortunate commanders, he pointed out, was that "Burgoyne thought he was acting in strict obedience to the King's Commands; Lord Cornwallis knew he was acting in positive disobedience to the orders of the Commander in Chief."

Greene refused to be diverted from the reconquest of the Southern states by Cornwallis's march to Virginia. Instead, he moved deeper into the South and thereby prevented the British from drawing reinforcements from the Carolinas and Georgia for their army in Virginia. York-town was thus made possible by Greene's strategy: while he kept the British occupied in the South, Washington and Rochambeau were able to move upon Yorktown with the French and American armies.

⌢ ⌢ ⌢

Several years before Cornwallis decided to invade Virginia, the British had turned their attention to the Old Dominion. Here, said Sir George Collier, was "the province which above all the rest has strung the sinews of rebellion." By exchanging its tobacco for military supplies in Europe and the West Indies, Virginia contributed mightily to the success of the Revolution. Tobacco was one of the main props of American credit in Europe; could this commerce be cut off, the British confidently looked forward to the collapse of the rebellion. And the means of accomplishing this objective seemed to lie immediately at hand. By establishing a naval station in Virginia, the Chesapeake could be effectively blockaded, the port of Baltimore closed to rebel shipping, and the tobacco of Virginia left to rot in warehouses. There were few opportunities open to the British to accomplish so much by the expenditure of so little effort.

Drawn southward by this fair prospect, the British early in 1779 took possession of Portsmouth, Virginia, and, from this vantage point, bottled up American shipping in the Chesapeake. So little resistance was encountered that Sir George Collier, the British admiral in charge of these operations, informed the home government that in his opinion the entire state might easily be overrun — "the people seem importunately desirous that the Royal Standard may be erected, and they give the most positive assurances that all ranks of men will resort to it." Small parties of men were sent out to forage for food and destroy tobacco warehouses; and they returned laden with plunder without having encountered serious resistance. Virginians screamed that the British were "plundering women and children, burning houses and committing every kind of outrage that could enter the heads of a licentious soldiery," yet they submitted with surprising tameness to this treatment. Washington was dismayed by the facility with which the British ravaged his home state. "Riches so easily and cheaply purchased will be a powerful inducement to another visit," he warned Virginians. "Wealth even among the boasting sons of Britain has charms more powerful than honor and glory acquired by hard knocks."

Despite this auspicious beginning, almost two years were allowed to elapse before the British seriously attempted to knock Virginia out of the war. Until late in 1780, few troops were dispatched to the Old Dominion and they were employed chiefly in protecting the naval station at Portsmouth. Indeed, for some months in 1780, the British left Virginia in peace, withdrawing their troops from Portsmouth in order to concentrate their forces against the Carolinas.

Late in 1780, however, as a diversion to Cornwallis's operations in the Carolinas, the British again invaded Virginia in force. They found Virginia a remarkably weak sister of the Confederation. Portsmouth was taken without the loss of a man; and as the British troops spread out over the countryside, they burned and plundered with impunity. Portsmouth was not a strong post, a British officer admitted; and "had we a formidable Enemy," he said, "we should be unequal to the defence of it. Against the force of this country we are under no apprehensions." Americans beheld "fourteen hundred troops shaking the Dominion of Virginia to the centre, — they who boasted that they could singly maintain the contest with Great Britain." The governor acknowledged that the state could not protect itself against one hundred British cavalry, although Virginia contained some of the finest horseflesh in the country.

To follow up this success, Clinton unleashed upon Virginia the Brigadier General whose services he had just purchased. Benedict Arnold was perhaps a costly acquisition to risk in these operations, but Clinton wished to commit the turncoat irrevocably to the British side; and there was hardly a better way of making it impossible for him ever to return to the Americans than to let him ravage the country he had betrayed.

Given scope to his talents for plundering and spreading devastation, Arnold wrote another black chapter to his career. "His genius leads him to harrass and distress the enemy," exclaimed one of his admiring subordinates. He sent back so much loot to New York that it was said he would soon be rich as a nabob; huge quantities of tobacco were put to the torch; plantations were burned and slaves carried off by the hundred.

It was Thomas Jefferson's misfortune to be governor of Virginia at the time of Arnold's invasion. Few leaders could have galvanized citizens who had suffered a handful of redcoats to remain within the state, or could have overcome the cumulative effects of five years of inflation which had utterly ruined the currency; but it is certain that Jefferson did neither. He won little honor in the governorship, and when he retired from office some Virginians blamed him bitterly for a failure the true causes of which were to be found in the lack of patriotism of the people themselves, the weakness of the state government, and the collapse of the currency.

The government of Virginia was weak to the point of debility. Most of the state governments established during the war were fit only for the piping days of peace and prosperity; but Virginia was doubly unfortunate because the war fell upon the state after its government had lost much of the authority with which the people had originally invested it. The legislature, having failed to sustain the value of the state's paper money, had fallen into low repute; and the executive was so hedged by constitutional restrictions as to be little more than a figurehead. The burgesses could agree upon nothing: while the British were plundering at will, the legislators were debating the state of the finances; apparently unable to deal with two emergencies at the same time, they grappled with inflation and left the redcoats to be disposed of by Providence. "Does not your indignation rise against such obstinate lethargic torpid wretches?" exclaimed a Virginian to a friend. "If the other states have no more energy or patriotism among their leaders than Virginia, all the blood, treasure, oaths and exertions which have been expended during this war will be utterly in vain, for we shall soon be converted to Hewers of Wood and Drawers. May Heaven or a Halter mend them."

Jefferson was obliged, moreover, to raise an army and fight a war without money. The treasury was a void where a microscopic examination in 1780 had failed to turn up a shilling. No state had issued more paper money than had Virginia, and the paper money of no state had depreciated as precipitously; now the Old Dominion, having quaffed deeply of the heady wine of inflation, was tasting the gall and wormwood which lay at the bottom of the cup. The state had lost its credit with its citizens;

there was hardly a bankrupt in the country who could not raise money on easier terms than could the government. Owing millions, its promise to pay repeatedly broken, and without a shilling in hard cash, the state of Virginia had ceased even to be a poor risk — it was a virtual certainty that it would never pay its debts. Almost the only resource left to the government to procure supplies was to employ force against its own citizens.

From his predecessor, Patrick Henry, Jefferson inherited many of the difficulties by which he was beset. As governor, Henry had courted popularity and had tried to ease the burdens of the citizens rather than to inure them to the hardships of war. He had opposed enlistments for the war, favoring instead the more popular system of voluntary enlistments for short terms. And when he resigned the governorship to Jefferson and the British descended upon the state, Henry declined to call a truce in politics. Henry dominated the legislature and he did not scruple to plant thorns under his great rival in the governor's chair. When the counties were summoned by Governor Jefferson to send reinforcements to the army of General Greene in South Carolina, some counties refused to obey and Henry abetted the recalcitrants.

The state had been stripped bare of guns and military stores, Jefferson having sent large quantities of supplies of war to the Carolinas to aid Gates and Greene in their struggle with Cornwallis.[4] In 1780, Jefferson found that there were so few guns in the state that many citizens "able and zealous to contend with the enemy" were "reduced to fold their arms for want of the means of defence." There were not enough guns even to supply the militia; whole companies turned out with hardly a musket among them. Some carried ancient squirrel guns and blunderbusses brought out of honorable retirement; and although many guns needed repair, there was not a person in Williamsburg capable of repairing a gun. Without artillery, cavalry, and military magazines, Virginia was almost powerless. Agents sent to Philadelphia to buy arms and ammunition for the state were not given a farthing of cash. Congress spared what aid it could; but overland transportation from Philadelphia, difficult at best, ceased altogether when the wagon drivers went on strike during this critical period of the war.

Moreover, at the same time that Virginia was compelled to withstand invasion from the sea, the Indians on the frontier, under British instigation, took up the hatchet. This struggle occupied at least three thousand

---

[4] Jefferson acted in the belief that if Georgia and the Carolinas were subdued by the British they would become instruments of Virginia's destruction. "The British force may harass and distress us greatly," said Jefferson, "but the Carolina's alone can subdue us. The Militia of North Carolina is very nearly as numerous as that of this State. Out of that our enemy will be able to raise great Armies. We therefore think it our first Interest to keep them under in that Quarter, considering the war in our own country but as a secondary Object."

men. Also, the state was engaged in conquering the West, Jefferson having sent out George Rogers Clark to dislodge the British from their strongholds north of the Ohio. But, above all, the springs of patriotism in the Old Dominion, as elsewhere in the confederation, had grown exceedingly rusty. "The war being distant and money plenty had produced a vicious kind of apathy," said Richard Henry Lee; the war was in danger of being forgotten in the pursuit of easy money.

Bounties of thousands of dollars in cash, land, and clothing were offered with few takers. In April 1781, General Steuben expected a reinforcement of five hundred men, yet only seven arrived in camp on time; and of these, two promptly deserted — probably to re-enlist and get another bounty before striking out for a cozy little home in the West. In Virginia, it was said, enlisting and deserting had been made "a kind of business. A man enlists himself for six or Eight thousand pounds this Spring, deserts, and in the summer a law for raising Men is passed, he enlists in another part of the State for eight or ten thousand more, deserts . . . and practices the same Villainy over again in some other part of the Country."

As a war leader and organizer of resistance, Jefferson was out of his element; in the Declaration of Independence he had awakened the patriotism and idealism of his countrymen, but no such clarion calls to action issued from the governor's office during the British invasion of Virginia. What was needed was a strong hand and an iron will — but Jefferson provided neither. Instead, when the militia were called out it often happened that the arms were sent to some other part of the state, with the result that the men, disgusted by such inefficiency, went home and refused to muster again. In consequence, the central government began to lose what little authority it still possessed: each county tried to save itself regardless of what happened to its neighbors, and finally each individual began to think only of the safety of himself and his family.

The great champion of the common man could not bring himself to bear down upon the people he loved; even in time of war and despite their remissness in support of the cause of liberty, he declined to speak with the authority and sternness that the situation deserved. "Mild Laws, a People not used to prompt obedience, a want of provisions of War and means of procuring them," he explained, "render our orders often ineffectual, oblige us to temporize and when we cannot accomplish our object in one way to attempt it in another." He leaned upon the legislature for advice; but the bewildered burgesses, many of whom looked to Patrick Henry for leadership, could give him no answer.

On the other hand, Jefferson was vigorous in defending the rights of citizens against exactions by the military authorities; civil liberties had not ceased to be precious in his eyes. He never forgot that a true republican was inexorably jealous of military power, and upon several occasions he put his principles to the proof by placing obstacles in the path of American generals engaged in trying to drive the enemy from Virginia. "We did not think proper to resign ourselves and our Country implicitly to the Demands of a Quartermaster," he said, "but thought we had some right of judgment left to us." Although the Continental Congress had given Wayne authority to impress provisions, Jefferson challenged the exercise of this power. Like many other republicans of this period, he devoted to the militia an affection which might more properly have been bestowed upon the Continental army and its commanders; he had not yet learned the truth of General Greene's aphorism: "Support the Army and that will support government. Without . . . all will fall together." [5]

When Arnold and the British fleet were reported off the capes of the Chesapeake, it was moved in the Virginia Assembly that the militia be called out, a strong force of cavalry raised, the rivers fortified, and the military stores removed to a place of safety in the interior. But this motion was "reprobated and deemed to be very absurd by the *Honourable Houses*"; nor was the governor more apprised of the danger. In consequence, Arnold found the state open to attack. He and his troops came up the James River and were in Richmond early in January, 1781, marching thirty miles from their ships to the capital "without a single grain of powder being flash'd at them or any kind of opposition of Obstruction thrown in their way." Just outside Richmond they met two hundred militia whom they dispersed without loss to themselves. Governor Jefferson, the burgesses, and most of the citizens fled the town, which Arnold shortly after plundered and burned. So meager were American supplies that the loss of five tons of powder at Richmond was reckoned a serious blow.

The spectacle of Virginia ravaged by the "Arch-Traitor and Parricide Arnold" at the head of fifteen hundred British troops made Virginia patriotism a byword in the United States. It was called a "Negro State," a "lifeless and inactive State," a state, said Washington, in which "the spirit of the people is certainly departed from them." Had Virginians a spark of patriotism, it was said, they would drive the British into the

---

[5] Jefferson's offense, however, was slight in comparison with that of the Virginia Legislature, which, in the height of the campaign, passed a law requiring that all horses impressed and valued at more than five thousand pounds (Virginia money) should be returned to their owners. As Jefferson admitted, this was in fact requiring all the horses to be returned. The meanest nag in the state was selling for triple that sum, and a good horse cost at least thirty thousand pounds. This law effectively prevented Lafayette and Steuben from raising a strong cavalry. The American army had so few horses that Lafayette was forced to use oxen to transport supplies, and on several occasions he was obliged to leave his artillery behind because he lacked transportation. The British, on the other hand, seized hundreds of horses in Virginia — with the result that Tarleton soon possessed a cavalry that threatened to overrun the country. General Greene acidly inquired: "Are horses dearer to the people than their liberties or lives?"

sea and swing Arnold from the highest gibbet in the state; but instead, following the example of their statesmen, they burned up the roads fleeing from this Attila. "I should be wretched, indeed," said Thomas McKean of Delaware, "if the Dregs of the British Army, they the Dregs of all Mankind, could truly boast of the like, even in the small State of Delaware." The Old Dominion had fallen so low in public esteem and was "so reproached by everybody," said a Virginia officer, "that it is almost dishonourable to be a Virginian. Scarce a day passes but I have my feelings hurt, and yet not dare say a word, because I can find no excuse for neglect." [6]

It was Britain's command of the sea that enabled Arnold, Phillips, and later Cornwallis, to despoil Virginia almost at will. British gunboats ranged up and down the rivers, throwing landing parties ashore to wreak destruction and then whisking them away before resistance could gather. As long as Americans were without naval power, it was almost impossible to devise defenses against these hit-and-run raids. Even Washington's own estate at Mount Vernon was laid under tribute by the raiders: threatened with the destruction of the plantation, Lund Washington agreed to supply provisions to the British ships. When Virginians finally succeeded in raising a superior force, the British beat a retreat to their ships and sailed away to another river — "and so on," lamented a Virginian, "keeping us in continual hot water."

Jefferson despaired of casting out the invaders unless Washington and the Continental army came to the rescue of the Old Dominion. The North, he complained, had long enjoyed the protection of virtually all the Continental army — "The Northern States are safe: their independence has been established by the joint efforts of the whole" — yet in March 1781, there was not a Continental soldier in Virginia, the only outside aid consisting of five hundred Marylanders. It was now time to share the resources of the continent, declared Jefferson; and putting his words to action he insisted that Congress bear part of the burden of defending Virginia by paying the cost of provisions for the Virginia militia. Provided that Congress repaid the arms that had been loaned it by Virginia, Jefferson promised that the Old Dominion would dispose in short order of the "British barbarians." But lend-lease, Virginians found, did not work in reverse: Congress now had little to send the beleaguered state.

At the same time, Southerners complained that the United States navy

[6] The military weakness of Virginia became a matter of concern to the French as well as to Americans. In February 1782, with less than one hundred soldiers in Washington's army and only a few hundred with Greene in South Carolina, the French minister undertook by a personal visit to the state to rouse the people from their lethargy. Madison admitted in 1782 that the Virginia Line was in a more disgraceful condition than that of any other state.

was made to serve the interests of the North while the South was left to find its own salvation.[7] In 1779, for example, Jefferson pointed out that the United States navy was never seen in Virginia waters and that "a British prize would be a more rare phenomenon here than a comet, because the one has been seen, but the other never was." If the United States navy did not soon put in an appearance and drive off the British ships that were preying upon Virginia's commerce, Jefferson declared that he would consider himself at liberty to appeal to France for separate naval aid.[8]

Strong pressure was brought to bear upon Washington by Southern congressmen to lead at least part of the Continental army to Virginia, but eager as he was to defend his "country," Washington refused to move from his position at Morristown. One of his cardinal principles of war was never to divide his army, despite the clamor raised on every side for protection. "Not a State upon the Continent," he said, "but thinks itself in danger, and scarcely an Officer at any post, but conceives a reinforcement necessary." Instead of gratifying these demands, he bluntly told his countrymen that they must endure enemy raids as long as the British held control of the sea, for if he divided his army, the British would be in a position to beat him by detachments. Moreover, he apprehended that to march his army south would entail the loss en route of at least one third of his men by sickness and desertion — a loss which would irreparably cripple the Continental army. As an alternative, Washington offered in 1780 to attack New York — a diversion which, he supposed, would relieve the South of its unwelcome visitors. In actuality, however, he had not sufficient arms, ammunition, and clothing for offensive operations in any sector of the country.

Nevertheless, Virginia's helplessness in the face of British marauding expeditions demonstrated to Washington the necessity of sending some succor to the Old Dominion. Keenly appreciative of the importance of sea power, the American commander drew up plans for combined land and sea operations in the Chesapeake. Lafayette was sent to Virginia in March 1781 to attack Arnold by land at the same time that part of the French fleet, lying inactive at Newport, sailed to the Chesapeake to cut off the escape of the British by sea. Lafayette did not reach Virginia in time to co-operate with the French fleet; but four thousand Virginia militia besieged Arnold in Portsmouth while French men-of-war patrolled

[7] In 1780, however, a considerable part of the Continental navy was lost in the fall of Charleston, South Carolina.

[8] In October 1775, Samuel Chase of Maryland declared in Congress that "it is the maddest idea in the world to think of building an American fleet. . . . We should mortgage the whole Continent. . . . We should provide, for gaining intelligence, two swift sailing vessels." Of the Southern attitude toward a navy, John Adams observed that the Southern delegates in Congress "agree that a Fleet, would protect and secure the Trade of New England but deny that it would that of the Southern Colonies."

the entrance to the Chesapeake. The British were caught in the same kind of trap that the French and Americans snapped shut at Yorktown; but Arnold was more fortunate than Cornwallis. The British admiral, Arbuthnot, came to his rescue and drove the French fleet back to Newport; and with control of the Chesapeake regained, the British strongly reinforced their army in Virginia. General Phillips was placed in command of the army in that state, and Arnold went back to New York to lead an attack upon his native town of New London, which he burned "by accident."

Thus was chalked up another failure for the allies; their combined operations, however well planned, always seemed to end in disappointment and frustration. Washington blamed the French for this latest miscarriage — they had refused to follow his wishes by sending their entire squadron to the Chesapeake; they had not carried troops with them to assist in the land operations; and after the battle they returned to Rhode Island, where, an American acidly remarked, they remained "spectators of very affecting tragedies in these states." The failure was particularly difficult to bear because, as Washington said, the country was "disappointed at not seeing Arnold in Gibbets." Nevertheless, Washington swallowed his chagrin, esteeming it "true policy to make the most of their [the French] assistance without censuring their Mistakes."

With Cornwallis's arrival in Virginia, there were almost as many British troops in the Old Dominion as in New York, the headquarters of the British army. That the Chesapeake had become, for the moment at least, the central theater of the war could not be denied; but Washington refused to be distracted from what he conceived to be his main purpose: keeping an eye upon Clinton in New York and preparing for the day when the allied fleets and armies would drive the British from that city. However, to reinforce Lafayette, he sent Anthony Wayne to Virginia with what remained of the Pennsylvania Line. The troops took advantage of the emergency to demand a cash payment with interest on the back pay owing them, and before they marched they had won the "strike."

Against Cornwallis's well-equipped army of seven thousand men, Lafayette and Wayne could bring to bear only five thousand hungry, ragged, and ill-armed troops, the great majority of whom were militia. Virginia could not supply them with shirts, shoes, clothing, and other necessities; the state quartermaster and commissary departments were almost useless — supplies, after being gathered by dint of great exertion, disappeared no one knew where. "Think of this poor body of men camping in the woods," exclaimed General Steuben, "perishing without seeing the enemy, without even being drilled, as they are destitute of shirts and shoes!" [9] Suffering from a shortage of clothing and shoes, a body of

---

[9] In 1780, Steuben was sent to Virginia with instructions "to collect, organize, discipline and expedite the recruits for the Southern army" — one of the most difficult assignments of the war.

militia were brought to the verge of mutiny, until Jefferson stepped into the controversy and ordered them home. General Wayne complained that many of his troops were "bare legged rather too high up for a modest eye to view." To crown these misfortunes, the credit of the Continental army had sunk almost as low as that of the states. "If my life . . . had depended on it," said General Steuben, "I would not have been able to raise ten dollars on credit. The certificate for $6000 which I held from the United States, I offered in vain for one tenth of its nominal value."

Against an enemy so destitute, it might be supposed that Cornwallis would have made short shrift of Lafayette. Yet when Cornwallis went into summer quarters at Yorktown, Lafayette and Wayne were still dogging his heels, still very much in the fight. Although a back-pedaling kind of warfare ran much against Lafayette's grain, he saved himself only by adopting the Fabian strategy of his master. "We manoeuvred rather than fought," he reported. Recognizing that the consequences of defeat might be the loss of Virginia and the war itself, he contented himself with a cautious sparring against his powerful adversary. Indeed, he had no hope of victory in hazarding battle; as Steuben said, American generals had not yet learned how to beat regular troops with one third their number of militia. At the height of the campaign, Lafayette's army was weakened by the necessity of giving furloughs to the troops in order that they might go home and harvest their crops. If balked in their desires of going home, they deserted in shoals. General Steuben, wearied by the clamor and undependability of the militia, declared that he would always regret that he had consented to undertake the defense of a country "where Caesar and Hannibal would have lost their reputation, and where every farmer is a general, but where nobody wishes to be a soldier."

Without the aid of the French fleet, Lafayette perceived that he could hope only to avoid a crushing defeat at the hands of Cornwallis. "I am lost in the sands of Virginia," he lamented, "employed in living by my wits only. . . . There is no fighting here unless you have a naval superiority, or an army mounted upon race-horses." But Lafayette had neither ships nor race horses.

So Cornwallis found himself in the familiar situation of British generals in North America: waging war against an enemy who declined to do more than skirmish. His pursuit of Lafayette failing to bring about the general action he sought, he was obliged to content himself in plundering the country, destroying stores of tobacco and military supplies. With almost a thousand cavalry at his disposal (Lafayette had virtually none), Cornwallis was able to spread devastation far and wide over the state. In June 1781, Tarleton's raiders swooped down on Charlottesville, routed the Virginia Assembly, captured seven burgesses and one congressman, and, for the second time, almost caught Governor Jefferson. Scores of barrels of powder were destroyed at Charlottesville, and the state was thrown into a panic by the exploits of the hard-riding British cavalry.

In this critical hour of the war, Jefferson retired from the governorship of Virginia with almost as much relief as he was later to quit the Presidency of the United States. The pursuit of happiness, Jefferson was prepared to acknowledge, did not lie in attaining political office in the republic. In 1781, he handed over the reins to "abler hands" and sought in private life "that happiness from which no slave is so remote as the minister of a commonwealth." Although the enemy was at the gates, Jefferson buried himself in his books and in the affairs of his estate, having learned that as a war governor he made a good philosopher and student. He believed that his retirement from the world of public affairs would be permanent, for, as he admitted, he had lost almost all public esteem. But he was not happy among his books: he yearned to redeem his reputation by again holding public office. A motion to impeach him, although promptly quashed by the burgesses, rankled deeply. Once he had silenced his critics, however, he was ready to quit politics forever — but what politician ever attains that Elysium?

The raid upon Charlottesville also marked the end of Cornwallis's exploits in Virginia. He abandoned Richmond and retired to Williamsburg, leaving Lafayette and Wayne hanging grimly upon his heels. At Green Springs, a sharp engagement was fought between the two armies, and although the Americans were driven from the field, their army was not shattered.

In Virginia, Cornwallis won the same successes — and met with the same failures — that had marked his career in the Carolinas. The decisive battle of the campaign still remained to be fought.

CHAPTER XXVI

The Diplomatic Front

To Washington, the campaign of 1781 seemed destined to end in disappointment and frustration as had his every undertaking since 1778. Congress had asked the states to put thirty-seven thousand men in the field; yet, by June 1781, Washington's effective force was under five thousand men, and some of the states even declined to reply to his requests for reinforcements. He feared that the year would be frittered away in a futile search for manpower; by midsummer, he lamented, things dragged on "like a Cart without wheels." The states were so backward in filling their quotas of troops that he declared he could do nothing unless the French sent, besides naval aid, a large army to the United States. Three weeks before the march to Yorktown, he warned that "we must end our Operations in Languor and disgrace, and perhaps protract the War to the Hazard of our final Ruin."

In contrast to the low state of the American army, business was booming throughout the country. In May 1781, the Philadelphia water front was a beehive of activity and the stores and shops of the city were filled with goods; business, reported a citizen, was "going on as brisk as ever, houses, stores are building, our markets affording the greatest plenty of every article one can desire and as for luxury and extravagance in dresses, equipages and entertainments, it is carried to the highest pitch." In the cities, pleasure-seeking went on as though the republic were in a state of peace and security; and in the country, harvests had seldom been better. Not without bitterness, Washington said that "the bountiful hand of Heaven is holding out to us a Plenty of every Article."

Despite this bounty, the country still hovered on the edge of disaster. Its currency worthless, its army suffering from shortages of every essential, and public spirit blighted by inflation, this lame and halting republic hardly seemed the conqueror of Great Britain.

Nor was the diplomatic front much brighter: although the United States had assiduously courted the powers of Europe, only France had seen fit to ally itself with the republic. American diplomats were sent by Congress to Austria, Spain, Prussia, Holland, Russia, and Tuscany but invariably they returned empty-handed — if, indeed, they were permitted to enter the country. Europeans still preserved a healthy respect for the British lion and were by no means inclined to take Americans' word that he was decrepit. As a result, exclaimed an American diplomat, America was left "like Hercules in his cradle, to strangle the serpent that annoys all Europe." This was hardly true, but with only one alliance to their credit, American diplomats were eager to win fresh laurels.

In sending its agents abroad, Congress did not pause to inquire how they would be received. Instead, it rushed into the arena of European politics with valor but without arms. A report that a European country was favorably disposed towards the United States was almost certain to produce a visit from an American diplomat bearing treaties ready for signature. Even such a pip-squeak sovereign as the Grand Duke of Tuscany was thus honored; and he repaid the courtesy by refusing to permit American emissaries to enter his country.

The experiences of two American diplomats abroad — John Jay and John Adams — profoundly affected the course of American diplomacy, not only during the War of Independence but for many years beyond. From a survey of their careers, it might be supposed that the shortest way to make an American an isolationist was to send him to Europe.

John Jay was sent to Spain in 1779 to follow up the promising lead opened by Spain earlier in that year. It had been understood by the Continental Congress that if Spain's offer of mediation was refused by Great Britain, Spain would enter the war, presumably as an ally of the United States. Spain had entered the war but the alliance with the United States still hung fire. To persuade His Catholic Majesty to take the leap was John Jay's assignment.

Jay went to Spain with high expectations of carrying off a fat loan, a commercial treaty, and a military alliance. The mines of Mexico and Peru, treasure fleets, the Spanish treasury piled high with bullion — these visions floated pleasantly before Jay when he embarked upon his mission. If Gérard, the French minister in Philadelphia, was to be believed, all this might be vouchsafed the United States if the republic but adopted a conciliatory attitude toward His Catholic Majesty.

In 1779, Jay was accounted among the staunchest friends of France in Congress. He spoke feelingly of the French blood that ran in his veins (he was a descendant of French Huguenots); his speeches in Congress earned for him the regard of the French minister; and he bore the repu-

tation among the patriot leaders of being one of the most irreconcilable
enemies of Great Britain.

Jay especially endeared himself to the French and Spaniards by his
views upon the American claim to navigation of the Mississippi. Arguing
that it was a privilege "which we would not want this age," Jay in 1779
was prepared to barter this claim for a Spanish recognition of American
independence.

It was a peculiarity of Spanish policy towards the United States that,
having brought Americans to agree to its demands, it invariably insisted
upon new concessions. The more Spain contemplated the American republic, the less desirable as a neighbor it appeared to be and the more
necessary became the erection of barriers against its intrusions. In 1779,
the government of Charles III had been willing to permit the boundaries
of the United States to extend to the Mississippi River, denying only
Americans' rights to navigate the river where it flowed through Spanish
territory; but it soon recognized that the river was not a defensible
boundary against the onrushing tide of American frontiersmen. When
this tide reached the Mississippi, Spaniards feared, it would leap the river
and turn toward Mexico City and points south. Spanish Louisiana, the
Floridas, and Mexico would be overwhelmed; and Spain, stripped of its
empire, would be turned naked into the world by the covetous Yankees.
Rather than suffer such a catastrophe, Spain determined to keep the
Americans several hundred miles east of the Mississippi River and to
erect a *cordon sanitaire* against American republicanism by making a
large part of the Middle West a perpetual hunting ground of "free and
independent Indians." Thus the hemisphere would be made safe for
Spanish monarchism, and the Mississippi would flow to the sea unvexed
by the Americans. The interior of the continent would become a vast
Indian reservation where, for centuries to come, the Indian brave might
stalk the deer — and any intruding Americans — and salute His Catholic
Majesty as the Great White Father to whom he was indebted for these
blessings.

As for persuading Spain to recognize the independence of the United
States, John Jay was pleading a cause in which judgment had already
been rendered against him. In 1779, Charles III of Spain declared that he
would not accord recognition to the republic until the British themselves
had done so. Nevertheless, it did not suit the purposes of the Spanish
government to tell Jay candidly that his efforts were hopeless and that
he might as well go home. Jay was kept dangling in Madrid in the hope
that the United States, wearied by fruitless negotiations, would give way
to Spain on the points in dispute between the two countries.

From Jay, Florida Blanca demanded a promise of payment for all aid
furnished by his government to the United States during the war, and he
bluntly asked the American diplomat how the republic proposed to liqui-

date the obligations it had incurred, dwelling at length, and with manifest relish, upon the financial embarrassments of the Continental Congress. He complained that for all assistance given the Americans, Spain had received from Congress "nothing but good words and fair assurances." Asking an American diplomat for a financial statement of the United States government was likely to bring on a choking fit; yet Jay was obliged to cover the entire painful ground for the benefit of the implacable Spanish minister. Nevertheless, Florida Blanca continued to regard the United States as a charity case, and he strongly intimated that the United States was not only a pauper but a swindler. By repudiating its paper money, Congress gained no honor in European chancelleries; and Florida Blanca made clear that Spain was in no financial condition to underwrite the American rebellion.

These pleas of poverty were not altogether fabrications designed to put off the importunate Americans. In actuality, the Spanish treasury was bare and the credit of the government severely strained: Jay learned that it was occasionally obliged to pay as high as 30 to 40 per cent interest on its borrowings. Graft-ridden and inefficient, Spain belied, as Jay found, "the extensive ideas entertained of Spanish opulence in America."

Jay's salary was always in arrears, and he was forced to look to Franklin (that is, the French court) for support. Yet, dunned as he was by the butchers and bakers of Madrid and completely dependent upon the charity of France, the unhappy diplomat was presented with bills for hundreds of thousands of dollars, drawn by Congress in the expectation that he would be successful in floating a loan from the Spanish government. These bills did not make Jay more welcome at Madrid. The government refused to honor most of these drafts, leaving Jay no recourse but to send them along to Franklin, who in turn passed them on to the French government. For all the help the Spanish government seemed disposed to grant, the United States might slip into bankruptcy and ruin.

To swell the measure of Jay's vexations, he was obliged to match wits with Richard Cumberland, a British agent who in 1779 began to intrigue in Madrid for a separate peace with Great Britain. While Jay beat vainly upon the door of the Spanish court, Cumberland was inside, enjoying the confidence of Florida Blanca and quietly counterworking every move made by the American diplomat. To the British agent, Florida Blanca let it be known that Spain would never recognize the independence of the United States as long as hope remained that Great Britain would surrender Gibraltar as the price of a separate peace. In short, the United States was becoming a counter in the game of international politics, and Spain was seeking to buy Gibraltar with American independence as the down payment.

In the war, as in diplomacy, Spain displayed a wholehearted devotion to its own interests and a minimum of concern for the welfare of the

United States. Spain was bound by no ties with the United States and gave it to understand that it ought not to presume too much from the fact that both countries happened to be at war with Great Britain. Spain insisted upon fighting the war in its own way, sometimes paying as little heed to the wishes of France as to those of the United States. In particular, Spain expended its energies in attempting to conquer Gibraltar, beating its head against the Rock for over three years.

Probably no American diplomat would have met with much favor from the Spanish government; but John Jay settled his fate by bringing to the Spanish court the proud, mettlesome, and uncompromising demeanor of an American republican. There was not a drop of humility in John Jay and, as he said of himself, he was never less disposed to humility than when confronted by adversity. He was profoundly convinced of the "glorious and laudable" work in which the United States was engaged — the defeat and humiliation of Great Britain, he said, merited "the approbation of all who wish well to the tranquility of Europe and the rights of mankind." Jay was therefore hardly the man to approach the Madrid government with the deference and subservience it believed to be its due. He spoke, instead, with a firmness and dignity that grated upon Florida Blanca — "Spain, recognize our independence; Spain, give us more money," was the way the flabbergasted Spanish minister summed up Jay's conversation.

Meanwhile, Americans' enthusiasm for a Spanish alliance waxed ever stronger as the British pushed their successes in the Southern states. It was in the power of Spain, Congress was persuaded, to draw the enemy from the back of the United States by making a diversionary attack upon the Floridas.[1] If this were true, how could the United States stand firm upon its claim to the navigation of the Mississippi — so far as Americans knew, the only obstacle to a Spanish alliance?

It was well known in Congress that, as a preliminary to any negotiations for an alliance, the Spanish court insisted upon the renunciation by the United States of all claims to the navigation of the Mississippi — "an object," said Florida Blanca, "that the King had so much at heart that he would never relinquish it." Congress had long insisted upon this right, yet in February 1781, it instructed Jay to yield the navigation of the Mississippi in exchange for an alliance with Spain.

Although eager to consummate an alliance between Spain and the United States, and at one time in favor of the renunciation he was now authorized to make, Jay declined to offer the price Congress was ready to pay. The American minister was in no humor to cast pearls at the feet of His Catholic Majesty; the close connection between the two countries which had once seemed to him so desirable had now begun to lose its charms; and a Spanish loan, if the Spanish monarch could be shaken loose

[1] East and West Florida had been British territory since 1763.

from his doubloons, promised to be a niggardly reward for the effort Jay had made in extracting it. Spain, he reasoned, being already in the war, had lost in consequence much of the attraction it had possessed as a neutral; there was no occasion to waste bait upon a fish that had already been landed. Therefore, he held back from Florida Blanca the instructions of Congress regarding the Mississippi, declaring instead that "the Americans, almost to a man, believed that God Almighty had made that river a highway for the people of the upper country to go to the sea by."

Jay's attempt to conceal his instructions did not deceive Florida Blanca: the Spanish minister was well aware of Congress's decision to abandon the navigation of the Mississippi — in fact, he knew Jay's instructions before Jay himself did. The American minister lived in a glass house; spied upon, his mail opened and read before it reached him, he could preserve few secrets from prying foreign governments. A letter bearing the seal of the United States enjoyed no sanctity — indeed, in the Spanish post office, it was regarded as an invitation to open and to transcribe the contents for the perusal of the Spanish foreign office. So regularly was his mail opened that Jay, in writing letters in Spanish, requested the inspectors at the post office to correct his faulty Spanish. In any event, Jay's correspondence from Congress was an open book to Florida Blanca, and the Spanish minister, thoroughly enjoying the situation, sometimes chose in his interviews with Jay to give the American diplomat advance information regarding the intentions of the American government. Jay, however, failed to see the humor — if any there was — in this state of affairs.

In experiencing the disadvantages of irregular correspondence with his home government, Jay was not unique among American diplomats of the revolutionary period. It frequently happened that American ministers abroad were without official news from Congress for periods as long as six months; as to the progress of the war and proceedings of the Continental Congress, a virtual blackout prevailed. Because his instructions were many months out of date, a diplomatic representative of the United States rarely knew whether he was carrying out the wishes of his government in dealing with foreign powers. Another unhappy effect of this lack of up-to-date news was that Americans abroad had little positive information with which to counteract British propaganda disguised as news. "Such accounts of our affairs as arrive in Europe at all," they protested, "come through the hands of our enemies and, whether defeated or victorious we are the last who are acquainted with events which ought first to be announced by us." Unable to check British reports in France that the American army had been routed and Congress was on the point of making peace, Silas Deane besought Congress: "For Heaven's sake, if you mean to have any connection with this kingdom, be more assiduous in getting your letters here." In 1781, Franklin pointed out that in his long diplomatic career he had received but few letters from Congress. "I know nothing of what passes in America," he said, "but what I learn from their newspapers or the English or from the [French] minister here, who are more early informed than I am even of what relates to myself." It was, for example, from Vergennes that Franklin first learned that Congress had refused his request to be relieved. In view of the fact that for a considerable period of time the Committee of Foreign Affairs in Congress consisted only of one member, James Lovell of Massachusetts, upon whose shoulders rested the responsibility of communicating with American diplomats abroad, the silence of Congress is not surprising.

American diplomats complained that they seldom heard from Congress, and Congress complained that it almost never heard from the diplomats. Each upbraided the other for neglect of correspondence, and each suspected that the other was putting pleasure before business. John Jay, kept hanging in suspense in Madrid for word from Congress, was prepared to believe that congressmen were taking life easy and letting correspondence lapse. "What with clever wives, or pleasant walks, or too tired, or too busy, or *do you* do it," he wrote, "very little is done, much postponed, and more neglected." On the other hand, it was not difficult for congressmen to leap to the conclusion that the gay life of foreign capitals had something to do with the failure of American representatives abroad to tend to their correspondence. Their silence, in fact, seemed eloquent, but when Congress did not receive a letter for six months from Franklin, the members might reasonably have supposed that the old philosopher was carrying the gay life a bit too far.

Probably over half the letters sent across the Atlantic by Americans during the War of Independence failed to reach their destination. Thanks to the vigilance of British cruisers, the Atlantic became for Americans a vast dead-letter office. Washington found that of nine letters he had written Lafayette in 1779 and 1780, not one had been received. John Adams, during 1778, wrote Mrs. Adams more than fifty letters, of which she had the satisfaction of reading only a few. For every three letters he sent to America, John Adams received one — a ratio which convinced him that only a small part of his mail was being delivered. So many of Franklin's letters disappeared en route that he was almost discouraged from writing; and he urged his correspondents to write often, because, he said, "the Chance is greater that one Letter out of many should arrive than one out of a few." The ship carrying the text of the Declaration of Independence to France left Philadelphia in July 1776 and was never heard of again.

To remedy this situation, the American ministers abroad proposed early in 1777 that a system of packet boats, with regular monthly sailings between the United States and France, be established. At the end of the war, the packets still remained a dream: in December 1782, Franklin declared that letters sometimes lay for months in the post office waiting for ships

to the United States. To get a reply from Congress during the peace negotiations in 1782 required at least six months.

❧   ❧   ❧

The knowledge that the United States had yielded its claims to the
Mississippi did not incline Florida Blanca to an alliance: when Congress
met his terms, he promptly raised them. The purpose of the Spanish government, as Jay discerned, was to spin out the negotiations by means of
evasions and palliations — "Delay is their system." Jay had come to Spain
"to make propositions — not supplications," but apparently even abject
surrender upon every point in dispute would not satisfy His Catholic
Majesty.

Under the treatment he received in Spain, John Jay's back stiffened
remarkably. From an American patriot of international sympathies, he
became an extreme nationalist of a deeply isolationist hue. On the strength
of his experiences in Spain, Jay concluded that the United States ought to
mix as little as possible in European affairs and to trust only in God and
its own armed might. "It will always be necessary for the United States
to be formidable at home, if they expect to be respectable anywhere,"
he declared. "We shall always be deceived if we believe that any nation
in the world has, or will have, a disinterested regard for us, especially
absolute monarchies. . . . In my opinion, we should endeavour to be as
independent of the charity of our friends, as of the mercy of our
enemies." Between monarchism and republicanism he saw no common
ground upon which a meeting was possible; even an alliance such as that
between France and the United States seemed likely to prove no better
than an uneasy marriage of convenience.

Jay was soon suffering from an incurable case of homesickness which
blinded him to the merits, but not to the shortcomings, of Europe. Aranjuez, he admitted was "a charming place," but, he added, "it is not America.
. . . I find little here," he went on, "that resembles, and nothing that can
compensate for, the free air, the equal liberty, and the other numerous
blessings which God and nature, and laws of our own making, have given
and secured to our happier country." He confessed that he had never
loved America half so well as since he had left it. "My eyes and affections
are constantly turned towards America," he declared — an orientation
which, while not reprehensible in an American minister abroad, was
hardly calculated to make him sprightly company for European statesmen. Travel sometimes narrows the mind; and John Jay, had he wished
to find happiness, ought to have remained at home, admiring Frenchmen
and hating Englishmen, instead of going abroad and putting his affections
and prejudices to the strain of experience. At home, shielded from the
deplorable realities of European power politics, he could perhaps have

loved all mankind; but after a year in Europe he indignantly spurned the suggestion that he was a citizen of the world. He was, he stoutly declared, a good American.

Jay's experiences in Spain even helped to poison his mind against the French, who, he believed, were seeking to thwart his efforts to procure a loan and alliance in Madrid and backing Spain's claims to the exclusive right of navigating the Mississippi. These suspicions and resentments Jay carried into the peace negotiations between Great Britain and the United States — with far-reaching effect upon the peace terms and the international relations of the republic.[2]

By the time Jay left Spain, the patience of Congress with Charles III — "his most Supine Majesty" — had been exhausted. The offer to surrender the navigation of the Mississippi was rescinded in 1782, and Congress again resolved to stand upon its rights to that waterway. The fickleness of Spain had created a spirit in the United States which boded no good to future relations between the two neighbors upon the North American continent — indeed, Spain seemed to have succeeded in raising up in the republic the very spirit it most dreaded. The Secretary of Foreign Affairs complained that the money received from Spain had scarcely paid Jay's expenses. "Spain," said Franklin, "has taken four years to consider whether she should treat with us or not. Give her forty, and let us in the meantime mind our own business."

⌢   ⌢   ⌢

John Jay began with leanings toward internationalism, but John Adams was from beginning to end a staunch nationalist. He went abroad as a knight-errant to do battle for the cause of republicanism; and although he received many hard knocks in the process, his Americanism grew stronger with adversity.

In 1779, many congressmen hotly resented the interference of the French minister in the domestic concerns of the United States, and their displeasure was evident in their choice of a plenipotentiary for conducting peace negotiations with Great Britain. Although Spain's efforts at mediation had come to naught, a new mediator had appeared in Austria, and Congress again turned its attention toward making peace upon advantageous terms. France wanted Franklin appointed peace commissioner, but some congressmen objected to Poor Richard as too subservient to France, favoring instead the candidacy of Arthur Lee. Because neither Franklin

---

[2] In this connection, it ought to be observed that Jay's best friend in the diplomatic circles of Madrid was Montmorin, the French ambassador. It was Montmorin who interceded with the Spanish government in Jay's favor, helped to tide him over his financial crises, and, on his personal credit, procured the money that enabled Jay to pay off some of the bills drawn upon him by Congress. Montmorin was a friend in need — and John Jay was seldom without need.

nor Lee was acceptable to a majority of Congress, a compromise was reached by appointing John Adams, a paladin of American rights who was not *persona non grata* at Versailles. But Congress did not oblige France by fettering Adams with instructions which would place him under the control of the French government: although enjoined to follow the advice of the Bourbon court, Adams was left in large measure to his own discretion.

John Adams was an upright, proud, and contentious republican. His patriotism was beyond doubt; but like many people who hold convictions strongly, he was apt to assume that those who differed with him were not merely wrong but somehow leagued with the powers of darkness. Armed in his own virtue, he was intolerant of others' ideas and methods; and he censured his opponents with a vigor reminiscent of a New England Puritan denouncing the flesh and the devil. Lacking both intellectual humility and a sense of humor, yet withal industrious, able, and honest, he won the respect but hardly the affection of his contemporaries. He was so devoted to his country's interests that he could ill bear to see anyone else do more in its behalf than he himself. This jealousy caused him great unhappiness and repeatedly put him in a false position.

Knocking about the courts of Europe did not smooth the rough edges of John Adams's character: eschewing the ways of courtiers, he remained the same simple, forthright, testy, and stubborn republican that Braintree and Boston had known. His boundless pride of country took the form, his critics complained, of the "fierce and haughty manners of the Lacedemonians and first Romans"; certainly, he was ever ready to mount his high horse and sally forth to slay the enemies of republicanism. Keenly aware of the grandeur that lay in store for the United States, he was impatient with all who refused to accept the republic at his value. In Europe, he was the irrepressible American, proclaiming the power and the glory of the United States. He stood before the ministers of some of the proudest monarchs of Europe and addressed them with the condescension that a representative of a new and vigorous country might employ toward the statesmen of a worn-out world. Uncompromising and bellicose, he served notice upon the nations of Europe that a new nation had arisen in the Western Hemisphere that would soon eclipse them all.

Adams's rugged Americanism did not admit of any doubt that, if necessary, the United States could withstand successfully all Europe. This country, he declared, was "the very centre and axis of the whole; . . . in a Land War America could defend herself against all the world." That Europe was hostile to the rising republic of the West he did not doubt: the United States, merely by its existence, menaced the rule of kings and nobles. He was convinced that this country would one day rise upon Europe's ruin. "Europe," he said, "is generally sensible that the United States in half a Century will, if they keep together, give the Tone to the World"; therefore, it could be presumed that the Old World would labor unceasingly to destroy this usurper of its greatness. "We must," said Adams, "defend ourselves against the wiles of Europe." The winning of freedom was not the end but the beginning of the struggle of the United States for survival; and there was no security anywhere save in self-reliance. Europe was the enemy's country; wherever Adams looked, he saw "enmity to the principle of our governments, to the purity of our morals, the simplicity of our manners, the honest integrity and sincerity of our hearts." There were "two worlds" — and one or the other must triumph.

Adams was no foe of the French alliance and he did not contemplate breaking faith with our ally — that faith, he declared, "is our American Glory, and it is our bulwark." Nevertheless he staunchly resisted every effort on the part of France to interfere in the internal affairs of his country and to influence its foreign policy — which caused Vergennes to suppose that Adams was ready to cast himself into the arms of Great Britain. In this, the French minister did the New Englander an injustice. Adams had lost faith in Englishmen — apparently the breed had begun to decline shortly after the Puritan emigration to New England. The proud, imperialistic Britons of George III's reign were not the bluff, hearty, good-humored John Bulls of happier days; when he was told by a Boston Tory that "God loves that little island of Old England and the people that live upon it," Adams's rejoinder was: "Who can be persuaded to believe that he loves so degenerate and profligate a race?" He believed that Englishmen, if given the opportunity, would persecute Americans as they had once harried the Puritans; the only security for Americans was to stifle whatever affection they still felt for that benighted people.

To those who had been offended by John Adams's militant personality — and they were legion — he was a "churlish republican" and a born curmudgeon. Even those who loved him for his honesty and forthrightness sometimes deplored the militant rectitude and harshness of manner that robbed him of much of the influence he might otherwise have enjoyed.

From his observation of Benjamin Franklin at work in Paris, Adams concluded that the venerable philosopher was bungling matters badly and that a wholly new approach to the French court was called for. To his mind, there was altogether too much humility in the tone adopted by the American representative: France was more indebted to the United States than this country was to France, and Americans ought to show a proper sense of their importance when addressing His Most Christian Majesty. As he told Franklin, "a little apparent Stoutness, and greater air of Independence and Boldness in our Demands, will procure us more ample Assistance" than would Franklin's policy of waiting upon French ministers and picking up any favors they might be disposed to drop. Unless American ministers abroad acted "a manly, honest, independent, as well as sensible part," Adams feared that they would become "the Sport of every intriguing Minister at every foreign Court." As a new nation, the United States must make its own way, judge for itself, insist upon equality with the most ancient monarchies in Europe, and cast off the subservience of colonists — and John Adams took it upon himself to show the world what this new man, the American, was like.

Since the United States had taken a dive into the murky waters of European politics, Adams wished to strike out boldly for deep water. He wished to secure alliances, loans, subsidies, and all other favors which European powers might grant the struggling republic; and to accomplish these objectives, he urged the United States to send ministers to every important country in Europe. Franklin, on the other hand, was disposed to be more sparing of the favors of the republic: it was folly, he insisted, for the United States to lay itself open to humiliation and insult by sending diplomats to countries that would not receive them. "A Virgin State," Franklin said, "should preserve the Virgin Character, and not go about suitoring for Alliances."

Impatient with all coyness and self-depreciation, Adams had no reluctance in asking for loans and other favors from foreign governments. For three years, he pointed out, the United States had withstood alone the full might of Great Britain — "the Scourge of God and the Plague of Mankind" — thwarting the efforts of that nation to rule the world. Europe thus owed the United States much more than it could ever repay. "England would have all the Mountains of Mexico and Peru in a few years if America should join her," he said in 1781. "Yet we are slighted. God forgive them, and enable America to forget their ungenerosity."

Adams's forthright, table-banging diplomacy was utterly foreign to Franklin's cool and circumspect methods. To Franklin, diplomacy was akin to dueling with a rapier; swinging a big stick was utterly foreign to his nature. France, he believed, ought to be handled with "Decency and Delicacy"; if the King found pleasure in regarding the aid he gave an oppressed people as part of the glory of his reign, Americans ought to enhance his pleasure by "thankful acknowledgments." A little flattery wonderfully greased the ways of diplomacy. As for being outwitted by astute European statesmen, Franklin deemed himself capable of taking care of himself and of his country's interests in any company. But he suspected that Adams, for all his bluster, would end by losing the game.

From the moment he reached France, Adams began to put his principles into practice. To demonstrate his dignity as the representative of a sovereign state, he remained in Paris for several weeks without paying a call upon Vergennes — until finally the French minister sent round to inquire what was keeping the American diplomat from Versailles. Vergennes charitably supposed that Adams was modestly waiting to be fitted by Parisian tailors, and he graciously signified that he would be happy to receive Adams in his American coat. Having made the French government come to him first, Adams consented to make a journey to Versailles.

A brief acquaintance with Adams made Vergennes regret that he had been so pressing in his invitation. The American lectured Vergennes upon naval and military strategy with an assurance that grated upon that states-man's already taut nerves. The substance of Adams's remarks was that France ought to send a large fleet to United States waters — "attacking the bull by the horns" rather than pricking its flanks with darts. The Bourbons were wrong in concentrating their forces against the British West Indies; no telling blow could be struck in that quarter because the British, Adams told Vergennes, were "in such a sulky, mulish, suicidal temper, that they would not make peace, if you took every island they have." Nothing was to be gained by besieging Gibraltar or trying to invade Great Britain — the war would be won or lost in North America and the decisive factor would be naval power. The idea was not new to Vergennes, but John Adams had a knack of making even truisms seem unpalatable to the French minister. Vergennes remained noncommittal and the New Englander was driven to the conclusion that his energies had been expended to little purpose. "There is something in the European understanding," he observed, "different from those we have been used to. Men of the greatest abilities, and the most experienced, are with great difficulty brought to see what appears to us as clear as day."

Given such irreconcilable points of view, there was no lack of topics for disagreement. Among other things, Adams and Vergennes tangled over the question of the repudiation of its paper money by Congress. The French minister insisted that Congress's action worked unmerited hardship upon French merchants, and announced his intention of pro-testing to the American government. Adams objected that such action would give aid and comfort to the Tories and speculators and do great disservice to the war effort. What right, demanded Adams, had for-eigners to expect better treatment than citizens from the United States? And he did not hesitate to assert that French merchants had already made such huge profits by selling to Americans that they could easily afford to absorb any losses they might sustain as a result of Congress's action.

Although much of his time had been occupied in brushes with Ver-gennes, John Adams did not intend to allow his peacemaking powers to lie idle: instructed by Congress to open negotiations with the British when an opportunity presented, Adams judged that in a business of this kind there was no time like the present. Without taking Franklin into his confidence, he proposed, therefore, to inform the British of his authority to make peace and to conclude a commercial treaty, and to signify his willingness to go to London at the earliest moment.

Vergennes was staggered by Adams's decision: to open peace negotiations with the British would, he pointed out, "announce to that power that her system of tyranny, her cruelties, and her perfidy are forgotten. . . . It is inviting her to believe that the Americans have an irresistible predilection for her." Scarcely less disquieting was Adams's eagerness to make a treaty of commerce with Great Britain: Vergennes guessed that the treaty would deprive France of all the commercial benefits she had expected to derive from American independence.

Vergennes therefore asked Adams to keep secret his commission to make a commercial treaty with Great Britain. A stormy scene ensued between the two men. Stung by Adams's imperious tone, Vergennes gave him a dressing-down which the New Englander did not long forget. The French minister did not mince words — two, he made clear, could play at the game of plain speaking. He told Adams not to meddle in the matters pertaining to the relations of the United States and France; His Most Christian Majesty, he snapped, had no need of Adams's advice to run his kingdom. Adams was never one easily to suffer a lecture; in his way, he was quite as proud and sensitive to slights as was Vergennes himself. Nevertheless, he was compelled to accept at the hands of the French minister a humiliation endured by few American diplomats.

Having thus smartly rapped Adams's knuckles, Vergennes began to pull wires in Philadelphia to induce Congress to recall its objectionable minister. "He will do nothing but provoke embarrassments and mischiefs," said the French foreign secretary, "because he has an inflexibility, a pedantry, an arrogance and a flatulent conceit which render him incapable of negotiating political matters." As the crowning injury, Vergennes persuaded Franklin to write to Congress supporting the French court in its dispute with Adams.

Franklin attempted to keep this "most unkind and stabbing" letter secret from Adams, but it was not easy to pull the wool over the eyes of his vigilant colleague. Adams soon learned of Franklin's part in the affair, but, although bursting with resentment, he gave no hint of his inner state when he encountered Poor Richard. Whereupon, Adams recounted, "the hypocritical old scoundrel received me here with smiles and complaisance and catched me in his arms, not knowing I was informed of his conduct." Franklin's embraces, needless to say, did not make Adams forget the ill turn he had received.

When he first came to France, John Adams was scandalized by Franklin's moral laxity and was envious of the celebrity enjoyed by the older statesman. Now, in Adams's somewhat jaundiced eyes, Franklin became a dishonest dotard who had sold himself, body and soul, to the French Ministry. Hand in glove with Vergennes, Franklin was mismanaging

American affairs abroad: he took his orders from Versailles rather than from Philadelphia and, by dint of long currying the favor of the French court, had become himself more than half a Frenchman. John Adams pronounced Franklin more false and deceitful than Vergennes himself; after five years of experience with Poor Richard, Adams swore that he had no faith whatever in his word — "I never know when he speaks the truth, and when not," said the New Englander. Franklin was a "Demon of Discord among our Ministers, and the Curse and Scourge of our foreign affairs" in Adams's opinion. "I wish with all my soul," he exclaimed, "he was out of public service, and in retirement, repenting his past life, and preparing, as he ought to be, for another world." Yet Franklin hung on, seemingly determined to live forever to spite any other Americans who sought to win fame by serving their country. And the longer he lived, the greater grew his reputation — which, said Adams, was already "one of the grossest impostures, that has ever been practised upon mankind since the days of Mahomet." It afforded some consolation to reflect that Franklin's popularity in France was owing to his immorality. "No man," remarked Adams, "will ever be pleasing at a court in general who is not depraved in his morals" and who did not stand ready to sacrifice his country.

Sore from this rough handling by Vergennes, John Adams went to Holland, vowing that he had been humiliated in a manner which proved that France was determined to break every American minister that it could not bend to its will. To Adams's mind, his unpopularity at Versailles was a tribute to his stainless Americanism and his refusal to tread the primrose path with Benjamin Franklin.

The year 1781 saw the neutrals — particularly Russia and Austria — working, for the third year in a row, to bring about peace by mediation. Again hope ran high on both sides of the Atlantic that the struggle would be ended at a peace conference rather than fought out to the finish. France, its treasury almost exhausted, was eager for peace. But if peace was to be made by diplomats meeting around a table in Vienna, it was clear that the French had some unfinished business in the United States to attend to. John Adams was still the sole American peace commissioner. What John Adams would do in Vienna to European diplomacy was something Vergennes did not care to think about. The breakage of diplomatic conventions — and perhaps of the furniture itself — promised to be spectacular.

Therefore, the French minister brought pressure to bear upon Congress to change its peace plenipotentiary, reduce its demands upon Great Britain, and permit France to handle its affairs at the forthcoming peace conference. John Adams, it was made clear, was unwelcome at Versailles and must be replaced by a statesman better fitted to grace the councils of Europe — Benjamin Franklin, Vergennes intimated, would do nicely.

And, the French minister explained to Congress, the United States was in no position to trump up extravagant claims against Great Britain — the enemy was not yet beaten and the military achievements of the republic hardly warranted an attempt at dictating peace. Above all, Congress ought to instruct its peace plenipotentiary to show "a perfect and open confidence in the French ministers and a thorough reliance on the King, and should direct him to take no step without the approbation of His Majesty."

While recognizing that John Adams had "more zeal than good manners," Congress nevertheless hesitated to remove him at Vergennes's bidding. He had given offense because of his outspoken defense of American rights and prestige abroad; he was a good American if not a wholly discreet one. Therefore, to recall Adams would argue a humiliating obsequiousness to France and deliver a rebuke to the patriotism and honesty of an American diplomat who had sought to serve his country by blunt, shirt-sleeves diplomacy. Congress could not altogether suppress a certain admiration for John Adams, the David who had braved the wrath of Goliath. And it could not deny the truth of Adams's remark that "to betray me in such a case would be an eternal opprobrium to our country."

Therefore Congress made John Adams a member of a five-man commission to make peace, but shackled the commissioners with instructions which effectively placed them under the control of the French Ministry. In this way, Congress sought to render harmless John Adams's tendency to kick over the traces, and at the same time to placate the French court, which had set its heart upon Adams's removal.[3]

The instructions drawn up by the Continental Congress for the guidance of American peace plenipotentiaries could hardly have been more favorable to France had they been written by Vergennes himself. Previously, American ministers had been usually directed to follow the advice of France, but they had been left a certain margin of discretion; now, because the French government did not trust John Adams, they were instructed to "make the most candid and confidential communications upon all subjects to the ministers of our generous ally, the King of France; to undertake nothing in the negotiations for peace or truce without their knowledge and concurrence"; and ultimately to govern themselves by the advice and opinion of the French court. This last provision of the instructions was procured through the direct intervention of La Luzerne and was carried in Congress only by a small majority.

The instructions did not go down easily either in Congress or in the country as a whole. They were called a disgraceful abnegation of American independence; America had not rebelled from Great Britain

[3] Franklin, Jay, and Adams were the only members of this commission who engaged actively in the peace negotiations.

to throw itself at the feet of France. The language of the instructions of June 1781, Arthur Lee declared, "was not the sentiment or language, that commenced the Revolution." Lee darkly predicted that between Vergennes and that "old serpent" Ben Franklin the vital interests of the United States would fall a sacrifice; it was, he said, as though Congress had stretched John Adams "upon an iron bed of torture and left the old man [Franklin] at full liberty to glut himself with tormenting him." Delivered bound and gagged to the French Ministry, the American commissioners could only accept whatever bounties France thought fit to dole out to the republic. It was a complete victory for French diplomacy. Nothing was withheld by the United States from its ally; the most implicit confidence was reposed in France; and the conditions of peace were left entirely to the decision of the Bourbon court.

However much congressmen might attempt to put a favorable face upon this transaction, the fact seemed self-evident that, as one member put it, "our allies are to rule the roost." It was no longer an alliance of equals as the treaty of 1778 had predicated: the United States was definitely the junior partner and practically surrendered the direction of affairs to the senior member. In making its own peace terms, France was not bound to consult with and secure the approval of the United States; but the United States could not make a move in peacemaking without the prior approbation of the French Ministry.

While admitting that the instructions of June 15, 1781, were a sacrifice of national dignity, James Madison insisted that they were justified by policy and by necessity. Congress was in no position to resist French pressure — its prestige and authority had reached the vanishing point; the Southern states seemed lost to British arms; and only France could supply the money and matériel that would keep the United States in the war. Nor could it be foreseen, in June 1781, that final and conclusive victory over the enemy was only four months away. Under these conditions, for Congress to stand upon its dignity was to risk having the ground cut from beneath its feet and losing the peace. The United States, observed Madison, was "more in danger of being seduced by Britain than sacrificed by France"; and, above all, it could not afford to lose the good will of the Bourbon government in order to preserve its freedom of action at the peace conference.

Despite all efforts to procure the repeal of the instructions, Congress stood firmly by its decision of June 1781. In October 1782, while the American commissioners were sitting down to peace talks with the British and making terms behind the back of France, Congress resolved that it would not "enter into the discussion of any overtures for pacification, but in confidence and in concert with his Most Christian Majesty." Congress, it is clear, expected the American peacemakers in Paris to make the instructions of June 1781 a basis of action.

Acknowledging that the instructions were a vote of "unreserved confidence" by the United States in France, Vergennes pledged that the republic would never have cause to regret its trust in the disinterested benevolence of His Most Christian Majesty. He assured Franklin that the King had "the honor of the United States at heart, as well as their welfare and independence," and that France could do more for the United States than the United States could do for itself. Franklin himself was convinced, at least outwardly, that the United States had done well to entrust its fate to "this upright and able minister [Vergennes], who never promised me anything which he did not punctually perform."

It is significant that even with these instructions in his pocket, Vergennes did not feel wholly secure. Plagued by apprehension that the United States would yet make a separate peace and return to the British Empire, Vergennes was like a fretful husband who fears that his bride will pack up at any moment and go home to mother. He constantly sought promises from the United States that it would remain true to its engagements; and, as an added precaution, he wished the states separately to ratify the Franco-American alliance. In 1782, he instructed La Luzerne to press the United States for additional assurances that it would not leave France in the lurch. "See to it, I beg of you," he directed La Luzerne, "that we be not taken for dupes." Honor among republicans was not a commodity by which Vergennes set much store.

WHILE Washington was fretting over the lack of patriotism of the people and Congress was surrendering its diplomatic autonomy to France, two events occurred which were to have far-reaching effect upon the outcome of the war: the appointment of Robert Morris as superintendent of finance, and the involvement of Holland as a belligerent in the war. Unrelated as they were, these two incidents contributed vitally to set the stage for the last act at Yorktown.

Congress was at last driven to face the hard facts: despite all its efforts, the country was sinking deeper into the financial morass. As a discouraged member observed, Congress appeared "to know nothing about either getting Money or saving it." For many years, congressmen had wrestled with this odious problem, only to find themselves in the end bruised and beaten. "What a pity it is," exclaimed a patriot, "that some Locke or Colbert could not start up and teach us the Art of Financing." Hopefully casting about for such a guide, in 1778 Congress invited Richard Price, the English radical who enjoyed considerable repute as a writer upon financial subjects, to come to the United States to save the Continental dollar. Price refused to leave England, however, and in 1780 the name of Alexander Hamilton was put forward in Congress as a financial expert who might restore the currency. Congress was slowly being converted to the view that the control of the country's finances must be "the work of *one Mind*."

It went against the grain of the revolutionary patriots to look to one man for salvation: the wisdom of legislative bodies rather than the talents, however pre-eminent, of an individual was regarded by these republicans as the mainstay of the state. When that individual happened to be a war profiteer, the case against one-man rule was clinched. Nevertheless,

Robert Morris seemed to be the only man with sufficient wealth and ability to save the country from the consequences of five years of uncontrolled inflation. The economic masters of the country were not the states to which Congress futilely appealed, but the merchants who had grown rich and powerful from the war; and none had grown richer or more powerful than had Robert Morris. Reluctantly, therefore, the patriots broke with their philosophy in order to preserve the state: in 1781, Robert Morris was elected superintendent of finance with sweeping powers over the country's finances.

Morris's better judgment told him to decline the proffered honor and to go about his business, which was rapidly making him the richest man in the United States. He was well aware that public office exposed "an honest man to the envy and jealousy of mankind at the same time that it lays him open to the malicious attacks of every dirty scoundrel that deals in the murther of reputations. . . . My opinion of mankind is grown worse from my experience of them," he declared in 1780; and he had little hope that if he saved the country, the people would prove grateful. On the other hand, the country had done well by Morris; and conditions had now reached the point where, as perhaps Morris would have put it, businessmen must step in and clean up the mess left by the mismanagement of the politicians. Certainly the affairs of the government needed the firm hand and executive ability that Morris could bring to them. If Morris could make the government of the United States half as prosperous as was Willing, Morris and Company, it would be a job well done.

When he assumed the post of superintendent of finance, Morris stipulated that he should not be asked to procure supplies for the army until 1782, when, he supposed, the finances of the country would be well on the road to recovery. But the crisis would not wait for Morris to set the republic's affairs in order: in 1781, he was called upon to find money and supplies for the troops, with the understanding that he was to have control of all money given or loaned by France to the United States.

Robert Morris struck the rock of American resources, and there was released, if not exactly a torrent, a sizable trickle of supplies for the army. What energy there was in the government of the United States stemmed largely from Morris; but it was French gold and his private credit as the richest American merchant of the day, rather than any confidence in the financial solvency of the Continental Congress, that enabled him to set the wheels in motion. By dint of begging and borrowing, he succeeded in eking out enough supplies to see the army through the Yorktown campaign. Meat, flour, and rum were stored along the line of march; and when the troops refused to march without pay, it was Morris who borrowed twenty thousand dollars from Rochambeau and a like sum from his fellow businessmen in Philadelphia. Thus a miracle was worked; on September 8, 1781, a major in the Continental army made the following entry in his diary: "This Day will be famous in the Annals of History for being the first on which the Troops of the United States received one Month's Pay in Specie." From the states, Morris received nothing until after Cornwallis's surrender: the campaign was financed entirely by credit and the hard cash supplied by the French. In fact, the states, in this decisive year of the war, busied themselves in devising means of drawing from Morris the small amount of cash he had been able to collect. Everywhere, he complained, he found greater willingness on the part of the states "to take money from the public treasury than to place any in it."

Largely through Morris's exertions, the American army was held together and enabled to fight a successful campaign. The year that began with the mutiny of the Pennsylvania Line and the seemingly hopeless paralysis of the country as a whole became the *annus mirabilis* — the year of Yorktown. Washington said in 1782 that "instead of a charge of having done too little, it will soon be a matter of wonder how Mr. Morris has done so much with so small means." The same might be said of Washington himself.

⌒ ⌒ ⌒

England could hardly hope to emerge triumphant from the struggle with France, Spain, and the United States unless the Bourbons were forced to fight a war on two fronts. In previous wars between France and England, the islanders had succeeded in raising formidable enemies on the continent against His Most Christian Majesty, with the result that France had usually been overborne by Great Britain and its allies. By means of these tactics, France had lost its empire. Menaced by enemies on their frontiers, the Bourbons had been forced to fight both on land and sea in two hemispheres; while they grappled with Austria or Prussia, the British conquered Canada and India. This, in essence, became traditional British policy — to fight France at sea with the British navy and to fight her on the European continent with British guineas.

It was to be expected, therefore, that during the War of American Independence the British should have reverted to this plan of action. If Russia, Austria, or Prussia could be induced to engage France upon the continent, the entire complexion of the war would be changed: while France was fighting for its existence in Europe, the British would be left free to subjugate the Americans without outside interference.

To this end, Great Britain attempted to persuade the countries of Europe that it was fighting their battle in maintaining its authority over its overseas dependencies. It was the Old World against the New, monarchism against republicanism, empire against the freedom of colonial peoples. Lord North warned that "if America should grow into a separate empire, it must of course cause . . . a revolution in the political system of the world." If Europe, out of hostility to Great Britain, supported the cause of American freedom, it would one day find itself ruled by America: imbued with democratic fanaticism, the armies of the United States would spread the American gospel of liberty over Europe. In a century or less, it was predicted, no power on earth could contend with the United States. It must be acknowledged that the English saw more clearly the course of America's destiny than did most Americans. Essentially, the British took the ground that only by presenting a united front to the revolutionary forces stemming from the Western Hemisphere could the old order survive. "Europe, wishing for the independence of America," they said, "resembles a man asleep on ice, and not sensible that ice thaws." By this reasoning, Europe ought to lose no time in joining forces with Great Britain against France and Spain.

It was England's misfortune that the War of American Independence occurred during one of those breathing spells in European wars when the contending powers took time out for the next round. The continent was at peace — and, what was more surprising, seemed disposed to remain so. At least, English guineas no longer worked their magic of raising allies in Europe: Russia was preoccupied with its expansionistic ambitions, Austria was allied with France, and Prussia would not touch an English alliance at any price. Although Prussia and Austria came to blows in a short and almost bloodless war in 1778, France was not drawn into the conflict; and the two warring powers soon made peace the better to devour helpless Poland. During the whole of the War of American Independence, France was able to devote all its strength to the struggle with Great Britain; Napoleon, on the other hand, was obliged to fight Great Britain with one hand while he kept Europe down with the other hand.

For Great Britain, the only cheerful spot in Europe was Portugal, the traditional ally of His Britannic Majesty. The use of Portuguese harbors, together with Gibraltar, by British armed vessels enabled them to maintain close guard over the entrance to the Mediterranean and to capture hundreds of American ships on their way to France and Spain. On the other hand, the Portuguese government refused to permit American vessels to enter its ports and even shelter was sometimes denied them. In its way, Portugal was as unneutral as was France — but its unneutrality was at the expense of the United States. It was for this reason that Americans were prepared to use Portugal as bait to bring Spain into the war, promising to aid Spain in conquering Portugal. "This little impotent morsel of a State ought not to do so much mischief so unjustly," exclaimed John Adams. "If she is neutral, let her be neutral; not say she is neutral, and be otherwise." This was no more than what the British were asking of France before the formation of the Franco-American alliance.

England's isolation was almost complete; she stood alone, groaned the Whigs, "like the stricken deer, deserted and abandoned by all the herd." The Whigs ascribed England's friendless state to Lord North's Ministry — as long as Tories remained at the helm, they predicted, England would be "abandoned by mankind." "No power in Europe," exclaimed Charles James Fox, "is blind; none stupid enough to ally itself with weakness, to become partner in bankruptcy, to unite with obstinacy, absurdity, and imbecility." Nevertheless, George III refused to despond: if England must stand alone, she would prove to the world that even without allies, England was terrible to its enemies.

Of all the great powers, Russia seemed the best disposed towards Great Britain. But the Russians, unhappily for the British, were engaged in a struggle with Turkey which tied up their manpower at home — manpower which the British government had hoped at the beginning of the war to hurl against the American rebels. Still, Russia was a power worth courting: Edmund Burke, contrasting the amazing rise of Russia with the decline of his own country, declared that this newcomer among the great nations stood "supreme between Europe and Asia, and looks as if she intended to dictate to both. We see in her a great but still growing empire." Silas Deane, the American diplomat, predicted in 1777 that the time would come when Great Britain, the United States, and Russia would dominate the world. "Russia," he remarked prophetically, "like America is a new state, and rises with the most astonishing rapidity." Lord Sandwich began hopefully to speak of Russia as England's "natural ally," and in 1780 the British government attempted to procure an alliance with Russia by offering to cede the Mediterranean island of Minorca. But this the Russians could hardly suppose a bargain: Minorca was besieged by the Spaniards, into whose hands it fell a short time later.[1]

Russia, like the other maritime powers of Europe, had felt the prick of John Bull's trident: as the dominant sea power, England was feared and respected, but seldom loved. Under Lord Sandwich, the British navy had adopted the policy, during the American war, of "intercepting all military or naval stores destined for the use of our enemies, be the consequence what it might in respect to the neutral powers." This order had been carried out to the full: neutral ships had been stopped by British cruisers, their cargoes condemned as contraband in British courts; and in 1779 an entire Dutch convoy carrying naval supplies to France had been seized by the British. Angered by these highhanded practices, European maritime powers were ready to take action against a nation they had come to regard as "the highwayman of the seas."

France worked so skillfully upon this resentment that she succeeded

[1] Lord Sandwich made clear that if Minorca were ceded to Russia, that power must engage to secure Great Britain "such a peace as we can with honour and safety accept" — including, of course, the return of the revolted colonies.

in uniting the principal European maritime powers in the so-called Armed Neutrality — a league composed of Russia, Sweden, Denmark, and Holland designed to uphold the rights of neutral shipping against British sea power. These powers pledged themselves to maintain the principle that free ships make free goods — British cruisers and men-of-war to the contrary. As protection against marauding British men-of-war, the neutrals began to convoy their merchantmen and to open their ports to American vessels; and in 1780, a Russian fleet appeared in the English Channel. The presence of the Russian flag in these waters was anything but reassuring to the British.

The Armed Neutrality might, Englishmen were aware, drop its neutrality at any moment and begin a shooting war. For England, this meant disaster: Lord Sandwich admitted that if the Russian fleet were joined to that of the Bourbons, England would probably have to strike her colors. Moreover, the powers of the Armed Neutrality controlled the only considerable supply of naval stores at the disposal of Great Britain after the loss of the American colonies. And it all came, exclaimed an English official, from the perversity of Catherine of Russia — "a b — of a queen, who could murder her husband and mount his throne — there's no trusting such a jade." He protested that he had no personal enmity against Catherine "except a little for the murder of her husband," which, he thought, concerned all husbands.

To Americans, the Russian bear began to appear so tame that, with a little stroking, it might become an ally of the United States. John Adams was for stepping up boldly to the Russians and asking them to sign a treaty; the cause of the United States, said Adams, was the cause of all nations and all men, so why be backward in telling the world — "it needs nothing but to be explained to be approved." And at least one American diplomat was eager to go to Russia "to make a Conquest of the Empress, who loves he says handsome Men, & may have a Curiosity for an American Gallant" — a curiosity which he proposed to gratify to the full. There was no more despotic power in Europe than Russia, but the United States was perfectly willing to league itself with tyranny in fighting Great Britain. The Continental Congress assured Catherine the Great that it was offering her an opportunity to attain "a distinguished place among those illustrious personages of ancient and modern times, who have delighted in promoting the happiness of mankind, and in disarming tyranny of the power of doing mischief." In fact, the United States itself tried to join the Armed Neutrality, although it was difficult to see how the republic, after five years of war with Great Britain, could qualify as a neutral.

Catherine of Russia was an enlightened despot who attempted to clear away the rubbish of feudalism that encumbered Russia, but her enlightenment did not take the form of enthusiastic good will toward American republicans. Nor was Francis Dana, the American diplomat entrusted with the negotiations in St. Petersburg, a gallant to her liking; Dana spent most of his time in Russia cooling his heels outside the antechambers of important personages. Although Dana reported in 1783 that the United States might consummate a treaty with Russia if it was willing to pay the price demanded by the Russian ministers, the United States declined to buy its way into the family of nations. As a result, it was not until 1809 that Russia finally recognized the United States as an independent nation, twenty-five years after the British themselves had acknowledged the fact.

⌢ ⌢ ⌢

In their quest for loans and alliances, Americans could scarcely overlook Holland, then the financial center of Europe and moneylender to the world. No European power, it was said, could safely embark upon war without first making sure of loans from Holland, "the treasury of Europe." "Would you know the credit and situation of the affairs of the different kingdoms," said a European, "consult the books of the Dutch banks." Naturally, Americans were eager to stand in the good graces of such potent capitalists, and accordingly John Adams was sent to Holland to persuade the Dutch bankers that the United States was a worthy investment.

Adams discovered that the Dutch were quite as stubborn as they were rich. Like all bankers, they demanded security before parting with their money — and of this commodity, the Americans could offer little. As a result, although the bankers of Amsterdam loaned large sums to the British government, they had not a guilder to spare for the Americans — they were not in business, they reminded John Adams, to help struggling republics to get on their feet. They wished well to the United States, but while their hearts went out to the Americans, their purses remained tightly closed. "Such a Nation of Idolators at the Shrine of Mammon never existed I believe, before," Adams exploded. "The English are as great Idolators, but they have more Gods than one." "Holland is no longer a Nation," said Benjamin Franklin, "but a great *Shop;* and I begin to think it has no other Principles or Sentiments but those of a Shopkeeper."

This hands-off policy pursued at least officially by the Dutch toward the American rebellion did not spare them from involvement in the war. The chance discovery of negotiations between the merchants of Amsterdam and the American revolutionists furnished the pretext upon which Great Britain declared war. The "menace" to Great Britain of the powerful and warlike Hollanders was much insisted upon by the British government to justify its action, but actually it was Holland's adherence to the Armed Neutrality and the tempting vulnerability of its trade and empire that prompted Britain's move. Moreover, as neutrals trading with all belligerents impartially, the Dutch merchants had incurred England's wrath: they played all sides and seldom troubled themselves about the color of their customer's money — and this Great Britain could not tolerate.

Although Holland was a member of the Armed Neutrality, not one of the nations composing that league raised a finger to save her from the vengeance of Great Britain. Thus the Armed Neutrality, as is frequently true of alliances, proved to be more formidable on paper than in deed. Catherine the Great remarked bitterly that it ought to have been called the Armed Nullity.

"The English have got another war," said Benjamin Franklin, "and perhaps not the last, upon their Hands. They are making large Strides towards becoming what Pirates are said to be, Enemies to all Mankind." Nevertheless, the King and his ministers were firmly entrenched in Parliament and stood high in the graces of the English people; another war, more or less, did not visibly shake their power. Moreover, the war against Holland promised to be a profitable venture which might yield territory and plunder to compensate for the losses sustained in North America.

There was no sign that England was weakening as the number of its enemies increased. If the American war had not gained in popularity, the dogged determination of Englishmen to snuff out the rebellion had hardly abated a jot in six years of war. Charles James Fox, while lamenting that it was intolerable that "it should be in the power of one blockhead to do so much mischief," was obliged to acknowledge that blockheads, if they but flattered the prejudices of Englishmen, could lead them where they would. "The people of this country in general," he declared, "deserve no pity, and certainly the King still less."

Every success of British arms strengthened the conviction of George III that the rebellion was on the point of collapse. Disappointed in the Howes, and later in Clinton, he found in Cornwallis the fair-haired knight who would slay the dragon of rebellion and restore the good king to his rightful possessions. For George, hope of victory sprang eternal: repeated disappointments did not lessen his faith or abridge his zeal, and long deferment of his hopes merely whetted his resolution to pursue the war to a finish. In May 1780, he was satisfied that, barring unforeseen developments, the rebels must sue for peace within six months. When those six months had expired, he was still predicting the speedy end of the rebellion. "I think success must ensue," he wrote just before Cornwallis surrendered at Yorktown.

The King's confidence was reinforced by the fact that he had finally found an admiral of impeccable Tory views who gave promise of winning the smashing kind of victories which England expected from its naval officers. George Rodney, the latest object of the King's affections, was a vigorous, dashing, colorful sea dog who recaptured something of the spirit of Drake and Hawkins. Unfortunately for England, however, the cost of winning his election to Parliament and his heavy losses at cards ruined him financially, and in 1774 he was obliged to flee the country and take refuge in Paris from his creditors. Had Rodney stood well in the graces of Lord Sandwich, the government might have bailed out the fugitive admiral, but the First Lord of the Admiralty, having quarreled with Rodney, was not disposed to recall him. And George III feared that Rodney, if restored to his post, would attempt to recoup his fortune by dishonesty in purchasing stores for his ships or by seizing enemy shipping at the expense of strategical objectives. It was Lord George Germain who finally succeeded, in 1779, in bringing back Rodney from exile. Although he was given a command, a commissioner was appointed to accompany Rodney at all times to make sure that he did not attempt to turn his post into a source of personal emolument.

Rodney injected into the war of maneuvers and bloodless battles that had hitherto characterized the struggle at sea something of the fire and dash that had characterized the British navy in its great days. To a people long starved for naval victories, Rodney became the hero of the day, and his name became as proverbial for victory as that of "Foul Weather Jack" Byron was for bad luck. As England's enemies soon learned, Rodney "meant mischief, not idle flourishes." In January 1780, he relieved Gibraltar, destroying part of the Spanish fleet that attempted to contest his passage. In April 1780, he attacked the French fleet under De Guichen in the West Indies, and although robbed of victory by a misreading of a signal by one of his captains, he held in check the superior French fleet until De Guichen returned to France in the summer of 1780.[2] Rodney's career quenched John Adams's hopes of an early peace: with a successful admiral riding the seas, Englishmen would never come to terms because, he remarked, "Naval Victories intoxicate them to Frenzy."

It fell to Sir George Rodney to carry out the British plan of attack upon the Dutch possessions in the West Indies. St. Eustatius, in particular had become a thorn in British flesh. In order to profit from the broils of Englishmen and Americans, the Dutch had made St. Eustatius a free port; and, under this dispensation, vessels of all nations came to the haven to exchange guns and European-manufactured munitions for American tobacco, indigo, flour, and naval stores. Even British merchants maintained branch offices at St. Eustatius; several hundred English businessmen, including a member of Parliament, were engaged in trading with the enemy

[2] It is revealing of the extent to which factionalism and party politics had permeated the British navy under Lord Sandwich that Rodney should have accused some of his captains, members of the Whig Party, of "barefaced disobedience to orders and signals" in order to discredit him, a staunch Tory. For their part, the accused captains swore that Rodney was "an old Woman"; "in fact," said one of the captains, "he despises them, and they him."

under the shelter of Dutch neutrality. When British convoys reached the West Indies, it was not uncommon for some ships to break formation and head for St. Eustatius, where they disposed of their cargoes at fancy prices. This island, indeed, became the Americans' chief source of British goods during the war. Of course, this traffic aided the rebels, but Lord Sandwich declared that no laws could restrain the "rapacity of merchants." Gun runners from all the seven seas came to St. Eustatius to bargain by day and carouse at night in water-front dives with the rebels. It was the liveliest spot in the Caribbean — twenty-four hours a day. The Dutch governor of the island went out of his way to be helpful to Americans; in fact, he conducted himself throughout the struggle more like the head of a chamber of commerce than the administrator of a supposedly neutral island.

For its size, St. Eustatius was no doubt the richest island in the world: every storehouse was crammed with goods, and "every part of a very extensive beach covered with sugar, tobacco, and cotton." Moreover, being almost defenseless, it could easily be scooped up by a hostile fleet. To Rodney, still haunted by his creditors and resolved at all costs to repair his fortunes, St. Eustatius looked like the answer to his prayers. Seldom has a man been presented with a more tempting opportunity of doing his duty and lining his pockets at the same time.

Rodney struck St. Eustatius before the islanders knew that they were at war. He sailed into the harbor flying the French flag; not until his guns opened fire did the Dutch realize that they were dealing with a hostile fleet. By that time, however, resistance was too late; the entire island, its warehouses crammed with merchandise and its roadstead filled with ships of every nationality, fell to the British almost without opposition.

Having taken St. Eustatius by ruse, Rodney continued to play the game of deception. The Dutch flag was kept flying over the fort — with the result that scores of French, Dutch, and American vessels sailed into the trap to add their cargoes to Rodney's booty. "Not a night but an American arrives loaded with tobacco," jubilantly reported the British admiral, "the morning surprizes them with being taken."

Rodney treated St. Eustatius as he might a nest of pirates, and conducted himself as though he were a rival pirate. The merchants were, he swore, "adventurers preying upon the vitals of Great Britain" who had no right to expect any immunities; he came as "the instrument of a great, powerful, but injured nation to scourge them for their perfidy, and," he added, "scourged they shall be." He seized whatever caught his eye; a heavy tax was levied upon the inhabitants; and more than a million pounds of loot were put aboard the British fleet.

Temptation proved too great for Rodney: as George III said, the British admiral "lost all his powers the moment he made the capture of St. Eustatius." Distracted by his sudden wealth, he lost all interest in conquering the other Dutch islands in the West Indies as the Admiralty had ordered. Yet, although Rodney did not seem to realize it, he had better things to do than gorging himself with the spoil of St. Eustatius. The French fleet was on the move.

⌢ ⌢ ⌢

The French government, in response to the pleas of the Continental Congress, had promised in 1780 that a large fleet would be sent to United States waters the following year. It was upon this naval armament that Washington largely pinned his hopes of victory; indeed, the prospect of French naval aid was the only rosy spot in an otherwise bleak picture.

Vergennes left Americans under no misapprehension as to the extent of future French aid. France, they were told, could spare no troops or ships after 1781; even financial aid would be cut off. The war had proved costly beyond the calculations of the Bourbon government; already it had spent a sum far exceeding anything that "Congress had a right to expect from the friendship of their ally." For the United States, it was therefore a question of now or never: they must make the most of French aid in this year of decision or depend upon their own resources to see them to victory.

Vergennes felt that France had been badly let down by its ally: instead of setting their house in order and buckling down to the business of winning the war, Americans seemed to be drifting into ever greater confusion, with the war steadily becoming more and more of a side issue. They importuned France for money and supplies, he testily pointed out, while they refused to pay taxes themselves, with the result that a disproportionate share of the burden was thrust upon France. Already fully occupied in waging global war against Great Britain, France could not fight Americans' battles for them while they calmly took their ease.

To enable the United States to wage war effectively, Vergennes sought to strengthen the central government established under the Articles of Confederation. In a few centuries or so, he admitted, American republicanism might menace the established order in Europe; but the immediate danger was not that the United States would conquer the world, but that it would expire of anemia. In allying his country with the United States, the French foreign minister had hardly expected to be called in as state physician to the republic and to be obliged to keep it alive with frequent transfusions of French money. Seeking a fighting ally, he had seemingly acquired a cripple that might expire on his hands. To remedy this evil, Vergennes urged Americans to ratify the Articles of Confederation, create a stronger Continental army, and place the administration of finance, war, marine, and foreign affairs under permanent departments instead of fluctuating congressional committees. Yet, as Vergennes was soon to learn, all the horses and men of the King of France could not restore the authority of the Continental Congress.

The French government had almost ceased to hope that a decision could be reached in the United States; perhaps it was for this reason that the French fleet which was ordered to proceed to North America in 1781 was intended primarily to aid the Spaniards rather than the Americans. Admiral de Grasse was ordered to co-operate with the Spanish fleet and army in capturing the British West Indies; only such ships as the Spaniards could spare from these operations were to be dispatched to the United States. Fortunately for his peace of mind, Washington did not know what his allies intended to be his portion of naval aid in the campaign of 1781.

While Rodney busied himself with the spoil of St. Eustatius, De Grasse reached the West Indies with a powerful fleet. But Rodney could not tear himself away from his newly won riches long enough to attend to this new danger: he failed to waylay De Grasse, who, with a large convoy under his protection, reached Martinique without interference. Here he joined forces with another French squadron which gave him a decided superiority over the British fleet in the West Indies. De Grasse had twenty-five ships to Rodney's eighteen, but when Rodney was finally ready to fight, the French admiral declined to be drawn into an engagement. Indeed, De Grasse made slight use of his superiority: he captured the island of Tobago but failed to reduce St. Lucia — a small return for the heavy investment France had made in her fleet. Actually, De Grasse was waiting for the Spaniards with whom he had been ordered to co-operate; but in Rodney's eyes the French commander appeared to be one of those poopdeck admirals who turned tail at the sight of a British squadron. Thus Rodney's experience with De Grasse in the Caribbean during the spring and summer of 1781 did not incline him to regard the Frenchman as a serious threat to British security.

With riches surpassing the dreams of Drake and the buccaneers, Rodney found it impossible to remain longer in the West Indies. No doubt his health was bad, but the compelling reason for his return to Great Britain was his desire to supervise the sale of the rich haul he had sent to England under convoy. Rodney knew that many of his acts at St. Eustatius would not bear daylight, and he particularly feared a parliamentary inquiry that might strip him of his riches.

But Rodney made the fatal mistake of counting his guineas before they were safe in England. The convoy laden with the spoil of St. Eustatius was set upon by a French squadron which carried off most of the transports. And even though part of the convoy reached England, Rodney profited little from the wealth he had seized at St. Eustatius; in fact, he was almost bankrupted by the lawsuits brought against him by the British merchants whose goods he had confiscated in the island.

The British Admiralty was deeply disturbed by this unfavorable balance of naval power in the West Indies, but Sandwich reposed complete confidence in the redoubtable Sir George Rodney to cope with the danger. Rodney himself had no doubt of his ability to handle De Grasse; he repeatedly assured the Admiralty that everything was under control in the West Indies, that he was keeping a close watch upon the French fleet, and that he was prepared to follow it to the coast of the United States if necessary. It came therefore as a distinct shock to learn that Rodney had decided to come home. Lord Sandwich begged him to reconsider: the French fleet would almost certainly sail northward during the hurricane season, and England relied upon Rodney to save the day. But Rodney was adamant; his health had been undermined, he declared, and only an English surgeon and the restorative waters of Bath could effect a cure.

If ever Rodney was needed by his country, it was in the summer of 1781 while he took time out from the war to return to England. In this fateful year for its empire, Great Britain was threatened with loss of the command of the sea in every quarter: the Mediterranean, the West Indies, India, and even the English Channel. At the very time that the French fleet was threatening to upset the British military position in North America, a combined Spanish and French fleet rode the Channel and again threatened Great Britain with invasion. England was spared for the third time: the French and Spanish commanders fell out and the fleets divided without having done more than parade through the Channel. But in America and in the Mediterranean, fortune forsook the British, and the empire crumbled into ruin.

That De Grasse intended to bring a French fleet to the United States during the autumn of 1781 was no military secret; in fact, it was one of the best advertised maneuvers of the war. From intercepted letters, the British commanders knew De Grasse's plans and they correctly deduced that he would sail northward during the fall of the year when hurricanes made the West Indies dangerous to shipping. They were certain, moreover, that his destination would be New York. The only circumstance of which they were in doubt was the size of the force the French admiral would bring with him.

Just as Rodney was about to leave the West Indies, he learned that De Grasse had slipped away and was making for the coast of the United States. But even this event, portentous as it was for the British cause, did not induce Rodney to change his plans. He contented himself with ordering Admiral Hood to follow De Grasse, warning Admiral Graves, commanding the British squadron in New York, of his danger and directing Graves to meet Hood in the vicinity of the Chesapeake in order to intercept the French squadron. That Rodney grasped the situation there is no doubt; but in seeking to send word to Graves of the approaching danger he underestimated the hazards of winds, weather, and enemy cruisers. And he took with him, as protection to the merchant ships he was convoying back to England, several ships of the line that might have spelled the difference between victory and defeat for the British fleet when Cornwallis was trapped at Yorktown.

Admiral Hood carried out Rodney's orders without delay: he set out in pursuit of De Grasse and sent word to Admiral Graves that the French fleet was on its way northward. But Hood failed to fall in with De Grasse, and the ship carrying the dispatches to Graves was captured at sea by the enemy. As a result, it was not until September that Graves finally learned the true state of affairs — too late to avert disaster.

That De Grasse sailed north in August 1781 with practically his entire fleet, and thereby made possible the victory at Yorktown, was owing to the dilatoriness of the Spaniards and to the initiative of the French commander himself. Shortly after arriving in the West Indies, De Grasse had written to Rochambeau asking for detailed plans how best he could aid the allied army in the United States; and at his request, American pilots were sent to Santo Domingo. Fortunately for the United States, the Spaniards were unprepared to embark upon large-scale operations in the West Indies, thus freeing De Grasse from instructions which would have tied the greater part of his fleet to the Caribbean. But it was De Grasse himself who decided to gamble everything upon a blow against the British in the United States by taking almost his entire fleet northward, leaving even French merchant ships to go home unconvoyed. Among the architects of victory at Yorktown, De Grasse takes first rank.

EARLY in 1781, when Clinton learned of Cornwallis's retreat to Wilmington, he little imagined that his subordinate — headstrong as Sir Henry knew him to be — would leave the scene of his victories to go to Virginia. Clinton expected that the war in the South would go on and that the loyalty of the people would be put to the final test which would determine whether Great Britain could reclaim the allegiance of Americans anywhere in the revolted colonies. It was still too early, he believed, to write off the great experiment upon which the British had embarked in the South; and he expected that Cornwallis, despite the disappointing turnout of the Loyalists, would retreat to South Carolina where, after re-forming and resting his army, the struggle with Nathanael Greene would be resumed.

It came therefore as a shock to Clinton to find that Cornwallis had brought his army in headlong haste to Virginia with the intention of making that state the principal theater of war. By this maneuver, Clinton exclaimed, Cornwallis had imperiled the entire British military position in the South and doomed to failure the experiment upon which the commander-in-chief rested his hopes of victory. Once again, Great Britain had abandoned her friends to the mercy of their enemies. Cornwallis's action was more censurable than the evacuation of Philadelphia and Boston — on those occasions, many thousand Loyalists had been evacuated with the British army, whereas the North Carolina Loyalists were abandoned to their fate.

Nor was the commander-in-chief pleased to discover that as a result of Cornwallis's dash northward, Virginia had become the chief battleground of the war. Sir Henry was not disposed to put the British cause to hazard in the Old Dominion: except as a base for British cruisers and a field for diversionary operations to aid Cornwallis in the Carolinas, the region of the Chesapeake had few attractions in his eyes. In fact, in April 1781, he planned to withdraw from Virginia in order to strengthen the defenses of New York, and only the insistence of Germain that the Chesapeake be held by a strong British army dissuaded him from reducing the size of the British force in Virginia. This fever-ridden state, Sir Henry believed, was "the graveyard of armies"; yet it was here that Cornwallis had established himself in the hot, unhealthy season when military operations were most hazardous.[1]

As Clinton feared, after Cornwallis's abandonment of North Carolina, the British position in the South rapidly deteriorated. With their forces spread thinly over an immense region, the invaders were vulnerable to attack in many quarters: Camden and Ninety-six were lost to Greene, and after the battle of Eutaw Springs (September 1781), the last important battle to be fought in the South during the Revolutionary War, the British retreated to Charleston and Savannah, where they were closely besieged by the Americans. The war between Whigs and Tories went on, however, with undiminished ferocity, massacres and countermassacres being the order of the day.

Clinton had long suspected that Cornwallis was angling for the post of commander-in-chief, and this unauthorized move to Virginia confirmed all his mistrust. Clinton felt acutely his lack of the qualities that made Cornwallis loved and admired — a dashing, devil-may-care, swashbuckling air and a willingness to take long chances that somehow always seemed to end successfully. Moreover, he was distressed by the obvious favoritism shown by Germain to Cornwallis. Sir Henry, it is plain, felt very sorry for himself; misunderstood, unappreciated, and cast into the shade by a younger man, he had come to regard his command as an almost unsupportable burden. "I am neglected, and ill treated, every opinion but mine taken, any plan but mine adopted," he grieved. "I am forced into operations planned by others, promised support, and unfortunate from that being wantonly withheld from me."

But, rallying from his despondency and self-pity, he resolved that Cornwallis should not be permitted to steal the limelight. If he must resign his command, he was determined to go out in a burst of glory: not until he had won a victory over the rebels would he make way for Cornwallis. Until his final blow, he would occupy the center of the stage while Corn-

[1] It seems evident that Clinton late in 1780 favored making the Eastern Shore of Maryland and Baltimore the route of an invasion of Pennsylvania. But in all these plans, Clinton was to be the commander, not Cornwallis. Clinton's interest in the Chesapeake rapidly cooled after Cornwallis's arrival there. See "Substance of Opinions given to Major General Phillips." 1780. Phillips MSS. Clements Library. Clinton had regarded Virginia as a proper field for a diversionary attack in aid of the war in the Carolinas and as the base of operations for an expedition against Baltimore or Philadelphia.

wallis, who had consistently played to the galleries, would be compelled to cool his heels in the wings. This, at least, was the way Clinton would have played the last act of the American war had not fate taken a hand in the proceedings.

And so, hedged round with difficulties, bedeviled by anxiety and despair, and incapacitated by temporary fits of blindness, Sir Henry Clinton clung to the command. Of all his afflictions, the most mortifying was the conduct of Lord Cornwallis.

Cornwallis wished to make Virginia the scene of the decisive battles of the American war; Clinton favored joining the issue in Pennsylvania. The commander-in-chief had little hope of finding any considerable number of Tories in the Old Dominion, but he still hoped that Pennsylvania would yet prove to be the Land of Tories he had sought unremittingly for the past six years. He proposed to put matters to the test by invading the state with five thousand men, aided by Cornwallis's army moving up from Virginia; and when he had captured Philadelphia and routed Congress, the people were to be invited to make their submission. This would be the final experiment in testing the loyalty of Americans; if it failed, said Clinton, "I shall . . . have little Hopes of afterwards reestablishing Order on this Continent; — which, I am free to own, I think can never be effected without the cordial Assistance of numerous Friends."

To assist the attack upon Philadelphia, Clinton advised Cornwallis to move his army to Baltimore. But Cornwallis, unwilling to place himself and his army at the disposal of the commander-in-chief, declined to leave Virginia, delicately suggesting that if Clinton felt that he must have Philadelphia, let him take it himself. He pointed out, for his superior's edification, that the expedition against Philadelphia was certain to fail since it would lack the indispensable element of surprise; and as for the support of the Loyalists, he had learned from his experiences in Carolina never to trust them — they protested their loyalty too much, he had found, and "when a Storm threatens, our friends disappear." Cornwallis continued to insist that there was no quicker and more certain way of ending the rebellion than by conquering Virginia.

Instead of falling in with Cornwallis's plans of strengthening the army in Virginia, Clinton asked his subordinates to send as many troops as possible to New York in order that the main army might take the offensive. As late as the middle of August, 1781, Clinton continued to count upon troops drawn from Cornwallis to execute his plans against Philadelphia. Clinton pointed out that Cornwallis could easily spare these men since he was confronted only by Lafayette and a handful of Continentals, together with "a small body of ill armed peasantry, full as spiritless as the militia of the southern provinces" — which Cornwallis might well have construed as a censure upon his failure to eliminate Lafayette and his contemptible army. In any event, Cornwallis was made to see that by coming to Virginia he had not forced the hand of his commander and that Clinton intended to direct the strategy of the war.[2]

With the approach of summer, Clinton ordered Cornwallis to take up a position at Yorktown until the weather should again permit campaigning. Now, if there was one thing that Cornwallis had not come to Virginia for, it was to remain on the defensive while the Americans collected their forces against him. To Cornwallis's way of thinking, the bane of British military strategy was its tendency to rely upon the defensive to win the war. Temperamentally, he was ill suited to such strategy; instead of waiting for the rebellion to collapse from internal weakness, he yearned to fall upon it with hammer blows. Rather than remain inactive at Yorktown in "an unhealthy swamp . . . for ever liable to become a prey to a foreign Enemy, with a temporary superiority at sea," he told Clinton that he would prefer to go back to Charleston; but the commander-in-chief declined to sanction such a move. Cornwallis must stay where he was and build a fortified camp at Yorktown.[3] Grudgingly, Cornwallis complied, but he made clear that he had no heart in the enterprise and that it was against his better judgment.

Deprived of the reinforcements he had expected, and frustrated in his ambition of giving the rebellion its deathblow in Virginia, Cornwallis lapsed into sullen ill-humor. He was still outwardly polite to Clinton but he made plain that, while he carried out the commander-in-chief's orders, he considered that Clinton was bungling matters woefully. English gentlemen do not lash out at each other with unrestrained abuse, yet it is clear that during the summer of 1781 relations between the two men were becoming dangerously strained. They wrangled over the question of reinforcements, plans of campaign, the wisdom of Cornwallis's march to Virginia, and the establishment of a naval base in Virginia. There was no harmony in the British command — a circumstance which redounded to the advantage of the French and Americans.

Inevitably, the rivalry between Clinton and Cornwallis permeated the lower ranks of the army; in the officers' mess, the merits and shortcomings of the two paladins were exhaustively canvassed. Clinton was said to be an "old Woman" maundering about his grievances while his opportunities to crush the rebellion slipped away. As long as Clinton was in command, the British army seemed destined to stand "like the hungry Ass between two Bushels of hay and for want of preference starves." He had once

[2] On August 14, 1781, twenty-five hundred German troops arrived at New York. Clinton wrote that he now had five thousand men with which to take the offensive — a number too few to ensure success. Therefore he must be content to remain on the defensive, he said, "at least till I see what Ld. Cornwallis can spare." On July 28, 1781, Clinton had written: "I am the more distress'd by Ld. Cornwallis' keeping all he had in Chesapeake defensive, as with what I expected from his Lordship, I did intend to have made a move against Philadelphia, and waited only its arrival."

[3] By fortifying Yorktown and a position across the York River at Gloucester, Clinton intended to protect the British base at Portsmouth.

been an able general, it was admitted, but long residence in America had afflicted him, as it did all British commanders, "with a Numbness very unfit for the active scenes they were sent here to fill." As for Cornwallis, he was held to be rash and vainglorious — a man who would bring all down in ruin to gratify his ambition.

Had Cornwallis succeeded in putting Virginia out of the war, he would, of course, have been acclaimed (as later he was to be on the strength of his achievements in India) one of England's greatest soldiers. His strategy is always judged in the light of its failure; but in the spring of 1781 there was much to be said for making Virginia the chief theater of war. Virginia was weak, distracted, and floundering in a financial morass; and its conquest would have had momentous repercussions upon patriot morale and might, indeed, have resulted in the submission of the entire South. On the surface, at least, there was nothing to condemn Cornwallis's strategy, but he required strong reinforcement and continued command of the sea in order to make his position secure.

Although Germain had been firmly convinced that Cornwallis would not, as other British commanders had done all too frequently, engage in "desultory enterprises, taking possession of places at one time and abandoning them at another," he did not rebuke his favorite for abandoning the Carolina Loyalists. Germain was content to let the man on the spot — provided the government had confidence in him — act as he saw fit; and Cornwallis's move to Virginia by no means shook Germain's faith in Cornwallis as the conqueror of America. The British minister had long wished to transfer the war to Virginia, for there, he believed, the rebellion was finally to be conquered. "To recover those [Southern] Provinces in preference to all others and to push the War from South to North" was one of Germain's favorite prescriptions for crushing the revolt. Yet, at the same time, he approved Clinton's plan of an expedition against Philadelphia. Apparently Germain had not learned from the Howe-Burgoyne misunderstanding not to give contradictory orders to commanders whom he expected to work together.

෴   ෴   ෴

The American campaign against Yorktown worked with such perfect co-ordination of land and sea forces that it appeared to be the result of long and careful planning. Actually, the strategy was improvised, almost conceived upon the spur of the moment, and undertaken contrary to Washington's inclinations. Not until the middle of August, 1781 — less than a month before the trap was sprung on Cornwallis — was it finally decided that Virginia rather than New York should be the scene of the combined operations of the allied army and navy.

In Washington's opinion, as in that of Sir Henry Clinton, the campaign in Virginia was secondary to the war in the Northern states. The decisive battles of the war, both commanders agreed in thinking, would be fought for the possession of New York City; the Chesapeake was little more than a side show.

At the conference held at Weathersfield, Connecticut, in May 1781, Washington and Rochambeau drew up plans for an attack upon New York City by the Franco-American army. A full transcript of the proceedings of the allied commanders fell into Clinton's hands. Thus the most jealously guarded secrets of the allies were known to the British commander — with fatal results, singularly enough, to the British.

The French did not share Washington's enthusiasm for an attack upon New York. In 1780, when John Laurens was promised naval aid, he was told that the French government regarded a siege of New York as too costly and hazardous. To the French, the Chesapeake seemed a much more promising field of operations than New York. In the spring of 1781, a French fleet had almost succeeded in cutting off Arnold in Virginia; why could not the same tactics be employed on a larger scale against Cornwallis? Moreover, since De Grasse's stay in United States waters was to be of short duration, an enterprise of less magnitude than an attack upon New York seemed advisable. Both Rochambeau and De Grasse urged these arguments upon Washington who, although nominally in chief command of both the American and French armies in the United States, had no control over the French navy and was therefore not in a position to dictate the strategy of the campaign of 1781.[4] Nevertheless, Washington so stubbornly insisted upon an attack upon New York that a serious breach between him and Rochambeau was averted only by the intercession of Lafayette.

So intent was Washington upon gaining New York that on July 2, 1781, without waiting for the arrival of the French fleet, he opened an attack upon the north end of Manhattan Island. After the first assaults had been beaten back, however, he decided to postpone his main attack until a more favorable moment. For weeks he remained at White Plains, probing the British defenses, hoping to find a weak spot that would deliver the city to him. That he could contemplate an attack upon New York without first pinning down the British fleet with a superior French force reveals how keenly he felt the necessity of action; that his attempt should fail was, under the circumstances, a foregone conclusion.

It was fortunate for Washington and the American cause that he was at last persuaded to abandon the assault upon New York in favor of putting a noose about Cornwallis in the Chesapeake. In New York, the British

---

[4] Although commander-in-chief of the allied army, Washington generally used his powers with such restraint that Lafayette, upon several occasions, urged him to be more forceful. To which Washington replied that "the confidence with which the King [of France] honoured him demanded redoubled delicacy and prudence."

were prepared to sustain an assault, and for that reason an attack was perilous and doubtful, if not hopeless. In view of De Grasse's orders, which obligated him to return to the West Indies after remaining only about six weeks in the United States, there cannot be much doubt that the British would have held New York against an assault by the allies. The credit for planning the triumph at Yorktown belongs clearly to the French; Washington's merit consists chiefly in his skillful execution of the strategy devised by the Bourbon commanders. The palms of victory had almost to be thrust upon the reluctant Washington.

The fact that in the summer of 1781 the British were braced for an attack upon New York, and were unprepared to sustain an action in the Chesapeake, apparently did not enter into the calculations of either Washington or the French commanders. Yet, by unexpectedly diverting their strength to the Chesapeake after convincing Clinton that their objective was New York, they gained the inestimable advantage of surprise. It was surprise, together with Franco-American naval and military superiority, which made Yorktown possible. None of the allied commanders, however, seems to have appreciated fully the benefit of such a last-minute change of strategy. They changed their plans, it is true, but for reasons other than taking the enemy off his guard.

Nevertheless, the knowledge that the French had decided to seek a decision in 1781 and that a French fleet was on its way to the United States did not save the British from disaster. Clinton was forewarned but not forearmed. Fundamentally, the trouble was that the British knew — or believed they knew — the enemy's plans so thoroughly that it was necessary to guard against attack at only one point — New York. It was not lack of knowledge of the enemy's intentions that upset the British in the campaign of 1781: their misfortune came from knowing too much about Washington's intentions of attacking New York. Had they known less, they might have been more upon their guard at such a vulnerable point as Yorktown.

Sir Henry Clinton rested secure in the knowledge that the allies intended to attack New York. That the allied commanders would change their plans, he seems not to have envisaged. It was comparatively easy, therefore, to deceive a man as firmly convinced as was Clinton that he knew the truth. True, he was worried by the prospect of a French fleet coming to the United States, but his concern was largely owing to the appalling inefficiency of the admirals who now commanded the British navy in North American waters.

While Lord Howe had commanded the British fleet and Sir William Howe led the British army in North America, the two services as a matter of course had worked closely together in combined operations. With the retirement of the two brothers, however, friction began to spring up between the army and navy until finally, in 1780 and 1781, the British general and admiral in North America were openly at odds, bitterly complaining of each other to the home government and endangering the success of military and naval operations by their quarrels.

Largely because Sandwich insisted upon making the navy a political football, a succession of weak and nondescript admirals successively assumed the command after the retirement of Lord Howe. Each commander bewailed more loudly than had his predecessor the critical state of the navy. Sir George Collier, for example, declared in 1778 that his lack of seamen would shortly oblige him to lay up half his vessels to man the rest. Admiral Gambier reported that there was not a single coil of rope and scarcely a store of any kind available: the ships were foul and so unseaworthy that even the Continental navy, contemptible as it was to British sea dogs, had begun to worry Gambier. But these admirals had scarcely an opportunity to reveal even their incompetence: the war had settled down to a more or less steady routine of convoying and commerce raiding. None of them had the satisfaction of defeating the Continental navy, for it remained, for the most part, prudently tied up in port. Collier alone won a victory over the rebels when he defeated a Massachusetts fleet off the coast of Maine. "No one," he reported, "could feel more happiness than I did during the time I was driving a squadron of the King's rebellious subjects before me, of more than double my force." To British naval officers, it was an all too rare pleasure.

Admiral Arbuthnot, in command of the British fleet in North American waters in 1781, was one of those grizzled sea dogs that Sandwich had fished out of retirement in his quest of naval officers. Obviously, Arbuthnot was well past his prime: indeed, he was verging upon decrepitude, and although the spirit was still strong, the flesh was superannuated. To Clinton, it was intolerable to be yoked with this doddering commander; he lectured Arbuthnot upon the importance of sea power but, as far as he could see, the admiral absorbed not a word. "He forgets from hour to hour," lamented Clinton; " — he thinks aloud — he will not answer my Letters, holds Conversations with my Aides de Camp, and afterwards denies it, as indeed he has done once or twice with myself. . . . His head is in my opinion gone." He concluded that this ancient mariner was under the thumb of his secretary who, Clinton suspected, was a traitor. Rather than serve with this "fine brave superannuated old Gentleman" with the conveniently short memory, the exasperated general asked to be relieved of his command, pointing out that he could not risk his reputation by engaging in any enterprises where the aid of the navy was necessary. Twice he was obliged to cancel expeditions against Rhode Island because the admiral was not ready to sail on schedule; to Clinton's pleas for action, Arbuthnot remained blissfully deaf.

Harnessed to this querulous valetudinarian and denied the reinforcements he deemed essential, the distraught general began to fear for the security of the army in his command, divided as it was into three large bodies in New York, Virginia, and the Carolinas. Clinton knew that the existence of these forces hung upon the slender thread of naval superiority; if the command of the sea were ever wrested from Great Britain, he said, "all our golden dreams will vanish" in ruin and defeat. As long as the French maintained a strong squadron at Newport, Rhode Island, and the British fleet was strung out from Nova Scotia to the West Indies, Clinton could enjoy no peace of mind. In June 1781, he pointed out to the home government that a French fleet of ten ships of the line in addition to the ships already at Newport would give the French control of the sea.

Despite his age and infirmities, Arbuthnot saw the menace created by De Grasse's presence in the West Indies more clearly than did younger and more active British naval officers. When it was pointed out to the old admiral that De Grasse and Barras (Commander of the French fleet at Newport) would probably attempt to unite their forces in United States waters during the autumn, he declared that it was impossible "for the Commander in Chief of the British fleet in the West Indies (be his Vigilance ever so great) to procure so early Intelligence of the Enemy's departure as to be able to send a reinforcement to this Country in time enough to be here before them." He warned that De Grasse would enjoy decisive superiority over the British fleet in United States waters and that the Chesapeake was one of the most vulnerable spots upon the chessboard of war. But Arbuthnot, in the summer of 1781, was succeeded in command by Admiral Graves, and Clinton breathed a sigh of relief upon being freed from the old man of the sea.

Admiral Graves took lightly the French threat to British naval supremacy. In August 1781, for example, he assured Clinton that the reports that a French fleet was on its way to the United States were probably the work of "a heated imagination." From the letters intercepted from the French, Graves knew that a strong naval armament was to sail north from the West Indies, but he wrote this off as French gasconading. "I conclude upon the whole that something is intended and much more talked of," he remarked.[5] As for the British troops in the Chesapeake, they were in no danger whatever he assured Clinton; cruisers had been stationed for their protection — and, in any event, if the French came to United States waters, was it not well known that their destination was New York?

Upon Clinton, the breezy self-assurance of Admiral Graves had the effect of lulling his apprehensions. Assured of the safety of Cornwallis and his troops, and certain that the French, if they came, would strike at

[5] In this connection, Graves wrote Clinton: "We are told that some of the Rhode Island squadron are going to Europe, which will necessarily call for some fresh ships here." But that De Grasse would come northward with a fleet larger than any the British could command against him, Graves did not believe. Admiral Graves to General Clinton. August 18, 1781. Clinton MSS. Clements Library.

New York, Clinton gave little further thought to the Chesapeake. He regretted only that he had not drawn more troops from Cornwallis to
reinforce New York, because in August 1781 he saw opening before him
an unexpected opportunity to deal the French forces in North America
a stunning blow.

Although largely neutralized by superior British sea power, the French
squadron at Newport was a constant menace to the far-flung British
supply lines, for, could it break out into the Atlantic as it had in March
1781, serious damage might be done British military operations upon the
continent. Clinton was eager to eliminate this thorn in his flesh and, at last
given an admiral with whom he could work in harmony, he saw his
opportunity. To co-operate with the Americans in the expected attack
upon New York, the French troops had been withdrawn from Newport,
leaving only a weak force of French regulars and American militia to
protect the fleet from a land attack. Clinton and Graves determined to
exploit this advantage by launching a combined land and sea attack upon
Newport. To that end, in August 1781, three thousand men were placed
aboard transports and the British fleet was prepared for action. By the
first of September, everything was in readiness: at the first favorable wind
Clinton and Graves were prepared to descend upon Newport and annihilate the French fleet.[6]

By this means, Clinton and Graves hoped to break up the Franco-
American attack upon New York before it could begin. Knowing that
the French fleet at Newport was expected to play an important part in
that operation, they set out to weaken French naval power to such a
degree that De Grasse and Washington would be forced to abandon the
assault upon New York City. In all their calculations, it will be seen, the
British commanders thought of the security of New York; for them, the
Chesapeake had ceased to be a theater of operations — indeed, it had
almost completely dropped beyond their horizon, and Cornwallis and
his seven thousand men were hardly more than spectators of the impending engagement in the North.

Clinton and Graves could undertake such an enterprise because they
felt sure of their continued command of the sea. From every quarter,
Clinton had been told that he need not worry about De Grasse, who,
from the latest information, was being carefully watched by the British
commanders in the West Indies.[7] Much of Clinton's earlier alarm had

[6] That there was sound military policy behind Clinton's intended attack upon
Rhode Island is seen from the remark of the Duc de Lauzun: "After the departure
of the army, it would have been sufficient to attack the French squadron at Rhode
Island to destroy it."

[7] Germain, for example, told Clinton that he had nothing to fear from De Grasse.
"As Sir George Rodney's Force is but little inferior to his [De Grasse's fleet]," wrote
the British minister, "and he will be watchful of his motions, I am not apprehensive
he will give him time to do you any material injury before he comes to your succour."

therefore subsided; for the first time in many months, he began to feel cheerful about his prospects. Every day that passed without news of De Grasse strengthened the British commander's confidence that the American war might yet be brought to a glorious end.

Clinton quickly learned the error of giving way, even momentarily, to optimism. On August 28, 1781, the British fleet under Hood which had left the West Indies in pursuit of De Grasse arrived at New York. Clinton at first supposed that this was a stroke of good fortune — he could use Hood's fleet on the expedition against Newport. But this hope was dashed when, on the evening of the same day that Hood sailed into New York, word was received that the French squadron had left Newport three days before and was now on the high seas. Without the French fleet, Newport was hardly a prize; so Clinton dropped all thought of an attack upon Rhode Island.

For Clinton, this was only the beginning of a series of blows of fortune. The escape from Newport of the French squadron under Barras was an important link in the chain of events that led to Cornwallis's surrender at Yorktown. Yet Clinton was at this time alarmed only for New York; Barras, he feared, would join the French fleet under De Grasse coming up from the West Indies and their combined strength would be thrown against the British army and fleet in New York.

Clinton did not yet know the worst. While he fretted over the safety of New York, the American and French armies began their march to the Chesapeake. The American general tried to create the impression that he was marching to Sandy Hook to meet the French fleet, and Clinton was completely taken in. Even when an American girl, the mistress of Colonel Rochambeau (the son of Count Rochambeau, the French commander), told a British spy that the French troops were marching to the Chesapeake, Clinton scoffed at such idle tales. Deserters from the American army informed the British as early as August 20 that Washington had given orders to cross the Hudson; and although some British officers believed that this indicated that the Americans were bound for the Chesapeake, Clinton retorted that it meant merely that Washington was going to his old headquarters at Morristown. New York was Washington's objective, and Clinton would credit no information to the contrary.

It was not until September 1, 1781, that it dawned upon Clinton that Washington was by-passing New York and that Cornwallis was in danger. Against this eventuality, Clinton had made few preparations: seldom has a British commander been caught more flat-footed.

As yet unknown to Clinton, De Grasse had sailed directly to the Chesapeake, arriving off that estuary on August 30. On September 1, about four thousand French troops were landed near Yorktown to aid Lafayette in preventing Cornwallis from retreating to the Carolinas before the

arrival of Rochambeau and Washington with the allied army closed the
trap upon the British commander.

Seeking Barras and the French squadron from Rhode Island, Admiral
Graves sailed early in September to the Chesapeake where, although there
was no sign of Barras, the British did find De Grasse's fleet of twenty-eight
ships of the line. Graves had only nineteen ships of the line. The odds
were more than Graves had bargained for, but before he had recovered
from his shock the French were upon him. The two fleets fought an
indecisive action off the Capes of the Chesapeake. It was, reported Graves,
"a pretty sharp brush" but it ended with the British sustaining more
damage than did the French and with the British limping back to New
York. During this engagement, Barras with eight ships of the line from
Rhode Island, carrying siege artillery to the French army, slipped into
the Chesapeake, where he joined De Grasse and thereby further upset the
balance of sea power to the disadvantage of the British. Now, for the
first time, allied strategy became clear to Clinton: Cornwallis was to be
invested by land and sea while New York and the main British army
were left undisturbed. The revelation did not come to Clinton until after
the French had gained command of the sea and Cornwallis was in desperate danger.

Meanwhile the French and Americans crossed the Hudson and began
to move across New Jersey. The destination was kept secret even from
the men: it was not until September 5, when the army lay at Chester,
Pennsylvania, that Washington, learning that De Grasse had actually
arrived in the Chesapeake, let it be known that they were on their way
to Yorktown.

Although ten lovesick French soldiers had to be forcibly removed from
their sweethearts at Newport, the French army marched to Virginia
without incident: during the long trek, the French troops preserved
perfect order and discipline — "a prodigy," said the Duc de Lauzun,
"which neither the English, nor the American army, had ever given an
example of." As they swung down the streets of Philadelphia, lined on
every side with spectators, past the State House where members of Congress stood at the door, Rochambeau ordered his men "to salute Congress
as a crowned head, and the President as the first prince of the blood." It
would not have been surprising had several congressmen dropped in a
dead faint at this demonstration: Congress, in these days, seldom received
such honors. The smart military appearance and exemplary behavior of
the French troops greatly impressed Americans and revealed how futile
were British hopes that the alliance would be ruptured by national and
religious discord. "The French are the finest body of troops I ever
viewed," said Anthony Wayne, "and harmony and friendship pervades
the whole." At the French camp, the Americans were hospitably received.
"Officers, soldiers and Americans," said the Abbé Robin, "all mix and

dance together; it is the feast of equality; the first fruits of the Alliance which should reign between the nations."

For the American army, the march to Virginia proved almost as difficult as Washington had feared: although the heavy artillery (loaned to the Continental army by the New England states) and some of the troops were able to go down the Chesapeake by boat from Head of Elk, for most of the men it was hard going over bad roads and across unbridged rivers. These obstacles so greatly hindered the army that Washington began to fear that Cornwallis, profiting by the delay, might yet escape or strengthen his defenses to such an extent that the allies could not break through. Food, as usual, was scarce; the French troops, for the first time, began to experience the hardships incidental to campaigning in the United States.

Early in September, Washington and Rochambeau reached Yorktown, where Lafayette and the troops landed by De Grasse hemmed in Cornwallis. The first Americans to make contact with the French found themselves "kissed by about 30 officers." Washington rode into camp without pomp or ceremony, attended only by a few horsemen, while Lafayette, who had long waited for this moment, "rode up with precipitation, clasped the General in his arms, and embraced him with an ardor not easily described." A few weeks later, on October 6, 1781, the Franco-American land forces began to move against Cornwallis's works.

In the meantime, Clinton was making frantic efforts to save Cornwallis from the forces that were closing in upon him. At first, he thought of making a diversionary attack upon Philadelphia in the hope of drawing Cornwallis's besiegers away from Yorktown, but the failure of Admiral Graves to prevent the junction of the fleets of De Grasse and Barras convinced him that anything short of direct aid to Cornwallis would be futile.

Clinton therefore worked feverishly to organize a rescue expedition but, as usual, he was obliged to wait upon the navy. The British had only twenty-three ships of the line, many in need of repairs, to send against the French fleet of thirty-seven ships of the line. In view of these odds, many naval officers were inclined to give up Cornwallis for lost. "The general conversation among them from the Captains downward," said a British officer, "is of the great superiority of the French fleet, the impossibility of destroying any of them by fireships, or forcing them in the position they have taken, and the certainty that they will come out immediately on the appearance of the British fleet." Everything conspired to retard the sailing of the fleet: there were shortages of ship stores, lumber, and ammunition, and in the midst of preparations Prince William, the son of George III, arrived in New York and two days were devoted to parties, parades, and receptions for the distinguished visitor. The troops were put aboard two weeks before the fleet was ready to sail. It was not until October 19 that the expedition finally put to sea — the day that Cornwallis surrendered at Yorktown.

These delays told heavily upon Clinton's already overtaxed nerves. The outcome of the war depended upon saving Cornwallis, and every day's passage made that hope more remote. Chafing at the slowness of the navy, Clinton at one time reconsidered his earlier plan of attacking Philadelphia in the hope of drawing the allied armies away from Cornwallis. He blamed Cornwallis bitterly for having brought this calamity upon British arms. His last act as commander, he told himself, would be to rescue his headstrong subordinate — then let Germain and Cornwallis conquer the Americans if they could. Yet, as the days passed without action, Clinton began to doubt that he would ever have the satisfaction of gloriously winding up his career in America. "I had," he wrote, "little more to expect in case of success than the saving part of his Lordship's troops with the loss of part of my own." Actually, nothing was either saved or lost: arriving off the Chesapeake on October 24, the British fleet and army turned back to New York upon learning that Cornwallis had surrendered five days before.

Instead of attempting to break out of the trap which he saw closing about him, Cornwallis chose to stand his ground at Yorktown. With the aid of some two thousand Negro slaves who had fled to his lines [8] he rushed work upon his fortifications at Gloucester and Yorktown. His position — on the tip of a peninsula almost surrounded by water — offered no hope of successful retreat once the allied army had laid siege: Cornwallis's only succor could come by sea. He trusted to British sea power to extricate him; confident that he would be relieved by an expeditionary force out of New York, he spurned suggestions of retreat.

For one who had won the name of a "modern Hannibal" and the reputation of being the hardest fighter among British generals, Cornwallis made a surprisingly weak defense of Yorktown. Although it had been said that he would never surrender as had Burgoyne — "he would rather die sword in hand" — Cornwallis offered less resistance than did Burgoyne and made no effort whatever to die gloriously. Instead of testing the gallantry of British troops in bold, spirited sorties, he made only one sally from his lines and that a trivial one. At the first appearance of the allied army he abandoned his outworks at Gloucester, leaving the enemy in possession of his redoubts, which they used for artillery emplacements. From this advanced ground they pounded the British lines with shells and mortars until Cornwallis was compelled to pull back his entire army to Yorktown. After seven days of trench warfare he was ready to quit — at least a week before the Americans had expected his surrender. When he ran up the white flag his works were still intact and he had a week's provisions on hand.

Cornwallis's halfhearted defense of Yorktown sank British military prestige among the Americans. The British fought well, remarked an

[8] Many of Washington's slaves ran away from Mount Vernon to join the British in the hope of gaining their freedom.

American soldier, "while there is a prospect of superiority; but losing this prospect, they do beg their lives with a meanness that would shock you. . . . All ranks of them discover a condescension and humility bordering on that of a Spaniel." The American Secretary of Foreign Affairs pronounced Cornwallis's defense "a most contemptible series of blunders" and declared that the best thing that could happen to the Americans would be to have him placed in future in command of the British army. On the other hand, Cornwallis was outnumbered two to one; his defenses were unfinished and constructed of fresh earth; the allies had heavy artillery and were in a position to open a flanking fire upon his lines; his troops had been pressed into a small area; and the prospect of relief which had prompted Cornwallis to maintain his position despite its disadvantages had grown dim. His position was not naturally strong — "nothing but the necessity of fortifying it as a post to protect the navy," he said, "could have induced any person to erect works upon it." But, had he held out a week longer, he would have stood a chance — albeit a slim one — of rescue by Clinton and the British fleet.

On October 19, 1781, the surrender took place at Yorktown. While Cornwallis sulked in his tent, leaving General O'Hara to conduct the distasteful formalities, the British marched out of their lines in military array, officers carrying their side arms, preceded by furled flags. The march played by the band was "The World Turned Upside Down." On either side of the British were their conquerors — French on the right and Americans on the left. The French troops, clothed in white regimentals, made an impressive military show; and even the Americans, at the head of whom stood Washington, Steuben, and Wayne, made a respectable appearance. The first line was composed of Continental troops most of whom were in uniform; but those who stood behind them were, said General Steuben, "but a ragged set of fellows, and very ill-looking." As they marched between these two lines, the British kept their eyes steadily turned toward the French: to surrender to French gentlemen was endurable, but to strike the flag to rebellious peasants was a humiliation not to be borne. Lafayette, however, did not spare Britons' sensibilities: he ordered the band to strike up "Yankee Doodle" to remind the vanquished Britons that this was an American as well as a French victory.

When the British troops reached the spot at which they were to surrender their arms, they cast them down violently. Up to this point, the allied soldiers had preserved perfect discipline, but when the British began the return march they were jeered at by the rebels in retaliation for the contempt they had shown the American army. British naval officers who surrendered to De Grasse were given a captain's guard of grenadiers to protect them from the insolence of the American soldiers, "who otherwise," said a British officer, "would have robbed us of the few things we had left at the end of the siege." Yet it is noteworthy that some Americans

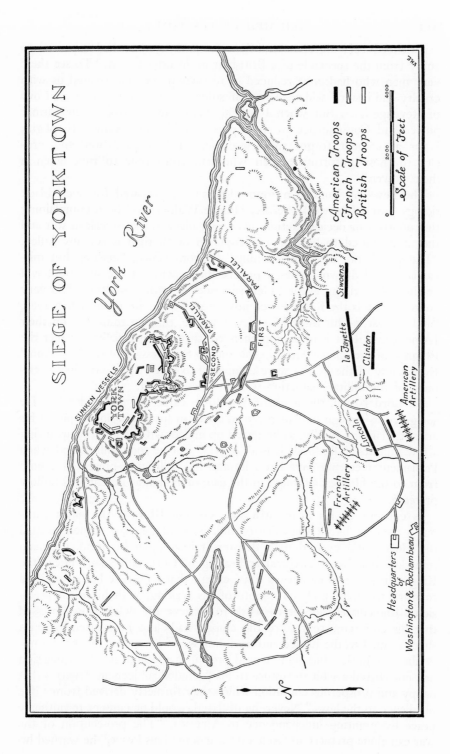

SIEGE OF YORKTOWN

York River

SUNKEN VESSELS

YORK TOWN

SECOND PARALLEL

FIRST PARALLEL

Siwoens

la Fayette

Clinton

Lincoln

American Artillery

French Artillery

Headquarters of Washington & Rochambeau

American Troops
French Troops
British Troops

Scale of Feet

0   2000   4000

experienced very different emotions from those they had expected to enjoy from the spectacle of a British army in utter defeat. "To see these very men who had once reduced us to their power and treated us with cruelty and insult," said an American soldier, "I was prompted by a Love of Revenge. . . . But when I beheld them reduced from their former power and Consequence to their present miserable melancholy plight, I for a moment forgot their insolence, their depredations and cruelty to those unfortunate men who had from time to time fallen in their power."

The news of Yorktown found England unprepared for such black tidings. Just a few weeks before, Horace Walpole had been complaining that no great or decisive actions ever took place in the American war and that it promised to bore more people to death than it actually killed. "The war is not even entertaining," he complained, "nothing but miscarriages and drawn battles. I believe the expense of the sum total will be the only striking event." Germain swelled with confidence. "So very contemptible is the Rebel Force now in all Parts," he remarked in 1781, "and so vast is Our Superiority everywhere, that no resistance on their [Americans'] Part is to be apprehended, that can materially obstruct the Progress of the King's Army in the Speedy Suppression of the Rebellion." Even many of the Whigs were compelled to agree that Germain's assessment of the military situation was for once correct.

To Lord North, the news of Yorktown came like a thunderclap. He staggered as though he had received a ball in his breast and "opened his arms, exclaiming wildly, as he paced up and down the apartment during a few minutes: 'Oh, God! it is all over!' " But he soon rallied, and when Parliament met two days later, he and his colleagues presented a bold front to the Houses, although in the case of North at least it was hollow pretense.

In contrast to his Prime Minister, George III took the news without a tremor: like a Crusader of old, he kept his face turned toward the Holy Land even though disasters rained upon his head. Germain remarked that immediately after hearing of Cornwallis's surrender "the King writes just as he always does, except that I observe he has omitted to mark the hour and the minute of his writing, with his usual precision." Immediately he set to work to retrieve the defeat; he confessed that his endeavors to restore the empire had "not been attended with success equal to the justice and uprightness" of his views, but he did not doubt that justice and right would prevail in the end; his determination had not abated a whit to restore to his "deluded subjects in America that happy and prosperous condition which they formerly derived from a due obedience to the laws." Never, he declared, would he consent to purchase peace by granting independence to America. "The prosecution of the war can alone preserve us from a most ignominious Peace," he warned his

countrymen; "if we recede no one can tell to what a degree the consequence of this country will be diminished."

George III was never greater than when confronting disaster: he was
the eternal Englishman, his back to the wall, fighting to the bitter end
for the survival of his country. The conservatism as well as the liberalism
of England has produced its heroes; nor was he the last renowned English Tory to rise to greatness in the face of defeat and overwhelming
odds.

In this crisis, the King turned to Benedict Arnold, who had come to
England after his forays in Connecticut. Arnold won the King's favor by
his advocacy of war to the death against the rebels: at the royal levee it
was observed that Arnold stood close to the King, and it was court gossip
that the American traitor might become the King's closest adviser. Certainly Arnold remained true to his new allegiance: Yorktown did not
shake his conviction that the war could be won if Great Britain would
but make another effort. Congress and the French, he asserted, were detested by the majority of the people — in short, he rehearsed all the arguments that for the past few years had kept Englishmen in the fight. The
Prince of Wales showed great admiration for Mrs. Arnold; but Arnold
did not stoop to the final ignominy of selling his wife, as he had sold his
country, for personal advancement.

Nevertheless, as the King had so often lamented, his subjects were not
made of the same stern stuff as was the royal person. Yorktown accomplished what no other defeat suffered since 1781 has done: convinced a
majority of Englishmen that they had lost a war. Taken with Burgoyne's
surrender, Yorktown drove home even to many of the most obstinate
supporters of the war the bitter realization that the colonies were not to
be reconquered by force; it seemed, it was said, "to have opened the eyes
of the blind themselves." For the edification of Englishmen, Franklin
pointed out that it was "a rare Circumstance, and scarce to be met with
in History, that in one War two Armies should be taken Prisoners completely, not a Man in either escaping." Even Henry "Starvation" Dundas,
a cabinet member who had won his nickname by his zeal to starve Bostonians into surrender in 1774, now publicly admitted that to send another
army to America would be to doom it to massacre or capture.

To the English Whigs, Yorktown was the finishing stroke to a war
which had been a disaster from beginning to end. Some even refused to
be cast down by an event which they had long predicted. "I cannot put
on the face of the day, and act grief," said Horace Walpole. "Whatever
puts an end to the American war will save the lives of thousands —
millions of money too." It promised also to bring down the Ministry and
put the Whigs in power: Lord Derby talked at Brooks's of "scaffolds for
the King, for his Ministers etc., as if he had nothing to do but to order
them."

Yorktown stirred up a bitter controversy over the question of responsibility for the disaster. Lord Sandwich whitewashed the Admiralty by remarking that "the hand of Providence did not seem to favour us," but this theory of divine accountability did not satisfy many Englishmen; and it is only fair to observe that when victory graced British arms, Lord Sandwich did not hesitate to take most of the credit upon himself, awarding the Almighty little more than honorable mention. The chief controversy, however, lay between Clinton and Cornwallis and their partisans. Clinton was charged with culpable neglect in permitting Washington and Rochambeau to by-pass him in New York; Cornwallis was denounced for having gone to Virginia without the approval of the commander-in-chief.[9]

In this controversy, Clinton came off second best. Cornwallis, whom Clinton held chiefly responsible for the disaster at Yorktown, was welcomed in England like a conquering hero, smiled upon by the court, awarded high honors, and given a new command. He lived to redeem his reputation and win the applause of his countrymen during the War of the French Revolution.

As for Clinton, he left for England early in 1782 "laughed at by the rebels, despised by the British, and cursed by the loyalists." There was no fanfare for him: only a handful of friends were on hand to bid him Godspeed, and his reception in England was on much the same scale. He quickly passed into that oblivion that usually swallows unfortunate generals: he was not even accorded the satisfaction of being called before Parliament to give his version of the defeat at Yorktown. As a matter of fact, he might have been killed in battle, for all that England heard of him; and indeed, there seems to have been a fairly general feeling that Clinton would have done better to have died sword in hand than to have returned to England after he had been beaten by rebels.

By the victory at Yorktown, said Franklin, "the infant Hercules in his Cradle has now strangled his second Serpent." But without the aid of his good friends the French it is evident that the infant Hercules might have furnished a tasty tidbit to the serpent. There were more French than Americans at Yorktown and twice as many French troops as Continentals; and without the presence of the French fleet the victory would not have been possible. At Saratoga, France furnished the guns and ammunition that led to Burgoyne's surrender; at Yorktown, it was French money, troops, and ships that brought Cornwallis to a like fate. As Anthony

[9] The Clinton-Cornwallis controversy might be thus summarized: Did Clinton consent to Cornwallis's march to Virginia? When Cornwallis arrived in the Chesapeake, ought Clinton to have strongly reinforced him, even, if necessary, abandoning New York to make the Chesapeake the principal theater of the war? Ought Clinton to have ordered Cornwallis back to Charleston or withdrawn the entire army to New York? Who was responsible for choosing Yorktown, admittedly an improper base, for Cornwallis's army? Could Cornwallis have conducted a better defense of Yorktown? Did Clinton devote all his efforts to rescuing Cornwallis?

Wayne wrote to a friend: "Believe me it was not to the exertions of America, that we owe the Reduction of this modern Hannibal, nor shall we always have it in our power to Command the aid of 37 Sail of the Line and 8000 Auxiliary Veterans." Perceiving these truths, the American Secretary of Foreign Affairs expressed his apprehensions lest the world draw the conclusion that Americans were "weak, divided and weary of the war and that they were content to receive their independence as a gift from their ally rather than to establish it by their own exertions."

CHAPTER XXIX

The Peace Settlement

DESPITE military defeats and diplomatic reverses that might easily have overturned another ministry, Lord North remained in power, picking his way from disaster to disaster. As the war spun itself out, North and his colleagues seemed riveted to their seats; through good news and bad, the Ministry stood firm, invulnerable to the slings and arrows of the opposition. Burke lamented that every event of the war, whether victory or defeat, the appointment of new generals or the recall of old generals, towns captured or towns surrendered, "all spurred us on to this fatal business. Victories gave us hopes, defeats made us desperate, and both instigated us to go on." "Everything has miscarried that has been undertaken," exclaimed Horace Walpole in 1779, "and the worse we succeed, the more is risked; — yet the nation is not angry."

Lord North owed his long tenure of power primarily to the determination of Englishmen to restore the revolted colonies to the empire. As the leader of the war party, North possessed the confidence of the country to a greater degree than did any Whig statesman; in general, Englishmen opened their hearts to the man who stood for the integrity of the British Empire against rebels and republicans. In his hours of discouragement — and they were many — Lord North took comfort in the reflection that there was "a very great majority of the nation at large, who were for prosecuting the war against our rebellious subjects in America"; he had not only the King, but the people, on his side.

At the beginning of the war, the Duke of Richmond had predicted that nothing except defeat and hardship would induce the people of Great Britain to make peace. "Injustice, rapine, murder, desolation, loss of liberty, all these we can inflict, or suffer our fellow-subjects to endure," he declared, "but when we are to pay, we shall grumble; . . . it will only be if our troops fail we shall feel the impracticability, absurdity, and wickedness of our present proceedings." The Duke's prophecy was borne out: what finally convinced Englishmen of the futility of continuing the struggle in America was not the eloquence of the Whigs but the ill-success and expense of the war.

After Yorktown, the hopes of the squires for an American revenue faded fast. Instead of easing their own burden by taxing the colonists, Englishmen were now confronted with the prospect of paying largely out of their own pockets the entire costs of the war, some one hundred and forty million pounds. Moreover, they had lost colonies which brought them a profit through commerce and trade of over a million pounds a year. All that the country gentlemen seemed destined to get from the struggle was pinched pocketbooks.

With the national debt almost doubled by the war, the navy weakened and undermanned, and the army thirty thousand men below its required strength, England seemed to have little choice but to abandon the war with the United States. On every side, the empire appeared to be crumbling to ruin; Minorca had been lost, Gibraltar was besieged, the British fleet in the West Indies was outnumbered by the French, and in India, Hyder Ali seemed on the point of driving the British from the country. Lord North would be remembered in history, said the Whigs, for having "in seven years, dismembered the most powerful state in the modern world."

Parliament reflected the chastened mood that had taken possession of the English people. The administration's parliamentary majorities steadily dwindled until finally, late in February, 1782, a motion to renounce all further efforts to subjugate the United States was adopted by the House of Commons. To all intents and purposes, the House had put an end to the American war.

Nothing more sorely taxed the King's fortitude than to see Englishmen throwing in the sponge; he could take defeats and even catastrophes in his stride, but he had always counted upon the bulldog courage of his countrymen to get the better of their enemies. Now, he found, Englishmen were sadly shrunken from the heroic stature they had attained in Elizabethan days. In his eyes, they had become merely the puny and ignoble shadows of their ancestors; indeed, George believed that his misfortunes were largely owing to the fact that he ruled over a singularly spineless generation of Englishmen. Public spirit, he complained, seemed "actually destroyed in this selfish and unprincipled age"; when unanimity alone could save the country, the people were divided and supine. The vote in Parliament demonstrated that the old fighting spirit had vanished from England, and this, more than anything else, convinced George that "it would be madness not to conclude Peace on the best possible Terms we can obtain."

One by one, the stalwarts of the administration began to drop away from Lord North. Lord Advocate Dundas resigned and was rewarded for his services with a pension of six thousand pounds a year. Lord George Germain, unnerved by defeat, had lost, it was remarked, "the only good part of his speaking, his arrogance and presumption," and now displayed a quite unaccustomed humility. He resigned early in 1782 receiving as reward the title of Lord Sackville — which prompted Burke to ask sarcastically: "What had the American war produced? What but peerages and calamities?" Lord Sandwich, likewise, was in low spirits; he appeared "near to death with fatigue and mortification." Some said that his perturbation was owing to the many attacks made upon him by the Whigs and the prospect of a naval inquiry by Parliament, but gossip reported that it was owing to "some attacks of his Lordship above the rate of his vigor." In any event, Sandwich informed the King that his ability to do "any service to this distressed country" was at an end and that he, too, must leave the government.

In this crisis, the King clung to Lord North with an affection dismaying to the bewildered Prime Minister. As the specter of a Whig ministry loomed ever larger, the more ardent became George's affection for Lord North, his shield and bulwark against the enemies of kingly power. The Prime Minister began to fear that he would become the subject of a civil war — and all because the King did not know when it was time to drop his friends.

But even George III could not forever keep Lord North in power against the wishes of the Prime Minister himself and of the people of Great Britain. The parting had to come; from North's point of view, it was long overdue. In March 1782, the King permitted the Prime Minister to surrender the seals; and as a reward for his war leadership, North was given his heart's desire of the wardenship of the Cinque Ports — a sinecure which brought him four thousand pounds a year.

And, despite the threats of the Whigs, Lord North escaped punishment for his part in the American war. Obviously, if the Prime Minister were to stand trial, the King himself would be involved; and besides, it was impossible to bear a grudge against so good-natured a man as Lord North. Shortly after his fall from power, he attended the fete of the Prince of Wales, dressed in blue and buff, and surrounded by the very men who a few months before had been clamoring for his head. "They now crowded round him," it was observed, "to admire the sallies of his wit, or to applaud the playful charms of his conversation."

Yet even after he had sacrificed North to harsh necessity, George could not bring himself to call in the Whigs. He had always believed that the opposition was resolved to reduce him to a cipher in the government; men who were willing to tear down the empire in order to humble the pride of kings were not likely, he judged, to leave him a shred of power once he was at their mercy. Although he struggled against his fate and risked plunging the country into chaos by his long delay in summoning the Whigs to form a government, he could not avert the inevitable. In April 1782, Lord Rockingham and Lord Shelburne formed a cabinet and the Whigs cast off their blue and buff uniforms to don the swords, lace, and hair powder of courtiers. Thus, said the Whigs, did the monarch submit "to the hard necessity of taking for his Ministers the most virtuous set of public men that ever appeared in this country." But George III always regarded it as "the fatal day" when he was delivered into the hands of his enemies.

The King was spared no humiliation: he was obliged to accept his worst enemy, Charles James Fox, as a cabinet minister. Fox, the King had learned from long and painful experience, was as troublesome as any American republican and a great deal more difficult to bear since he was not, unhappily, three thousand miles across the Atlantic; for his part, Fox compared the monarch to Satan — "a comparison, which," it was observed, "he seems fond of," although it could hardly be said to be original, the Americans having frequently pointed out the resemblance. The King and the cabinet minister remained at swords' points; at the royal levee, when Fox presented to the sovereign an address from Westminster, "the King took it out of his hand without deigning to give him a look even, or a word; he took it as you would take a pocket handkerchief from your *valet de chambre* . . . and passed it to his Lord-in-waiting."

Fox, however, bore up bravely under the monarch's displeasure and applied himself diligently to business, to the joy of friends who believed that this regimen of hard work might "preserve his life, which his former dissipation constantly endangered." The responsibilities and cares of office were as nothing compared with the debilitating effects of the gaming, slow horses, and fast women with which Fox had hitherto busied himself.

In accordance with their promises, the first step of the Whigs was to open peace negotiations with the Americans. In this, however, they had been anticipated by Lord North; moreover, England's position at the peace table had been greatly strengthened by a naval victory for which Lord North was in part responsible.

Yorktown seemed to be merely the beginning of a series of disasters that would strip Great Britain of the last shreds of empire. "One Battle at Sea," Franklin had warned, "their Credit is gone, and their Power follows." The West Indies lay at the mercy of De Grasse's victorious fleet — "and it is their [the French government's] fault," said an Englishman, "if any possessions whatever, either in North America or in the West Indies, remain under the British Empire."

De Grasse remained in the United States only until Cornwallis had been brought to surrender. At the beginning of the siege, he had informed

Washington that he must return to the West Indies by the middle of October, thus giving the American commander-in-chief six weeks of grace to dispose of Cornwallis. He was as good as his word: after the capitulation, Washington urged De Grasse to join the Franco-American army in an attack upon Charleston — a measure which if successful would have broken the British hold upon the Southern states — but De Grasse politely explained that he was already overdue and that his obligations to the Spaniards and the orders of his government compelled him to return to the West Indies and join in the attack upon Jamaica. As a result, except for two frigates left to protect the French troops at Yorktown, there was hardly a French warship in United States waters by November 1781; the British navy ruled the coasts of the republic almost as absolutely as before. Washington therefore relinquished any ideas of operations in the Southern states; without the aid of the French navy there would be no more Yorktowns in the war. "A constant Naval superiority would terminate the War speedily," he said; "without it, I do not know that it will ever be terminated honourably."

In the West Indies, De Grasse gave the hard-pressed British no respite. Three islands fell in quick succession to the French fleet, and early in 1782 the French and Spaniards prepared to attack Jamaica, the largest British possession in the Caribbean. But Rodney came to the rescue, and the celerity with which he acted made Englishmen regret the keener that their fighting admiral had not been in action the previous year when Cornwallis was hemmed in at Yorktown. His health restored by an operation and the waters of Bath, Rodney, in April 1782, defeated the French fleet, took De Grasse himself prisoner, and saved Jamaica. Although the Battle of the Saints was far from a crushing victory over the French fleet, it brought the war to a close in North America in a burst of glory for the British navy and put an end to French hopes of dictating peace to a beaten England. As for Rodney, his grateful countrymen forgot his equivocal conduct at St. Eustatius and he was raised to the peerage.

In India, likewise, the fortunes of war favored the British. By 1779, Warren Hastings had conquered the last French stronghold in India, giving Horace Walpole occasion to remark that "while we break in Europe, we may pack up and remove to India, and be emperors again!" [1] Vergennes, however, was not willing to leave the British in undisturbed possession of the riches of the East; he was well aware that India was a prize of war which might prove the decisive element in the struggle

[1] India was at this time under the jurisdiction of the East India Company rather than of the British government itself. Burke and other Whigs opposed all efforts to bring India under the direct rule of the British Crown. "I fear," said Burke, "if our East India possessions are to come under the patronage of the Crown, and are to be governed as a military province, that they will follow the fate of our dominions in the West, and will finally be wrested from this country."

between France and England for mastery. A large French fleet was dispatched to wrest control of India from the British. The French succeeded for a short time in gaining control of the sea, but they were unable to exploit their advantage. At almost the same time the British were confronted by a formidable rebellion led by Hyder Ali. This danger was likewise surmounted, and by the end of 1782 the British were more firmly planted in India than before.[2]

Lord North, having served seven years as a war minister, was prepared to essay the role of peacemaker. An emissary was dispatched to Franklin in Paris, and John Bull dropped his grim and forbidding visage and became again, for Americans' benefit, the hearty, good-humored, beef-eating, somewhat bumbling old gentleman they had known in colonial days. It was a quick change, but hardly convincing to a people fed upon British atrocities for seven years. Moreover, the presence of Lord North was certain to curdle any peace negotiations with which he was connected. Nevertheless, the Prime Minister believed himself eminently qualified to restore peace to the empire; and he vigorously pursued this objective until his activities were abruptly terminated, in March 1782, by his fall from power.

The Whig government that came into power in April 1782 was an uneasy coalition of factions, and from its advent it was racked by the jealousy and quarrels of its leaders, Rockingham, Shelburne, and Fox. Fox and Shelburne in particular jostled each other as they struggled to bring the peace negotiations under the control of their respective departments. Despite friction in the cabinet, England was now committed to peace with the United States, and the negotiations begun by North were pushed forward without remission.

Since 1778, Great Britain had left no stone unturned to destroy the "unnatural alliance" between France and the United States. Lord North declared in Parliament that "there was nothing he more ardently sought than to disunite France and America, and that he should use every effort in his power to effect it consistent with the interests of the empire, and the dignity of a great nation." It was difficult for Englishmen to believe that France would supersede them in the affections of their erstwhile colonists. Religious and ideological differences militated against a permanent union of the two countries unless, as some Britons feared, the United States had become a strumpet, picked up promiscuously by Frenchmen, Dutchmen, and Spaniards. In that case, the United States would find herself "a common prostitute in the world, where those who

[2] "By mismanagement we may lose the empire of India as speedily as we conquered it by accident," wrote Alexander Macaulay in 1783. "There never was a national object that required and deserved more serious consideration and dispassionate decisions than the manner in which we are to secure and govern India, and I hope in God we shall deal no longer in temporary expedients and dangerous experiments."

might seduce her, after she had served their turn, would naturally leave her to her fate, when it would be too late to return to her old and steady friend JOHN BULL." However, the zeal with which John Bull continued to prosecute the war suggested that he was ready to take back America, tarnished virtue and all.[3]

Those who dwelt upon the incompatibility of France and the United States overlooked the fact that the Puritans of Cromwell's England had allied themselves with France and that, when necessity prompted, the Bourbon kingdom had joined hands with Lutherans and Mohammedans. During the period of the American Revolution, His Most Christian Majesty was allied with Sweden, one of the most staunchly Protestant countries of Europe. Obviously, expediency was a higher law in Bourbon councils than religious or ideological differences. As for religion's serving as a bond between America and Great Britain, John Adams observed that there was "not enough of religion of any kind to make the Americans very fond of them. . . . What religion there is in England, is as far from being the religion of America as that of France."

The objective of the British government was to make a separate peace with either France or the United States; it little mattered which power made peace so long as it acted independently of the other and thereby broke the alliance that had been forged against Great Britain. To this end, the government approached both France and the United States with peace offers — making it clear to each that only by selling out the other could it reap the full reward of Britain's generosity.

But the French disdained the lure: they would enter into no peace negotiations that did not include the United States as a full partner in the treaty. If the British truly wanted to make peace with the United States, Vergennes advised them to go to the American commissioners in Paris — they alone were authorized to act for the United States. France would never talk terms with the British behind the back of her ally. In this unequivocal manner, Vergennes rebuffed the British emissaries and they left Versailles convinced that a separate peace could not be effected there.

Vergennes suspected that the British, rebuffed in their efforts to make peace with France, would turn to the United States; accordingly, he informed Franklin of the British overtures and warned him to be on his

[3] Likewise, the American Loyalists had screamed that this "unnatural alliance with perfidious Frenchmen" was designed to bring about "the universal re-establishment of Popery through all Christendom." By 1789, they predicted, the Inquisition would be firmly established in the United States; the country would be swarming with priests and friars; the Old South Meeting House in Boston would be converted into a Romanist cathedral, and the other meetinghouses would be made convents; Sam Adams would enter the priesthood and preside over the autos-da-fé celebrated in Boston. In preparation for this career, Adams was said to be boning up on the works of Ignatius Loyola.

guard against the honeyed words of British agents. No doubt, the French minister delighted in taking this opportunity to prove how open and straightforward was the conduct of the French government towards its ally. Franklin reciprocated by telling Vergennes that he, too, had been approached by enemy agents; and the two men again pledged themselves never to make a separate peace. Thus, in April 1782, the alliance seemed to be firmly cemented; there was hardly a crack through which the British could insinuate a peace feeler.

Nevertheless, Dr. Franklin did not slam the door completely upon these British overtures. Although he turned a cold shoulder upon the idea of a separate peace, Franklin seemed willing to talk peace without the participation of the French, and to British agents he employed the word "reconciliation" in speaking of Anglo-American relations. "I do not cease to try what can be done with Franklin," wrote a British agent in Paris, "and though he never gives any hope of a separate treaty which might detach them from France, he certainly expresses every intention and wish of making a solid union."

Franklin already had Vergennes's consent to opening peace discussions with the British — the French minister had, in fact, referred the British agents to Franklin when they proposed a separate peace to France. "You will treat for yourselves," the French minister told Franklin at this time, "and every one of the powers at war with England will make its own treaty. All that is necessary for our common security is that the treaties go hand in hand and are signed all on the same day." Vergennes claimed no right of negotiating for the Americans; he hoped, rather, to superintend the various peace discussions being held in France between the British, on the one hand, and the allied powers on the other. The Americans were to be free to deal directly with the British; but they were expected to keep the French government informed of developments and to ask its advice upon all important matters.

As has been seen, the American commissioners were obliged by the instructions of June 1781 to consult with and to be guided by the French court in all matters pertaining to the peace negotiations. Vergennes was to be a sort of father confessor to the American diplomats. What raised British hopes of making a separate peace with the United States was Franklin's profession of willingness to conduct peace talks *in secret*, although by so doing he violated his instructions and broke his word to Vergennes. If Franklin would go that far, perhaps he could be persuaded to go all the way and make a separate peace with Great Britain.

This, no doubt, was the impression Franklin wished to convey. He was well aware of the eagerness of the British to detach the United States from France and he believed that they might be persuaded to pay a high price in the form of territorial concessions. In short, much advantage might be gained by playing upon Britons' weaknesses; but that Franklin would have gone the length of jeopardizing the French alliance is extremely unlikely. At no time did he utter a word against France to the British negotiators; if he had any doubts of France's good intentions towards the United States, he kept them strictly to himself.

After the French alliance was safely in his pocket, it had no more ardent defender than Benjamin Franklin. He devoted himself to persuading his countrymen that their security depended upon maintaining the entente with France inviolate; John Bull, he said, was America's most dreaded enemy but the United States had happily made an alliance "that will help to keep the Bull quiet and make him orderly." Franklin felt a romantic regard for "our first and our faithful Friend." There was hardly an American, he said, who would not "spurn at the Thought of deserting a noble and generous Friend, for the sake of a Truce with an unjust and cruel Enemy." Such treachery would cost the United States its honor among nations; none would ever again aid the republic in its hour of necessity. If Congress ordered him to commit such perfidy, Franklin declared that he would immediately resign his position and never set foot again in so infamous a country.

Franklin looked beyond the Franco-American alliance to a world organized for peace. To establish machinery for the peaceful arbitration of disputes between nations was his ultimate goal, and as the first step in this direction he urged the formation of a "family compact" between Great Britain, the United States, and France.[4] Despite the fact that the United States had made good its independence by war, Franklin considered that wars were "Follies, very expensive, and very mischievous," and it grieved him to see nations wasting their resources in senseless and unprofitable wars when they might be increasing their wealth and the happiness of mankind by constructing bridges, roads, canals, and other public works. "There hardly ever existed such a thing as a bad Peace, or, a good War," he declared. Mankind's greatest problem, he believed, was "the Discovery of a Plan, that would induce and oblige Nations to settle their Disputes without first Cutting one another's Throats"; he prayed that "men would cease to be Wolves to one another, and that human Beings would at length learn what they now improperly called Humanity!"

In 1782, therefore, he hoped to make an enduring peace and to eradicate "the idea of any nations being natural enemies to each other." Yet privately he feared that the British, of all nations, would be the least

---

[4] "I am convinced that the chief reason why Dr. Franklin wishes for reconciliation [with Great Britain]," wrote Benjamin Vaughan in 1782, "is that America may be kept out of all wars. For if England disarms herself, America need not fear England, and not fearing England she need not cultivate France; and as a lover of Mankind, the Dr. may be happy in thinking that when England and France lose this Motive for War, their Wars may be less frequent." Benjamin Vaughan to Shelburne, August 6, 1782. Vaughan MSS. Clements Library.

amenable to the doctrine of peace on earth and good will to men; even though they were beaten, he pointed out, "a little success may make them as insolent as ever." The British had to be thoroughly humbled before they would become good neighbors. "I remember that, when I was a boxing boy," said Franklin, "it was allowed, even after an adversary said he had enough, to give him a rising blow. Let ours be a douser." Such sentiments were hardly calculated to give comfort to the British in their efforts to wean the old philosopher from his love of France.

Divested of all the subterfuge to which Franklin was addicted, his purpose was to extract concessions from the British by dangling before them the hope of reconciliation. If Englishmen were sufficiently generous, he seemed to be saying, Americans might be persuaded to forgive them for having begun an unjust war and waged it with unexampled barbarity. To the British commissioners he "expressed himself in a friendly way towards England, and was not without hopes that if We should settle on this occasion in the way he wished, England would not only have a beneficial Intercourse with the Colonies, but at last it might end in a federal Union between them." But this, he made clear, must be left to time and to the magnanimity of the British.

Charles James Fox was so elated by Franklin's conciliatory attitude that he began to talk of making a separate peace with the United States and employing the British army in New York against France and Spain in the West Indies — a favorite project of that stout foe of the Bourbons. Fox ardently urged an Anglo-American alliance. "Through that alliance," he predicted, "the sun of Britain might rise again, and shine forth with dazzling lustre." [5]

Still, as Franklin took pains to point out, the affections of America were not to be bought cheaply. The memory of the war and its atrocities could not be erased without heavy cost to the remainder of the British Empire. The restoration of Canada, the fisheries, an admission of war guilt, and many of the privileges in empire trade Americans had enjoyed prior to the Revolution — these were the price of Anglo-American amity. If Great Britain yielded these points, then, said Poor Richard, Americans might again hold in esteem the people they had been calling "butchers" and "barbarians" for the past seven years and they might, in time, admit Great Britain to the circle of civilized nations.

Franklin had long yearned to bring Canada into the fold. In 1776, he had gone to Canada as a member of a congressional committee in the hope

[5] Fox assumed that Americans would always remain farmers and consumers of British manufactures; politically independent of Great Britain, they would be economically dependent upon the former mother country. British manufacturers and merchants, therefore, might continue to eat the colonial cake without being obliged to pay for it in the form of taxes for imperial defense. America, he predicted, "might, in some future and distant period, be the Arcadia, but could never be the Britain of the world."

of restoring by diplomacy the losses incurred by military defeat, and he had never been reconciled to the failure of that mission. Canada, he knew, would be writ upon many American hearts and upon his own not least of all. Now, in the peace negotiations of 1782, he plunged into an experiment comparable to his feat of drawing lightning from the clouds: drawing Canada out of the British Empire and at the same time making the British enjoy presenting the United States with the gift. He made the restoration of Canada appear to be an act of wisdom on Britain's part — a step toward reconciliation with the United States which would help materially toward wiping out memories of the war. The British must expect to pay heavily for American good will, Franklin argued, because of the barbarous manner in which they had waged war; the surrender of Canada was no more than fair reparation for the devastation wrought by the British army in the United States. Moreover, such atonement on the part of the former mother country would ensure peace: if Great Britain held no territory on the continent of North America there would be little likelihood of future wars between the two countries. On the other hand, if England chose to keep Canada, Anglo-American reconciliation would be impossible; the United States would cling more closely than ever to France to defend itself against British wars of aggression.

As Franklin knew, France had always opposed the cession of Canada to the United States and was not likely to look with favor upon his attempt to carry off that province in the peace negotiations. Therefore, he discreetly concealed his plans from Vergennes; when he gave his peace terms to Richard Oswald, the British agent appointed by Shelburne to conduct negotiations, he did so "with many precautions, for fear of its being known to the French court, to whom it was supposed not to be agreeable." To carry off Canada from under the noses of the French ministers necessitated the greatest skill and circumspection, but it was the kind of game Franklin loved and in which he had yet to meet his match. No one knew better than did Poor Richard how to play the game of diplomacy with his cards close to his chest and a bland, innocent expression on his face.

If the cession of Canada was known to be disagreeable to France, it might be supposed to be downright insupportable to Englishmen. Having lost thirteen colonies, they were now asked to throw in a fourteenth for good measure. Nevertheless, Franklin so succeeded in convincing Oswald of the necessity of ceding Canada in the interests of Anglo-American amity that the British agent undertook to urge this measure upon Rockingham, Shelburne, and Fox.[6] Rockingham and Shelburne

---

[6] David Hartley, the British commissioner in charge of making the definitive treaty of peace with the Americans, advocated giving Canada to the United States in the interests of Anglo-American friendship. "After that [the cession of Canada]," he observed, "common reason assures, that for their own security, they must desire the

seemed not averse, but Fox was thunderstruck at the idea of purchasing American friendship by such a princely gift.

That Franklin could have made off with Canada while Shelburne and Rockingham were in this benevolent and openhanded frame of mind seems improbable. Since the beginning of the peace negotiations, the British military position had steadily improved. The siege of Gibraltar had been raised, and in the West Indies De Grasse, the conqueror of Cornwallis, had come to grief at the hands of Rodney and had been brought to England as a captive. The struggle seemed to be following the usual course of England's wars: after suffering heavy losses and grievous reverses in the field, the islanders were staging a fighting comeback that in the last round promised to lay their adversaries low. Except upon the American continent, the war had never looked brighter for the British, and in May 1782 the British cabinet, its hopes bolstered by these favorable developments, decided against surrendering Canada. As John Adams had often warned, victory was certain to stiffen the backs of Britons; now, in 1782, he gave up all hope of making peace until final and irretrievable disaster had overtaken them. "The persevering Obstinacy of the King, the wickedness of his Ministry, and the haughty Pride of the Nation" inflamed by victory, he pointed out, made peace remote. And Franklin had not yet broached the subject that later was almost to break up the peace conference — the compensation of the Loyalists.

In July 1782, Lord Rockingham died and Shelburne succeeded as Prime Minister. With these events, the Whig government dissolved into its component factions: Fox, unable to endure the command of Shelburne, "the Jesuit of Berkeley Square," resigned office and went into opposition, where he held forth in such unbridled language against his former colleague that it was expected that the two would shortly meet in Hyde Park to settle their differences in the manner of gentlemen. Out of office, Fox reverted to his earlier untidiness in dress. "His bristly, black person, and shagged breast quite open and rarely purified by any ablutions," remarked a friend, "was wrapped in a foul linen nightgown, and his bushy hair dishevelled." He consoled himself for his political reverses by taking as mistress Perdita Robinson, an actress fresh from a conquest of the Prince of Wales and other less notable personages. Fox's friends mourned his backsliding. "Who should the *Man of the People* live with," they asked, "but with the *Woman of the People?*"

Of all the Whigs, Lord Shelburne was by far the least objectionable to the King. Shelburne, the devoted follower of Lord Chatham, shared the monarch's views regarding the inviolability of the empire and was not so ardent as were Burke and Fox in demanding reform. The new

alliance and friendship of the only power who can in any degree be a terror or restraint to them." David Hartley to Fox, June 5, 1783, Hartley MSS. Clements Library.

Prime Minister, for his part, found that the King, when viewed from the perspective of the cabinet, appeared very different than when seen from the opposition benches; he was amazed, he declared, "at the genius he found in the King!"

The monarch, reluctantly persuaded of the necessity of recognizing American independence, hoped to make such recognition the price of a peace otherwise advantageous to Great Britain. To acknowledge American independence without exacting concessions in return was, in George's opinion, to "give everything without any return and then receive Peace if America will grant it." The King hoped to make France as well as the United States pay for American freedom, but he dreaded the prospect of sitting down to a peace table with those sinister customers, Vergennes and Franklin. Of France, he said that England had "never known how to treat with that crafty Nation." As for Franklin, the King had learned to hold him in respect and he greatly feared that in dealing with him Englishmen would be overreached. From the beginning of the war, said George III, England had piled mistake upon mistake, "whilst caution and system have been those of Dr. Franklin."

George might have set his fears at rest: the conduct of Franklin's own colleagues as well as the fortunes of war were working against his efforts to make Canada the fourteenth state. He was, in fact, never given a chance to show what his secret diplomacy could do, because in the midst of his negotiations with the British, John Jay stormed upon the scene very much like the proverbial bull in the china shop. Amid the clattering of crockery, the French alliance itself was in danger of being smashed. It required all Franklin's skill to keep that precious vessel from being broken beyond repair; despite all his precautions, it received several serious cracks. And while he was frantically attempting to save the alliance, Canada was irrevocably lost.

The disadvantages of fighting a war of coalition were never more evident than in making peace. The allies, fighting for different, and sometimes conflicting, objectives, were in peril of falling out over the terms for ending the struggle. If it had been difficult for the alliance to wage war effectively, it was found almost impossible to make peace harmoniously. Suspicion and distrust had eaten deeply into the coalition; as a result, when the peacemakers convened in Paris in 1782, the atmosphere was poisonous with jealousy and secret hates.

Up to this time, the British government had made no move to recognize the independence of the United States. The commission under which Richard Oswald entered into negotiations with the American commissioners scrupulously refrained from mentioning the *United States;* Oswald was empowered only to discuss peace terms with commissioners representing the *colonies.* Franklin had no objection to humoring Englishmen's reluctance to down the bitter pill; Canada was surely worth a little sacrifice of ceremony. But to John Jay's mind, the British failure to acknowledge the United States by name indicated a plot to cheat his country of its independence: while the Ministry pulled the wool over the eyes of the Americans by pretending to draw up peace terms, it was preparing to crush the rebellion. Not until the British Ministry expressly recognized the independence of the United States would John Jay consent to negotiate with the British emissaries in Paris.

If there was one thing upon which Vergennes had set his heart, it was to get the peace discussions started. (He did not know what a promising beginning the astute Dr. Franklin had already made in that direction.) Therefore, in the hope of speeding up the conferences, which according to the plan of procedure adopted by Versailles were to be held separately by the French, Spaniards, and Americans with British peace commissioners, he urged the Americans to negotiate with Oswald even though the British government still persisted in referring to the United States as "colonies." Fearing that the British would not agree to Jay's demand that the United States be expressly recognized as independent prior to treating, he foresaw endless delays and complications before the American commissioners could hope to carry their point. In this view Franklin agreed — he was willing to follow the advice of the French minister in the matter; but upon John Jay, Vergennes's counsel had a very different effect.

In Vergennes's advice to negotiate with the British without the formality of a prior acknowledgment of independence, John Jay discerned confirmation of his suspicions that France was working against the interests of the United States. Vergennes, he believed, was trying to delay, if not to defeat, American independence, and in this work he was hand in glove with the British.

Jay was doing the French statesman an injustice. Vergennes's only concern was to speed up the peace negotiations, not to defeat the aspiration of the United States for independence. Had Jay's suspicions ended there, Vergennes's good faith might have been quickly vindicated. But John Jay was not disposed to let the French minister off so easily: he believed that Vergennes was counterworking the United States in the fisheries, the western boundaries, and the matter of compensating the American Loyalists.

France, it has been seen, had a vital interest in the Newfoundland fishery, having been awarded by the Treaty of Utrecht (1713) the exclusive right of drying fish on a part of the Newfoundland coast. Now, in 1782, France made such extensive demands for fishing rights that George III began to fear that if the United States were also admitted, "between the two, poor England must have the worst share." Realizing that Great Britain was unlikely to gratify both France and the United States, Vergennes resolved to strengthen the position of his own country at the expense of its ally. Moreover, the French did not overlook the fact that the fisheries, if the United States were excluded from participation, might become a fertile source of future discord between Great Britain and the United States.

In September 1782, Vergennes sent his secretary, Rayneval, upon a secret mission to London. In his conference with Shelburne, Rayneval deliberately arrayed France against American claims to the fisheries and to the Mississippi River boundary; on the other hand, he insisted upon the surrender of Gibraltar to Spain. After Rayneval had spread his cards upon the table, Shelburne might reasonably conclude that, except for independence, he might write his own terms with the United States. It seemed evident that the fewer concessions made to the United States, the better pleased the French government would be. France deliberately invited the British to make a stiff peace with the Americans and indicated that she would not take amiss the disappointment of her ally's hopes.

In thus letting down his allies, Vergennes was not guilty of any violation of the terms of the Franco-American alliance. The treaty pledged France only to procure the independence of the United States; it was silent regarding territorial limits and fishing rights. Upon the letter of the treaty Vergennes took his stand; to the spirit of the treaty, it seems clear, the French minister paid scant homage.

Vergennes could always justify this ungenerous treatment of his ally on the ground that the demands of the United States were excessive and would never be granted by Great Britain. If this was true, he was doing the Americans a favor by whittling down their claims to more acceptable dimensions. As Vergennes knew, it would be fatal to press the British too hard: they were far from humbled, the war had begun to turn in their favor, and France, desperately in need of peace, could send no more fleets or armies to the aid of the Americans. From his viewpoint, the Americans were in danger of losing everything, including their independence, by making impossible demands upon a still unconquered enemy; and France, although threatened with financial ruin, might be obliged to continue the war merely because of the intransigence and greed of its ally.

French policy was also influenced by the necessity of preserving the friendship of Spain; and, as usual, His Catholic Majesty was placated at the expense of the United States. Vergennes made little effort to conceal from the American commissioners his sympathy for Spanish territorial claims. In July 1782, his secretary, Rayneval, bluntly told Jay that the United States had no claim to the West and that Spain's title was unimpeachable. As for the navigation of the Mississippi, how could the United States expect to enjoy this privilege when its frontiers lay several hundred miles east of this river? Rayneval advised the United States to make the best terms it could with Spain; and he strongly implied that whatever the United States received west of the Appalachians would be entirely owing to Spain's generosity. Most of the trophies of war, it was made plain, were to be decked upon Spain, despite its disappointing showing in the struggle.

As Vergennes knew, the British were attempting to make a separate peace with Spain; and he was far from certain that the Franco-Spanish alliance would hold firm in the face of an attractive peace offer from Great Britain. To forestall British intrigue, he felt obliged, at least ostensibly, to underwrite Spain's territorial aspirations and to play the part of a dubious friend to the United States. Nevertheless, behind the scenes, Vergennes tried to moderate Spain's demands upon the enemy, remarking that Spain's conduct in this matter was "like that of a petty shopkeeper, who thinks that the only way to get a fair price for his goods is to begin by asking ten times more than they are worth," while the United States made a practice of unblushingly demanding everything in sight. Unknown to the Spaniards, the French foreign minister later in the negotiations gave the British to understand that France was willing to see the Union Jack continue to float over Gibraltar — on the principle that such possession promised to keep Spain and Great Britain permanently embroiled. To compensate His Catholic Majesty for this deprivation, Vergennes was disposed liberally to award him territories claimed by the United States.

The obvious danger in this policy of favoring one ally over the other was that if Great Britain yielded the fisheries and the West to Americans, France might forfeit the gratitude and good will of the United States. In that case, clearly, France's loss would be Britain's gain. Nevertheless, Vergennes took this risk, preferring the aggrandizement of Spain to that of the United States and confident that Great Britain would never concede these disputed points to the United States.

John Jay won two allies in his stand for an unconditional acknowledgment by Great Britain of the independence of the United States: John Adams refused to leave Holland to take part in the peace negotiations in Paris until Jay's demands had been fulfilled, and Vergennes, recognizing that these stubborn republicans would never sit down to a peace table until they had carried their point, urged the British government to yield. The British Ministry was no more disposed than Vergennes to see the peace negotiations retarded by a punctilio; a new commission was issued to Oswald, and the Americans declared themselves satisfied. At last the decks were cleared for action.

But the dry rot of distrust had penetrated too deeply to be thus easily dispelled. Satisfied that Vergennes was double-crossing the United States, Jay came to a momentous decision: he would violate his instructions from Congress by negotiating with Oswald behind the back of the French minister. Perhaps Jay would have come to this decision sooner had he known of Franklin's secret negotiations with Oswald; but the doctor characteristically did not take even his colleagues into his confidence and, in consequence, Jay knew nothing of Franklin's efforts to extract Canada from the British Empire. Certain it is, however, that the instructions of June 1781 had long grated upon Jay and John Adams. In their eyes, these instructions were an insufferable humiliation and a relinquishment of America's vital interests to the custody of a dubious friend. Jay and Adams were fiercely patriotic and quick to resent a slight upon their country's honor; they wished to make their own virtues of self-reliance and pride the basis of their country's foreign policy. It was his object, said Adams, to make his countrymen proud — "to make them hold up their heads, and look down upon any nation that refused to do them justice."

But, in this matter of the instructions, pride and honor were secondary: they must be broken if the republic was to be preserved. "Congress," the two commissioners said, "surrendered their own sovereignty into the hands of a French minister. . . . It is glory to have broken such infamous orders." Admitting that Vergennes was prepared to carry out the letter of the treaty by insisting upon the independence of the United States, they believed that he begrudged the republic every accession of strength by which its independence could be ensured. Vergennes's idea of doing the United States a friendly turn, said John Adams, was "to keep his hand under our chin to prevent us from drowning, but not to lift our heads out of water."

Moreover, Adams and Jay were supremely confident that they knew how to handle Englishmen without calling upon Frenchmen for help. To American revolutionaries, getting the better of Englishmen was all in the day's work. "There is but one way to negotiate with Englishmen," explained John Adams; "that is clearly and decidedly; their fears only govern them. . . . The pride and vanity of that nation is a disease, it is a delirium; it has been flattered and inflamed so long by themselves and by others that it perverts everything." In short, the islanders understood only force; to attempt to reason with them was futile. Americans ought to sit down at the peace table carrying a big stick: Englishmen were apt to construe the slightest sign of cordiality to mean that Americans were weakening and might yet be brought back into the empire as subjects of George III.

Neither Jay nor Adams carried his suspicions to the length of believing that France was seeking undue advantages in the peace. France, indeed, set her allies an example of moderation in her territorial demands upon Great Britain; asking for little for herself, France could properly recommend moderation upon her allies. To the American commissioners, France's clean record in this regard did not entitle her to the confidence of the United States; for, by supporting Spain's extravagant claims, France was in effect taking sides against the United States, and by throwing her weight into the scale against American rights in the fisheries, she was actively opposing the interests of her ally. In their opinion, France was not acting the part of an honest broker. Jay believed that the war was being protracted for the attainment of Spanish objectives; and Jay's experiences in Spain had revealed to him the depths of that country's hostility to the United States. Moreover, the French seemed to have taken upon themselves the role of champions of the integrity of the British Empire — for example, Canada, they insisted, must remain under British sovereignty. Apparently they subscribed heartily to the view that there would always be an England and that this was in the best interests of France. Those Americans who had looked forward expectantly to the day when France would dictate a crushing peace in London reckoned without their Bourbon hosts.

John Adams, to whom Franklin was little better than a tool of the French court, anticipated difficulty in persuading Franklin to follow his fellow commissioners in shelving the instructions of the Continental Congress. Much more hostile to Franklin than was Jay, Adams persisted in regarding the old philosopher as the personification of all the evils of senility and corruption. By this time, Adams had slipped into the habit of linking Vergennes and Franklin as enemies of the United States. "I will not be horse jockeyed," he exclaimed on one occasion. "At least, if I am, De Vergennes and Franklin shall not be the Jockies."

Nevertheless, when Jay proposed to initiate secret negotiations with the British, Franklin exclaimed: "I am of your opinion, and will go on with these gentlemen without consulting the [French] court." Yet Franklin was not without misgivings that Jay and Adams would upset his own carefully laid plans. Poor Richard trusted in his own skill to weave safely through the diplomatic maze, but he had little confidence that Adams and Jay could penetrate its mysteries; so, throughout the negotiations, he held tightly to their coattails lest they stumble into the pitfalls he saw on every hand.

Vergennes invited Great Britain to drive a hard peace with the United States, but it remained to be seen whether the British government would make conciliation or vengeance the polestar of its policy. On the one hand, outraged pride urged Englishmen to treat the United States as an enemy; on the other hand, the importance of winning the good will of Americans and of disrupting the Franco-American alliance counseled them to deal generously with the rising state across the Atlantic.

Lord Shelburne, the Prime Minister of Great Britain, was one of the most enlightened statesmen of the eighteenth century. Resolved to make the empire a stronghold of free institutions, he could not easily bring himself to admit that Americans had been irrevocably lost to the mother country. Charles James Fox favored an immediate and unconditional recognition of American independence, but Shelburne sought to avert the parting; he frequently spoke of "the dreadful consequences that must ensue to this country, if America should be separated from it." Hoping to the last that he would not be called upon to preside over the dissolution of the empire, he toyed with all sorts of schemes — imperial federation, common citizenship, a close-knit alliance — to stave off the evil hour of independence. He yearned for the Americans, if not as subjects equal in every respect to true-born Englishmen, at least as friends and allies; and he urged upon them "the ideas of cordial, perfect friendship, of entire reconciliation of affections." Already, he said, the British and American peoples were united "by blood, by principles, habits, and every tie short of territorial proximity"; to unite them in friendship was the great challenge to British statesmanship.[7]

But by September 1782, when Vergennes sent Rayneval to London to acquaint Shelburne with the kind of peace terms with the United States that would be acceptable to France, the British Prime Minister had recognized the futility of attempting to retain Americans within the empire. Independent they must be, he reluctantly acknowledged, yet he did not cease to hope that by generous treatment Americans might some day become allies of Great Britain or even form a federal union with the former mother country. After many years of dealing with Americans as mere colonists or provincials, the British government, under Lord Shelburne's leadership, began to treat them as equals and as friends. Shelburne, said Edmund Burke, wished to prove to Americans that "we were really cured of our follies, and were brought to think and act like men." In this way, Shelburne hoped, would the miracle of the Atlantic be wrought: bridged by common purposes and honest understanding, the United States and Great Britain would carry on the chief purpose of the British Empire — the purpose which George III and his ministers had forgotten — the enlargement of the boundaries of freedom.

Shelburne therefore did not fall in with the urgings of the French court to deal rigorously with the United States. Although adamant on compensation to the Loyalists, he was disposed to make a generous

---

[7] Shelburne's policy was summarized by his friend Benjamin Vaughan as follows: "America was not to be wantonly thrown away and yet not to be attempted to be kept by force. Great Britain will be wonderfully reduced by the separation, and America not much benefitted by it." Therefore, Great Britain ought to withhold the grant of independence from the United States, not from any desire to hold America in subjection, but because it ought not "throw away the chance of an affectionate reunion with America by a wise negotiation." And "if we cannot regain America as a part of the empire, we may at least by this method get some recompense when we surrender her the title deeds." Benjamin Vaughan to John Vaughan, December 15, 1782; Benjamin Vaughan to James Monroe, September 18, 1795. Vaughan MSS. Clements Library.

Benjamin Vaughan, however, counseled Shelburne: "You must depend upon America, only for trade, good wishes and peace; and take your chance about having her alliance in war."

peace with the Americans.[8] True, he encouraged the French to believe that he had embraced their policy of keeping the republic weak, but actually he drove a wedge between the allies by giving the United States far more liberal terms than the French themselves were known to favor. It was Vergennes who was duped: relying upon British inveteracy toward the former colonies, he rested his policy upon the assumption that Shelburne would never yield to the Americans on the boundaries and fisheries.

The peace commissioners sent by Shelburne to negotiate with the Americans in Paris were men of a very different stamp from those Englishmen of cramped vision who had lost the colonies. Richard Oswald, in particular, although almost eighty years old, was in touch with the most progressive ideas of the age. A follower of Adam Smith and himself a merchant, his memories went back to the era of "salutary neglect" when America had poured wealth into the coffers of British merchants and manufacturers and Great Britain had not asked for more. He foresaw that the United States was destined to be a great and powerful country and he urged his countrymen to link their fortunes with those of the rising republic of the West. In eighty years, he predicted, the United States would have eighty million people, and the welfare of Great Britain might depend upon the attitude of these eighty million Americans toward their former mother country. England sorely needed an ally — and where was she more likely to find one than among the English-speaking people of North America? As might be expected, it was soon objected to Oswald that he had turned American and was pleading the cause of the United States more vigorously than he was defending the rights of Great Britain. Nevertheless, he exercised profound influence upon the peace; more liberal than Shelburne himself, he induced the minister to make concessions to the United States which went beyond Shelburne's original intentions.

Vergennes knew, of course, that the American commissioners were engaged in negotiations with the British peace emissaries, but of what went on behind the locked doors of their meeting place, the French minister knew next to nothing. When he asked the American commissioners for information, he usually received vague, noncommittal answers. The Americans could not truly say, however, that Vergennes made a nuisance of himself; he never wearied them with his curiosity. On the other hand, the American commissioners saw little profit in talking with Vergennes because, whenever the subject of peace was brought up, he tried to convince them of the necessity of surrendering the fisheries and the West — advice which was wasted upon the commissioners. He did not dream that the Americans would violate their instructions; Franklin, in

[8] It was probably for this reason, rather than because of the conquests of George Rogers Clark, that Shelburne was prepared to give Americans the West.

particular, he relied upon to keep him in touch with important developments.

While conducting these secret negotiations, the American commissioners saw no impropriety in accepting freely of the hospitality of the French ministers whom they were deliberately keeping in the dark. At a dinner given by Vergennes, John Adams was introduced to the wife of the French minister. "She made me sit next to her," reported Adams to his American friends, "on her right hand, and was remarkably attentive to me the whole time. The Count, who sat opposite, was constantly calling out to me to know what I would eat, and to offer me gateaux, claret, and Madeira, etc." If Vergennes hoped that the wine would loosen Adams's tongue, he was disappointed: as always, Adams kept mum about the peace negotiations. However, in asking for another large loan from France, the American commissioners found their tongues; but this was a subject distasteful to the French minister.

Even though the proceedings were kept secret from Vergennes, the course of the peace parleys between the American and British commissioners ran far from smoothly. Almost immediately, two obstacles were encountered which threatened to prevent the peacemakers from reaching an agreement. For a time there was serious danger that the deadlock would force the commissioners to call in the French to arbitrate their differences.

Many times during the war, Great Britain had abandoned the American Loyalists, but she could not afford to forsake them in the treaty of peace without jeopardizing the stability of the British Empire. If those who defended the sovereignty of the mother country received only banishment and confiscation of property for their pains, how could it be expected that, in future rebellions in the empire, any provincials would dare to espouse the cause of Great Britain? In Shelburne's eyes, to leave the American Loyalists to their fate might well prove the deathblow to the British Empire. Moreover, no treaty that failed to make provision for the Loyalists could win the approval of the House of Commons; rather than leave the Loyalists in the lurch, the members would prefer to continue the war. For these reasons, Shelburne demanded that the Loyalists be restored to the rights and property of which they had been deprived by the patriots during the war.

To the Americans, compensating the Loyalists was tantamount to admitting that the Revolution had been wrongful from the outset and that those who had opposed it were in the right and ought to be repaid for their losses. It would put the patriots in the light of miscreants who, said John Adams, "by a fortunate coincidence of events, have carried a wicked rebellion into a complete revolution." At the same time, it would deprive Americans of a great deal of property confiscated from the Loyalists. Surely, the spoils of war belonged to the victors.

By the end of October, 1782, the negotiations had completely bogged down. The Loyalists, it appeared, would at least enjoy the gratification of keeping the rebels from the peaceful enjoyment of their independence. Prepared to deal generously with the United States in the matter of boundaries, the British insisted that every concession made to the Americans was conditional upon full reparation to the Loyalists. This, the American commissioners declared, left them no alternative but to prolong the war. And so matters rested, each side claiming that its honor was at stake and each refusing to budge an inch from its position. The British negotiators threatened to throw the peace discussions into Parliament where, presumably, every member would demand full restitution to the Loyalists. John Adams countered with a warning that if peace was delayed over the Loyalists, he and Jay would be recalled and new ministers, probably under Vergennes's thumb, would be appointed by Congress.

Confronted by the Americans' obduracy, Shelburne's good will toward the United States evaporated: in October 1782, the cabinet demanded that the United States renounce its claims to all territory west of the Appalachians and surrender part of Maine, including Penobscot, to Great Britain. At the same time, the British seemed bent upon excluding Americans wholly from the Newfoundland and Nova Scotia fisheries. Indeed, Shelburne was heard to say that he trusted the French more than he did the United States; for a moment, he doubted the wisdom of attempting to win the esteem of these obstinate republicans who refused to do common justice to the Loyalists.

In this crisis, Franklin proved a tower of strength to the Americans. Acting upon the principle that the best defense is the offense, Franklin declared that if England insisted upon compensation for the Loyalists, he would advise the states to draw up bills for damages perpetrated by the British and Loyalists in the United States. If Americans began delving into these war crimes, the doctor warned, it would "form a record that must render the British name odious in America to the latest generations." What would become then of Shelburne's hope of reconciliation between the two countries? Here was the weak spot in the British armor and Franklin hammered it remorselessly. When the British commissioners, their patience exhausted by the Americans' inflexibility on the fisheries and Loyalists, threatened to send home for instructions, Franklin whipped out of his pocket a sheaf of papers which contained his own estimates of war damages done by the British in America and demanded that it be presented to the British government. Rather than see Franklin rake up the embers of war hatreds, the British commissioners advised Shelburne to accept a compromise.[9]

[9] Franklin actually requested Congress to forward estimates of the damage done by the British during the war. Congress, in turn, asked the states to draw up their claims, but the states were laggard in complying with this request and only Connecti-

Throughout the negotiations, Franklin proved himself more unyielding than either Jay or Adams. When his colleagues seemed disposed to give way, the doctor remained adamant, countering British demands by rehearsing the well-worn atrocity stories. For example, Shelburne's agents demanded an acknowledgment of the rights of British subjects to collect debts contracted by Americans before 1775. Franklin strenuously demurred, but the British insisted and Jay and Adams deserted Franklin — with the result that the British were given the privilege of collecting the debts, if they could. Even John Adams acknowledged that Franklin had been "able and useful" in the peace talks — a somewhat temperate appraisement of Franklin's services.

Against British demands for compensation of the Loyalists, the Americans put forward one insuperable objection: the powerlessness of Congress. For once, the weakness of Congress stood Americans in good stead: the estates of the Tories had been confiscated by the states and Congress had no authority to interfere. The commissioners gladly pleaded the insufficiency of Congress, pointing out its inability to bind the states to any agreement that infringed upon their sovereign rights.

Thus the British had to content themselves with considerably less than half a loaf by way of reimbursement to the Loyalists. Congress was committed in the peace treaty merely to "earnestly recommend" to the states that confiscated estates be restored and the Tories permitted to return to settle their affairs — but the states were free to reject this recommendation if they chose, and their past conduct was anything but a good augury.

The American commissioners were of one mind regarding the fisheries, western boundaries, and the Loyalists, but it was John Adams who distinguished himself in the battle for the fisheries. In fighting for the fisheries, New England was battling for its life; and it could not have asked for a stouter champion than John Adams. The attitude of the French court encouraged the British to exclude the Americans entirely from the Newfoundland fishing banks, but John Adams treated the fisheries as though Congress had made them an ultimatum, refusing to consent to any peace that did not include them. That Americans should fish off Newfoundland and Nova Scotia and dry their fish along the shore was, to Adams's mind, a law of nature; the same dispensation that had placed the fishes in the sea had intended that New Englanders should remove them. And if the British failed to recognize this ordinance of Heaven, they would again find themselves plunged into war with the United States; in seven years or less, Adams predicted, "we should break through all restraints and conquer from them the island of Newfoundland itself, and Nova Scotia, too."

---

cut and Rhode Island sent in their account. Even these came much too late to be used in the peace negotiations.

The Americans, having given way, however slightly, in the case of the Loyalists, insisted that the British do likewise in the matter of the fisheries. In contrast to the concessions made the British regarding the Loyalists, they received concrete advantages, although not, it is true, everything they asked. The settlement ultimately agreed upon gave the Americans permission to fish off Newfoundland and to dry or cure their fish in un-settled parts of Nova Scotia and Labrador.[10] "Thanks be to God," ex-claimed John Adams, ". . . our Tom Cod are safe in spite of the malice of enemies, the finesse of allies, and the mistakes of Congress." In his eyes, it was a victory of Yankee shrewdness over French cunning and British obduracy.

In all the obstacles to peace met with during these protracted negotia-tions, Jay and Adams saw the "slippery craft" of Vergennes. Left to themselves, the British might concede American demands, but assured as they were of Vergennes's support, they were uncompromising. British ideas, said John Adams, came "piping hot from Versailles."

By supporting the British position on the Loyalists, Vergennes con-firmed the blackest suspicions of the commissioners. Less vigilant men might have assumed that Vergennes intended merely to remove a par-ticularly annoying obstacle from the path of the peacemakers; but to Jay and Adams, the assertion by the French minister that "England's honor" necessitated fair treatment of the Loyalists was proof that he was up to his old tricks of planting apples of discord between England and the United States. John Adams's Francophobia became so strong that he was ready to charge his ally with the final iniquity: trying to swindle the United States of its independence. France, he said, in December 1782, was as averse to seeing the United States independent as was Great Britain itself: in every chancellery in Europe, the Bourbons were raising up obsta-cles to the recognition of the United States as an independent power. John Jay now claimed that France, failing to secure the West for Spain, would favor British claims to the region rather than see the United States come into possession. When Vergennes, disturbed by Jay's long absence from Versailles, sent Lafayette to inquire what was keeping the American diplomat away, Jay exclaimed: "How can he expect it, when he knows he has endeavored to play us out of the fisheries and vacant lands?" The rift with France was becoming a dangerous breach in the alliance itself.

This atmosphere of distrust and suspicion encouraged British hopes of wholly detaching the United States from its ally. Dr. Franklin had always stoutly defended France in the presence of the British peacemakers, how-ever willing he might have been to negotiate a settlement behind Ver-gennes's back. But Jay and Adams railed against Vergennes and poured

[10] Permission to dry or cure fish on the coast of Newfoundland was denied Ameri-cans. Moreover, Americans were given the "liberty" to fish these inshore waters; there was no acknowledgment of right.

their suspicions into the receptive ears of Shelburne's emissaries. Delighted to find the Franco-American alliance cracking, the British set out to enlarge the fissure by playing upon Jay's suspicions. They obligingly turned over to the American commissioners an intercepted letter written to Vergennes by Marbois, a French diplomatic agent in the United States, in which the French official expressed opposition to the participation of the United States in the fisheries. If given the fisheries, Marbois predicted, Sam Adams and other expansionists in Congress would demand Canada and Nova Scotia — therefore he advised that the Americans be excluded from the fisheries as well as from Canada and Nova Scotia. Written in code, the Marbois letter was translated by the British; and although Jay never saw the original, he had no doubt of its authenticity.[11] But when Oswald took Jay and Adams aside to "reveal" to them a plot by Vergennes to divide America between France and England (France to take New England among other choice parts of the continent), Jay's credulity balked. Nevertheless, he was prone to believe most tales of Vergennes's villainy and to base his conduct upon the assumption that the French court was a secret enemy. And so little disposed was he to keep his suspicions to himself that he asked Benjamin Vaughan, one of the British commissioners in Paris, to convey to Shelburne the apprehensions of the American commissioners that the French court was harboring treacherous intentions. On one occasion, when Jay and Vaughan were alone together in the former's carriage, Jay exclaimed to the British commissioner: "Why will not your court cut the cord that ties us to France?" Unlike Franklin, Jay was holding up more than friendship in exchange for British generosity: for a price, he seemed willing to put even the Franco-American alliance on the block.

At the same time that the British emissaries quickened the American commissioner's suspicions of France they sought to awaken the "ancient affection and regard for old England" which, Englishmen liked to believe, was dormant in all Americans. Leave the embrace of France, they counseled, and return to the maternal affection of Great Britain; no more family rows, they promised, would disturb the empire. One British peace emissary told Franklin that he believed that Englishmen would henceforth "be more or less cured of fighting and monopolizing notions, and look to Americans' friendship." "We never can be such damned sots," said Oswald, "as to think of differing again with you." "Why," answered John

[11] Marbois denied that he had written the letter in question and Vergennes declared that the views expressed therein did not reflect his own. But Marbois was at this time urging Congress to renounce its claim to the fisheries and Vergennes was telling the British government that the United States ought to be excluded.

In London, Vaughan found that Shelburne "put all Suspicion of a collusion with France out of the question by showing that he thought no policy with America rational, but that of a permanent and affectionate peace, instead of a truce." Benjamin Vaughan to James Monroe, September 18, 1795, Vaughan MSS. Clements Library.

Adams, "in truth I have never been able to comprehend the reason why you ever thought of differing with us."

Naturally, the British commissioners were charmed with John Jay: it was a new and delightful experience to deal with a diplomat who took them unreservedly into his confidence. Moreover, they found Jay sympathetic to their suggestions of a future connection between the two countries — Jay, reported Benjamin Vaughan, seemed "for returning to an *attachment* to England, and is very bigotted to the English constitution; and indeed was one of the very last to join in independence." Jay informed the British commissioners that all that Great Britain had to do to win the good will of Americans was "to *ease off*." Yet Benjamin Vaughan preferred Benjamin Franklin rather than John Jay as United States ambassador to the Court of St. James's. "If Mr. Jay takes disgust at the vices or corrupt public ideas of the English," observed this sage diplomat, "he will be more difficult to manage than the Dr., as he is very honest and very active with his pen. Dr. Franklin knows the worst of us, and I think Mr. Jay will think better of us at a distance than near." Jay had been fond of Frenchmen before he came to France; let him preserve his illusions about Englishmen, counseled Vaughan, by keeping him out of England.

By exhibiting their suspicions of France to the British commissioner, it is doubtful whether Jay and Adams served the cause of their country. Whereas Franklin had coyly hinted that the British might win the favor of Americans by making a generous peace, Jay and Adams, by their impetuous and unguarded conduct, let it be known that the United States could be won without the necessity of making a costly good-will offering.

Jay, once satisfied of Shelburne's sincerity regarding American independence, was eager to hasten the negotiations before Vergennes's treachery could do its work. In his desire to make peace in haste, he was little disposed to haggle over Canada — America, he said, would not permit "a few acres" to stand in the way of a speedy settlement with Great Britain. Jay thereupon rushed into the negotiations and, somewhere along the road, Canada was jostled off — to the dismay of Dr. Franklin.

During these eventful weeks in the autumn of 1782 when the Americans were meeting secretly with the British peace emissaries, the French and Spaniards were likewise conducting peace negotiations with another set of British peacemakers. The details of these negotiations were not divulged by France or Spain to the Americans — the junior partner was not trusted with such important state secrets. To Adams and Jay, this treatment justified their decision not to take Vergennes into their confidence. If the allies were equal — and the American commissioners insisted that they were — then Americans were no more obliged to reveal their proceedings than were the French.

For these reasons, it was made the easier for the American commissioners to take the final step of signing the preliminary peace treaty with Great Britain without the knowledge or approval of Vergennes. To the last, Jay and Adams believed that if the French minister learned its terms he would attempt to wreck the treaty. By signing the document without so much as a word to Versailles that negotiations had been completed, the American commissioners more flagrantly violated their instructions than in carrying on peace talks with the British behind Vergennes's back. The Americans here gave unmistakable evidence of their distrust of the French court; it was an affront which Vergennes could not be expected to overlook. But it was, after all, merely an affront, not the breaking of the alliance that the British had hoped for: the treaty signed by the Americans was expressly declared to be a preliminary treaty and it was not to go into effect until France had made its terms with Great Britain and a general peace had been drawn up.

It was left to Franklin to break the awkward news to Vergennes. The doctor, it is true, was experienced in smoothing over the rough passages in Franco-American relations, but never before had his talents been put to greater stretch. He went, therefore, to Versailles prepared to dispense soothing syrup liberally to the French minister in what he feared would be a stormy interview.

Yet Franklin came off in this encounter better than he had expected. Vergennes was stunned to find that the Americans had signed the treaty without consulting him — that was the unkindest cut of all — and he hotly resented the commissioners' suspicions of his good intentions toward the United States. But to a diplomat of Vergennes's long experience, duplicity was not unfamiliar. "We have never based our policy towards the United States on their gratitude," he remarked. "This sentiment is infinitely rare among sovereigns, and unknown to republics." He concluded that there was a fatal predilection in Americans for Englishmen — no matter how badly they were treated, these republicans always came back for more. No foreigner, however honest or worthy, could long come between them. France, Vergennes began to fear, had won the war but lost the Americans. "If we may judge of the future from what has passed here under our eyes," he said, "we shall be but poorly paid for all we have done for the United States and for securing to them a national existence."

If Vergennes could not comprehend the motives of the Americans, neither could he fathom the policy of the British. They had bought rather than made peace, he exclaimed; it was more like a dictated than a negotiated settlement. If only the British would prove equally kind to France, Spain, and Holland! Still, from Vergennes's point of view, the treaty might well have been worse. At least, the British had not made a commercial treaty with the Americans which might rob France of the material benefits of American independence. And the French minister could always hope that the British would revert to the same policy toward the United States that had precipitated the American Revolution. There were many Englishmen who had learned nothing from the American Revolution, and in them he placed his chief reliance.

Vergennes knew that if Americans were to be kept out of the clutches of John Bull, he could not afford to give way to pique at their good fortune. If France expected to retain their friendship, she could hardly show resentment at their prosperity. So, although it was beginning to dawn upon Vergennes that the quickest way to lose a friend is to loan him money, the French government made another loan to the United States after the commissioners had dropped their bombshell at Versailles.

By making peace without the concurrence of the French court, the American commissioners secured much more advantageous terms than if they had followed the lead of France. British generosity was owing in large measure to the hope of reconciliation held by the Americans in negotiating without the privity of France. The Dutch, who stubbornly refused to detach themselves from France despite British blandishments for a separate peace, and who permitted France to negotiate a peace for them with the British, fared far less well than the United States. As in the case of the United States, the French tried to moderate the demands of the Dutch; in London, Shelburne observed in Rayneval, Vergennes's secretary, no "disposition to make a greater stand than Decency required in favour of the Dutch." The loyalty of the Dutch to France did not dispose the British to grant favorable terms; as a broker, France could do little in London for its clients.

Viewed in any light, the manner in which the treaty was made was a blow to French prestige. France had planned to preside over the peace negotiations and to pass out the presents to her happy circle of allies. The American commissioners had rudely deprived France of this role: like unruly urchins, they had snatched the presents for themselves and had made off with more than France had intended to give them.

The fact that the American commissioners had signed only a preliminary peace with the British deceived no one. Such palliation, said Vergennes, did not wipe out the stain of having signed a peace contrary to the agreement between the two allies. And Shelburne was careful to explain in the House of Lords that one of the prime virtues of the treaty was that it had been consummated without the knowledge of France and might, therefore, prove to be the means of dividing the allies. The preliminary peace came strongly recommended to Englishmen as virtually a separate peace; and if much seemed to be given America, Shelburne argued that by generosity he had weakened a union of powers dangerous to Britain's security.

After the signing of this treaty, only Franklin, of the American commissioners, continued to enjoy favor at Versailles. The doctor's relations with Vergennes remained amicable: he showed no resentment when the

French minister rebuked him for his part in the deception. Convinced as he was that Great Britain would never cease trying to disunite France and the United States, he devoted himself to counteracting British intrigue and the no less dangerous work of "a certain mischievous madman" — John Adams. John Adams would bear watching by all friends of Franco-American amity.

Before the final treaty of peace was signed, Adams was considering the possibility of a future war with the Bourbons. "To think of Gratitude to France is the greatest of Follies," he declared, and "to be influenc'd by it would ruin us." Everywhere he saw the hand of France raised to thwart and cripple its ally. The French ministry, he charged, had done more than even Great Britain toward preventing the United States from concluding treaties with other European powers; even in the refusal of Great Britain to make a commercial treaty with the United States, he detected French influence. His lively fears of French influence made Lafayette appear to be a menace to the United States. "I see in that Youth the seeds of Mischief to our Country if we do not take Care," said Adams. ". . . He has gained more applause than human nature at twenty-five can bear. It has kindled in him an unbounded Ambition which it concerns Us much to watch."

Despite the high hopes of the British peacemakers, neither Jay nor Adams was ready to break the Franco-American alliance and fling himself into the arms of the late mother country. Heaven preserve the United States from the mercies of England, was still the prayer of these republicans: the last drop of human kindness seemed long since to have been wrung from that nation. "If we entertain an idea of their generosity or benevolence towards us, we are undone," said John Adams. "They hate us universally from the throne to the footstool, and would annihilate us, if in their power, before they would treat us in any way." The only safe course for the United States was to be independent of all nations: Americans must recognize that one European power was no better than another, and that Great Britain set the standard.

Despite this bleak international outlook, the growing coolness of Adams and Jay toward France tended to moderate their hostility toward England. After the signing of the preliminary peace treaty, John Adams said that his purpose was "to hurt Great Britain no farther than should be necessary to secure our independence, alliance, and other rights." And one of the British commissioners, Benjamin Vaughan, was struck by the partiality displayed by Adams and Jay for things English: they dearly wanted to see English trade and manners restored and, he believed, would consider an "intimate union" with the former mother country. "They have tried to restore English and eradicate French connections," wrote the English diplomat, "by giving the leaders of Congress a history of French intrigues." When the subject of a federal union with Great Britain was brought up by the British commissioners, Jay remarked that "as for regaining the affections of America, time, he thought, would be required . . . but in a few years things would become right probably for some wise association or other, because common interests would generate it." In comparison with Adams and Jay, Franklin seemed to be an unreconstructed rebel and the chief stumbling block in the way of reconciliation between Great Britain and her former colonies.

There was one point upon which the patriot leaders were agreed: the United States must stay out of Europe's wars. To Americans, the Declaration of Independence was a charter of peace as well as of liberty; by breaking away from Great Britain, the United States, it was supposed, freed itself not only from the wars of the mother country but from all wars. Thomas Paine declared that the American republic shook hands with the world in declaring its independence; never again, he prayed, would the republic "dip her hands in the bloody work of Europe." The American Secretary of Foreign Affairs said in 1783 that the United States intended to be "totally disengaged" in European disputes. When the Swedish ambassador remarked to John Adams in 1784 that he "took it for granted, that you [Americans] will have sense enough to see us in Europe cut each other's throats with a philosophical tranquillity," Adams heartily joined in the sentiment.

From staying out of Europe's wars, Americans advanced to the proposition that they ought to stay out of Europe's affairs altogether — to keep that unhappy continent at arm's length and, whenever possible, close their eyes altogether to its existence. Jay and Adams, for example, would have had the United States remain apart, preserving only a commercial connection with the outside world. We could do business with Europeans but we ought not to permit our intimacy to extend beyond business hours lest we be compromised by intriguing continental statesmen. In a world of bad neighbors, it was the part of wisdom to stay at home. America — so ran this theory — was a world in itself and needed only privacy to enjoy its felicities. With this idea in mind, Charles Carroll moved in Congress in 1780 that the United States should send no ministers abroad except in emergencies and should itself receive no foreign ministers.[12] This act of withdrawal, said Carroll, would "not only be economical, but would withhold our distinguished Citizens from the corrupting scenes at foreign Courts, and what was of more consequence would prevent the residence of foreign ministers in the United States whose intrigues and examples might be injurious both to the Government and the people."

Jay and Adams had come to speak the language of isolationism; in their dispatches from France were foreshadowed the doctrine later to be em-

---

[12] This idea crops up again in American history during the administration of Thomas Jefferson. As President, Jefferson proposed to call in virtually the entire diplomatic staff.

bodied in Washington's Farewell Address. To "defend ourselves against the wiles of Europe," to guard against treachery from a faithless friend, and to remain aloof from European affairs seemed to be their testament to the American people. "Let us, above all things," said John Adams, "avoid as much as possible entangling ourselves with their wars or politics. Our business with them, and theirs with us, is commerce, not politics, much less war."

Yet their isolationism was not an inflexible policy which held true for all times and for all occasions: in their distrust of European monarchies, they did not overlook the possibility that one day the United States might stand in need of allies upon the European continent. They saw the necessity of creating a balance of power that would prevent Great Britain — or any other country — from attacking these shores. John Adams, for example, suggested that if, at some time in the future, France should make inadmissible demands upon the United States, "we may find in the alliance of Austria, England and Holland, a resource against the storm." Isolationism, yes — but only so long as it served the interests of the United States.

The American commissioners offered no apologies for having broken their instructions. Jay and Adams gloried in having saved their country from a disastrous French-dictated peace which, said Adams, "would have made Us long the miserable Satellites of some great European Planet." They had no fear that their countrymen would seriously rebuke them for having acted in the best interests of their country; and they expected to silence faultfinding by stuffing the mouths of their critics with the good things they had brought home from Paris. "Our countrymen love buckskins, beaver-skins, Tom-cod, and pinetrees too well," said John Adams, "to hang their ministers for accepting them." The American people, they believed, would not look a gift horse in the mouth. As for American honor, it too was intact: John Jay remarked that the rectitude of the American commissioners was evident in every stage of the negotiations.

As the commissioners had foreseen, Congress did not disdain a treaty, however irregularly procured, which fulfilled its highest hopes. Americans were astonished by Great Britain's unaccountable liberality; the peace terms, it was said, exceeded "the most sanguine Expectations of the most Sanguine." The boundaries of the United States were exceptionally gratifying: on the west, the republic was bounded by the Mississippi River, and on the north by the river and lake line which still separates the two countries. Nevertheless, the manner in which the commissioners had acted was not condoned: rightly, the honor of the United States and the existence of the French alliance were judged to be at stake. If the treaty was accepted, the friendship of France might be sacrificed; on the other hand, if it was rejected and the American plenipotentiaries publicly censured, an excellent peace would be lost. Vergennes complained to Congress of the commissioners' conduct, making plain his displeasure at being ignored in the peace negotiations. At the same time, the commissioners cited the opposition of the French court to American aspirations to justify their decision to act independently of its advice. Thus wrapped in a dilemma, the peace treaty was presented to Congress.

But the statesmen in Philadelphia had yet to learn the worst. By a secret article appended to the treaty, it was agreed that in exchange for a renunciation by Great Britain of its title to territory above the Yazoo River claimed by the United States, the commissioners promised to recognize British sovereignty over the Floridas should the British possess that region at the end of the war.[18] This article strongly revealed the anti-Spanish bias of the commissioners, but it is doubtful whether they were wise in preferring Great Britain to Spain as a neighbor to the south. Later it proved much easier to acquire the Floridas from Spain than it would have been from Great Britain. But in 1783, Congress was alarmed by the effect this article might have upon Franco-American relations, once the French got wind of it. Clearly, the United States could not stand revealed as secretly favoring the claims to the Floridas of Great Britain, an enemy, to those of Spain, a friendly power. Therefore Congress insisted that the secret article be divulged to France before the French learned of its existence for themselves, which they were sure to do, since it was published in a Philadelphia newspaper. Fortunately for the United States, the secret article never came into operation, because the British failed to conquer the Floridas and, as a result, Spain held the region until it was acquired by the United States.

Upon only one other point were the commissioners loath to claim credit: the provision for the Loyalists. They seem to have suffered more remorse over what they had done toward compensating the Loyalists than over their disregard of the instructions of Congress. Expecting to be reprimanded upon this score, they prepared their defense beforehand: unless they had yielded on the Loyalists, they could not have procured the many advantages contained in the treaty. Even so, Franklin expected the worst — he was well aware that peacemakers were seldom blessed by the people they served. "BLESSED are the peace-makers, is, I suppose," he said, "to be understood in the other world, in this they are frequently *cursed*. . . . I have never known a peace made, even the most advantageous, that was not censured as inadequate, and the makers condemned as injudicious or corrupt. . . . War," he added, "is made according to

[18] The British had asked for the privilege of evacuating New York without interference in order to turn their army against the Floridas, but this the commissioners had refused, although John Jay was willing.

the mistaken imaginations of the people, and peace, according to their real necessities as seen by the peace-makers, and hence the frequent idea that they were bribed."

These forebodings proved correct: the commissioners received no thanks from their countrymen for having given way on the Loyalists. Agitated patriots declared that if the Loyalists were permitted to return, "if we do not look about us, they will be on our backs booted and spurred before we know where we are," and Americans would be compelled "like a drove of tame asses, to take up our old burdens at the hands of the British King and Parliament." It was quickly perceived, however, that the treaty contained a saving clause: the states were not bound, except in so far as they saw fit, to carry out the recommendations of Congress; and, as might be expected, they saw fit to do little in favor of the Loyalists. Most states ignored the recommendations of Congress regarding the Tories as they did upon virtually every other subject. Some states even continued to confiscate Tory property after the peace treaty had gone into effect. For years after the Revolution, in many parts of the country, a Tory had only to show himself to provoke a riot; as for the provision that their estates be returned, it remained a dead letter. This treatment was justified by Americans on the ground that even the British government had no real intention of doing anything for the Loyalists: the provision regarding Loyalists was inserted merely to salve the consciences of the King and Parliament. The American Secretary of Foreign Affairs took upon himself to point out that it was designed rather "to appease the clamor of these poor wretches [the Loyalists] than to satisfy their wants."

The Loyalists themselves were not under any illusion that a new day had dawned for them; they had won only an honorable mention in the treaty — to receive justice at the hands of the rebels was, they knew, a forlorn hope. Their fate, said one, was a "striking lesson to future generations never to support the views of government against the determined resolution of a very numerous people." Although Great Britain recompensed them for part of their losses and opened a haven for them in Canada and Nova Scotia, in general they met with the unhappy fate of those who choose the losing side in civil wars.

The Tories proved to be an expensive burden to the British government. Their claims for losses resulting from confiscations and from deprivation of office and professional income were so high that the government paid only a small part of their demands; nevertheless, it cost the mother country over forty million dollars before it had done with the Loyalists.[14] Surveying the expense of settling Nova Scotia with Loyalists, Edmund

[14] Three million pounds was awarded them as compensation for property losses sustained as a result of the Revolution. The Loyalists claimed eight million pounds damages.

Burke exclaimed: "Good God! What sums the nursing of that ill-thriven, hard visaged, and ill favoured brat, has cost to this wittol nation!" On both sides of the Atlantic, it was the treatment of the Loyalists which caused the loudest outcry against the treaty of peace: Englishmen exclaimed that too little had been done for them, while Americans objected that too much had been given them.

The provisions of the peace treaty regarding the recovery of debts owing British subjects by Americans likewise incurred much unpopularity in the United States. Many states declined to carry out this part of the treaty; particularly in the South, where the planters were heavily in debt to British merchants, was this part of the treaty flouted. During the war, the planters had sought to extricate themselves from their obligations by making payments in depreciated paper money — a method of settlement which, of course, was unacceptable to their British creditors.[15] Many Americans had assumed that the annulment of all debts owing British subjects would be written into the peace treaty; and when they found that they were specifically obliged to honor those debts, they simply nullified the objectionable portion of the treaty, justifying their action on the ground that the British had carried off thousands of Negro slaves belonging to Americans.

In short, neither side enforced the provisions of the treaty of peace to which it objected. Each alleged that the other was the first transgressor and thereby justified its own breaches. The Americans violated the clauses regarding Tories and debts; the British, in order to preserve the fur trade and Indian alliances, refused to give up the Northwest posts lying within the borders of the United States. It was not until 1796 that these posts were finally surrendered to the United States; the British, however, never received from the United States a satisfactory settlement of Loyalist property. The treaty of 1783 ended the war between the United States and Great Britain, but it failed to bring the kind of peace to which Benjamin Franklin and Lord Shelburne looked forward.

[15] An act passed by the Virginia Legislature in 1777 provided that money owing British subjects could be paid to the state in paper money; in exchange, the state auditor gave the debtor a certificate of payment, discharging him from all further obligations. James Madison and many other leading citizens (with the conspicuous exception of Patrick Henry) protested against this method of settling debts owing British subjects.

CHAPTER XXX

❈

The Problems of Peace

N O DOUBT the impoverishment and exile of large numbers of Loyalists, the natural conservatives of the country, markedly weakened the forces opposed to democracy in the United States. The confiscation of Loyalist property and the passing of large estates into the possession of hundreds of small owners tended further to advance the cause of economic equality. Likewise, the abolition of the restrictions on the acquisition of land formerly exercised by the King and proprietors; the seizure of Crown lands by the states; the abolition of quitrents, primogeniture, and entail; the granting of bounty lands to soldiers; and the large-scale sale of lands by the states to pay debts incurred during the war materially aided toward creating a system of democratic land tenure. And lastly, by opening the trans-Appalachian West the American Revolution guaranteed that the republic would remain for generations a land of independent farmers and that democracy would be firmly rooted in the soil that had given it birth.[1]

Nevertheless, the aristocratic tradition did not fall at the mere blast of the democrats' trumpets: proclamations of the sovereignty of the people and the equality of all men made little impression upon its battlements. The radicals were obliged to reduce it by slow siege, and at the end of the Revolutionary War its citadel still stood. In Philadelphia, for example, its was evident that equality — social and economic — was not brought appreciably nearer by the Revolution: the constitution of 1776 did not succeed in forcing democracy down the throats of unwilling citizens. It was observed in 1782 that the citizens who were able to "trace back their

---

[1] By the end of the war, there were about twenty-five thousand settlers west of the Alleghenies, Kentucky containing the largest number. A more detailed study of this population movement and its consequences will be made in the next volume of this history.

families to the foundation of the city, assume to themselves certain privileges, and this pretension is much more notable amongst those who join to the possession of this great advantage the possession of great riches." At a ball in Philadelphia, the Chevalier de la Luzerne, the French minister, "presented his hand to Mrs. Morris (wife of the financier), and gave her the precedence, an honor pretty generally bestowed on her, as she is the richest woman in the city, and all ranks here being equal, men follow their national bent, by giving the preference to riches." A Swedish observer, De Fersen, said in 1782 that the struggle between aristocracy and democracy had just begun; and Benjamin Rush of Pennsylvania declared that "it will require half a century to cure us of all our monarchical habits & prejudices"; the only hope lay in the re-education of the American people and in the probability that republican forms of government would in time "beget republican opinions & manners."

In general, it is fair to say that the spirit of aristocracy outlived the institutions in which it had found expression. In abolishing primogeniture and entail, Jefferson believed that he was striking a blow at the root of aristocracy but he soon found that he had merely lopped off one of its limbs. The end of great estates was not yet: vast amounts of Western lands, for example, passed under the control of speculators and land jobbers. The Revolution weakened the social position and political influence of the Virginia aristocracy but it left almost untouched the economic basis of their power. Tidewater Virginia remained a region of great estates, Negro slaves, and poverty-stricken whites clinging to the fringes of the plantation system. It was in Virginia that European travelers, proceeding southward from New England, saw for the first time signs of destitution among large numbers of white Americans.

The most inflexible opposition to the attainment of the ideals of the Revolution came from the new aristocracy spawned by the Revolution itself. The personnel of the aristocracy, particularly in the Northern states, was greatly altered by the Revolution, yet there was little change in the ideas or attitudes of the upper class. The ferment brought to the surface a new class which quickly aped the ways and occupied the houses of the aristocrats they had dispossessed. Instead of furthering democracy, they marshaled their strength in defense of the prerogatives and ideals of which the Tory upper class had been the custodians. Many of the men who were indebted to the Revolution for their rise revealed themselves to be uncompromising foes of its democratic ideals: children of the Revolution, they denied their own mother. "Men who could scarcely maintain their families," it was pointed out in 1777, "now live in splendor . . . raised to immense wealth, or at least to carry their appearance of a haughty, supercilious and luxurious spendthrift."

In this fashionable company, the patriots of '75 found themselves regarded as old-fashioned revolutionists — "those bawling, brawling patriots who bluster and bellow" — who had outlived their usefulness. It was said of Sam Adams, for example, that "tho' he might pull down a bad Government, yet [he] was not able to support a good one"; thriving only upon contention, he insisted even upon disturbing honest Whigs in their pleasures with his out-of-date Puritanism and equalitarianism. By the end of the war, some patriots were asking themselves in despair to what end they had labored. In 1776, they had not dreamed that the fruits of independence would fall into the unworthy hands of profiteers and parvenus.

⌒   ⌒   ⌒

The authority of the Continental Congress was one of the casualties of the war and the inflation. As the struggle drew to a close, the body that had thundered the Declaration of Independence across the Atlantic and had concluded a treaty of alliance with Bourbon France was relegated to the position of a needy dependent of the sovereign states that composed the American union. "We, mighty Men," exclaimed a congressman, "totally dependent upon 13 Legislatures different in Views, for Support in our smallest Endeavors to carry on the War" — how fallen now that Congress's money was worthless.

Nor did the belated adoption in 1781 of the Articles of Confederation restore to the Continental Congress its lost influence and prestige. Congress was a greater power in the land while its ascendancy rested upon popular consent than when it drew its authority from a written constitution.

The Articles of Confederation, it will be remembered, had been submitted to the states for ratification in 1777; yet it was not until almost four years later that they were formally adopted. Requiring the unanimous approval of the thirteen states, the Articles remained in abeyance because three small states — New Jersey, Maryland, and Delaware — refused to accede. Of these refractory states, New Jersey and Delaware concurred in 1778 and 1779, leaving Maryland as the sole holdout. "There now only remains Maryland who has seldom done anything with a good Grace," exclaimed a disgusted congressman, "she has always been a forward hussy."

In Maryland's conduct there was something more than met the eye. Certainly it was not merely a perverse fondness for upsetting the best-laid plans of American statesmen that accounted for its steadfast opposition to the Articles of Confederation. Nor were its spokesmen merely concerned with the rights of small states in the union. The fate of the American West was at stake and, whatever their motives, the leaders of Maryland were upholding the cause of nationalism in the West. Their fight against the Articles of Confederation was a filibuster designed to break the grip of the great landed states upon what ultimately became the national domain of the United States.

One of the most important achievements of the American Revolution was the opening of the West to expansion. Fearful of provoking war with the Indians and reluctant to permit its colonists to move across the Appalachians beyond the immediate reach of its authority, the British government had in 1763 closed the West to settlement; and for more than a decade, the so-called Proclamation Line marked the terminus of westward-bound frontiersmen. Finally, in 1775, the British government determined to relax these restrictions and to permit gradual, orderly settlement in the region west of the mountains. But there was to be no free land — quitrents were to be imposed upon all land open to settlement, and the region was to be turned over to the control of large land companies dominated by wealthy businessmen in Great Britain and the colonies. This was not the kind of settlement that the plain people of America wanted; rather, it was designed for the benefit of capitalists and the government. The outbreak of the Revolution put an end to these schemes, and the problem of administering the West was inherited by the Continental Congress.

In *Common Sense*, Thomas Paine pictured these Western lands as a national domain in which all Americans would share. Since all the states were waging war against Great Britain, ran Paine's argument, all should benefit from the acquisition of lands once belonging to the British Crown. Western lands were deemed a source of almost inexhaustible riches by which Americans would be enabled to pay for the war and be relieved for many generations of the necessity of paying taxes. From the proceeds of the sale of these lands, it was expected, the American governments could function without recourse to any other means of raising revenue. "They seem made by our benevolent creator to reward our efforts." Moreover, Congress and the states had promised land to the soldiers in reward for their service, and much of this land was located in the region lying to the west of the mountains. Thus this territory came to be regarded as "a common stock . . . purchased by the joint blood and Treasure of the confederacy."

But to make it so was another matter. By virtue of charters granted by the King of England in the seventeenth century, when it was assumed that the South Sea (Pacific Ocean) lay a few hundred miles to the westward, some colonies claimed to extend across the entire continent to the Pacific. Virginia, in particular, advanced claims to a domain of imperial extent, a huge bloc of territory drained by the Ohio and Mississippi rivers. By right of conquest and title devolving from its colonial charter, the Old Dominion aspired to extend its boundaries over a large part of what is now the Middle West. Already the largest state in the union, Virginia, if its claims were made good, would become a colossus bestriding the continent. Then, truly, the motto of the arms of Virginia would be realized: "Virginia gives a fourth quarter to the world."

These claims of "boundless empire" terrified the small states, already worried over their status in a union of unequals; inevitably, the contest over Western lands became essentially a struggle between have and have-not states. The Articles of Confederation bestowed upon Congress neither jurisdiction over the West nor authority to limit the western boundaries of the states. Yet it was plain that if any body could be said to represent the American people as a whole, that body was the Continental Congress. So the small landless states became the champions of congressional control over the West — not because they loved the Continental Congress and the centralized government for which it stood, but because they feared the ambitions of the large states. Hitherto among the chief opponents of congressional authority, the small states now hailed the Continental Congress as "the SOVEREIGN POWER of America" and sole custodian of Western lands.

Rivals with the states for control of the West were the land companies organized by British and American capitalists. If these land companies were to enforce their titles to Western lands, it was essential for them to defeat the claims of Virginia to ownership of the region, for Virginians would not permit the intrusion of outside land companies upon their domain. Therefore, the land companies urged that the Continental Congress be invested with the stewardship of this region. Presumably, the land companies would know how to handle the Continental Congress to the best advantage once the West was placed under its jurisdiction.

It is true that some of the Maryland delegates to the Continental Congress were personally concerned in these land companies and therefore could not pretend to disinterestedness. Nevertheless, they did good by stealth and indirection; regardless of their motives, they served the best interests of their country. Had the states been permitted to expand westward indefinitely, the future of the American republic would have been jeopardized, and nationalism might have been submerged by the rise of powerful, aggressive states, each aspiring to make itself master of the union.

Although all the states wished to share in Western lands, few took action to make good their title against the British and Indians. Maryland, for example, refused to assist Pennsylvania and Virginia in defending their frontiers, on the ground that this was a duty devolving solely upon the states directly concerned.

Virginia, as the chief claimant to the West, was fully alive to its responsibilities. In 1778, George Rogers Clark, "the Hannibal of the West," was placed in command of an expedition to eliminate British power in the Mississippi and Ohio valleys. It is important to observe that this was almost wholly a state enterprise, the Continental Congress having declared its inability to aid the Old Dominion in its efforts to conquer the West.

At the head of a few hundred men — frontiersmen dressed in buckskins, with moccasins on their feet, and carrying tomahawks and rifles — Clark descended the Ohio in flatboats and captured the British post of Kaskaskia. Alarmed by Clark's success, Lieutenant Governor Hamilton, the British commander at Detroit, set out with a small British force accompanied by Indians to wrest the Illinois country from the Americans. But in May 1779, Hamilton and his men were captured by Clark at Vincennes and the entire British position in the West began to totter.

It assuredly would have collapsed had Clark been able to follow up his victory with the capture of Detroit. But Clark ran short of supplies; Oliver Pollock, the New Orleans merchant who had largely financed the expedition, was compelled to default on bills drawn upon him; the Indians, instigated by the British, rose against Clark; the French inhabitants of the Mississippi Valley, after first warmly welcoming the Americans, turned against them and refused to accept Continental paper money; and Americans became engrossed in land jobbing and speculation rather than in completing the conquest of the West. As a result, the war ended with Clark vainly attempting to organize an expedition against Detroit.

Virginians' preoccupation with Western lands reacted disastrously upon the Old Dominion's contribution to the war effort in the East. Such a frenzied scramble for real estate followed the opening of the Land Office in 1779 that, for the moment at least, the energies of many Virginians were completely absorbed in making their fortunes. The Old Dominion lost its position of leadership in the struggle against Great Britain; its quota of troops for the Continental army was left unfilled, and even Maryland seemed to be making more vigorous exertions than Virginia. So many soldiers deserted or left the army upon the expiration of their terms of service to stake out claims in the West that Washington began to fear that the Virginia Line would be broken up. But it was the stay-at-home speculators who really profited: several tracts of over a million acres each passed into the hands of private purchasers who paid for this land with depreciated paper money at the rate of fifty cents for one hundred acres of land.

Virginia denied that Congress — "a foreign tribunal" — had any authority to limit the western boundaries of the states and refused to submit to such "intolerable despotism." Rather than consent to any diminution of its domain, Virginia attempted to form a confederation of twelve states, leaving Maryland, the obstinate sister, outside the fold. But Virginia's bid for empire had aroused the jealousy and apprehension of other states, even including those claiming Western lands. The solid front of the landed states began to crack, and in 1780 New York deserted its former allies by relinquishing to the Continental Congress part of its Western lands. Connecticut shortly after followed suit. The claims of these states, it is true, were highly controvertible and Virginia could say with considerable justification that New York and Connecticut had surrendered nothing that they really owned. Nevertheless, the position of the Old Dominion was seriously weakened by the decision of the other states to turn over their land claims — good, bad, or indifferent — to the Continental Congress.

Many Virginians themselves feared that their state was grasping at inordinate dominion and that the West would revolt against its rule. It was unwise, said Washington, for Virginians to seek "more territory than they are competent to the Government of"; already, the state might be too large "for the energy of republican Government." That these apprehensions were not wholly visionary was demonstrated by the secession movement which broke out in 1780 in Kentucky, then a part of Virginia. The men of the Western waters made as troublesome subjects for Eastern rulers as did Americans as a whole for British imperialists. About three thousand men who were reported to be "perfect Tartars, for they live solely on meat," and were said to feed their children, as soon as they were weaned, with raw bear and buffalo meat, rose against the rule of the Old Dominion, demanding that the Continental Congress be vested with jurisdiction over the West and that separate states be carved out of the region as soon as the population warranted. Jefferson declared that he wished "to give them full participation of the benefits of our free and mild Government," but Westerners were content with nothing less than independence.

Virginians might have taken warning also from the experience of New Yorkers in attempting to bring frontiersmen under their control. The Green Mountain Boys of Vermont proved most intractable subjects, preferring to wage war against New York and, in the case of Ethan Allen and his brothers, to conspire with the British rather than surrender their claim to independent statehood. The New York landlords who sought to establish their claim to a large part of Vermont were soon appealing to Congress to save them from the Green Mountain Boys who began to swarm across the New York line and, musket in hand, take possession of choice New York real estate. The New Yorkers screamed that they must have protection against the Vermonters or their lives and property would be "at the Disposal of Ethan Allen which is more to be Dreaded than Death, with all its Terrors."

In the person of Ethan Allen, the Green Mountain Boys possessed a rugged and resourceful leader quite capable of carrying out his threat that he would "fight, nay even run on the mountains and live on mouse meat," before he would submit to the New Yorkers. But no New Yorkers ever raised the question whether Allen was a mouse or a man: his reputation west of the Hudson served to frighten unruly children into good behavior when the familiar "the Devil will get you" failed to produce the desired effect. A land speculator himself — he and his friends owned three hundred thousand acres of Vermont land — he kept the New York claimants at bay for many years. Pronounced a public enemy by New York and a price put on his head in 1772, Allen disdained this threat by offering a reward for the capture of prominent New Yorkers and inviting claimants to Vermont land to cross the Hudson and see "as good a regiment of marksmen and scalpers as America can afford."

Unwanted and insoluble problems the states gladly dumped into the lap of the Continental Congress, and here, in due course, the Vermont question arrived. Congress, however, found it much too hot to handle. It could not be kept apart from such burning issues as the claims of rival land speculators for choice Vermont real estate, the keen dislike of New Englanders and New Yorkers for each other, the fear of the small states of being swallowed up by the large states, the determination of many Americans to limit the land claims of large states like Virginia, and the rivalry between the Northern and Southern sections of the Union. As a result, it was not until 1791 that Vermont finally achieved statehood.

Meanwhile, in the case of Virginia's Western claims, Congress steadily veered towards Maryland's position. In 1780, it recommended that the states cede their Western lands to the central government and that these lands be settled and divided into separate states, enjoying the same rights as the original members of the confederacy. Whereupon Virginia, hoping to save most of its dominions by sacrificing part, agreed to cede its claims to the territory north of the Ohio River in exchange for a guarantee by Congress that elsewhere its jurisdiction would be upheld.

These concessions by Virginia did not evoke a like conciliatory spirit in Marylanders: they declared that they would not adhere to the confederation until the Old Dominion had receded further from its claims. Finally, the French minister was obliged to take a hand with the obdurate state. Early in 1781, finding itself unable to protect shipping on the Chesapeake from the depredations of British cruisers, Maryland asked La Luzerne for naval aid. La Luzerne took the opportunity to impress upon Marylanders the extreme concern with which his government viewed Americans' failure to agree upon a frame of government. Under this prodding, Maryland gave way: in January 1781, its representatives in the Continental Congress were instructed to sign the instrument of government and on March 1, 1781, ratification was celebrated with a collation at the house of the President of Congress and a fireworks exhibition at the State House and on board John Paul Jones's ship in the harbor.[2]

Congress thus came into a wholly unexpected inheritance: as administrator and trustee of a region larger than many European kingdoms, it could hold up its head in the proudest company. Here, moreover, was a bond of union: through the Continental Congress, all the states were concerned in the welfare and prosperity of the West. Thanks in large

[2] Virginia's price for renouncing its claims to the region north of the Ohio River was subsequently rejected by Congress but the cession was not withdrawn by the Old Dominion.

measure to the obstructions of Maryland, Congress's prospects brightened perceptibly.

It is also true that Congress was beginning to exercise powers which made it, if not a sovereign over the states, at least an umpire in their disputes. By the Articles of Confederation, Congress was authorized to arbitrate differences between the states; and under this authority, it settled the quarrel between Pennsylvania and Connecticut over the Wyoming region by awarding the disputed area to Pennsylvania. Congress seemed destined to become a court of justice to decide the claims of the independent states. "The day will come," predicted the Secretary of Foreign Affairs, "when all disputes in the great republic of Europe will be tried in the same way, and America be quoted to exemplify the wisdom of the measure."

For the Continental Congress, however, the immediate question was whether it could hold together long enough to enter upon its inheritance in the West. Riches and power perhaps awaited it; but Congress, to enjoy this future felicity, must first survive the critical period upon which it had now fully entered.

It has been seen that in its fall, paper money dragged down with it much of the authority and prestige of the Continental Congress. It could no longer be regarded as a rich uncle by the states: having fallen upon adversity, Congress was now a pauper, dependent upon the bounty of the states and whatever loans it could raise abroad. "We have no Money *now* to squander upon A, B, C, and all the Letters of the Alphabet under the sole Restriction of 'he is to be accountable,'" exclaimed a congressman; retrenchment and penny-pinching were now incumbent upon statesmen who had talked coolly in terms of millions and who had prodigally run through their purse without troubling to keep accounts. In its adversity, Congress was spared no humiliation: after it had been compelled virtually to let the army fend for itself, the ladies of Philadelphia collected donations for the troops — with such success that it began to appear that the ladies of Philadelphia were a greater power in the land than was the Continental Congress.

As might be expected, the states showed little affection towards an uncle without visible means of support. Congress's distress evoked little sympathy from the states; in any event, pity did not move them to give succor to the central government. For the most part, they left Congress to beg or borrow as best it could, disclaiming responsibility for any bills that had been run up by this tottering shadow of a government. No longer was there any doubt who was master in the household: the Continental Congress was moved down to the foot of the table and the thirteen sovereign states ensconced themselves in the seats of honor.

Few Americans wished to see Congress die, but many were content to let it remain an invalid, able to sit up and take nourishment from the states but incapable of superintending the affairs of the United States. Richard Henry Lee of Virginia declared that "he had rather see Congress a rope of sand than a rod of iron." That it must be either a rod of iron or a rope of sand was taken for granted by many patriots: there was no middle ground between tyranny and impotence. Thus, only if stripped of all real authority was the existence of the Continental Congress tolerable to these lovers of liberty.

Deprived of paper money — its prop and staff — Congress stumbled forward. If hitherto Congress had gone along on three wheels, now, said a congressman, "every wheel of the machine seemed stopped." It lavished upon the states a wealth of good advice which, like much of that commodity, was unpalatable and therefore rejected. When not addressing itself to this thankless task, Congress, having nothing better to do, fell into disputes about "diction, commas, colons, consonants, vowels, etc.," and other trivial irrelevancies. Often it was found impossible to proceed to business because of the absence of a quorum; and most of the able men had long since retired to their states to carve out their political fortunes. A seat in Congress was beginning to be regarded as an unimportant job to be wished off on some lesser luminary in state politics; in 1781, even the presidency of Congress went begging, so diminished was the prestige attaching to that office.

Bewildered and discouraged, even though the boundless resources of the West lay before it, Congress surrendered its powers almost with relief. As Hamilton said, congressmen were little inclined in these latter days to assert their powers: "timid and indecisive in their resolutions, constantly making concessions to the States, till they have scarcely left themselves the shadow of power," they sought only to throw off their unsupportable burdens.

Meanwhile paper money sank so low that it took almost a basketful to buy an equivalent amount of groceries. In Virginia, for example, a traveler was asked five hundred dollars in paper money for a bowl of apple toddy but the tavern keeper was overjoyed to settle for one dollar in silver. Tea sold in Philadelphia for ninety dollars a pound; wood for six hundred and thirty dollars a cord; a silk handkerchief for one hundred dollars; buttons for thirty dollars a dozen; and in 1781 Thomas Paine paid three hundred dollars for a pair of stockings. Continental paper money reached fifteen hundred to one in 1781, and continued to fall; it was now "fit for little else but to make the tail of a paper kite with."

By the middle of 1781, the inflation had run its course: the paper money of the Revolution had become little more than scrap paper — unhonored and unsung, it was consigned to the wastebasket. With the disappearance of Continental money there was no longer a national currency in the United States; thus another prop to the union had been kicked away. And, unfortunately, in its passing it had not left behind an effective substitute: at the end of the war Americans still lacked gold and silver. Free at last of the incubus of depreciating paper money, Congress could scarcely take joy at its deliverance: it was no less a pauper, and salvation still seemed as far distant as when paper money was flooding the land. For deflation brought no surcease to the tribulations of Congress and of the American people; the malady was different but the inevitable end seemed no less dismal. Whether the United States should expire from an overdose of paper money or from lack of any money at all; whether prices should soar skyward, as in an inflation, or plummet to the depths, as they were doing in the deflation that now gripped the country, was a choice of evils which afforded little consolation to the sufferers.

The American people awoke after their inflationary debauch to find that sometime during the course of the celebration their pockets had been picked and that they were suddenly poor. Those who had borrowed inflated paper dollars were now required to repay the loan in hard money, worth perhaps a hundred times or more the value of the money they had borrowed. Inflated debts had to be paid in deflated dollars; and farmers who had been accustomed to receiving high prices for their produce now found the market going down more rapidly than it had gone up. As in every inflation, the ascent had been exhilarating, but the descent was like falling into a bottomless pit.

The joy ride was over and it was now time to pay the piper – and not in depreciated paper money, but in hard coin. The taxes levied by many states were made payable only in specie; because the states were no longer printing paper money, they declined to accept it in discharge of obligations. This worked extreme hardship upon the people because little specie was to be found in the country and it was concentrated in the hands of a few individuals.[2a] Washington complained in 1781 that he was forced to sell part of his property to pay taxes on the rest. "This," he remarked, "I should do with cheerfulness if the taxes were equally laid, and judiciously applied. But flagrant partiality is enough to sour the minds of any people." Poll taxes – the method of taxation most generally employed – fell with particular force upon the poor man with a large family; and taxation of all land, regardless of quality or state of cultivation, at the same rate for every hundred acres, discriminated against the poorer farmers of the upcountry.

Those who had profited from the inflation now became champions of sound money. The profiteers and inflationists of the war years became the conservative and sound-money men of the postwar period. As men of property, these heirs of the Revolution staunchly upheld the status quo; another inflation threatened to wipe out their gains. "The depreci-

[2a] Probably much of the specie brought into the country by the British and French armies was spent by the people, particularly after 1780, upon foreign luxuries.

ation of money always did and will originate with debtors," they now said, "because it is their interest to depreciate." To those who had already profited to the full from inflation, stability and order became the primary needs of the day.

The hardships produced by deflation and the return to specie bred a dangerous spirit of revolt among the people which was appeased only by a resort to paper money. The debtor class — and for the first time there truly could be said to be such a class in the United States — hoped to ease its burdens and to recapture the prosperity of the early war years by again opening the dykes to paper money. Paper money now became a weapon in the hands of poorer citizens — chiefly farmers — in the struggle between rich and poor. The lines of battle were formed between radicals and conservatives with the currency as the great bone of contention. It was paper money versus specie, inflation as opposed to stability. When radicals succeeded in capturing control of state governments, they immediately set the printing presses in motion — Virginia, for example, late in 1781 issued twenty million pounds (Virginia money) in notes, soon to be devalued at the rate of one thousand to one.

It was Robert Morris's task to bring order out of this chaos and to reestablish the authority as well as the financial solvency of the Continental Congress. Many patriots, it has been seen, feared to entrust power to an individual lest he make himself master of the country, yet in this case they might reasonably have concluded that Americans stood in greater danger of losing their liberties as a result of internal collapse than of dictatorship.

Morris found congressional bookkeeping a labyrinth through which no man could find his way. It was impossible, for example, to determine how much had been drawn in bills upon American ministers abroad, because few records had been kept of these transactions. Invoices for clothing and other supplies sent from Europe had disappeared. How much was outstanding in the form of certificates could only be guessed: Congress had "attended not at all to those little circumstances of taking receipts, and vouchers, and keeping regular accounts." If Congress could have borne the entire burden of the war, said Jefferson, "I believe we should have done it and never dishonored our exertions by producing accounts." It was left to Morris to undo the damage of six years of negligence and to fight his way clear of "the cumbrous load of useless paper, the multiplied mass of certificates."

The success of Morris's program depended almost wholly upon the co-operation of the states: in this respect, the Superintendent of Finance was in no better position than had been the Continental Congress. Unless the states granted money to the central government, Morris could neither finance the war nor satisfy public creditors. He could not forever improvise or draw money out of his own pocket — sooner or later the states must do their duty or accept the consequence of a collapse of the Federal government. Until the states came to his aid, Morris was like a man who desperately borrows and mortgages in order to stave off the creditors swarming around his door — but is always sinking deeper into debt. As Washington bluntly told the states, Morris could not work miracles; only the citizens of the republic could save the country.

In supposing that the requisition system could be made to work by appealing to the honor and interests of the states, Morris overestimated the patriotism of his fellow citizens. Although Congress had failed before him, Morris believed that public opinion, if properly mobilized, might yet work wonders. After the people had been informed of the true state of affairs, he assumed that they would wholeheartedly support Congress and bring pressure upon their state governments to comply with its requisitions. Therefore he wrote his appeals for aid "for the public eye, so that the meanest individual may be in due time informed of those affairs in which as a free citizen he is interested." At first he hesitated to inform the people how bad matters really were lest he give hope to the enemy of a speedy end of the rebellion; but he soon decided that the unvarnished truth would do more good than harm. In a manner worthy of Thomas Paine, he pulled out all the stops in playing upon the dangers of "military pillage," anarchy, and British conquest. Eloquently he appealed to national feeling in the United States; it was "by generous grants of solid revenue, and by adopting energetic methods to collect that revenue," he declared, "and not by complainings, vauntings, or recriminations, that these States must expect to establish their independence and rise into power, consequences, and grandeur."

He soon found that he had grossly miscalculated the strength of provincialism in the United States. His eloquence fell on deaf ears — it was, he said, like preaching to the dead. Every state complained that its quota was too high and, added Morris, "would be very happy to apologize to the world for doing nothing, with the thin and flimsy pretext that it has been asked to do too much." Since the state legislatures were not to be moved by letters, Congress sent a delegation to lay the country's plight before these sovereign bodies. Supplication proved no more effective than letter writing; the indifference of the states was "unequalled, unless by the earnestness of entreaty with which those requests were made." Perhaps, as Washington suggested, the states believed "that the Army had contracted such a habit of encountering distress and difficulties, and of living without money, that it would be impolitic and injurious to introduce other customs in it!"

By 1784, after almost three years in office, Morris had succeeded in extracting about one million dollars from the reluctant states — a sum sufficient to run the government for only a few months. The country was deeper in debt than when he had assumed office, and the Continental

Congress was still dependent upon the states for the means of survival. From this record it can be seen that Morris had not succeeded any better than had the British Parliament or the Continental Congress in making the requisition system work. "It would be more manly," exclaimed Morris in 1782, "to declare at once for unlimited submission to British tyranny than to make specious declarations against it and yet take the direct road to bring it about by opposing the measures for our defence." Reluctantly, he was driven to the conclusion that in "Republican Governments, people often turn their thoughts to that part of the Constitution which bequeaths them their liberties; but too frequently forget that they ought to pursue measures for securing them."

Despairing of succor from the states, Morris turned in 1782 to its one unfailing source of revenue — foreign loans. Congress's greatest triumphs in finance had been scored in Europe; discredited at home, it still enjoyed a small measure of prestige abroad upon which it might capitalize. In any event, there was more to be hoped for from France, Spain, and Holland than from the sovereign states of the union. Congress therefore resolved to apply first to France; and if France proved unkind, "an experiment," it declared, "will be made on the liberality of our new friends." The new friends of Congress, upon hearing these ominous words, might well clutch at their pocketbooks: the "experiments" of the statesmen in Philadelphia ended, at least in the case of France, in delving deeply into the treasury of its ally.

Morris had hoped to restore American finances without leaning upon France, which, he admitted, had already done more than its share toward buttressing the finances of the republic; yet the backwardness of the states left him no alternative but to look abroad for salvation. As a result, Franklin's trips to Versailles became more and more frequent and his appeals for aid more importunate. In November 1782, Franklin flatly informed Vergennes that unless France gave the United States more money, the army would disband; and rather than see his ally quit the war, Vergennes advanced another six million livres to the republic. Morris, however, had already largely anticipated this loan by drawing drafts upon the American ministers abroad — a practice which, he insisted, was essential to the war effort. Indeed, he even drew drafts directly upon the governments of France and Holland in the hope that they would honor them rather than permit the United States to sink into bankruptcy. This financial legerdemain meant that Morris was usually a year or more ahead of the actual loans made by foreign countries. It was not sound finance, he admitted, but it was the only way of keeping the government above water.

Indeed, during the period of Morris's service as superintendent of finance, the United States was more dependent upon foreign largess than ever before. Up to 1780, the republic had received about nine million livres in gifts and loans from France; yet in 1781 alone, fourteen million livres were advanced by the French court. By 1783, John Adams, appalled by the quantity of drafts presented him for payment, was exclaiming that "the catastrophe must now come on." As for Robert Morris, he continued to hope that when Europeans saw "exertion on one hand and economy on the other they will be willing to assist us all they consistently can." Unfortunately, this cheering spectacle of Americans putting their united strength behind the national government remained unrealized. Although Morris cut expenses to the bone, put the nation's finances on a specie basis, and managed to stave off utter disaster, the exertions of his countrymen were still wanting.

The French government had welcomed the appointment of Morris as Superintendent of Finance; the financial distress of the United States had given French ministers almost as much concern as did the insolvent state of their own country. As has been seen, although Vergennes did not want the United States to become powerful and vainglorious, neither did he want it to grow so decrepit that it could subsist only on handouts from its ally. If Morris's appointment meant that the United States was to set its house in order and put itself upon a self-sustaining basis, the French government would be the first to rejoice.

In Morris, however, the French were badly disappointed: his financial jugglery failed to win their applause because, however skillful the exhibition, they knew that it was their money that the American financier was tossing about. They complained that Morris treated them as his cashier, and Vergennes remarked acidly that "it was easy to be a financier and draw bills when others provided the funds to pay them." Americans were in danger of killing the goose that laid the golden eggs; so, in January 1783, Congress finally announced that it would seek no more loans in Europe — at least not until its credit had been fully restored. This renunciation was accomplished, however, not by any improvement in the country's affairs, but by recognition of the dismal fact that further effort in that direction was likely to lead only to rebuff and humiliation.

A sound-money man, Morris deplored the almost worthless Continental paper money that still cluttered the country as "a monument of national perfidy"; and in June 1781, at his instigation, Congress broke entirely with paper money and went on a specie basis. Yet even the enemies of paper money admitted that it had served a valuable purpose and that Americans could not carry on business with specie alone. Robert Morris proposed to solve this problem by establishing in the United States a bank which, although under private control, would take over from the Continental Congress the financial powers it had so lamentably misused.

The war had demonstrated that one of the greatest advantages enjoyed by the British government over its enemies was the banking system which enabled it to borrow money from its citizens and to float loans in the financial centers of Europe. The lesson had not been lost upon Robert Morris, who had long been eager to set up in the United States an institution modeled upon the Bank of England. Yet how could a bank be established without capital? With its paper money expiring upon its hands, the Continental Congress was in no position to finance a bank; and Morris's private credit, already severely strained by his practice of underwriting the government's obligations, was inadequate to the purpose. It was the French who made possible the bank, as they did all things in the United States during this period. With four hundred thousand dollars in specie — part of a French loan to the United States — Morris organized the Bank of North America.

Some democrats did not relish seeing the cause saved by banks and bankers. In their eyes, the Bank of North America represented an effort on the part of individuals to usurp functions belonging to the state; the bank, they said, was intended to demonstrate that "Individuals could do more than the Government" and to persuade Americans to put their trust in bankers and merchants rather than in their own government. To this, Morris might have answered that when government had failed, it was time for capitalists to save the country.

With the aid of this bank, Morris sought to do what Alexander Hamilton was later to accomplish by means of the Bank of the United States: to centralize the financial power of the country and "indissolubly to attach many powerful individuals to the cause of our country by the strong principle of self-love and the immediate sense of private interest." "I mean to render this a principal pillar of American credit," Morris declared, "so as to obtain the money of individuals for the benefit of the Union, and thereby bind those individuals more strongly to the general cause." Let the government support the rich and the rich would support the government was the theory in which both Morris and Hamilton placed their hopes for the republic. The bank was not to be merely a temporary device to win the war and save "the liberties, lives, and property of the virtuous part of America": it was to be a permanent fixture in the American scene. Morris intended that the Bank of North America would be a highly influential institution, doing business in all the states and enjoying a monopoly of all the banking business in the country.

Although he did not attain his goal of monopolizing the country's finances, Morris did succeed in making the notes issued by the Bank of North America equal in value to gold and silver. Unlike the paper money of the states and the Continental Congress, the bank's notes did not depreciate, being secured by an adequate supply of specie. From the bank, the government was permitted to borrow short-term loans and to use the bank's vaults for the deposit of its funds and securities. So manifold, by 1782, had become the operations of the Bank of North America that Morris could claim that it had saved the country.

The apprehension of the friends of states' rights that despotism would rise in Philadelphia was given fresh plausibility by Morris's activities. To guard against this danger, every state was urged to pay its own troops directly rather than trust its money to the Superintendent of Finance, who presumably would devote it to his own nefarious purposes. Unless Morris agreed to give a monthly accounting of his expenditures, his enemies would have had the states withhold all contributions to the national government. What effect this might have upon the war effort, they did not deign to say.

Morris did not propose, as did some members of Congress, that Americans should put the war upon a pay-as-you-go basis by means of heavy taxation. Future generations, he said, ought to bear the greater part of the cost of independence because they would reap the full reward. Moreover, he realized that Americans' aversion to taxes made a good deal of coddling necessary when administering the unpalatable dose; the United States, he pointed out, "cannot be suddenly brought to pay all which might be spared from the wealth of her citizens." Like Alexander Hamilton, Morris believed that a public debt, if properly funded, might become a public blessing. "A public debt," he said, "supported by public revenue, will prove the strongest cement to keep our Confederacy together."

It was manifest, however, that unless Congress was given a source of income independent of the states, the public debt would be a disaster rather than a blessing. The first step, therefore, was to get Congress out of the poorhouse where the states had consigned it and give it financial standing in the community. This the nationalists proposed to do by means of an impost or custom duty on imports. Congress was to be given authority to levy a 5 per cent duty upon foreign goods brought into the United States, and the proceeds were to be used to defray the interest on the public debt. Essentially a tax upon consumers, the impost was expected to yield only a small part of the sum required by Congress for complete financial solvency, but it at least broke the ground for the sowing of future taxes by Congress.[3] As a tax, the impost was so light that it would scarcely be felt, and it had the added advantage of being hidden from the tax-wary American people. "I know of no Tax more convenient," said Washington; "none so agreeable, as that which

[3] The impost was expected to yield about five hundred thousand dollars a year — a sum inadequate for the needs of the government. Robert Morris therefore intended, once the impost had been accepted, to move for land taxes, poll taxes, and an excise tax upon whiskey. These taxes, he estimated, would produce about two million dollars a year, and would go far toward making Congress independent of the requisition system. The impost was not intended to pay the soldiers; the domestic civilian and foreign creditors of the United States were to receive the direct benefit of the money raised by this tax.

every man may pay, or let it alone as his convenience, abilities, or Inclination shall prompt."

First proposed in January 1781, it was not until after Yorktown that the states gave serious consideration to the impost. This delay did not work to its advantage: the military fortunes of the United States unexpectedly improved and hence the impost came before the country at a time when peace and prosperity seemed in the offing. True, the problems of peace promised to be no less perplexing than those of war, but there was no longer a conquering British army on hand to strengthen the arguments of the nationalists that the powers of Congress must be enlarged.

As a result, the impost encountered the opposition of Americans who were fighting the Revolution over again — this time, however, not against the British Parliament but against the Continental Congress. In the impost, they saw only a device to make Congress absolute and to rivet an aristocracy upon the United States. In 1775, Americans had risen against the centralization of authority in London; now they resisted as strenuously every effort to centralize authority in Philadelphia. Tyranny had merely moved its headquarters from London to Philadelphia — let not Americans be deceived by the change of address: it was the old enemy doing business at a different stand. Americans had rejected the British brand of despotism; now they must beware of the "Made in America" variety. As James Madison said of his countrymen: "It is one of our greatest misfortunes that men are apt to reason from one thing to another that is very dissimilar."

On the other hand, many prominent Americans supported the impost. Washington declared that unless the authority of Congress was strengthened, "the Blood which has been spilt, the expense that has been incurred, and the distresses which have been felt, will avail us nothing; and that band, already too weak, which holds us together, will soon be broken; when anarchy and confusion must prevail." James Madison predicted the breakup of the Confederacy, the formation of Northern and Southern confederacies, and civil war between the two. And Thomas Paine, under the signature "Common Sense," vigorously championed the cause of "a more compact union."

But the most compelling argument for the adoption of the impost was the state of the Continental Congress itself. Unless Americans were prepared to yield up the ghost of nationalism, it was apparent that they must take measures to keep the Continental Congress alive. This was so plainly evident that twelve states voted to grant Congress the impost.[4] Only one state, Rhode Island, withheld ratification; and because the Articles of

---

[4] Most of the states agreed to the impost only on condition that the measure should be approved by every state in the confederation. Some appended other qualifications designed to guard against possible tyranny by Congress.

Confederation required unanimity in effecting changes in the fundamental law, the indecision of Rhode Island promised to prove fatal.

The blow fell in November 1782: "unanimous and final veto by the Assembly of Rhode Island" of the impost. Congress immediately sent a delegation to persuade the "perverse Sister" to reconsider, and Thomas Paine borrowed a horse and rode off to Rhode Island hoping to turn the tide singlehanded, but he found himself denounced as an agent of Congress. Before the delegates reached Rhode Island, Virginia repealed her ratification of the impost. In the face of these setbacks, Congress recalled its delegation. The impost was dead, a victim of that malady known as states' rights.

Rhode Island accompanied its rejection with the recommendation that Congress adhere to the requisition system — the only tax to which a liberty-loving people would submit. Yet, at this very time, Rhode Island was deeply in arrears to Congress, having shown its requisitions the same kind of sovereign contempt as had the other states. Foreign loans were also urged upon Congress: "*Why don't Congress borrow — why don't Congress borrow?*" asked the Rhode Islanders. The answer was, of course, that Congress had borrowed up to the hilt and that no one was willing to loan money to a bankrupt.

By this action, Rhode Island conceived that it was plugging the dyke against tyranny and that future generations would cherish the memory of its heroic stand for freedom. "Rhode Island," it was said, "deserves to be hailed as the saviour of America." Yet there was a strong admixture of commercial profit in Rhode Island's zeal for liberty. As an importing state, Rhode Island levied tribute upon the neighboring states, particularly Connecticut, which, possessing few important ports, imported hardly one tenth of the merchandise it consumed. Naturally, Rhode Island merchants and politicians were not eager to give the Continental Congress the right to tax this commerce; the effect of the impost, they predicted, would be to rob the state in order to enrich the Continental Congress.[5]

In slaying the dragon of centralized government, Rhode Islanders cleared the way for the no less menacing evil of civil war and anarchy. Perhaps foreign and domestic creditors could be put off with promises, but the army was not always to be denied. The temper of the veterans was unpredictable, and since they had guns in their hands and officers to lead them, they were not to be trifled with. The soldiers must be paid, yet every means of raising money, short of taxation, had been tried and found wanting.

[5] New Jersey was in much the same plight as Connecticut. Lying between two commercial states, New York and Pennsylvania, Jerseymen complained that their money floated off "in large cargoes to the neighboring states, whose ports are open for luxuries, gewgaws, and useless trinkets."

In 1783, partly because of the mutinous state of the army, Congress made another trial of the impost. In the hope of disarming opposition from the states, it was proposed to limit the impost to a fixed period of twenty-five years. The first impost had been intended mainly for the benefit of foreign and civilian creditors of the United States; and even now, despite the threatening attitude of the troops, Hamilton opposed making the army the sole beneficiary of the impost. "It was impolitic to divide the interests of the civil and military creditors," he said, "whose joint efforts in the States would be necessary to prevail on them to adopt a general revenue." But at least the army might expect some measure of relief if the states could be persuaded to endow Congress with a regular source of income.

It was now the turn of New York to cast the dissenting vote which, despite the will of the majority of the states, brought the plan to an untimely end. This action left the Continental Congress penniless and threadbare, seemingly joined to the requisition system until death did them part. Palliatives had failed and nature was left to take its course. To an ever greater degree, the states regarded themselves as independent sovereignties; after 1783, every state except New Jersey imposed duties upon imports in order to raise revenue for state purposes. Thus did the states take unto themselves the revenue that might have made the Continental Congress powerful and respected, and have prevented mutiny in the army.

While the states were debating the impost, the army was passing through the throes of demobilization. One of the strongest arguments advanced in favor of the impost was the necessity of paying the soldiers at least a small part of their back pay in order to induce them to lay down their arms and return to their homes peacefully. For the threat of mutiny and military dictatorship had never been more acute than in these last days of the war.

In May 1782, the Secretary of War informed Congress that because of the financial crisis the army could not possibly undertake another campaign. A quick glance into the treasury left little hope from that quarter: from those bare vaults could not be drawn the sustenance required by the army. In fact, Congress was so down at the heels that the Secretary of War was obliged to tell General Morgan that the medal promised the general would have to wait — the money was needed for feeding the army. General Morgan received his medal seven years later. General Knox, sent to Rhode Island to ask the legislature of that state to appropriate money for the support of the army, was "obliged to borrow a Johannes, to defray the expenses of his Journey."

Despairing of any supplies, specific or otherwise, from the states, Robert Morris turned over the feeding of the Continental army to contractors. Businessmen were invited to enter into contracts with the Con-

tinental Congress by which, at a handsome profit, they agreed to supply
the army with necessities. The profits were, of course, wholly contingent
upon the merchants' success in collecting their bills. Congress, at this
time, seemed a worse risk than ever: Timothy Pickering, the quartermaster general, was actually in hiding to escape the creditors of the
quartermaster's department.[6] Morris was obliged to pledge his personal
credit to repay merchants who entered into contracts with the United
States – and only upon these terms did he find men willing to risk their
capital in supplying the army.

Congress had long struggled with the problem of raising an army;
now it was hardly less embarrassed by the difficulty of disbanding the
army. Owing the troops over six million dollars in back pay, the government had no funds with which to make this sum good. Stated baldly,
Congress did not have enough money to get rid of the army or to keep
it mobilized; yet every day that the troops remained in camp added to
the debt for which Congress was responsible. The financial resources
of the United States seemed to have reached their lowest ebb: without
paper money or credit and dunned by a host of angry creditors, some
of whom had arms in their hands, Congress saw no way out of this
quandary. "Believe me," exclaimed a congressman in February 1783,
"that I would rather take the field in the hardest military service I ever
saw, than face the difficulties that await us in Congress within a few
months."

Inflation had wiped out the savings and property of many officers and
enlisted men: even a major general of the Continental army, St. Clair,
declared in 1782 that he had not a shilling to his name; after he had sold
his property, the money had become worthless in his hands. "Were it
not for the rations I receive," he lamented, "my family would actually
starve." Some soldiers faced imprisonment for debt when they returned
home, even though they incurred the debts while serving their country
in the field. But, whatever their financial prospects, all were going into

---

[6] Pickering was just in the act of handing Mrs. Washington into her carriage when
a sheriff presented him with a writ holding him personally responsible for debts contracted by his department. "What a cruel oppression is this!" exclaimed Pickering,
"that, when the public is unable to pay its debts, its innocent servants must be made
personally liable." The quartermaster general was saved from a debtors' prison by
the action of the New York Legislature in passing a law absolving public officials
from responsibility for public debts; but until the passage of this law, Pickering remained in seclusion, scarcely daring to go outdoors lest he be tapped on the shoulder
by a sheriff. But, as he said himself, he could have accomplished nothing had he
attempted to exercise the duties of his office: he was ordered to supply the army with
necessities of every kind – "and required to procure them *without money*." Pickering's plight was matched by that of General Nathanael Greene, who, in order to induce contractors to supply food to his troops, made himself a surety. The contractors
went into bankruptcy, the creditors demanded payment of Greene, and the unfortunate general was obliged to sell his estate in South Carolina, given him by the
legislature of that state as a token of gratitude for his services in the South.

the world at the mercy of "unfeeling, avaricious speculators" and as "the most wretched part of the Community, with the constant mortification before us of seeing every Body else in ease and plenty at our Expense." One veteran was apprehensive lest the war had doomed him to bachelorhood: "the young women dread us, the picture of poverty and the speculators, to our great Mortification is running away with the best of them."

The officers had been promised half pay for seven years or a cash settlement, but no funds had been provided by either the states or Congress for this purpose. Moreover, the continued hostility of the New England states toward half pay to the officers raised serious doubts that they would ever receive a farthing.[7]

Soldiers were also beginning to learn that their stock as heroes had fallen sharply since the early days of the war. Philadelphia, the officers found, was not as openhearted as it once had been to soldiers home from the wars: men in uniform were no longer sought after and the adage of "Out of sight, out of mind" could be verified on every hand. As one officer remarked, soldiers "seem to be a people left of themselves, and are evidently . . . considered as the *fag end* of creation." "We poor Dogs," exclaimed a heartbroken officer, "shall return with broken Constitutions and Empty purses, and the Cursed Sin of Ingratitude has taken such deep hold of our *Virtuous* Countrymen that I expect a chosen few only will know Us."

The morale of American soldiers seemed capable of enduring everything — except victory and inaction. With the fighting at an end, they became more vehement in their demands for arrears of pay, the lands that had been promised them as bounties, and an opportunity to go home to reap some of the fruits — which civilians had been enjoying for seven years — of victory. Hotheads were charging that Congress planned to disband the army and to defraud the soldiers of their pay; let the army assert its strength, they urged, and force Congress to do it justice.

Although the military situation was so quiet that Washington might safely have returned to Mount Vernon in the winter of 1782–1783, the danger of mutiny in the army kept him at his post at Newburgh. "The spirit of enthusiasm, which overcame everything at first," he said, "is now done away" and in its place was a grim determination to redress the grievances under which the army had long suffered. Washington found that the men were becoming increasingly callous to those "noble

[7] It was alleged that because the vote of half pay had been taken before the adoption of the Articles of Confederation, this legislation was not binding upon Congress. In 1783, the Massachusetts Legislature put itself on record as opposed to half pay, repeating the time-honored argument that the reward was too great to be tolerated by a people who believed in democracy. On the other hand, Washington declared that half pay was a "debt of honor" — a promise made by Congress when it had nothing else to give, to save the army from dissolution.

Sentiments" to which he had appealed time after time during the critical days of the struggle. The mutinous spirit among the officers was particularly alarming; previously, when the common soldiers had been restive, it was the officers who, sometimes at the risk of their lives, had restrained the troops. With disaffection spreading among the officers, the army was indeed in a desperate state.

The officers were resolved to keep the army together until justice had been done them by Congress and the states; from the attitude of civilians, it seemed plain that if the soldiers disbanded without first reaching a settlement, "no manner of regard would be paid to their claims, their services or their merits." Apparently the American people had to be gently nudged with bayonets before they could be brought to do their duty by the soldiers; otherwise they would try to save their money by holding out on their defenders. This point of view, however unflattering to civilians, was based upon seven years' harsh experience. Recognizing that the people would be more indifferent to the necessities of the soldiers after peace had been made than they had been during the war, General Knox advised the army to remain under arms until satisfaction had been guaranteed by the people — and then, he said, "we shall demand a very small pittance of their gratitude and little shall we receive."

Washington lent his support to the soldiers' demands for a settlement of accounts prior to disbandment; no soldier, he declared, ought to leave camp without a guarantee that the balance due him for services rendered would be paid. The minimum cash payment, in his opinion, ought to be three months' pay — a smaller sum would hardly enable the men to get home, find a job, and stave off their more insistent creditors. "To be disbanded at last, without this little pittance," he said, "like a Sett of Beggars, Needy, distressed, and without Prospect will not only blast the Expectations of their Creditors, and expose the Officers to the utmost Indignity and the Worst of Consequences, but will drive every Man of Honor and Sensibility to the extremest Horrors of Despair."

That serious trouble was brewing in the "rugged and dreary Mountains" around Newburgh where the army lay encamped could hardly escape the notice of the most complacent member of Congress. The long-predicted showdown between civilians and militarists was evidently at hand. This state of affairs, far from representing a vindication of those who had feared military dictatorship, was rather the consequence of years of neglecting the elementary needs of the army and thrusting the burdens of the struggle for liberty upon the shoulders of a few devoted defenders. American soldiers could not be brought to see "why they should be made a certain sacrifice of, for the common good." The question which had been raised almost at the beginning of the Revolution no longer admitted of equivocation: "How long will one part of the community bear the burden of the whole?"

So tense had the situation become that when Washington suggested that the discharged soldiers be permitted to keep their guns as souvenirs to hand down to their children, it was objected that the veterans might use their guns for other purposes and "become a great terror to the Inhabitants." Men with such palpable wrongs to redress could hardly be trusted with arms, and many citizens trembled in their boots at the very thought of turning them loose upon the country. Nevertheless, Congress voted to permit the men to retain their guns; indeed, it might have been difficult to part them from their weapons.

The discontents of the army found expression in the Newburgh Addresses written in March and April, 1783, probably by Major John Armstrong, Jr., of the Continental army. In these manifestoes to his fellow soldiers, Armstrong contended that the army had the power to write its own terms with the Continental Congress by turning its bayonets against the civil authority. It was not to establish a country that "tramples upon your rights, disdains your cries and insults your distresses," Armstrong told the officers, that the army had fought the Revolutionary War; the men who had opposed tyranny in monarchs ought now to rise up against the tyranny of a republic. These addresses were a negation of the whole concept of republican government; they called for a seizure of power by the army, and Washington was invited to be dictator.

But Washington was no more inclined to play the dictator in 1783 than he had been in 1776; after seven years of the shocks and buffetings of war, his veneration for the civil authority was unimpaired. Instead of hankering for a crown, he declared that for him to be King of America would be "the greatest mischief that can befall my Country." His ambition was not to mount a throne but to get back as quickly as possible to Mount Vernon and resume the life of a country gentleman. Having fought for seven years to establish the American republic, he was not prepared to admit that republican government, despite all the shortcomings of which he, perhaps more than any other man, had been the victim, was a failure and ought to be discarded.

Armstrong summoned the officers to assemble and agree upon a course of action, but before this meeting could be held, Washington called the officers before him in a last-minute effort to stop the spread of mutiny. Although it was hardly to be expected from such a plain, straightforward man, Washington proved himself a master of stagecraft. As he took his place on the platform, he put on his spectacles to read his address, saying as he did so: "Gentlemen, you will permit me to put on my spectacles, for I have not only grown gray, but almost blind, in the service of my country"; whereupon many of the officers shed tears unashamedly. After this superb opening, Washington went on to denounce those who sought to "open the flood Gates of Civil discord, and deluge our rising Empire in Blood," and to plead with the officers to send a petition to Congress instead of attempting to coerce the legislature. Washington's advice was adopted: a petition from the officers to the Continental Congress, their "head and sovereign," was shortly on its way from Newburgh.

Washington had temporarily quelled the disturbances in the main army, but Congress was rudely reminded that the soldiers' grievances were still unredressed. Early in June, 1783, the Maryland Line, few of whom by this time were native-born Americans, while marching through Philadelphia after being furloughed, insulted and threatened Congress. Then, unexpectedly, the troops garrisoning Philadelphia revolted, and almost before the astonished congressmen knew what had happened, the Pennsylvania State House was surrounded by soldiers with drawn bayonets. Both Congress and the President and Council of Pennsylvania, who shared the same building, found themselves virtually prisoners of their own army.

These insurgents were mostly short-term recruits who had experienced few of the hardships of the army; a congressman described them as "fellows who had never been in action, the off-scouring and filth of the Earth." Many had been employed in guarding prisoners of war in Philadelphia and Lancaster. Unlike the veterans in the army, they had not learned to suffer patiently; when they were faced with the prospect of being turned out with only a pittance of pay, they mutinied and, led by an unruly lieutenant and a mentally deranged captain, seized the arsenals in Philadelphia and marched upon the Pennsylvania State House. Their resentment was chiefly directed against the heads of the Pennsylvania government: to the President and Council of Pennsylvania they sent a message stating their grievances and "demanding an answer in fifteen minutes or they would let in an enraged Soldiery on them." Some of the soldiers, far gone in liquor, hooted and threatened Congress, much to the alarm of apprehensive members. Hemmed in by "a Lawless Band of Armed Desperado's," Congress sat for three hours until the members, taking their courage in their hands, marched out and passed through the files of the mutineers without molestation. General St. Clair persuaded the troops to go back to their barracks but they soon broke out again, drinking and carousing.

While Philadelphia remained in the grip of the mutineers, the Pennsylvania authorities made no effort to call out the militia to rescue Congress, on the ground that the sympathies of the militiamen were largely with the soldiers. Finally Washington ordered Continental troops to move into Philadelphia; whereupon the insurgents immediately laid down their arms and several of the ringleaders boarded ship for England. When the loyal troops reached Philadelphia, the situation was under control; but in the meantime, Congress had fled the city.

By its precipitate retreat from Philadelphia, Congress sacrificed almost its last remaining shreds of dignity and prestige. Some patriots called Congress cowardly in running away from this small tumult, pointing out that George III had frequently stood his ground in St. James's in the face of far worse riots; and such eminent personages as Lord North, Lord Sandwich, and Lord George Germain had braved the mobs of London, sometimes from the security of their rooftops. The British King and British statesmen seemed to be made of sterner stuff than American congressmen. In any event, the Continental Congress was again on its travels, this time to Princeton where nothing more formidable than undergraduates seemed likely to disturb its repose.

Philadelphia, after the bird was flown, sought to coax it back with honeyed words. The one hundred thousand dollars a year which, it was estimated, Congress brought the city was not to be lightly thrown away and to get it back Philadelphians were ready to put on sackcloth and ashes. It was pointed out that Congress ought to be located in a big city where its acts could be closely observed by "the greatest number of active, inquisitive, vigilant and jealous spirits, who will . . . give the speediest alarm to the continent, if ever they should abuse their power" — and where were such citizens to be found in greater number than in the City of Brotherly Love? One Philadelphian, however, declared that his home town was too pure to harbor Congress any longer — "expense and public amusements (so unfriendly to republicanism) will follow them wherever they go." He suggested New York as a proper place for Congress to settle down.

But Congress declined to be lured back to Philadelphia by fair words — they would rather continue their travels forever, exclaimed some members, than return to that "sink of Toryism and Extortion." The city of William Penn — "the Sink of America, in which is huddled and collected Villains and Vermin from every Quarter," the center of vice as well as of politics — was held to be too mobbish, corrupt, and expensive to give sanctuary to Congress. It was, exclaimed a delegate, "the most inhospitable scandalous place I ever was in. If I once more can return to my family all the Devils in Hell shall not separate us."

Southerners hoped to move the capital to the Potomac, where Southern influences might offset the greater wealth and power of the North. Here in "the Centre of the Empire" was the proper home of the Continental Congress; "posterity would laugh at our federal buildings and desert them," it was said, "if we should unwisely for selfish purposes fix them on a corner of the Empire." Although they had starved Congress, the states, now that it was homeless, bid against each other for the privilege of sheltering the waif. New York offered Congress a tract of territory on the Hudson; Maryland proposed to surrender Annapolis to its jurisdiction; and New Jersey harped upon the advantages of Princeton.

As the prestige and authority of Congress declined, its popularity seemed to reach a new high.

Congress yearned for a few acres it could call its own, safe from mobs and the corrupting influence of large cities. Some members favored New Jersey as a site — here was a small state, debarred by its situation, it was supposed, from ever becoming other than a community of farmers uncontaminated by commerce or industry.

Others looked to the West as Congress's best hope in a highly uncertain world. It is true that, after 1783, its most important acts dealt with the West, and that its principal occupation consisted in administering the national domain. In the states themselves, there was little evidence of Congress's authority; in the West, its power was paramount and pervasive. It is not surprising, therefore, that at one time Congress seriously considered going West itself and growing up with the country: some Congressmen dreamed of a Federal city rising on the banks of the Monongahela from which Congress should rule a vast domain of forest and prairie. The Continental Congress might be poor and despised, but its trusteeship of the West augured better days in store — provided it lived long enough.

Congress debated the question of a site for its deliberations with as much earnestness as though it really mattered where it betook itself. In actuality, however, the peregrinations of that poor paltry body had ceased to have much significance other perhaps than finding a place in which to expire as comfortably as possible. It seemed probable that Congress "like the traveller's coat in the fable, after having been hugged close through the stormy hour of danger, will be cast aside as a useless burthen in the calm and sunshine of peace and victory." The fugitive was growing progressively weaker, and wherever it chose to settle promised to be its last resting place.

Meanwhile, Robert Morris was desperately searching for ways and means of raising money with which to appease the soldiers. "The Financier says he is doing everything in his power to pay the army," it was said, "but while the grass is growing, the horse may starve." Morris had already overdrawn governmental funds in Europe to the tune of three and a half million dollars, he owed contractors for last year's supplies, he had been obliged to offer 30 per cent over the previous year's prices to tempt contractors to sell to the army, and he had overstrained his own credit. All the money received from France went to the contractors; nothing was left over for the troops.

Almost at his wits' end, Robert Morris raised enough money to pay the soldiers a few months of their back pay — a mere trifle of the sum owing them — by anticipating the proceeds of a loan the United States hoped to raise in Holland.[8] With this money, Congress decided to fur-

[8] The loan did not materialize and the bills were protested in Europe, with the result that the credit of the Continental Congress reached a new low. But, at least,

lough the troops (it did not have enough money to discharge them out-right, but everyone knew that the difference between furloughing and discharging was only in name). But the money consigned to the troops was so delayed in reaching the army that many soldiers struck off for home in disgust without waiting for their pay. Thus, said a Continental officer, the soldiers were *"sent about their business,* — without pay, and without even thanks, for eight years' toil and dangers!" Those who remained in camp, however, received the small sum promised them by Congress. The Secretary of War, deeply distressed by the wrong done the army, borrowed money from his friends "in order to give three or four dollars to some officers of his acquaintance . . . to enable them to get home." The password was "Go in peace" and in three days the sol-diers were so dispersed that it was said that they would not be found together again until the Day of Judgment. "Is not this the day," asked General Steuben, "that all the preachers say that all accounts will be settled?"

Civilians could at least congratulate themselves upon the courage and patience of their army; their own record was somewhat less edifying. "We believe," said a congressman, "there never was an instance of an army being kept together who were so ill paid as ours, much less of their being disbanded without pay." The full measure of devotion was exacted from the soldiers of the Revolutionary army; the men whose blood made possible the realization of American independence received but a trifling reward from their countrymen. "If justice, good faith, honor, gratitude and all the other qualities which ennoble the character of a nation" were to be applied to the United States, said James Madison, "the republic would be found sadly wanting." "No country or people ought to be free that will not Support the Army that is fighting for their Liberties," said a patriot; but Americans had proved that a few determined men could win freedom for an entire nation. Washington pointed out philosophically that "Ingratitude has been experienced in all Ages, and Republics in particular have been famed for the exercise of that unnatural and Sordid Vice." Plainly, the United States was disposed to take full advantage of this prerogative of republics. "From my Soul I pity the Army," said the commander-in-chief.

In the Southern states, the war went on throughout 1782, and American soldiers continued to suffer the same privations which had beset them from the beginning of the war seven years before. Hungry, ragged, and unpaid, they remained in the field, constantly on the verge of mutiny. Whereas the Northern army was supplied by contract, the Southern army was left to live off the land — which, in this devastated region, meant short rations

the crisis over the disbanding of the Continental army was safely passed with the aid of these protested bills. Ultimately, the soldiers were paid in notes which steadily depreciated until Hamilton's financial program was adopted in 1790–1791.

indeed. "Our beef was perfect carrion," said General Nathanael Greene, "and even bad as it was, we were often without any." "Our regimen," reported Anthony Wayne, "is rice, poor beef, and *Aligator* water, which in addition to the British bullet and bayonet, the tommyhock, or scalping knife of other less *Savage* allies . . . affords no very flattering prospect of seeing Pennsa. in health and safety." To these officers, it began to seem that the people were indifferent to their fate. "Have you all forgot us to the Northward?" they asked. "We have not had a drop of Spirits in Camp for more than a month." In August 1782, Greene reported that almost half his men were "entirely naked, with nothing but a breech cloth about them, and never came out of their tents, and the rest were ragged as wolves."

It did not need the failure of the Continental Congress to deal fairly by the soldiers of the republic to demonstrate to farseeing patriots the necessity of a stronger central government. For several years before the demobilization of the army, the inadequacies of the Articles of Confederation had been apparent to all who aspired to see the United States great and powerful. The movement toward a more perfect union which reached its consummation in the Federal Constitution of 1787 began during the Revolutionary War.

To many Americans, the decline of the Continental Congress was as great a catastrophe as a military defeat. All their experience during the war had pointed to the necessity of a strong central government, and they could not reconcile themselves to seeing the United States dwindle into insignificance. "We have the Melancholy prospect of having spent our best Days, our Fortunes, and our Blood to no purpose, or to a bad one," said Alexander McDougall; "and of becoming the most Wretched despicable People on the Face of the Earth."

Washington frequently said that no one in the United States was more acutely conscious than he of the necessity of strengthening the central government because "no Man perhaps has felt the bad effects of it more sensibly." To the defects of the Articles of Confederation he ascribed the length and enormous cost of the war, the distress of the army, and the difficulties he had encountered as commander-in-chief; the Articles he would have scrapped without ceremony for a stronger and more efficient form of government. "I think the blood and treasure which has been spent in it [the war] has been lavished to little purpose," he wrote, "unless we can be better cemented"; in its present state, the United States was "no better than a rope of Sand and are as easily broken asunder." As long as the United States insisted upon living under the Articles, he pointed out, there would always be danger that the whole structure of government would collapse at any moment. And when that occurred, anarchy would almost certainly follow, "and we may find," said Washington, "by our own unhappy experience, that there is a natural and necessary progression, from the extreme of anarchy to the extreme of Tyranny; and that arbitrary power is most easily established on the ruins of Liberty abused to licentiousness." Long before the last shot of the war was fired, Washington was calling for "a Convention of the People" to revise the Articles of Confederation.

To Washington, his countrymen's distrust of the Continental Congress was inexplicable. "For Heavens sake," he asked, "who are Congress? Are they not the Creatures of the People, amenable to them for their Conduct, and dependent from day to day on their breath?" Nevertheless, he put his faith in the good sense of the American people, who, though often wrong, could be counted upon to come right eventually, even if their progress was agonizingly slow. Admittedly, to set Americans' feet on the right road was "a Herculean task, and to effect which, mountains of prejudice must be levelled"; but, like Robert Morris, Washington looked forward to the time "twenty years hence, when time and habit have settled and completed the Federal Constitution of America."

As might have been expected in men who for seven years had experienced the pernicious effects of provincialism, the soldiers were far more nationalistic than were the mass of civilians. Despite the failures and shortcomings of the Continental Congress, the troops were not eager to turn authority over to the states and to make the Continental army in effect thirteen different armies; they asked to be "one continental body, looking up to one sovereign," and one of their favorite toasts was: "A hoop to the barrel and cement to the union." Through common suffering and the comradeship that comes to all men who serve together in arms, the troops had been fused into one body.[9] "Who," asked Washington in 1783, ". . . could imagine that the most violent local prejudices would cease so soon, and that Men who came from different parts of the Continent, strongly disposed, by the habits of education, to despise and quarrel with each other, would instantly become but one patriotic band of brothers?"

A rising chorus of complaint proclaimed the inadequacy of the Articles of Confederation. Alexander Hamilton, for example, declared in 1780 that the Articles were fit neither for war nor for peace. If the United States was long to endure, it must have a strong central government invested with the right of imposing taxes, a bank, and an independent executive and judiciary. This "solid coercive union," he declared, must be the work of a constitutional convention. To forward Hamilton's program, the Federal Society was organized in Philadelphia in 1780 by a group of army officers and citizens calling themselves Confederationists. These men, representing most of the states in the union, proposed to lay before

[9] For example, at Valley Forge, in celebration of the French alliance, the officers paraded arm in arm, thirteen to a line. The number of officers in each line signified the thirteen states "and the interweaving of arms, a complete Union and most perfect Confederation."

the country evidence of the alarming encroachments being made by the states upon the powers of the national government. Unless this drift toward anarchy was halted, they predicted, Americans would fall victim of the "antipathy of states against states, of counties against counties in each state, and of townships against townships." Congressmen who failed to support the rights of Congress were to be recalled; and as a warning to backsliders, the Confederationists in every state were to be organized and their influence exerted at the polls. Thus began the labors that seven years later were to bring forth the Constitution of the United States.

Some Americans were prepared to adopt more drastic measures. Meeting in convention at Hartford, Connecticut, in 1780, delegates from New England and New York proposed that Congress be given power to employ military force against states that refused to comply with its requisitions of men and supplies. And almost at the same time, a committee of Congress, returning from a tour of inspection of the Continental army, recommended that Washington be given dictatorial powers. Alexander Hamilton urged Congress to proceed upon the assumption that it enjoyed all necessary authority under the power to preserve the republic — a broad construction of the Articles of Confederation which Hamilton was later to apply with notable results to the Federal Constitution of the United States.

Benjamin Franklin reminded his countrymen that they were living in a world hostile to democracy and that not even the Atlantic could protect them from their enemies. John Adams predicted that if Americans failed to cement the union, unfriendly powers would quickly put an end to this experiment in republicanism. "We shall be the sport of transatlantic politicians of all denominations, who hate liberty in every shape," he said.

Nationalists wished to maintain a sizable army, strengthen the navy, and create a diplomatic corps that would make the United States respected abroad. Washington, although deploring a large standing army, insisted upon universal military training in the militia, "the Palladium of our security," and upon a powerful navy to keep hostile powers from our shores. But this advice was ignored by the war-weary Americans: in 1784, the army was disbanded except for about one hundred officers and men to guard the stores at West Point and Fort Pitt; and about this time Congress sold the last ship of the Continental navy. Americans' chief defense, it was clear, was to be the Atlantic Ocean and the special provi-dence which, it was supposed, watched over the republic.

⌢ ⌢ ⌢

On both sides of the Atlantic, the utmost forbearance was required if the peace of 1783 was to be more than a truce between two wars of the English-speaking peoples. All the passions engendered by war and propaganda taught that the two countries were eternal enemies. "I would as soon have an Alliance with a Band of Robbers as with the People of Great Britain," exclaimed Edward Rutledge of South Carolina. "They are . . . the Natural Enemies of this Country — their Pride and their Interest will keep them so, and whenever they can stab, they will." It was urged that the United States never permit the British flag to be flown on British ships entering American harbors — "this," it was observed, "would be a moderate mark of our resentments towards so bloody, so barbarous a nation."

Before the United States could be truly independent, said John Adams, it was necessary to eradicate "forever from the heart of every American every tender sentiment towards Great Britain." Independent in name, Americans would actually be in a state of colonial bondage if they permitted themselves to fall into the old habit of thinking well of the former mother country. The radicals vigorously combated the idea that there was "some justice, some honor, some humanity, and some reason in Great Britain"; on the contrary, there was hardly a respectable remnant of honest men remaining in England — who, if they were wise, would emigrate from that doomed island.

Although Franklin had completely lost that veneration for the British Empire which had made him before the Revolution a staunch champion of imperialism (of his own peculiar brand, to be sure), he saw no reason why Britain and the United States could not exist peacefully, if not as neighbors — for, it will be remembered, Franklin was eager to take over all British possessions in North America — at least as friends across the sea. If the English could only be made to see that the United States was destined to be one of the most powerful nations in the world, friendship between the two countries would, he believed, be assured, and "England, if she has at length gained Wisdom will have gained something more valuable, and more essential to her Prosperity, than all she has lost." After 1783, his watchword was: "Let us now forgive and forget."

Yet it did not come easily to Englishmen to take the hand of a people who had involved them in a long and costly war and who had broken away from the parent state. "These Miscreants," exclaimed an indignant Englishman, ". . . who led an indulging People into War" without provocation, merited the eternal hatred of every Briton. Republicans and revolutionaries to the end, they would not rest content until they had tumbled the throne and all other conservative institutions about the heads of Englishmen.

To vex Englishmen further, some Americans took this opportunity to lecture the erstwhile mother country upon how to regain her place in the world, lost through the folly of quarreling with her colonists. England could again be great, they declared, only by winning the affections of that "great and growing people" across the Atlantic, the prop of England's old age. John Adams, for example, informed the British peace commissioners: "Depend upon it, you have no chance for salvation but by setting up America very high." Such advice, however well meant, was not often accepted graciously by Britons: it grated upon them to be instructed by upstart republicans upon the importance of being in the good graces of the Americans. Having been compelled to recognize the independence of their colonies, Englishmen thought that they at least might enjoy the satisfaction of looking down their noses at the United States and all its works.

By the treaty of peace, England had gone far toward the reconciliation which Shelburne had so much at heart. As John Jay said, the peace terms had removed the causes of future variance between the two countries and "we may become as sensible to her [Great Britain's] future good offices as we have been to her former evil ones." Yet the decisive test of British good will toward the United States hinged upon the willingness of the former mother country to make a commercial treaty with the United States. In the preliminary treaty of 1782, an article had originally been included restoring the Americans to a privileged commercial position in the British Empire. Benjamin Vaughan urged his government to allow the Americans the same freedom of trade with the empire that they had enjoyed as colonists. Only by clearing away "the rubbish of Acts of Parliament" by which Americans were barred from empire markets, he said, could a firm foundation for Anglo-American friendship be laid. "If you make navigation laws against the Americans," he warned his countrymen, "the Americans will do the same against you" — with the result that Great Britain would find itself involved in a ruinous trade war with a people who, if they were but treated with consideration, would be its best customers and firmest friends.

Admittedly, the prosperity of the United States depended largely upon access to the markets of the British Empire. As British colonists, Americans had enjoyed the privilege of trading freely within the empire; now, as an independent people, they saw with dismay that they could not do without the protected markets of the empire from which they had rebelled. Americans, it would seem, could not be happy in the British Empire or wholly outside it.

English liberalism, momentarily in ascendancy during the administration of Lord Shelburne, counseled a policy of conciliation and friendship toward the republic. To the Whigs, the next best thing to preserving the empire was maintaining as close a union as possible with the United States. Accordingly, they endeavored to place the commercial relations of the two countries upon a mutually profitable basis. By the terms of the bill introduced into Parliament by William Pitt the Younger, the Americans would have been accorded many of the economic privileges they had enjoyed as British subjects. Among other things, this bill opened direct trade between the United States and the British West Indies in American ships — a trade as essential to the United States as it was to the British islands in the Caribbean.

At this critical moment, the weakness and disorder that prevailed in the United States under the Articles of Confederation encouraged many Englishmen to believe that the republic was on the verge of collapse and that pressure from Great Britain would ensure its ruin. The states, it was said in London, "are all in confusion, weary of their independence, and will soon return to Great Britain upon her own terms" — the same illusion that had led Englishmen to prosecute the war long after less obstinate men would have renounced the struggle. It was admitted that, for the time being, England must give up its efforts to force Americans to return to their allegiance, but much was expected from the happy effects of the civil wars, financial prostration, and economic collapse which were held certain to occur in the United States. *"The American States will break to pieces, and then we may still conquer them"* succinctly expressed this policy towards the United States. This, Americans themselves admitted, was but too probable; and it is perhaps not blameworthy in English statesmen that they acted upon so fair a calculation.

Spokesman for the irreconcilables in Great Britain was Lord Sheffield, in whom love of British maritime supremacy was joined with hatred for the rebels across the Atlantic. It ran against Lord Sheffield's grain to stoop to conciliations; rather, Americans ought to be taught that their vaunted independence was a bed of thorns — and Lord Sheffield conceived it to be England's duty to plant as many thorns as possible under these raffish republicans. To foster their commerce and thereby raise up a rival to England's maritime power was in Lord Sheffield's opinion to sign the death warrant of Great Britain and its empire. England, he declared, "was as tenacious of the principle of that Act [Navigation Acts] as it possibly could be of the principle of Magna Charta," and national interest required that Americans be denied vital trading privileges within the empire.

With these arguments, Lord Sheffield attempted to persuade his countrymen that they could treat Americans as inconsiderately as they chose and still enjoy a virtual monopoly of the trade of their former colonists. Whether in or out of the empire, ran his comforting philosophy, Americans could not do without British manufactured goods and, willy-nilly, must sell their raw products in the markets of the British Empire. Britain alone could provide Americans with acceptable credit facilities, supply their wants, and furnish a market for their goods; however Americans might struggle in the toils, they could not free themselves — economically, they were inextricably attached to Great Britain.

Thus the promising beginning in Anglo-American friendship manifested in the peace treaty of 1782 was wrecked by prejudice and ill will. England seemed to have exhausted its liberalism in making peace with America; little remained to sweeten relations between the two countries in the postwar period. Even Charles James Fox, the champion of American freedom, denounced the treaty as a surrender of England's vital interests; and Edmund Burke called it a "disgraceful concession" to the United States which abandoned the Loyalists without securing a single advantage in return.

That Americans, in their eagerness to retaliate upon Great Britain, would forgo their provincialism and sink their differences in order to form a more perfect union was apparently beyond the ken of many Englishmen. They had yet to learn, although their experiences of the last twenty years had afforded them ample instruction, that whenever Great Britain attempted to coerce Americans it succeeded only in uniting them.

Unmindful of this lesson, Great Britain, having done much to create an American union, unwittingly helped to cement that union when it seemed certain to disintegrate after the war. The United States owes a heavy debt to British ministers; George Grenville, Charles Townshend, Lord Hillsborough, Lord North, all helped to call a new world into being. It remained for Lord Sheffield to save Americans from their own errors. No wonder that Americans believed that Providence was on their side, when even their enemies worked in their favor. Washington rejoiced that British statesmen had not lost their old skill in awakening the dormant patriotism of his countrymen. Americans, said Gouverneur Morris, ought to be eternally grateful to the former mother country because "by seizing the critical moment when we were about to divide, she [Great Britain] has shown clearly the dreadful consequences of divisions." From this the moral could be drawn that Great Britain was America's best friend — and never more so than when trying to be its enemy.

⌒ ⌒ ⌒

Not even Lord Sheffield was more averse to accepting the United States within the community of nations than was His Britannic Majesty, George III. In March 1782, confronted with the decision of Parliament to abandon the American war, George had contemplated abdication, even going so far as to compose a farewell message to the English people: "His Majesty . . . with much sorrow finds He can be of no further utility to His Native Country which drives Him to the painful step of quitting it forever." Thinking better of such a drastic measure, George remained on the throne even though it had become for him a seat of misery. Never did he cease to be afflicted by the success of the rebels in making good their independence. To him, there were no compensations for Great Britain in the loss of the American colonies unless, perhaps, in the riddance of some uncommonly troublesome and ungrateful subjects. George sickened at the thought of independence, and the royal ears could not bear that horrid name, "The United States of America." All that remained to the unhappy monarch was the privilege of cherishing his antipathies and snubbing his former subjects. He carefully avoided reading any of the articles of the treaty of peace that mentioned the United States of America; and in 1783, he declared that he would receive no minister from the republic and that he would "ever have a bad opinion of any Englishman who would accept of being an accredited Minister for that revolted state." George arranged to be out of town when the heralds proclaimed peace in London. He could not bear to hear the trumpets which, to his ears, sounded "the Downfall of the lustre of the Empire." Other Englishmen might celebrate the end of the war, but the King feared that it would prove to be a wake for the British Empire.

While English statesmen repented of their liberality toward the American republic, the King's conscience remained clear and untroubled: he, for one, had never been guilty of advocating generosity or forgiveness toward the rebels. "One comfort I have," wrote the monarch, "that I have alone tried to support the Dignity of my Crown and feel that I am innocent of the Evils that have occurred, though deeply wounded that it should have happened during my Reign. . . . I should be miserable indeed," he said, "if I did not feel that no blame on that Account can be laid at my door, and did I not also know that knavery seems to be so much the striking feature of its Inhabitants that it may not in the end be an evil that they become Aliens to this Kingdom!" To George's mind, Great Britain could not be great and powerful without America, yet he could not bring himself to court the affections of the United States in order to win a friend and ally. He would go down, if go down he must, with his pride and prejudices intact. If he could not have Americans as subjects, they were as nothing in his eyes. No recognition of the future power of the United States affected his attitude toward his former subjects; yet he reluctantly acknowledged that the peace of 1783 was the best that Englishmen could expect in their fallen state. A nation divided into opposing factions and with "Religion and Public Spirit . . . quite absorbed by Vice and Dissipation" could hardly hope to win victory; it ought to be thankful it had escaped utter ruin.

To the King, the misfortunes of the nation were accompanied by personal afflictions which tried the hardihood of that already overburdened monarch. George III had reared the Prince of Wales with exacting care, even keeping him in the frilled shirts of infancy far into his adolescence, and exerting over him some of that strict parental authority which Americans had suspected would have been meted out to them had they remained in the empire. Like the colonists, the Prince rebelled against this regimen, and the royal household was thrown into the same kind of confusion that had overtaken the empire. He found a mentor in his uncle, the Duke of Devonshire, as accomplished a rake as ever graced the nobility. The duke, having quarreled with his brother, George III, was eager to take the young Prince under his wing if only for the satisfaction of bringing sorrow upon the King. The Prince showed as little contrition as did his uncle in causing his father grief: there was hardly a more apt pupil in all England in the ways of debauchery. "Such were the fruits," remarked Horace Walpole, "of his being locked up in the palace of piety!"

The wayward Prince and his uncle openly insulted the King in public; and in a letter to his mistress, the Prince was reported to have called his sister, the Princess Royal, *"that bandy legged b——h, my sister."* This was nothing, however, to what George III endured at the hands of his son and brother. "When we hunt together, neither my son nor my brother speak to me," lamented the King, "and lately when the chase ended at a little village where there was but a single post-chaise to be hired, my son and brother got into it and drove to London, leaving me to go home in a cart if I could find one." The escapades and heartlessness of the Prince brought such pain to the King that he declared he could not sleep for ten nights.

The most painful wound inflicted by this serpent's tooth came when the willful Prince joined the Whigs and began to frequent the company of Charles James Fox. The Prince was first attracted to Fox by his reputation as a man about town but, having sat at Fox's feet for instruction in vice, he began to take his politics from the same source. Becoming a regular habitué of Brooks's, he listened avidly to the wit and sallies of the Whig leaders and, learning to lose a small fortune during an evening at cards, he also learned to damn the Tories. So enamored of Fox did the Prince become that he campaigned in Westminster for Fox's re-election to Parliament; and the two men carried their intimacy to the point of exchanging mistresses.

Once the Prince of Wales had thrown off the traces, the King knew little domestic peace. The spirit of revolt spread alarmingly among his offspring: the seven-year-old Duke of Sussex had to be locked in the nursery for wearing the colors of a popular Whig admiral who had fallen from favor at court. The monarch seemed destined to suffer the unhappy end of King Lear in losing his empire and his children at the same time.

⌒   ⌒   ⌒

In November 1783, the British, who had clung to New York until the signing of the definitive treaty of peace, marched out of the city and the American army marched in. The city which over seven years before had been captured by Sir William Howe and had held out resolutely against every attempt to carry it by storm was once again in the hands of the Americans, and they sat down to celebrate the event in style. At a dinner given by Governor Clinton of New York to Washington and his officers, a good-sized cellar was drunk dry by the guests.

After this rousing celebration, Washington hurried to Annapolis to take formal leave of the Continental Congress and the duties he had borne since taking command of the Continental army on that midsummer day over eight years before. The general was in a hurry, for he had promised to spend Christmas Day with his wife and family at Mount Vernon. But in every town and village through which he passed, the citizens turned out to pay him homage. In Baltimore, he was escorted into the city by a company of gentlemen and greeted by "a brilliant collection of ladies assembled to entertain him through the evening." He entered heartily into the spirit of the occasion and led the dancing with his usual graceful skill. Next morning, however, Washington tore himself away from his admirers; had he tarried as long as the Baltimoreans wished, Martha Washington would have spent a lonely Christmas.

At Annapolis, on December 23, 1783, Washington bade farewell to the Continental Congress and resigned his commission as commander-in-chief of the American army. The scene was one of the most affecting in American history. His hand, in which he held his address, shook visibly as he spoke; and when he recounted the services of his officers and urged Congress to deal liberally with them, "he was obliged to support the paper with both hands. But when he commended the interests of his dearest country to Almighty God . . . his voice faltered and sunk, and the whole house felt his agitations."

The next day he came home to Mount Vernon.

⌒　⌒　⌒

The American Revolution marked a turning point in history: the principles of individual liberty and the sovereignty of the people, apparently about to suffer eclipse in Europe, were now firmly established in the Western Hemisphere. These ideas, though actually as old as the Greeks, began to appear as distinctively American, and under this guise they began to conquer the world. The American Revolution was, as Thomas Paine said, the accomplishment of an age — the fruition of eighteenth-century liberalism. In America were to be found religious and political freedom, an approximation to economic equality, active sovereignty of the people, and faith in the power of reason to solve all mankind's problems — the state of society, in short, of which the philosophers had dreamed and the people had come to regard as an almost unattainable ideal. The impact of this example had incalculable effect upon the history of the world. "The precepts, the reasonings, and example of the United States of America," said John Adams, "disseminated by the press through every part of the world, have convinced the understanding and have touched the heart." In this sense, Thomas Paine observed, the American Revolution had "contributed more to enlighten the world, and diffuse a spirit of freedom and liberality among mankind, than any human event (if this may be called one) that ever preceded it."

The American Revolution did not immediately establish a full-fledged democracy in the United States, but it did furnish Americans with ideals and aspirations which, however far from being realized, remain the goal of their endeavors. From the course set by the Revolution, Americans have never far deviated. Many citizens are sometimes in doubt just where the republic is headed, and find its progress rough and jolting. Yet, if the affairs of the United States seem unsettled and confused, Americans can say — as since 1776 they have never ceased to say — "This is a free country."

The keynote was freedom.

Bibliography

MANUSCRIPT SOURCES

Samuel Adams MSS., New York Public Library.
Elias Boudinot MSS., Historical Society of Pennsylvania.
Sir Henry Clinton MSS., William L. Clements Library, Ann Arbor, Michigan.
Annotations by Sir Henry Clinton in C. Stedman, *The History of the Origin, Progress, and Termination of the American War*, John Carter Brown Library, Providence, Rhode Island.
Papers of the Continental Congress, Library of Congress.
Lord Cornwallis MSS., Library of Congress.
Diary of N. Digby, British Museum Add MSS. 32413 LC.
William Duer MSS., New York Historical Society.
Benjamin Franklin MSS., American Philosophical Society.
Thomas Gage MSS., William L. Clements Library.
Horatio Gates MSS., New York Historical Society.
Lord George Germain MSS., William L. Clements Library.
Nathanael Greene MSS., William L. Clements Library.
—— American Philosophical Society.
David Hartley MSS., William L. Clements Library.
William Irvine MSS., Historical Society of Pennsylvania.
Thomas Jefferson MSS., Library of Congress.
Henry Knox MSS., Massachusetts Historical Society.
William Knox MSS., William L. Clements Library.
Alexander McDougall MSS., New York Historical Society.
Thomas McKean MSS., Historical Society of Pennsylvania.
Robert Morris MSS., Library of Congress.
Richard Peters MSS., Historical Society of Pennsylvania.
Joseph Reed MSS., New York Historical Society.
Benjamin Rush MSS., Library Company of Philadelphia.
William Shippen MSS., Historical Society of Pennsylvania.
Lord Stirling MSS., New York Historical Society.
Benjamin Vaughan MSS., William L. Clements Library.
George Washington MSS., Library of Congress.
Anthony Wayne MSS., Historical Society of Pennsylvania.
Jasper Yeates MSS., Historical Society of Pennsylvania.

CONTEMPORARY PAMPHLETS

I

Abingdon, Earl of. *Thoughts on the Letter of Edmund Burke*. London 1777.
—— *An Answer to Edmund Burke*. London, 1777.
Berkenhout, John. *Lucubrations on Ways and Means*. London, 1780.
Burgoyne, John. *A Letter from Lt. General Burgoyne to His Constituents*. Dublin, 1779.
—— *The State of the Expedition from Canada as Laid before the House of Commons*. London, 1780.
Chalmers, George. *Second Thoughts*. London, 1777.
Clinton, Sir Henry. *Observations on Mr. Stedman's History of the American Revolution*. London, 1794.
Hartley, David. *Letters on the American War*. London, 1780.
—— *An Address*. York, 1781.
Howe, Sir William. *The Narrative of Lieut. General Sir William Howe*. London, 1780.
Price, Richard. *Observations on the Importance of the American Revolution*. London, 1784.
—— *Two Tracts on Civil Liberty*. London, 1778.
Pulteney, William. *Thoughts on the Present State of Affairs with America*. London, 1778.
—— *Considerations on the Present State of Affairs*. London, 1778.
Robinson, Matthew. *Peace the Best Policy*. London, 1777.
Stewart, James. *The Total Refutation and Political Overthrow of Dr. Price*. London, 1776.
Tooke, John Horne. *Facts Addressed to the Subjects of Great Britain and Ireland*. London, 1780.

II

Candid Thoughts. London, 1781.
Characters. London, 1777.
A Letter to Lord Chatham. London, 1777.
Considerations Addressed to all Persons of Property. London, 1777.
A Letter to Lord George Germain. London, 1778.
A Journal of the March of a Party of Provincials. Glasgow, 1776.
A Letter to the People of America. London, 1778.
Remarks upon the Report of a Peace. Dublin, 1783.
The Remembrancer. London, 1775.
A Speech on Some Political Topics. London, 1778.
A Letter to the Whigs. London, 1779.

NEWSPAPERS AND MAGAZINES

Annual Register, 1763–1783.
Continental Journal and Weekly Advertiser, 1778–1783.

Essex Gazette, 1775–1783.
Freeman's Journal or North American Intelligencer, 1780–1783.
Gentleman's Magazine, 1776–1783.
Historical Magazine.
Independent Chronicle and Universal Advertiser, 1776–1783.
London Chronicle, 1776–1783.
Magazine of American History.
New England Chronicle, 1776.
New York Gazette and Weekly Mercury, 1778–1780.
Pennsylvania Gazette, 1775–1783.
Pennsylvania Magazine of History and Biography.
Pennsylvania Packet, 1777–1783.
Rivington's Royal Gazette, 1777–1782.
Royal Pennsylvania Gazette, 1778.
The Scot's Magazine, 1775–1783.
South Carolina Historical and Genealogical Magazine.
Town and Country Magazine, 1763–1783.
Tyler's Quarterly Historical and Genealogical Magazine.
Virginia Magazine.
William and Mary College Quarterly.

TRAVELERS' ACCOUNTS

Anburey, Thomas. *Travels Through the Interior Parts of America*. Houghton Mifflin. Boston, 1923.
Barbe-Marbois, François, Marquis de. *Our Revolutionary Forefathers*. Duffield. New York, 1929.
Chastellux, François Jean, Marquis de. *Travels in North America*. New York, 1827.
Hunter, Robert. *Quebec to Carolina in 1785–1786*. The Huntington Library. San Marino, California, 1943.

HISTORICAL COLLECTIONS

Manuscripts of the Marquis of Abergavenny. Historical Manuscripts Commission, Tenth Report, Appendix, Part 5. Eyre and Spottiswoode. London, 1885.
American Manuscripts. Vols. I, II, III. Historical Manuscripts Commission. His Majesty's Stationery Office. London, 1904, 1906, 1907.
Balch, Thomas, editor. *Letters and Papers Relating to the Provincial History of Pennsylvania*. Privately printed. Philadelphia, 1855.
—— *Papers Relating Chiefly to the Maryland Line*. Privately printed. Philadelphia, 1857.
John P. Branch Historical Papers. Vol. I. Privately printed. Ashland, Virginia, 1904.
Manuscripts of the Earl of Carlisle. Historical Manuscripts Commission, Fifteenth Report, Appendix, Part 6. Eyre and Spottiswoode. London, 1897.

Public Papers of George Clinton. State Printers. New York and Albany, 1899.

Journals of the Continental Congress (Gaillard Hunt, editor). Government Printing Office. Washington, 1910–1928.

Letters of Members of the Continental Congress (Edmund C. Burnett, editor). Carnegie Institution. Washington, 1921–1936.

Doniol, Henry. *Histoire de la participation de la France à l'établissement des Etats-Unis d'Amerique.* Imprimerie nationale. Paris, 1886–1892.

Durand, John, editor. *New Materials for the History of the American Revolution.* Holt. New York, 1889.

Essex Institute Historical Collections. Salem, Massachusetts.

Force, Peter, editor. *American Archives.* Clarke & Force. Washington, 1833–1851.

The Manuscripts of J. B. Fortescue. Historical Manuscripts Commission, Thirteenth Report, Appendix, Part 3. Her Majesty's Stationery Office. London, 1892.

Gibbes, Robert W. *Documentary History of the American Revolution.* Appleton. New York, 1853–1857.

Hastings Manuscripts. Vol. III. Historical Manuscripts Commission. His Majesty's Stationery Office. London, 1934.

Historical and Genealogical Register. Vol. I. Boston, 1876.

Hunt, Gaillard, editor. *Fragments of Revolutionary History.* The Historical Printing Club. Brooklyn, 1892.

Manuscripts of Lord Kenyon. Historical Manuscripts Commission, Fourteenth Report, Appendix, Part 4. Her Majesty's Stationery Office. London, 1894.

Collections of the Massachusetts Historical Society.

Proceedings of the Massachusetts Historical Society.

Meng, John J. *Despatches and Instructions of Conrad Alexandre Gerard.* Johns Hopkins Press. Baltimore, 1939.

Moore, Frank. *Diary of the Revolution.* Charles T. Evans. New York, 1863.

Morison, Samuel Eliot. *Sources and Documents Illustrating the American Revolution.* Clarendon Press. Oxford, 1929.

Niles, H. *Principles and Acts of the American Revolution.* Printed for the Editor. Baltimore, 1823.

The Parliamentary History of England, 1775–1783. T. C. Hansard. London, 1812.

Roberts, Kenneth. *March to Quebec.* Doubleday, Doran. New York, 1938.

Sparks, Jared, editor. *Correspondence of the American Revolution.* Little, Brown. Boston, 1853.

State Historical Papers:
   Archives of Maryland.
   Documents relating to the Revolutionary History of New Jersey.
   Documents relating to the Colonial History of New York.
   Collections of the New York Historical Society.
   State Records of North Carolina.
   Archives of Pennsylvania.
   Records of the State of Rhode Island.

Stevens, B. F., editor. *Facsimiles of Manuscripts in European Archives Relating to America, 1773–1783.* Privately printed. London, 1889–1895.
——The *Clinton-Cornwallis Controversy.* Privately printed. London, 1888.
Stopford-Sackville Papers. Vol. II. Historical Manuscripts Commission. His Majesty's Stationery Office. London, 1910.
The Sullivan-Clinton Campaign in 1779. The University of the State of New York. Albany, 1929.
Thwaites, Reuben Gold, editor. *Collections of the State Historical Society of Wisconsin.* Vol. 12. Madison, 1892.
Various Collections. Vol. VI. Historical Manuscripts Commission. His Majesty's Stationery Office. London, 1909.
Collections of the Vermont Historical Society. Vol. 1. Montpelier, 1870.
Wharton, Francis. *The Revolutionary Diplomatic Correspondence of the United States.* Government Printing Office. Washington, 1889.

MEMOIRS AND LETTERS

Abbatt, William, editor. *Memoirs of Major General William Heath.* Privately printed. New York, 1901.
Adams, Charles Francis, editor. *Familiar Letters of John Adams and His Wife.* Hurd & Houghton. New York, 1876.
—— *The Works of John Adams.* Little, Brown. Boston, 1851.
Albemarle, George Thomas. *Memoirs of the Marquis of Rockingham.* R. Bentley. London, 1852.
"Diary of James Allen." *Pennsylvania Magazine of History and Biography.* Vol. 9. Philadelphia, 1885.
Major André's Journal. Privately printed. Tarrytown, New York. 1930.
Andrews, Frank A., editor. *Philip Fithian: Letters to His Wife.* Privately printed. Vineland, New Jersey, 1932.
Ballagh, James C., editor. *The Letters of Richard Henry Lee.* Macmillan. New York, 1912.
"Baurmeister's Narrative." *Magazine of American History.* Vol. 1. New York, 1877.
Biddle, A., editor. *Old Family Letters.* Lippincott. Philadelphia, 1892.
"Letters of Robert Biddulph." *American Historical Review.* Vol. 29. New York, 1924.
Bolton, Charles Knowles, editor. *Letters of Hugh Earl Percy.* Charles E. Goodspeed. Boston, 1902.
Boudinot, Elias. *Journal.* Frederick Bourquin. Philadelphia, 1894.
"A British Officer in Boston." *Atlantic Monthly.* Vol. 39. Boston, 1877.
The Correspondence of Edmund Burke. Francis & John Rivington. London, 1844.
The Works of Edmund Burke. Little, Brown. Boston, 1880.
Campbell, Charles, editor. *The Bland Papers.* Edmund & Julian Ruffin. Petersburg, Virginia, 1840.
Chinard, Gilbert, editor. *George Washington as the French Knew Him.* Princeton University Press. Princeton, 1940.

Cornwallis-West, G. *The Life and Letters of Admiral Cornwallis.* Robert Holden. London, 1927.

Journal of Nicholas Cresswell. Jonathan Cape. London, 1925.

Curwen, Samuel. *Journals and Letters.* G. A. Ward. New York, 1842.

Cushing, Harry A., editor. *The Writings of Samuel Adams.* Putnam. New York, 1906.

"Journal of Captain John Davis." *Pennsylvania Magazine of History and Biography.* Vol. 5. Philadelphia, 1881.

Deux-Ponts, Count William de. *My Campaigns in America.* Wiggins & Lunt. Boston, 1868.

Drayton, John. *Memoirs of the American Revolution.* A. E. Miller. Charleston, 1821.

"Journal of William Ellery." *Pennsylvania Magazine of History and Biography.* Vol. 13. Philadelphia, 1885.

Epping, C. S. J., editor. *Journals of Du Roi the Elder.* Appleton. New York, 1911.

Field, Edward, editor. *Diary of Colonel Israel Angell.* Privately printed. Providence, Rhode Island, 1899.

Fitzpatrick, John C., editor. *The Writings of George Washington.* Government Printing Office. Washington, 1931–1944.

—— *The Diaries of George Washington.* Houghton Mifflin. Boston, 1925.

Foner, Philip S., editor. *The Complete Writings of Thomas Paine.* Citadel Press. New York, 1945.

Ford, Paul Leicester, editor. *The Writings of Thomas Jefferson.* Putnam. New York, 1892.

Ford, Worthington C., editor. *The Correspondence and Journals of Samuel B. Webb.* Privately printed. New York, 1893.

—— *The Letters of Joseph Jones.* Department of State. Washington, 1889.

Fortescue, Sir John. *The Correspondence of George III.* Macmillan. London, 1927–1928.

Francis, Sir Philip. *The Francis Letters.* Hutchinson. London, 1900.

The Letters of Moore Furman. Frederick H. Hitchcock. New York, 1912.

Gottschalk, Louis, editor. *The Letters of Lafayette to Washington, 1777–1779.* Privately printed by Helen Fahnestock Hubbard. New York, 1944.

"Diary of William Greene." *Proceedings of the Massachusetts Historical Society.* Vol. 54. Boston, 1922.

Hamilton, S. M., editor. *The Writings of James Monroe.* Putnam. New York, 1898.

Hammond, Otis G., editor. *The Sullivan Papers.* New Hampshire Historical Society Publications. Concord, 1930–1939.

Hannay, David, editor. *Letters of Sir Samuel Hood.* Publications of the Navy Records Society. London, 1895.

Heartman, Charles F., editor. *Letters Written by Ebenezer Huntington.* Privately printed. New York, 1914.

Hunt, Gaillard, editor. *The Writings of James Madison.* Putnam. New York, 1906.

"Letters of Ebenezer Huntington." *American Historical Review*. Vol. 5. New York, 1900.

Hutchinson, Thomas. *Diary and Letters*. Sampson Low. London, 1883.

Johnston, Henry P., editor. *The Correspondence and Public Papers of John Jay*. Putnam. New York, 1891.

Jones, E. Alfred, editor. *Journal of Alexander Chesney*. Ohio State University Press. Columbus, 1921.

"Journals of Lieut. Colonel Stephen Kemble." *Collections of the New York Historical Society*. Vol. 16. New York, 1884.

Kirkland, Frederick R., editor. *Letters on the American Revolution*. Privately printed. Philadelphia, 1941.

Lamb, R. *Journal of Occurrences*. Wilkinson and Courtney. Dublin, 1809.

Laughton, J. K., editor. *Journal of Rear Admiral Bartholomew Jones*. Publications of the Navy Records Society. Vol. 6. London, 1896.

Laurens, John. *Army Correspondence*. Privately printed. New York, 1861.

Memoirs of the Duc de Lauzun. Sturgis and Walton. New York, 1912.

"The Lee Papers, 1754–1811." *Collections of the New York Historical Society*. Printed for the Society. New York, 1872–1875.

Anecdotes of the Late Charles Lee, Esq. J. S. Jordan. London, 1797.

Lee, Henry. *Memoirs of the War in the Southern Department*. Bradford and Inskeep. Philadelphia, 1812.

Lee, Richard H. *Memoir of the Life of Richard Henry Lee*. Carey & Lea. Philadelphia, 1825.

The Life and Letters of Lady Sarah Lennox. John Murray. London, 1902.

Lewis, W. S., editor. *The Yale Edition of Horace Walpole's Correspondence*. Yale University Press. New Haven, 1937–1944.

Lincoln, James Minor, editor. *Papers of Capt. Rufus Lincoln*. Privately printed. Boston, 1904.

Lodge, Henry Cabot, editor. *The Works of Alexander Hamilton*. Putnam. New York, 1903.

Mackenzie, Frederick. *Diary*. Harvard University Press. Cambridge, 1930.

"Journal of Captain John Montresor." *Pennsylvania Magazine of History and Biography*. Vol. 6. Philadelphia, 1882.

Correspondence of Robert Morris. Printed by Stan V. Henkels. Philadelphia, 1917.

"Diary of Robert Morton." *Pennsylvania Magazine of History and Biography*. Vol. 1. Philadelphia, 1877.

Moultrie, William. *Memoirs of the American Revolution*. David Longworth. New York, 1802.

"Diary of Captain John Nice." *Pennsylvania Magazine of History and Biography*. Vol. 16. Philadelphia, 1892.

Parsons, Theophilus. *Memoir of Theophilus Parsons*. Ticknor and Fields. Boston, 1859.

Pettingill, Ray W., editor. *Letters from America, 1776–1779*. Houghton Mifflin. Boston, 1924.

Phillips, George Morris, editor. *Historic Letters* from the Collections of the West Chester State Normal School. Lippincott. Philadelphia, 1898.

"Diary of Ezekiel Price." *Proceedings of the Massachusetts Historical Society.* Vol. 7. Boston, 1864.

"Diary of Robert Proud." *Pennsylvania Magazine of History and Biography.* Vol. 34. Philadelphia, 1910.

Radziwill, Princess, translator. *They Knew the Washingtons.* Bobbs-Merrill. Indianapolis, 1925.

Read, William T., editor. *The Life and Correspondence of George Read.* Lippincott. Philadelphia, 1870.

Reed, W. B., editor. *The Life and Correspondence of Joseph Reed.* Lindsay & Blakiston. Philadelphia, 1847.

Diary of Samuel Richards. Privately printed. Philadelphia, 1909.

Letters and Journals of Mrs. General Riedesel. J. Munsell. Albany, 1867.

Diary of Captain Thomas Rodney. Historical Society of Delaware. Wilmington, 1868.

Ross, Charles, editor. *Correspondence of Charles, First Marquis Cornwallis.* John Murray. London, 1859.

Russell, Lord John, editor. *Memorials and Correspondence of Charles James Fox.* Blanchard & Lea. Philadelphia, 1853.

Ryden, George Herbert, editor. *Letters to and from Caesar Rodney.* Historical Society of Delaware. Philadelphia, 1933.

The Sandwich Papers (edited by G. R. Barnes and J. H. Owens). Publications of the Navy Records Society. Vol. 69. London, 1932.

"Letters of Alexander Scammell." *Magazine of American History.* Vol. 10. New York, 1893.

George Selwyn: His Letters and His Life (edited by E. S. Roscoe and Helen Clergue). T. F. Unwin. London, 1899.

"William Seymour. A Journal of the Southern Expedition." *Pennsylvania Magazine of History and Biography.* Vol. 7. Philadelphia, 1883.

Simcoe, Lieut. Colonel J. G. *Military Journal.* Bartlett & Welford. New York, 1844.

Smith, Albert Henry, editor. *The Writings of Benjamin Franklin.* Macmillan. New York, 1905.

Smith, William A., editor. *The St. Clair Papers.* Robert Clarke. Cincinnati, 1882.

Sparks, Jared, editor. *The Works of Benjamin Franklin.* Childs and Peterson. Philadelphia, 1840.

Stone, William L., editor. *Letters of Brunswick and Hessian Officers.* J. Munsell. Albany, 1891.

—— *Memoirs of Major General Riedesel.* J. Munsell. Albany, 1868.

Tarleton, Lieut. Colonel Banastre. *History of the Campaigns of 1780 and 1781 in the Southern Provinces of North America.* T. Cadell. London, 1787.

Tatum, Edward H., editor. *The American Journal of Ambrose Serle.* The Huntington Library. San Marino, California, 1940.

Thacher, James. *Military Journal.* Richardson and Lord. Boston, 1823.

Uhlendorf, B. A., and Vosper, Edna, editors. *Letters from Major Baurmeister.* University of Pennsylvania Press. Philadelphia, 1937.

Official Letters of the Governors of the State of Virginia. Vol. III. Richmond, 1927.

"Diary of Albigence Waldo." *Pennsylvania Magazine of History and Biography*. Vol. 21. Philadelphia, 1897.

Walpole, Horace. *The Last Journals*. J. Lane. London, 1910.

—— *Memoirs of the Reign of George the Third*. Putnam. New York, 1894.

Warren-Adams Letters. 2 vols. *Collections of the Massachusetts Historical Society*. Vol. 73. Boston, 1925.

Wilkin, Captain W. H., editor. *Some British Soldiers in America*. H. Rees. London, 1914.

Wilkinson, General James. *Memoirs of My Own Time*. Abraham Small. Philadelphia, 1816.

"Journal of Miss Sally Wister." *Pennsylvania Magazine of History and Biography*. Vol. 9. Philadelphia, 1885.

Wortley, Mrs. E. Stuart, editor. *A Prime Minister and His Son*. John Murray. London, 1925.

Wraxall, Sir Nathanael William. *Historical Memoirs of My Own Time*. Kegan Paul, Trench, Trubner. London, 1904.

"Journal of Sergeant William Young." *Pennsylvania Magazine of History and Biography*. Vol. 8. Philadelphia, 1884.

MONOGRAPHS

Abbott, Wilbur C. *New York in the American Revolution*. Scribner. New York, 1929.

Abernethy, Thomas P. *Western Lands and the American Revolution*. Appleton-Century. New York, 1937.

Adams, Charles Francis. "The Battle of Bunker Hill." *American Historical Review*. Vol. 1. New York, 1896.

—— "The Campaign of 1777." *Proceedings of the Massachusetts Historical Society*. Vol. 44. Boston, 1911.

—— *Lee at Appomattox and Other Papers*. Boston, 1903.

—— "The Weems Dispensation." *Proceedings of the Massachusetts Historical Society*. Vol. 44. Boston, 1911.

Adams, Randolph G. "A View of Cornwallis's Surrender at Yorktown." *American Historical Review*. Vol. 37. New York, 1932.

Albion, R. G., and Pope, J. B. *Sea Lanes in Wartime*. W. W. Norton. New York, 1942.

Anderson, Troyer S. *The Command of the Howe Brothers During the American Revolution*. Oxford University Press. New York, 1935.

Baker, William J. *The Exchange of Major General Charles Lee*. Privately printed. Philadelphia, 1891.

Baldwin, Alice M. *The New England Clergy and the American Revolution*. Duke University Press. Durham, North Carolina, 1928.

Becker, Carl L. *The History of Political Parties in the Province of New York*. Bulletin of the University of Wisconsin. Madison, Wisconsin, 1909.

—— *The Declaration of Independence*. Harcourt, Brace. New York, 1922.

Belknap, Jeremy. *The History of New Hampshire*. Bradford and Read. Boston, 1813.

Bingham, Hiram. *Five Straws*. Privately printed. Cambridge, 1901.

Bolton, Charles K. *The Private Soldier Under Washington*. Scribner. New York, 1902.

Bowman, Allen. *The Morale of the American Revolutionary Army*. American Council on Public Affairs. Washington, 1943.

Brown, Weldon A. *Empire or Independence*. Louisiana State University Press. University, Louisiana, 1941.

Brunhouse, R. L. *The Counter-Revolution in Pennsylvania*. Pennsylvania Historical Commission. Harrisburg, 1942.

Carrington, Henry B. *Battles of the American Revolution*. A. S. Barnes. New York, 1888.

Castro, J. P. de. *The Gordon Riots*. Oxford University Press. London, 1926.

Clark, Jane. "The Convention Troops and the Perfidy of Sir William Howe." *American Historical Review*. Vol. 37. New York, 1932.

—— "Responsibility for the Failure of the Burgoyne Campaign." *American Historical Review*. Vol. 35. New York, 1930.

Corwin, Edward S. *French Policy and the American Alliance of 1778*. Princeton University Press. Princeton, 1916.

Curtis, Edward E. *The Organization of the British Army in the American Revolution*. Yale University Press. New Haven, 1926.

Davidson, Philip. *Propaganda and the American Revolution*. University of North Carolina Press. Chapel Hill, 1941.

DeMond, Robert O. *The Loyalists in North Carolina During the Revolution*. Duke University Press. Durham, North Carolina, 1940.

Drake, S. A. *Bunker Hill*. Nichols and Hall. Boston, 1875.

Draper, Lyman C. *King's Mountain and Its Heroes*. Dauber & Pine. New York, 1929.

East, Robert A. *Business Enterprise in the American Revolutionary Era*. Columbia University Press. New York, 1938.

Eckenrode, H. J. *The Revolution in Virginia*. Houghton Mifflin. Boston, 1916.

Einstein, Lewis. *Divided Loyalties*. Houghton Mifflin. Boston, 1933.

Feiling, Keith. *The Second Tory Party*. Macmillan. London, 1938.

Flick, A. C. *Loyalism in New York*. Columbia University Press. 1901.

Fonblanque, Edward Barrington de. *Political and Military Episodes*. Macmillan. London, 1876.

Fox, Dixon Ryan. *Yankees and Yorkers*. New York University Press. New York, 1940.

French, Allen. *The Day of Concord and Lexington*. Little, Brown. Boston, 1925.

—— *The First Year of the American Revolution*. Houghton Mifflin. Boston, 1934.

Frost, Holloway H. *We Build a Navy*. United States Naval Institute. Annapolis, 1940.

Frothingham, Richard. *History of the Siege of Boston*. Little, Brown. Boston, 1903.

Gilbert, George A. "The Connecticut Loyalists." *American Historical Review*. Vol. 4. New York, 1899.

Gilson, James E. *Dr. Bodo Otto*. Charles C. Thomas. Springfield, Illinois, 1937.

Guttridge, G. H. "Lord George Germain in Office." *American Historical Review*. Vol. 33. New York, 1932.

Hancock, Harold Bell. "The Delaware Loyalists." Papers of the Historical Society of Delaware. New Series, Vol. III. Wilmington, 1940.

Harlow, Ralph V. "Some Aspects of Revolutionary Finances." *American Historical Review*. Vol. 35. New York, 1934.

Harrell, Isaac S. "Some Neglected Phases of the Revolution in Virginia." *William and Mary College Quarterly*. Vol. 5, Series II, Williamsburg, 1925.

Hatch, L. C. *The Administration of the American Revolutionary Army*. Longmans, Green. New York, 1904.

Holzman, James M. *The Nabobs in England*. Columbia University Press. New York, 1926.

James, Captain W. M. *The British Navy in Adversity*. New York, 1926. Longmans, Green. London, 1926.

Jensen, Merrill. *The Articles of Confederation*. University of Wisconsin Press. Madison, 1940.

Johnson, Walter Leroy. *The Administration of the American Commissariat During the American Revolutionary War*. University of Pennsylvania Press. Philadelphia, 1941.

Johnston, Henry P. *The Campaign of 1776*. Long Island Historical Society. Brooklyn, 1878.

Knollenberg, Bernhard. *Washington and the Revolution*. Macmillan. New York, 1940.

Lincoln, C. H. *The Revolutionary Movement in Pennsylvania*. For the University. Philadelphia, 1901.

Lossing, John B. *The Pictorial Field-Book of the Revolution*. Harper. New York, 1860.

Lowell, Edward J. *The Hessians and Other German Auxiliaries*. Harper. New York, 1884.

Lundin, Leonard. *Cockpit of the Revolution*. Princeton University Press. Princeton, 1940.

Macmillan, M. B. *The War Governors in the American Revolution*. Macmillan. New York, 1943.

Mark, Irving. *Agrarian Conflict in New York*. Columbia University Press. New York, 1940.

Morison, Samuel Eliot. *The Maritime History of Massachusetts*. W. Heinemann. London, 1923.

Moore, George H. *The Treason of Charles Lee*. Scribner. New York, 1860.

Murdock, Harold. *Bunker Hill*. Houghton Mifflin. Boston, 1927.

Myers, William Starr, editor. *The Battle of Monmouth by Wm. S. Stryker*. Princeton University Press. Princeton, 1927.

Namier, L. B. *The Structure of British Politics at the Accession of George III*. Macmillan. London, 1929.

Nickerson, Hoffman. *The Turning Point of the Revolution*. Houghton Mifflin. Boston, 1928.

O'Donnell, William Emmett. *The Chevalier de la Luzerne, French Minister to the United States, 1779–1784.* Desclée de Brouwer. Bruges, Belgium, 1938.

Pennypacker, Morton. *General Washington's Spies.* Long Island Historical Society. Brooklyn, 1939.

Petrie, Sir Charles. *The Jacobite Movement.* Eyre and Spottiswoode. London, 1932.

Phillips, U. B. *The Course of the South to Secession.* Appleton-Century. New York, 1939.

Pitman, F. W. *The Development of the British West Indies.* Yale University Press. New Haven, 1917.

Quaife, Milo M. *The Capture of Old Vincennes.* Bobbs-Merrill. Indianapolis, 1927.

Rosengarten, J. G. *The German Allied Troops, 1776–1783.* J. Munsell. Albany, 1893.

Schaefer, William A. "Sectionalism and Representation in South Carolina." *Annual Report* of the American Historical Association. Washington, 1901.

Selsam, J. P. *The Pennsylvania Constitution of 1776.* University of Pennsylvania Press. Philadelphia, 1936.

Shaw, Helen Louise. "British Administration of the Southern Indians." Ph.D. Thesis. Bryn Mawr, 1931.

Smith, Justin H. *Our Struggle for the Fourteenth Colony.* Putnam. New York, 1907.

Spaulding, Oliver L. *The United States Army in War and Peace.* Putnam. New York, 1907.

Stille, Charles J. "Beaumarchais and 'The Lost Million.'" *Pennsylvania Magazine of History and Biography.* Vol. 2. Philadelphia, 1887.

Stone, William L. *The Campaign of Lieut. General John Burgoyne.* J. Munsell. Albany, 1877.

Sullivan, Kathryn. *Maryland and France.* University of Pennsylvania Press. Philadelphia, 1936.

Swiggert, Harold. *War Out of Niagara.* Columbia University Press. New York, 1933.

Tornquist, Karl Gustaf. *The Naval Campaigns of the Count de Grasse.* Swedish Colonial Society. Philadelphia, 1942.

Turner, Frederick J. "Western State Making in the Revolutionary Era." *American Historical Review.* Vol. 1. New York, 1896.

Uhlendorf, B. A. *The Siege of Charleston.* University of Michigan Press. Ann Arbor, 1938.

Van Doren, Carl. *Secret History of the American Revolution.* Viking Press. New York, 1941.

—— *Mutiny in January.* Viking Press. New York, 1943.

Van Tyne, Claude H. *The Loyalists in the American Revolution.* Macmillan. New York, 1901.

Wead, Eunice. "British Public Opinion of the Peace with America in 1783." *American Historical Review.* Vol. 34. New York, 1934.

Weaver, Emily P. "Nova Scotia and New England During the Revolution." *American Historical Review.* Vol. 10. New York, 1905.

BIBLIOGRAPHY   701

Williamson, Hugh. *The History of North Carolina*. Vol. II. Thomas Dobson. Philadelphia, 1812.

Winstanley, D. A. *Lord Chatham and the Whig Opposition*. Cambridge University Press. Cambridge, 1910.

Wright, Colonel John W. "Notes on the Continental Army." *William and Mary College Quarterly*. Series II. Vol. II. Williamsburg, 1931.

Wrong, George M. *The Conquest of New France*. Yale University Press. New Haven, 1920.

BIOGRAPHIES

Austin, James T. *Elbridge Gerry*. Wells and Lilly. Boston, 1828.

Barry, Richard. *Mr. Rutledge of South Carolina*. Duell, Sloan and Pearce. New York, 1942.

Boardman, Roger Sherman. *Roger Sherman, Signer and Statesman*. University of Pennsylvania Press. Philadelphia, 1938.

Brooks, Noah. *Henry Knox*. Putnam. New York, 1900.

Dakin, Douglas. *Turgot and the Ancien Régime in France*. Methuen. London, 1939.

Fitzmaurice, Lord Edmund George. *The Life of William, Earl of Shelburne*. 2 vols. Macmillan. London, 1912.

Fitzpatrick, John C. *George Washington Himself*. Bobbs-Merrill. Indianapolis, 1933.

Frothingham, Thomas G. *Washington, Commander in Chief*. Houghton Mifflin. Boston, 1930.

Glenn, Thomas Allen. *William Churchill Houston*. Privately printed. Norristown, Pennsylvania, 1903.

Goodman, Nathan G. *Benjamin Rush*. University of Pennsylvania Press. Philadelphia, 1934.

Gottschalk, Louis. *Lafayette Comes to America*. University of Chicago Press. Chicago, 1935.

—— *Lafayette Joins the American Army*. University of Chicago Press. Chicago, 1937.

—— *Lafayette and the Close of the American Revolution*. University of Chicago Press. Chicago, 1942.

Greene, George W. *The Life of General Nathanael Greene*. Hurd and Houghton. New York, 1871.

Hall, Charles S. *Benjamin Tallmadge*. Columbia University Press. New York, 1943.

Henry, William Wirt. *Patrick Henry*. Scribner. New York, 1891.

Higginson, Thomas Wentworth. *The Life and Times of Stephen Higginson*. Houghton Mifflin. Boston, 1907.

Huddeston, F. J. *Gentleman Johnny Burgoyne*. Bobbs-Merrill. Indianapolis, 1927.

Hughes, Rupert. *George Washington: The Human Being and the Hero*. William Morrow. New York, 1926.

Irving, Washington. *The Life of Washington*. Putnam. New York, 1868.

James, James Alton. *The Life of George Rogers Clark*. University of Chicago Press. Chicago, 1928.

Kite, Elizabeth S. *Brigadier-General Duportail*. Johns Hopkins Press. Baltimore, 1933.

Lascelles, Edward. *Charles James Fox*. Oxford University Press. New York, 1936.

Leake, Isaac Q. *John Lamb*. J. Munsell. Albany, 1857.

Lee, R. H. *Life of Arthur Lee*. Wells & Lilly. Boston, 1829.

Lorenz, Lincoln. *John Paul Jones*. United States Naval Institute. Annapolis, 1943.

Low, D. M. *Edward Gibbon*. Random House. New York, 1937.

Lucas, Reginald. *Lord North*. Arthur L. Humphreys. London, 1913.

Martyn, Charles. *Artemas Ward*. Privately printed. New York, 1921.

Matheson, Cyril. *The Life of Henry Dundas*. Constable. London, 1933.

McHugh, Roger. *Henry Grattan*. Sheed and Ward. New York, 1937.

McRea, G. J. *The Life and Correspondence of James Iredell*. Appleton. New York, 1857.

Miller, John C. *Sam Adams, Pioneer in Propaganda*. Atlantic–Little, Brown. Boston, 1936.

Minto, Countess of. *The Life and Letters of Sir Gilbert Elliot*. Longmans, Green. London, 1874.

Monaghan, Frank. *John Jay*. Bobbs-Merrill. Indianapolis, 1935.

Morison, Samuel Eliot. *The Life and Letters of Harrison Gray Otis*. Houghton Mifflin. Boston, 1913.

Oberholtzer, Ellis P. *Robert Morris: Patriot and Financier*. Macmillan. New York, 1903.

Palmer, John McAuley. *General von Steuben*. Yale University Press. New Haven, 1937.

Rowland, Kate. *George Mason*. Putnam. New York, 1892.

Sparks, Jared. *The Life of Gouverneur Morris*. Gray & Bowen. Boston, 1822.

Spaulding, E. Wilder. *His Excellency George Clinton*. Macmillan. New York, 1938.

Stephenson, N. W., and Dunn, Waldo L. *George Washington*. Oxford University Press. New York, 1940.

Stille, C. J. *Major General Anthony Wayne and the Pennsylvania Line*. Lippincott. Philadelphia, 1893.

Tuckerman, Bayard. *The Life of General Philip Schuyler*. Dodd, Mead. New York, 1903.

Van Doren, Carl. *Benjamin Franklin*. Viking Press. New York, 1938.

Wallace, David D. *The Life of Henry Laurens*. Putnam. New York, 1915.

Warren, Edward. *The Life of John Warren*. Houghton Mifflin. Boston, 1878.

Williams, Basil. *The Life of William Pitt*. Longmans, Green. London, 1914.

Yarborough, M. C. *John Horne Tooke*. Columbia University Press. New York, 1926.

GENERAL

Because many of the books listed here extend over the entire period of the Revolution, 1763–1783, this section includes the bibliography for the preceding volume, *Origins of the American Revolution*.

Adams, James Truslow. *The Founding of New England*. Atlantic–Little, Brown. Boston, 1921.
—— *Revolutionary New England*. Atlantic–Little, Brown. Boston, 1923.
—— *The Epic of America*. Atlantic–Little, Brown. Boston, 1931.
—— *The Adams Family*. Atlantic–Little, Brown. Boston, 1931.
Adams, Randolph G. *Political Ideas of the American Revolution*. Trinity College Press. Durham, North Carolina, 1922.
Alvord, Clarence W. *The Mississippi Valley in British Politics*. Arthur H. Clark. Cleveland, 1917.
Andrews, Charles M. *The Colonial Period of American History*. Yale University Press. New Haven, 1934, 1936, 1937, 1938.
—— *The Colonial Background of the American Revolution*. Yale University Press. New Haven, 1924.
—— *Colonial Self-Government*. Harper. New York, 1904.
Bancroft, George. *History of the United States*. Little, Brown. Boston, 1874.
Beard, Charles and Mary. *The Rise of American Civilization*. Macmillan. New York, 1930.
Becker, Carl L. *The Eve of the Revolution*. Yale University Press. New Haven, 1921.
Belcher, Henry. *The First American Civil War*. Macmillan. London, 1911.
Bemis, Samuel F. *The Diplomacy of the American Revolution*. Appleton-Century. New York, 1935.
Burnett, Edmund C. *The Continental Congress*. Macmillan. New York, 1942.
Bridenbaugh, Carl. *Cities in the Wilderness*. Ronald Press. New York, 1938.
—— with Bridenbaugh, Jessica. *Rebels and Gentlemen*. Reynal and Hitchcock. New York, 1942.
Channing, Edward. *A History of the United States*. Macmillan. New York, 1928.
Coupland, Reginald. *The American Revolution and the British Empire*. Longmans, Green. London, 1930.
Dickerson, Oliver M. *American Colonial Government*. Arthur H. Clark. Cleveland, 1912.
Dorn, Walter L. *Competition for Empire*. Harper. New York, 1940.
Earle, Edward M., editor. *Makers of Modern Strategy*. Princeton University Press. Princeton, 1940.
Egerton, H. E. *The Causes and Character of the American Revolution*. Oxford University Press. Oxford, 1923.
Fisher, Sydney George. *The Struggle for American Independence*. Lippincott. Philadelphia, 1908.

Fiske, John. *The American Revolution*. 2 vols. Houghton Mifflin. Boston, 1891.

Frothingham, Richard. *The Rise of the Republic of the United States*. Little, Brown. Boston, 1910.

Gipson, Lawrence H. *The British Empire Before the American Revolution*. Caxton Printers. Caldwell, Idaho, 1936–1939.

Gordon, William. *The History of the Rise, Progress, and Establishment of the Independence of the United States of America*. Samuel Campbell. New York, 1794.

Greene, Evarts B. *Provincial America*. Harper. New York, 1905.

—— *The Revolutionary Generation*. Macmillan. New York, 1943.

Guedalla, Philip. *Fathers of the Revolution*. Putnam. New York, 1926.

Guttridge, G. H. *English Whiggism and the American Revolution*. University of California Press. Berkeley, 1942.

Hockett, Homer C. *The Political and Social Growth of the United States*. Macmillan. New York, 1925.

Hunt, William. *The History of England*. Longmans, Green. London, 1905.

Jameson, J. Franklin. *The American Revolution Considered as a Social Movement*. Princeton University Press. Princeton, 1926.

Larabee, Leonard W. *Royal Government in America*. Yale University Press. New Haven, 1930.

Lavisse, Ernest. *Histoire de France*. Paris, 1911.

Lecky, W. E. H. *History of England in the Eighteenth Century*. Appleton. New York, 1883.

Mahan, A. T. *The Influence of Sea Power upon History*. Boston, 1902.

McIlwain, Charles H. *The American Revolution*. Macmillan. New York, 1923.

Morison, S. E., and Commager, H. S. *The Growth of the American Republic*. Oxford University Press. New York, 1937.

Montross, Lynn. *War Through the Ages*. Harper. New York, 1944.

Morris, Richard B. *The Era of the American Revolution*. Columbia University Press. New York, 1939.

Namier, L. B. *England in the Age of the American Revolution*. Macmillan. London, 1930.

Nettels, Curtis. *The Roots of American Civilization*. Crofts. New York, 1938.

Nevins, Allan. *The American States During and After the Revolution*. Macmillan. New York, 1924.

Osgood, H. L., edited by Fox, Dixon Ryan. *The American Colonies in the Eighteenth Century*. Columbia University Press. New York, 1924.

Parkman, Francis. *A Half Century of Conflict*. Little, Brown. Boston. 1929.

—— *Montcalm and Wolfe*. Little, Brown. Boston, 1927.

Parrington, Vernon L. *Main Currents in American Thought*. Harcourt, Brace. New York, 1930.

Ramsay, David. *The History of the American Revolution*. Trenton, 1811.

Schlesinger, Arthur M. *The Colonial Merchants and the American Revolution.* Columbia University Press. New York, 1918.

—— *New Viewpoints in American History.* Macmillan. New York, 1926.

Schuyler, R. L. *Parliament and the British Empire.* Columbia University Press. New York, 1929.

Spaulding, O. L. *The United States Army in War and Peace.* Putnam. New York, 1937.

Stedman, Charles. *The History of the Origin, Progress, and Termination of the American War.* 2 vols. J. Murray. London, 1794.

Stephen, Sir Leslie. *History of English Thought in the Eighteenth Century.* Smith Elder. London, 1881.

Trevelyan, Sir George. *History of the American Revolution.* Longmans, Green. New York, 1899.

—— *George the Third and Charles James Fox.* Longmans, Green. New York, 1927.

Tyler, Moses Coit. *Literary History of the American Revolution.* 2 vols. Putnam. New York, 1897.

Van Tyne, Claude H. *The Causes of the War of Independence.* Houghton Mifflin. Boston, 1922.

—— *The War of Independence.* Houghton Mifflin. Boston, 1929.

The Cambridge History of the British Empire. Macmillan, New York, 1929.

Dictionary of American Biography. Scribner. New York, 1928–1936.

Dictionary of National Biography. Macmillan. London, 1885.

Index

ACKLAND, LADY HARRIET, 215
Ackland, Lord, 178, 215
Adams, John, 16, 19, 22, 55, 61, 70, 81, 91, 101, 106, 110, 118, 185, 190, 192, 194, 198, 202, 204, 220, 238, 240, 244, 246, 340, 343, 344, 375, 412, 446, 457, 467, 469, 470, 477, 489, 503, 526, 585, 587, 590, 622, 627, 664, 680, 687; at Lord Howe's peace conference, 131–132; against French alliance, 273, 275, 381; exponent of conservative views, 345–346, 353, 354; in Paris, 357–361, 370–371, 565, 570, 572–580; diplomat in Holland, 588; at peace settlement, 631–649 *passim*
Adams, Mrs. John, 70, 444, 457
Adams, Sam, 22, 190, 220, 241, 248, 259, 261, 330, 356, 362, 372, 379, 391, 469, 470, 475, 476, 622*n.*, 652; as propagandist, 281; as conservative democrat, 345; for state sovereignty, 426
Albany, 119, 149–151, 175, 176, 178, 179, 181, 183, 184, 185, 187–190, 194, 195, 198, 210, 211
Alexander, Lady Kitty, 232
Ali, Hyder, 617, 621
Allen, Ethan, 90–91, 656; marches to Quebec, 90–93; capture of, 169
Amboy, 160
American Revolution, *see* Independence, War of
Amphitrite (ship), 208, 280
André, Major, 206, 537–538
Annapolis, 200, 675, 687
Aranjuez, Agreement of, 390
Arbuthnot, Admiral, 167, 561, 603–604
Armand, Colonel, 287, 495
Armed Neutrality, the, 587–589
Armistead, Mrs., 31
Armstrong, Major John, 673
Army, British, 5–6, 36, 393; recruiting for, 7, 10–15, 337–338; supplies for, 7, 76, 86, 173–174, 176, 180–181; overconfidence of, 7–9, 47, 126; class distinctions in, 9–10; American attitude toward, 15, 75; in Boston, 46, 74–86,

91, 92; at battle of Bunker Hill, 49–53; fear of frontier riflemen, 72–73; evacuates Boston, 85–87; on Long Island, 116–117, 122–128; attempts to reach Albany from Canada, 149–151; cruel conduct of, 164–169; treatment of prisoners, 166–170, 174, 517; under Burgoyne, 174–185; under Howe in Pennsylvania, 191–207; at Germantown, 205–206; evacuates Philadelphia, 315–318; Lee's attitude toward, 321; in New York, 331; cavalry in, 494, 520, 547; deserters in, 506; in the South, Chapters XXIV *and* XXV *passim*; separation of, 604
Army, Continental, 57*n.*, 71; unmilitary appearance of, 8, 137, 148, 221, 485–488, 610; advantages of, 17, 19–20; recruiting for, 19, 83, 192, 431, 500–508; British attitude toward, 37–38, 52, 147, 159, 175, 177, 209, 216; commander-inchief for, 60–63; ammunition and supplies for, 66, 74–76, 82, 84–85, 93–94, 99, Chapter VII *passim*, 144, 176, 208, 218, 221–224, 241, 368, 443, 450, 454, Chapter XXIII *passim*, 518, 527–528, 540–541, 583, 669–670; under Washington, 67–69, 71–76; riflemen in, 72–74, 122–124, 127, 158, 179, 209, 212, 254, 325, 520, 547; in Boston siege, 74–86; permanence of, 80–81, 148–149, 161–162, 225, 233, 498–508; invades Canada, 90–100; deserters from, 131, 138, 505; captures New York, 133–138; rout of, in New Jersey, 152; treatment of prisoners in, 166*n.*, 169–170, 215, 320, 507; at Bennington, 182; at Fort Stanwix, 184; under General Gates, 189–190, 521–525; in Pennsylvania, 193–194, 195, 198, 200; at Valley Forge, Chapter XII *passim*, 481, 483; militia in, 237–238, 505, 513, 518, 521, 522, 548; French officers commissioned in, 285–289; at Monmouth Courthouse, 323–327; dissension with French, 330; state lines in, 431–432, 485, 486, 521, 544, 545*n.*, 655; ef-